AF412009

Neubau Forst Catalogue

Stefan Gandl
Benjamin Ganz
Christoph Grünberger
Daniel Cottis
Paul Heys

Lars Müller Publishers

ISBN 978-3-03778-435-8
© 2014, 1st Edition
Lars Müller Publishers

Printed on FSC® Certified Paper
Munken Print White 115 gsm
Multi Art Gloss 150 gsm
Hello Fat Mat 150 gsm

N3

N4

N1　B1　B3　　　　　　　　　　　　　　　　N11　　N12

A9　E4　A11

U1　N5　U3　　　　　　　　　　　　　　U7　　U10

A10　E5　A12

B9

A1

A3

B4　B10　　　　　　　A17　　A22

E2　A5　　　　　A15　E7　E10

E11

A18
E1　U4　A16　U8　E9
E3　A6　A19

B5　B13　B15

A2　A4

E6

B6　B14　B16

E8

A7　U5　A13　U9
A20
A21　N7　A23

A8　U6　A14

B11

B7

N2　B2　N6　B8　　　　　　　　　　　N10

N8

B12　　　　　　　　　　　N9

●52.525262,
13.392119
●52.524419, 13.396813
52.522991, 13.388233
● ●52.522862, ●52.522777,
13.391933   13.400872

●52.522827, ●52.522775,
13.445657   13.454659

52.516964,
13.421377
● ● ●52.51698,
52.517016, 13.425237
13.417667

52.514097, 52.514327,
●13.391811 ●13.40131
●52.514638,
13.39708

●52.514205, ●52.514162,
13.441764   13.450905

52.511419,52.511149,
13.417836 13.42484
●   ●   ●
52.511437,
13.421323

●52.508198,
13.421282

●52.506135,
13.393542

●52.504626,
13.40199
●52.503164,
13.400999

●52.502826,
13.42116

●52.502894, ●52.502727,
13.441345   13.450677

●52.498949, ●52.499584, ●52.499432,
13.392085   13.401113   13.411075

●52.499470, ●52.499613,
13.432120   13.442006   ●52.496656,
13.451107

52.494413,
●13.400975

●52.496656,
13.451107

52.494651, 52.494413,
●13.392208 ●13.400975   ●52.495167, 13.44199
●52.494188, ●52.494291, ●52.494602, 13.441848
13.401075   13.41086   ●52.494267,
13.44663
●52.494099,
13.432009
●52.492469,
13.44188

●52.490298,
13.401057

●52.490258, ●52.490369,
13.441899   13.450498

●52.488174, ●52.488113,
13.392141   13.401183

●52.48695,
13.437359
●   ●52.485903,
●52.48595,   13.451037
13.401082   52.485902,
13.44186

●52.483596,
13.444708
52.482295,
●52.482269,   ● ●13.425044
13.410997   52.482204,   ●52.481821, 13.441726
13.421527
●52.480711, 13.44181
52.479609, 13.445774
●   ●52.479361,
52.479399, 13.450728
13.441912

52.47680,   52.476821,
●13.41094   ● ●13.424727
52.476875,
13.42157

●52.473656,
13.421519

●52.47319,
13.40132
52.47083,
13.38851   52.47085, 13.39734
●   ●   ●   ●52.47090,
52.47078,   13.40115
13.39216

●52.470828,
13.454545
●52.469395,
13.446389
●52.46833,
13.450608
●52.468253,
13.421506

●Oranienburger Strasse 38

●Oranienburger Strasse 20
Friedrichstrasse 105
●   ●   ● Monbijouplatz 12
Tucholskystrasse 1

Auerstrasse 10
●
Richard-Sorge-
Strasse 80

Ifflandstrasse 2
●   ●   ●Singerstrasse 115
Alexanderstrasse 31

Jägerstrasse 19
●   ●Sperlingsgasse 1
●Jägerstrasse 41

●   ●Kadiner Strasse 19
Fredersdorfer Strasse 10

Ohmstrasse 11
●   ●   ●Michaelkirchstrasse 19
Michaelkirchstrasse 27

●Michaelkirchstrasse 2

●Markgrafenstrasse 66

●Ritterstrasse 44

●Ritterstrasse 77

●Waldemarstrasse 60

●   ●Ehrenbergstrasse 20
Gröbenufer 1

●
●Bergfriedstrasse 9
Alexandrinenstrasse 8
●
Mehringplatz 36

●   ●Wrangelstrasse 84
Skalitzer Strasse 95   ●Schleusenufer 6

●Am Flutgraben 1

Nostitzstrasse 60
●   ●Urbanstrasse 180
●   ●Böckhstrasse 54
Urbanstrasse 177

●Görlitzer Strasse 40
●Wiener Strasse 56
●   ●Jordanstrasse 36
Reichenberger Strasse 95
Lohmühlenstrasse 21

●Gneisenaustrasse 72

●   ●Bouchestrasse 83
Lexisstrasse 3

●   ●Jüterboger Strasse 3
Willibald-Alexis-Strasse 22

●Ossastrasse 13

●Züllichauer Strasse 1

●   ●Elsenstrasse 81
Weigandufer 9

●Wildenbruchplatz 5

Columbiadamm 128
●   ●Karlsgartenstrasse 1
Karlsgartenstrasse 9

●Finowstrasse 29

●Anzengruberstrasse 14
Roseggerstrasse 40
●   ●   ●Weserstrasse 133
Innstrasse 24

●THF   ●   ●Weisestrasse 51
Herrfurthplatz 7

●Lichtenrader Strasse 35

●THF

●THF ●THF   ●THF ●THF

●Niemetzstrasse 40

●Lahnstrasse 75

●Oderstrasse 4   ●Lahnstrasse 39

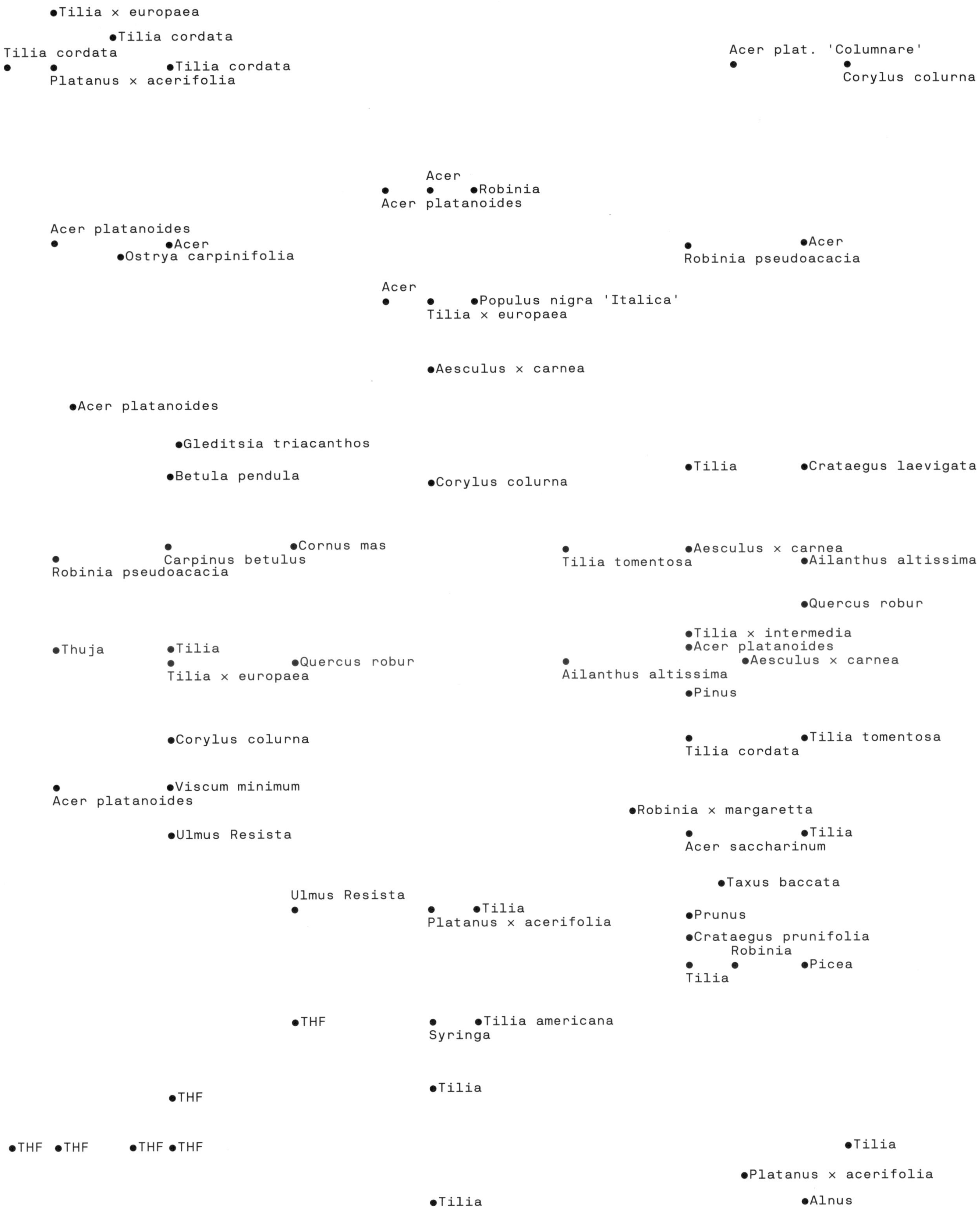

●Tilia × europaea
●Tilia cordata
Tilia cordata
●   ●   ●Tilia cordata
Platanus × acerifolia

Acer plat. 'Columnare'
●   ●
Corylus colurna

Acer
●   ●   ●Robinia
Acer platanoides

Acer platanoides
●   ●Acer
●Ostrya carpinifolia

●   ●Acer
Robinia pseudoacacia

Acer
●   ●   ●Populus nigra 'Italica'
Tilia × europaea

●Aesculus × carnea

●Acer platanoides

●Gleditsia triacanthos

●Betula pendula

●Corylus colurna

●Tilia   ●Crataegus laevigata

●   ●Cornus mas
Carpinus betulus
●
Robinia pseudoacacia

●   ●Aesculus × carnea
Tilia tomentosa   ●Ailanthus altissima

●Quercus robur

●Tilia × intermedia
●Acer platanoides
●Thuja   ●Tilia   ●   ●Aesculus × carnea
●   ●Quercus robur   Ailanthus altissima
Tilia × europaea   ●Pinus

●   ●Tilia tomentosa
Tilia cordata

●Corylus colurna

●   ●Viscum minimum   ●Robinia × margaretta
Acer platanoides   ●   ●Tilia
Acer saccharinum
●Ulmus Resista

●Taxus baccata

Ulmus Resista   ●Prunus
●   ●   ●Tilia   ●Crataegus prunifolia
Platanus × acerifolia   Robinia
●   ●   ●Picea
Tilia

●THF   ●   ●Tilia americana
Syringa

●Tilia

●THF

●THF ●THF ●THF ●THF   ●Tilia

●Platanus × acerifolia

●Tilia   ●Alnus

Contents

Introduction

Designer as Archivist – Archivist as Designer

For more than a decade, Neubau have occupied the vanguard of contemporary graphic design practice and studio production. As a studio, it continues to generate work that integrates critical design theory in exploring the relationships and potentiality of ordering and design systems, interrogating the discipline of graphic design as a 'programme management' application for system-based graphic production.

A rigorous level of self-discipline underpins these functionalist strategies and acts as a support mechanism, maintaining a high-level output and a clear studio philosophy. Working in this way assures all auxiliary roles – the viewer, user, and the designer – are valued equally as part of a demo-cratic graphic design process.

Inspired by dry transferable lettering systems [01] introduced and utilised within commercial graphic design throughout the 1960s–1980s, Neubau's detailed and systematic approach to creating publications and innovative software applications exemplifies the studio's desire to offer a resource, service, and purpose in addition to – or indeed beyond that of their own studio creations. The combi-nation of primary data; typographic design (text/image), vector silhouette, mathematical modular pattern generation (image), and publication (artifact) allows the reader or partici-pant the unique opportunity to access an infinite amount of visual possibilities and configurations. The new ideas generated through this process construct, control, and pre-serve the magnitude of the studio's own stored material and archive. Neubau's distinctive approach to graphic design production connects the maker, material, and user, leading to a universal creative language.

It is rare to find a studio that exploits digital technology and the common role of the graphic design workplace in order to enhance primary content, enable accessibility, and undertake the detailed task of combining and preserving its materials and artefacts. Through public publishing Neubau grants access to its digital and material collections, an em-bedded process of which populates, conserves, and sustains interest in the Neubau meta-archive.

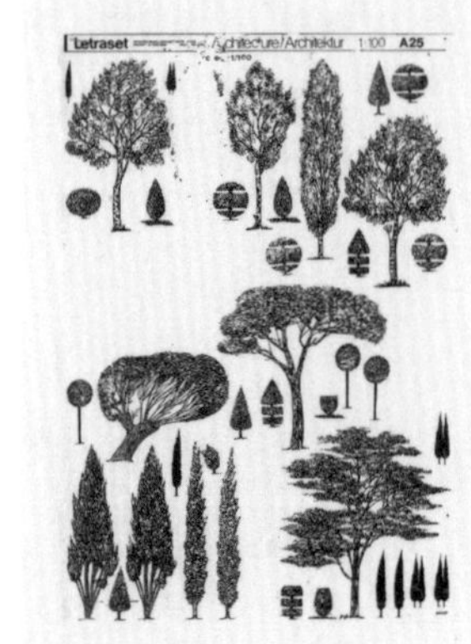

01.
Letraset, 'architecture'
dry transfer sheet
Letraset, UK 1982
letraset.com

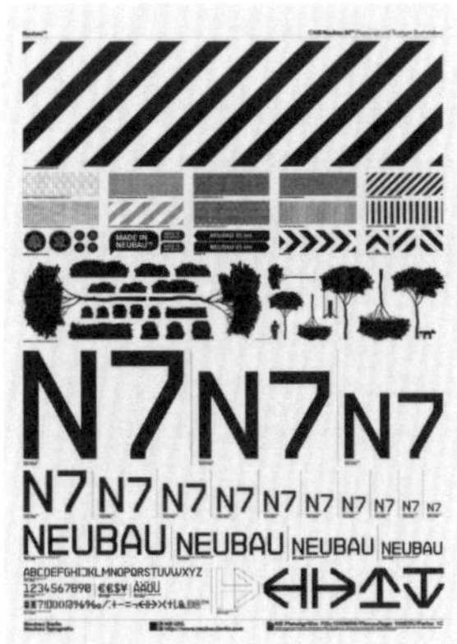

02.
'NB-55MS™ Specimen'
Poster, Gandl, S.,
Neubau, DE 2002
neubauberlin.com

03.
Fineder, M., Kraus, E.,
Pawlik, A.,
'Postscript: zur Form von
Schrift heute', A/CH/D
Künstlerhaus Wien,
10.10–1.12.2002,
Hatje Cantz, Ostfildern,
DE 2004

04.
Baudrillard, J.,
'The System of Objects'
(J. Benedict, Trans.)
The Marginal Objects:
'Antiques' (pp.77–90)
Verso, London, UK 2005

05.
Barthes, R.,
'Critical Essays'
Northwestern University
Press, Illinois, USA 1972

In 2002 Neubau published NB-55MS™ Postscript Specimen,[02] a commission presented at the exhibition 'Postscript: zur Form von Schrift heute', A/CH/D, Künstlerhaus Wien, Vienna. The project consisted of an exposition and successive publication[03] which questioned the future of postscript typefaces and poster design. 70×100 cm in size, Neubau's contribution resembled the dry transferable lettering system sheets known from a design past, consisting of seventy original components designed and edited by the studio. The specimen sheet included modular pattern swatches, the graphic representation of trees in vector silhouette, one typeface specimen and a selection of Neubau promotional transfers. Repurposed, reconfigured, and relocated, the audience were now faced with an image or object that positions itself somewhere between the past and present, establishing a commentary on the potentiality of graphic design publishing. Neubau had remixed its principle reference material with a combination of factual representations and original graphic content creating a system that generates objects of nostalgia from within. Turning to Jean Baudrillard's theory of the 'marginal object or antique',[04] Neubau had referenced the afunctional object present in the visual language represented in the dry transfer sheet, a technique that consistently appears in Neubau's design agenda as a means to signify time. This synthesis of dissection, articulation,[05] and communication relies on the viewer's memory to recalculate the presented text, image and/or artefact; in this case the example of content is the poster design and its relationship to the past. The reader is also made to consider how one connects with the present, whilst considering the function and meaning of a single, multiple, or interconnected element. The result – NB-55MS™ Postscript Specimen – manifests itself as an embedded, structuralist discourse on the future of postscript typefaces and poster design. Using these methods allows Neubau to scrutinise its own graphic design ideologies and develop a unique in-house graphic design research programme. Referencing and remixing the past positions Neubau at the forefront of designing for the present and declares the studio as a stakeholder in designing and building for the future.

In 2005 Neubau developed and released 'Neubau Welt';[06] a graphic pilgrimage in search of how a design studio could define and redefine its present environment and technological position using recognised historical design reference, contemporary graphic design techniques and digital technologies. Repurposing the culturally rich, urban landscapes of central Berlin alongside the studio's own permaculture,[07] Neubau created a material archive and digital database consisting of 1,247 vector objects and four original typefaces. 2007 saw the release of Neubau's second publication; 'Neubau Modul',[08] a critical review of mathematical principles applied to modular pattern construction and architectures. This included 2,031 patterns alongside a digital swatch library, which integrated seamlessly with industry standard creative software.

'Modul' also included two original typefaces and a NB-Modulmeter™, a clear, tangible substrate comparable to a typographic ruler or Typometer; a physical tool to aid the designer and determine the best possible overlays and offsets in the printed sections of the 'Modul' catalogue. Additionally, in 2008 Neubau created 'Neubauism',[09] the studios first showcase, exploring the complete works in an interactive, fully immersive exhibition that took place at Eindhoven's visual arts centre – MU, The Netherlands. Here the audience could control all Neubau content in real time, by overlaying typeface design from Neubau's self-generated type foundry with a carefully selected arrangement of vector objects from 'Neubau Welt' and infinite pattern overlays and offsets from 'Neubau Modul'. The user was in full control of the content. The exhibition supported Neubau's third publication also titled 'Neubauism'; both the publication and the exhibition served as a commentary on the studio's current position; somewhere between creator and curator and designer as archivist. 'Neubauism' also observed the studios global impact and created time to reflect and build primary material, accessible through the studio's current resource and digital archive.

06.
Gandl, S.,
'Neubau Welt' [1,247 HD Vector Objects]
DGV, Berlin, DE 2005

07.
The use of the term 'permaculture' relates to the development of a 'design' not agricultural ecosystems intended to be sustainable and self-sufficient.

08.
Gandl, S., Grünberger C., 'Neubau Modul' [2,031 Electronic & Analogue Patterns & Grids]
DGV, Berlin, DE 2007

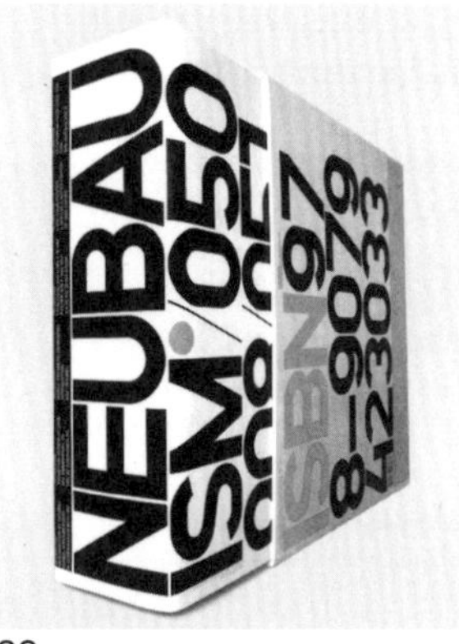

09.
'Neubauism Box'
Gandl, S., Grünberger C.,
Exhibition publication
[MU, 05.09.–05.10.08]
Stichting MU, Eindhoven,
NL 2008

10.
Martin, L.,
'The Grid as Generator'
In L. M. Martin & L. M. March
(Ed.), 'Urban Space and
Structures' (pp. 6–27)
Cambridge University Press,
Oxford, UK 1972

11.
The amount of edited
assets available in the
final edit of 'Neubau Forst
Catalogue'.

It was here in Eindhoven, six years ago that proposals of a fourth publication and database were discussed. As with 'Welt' and 'Modul' the discourse surrounding the new venture centred on developing a resource and service that was currently unavailable or unattainable to commercial artists, architects, and designers, putting the user first. The next repository to feature in the Neubau meta-archive series would undoubtedly follow similar frameworks to that of its prede-cessors, and would be the benchmark for future contributions. As always, the goal was to create an essential compendium that combined functionality with graphic appeal.

Neubau began to review, update, and design a com-pound of design systems that would govern the new repository refining the functionality of the Neubau archive and its data-base. This would redefine how the user would first receive and research Neubau content and how they would find and retrieve the content from both the material artifact and the digital database. Bespoke in-house 'grid generators'[10] were developed to capture, design, and edit the content, assuring the production quality and standards were proportionate in over 700 assets.[11] 'Forst' has redefined the search and stor-age system developed by Neubau over the last decade. In addition to advancements in digital hardware and software components, Neubau itself has advanced as a collective culture, able to offer a progressive, 'high-end' quality of prod-uct and service; the currency of Forst's content is matchless. 'Neubau Forst' offers the maximum in high-quality vector silhouette and high-definition bitmap modules and textures, an activity that has taken a disciplined team of twenty designers more than five years to complete, pushing the very limits of design studio and design software.

Located in the dynamic borough of Kreuzberg, Neubau are a microcosmic yet highly adaptive organism embedded in the cultural movements and changes within its geographic location and neighbouring borders; this position and locality forms the critical vantage point of 'Neubau Forst'. Forst's complete manufactured content uses a series of unique, purpose-built, multilayered grid systems. It is a hybrid of the conventional and the unique. The more comprehensible examples include typographic-based structures of which all Neubau typefaces are designed alongside grid constructs designed for desktop publishing software applications used in all Neubau's material and digital production. It is 'Forst' that introduces the unique; an intense, multi-layered, architecturally driven grid structure that complements the conventional and enriches the overall layout, arrangement, and development of the 'Neubau Forst Catalogue'.

The seventy-two 'dots' that penetrate the sleeve and the entirety of each artifact are critical guides to Neubau's systematic positioning that defines all content generated and created in 'Neubau Forst'. Asserting the role of city planner, the studio retrieved a scaled thematic map of central Berlin. The map was then scaled and edited for review. Further versions were re-edited, reviewed, and finalised. As a result, a reconfigured city map of Berlin spans a twenty-five-kilometre square plot and is now ready for development. A further grid is proportionally aligned over and against the parameters of the proposed development sight, the studio being the central focus of the map. Developing the 'locator grid',[12] generated using metrically spaced typography, the typographic specimen utilised is NB-Grotesk 55R™,[13] specifically engineered and originally developed for 'Neubau Forst'. This new typographically driven framework, meticulously composed, now offers the conventional landscape and a chance to redefine itself, to respond to growth and change. The grid consists of six individual letterforms. When distilled to their basic, mathematical construct these nodes or 'anchor points' represent seventy-two proportionally placed locators. Each represent a placeholder equipped for graphic content, a propoed regenerative plan of a city.

12.
A term, adapted by Neubau, derived from Leslie Martains' essay, Space and Structures. (See 07).

13.
NB-Grotesk Rund™ typeset Gandl, S., Neubau, Berlin, DE 2007 neubauladen.com

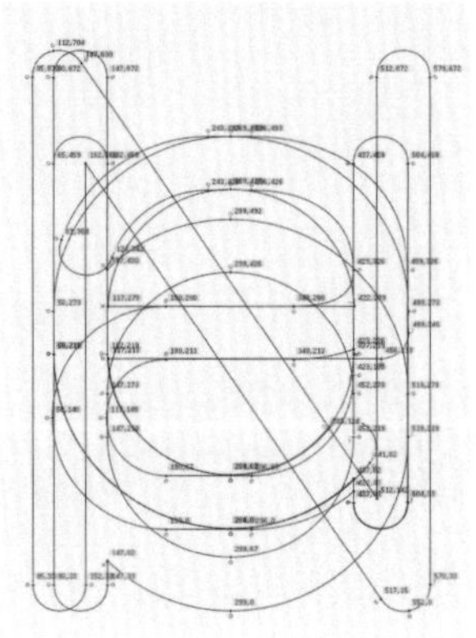

'NBF-Locator Grid'
A multilayered grid system derived from individual letters' construction points placed on a Berlin city map Neubau, Berlin, DE 2009

Typeface: NB Grotesk-55R™ Neubau, Berlin, DE 2007

14.
Chevrier, J. F.,
'A world without irony'
In H. Foundation, 'Tree Line'
(A. Waite, Trans., Vol. I, p. 104)
Steidl, Göttingen, DE 2009

15.
Chevrier, J. F.,
A world without irony
In H. Foundation, Tree Line
(A. Waite, Trans., Vol Ibid.,
p. 109) Steidl, Göttingen,
DE 2009

16.
Chtcheglov, I.,
'Formulary for a New
Urbanism: Sire, I Am from
Another London',
Psychogeographical
Association, UK 1997

The locator's typographic data extracted from the anchor points of each of the six typographic characters or forms, when reconnected represent a greater city agenda. This grid and agenda is: 'N' 'e' 'u' 'b' 'a' 'u'.

To assign responsibility to the 'Forst' repository, controlling the sum of content, considering both application and retrievable formats would take a great deal of time to perfect. 'Forst' now issued with the photographic image of each tree, enables the studio to update its image database adding faithful photographic reproduction and representation. The central objective was to produce a graphic design archival distribution system that would surpass all expectation. 'Without denying the legitimacy of a metaphorical interpretation of documentary reality'.[14]

In order for Neubau to fulfill the studio's outward-facing social agenda in providing exemplary quality in both service and product, it comes as no surprise that commitment to both could be problematical. Complex in nature, both Neubau and 'Forst' strive to sensitively produce and present clarity of all content and present systematic and structural order. A world in which 'fact and memory blend together'.[15] The addition of the photographic process now projecting itself to the forefront of Neubau's directory of editable assets and modules extends the overall potential of the archive, offering a greater range of graphic and photographic possibility. Transcending the abstract of the vector graphic silhouette, the option of the photographic image reinforces the association Neubau inherently assigns to its transformable landscapes offering a 'new vision of time and space'.[16]

'Neubau Forst' evolves the existing system of self-referential, publically accessible archival material. The seventy-two reference points now occupy Neubau's urban grid, a complex mapping system, effortlessly connecting the studio to the city.

However, content connects us all. It is here where Neubau pays tribute to the work of Joseph Beuys[17] in an attempt to clarify 'Forst's pure intension and transparency of concept as analogous to that of (past) artist and (present) designer. In 1982 Joseph Beuys presented '7000 Eichen' ('7000 Oaks') at documenta VII.[18] A five-year long community-driven project where by the artist and interested parties planted 7,000 trees throughout the city of Kassel in Germany. Each of Beuys' trees were planted and aligned with a solid stone marker in order to celebrate each of the natural object's significant beginnings. 'The solid stone form beside the ever-changing tree symbolically represents a basic concept in Beuys' philosophy, that these two natural and yet oppositional qualities are complementary and coexist harmoniously'.[19]

The living physical object – the tree – is the municipal object that connects all cities and their occupants. Both, studio and project, strive to express and recognise the potency of the tree in its own self-image. Neubau's interpretation of each tree transcends the archive and allows for it to be a stand-alone module.

In relation to 'Neubau Forst' the essay '7000 Oaks' by Lynne Cooke of the Dia Art Foundation, NYC relates to Beuys' efforts, which she argues, 'function as a small-scale, intimate project, the outcome of individual initiative, as well as a highly ambitious, potentially vast undertaking meant to be replicated elsewhere. [...] It accords well with Beuys' intensified focus during the 1970s on the production of multiples, that is, objects usually intended to be available at low cost in very large editions'. A position which could, and possibly should in this context, be assigned to Neubau's near decade of activity, the studio's archives, meta-archives and its past, present, and future projects fascinated with reproduction, quality, and accessibility.

17.
Beuys, J. H.,
(12 May 1921–23 Jan. 1986)
German Artist

18.
Cooke, L.,
Joseph Beuys, '7000 Oaks'
(Dia Foundation, Producer)
diaart.org

19.
'Joseph Beuys and his "7000 Oaks", Walker Art Center's 'Tree-Planting Project' Walker Art Center, USA 1997
walkerart.org

The reasoning behind Forst's concentration on a singular structure, the tree as a basis for all of its creation was a purposeful act, which served to bring clarity to the project. A tree, species, size, location, and role would now occupy each of the seventy-two locators, featuring on the front cover and operating as content holders for the inner pages of the book. These nodes or anchor points introduce the latest edition of the Neubau meta-archive, a spatial and temporal urban forest, engaged with its physical and geographical surroundings, remapped onto an adopted digital, transformative landscape. Nature is broken down into digital and modular data, the harmonious bond of the permanent and the ever-changing.

Paul Heys is an educator and graphic designer whose current research explores the theme of the 'designer as archivist' by examining the ordering of design systems. Heys is a Senior Lecturer and Course Leader of the BA (Hons) Graphic Design programme at the University of Huddersfield, UK.

```
N1    S   W      Linden            [Tilia cordata]
N7        W      Locust            [Robinia pseudoacacia]
N8    S   W      Plane             [Platanus x acerifolia]
N11   S          Maple             [Acer plat. 'Columnare']
N12   S          Hazel             [Corylus colurna]

E1    S          Thuja             [Thuja]
E3    S          Linden            [Tilia x europaea]
E4        W      Maple             [Acer]
E5    S   W      Linden            [Tilia x europaea]
E6        W      Locust            [Robinia x margaretta]
E9    S   W      Chestnut          [Aesculus x carnea]
E10   S          Tree of heaven    [Ailanthus altissima]

U4    S   W      Linden            [Tilia]
U6    S   W      Lilac             [Syringa]

B3    S   W      Linden            [Tilia cordata]
B9    S          Chestnut          [Aesculus x carnea]
B10       W      Hazel             [Corylus colurna]
B13   S   W      Linden            [Tilia cordata]
B14       W      Silver maple      [Acer saccharinum]
B15   S   W      Linden            [Tilia tomentosa]
B16       W      Linden            [Tilia]

A2    S          Maple             [Acer platanoides]
A9    S   W      Maple             [Acer platanoides]
A10   S          Maple             [Acer]
A12       W      Poplar            [Pappula Nigra 'Italica']
A14   S   W      Linden            [Tilia americana]
A16       W      Tree of heaven    [Ailanthus altissima]
A18   S          Linden            [Tilia x intermedia]

U7        W      Locust            [Robinia pseudoacacia]
U9        W      Morello Cherry    [Prunus]
```

Inventory
N1–U9
Trees

Inventory includes a total of 683 digitally editable compositions. 41 vector sculptures, 315 masked tree sculptures and 327 tree modules. Additional information included outlines each individual trees' species, which range from Linden, Chestnut, Hazel, Lilac, Locust, Maple, Plane, Poplar, Morello Cherry, Thuja to Tree of heaven and are documented seasonally throughout a four-year period during 2009–2013. A combination of the trees' modules and existing tree sculptures enable the user to create an indefinite number of new and individual tree variations.

— Printed on Munken Print White 115 gsm

```
N1    S  W      Linden          [Tilia cordata]
N7       W      Locust          [Robinia pseudoacacia]
N8    S  W      Plane           [Platanus x acerifolia]
N11   S         Maple           [Acer plat. 'Columnare']
N12   S         Hazel           [Corylus colurna]
```

N1–N12

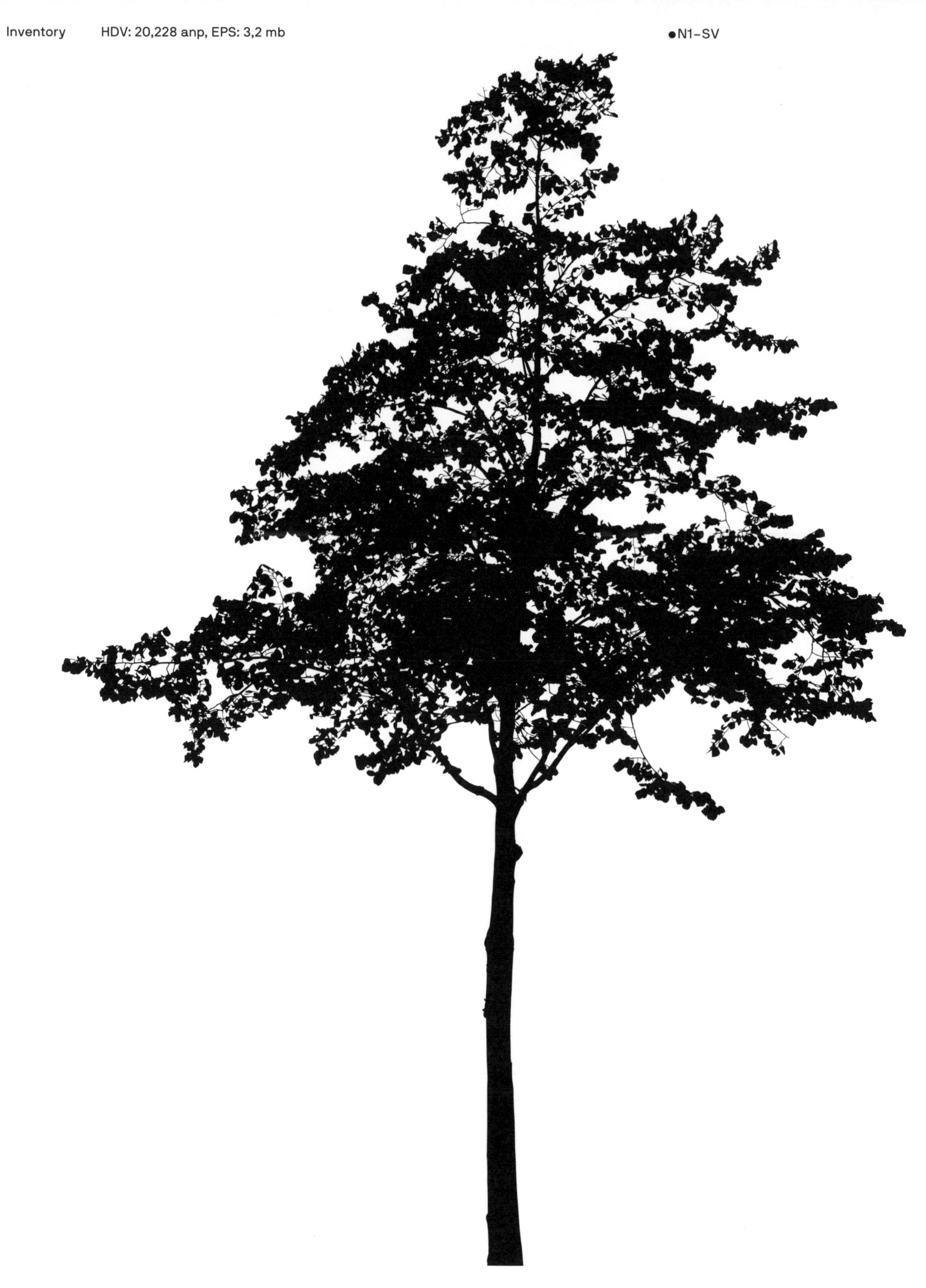

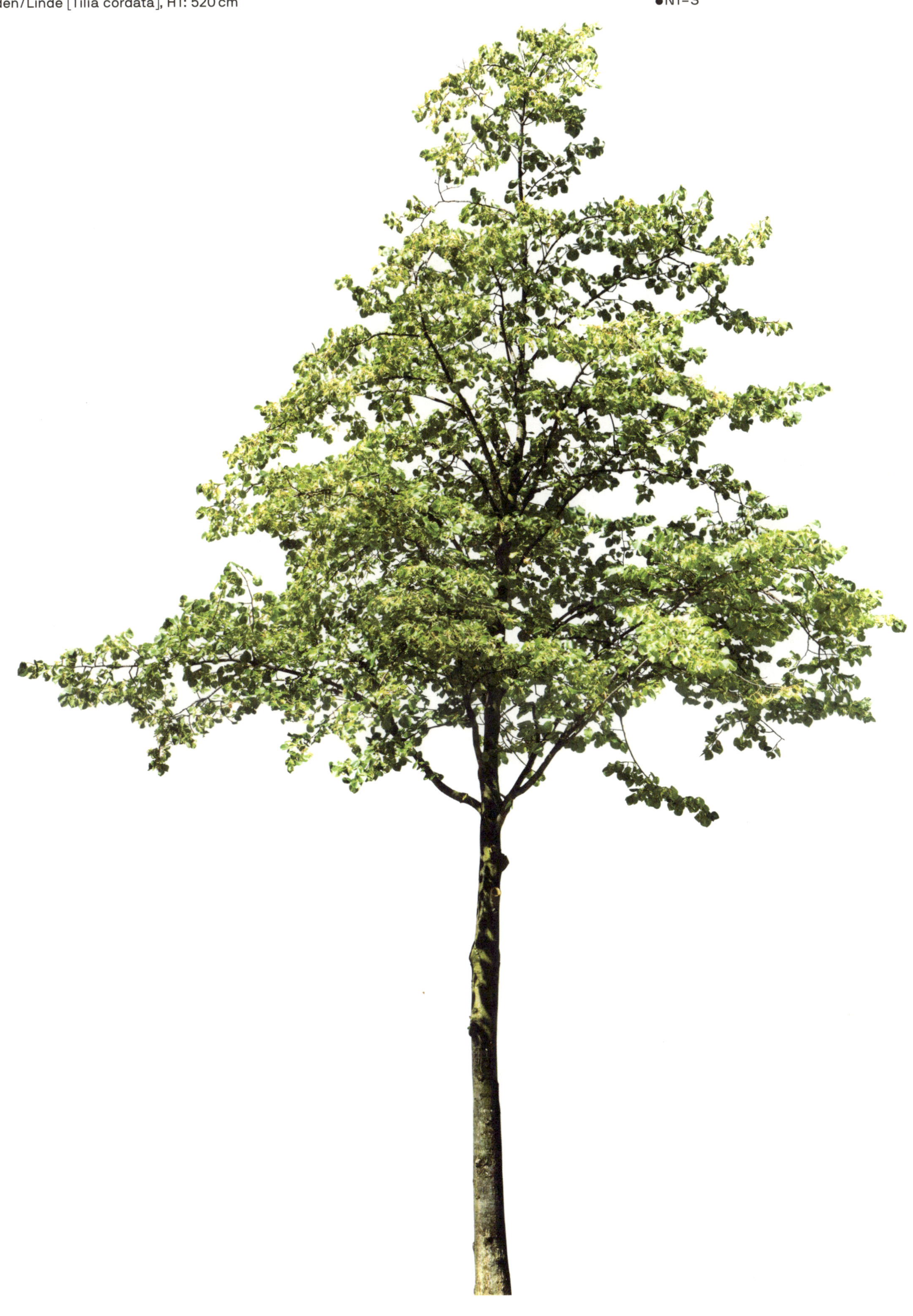

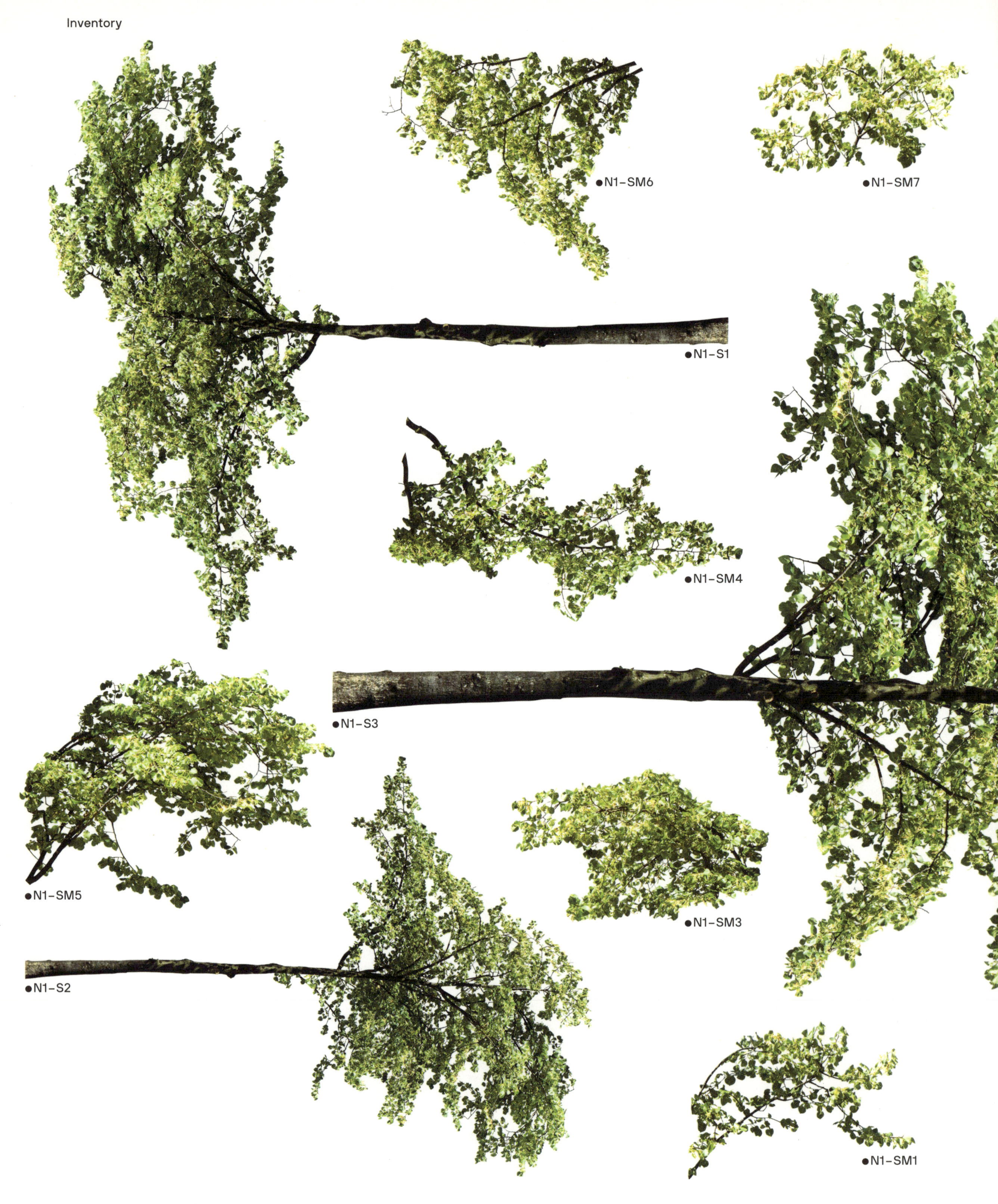

●N1–SM6
●N1–SM7
●N1–S1
●N1–SM4
●N1–S3
●N1–SM5
●N1–SM3
●N1–S2
●N1–SM1

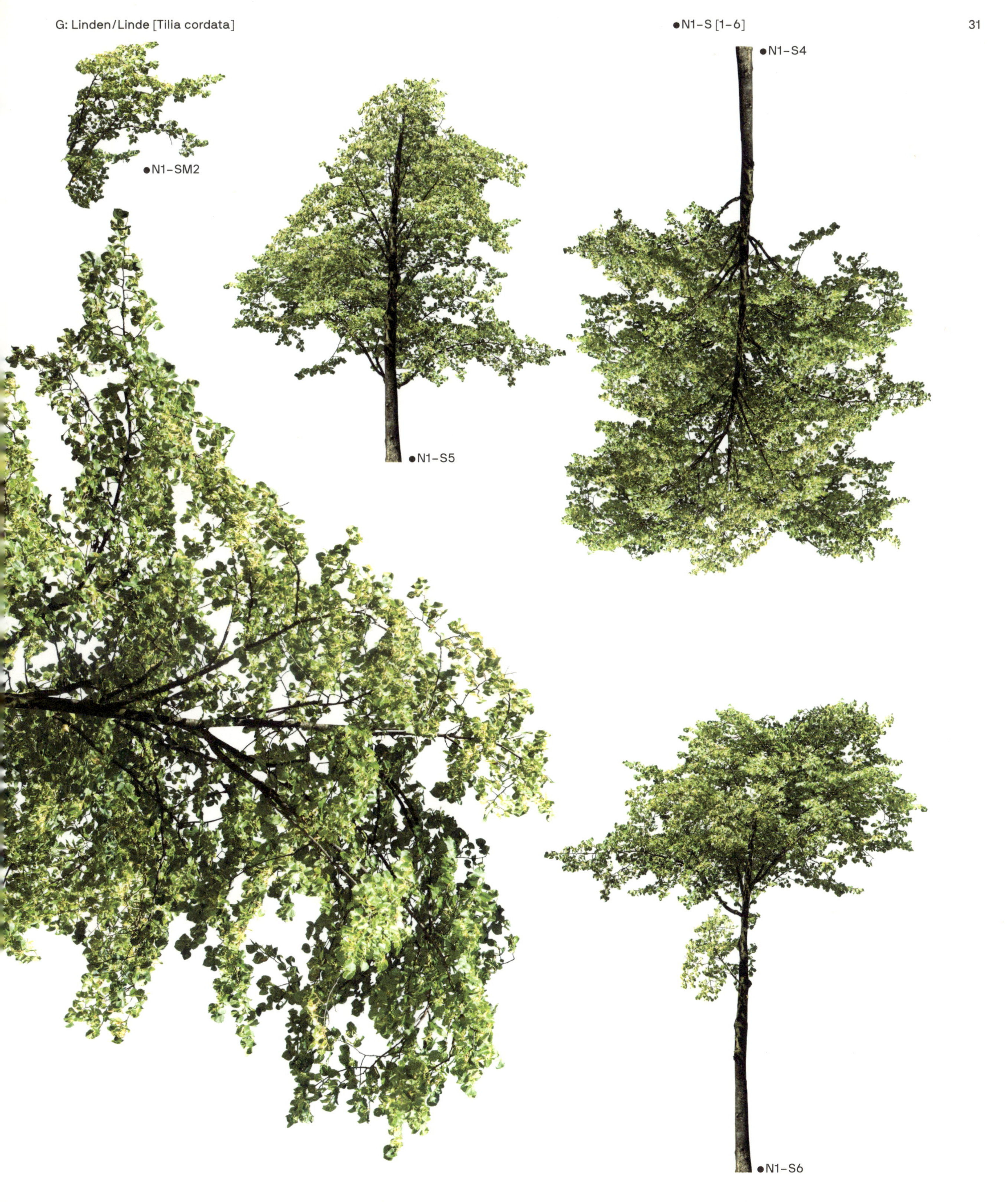

●N1–SM2
●N1–S5
●N1–S [1–6]
●N1–S4
●N1–S6

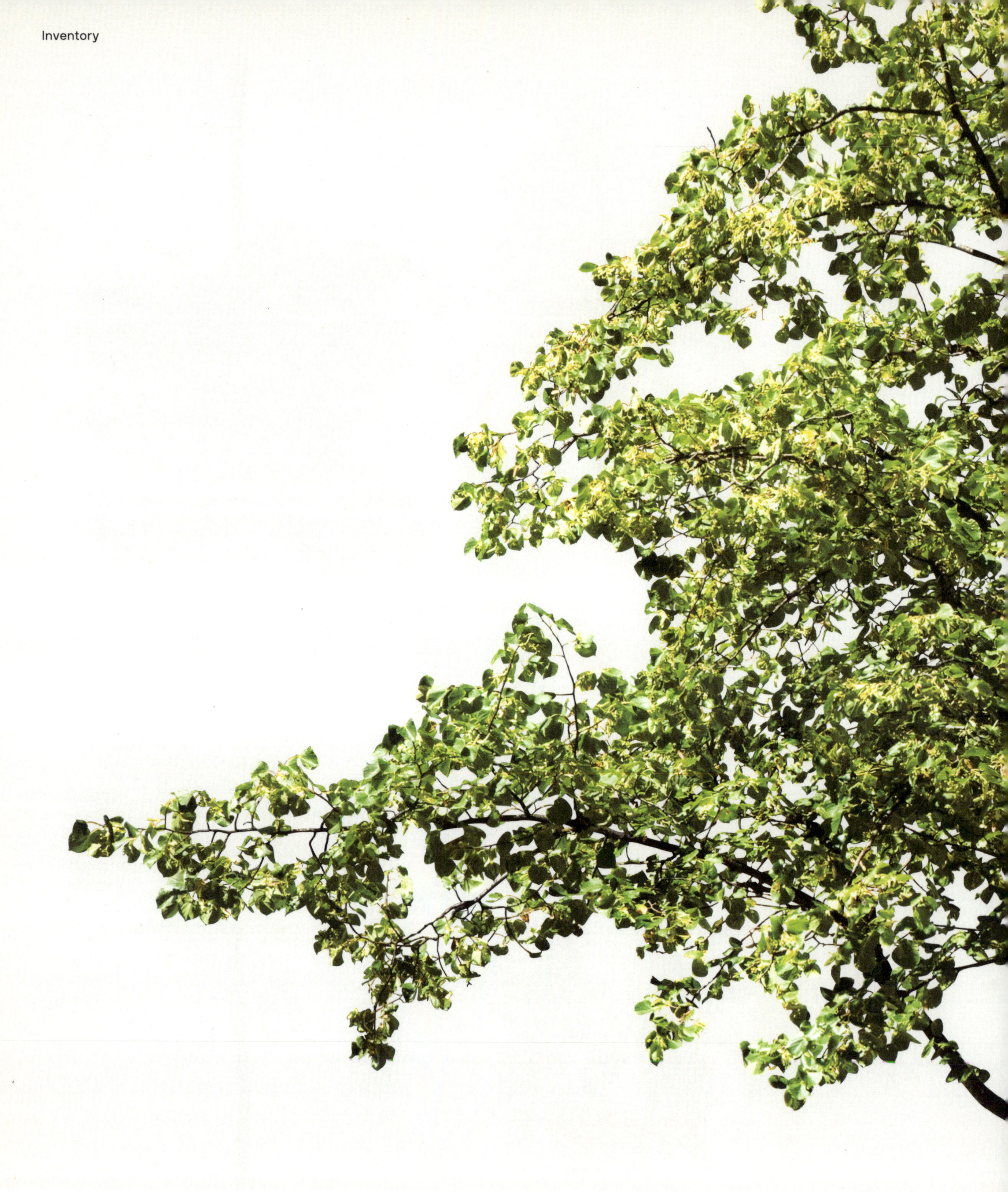

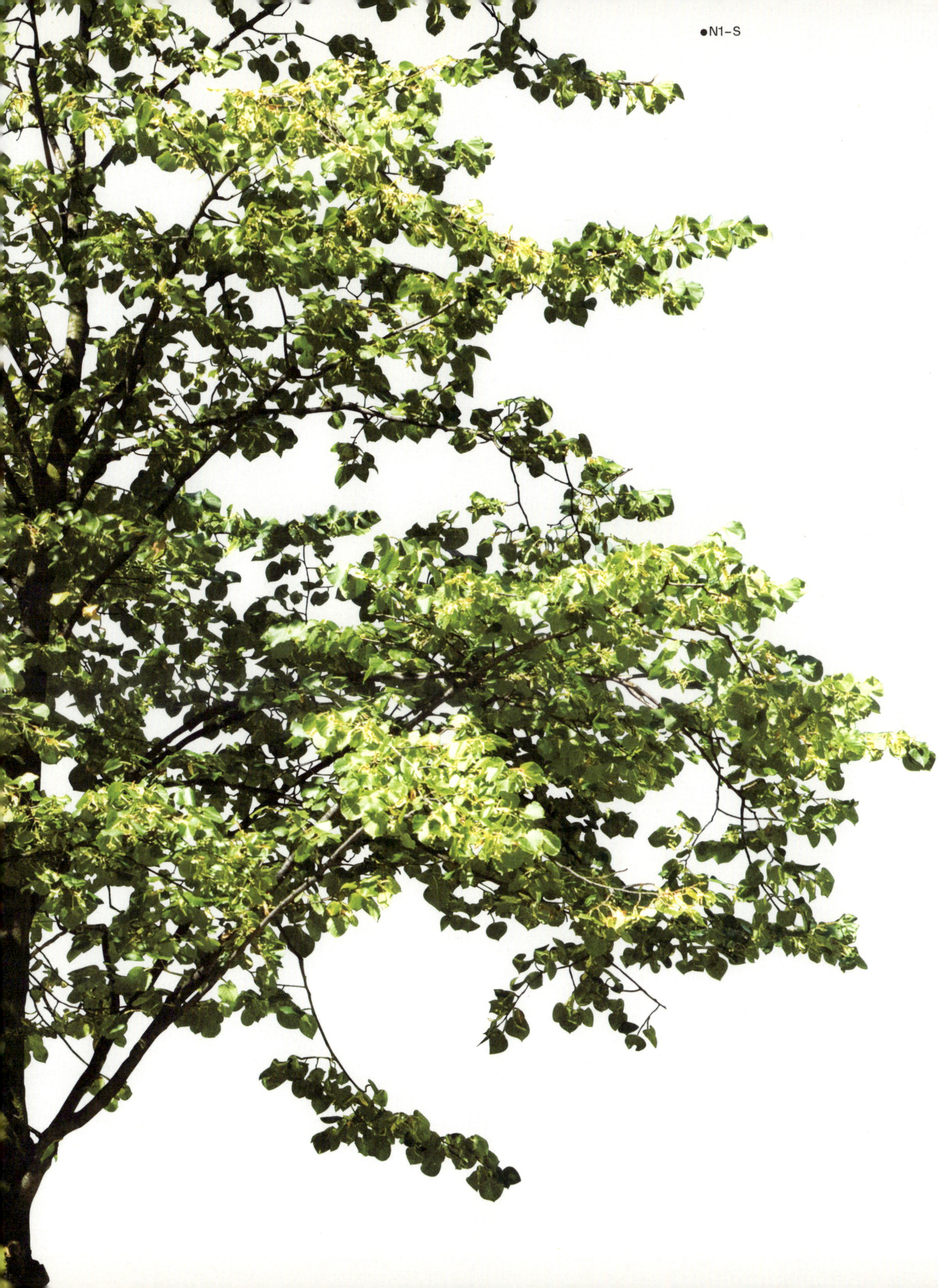

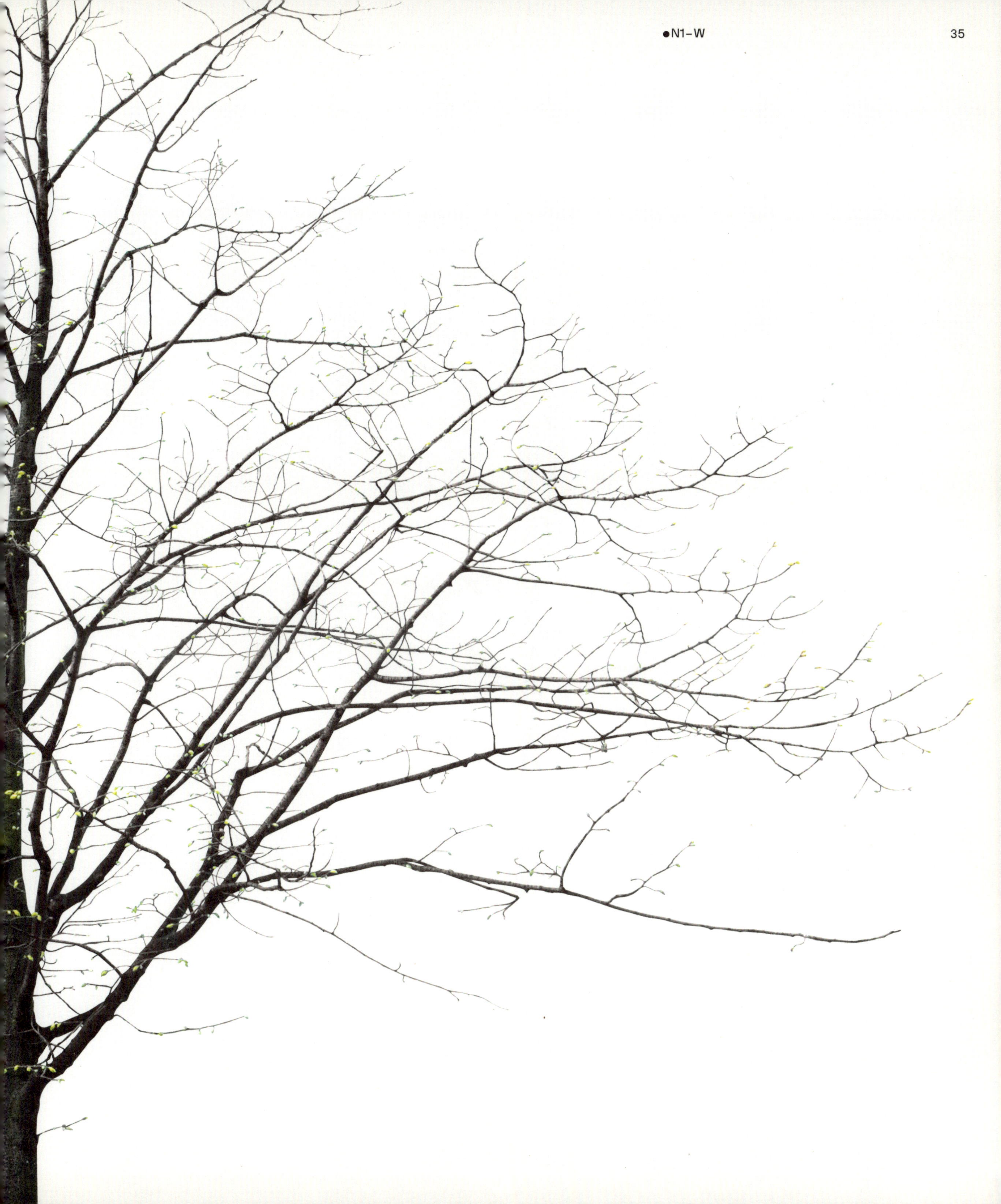

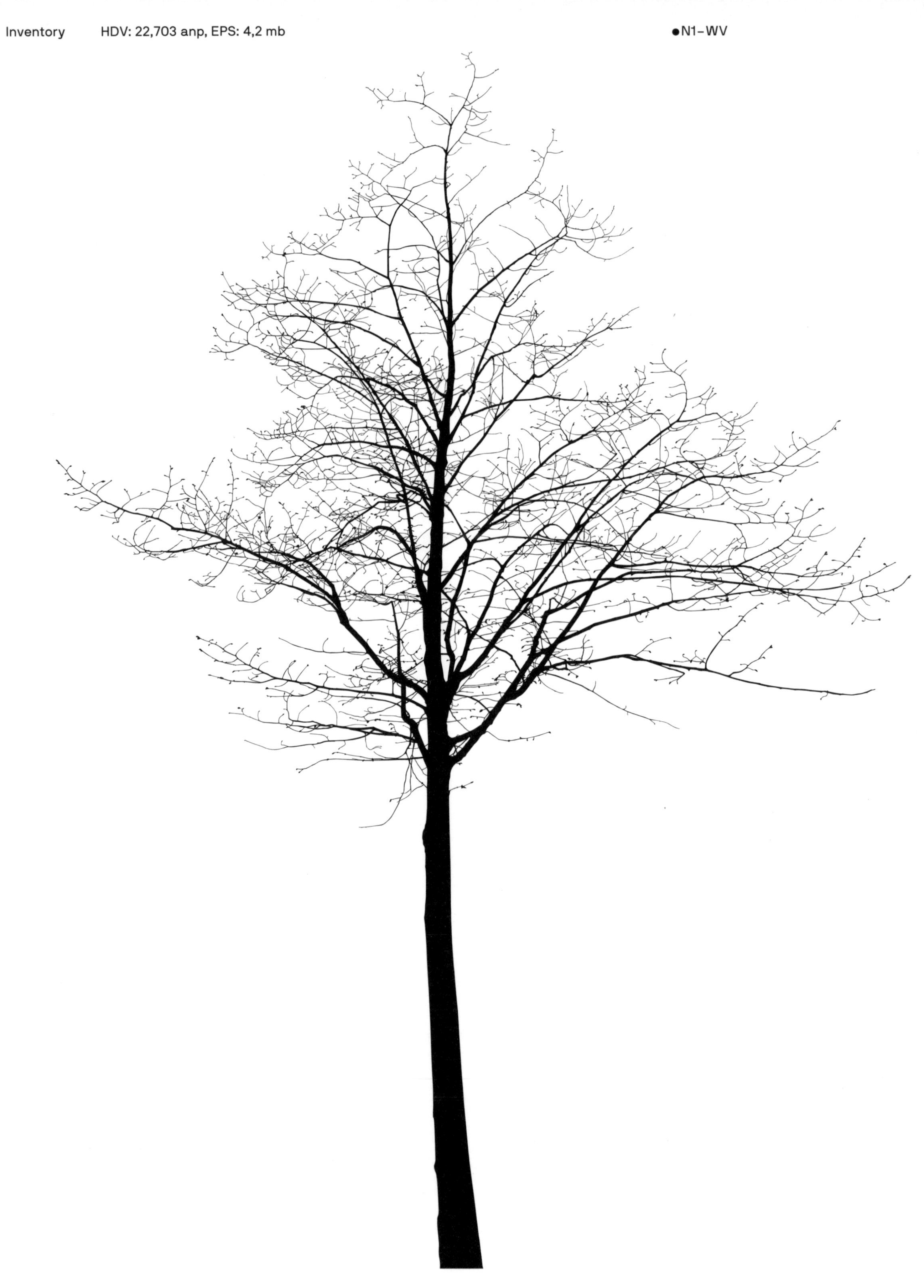

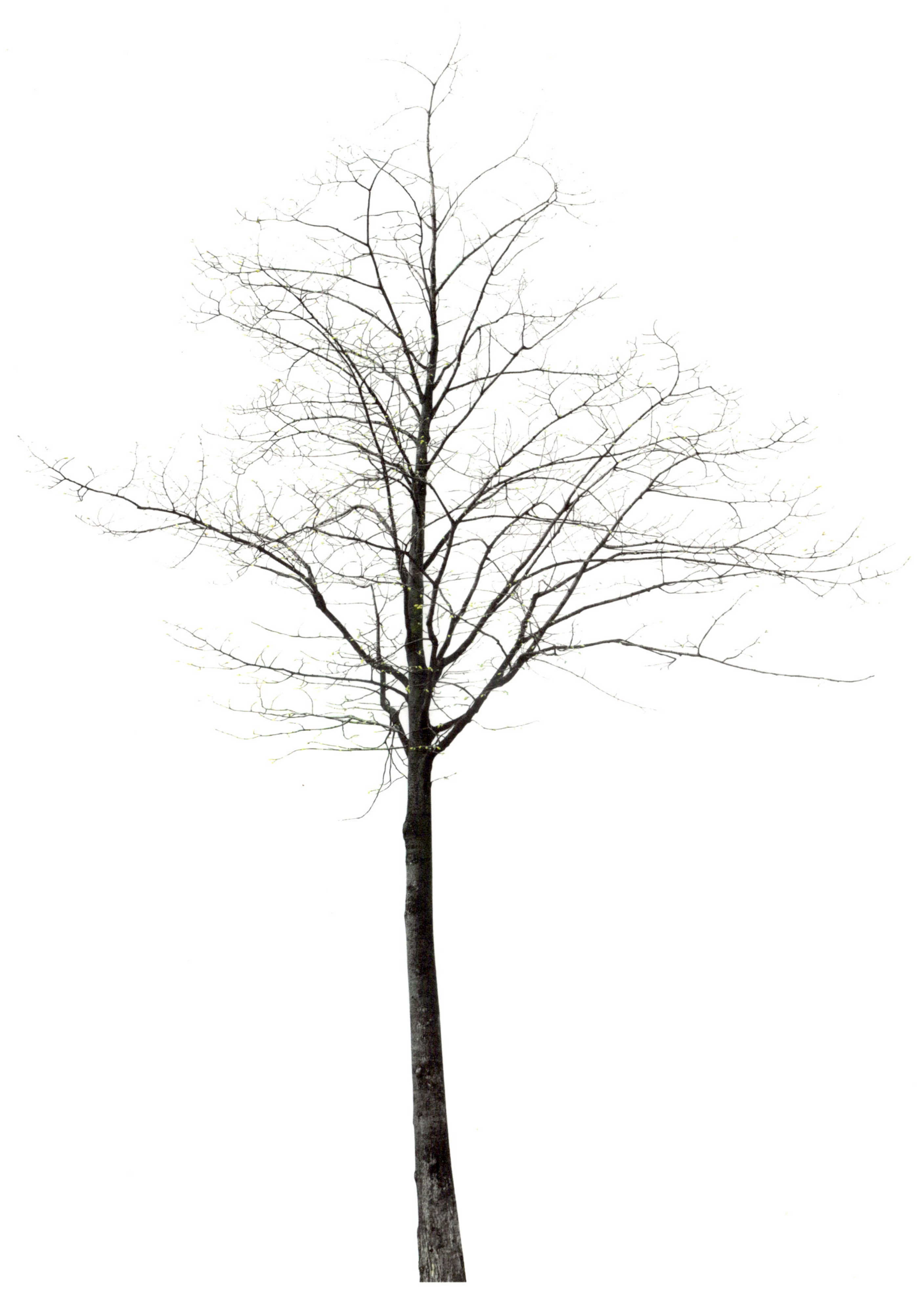

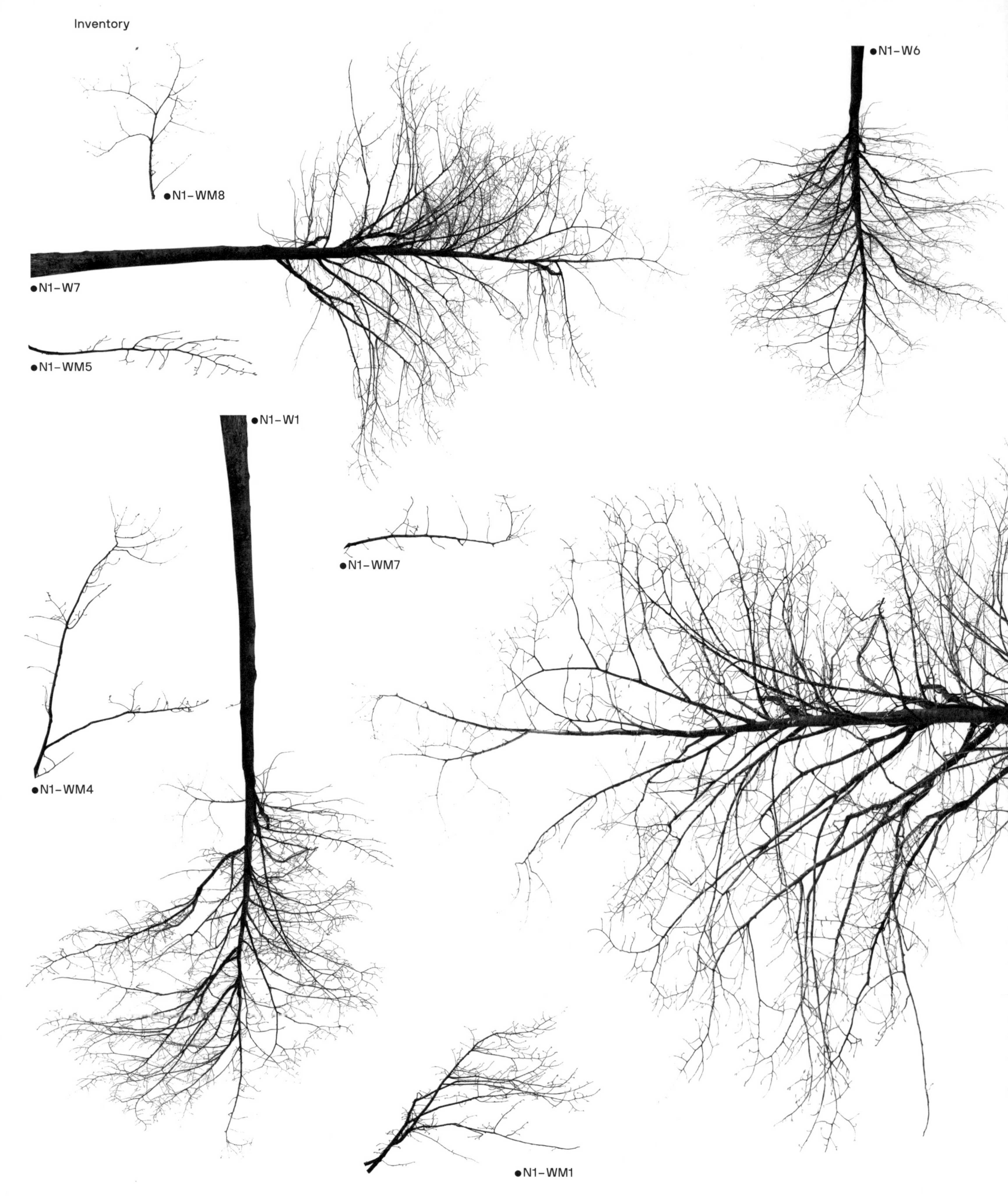

●N1–WM8
●N1–W7
●N1–WM5
●N1–W6
●N1–W1
●N1–WM7
●N1–WM4
●N1–WM1

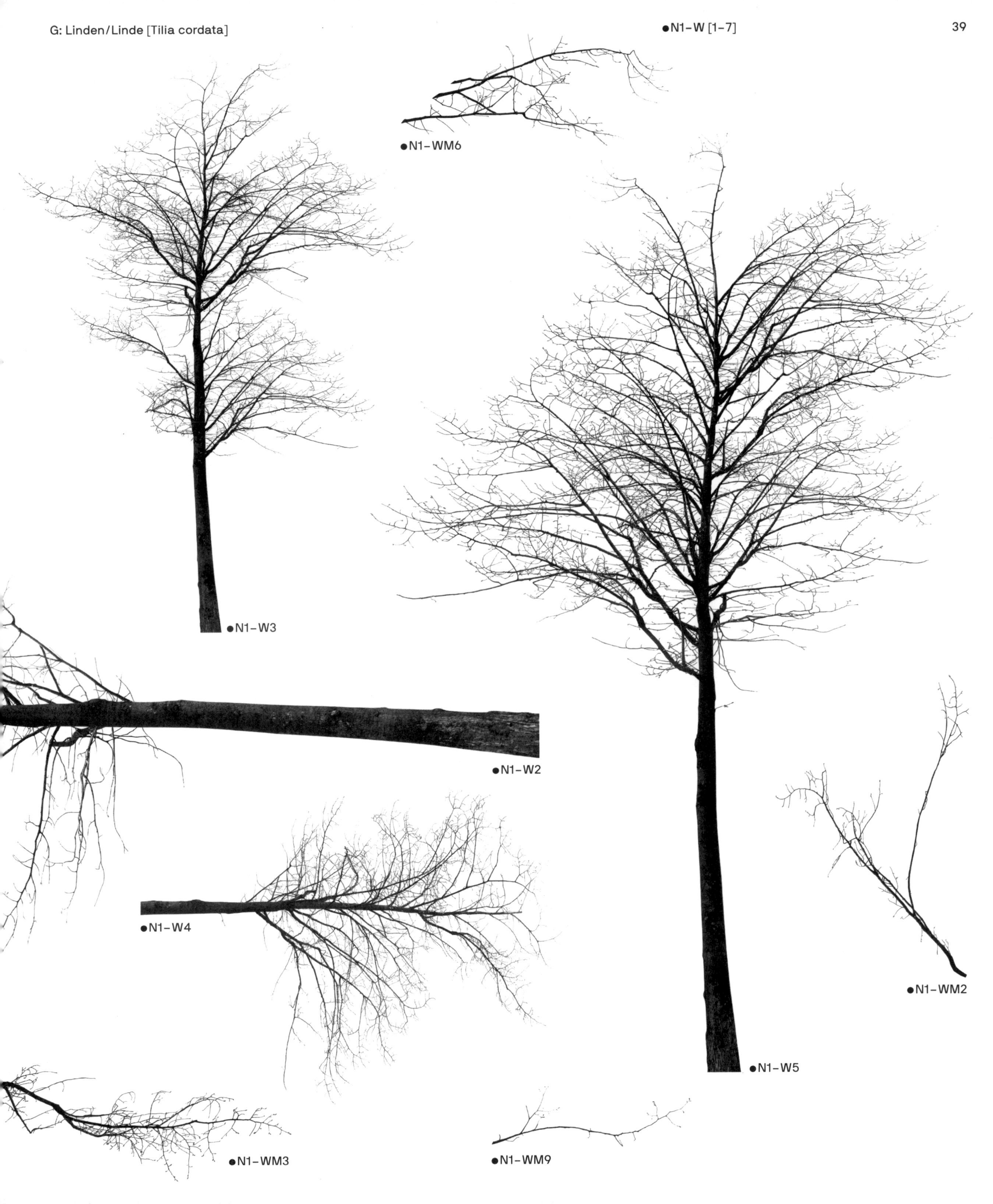
●N1–W [1–7]
●N1–WM6
●N1–W3
●N1–W2
●N1–W4
●N1–WM2
●N1–W5
●N1–WM3
●N1–WM9

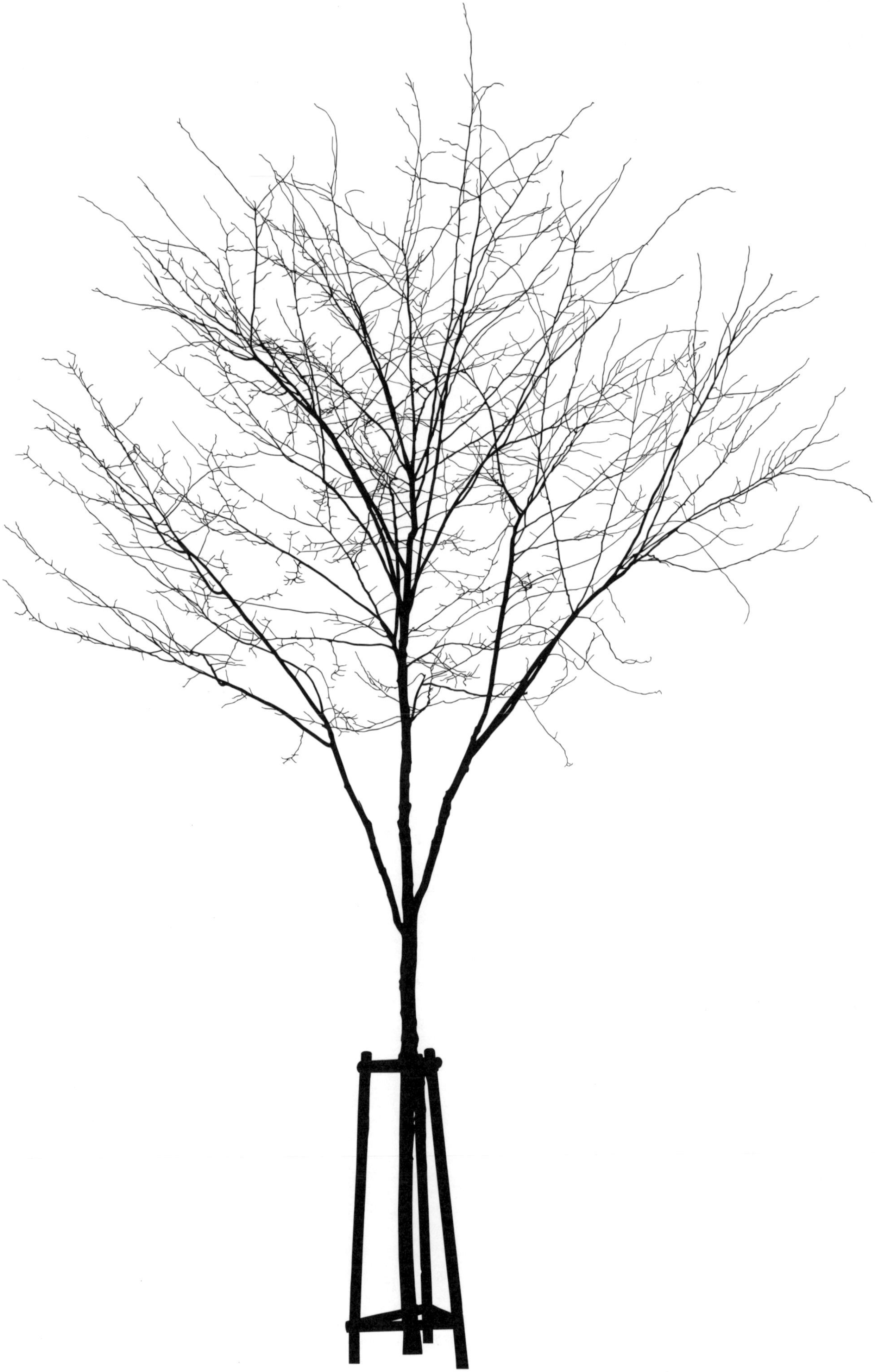

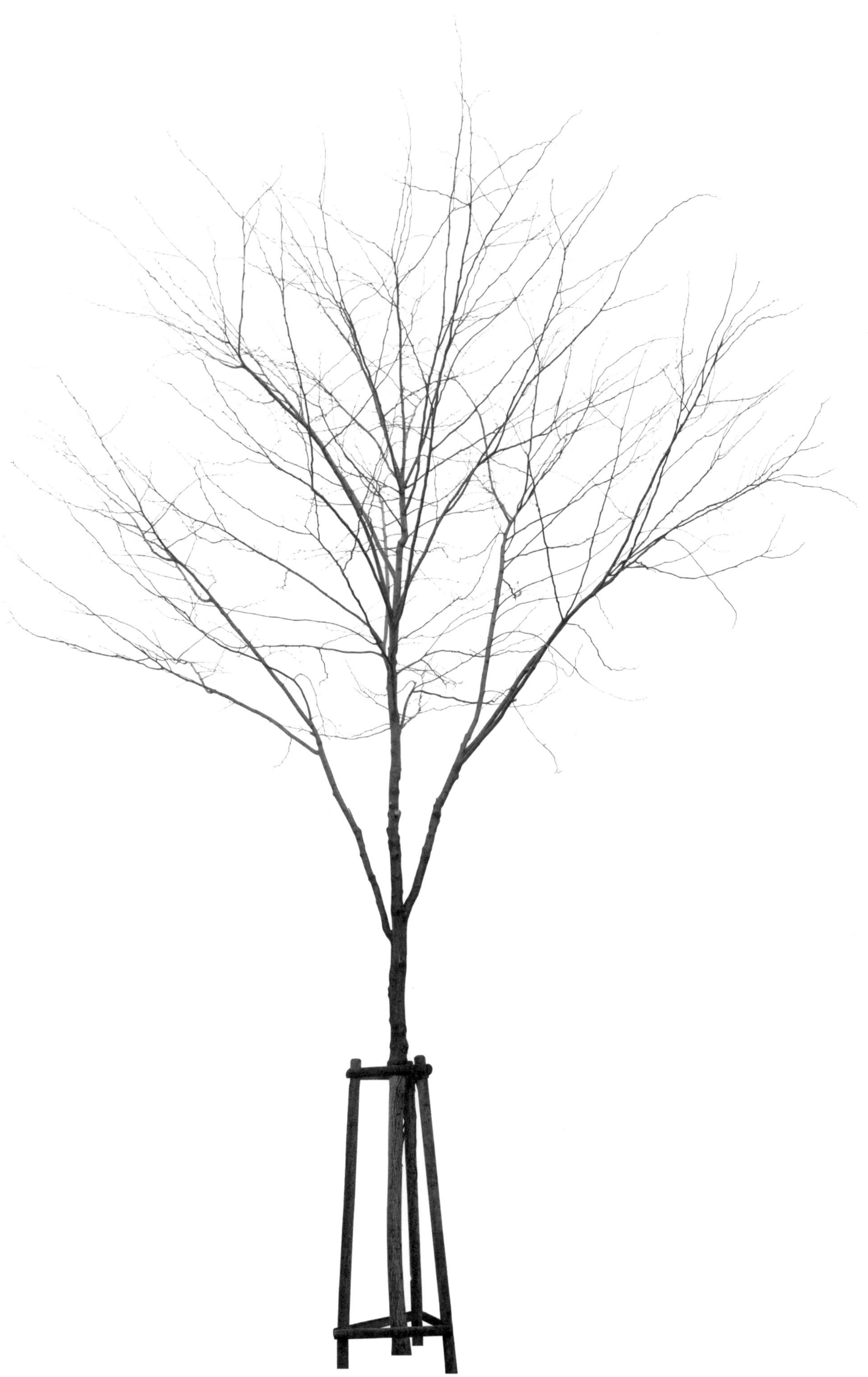

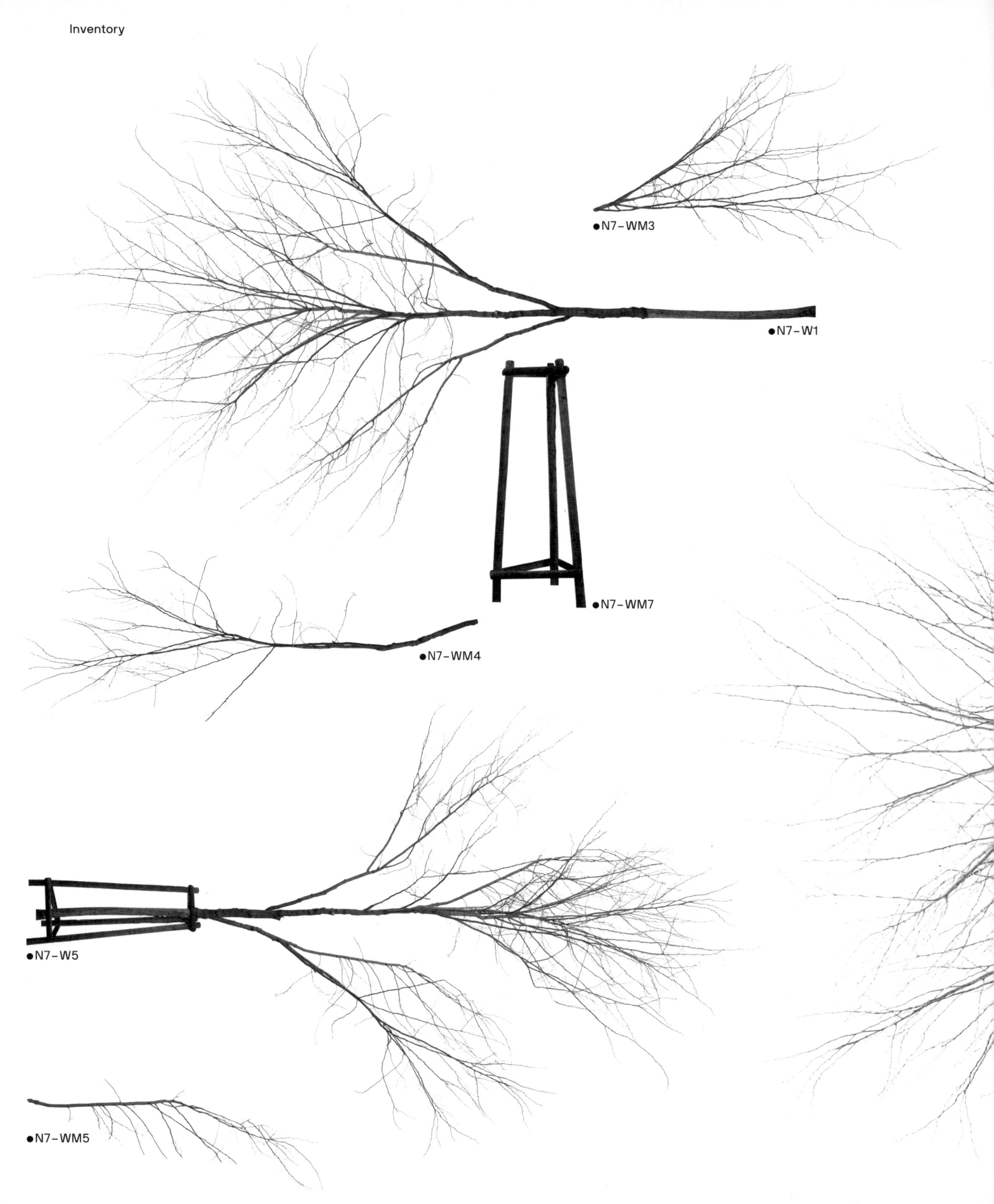
●N7–WM3
●N7–W1
●N7–WM7
●N7–WM4
●N7–W5
●N7–WM5

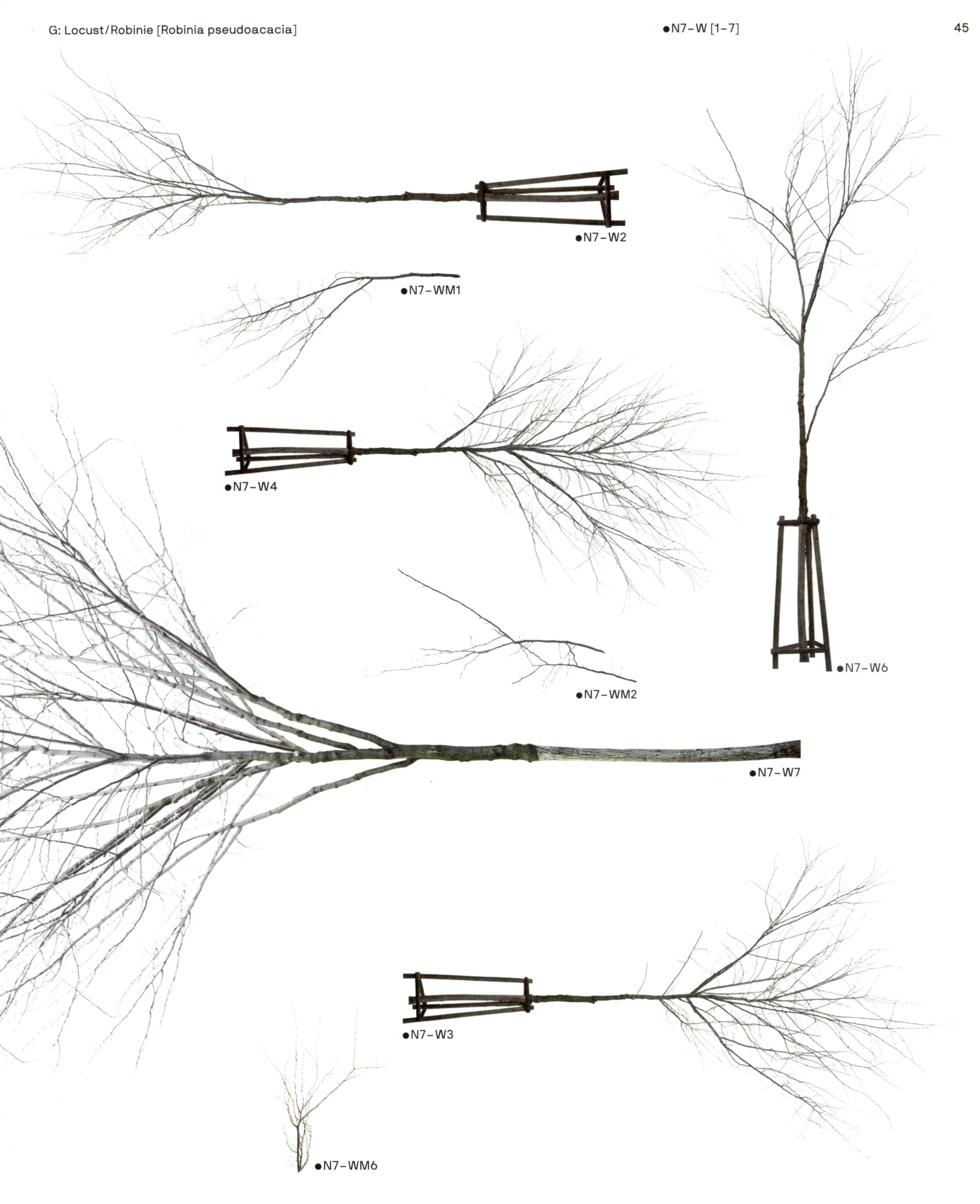

●N7–W2
●N7–WM1
●N7–W4
●N7–W6
●N7–WM2
●N7–W7
●N7–W3
●N7–WM6

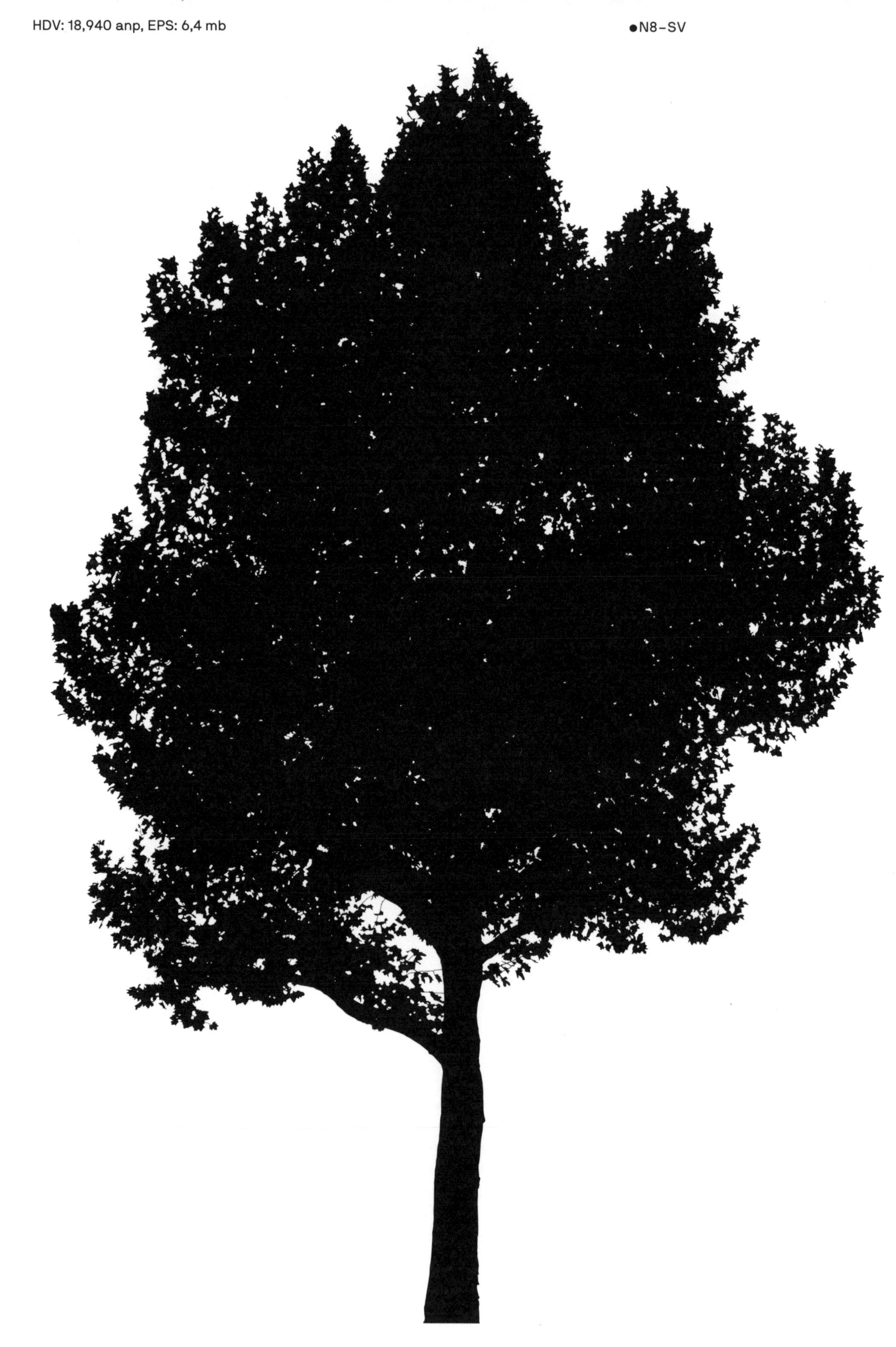

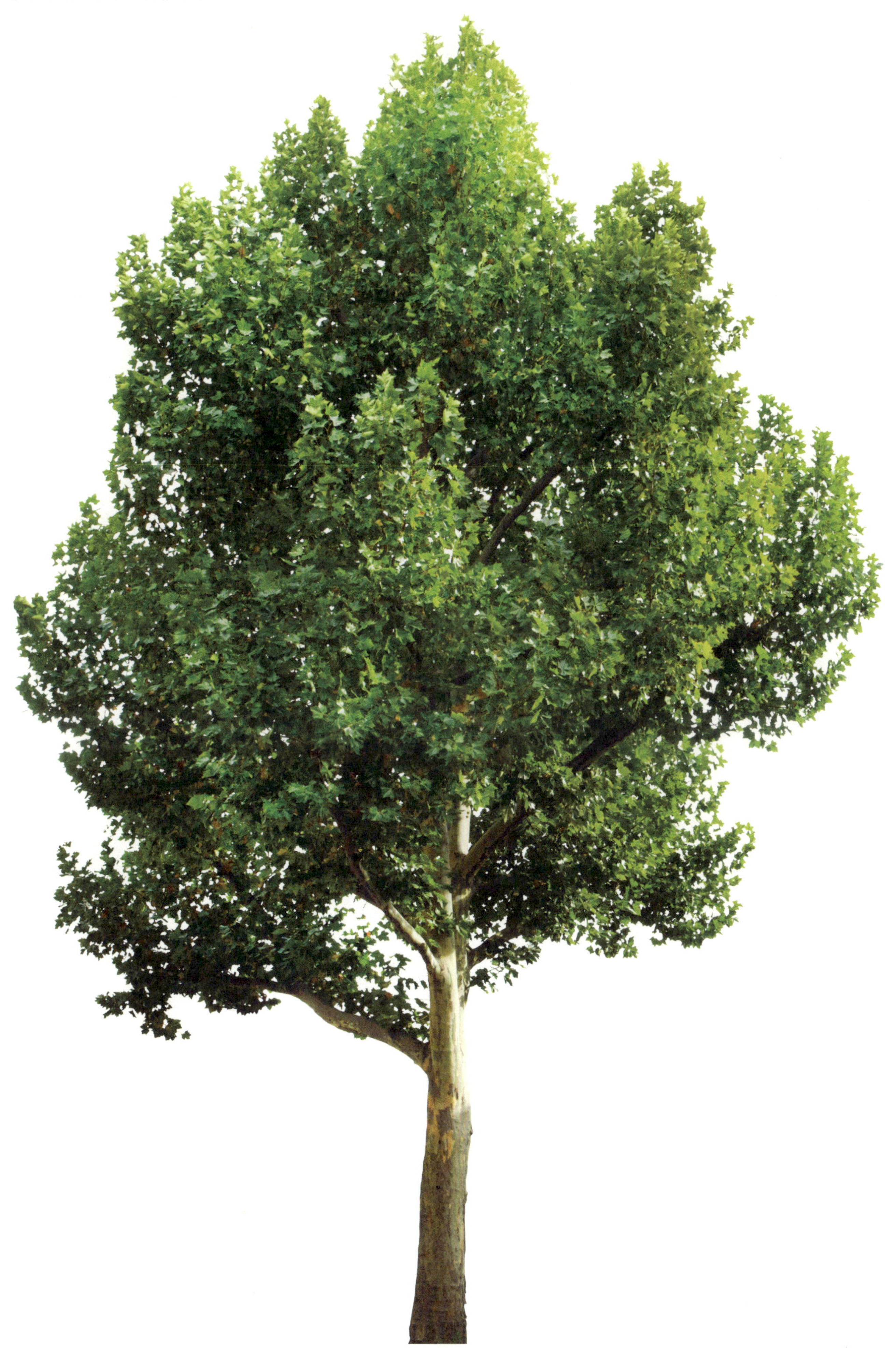

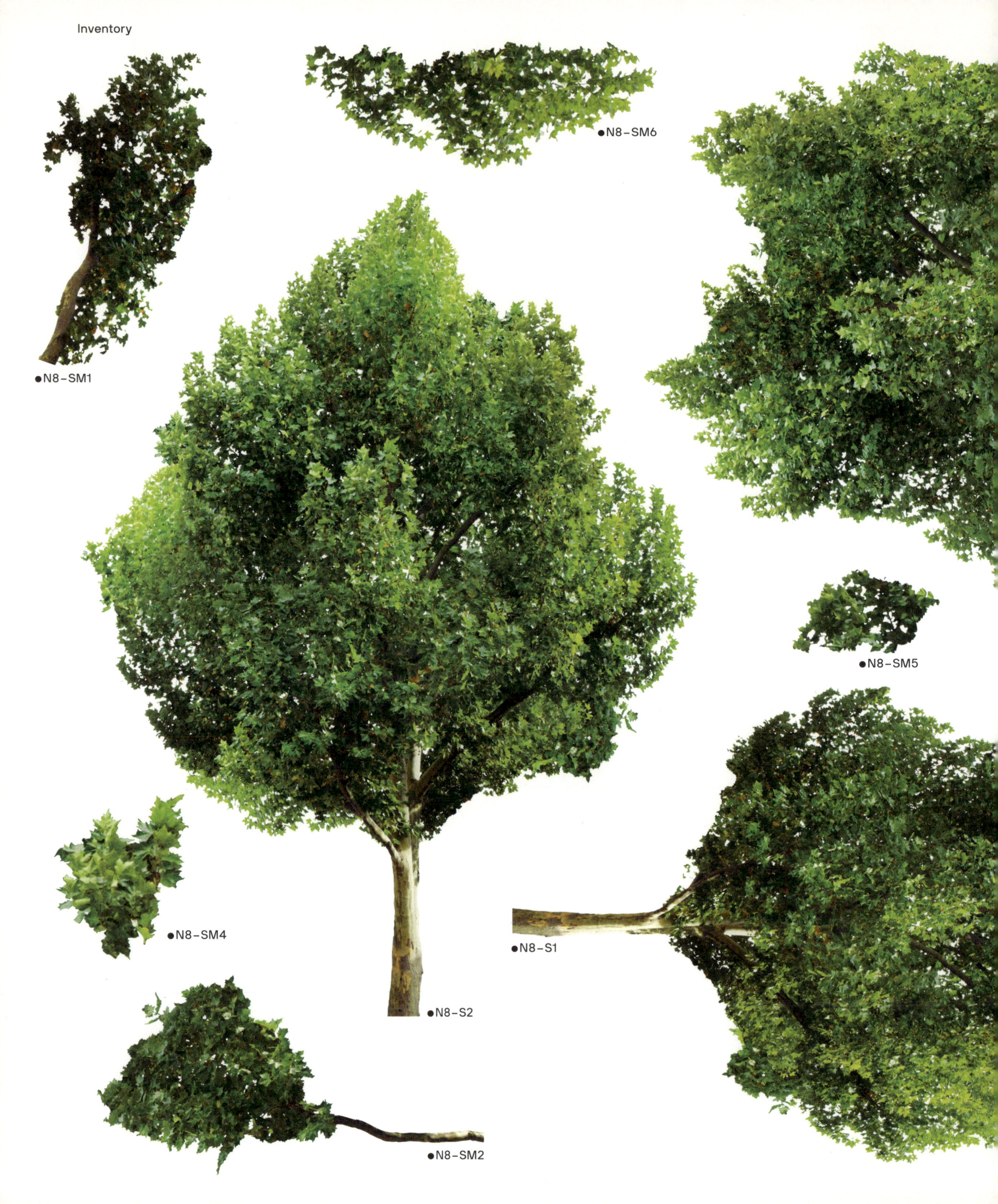

Inventory
●N8–SM6
●N8–SM1
●N8–SM5
●N8–SM4
●N8–S1
●N8–S2
●N8–SM2

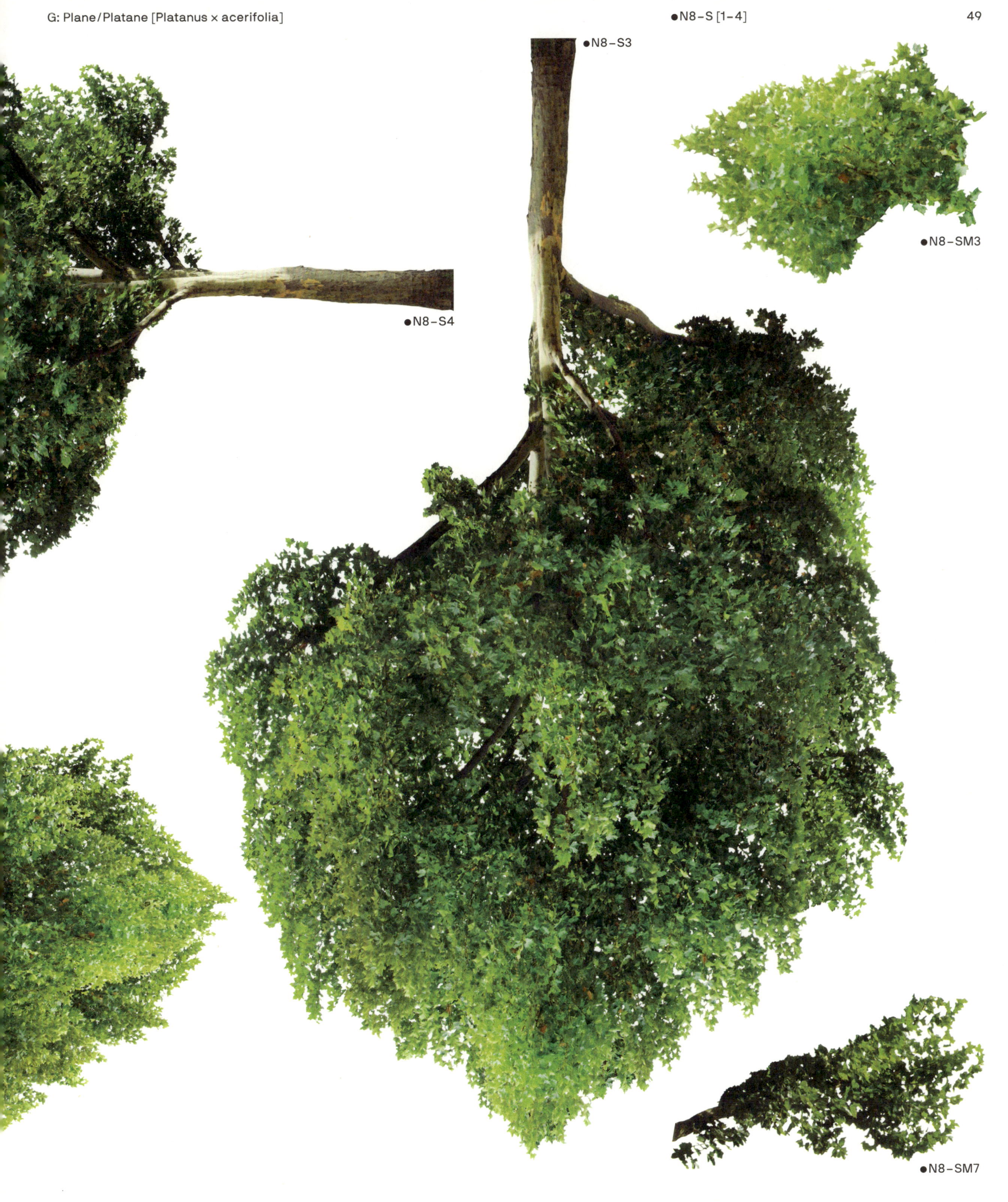
●N8–S3
●N8–S4
●N8–SM3
●N8–SM7

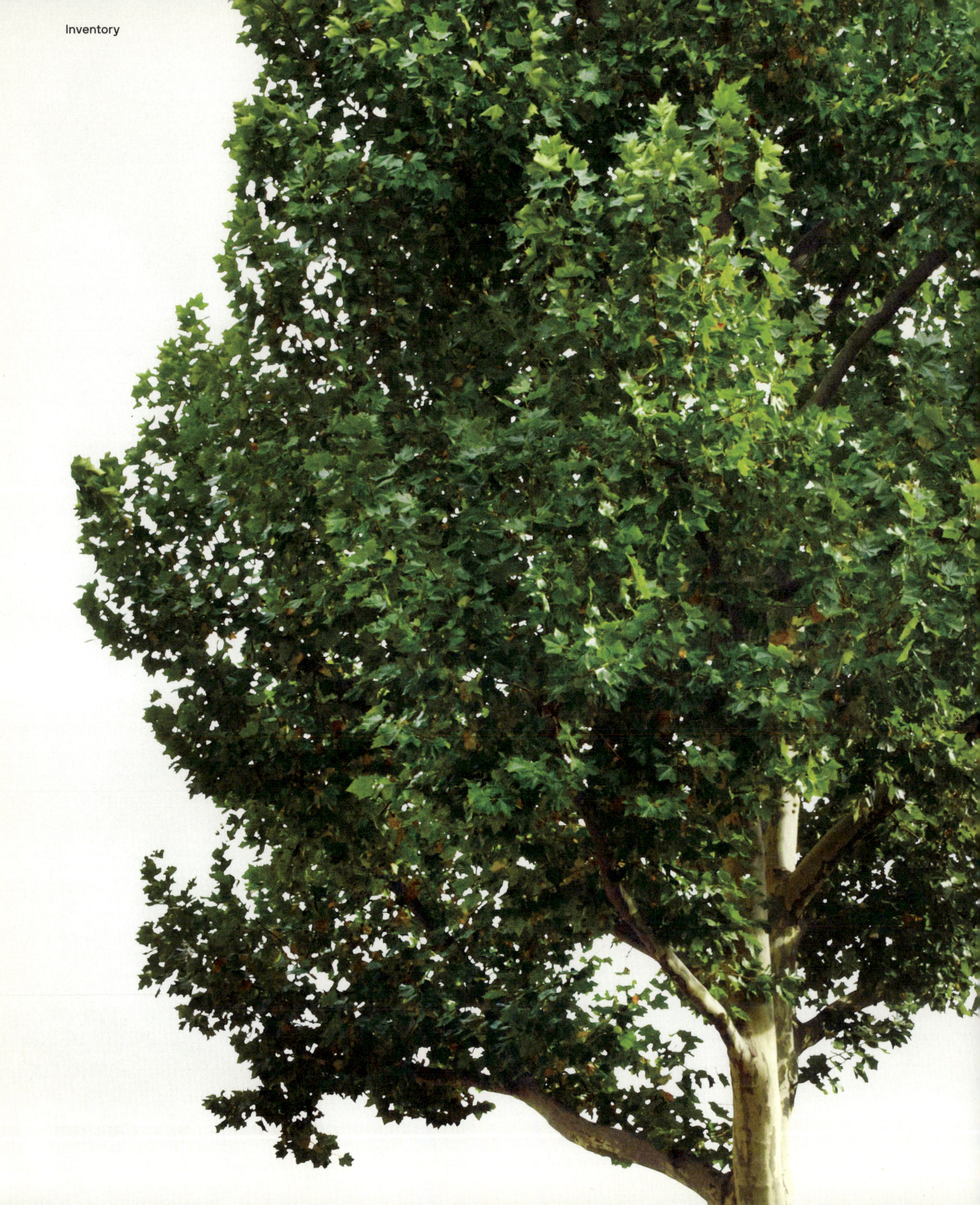

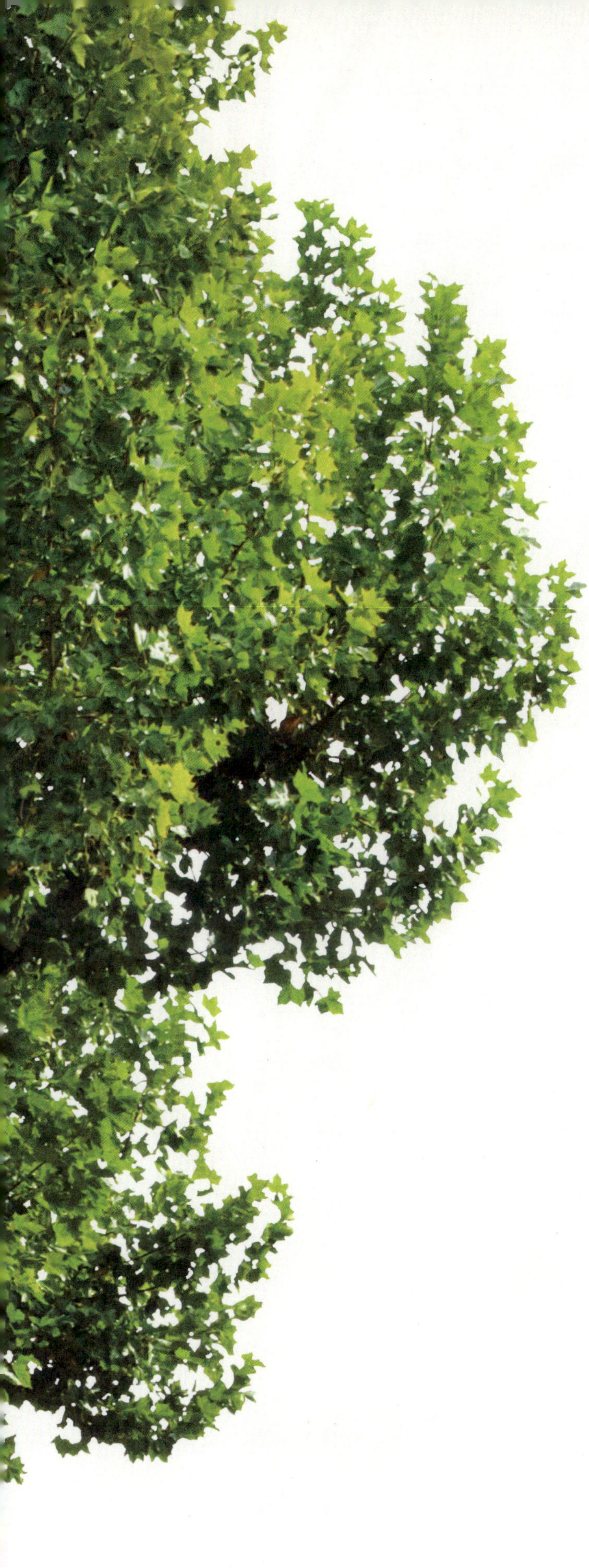

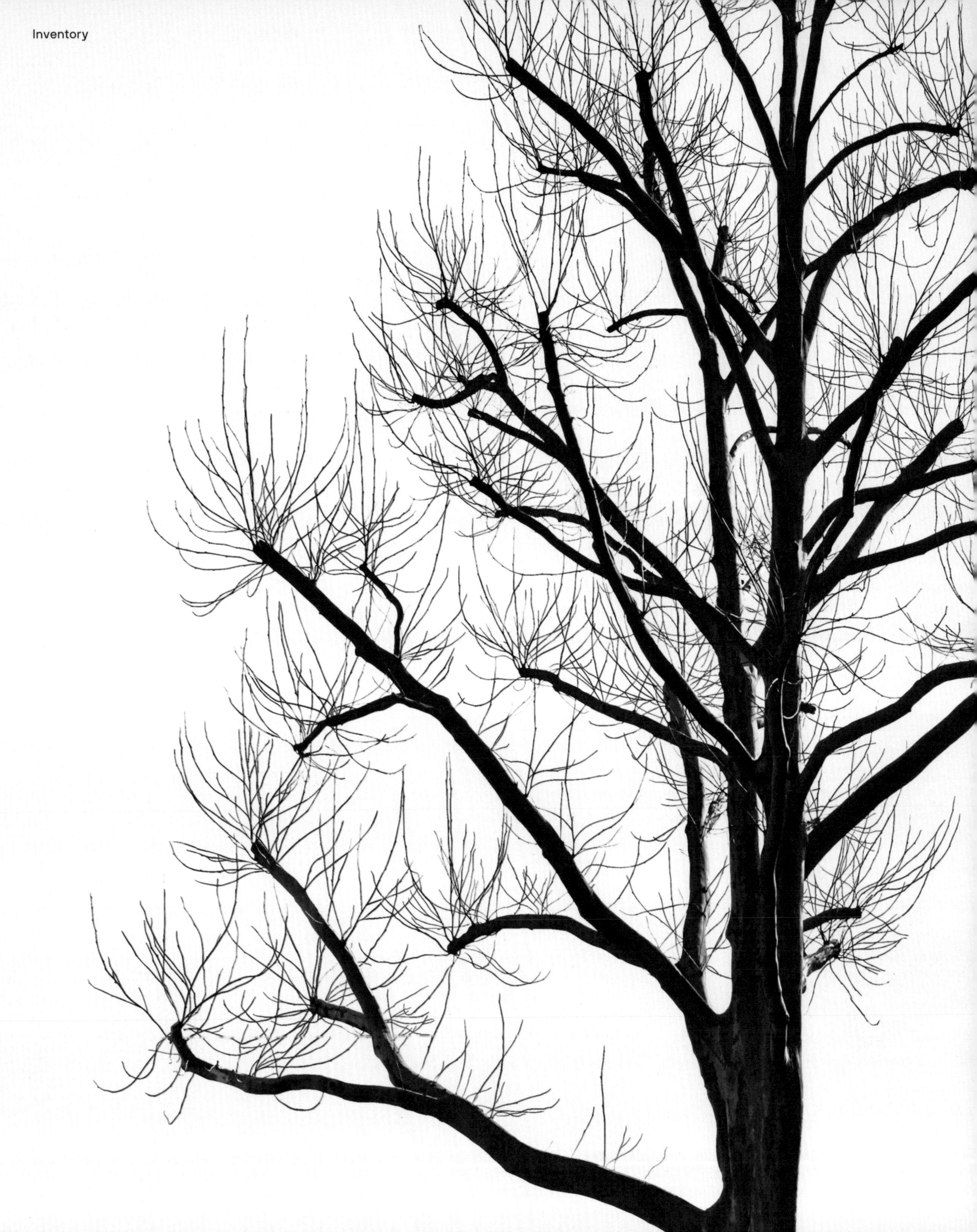

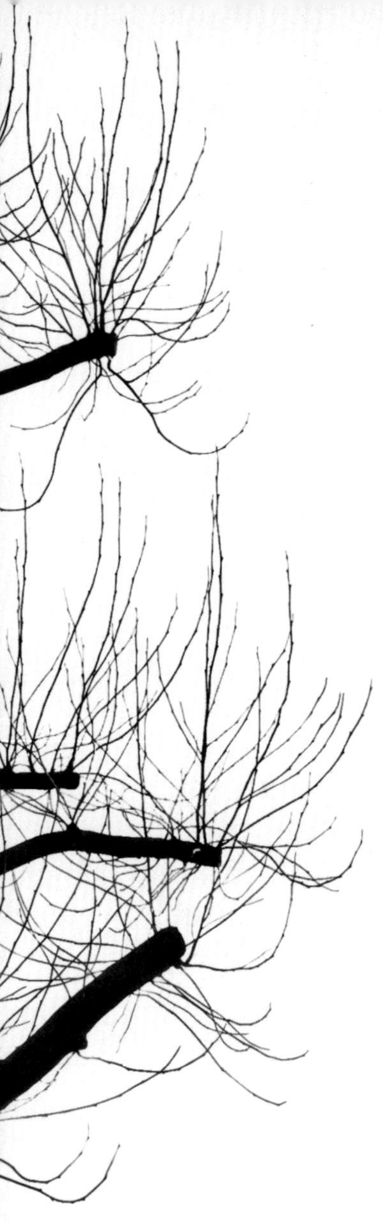

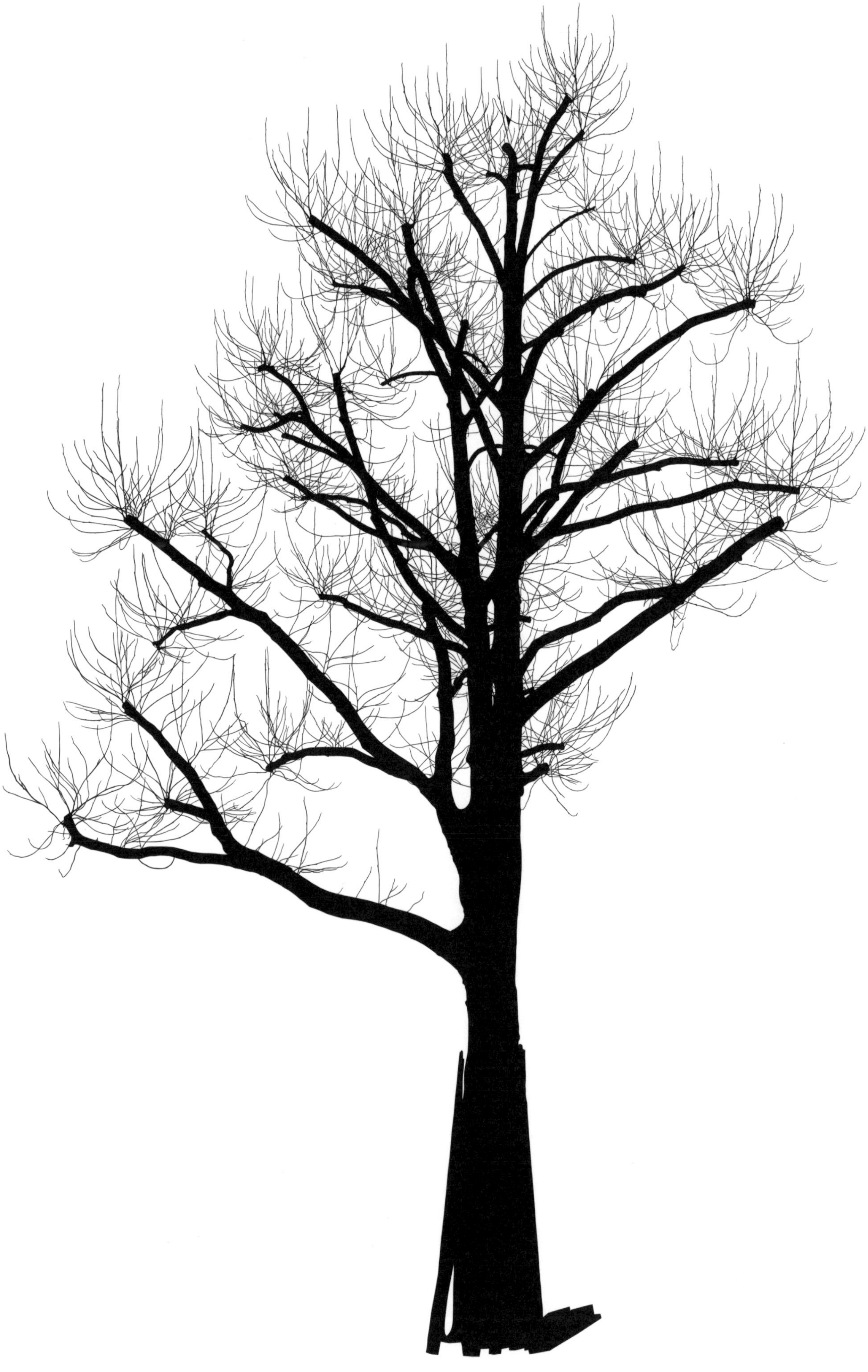

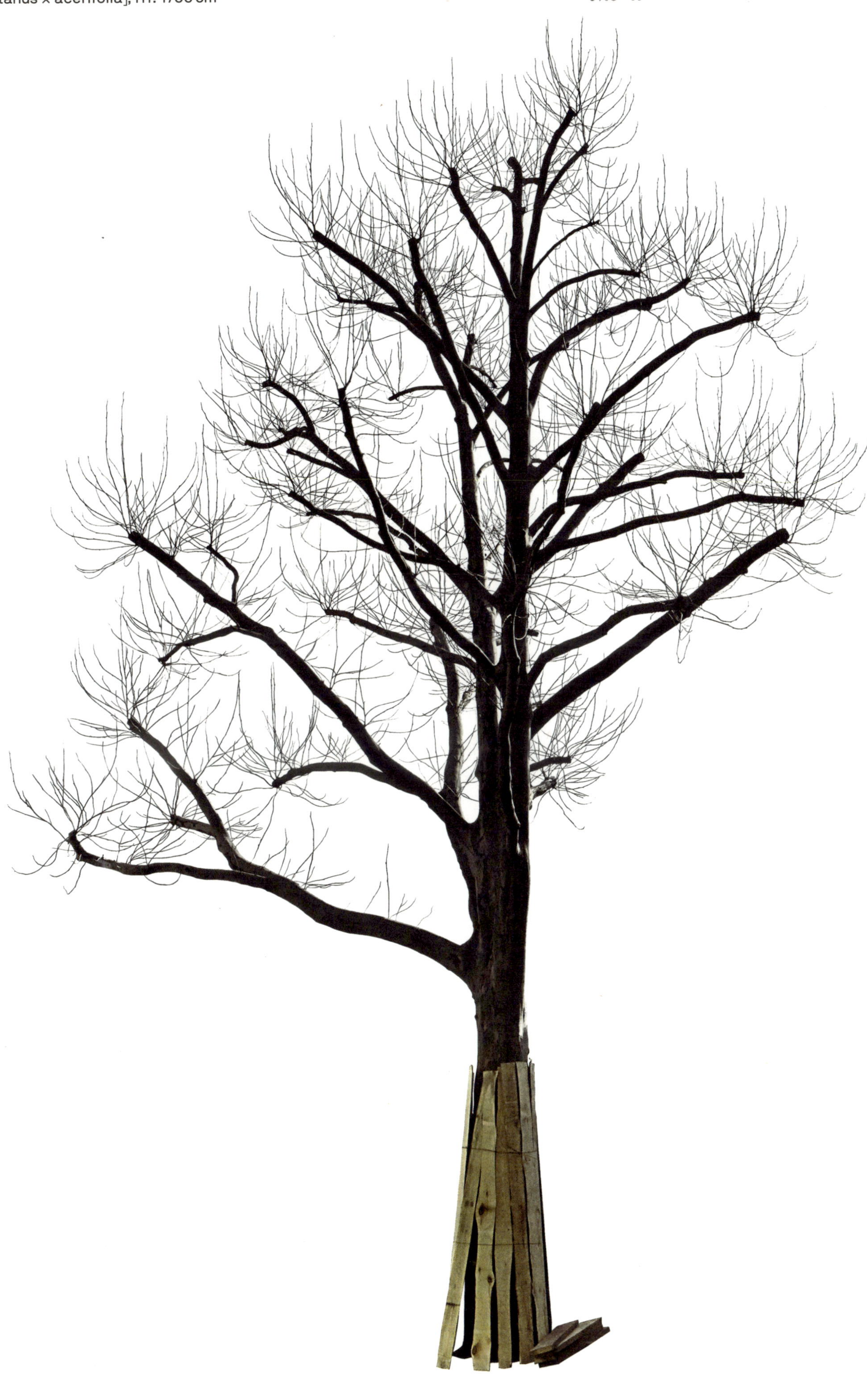

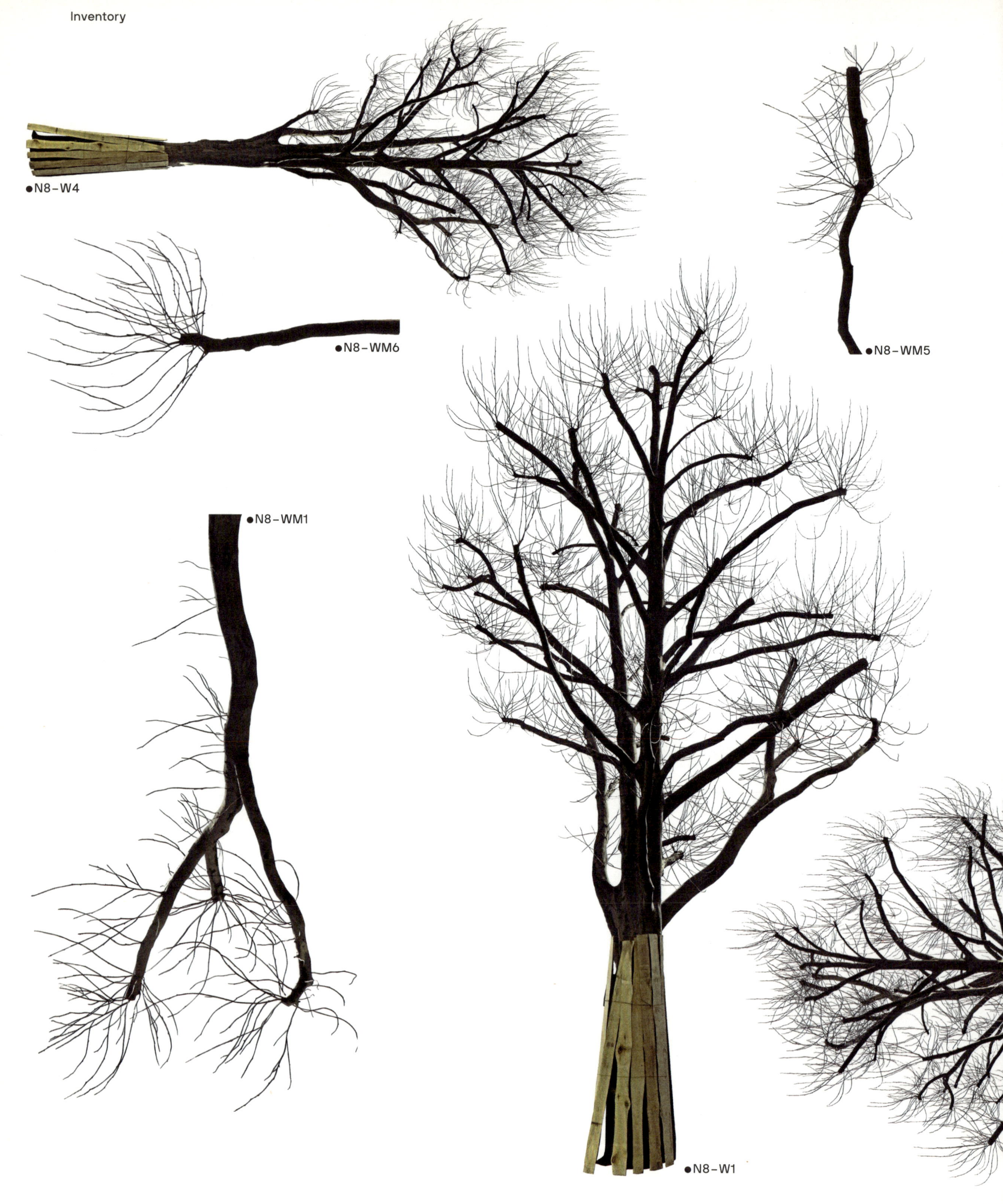
•N8–W4
•N8–WM6
•N8–WM5
•N8–WM1
•N8–W1

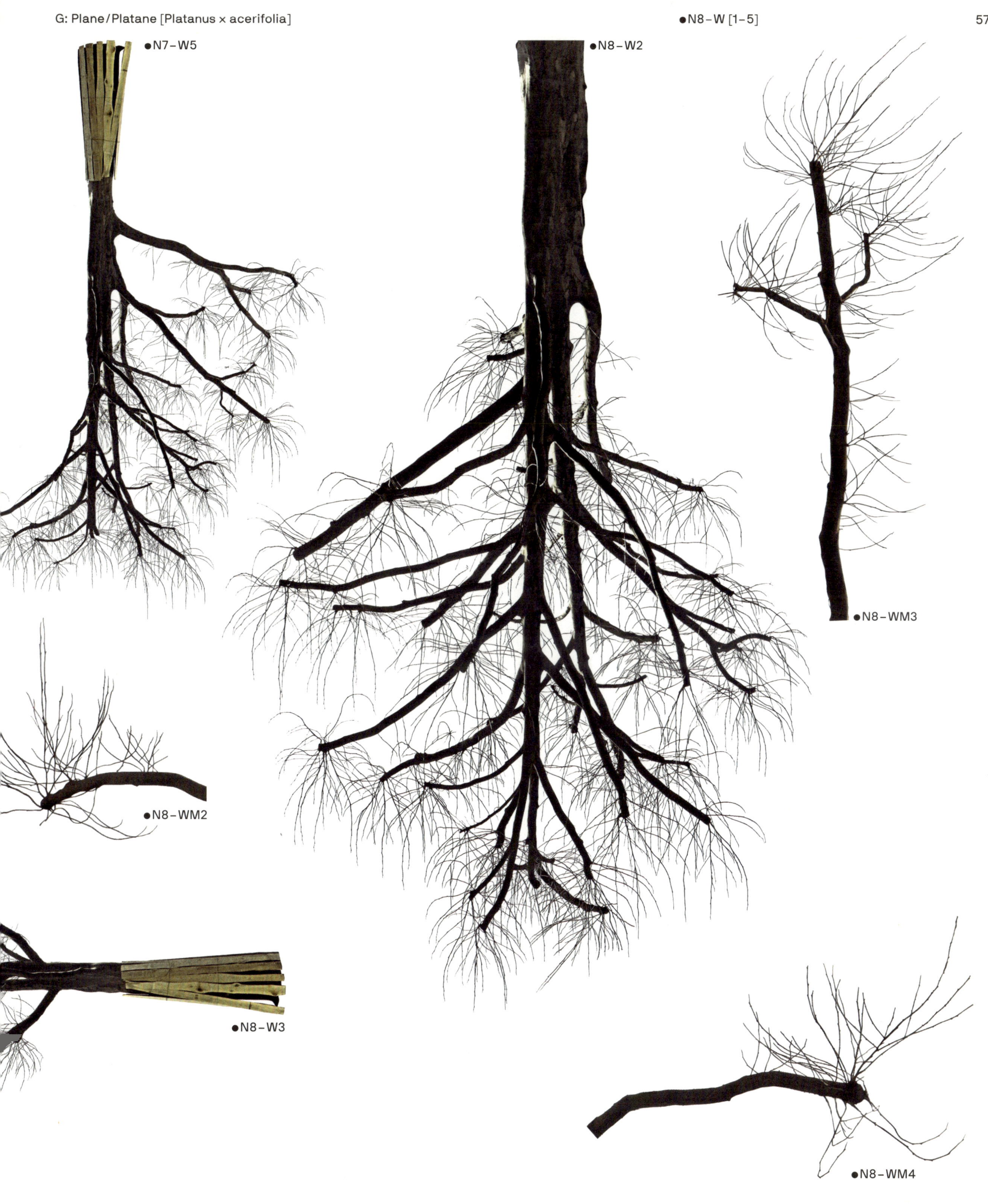
●N7–W5
●N8–W2
●N8–WM3
●N8–WM2
●N8–W3
●N8–WM4

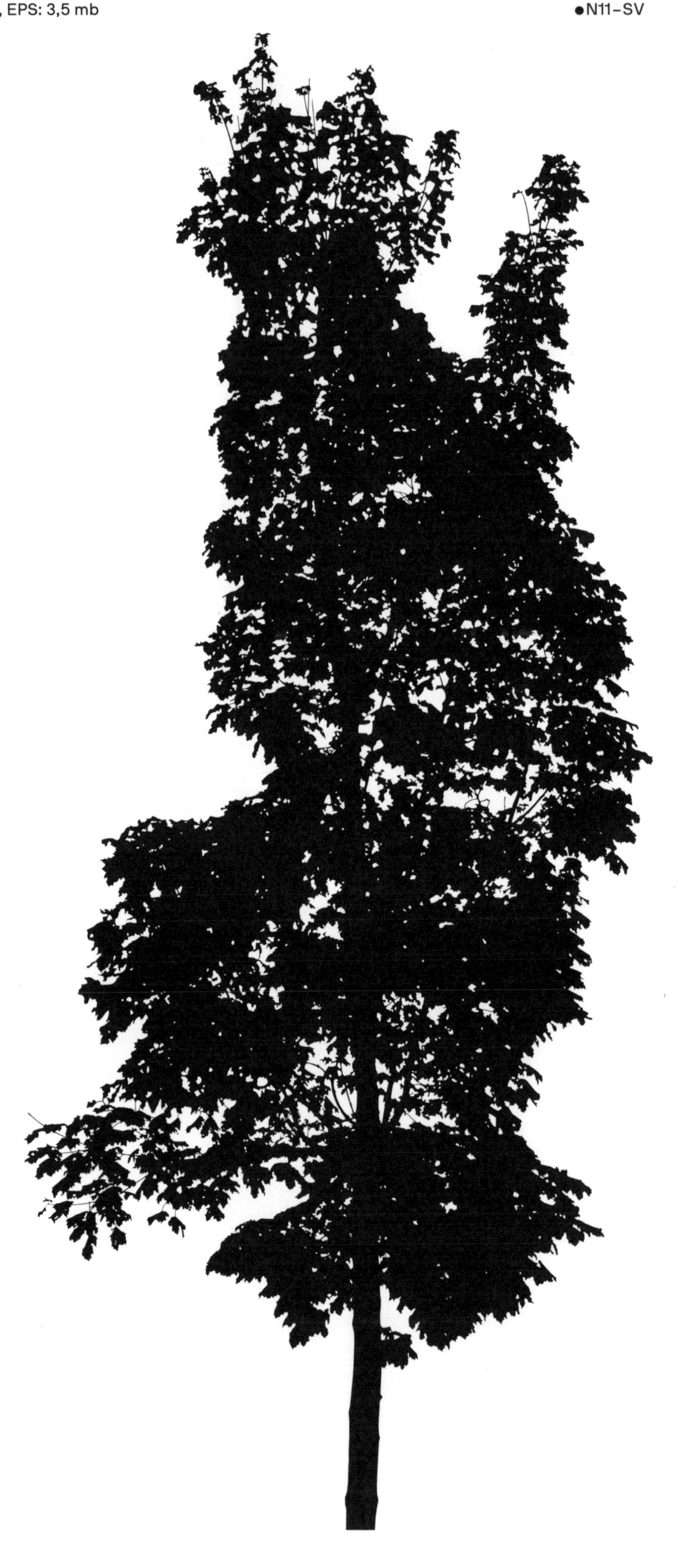

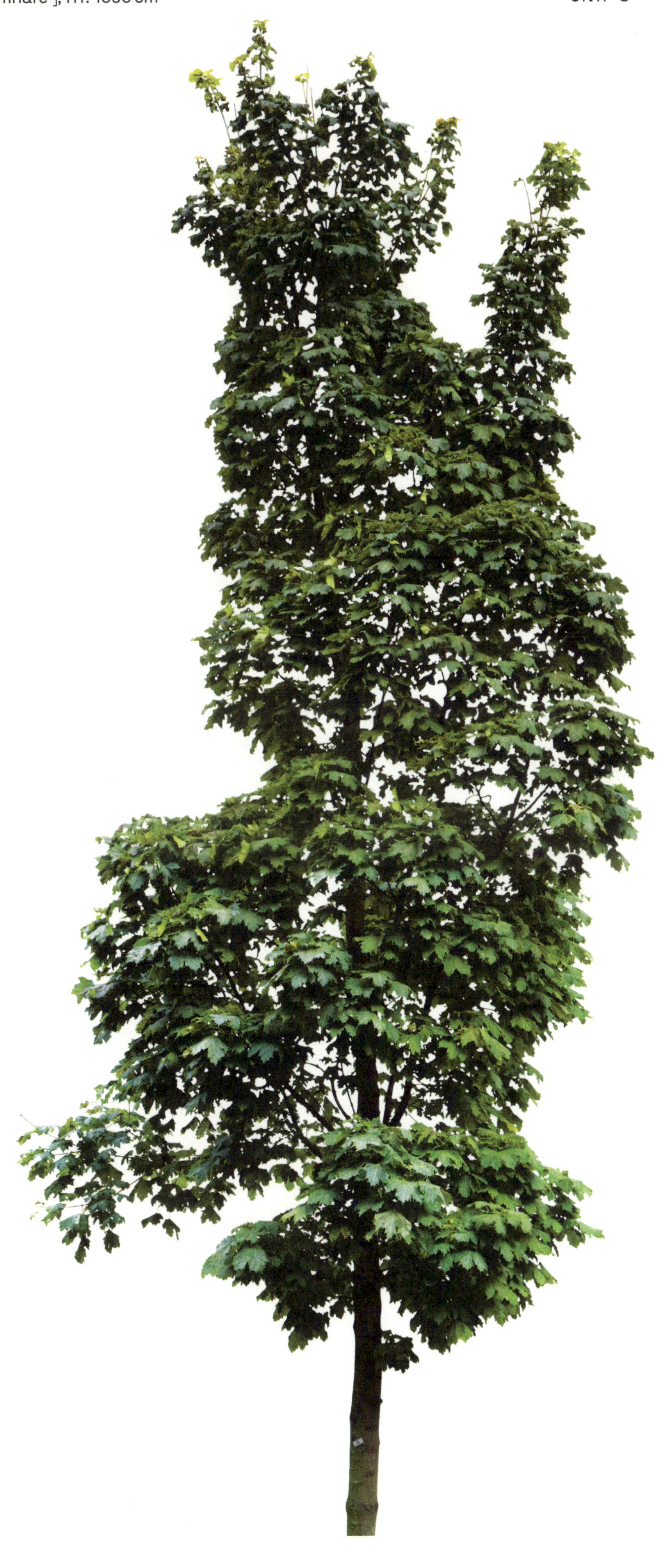

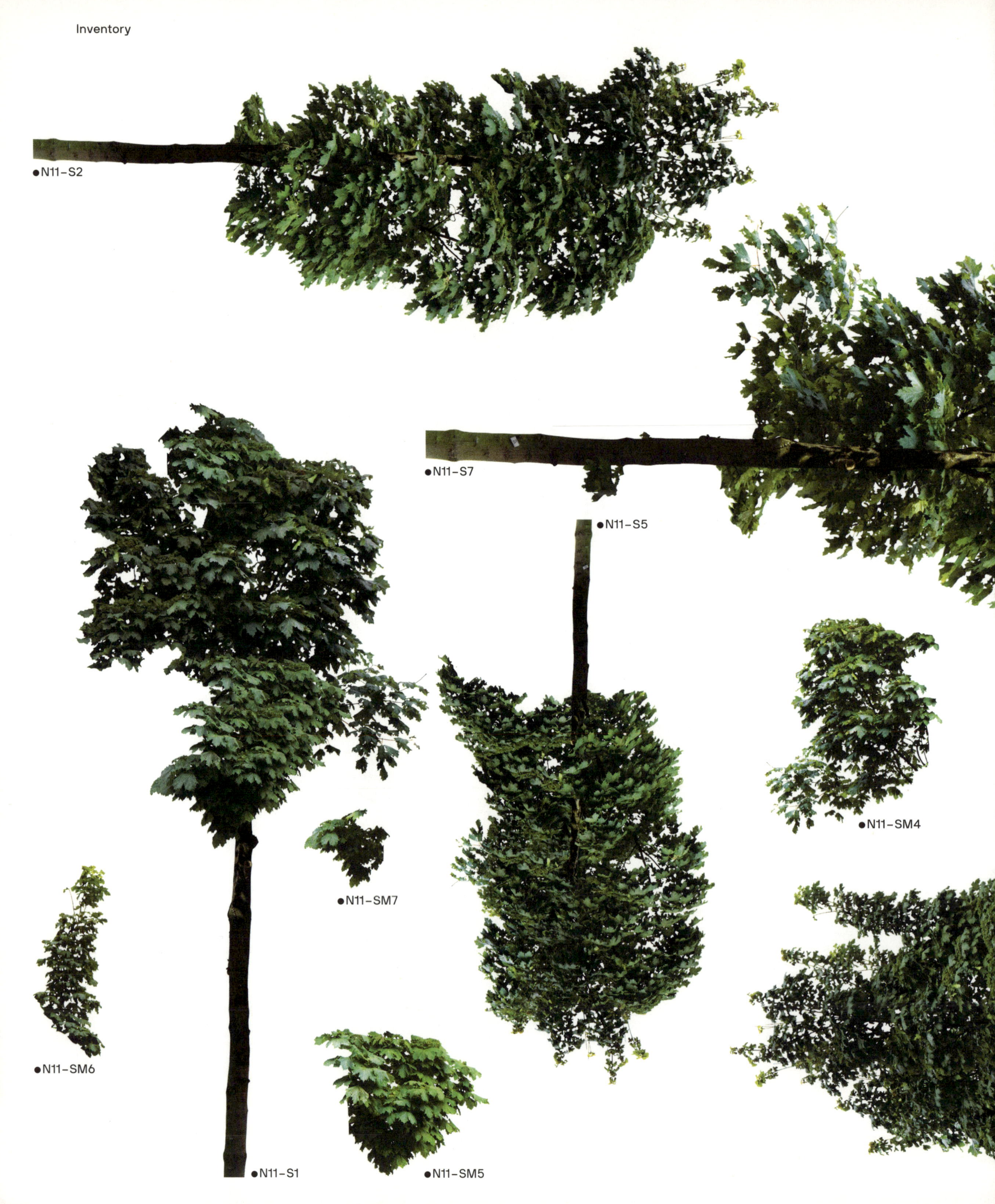

●N11–S2
●N11–S7
●N11–S5
●N11–SM4
●N11–SM7
●N11–SM6
●N11–S1
●N11–SM5

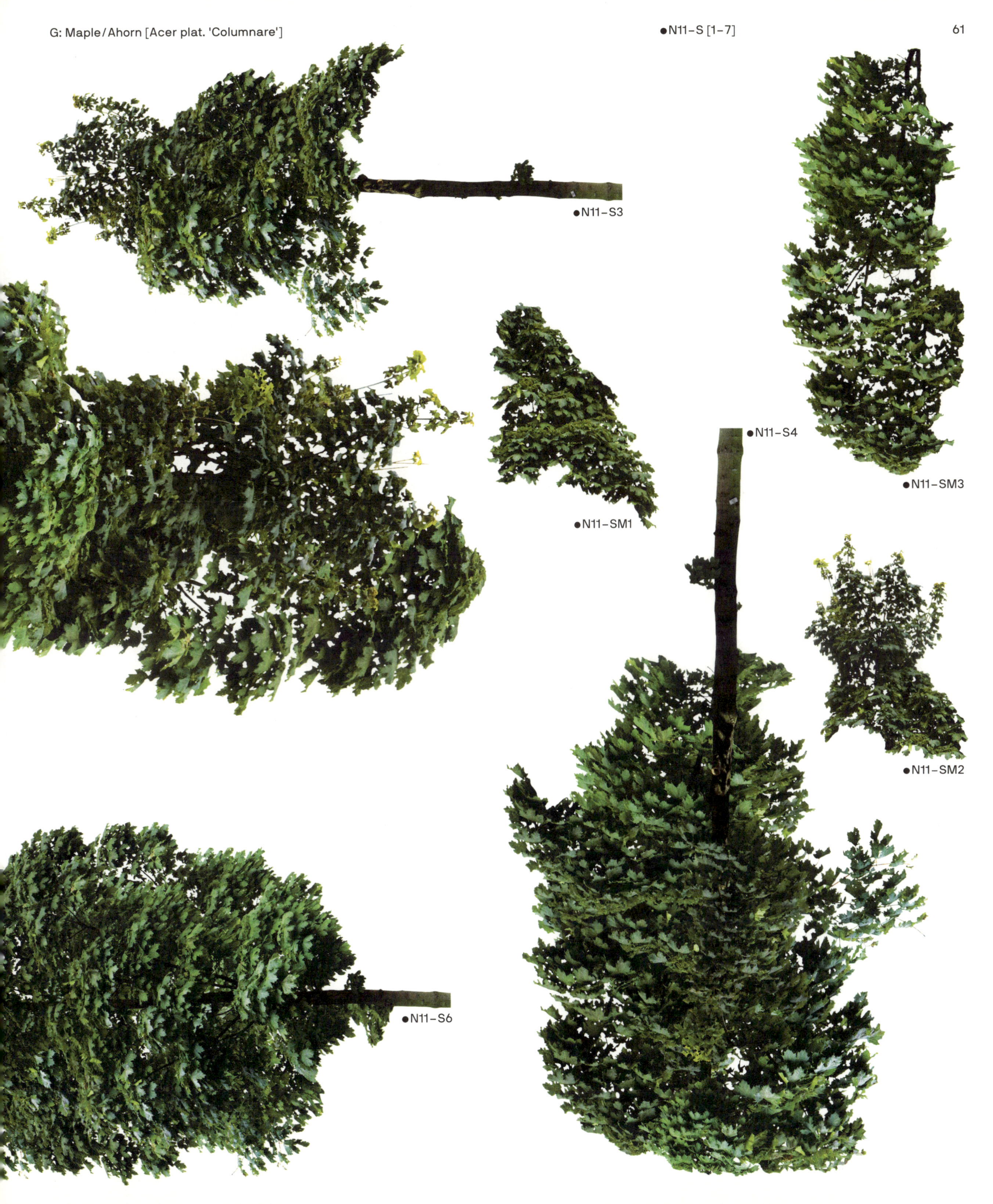
●N11–S3
●N11–S4
●N11–SM1
●N11–SM3
●N11–SM2
●N11–S6

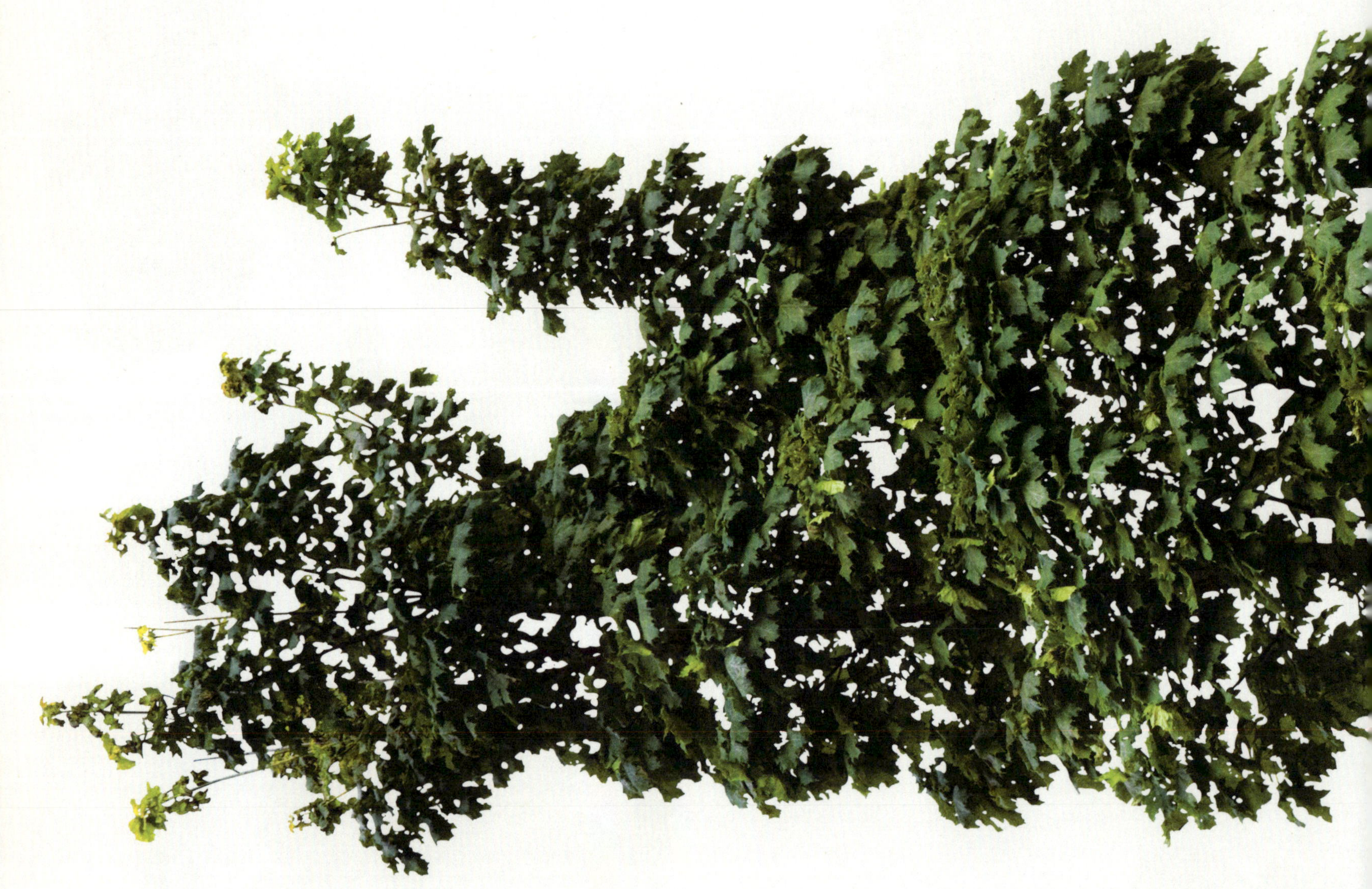

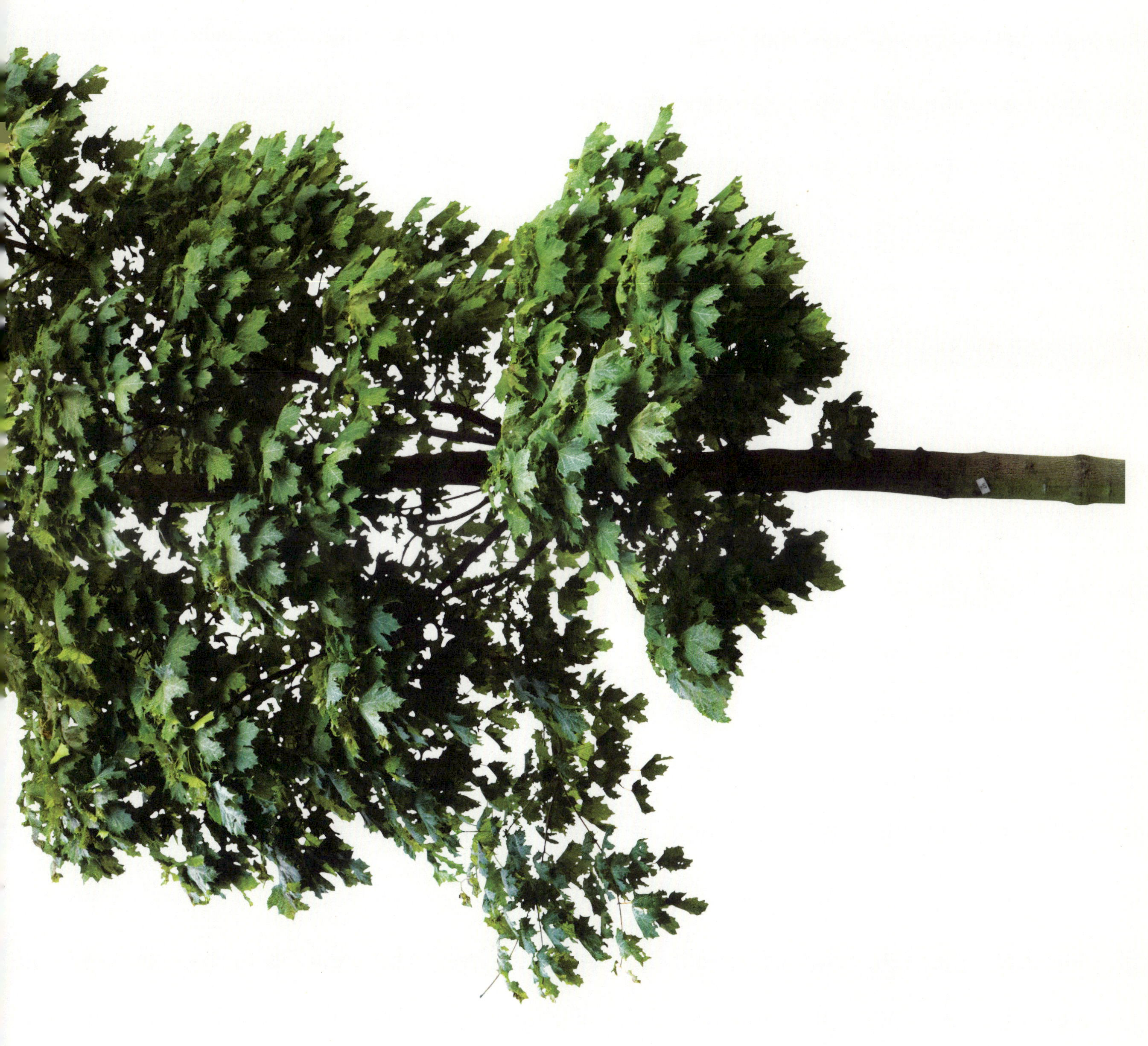

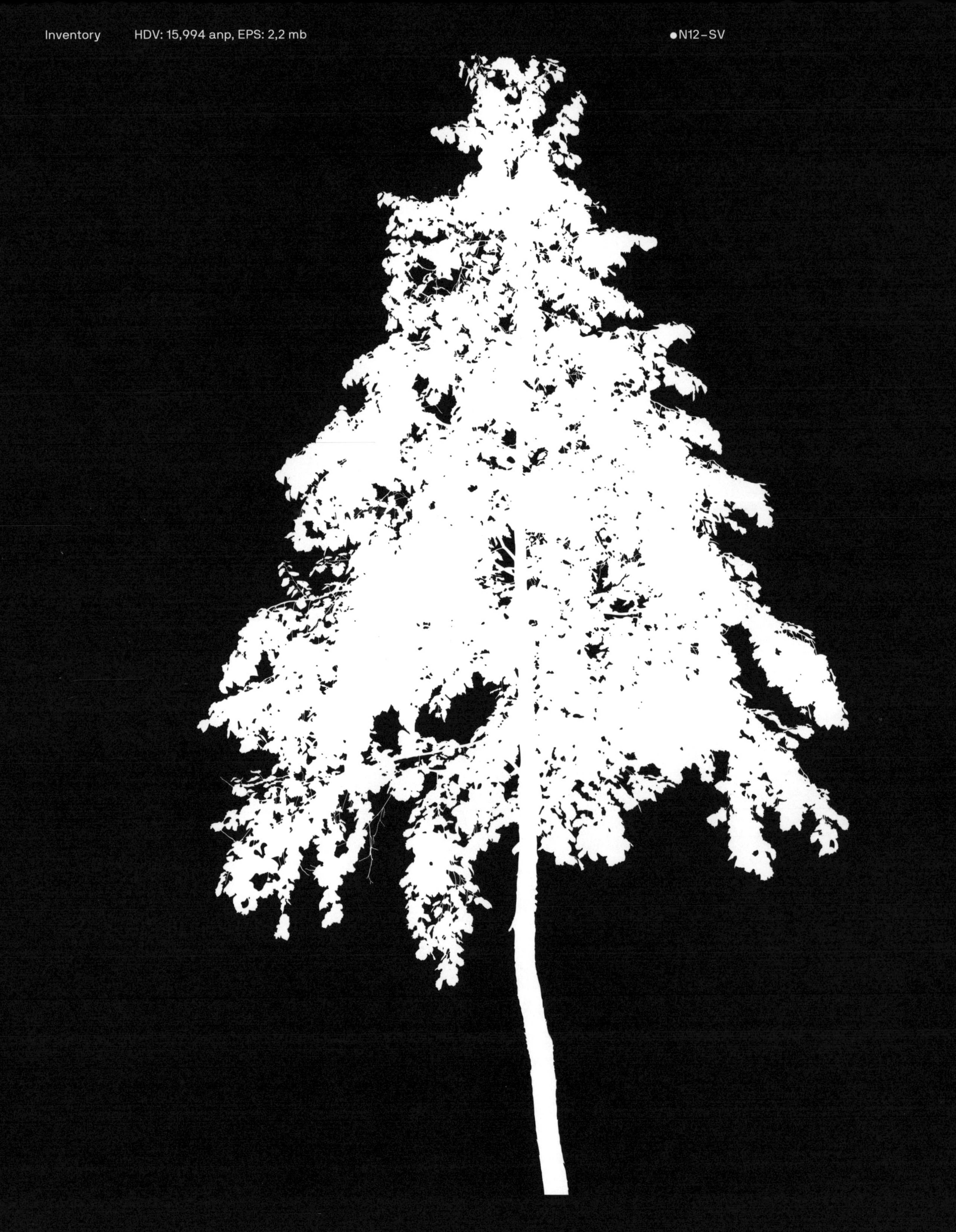

Inventory   HDV: 15,994 anp, EPS: 2,2 mb
●N12–SV

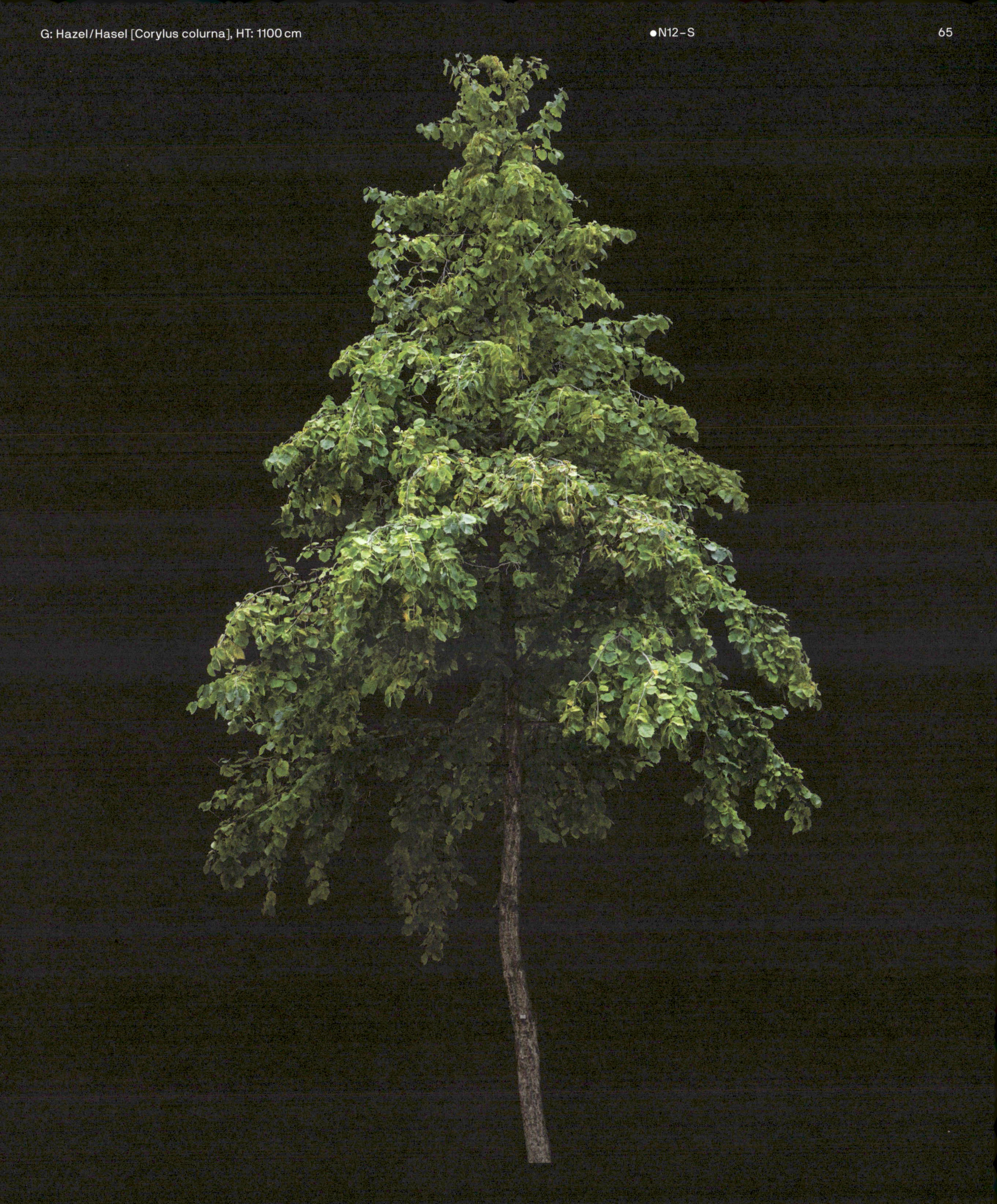

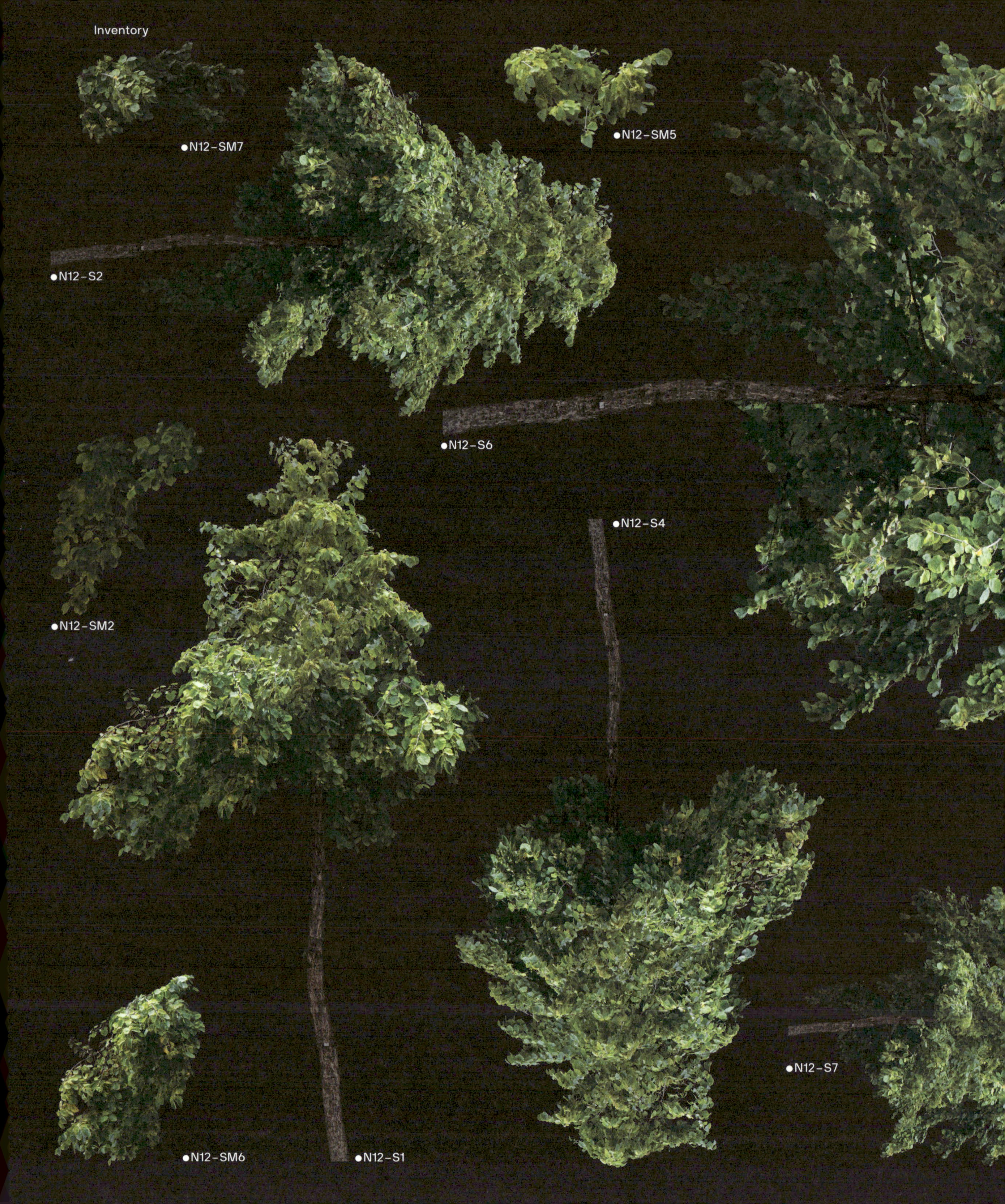

●N12–SM7
●N12–SM5
●N12–S2
●N12–S6
●N12–S4
●N12–SM2
●N12–S7
●N12–SM6
●N12–S1

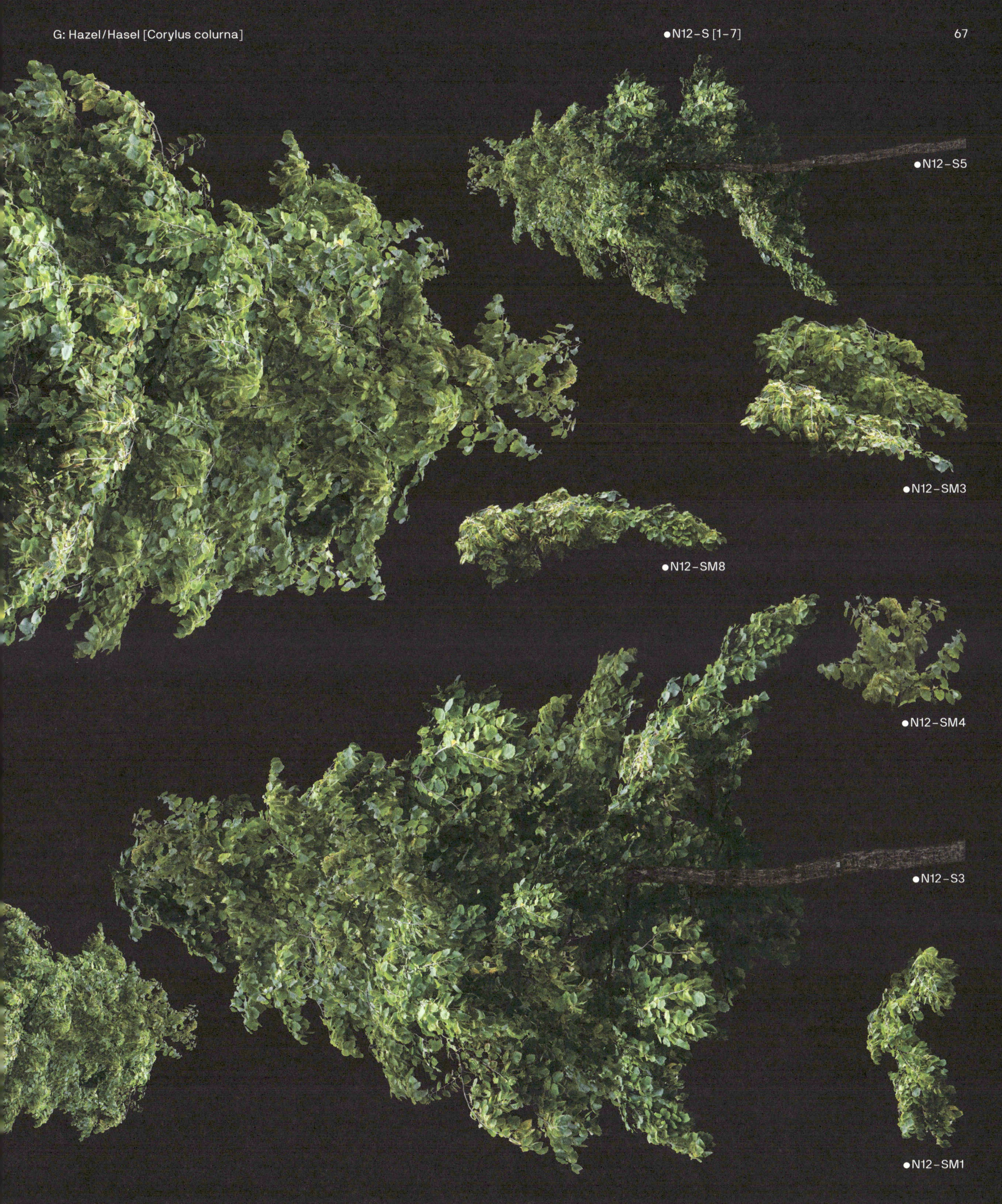
●N12-S5
●N12-SM3
●N12-SM8
●N12-SM4
●N12-S3
●N12-SM1

Inventory

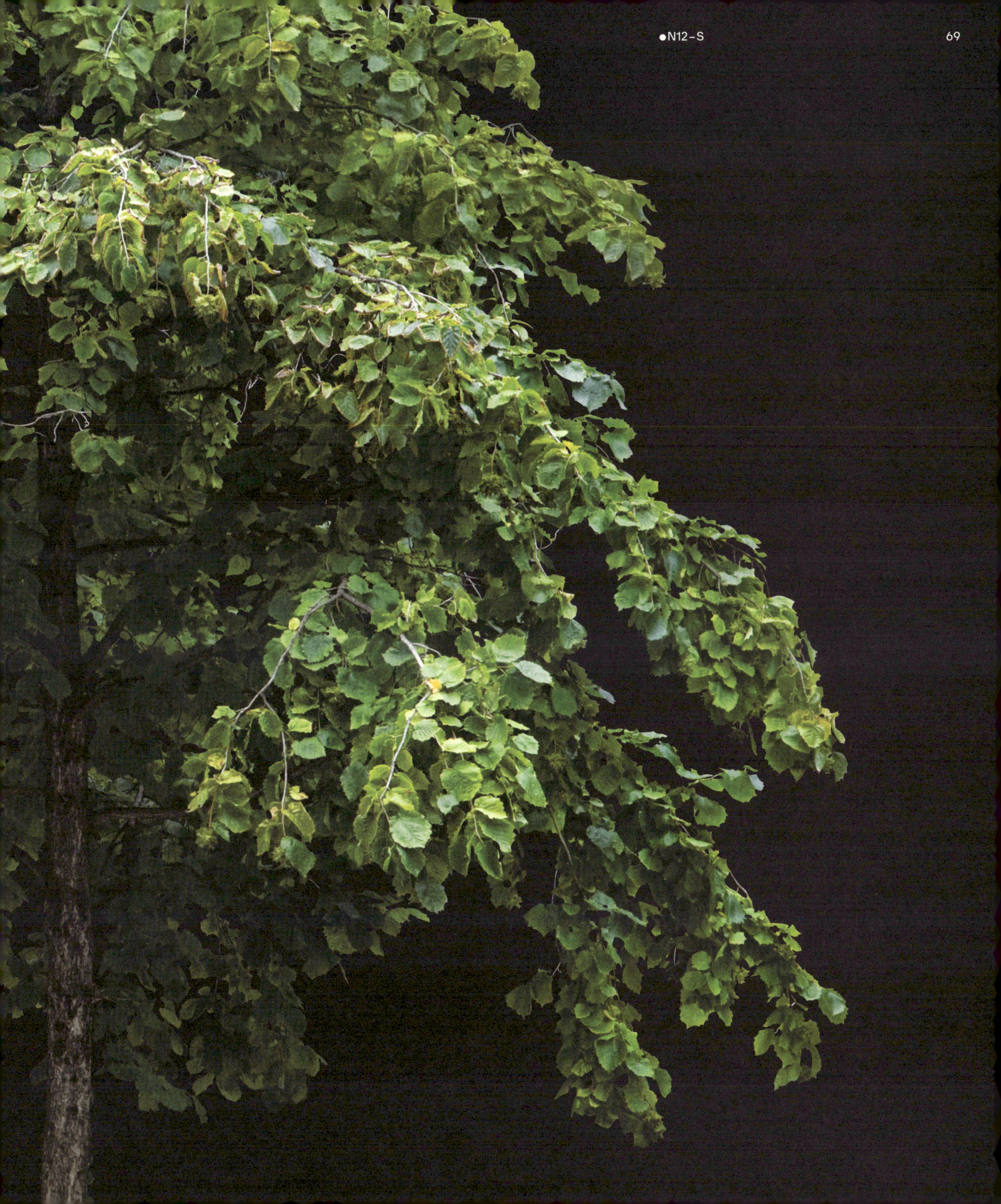

Inventory

```
E1    S  W      Thuja            [Thuja]
E3    S         Linden           [Tilia × europaea]
E4       W      Maple            [Acer]
E5    S  W      Linden           [Tilia × europaea]
E6       W      Locust           [Robinia × margaretta]
E9    S  W      Chestnut         [Aesculus × carnea]
E10      W      Tree of heaven   [Ailanthus altissima]
```

E1–E10

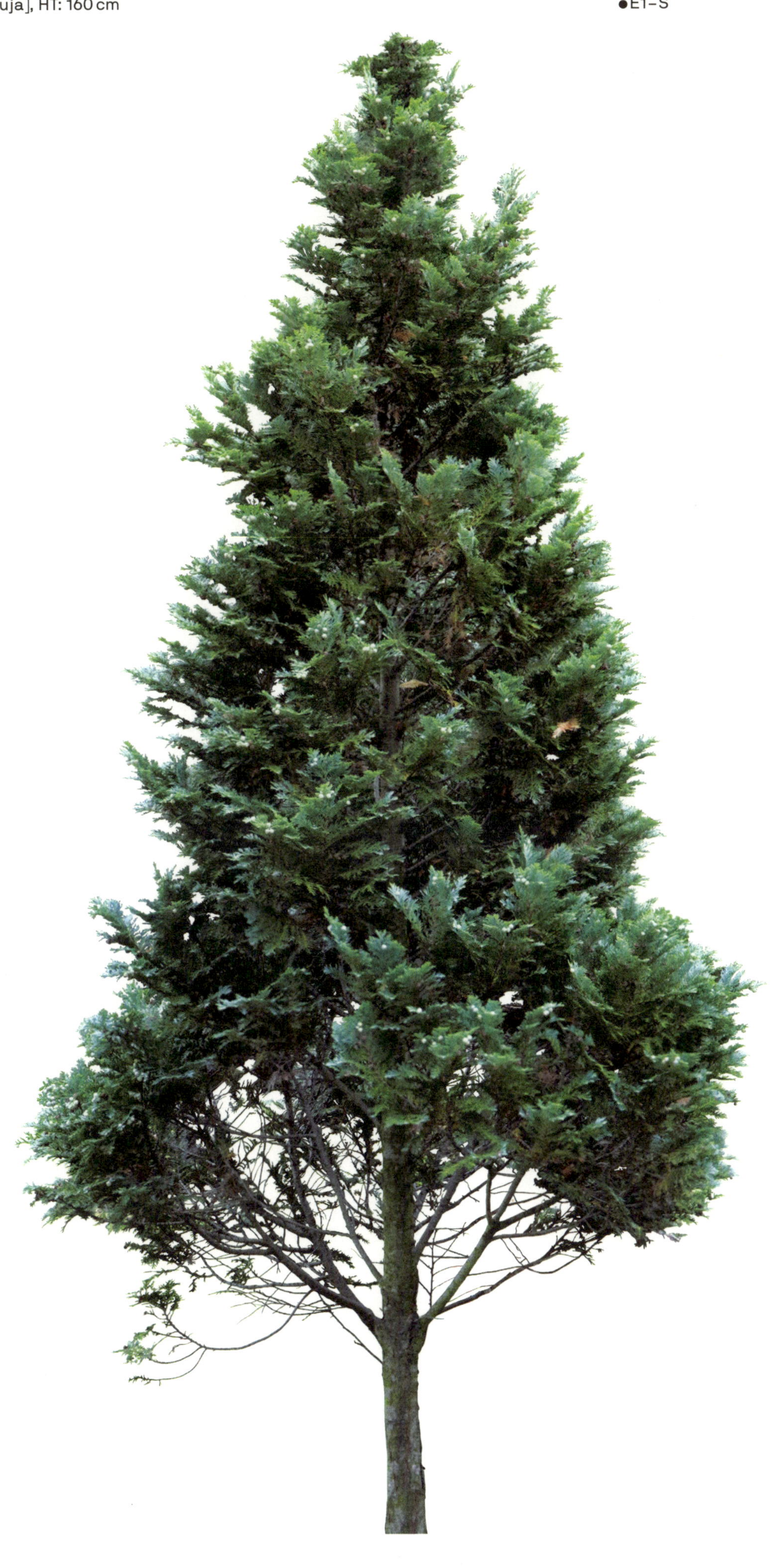

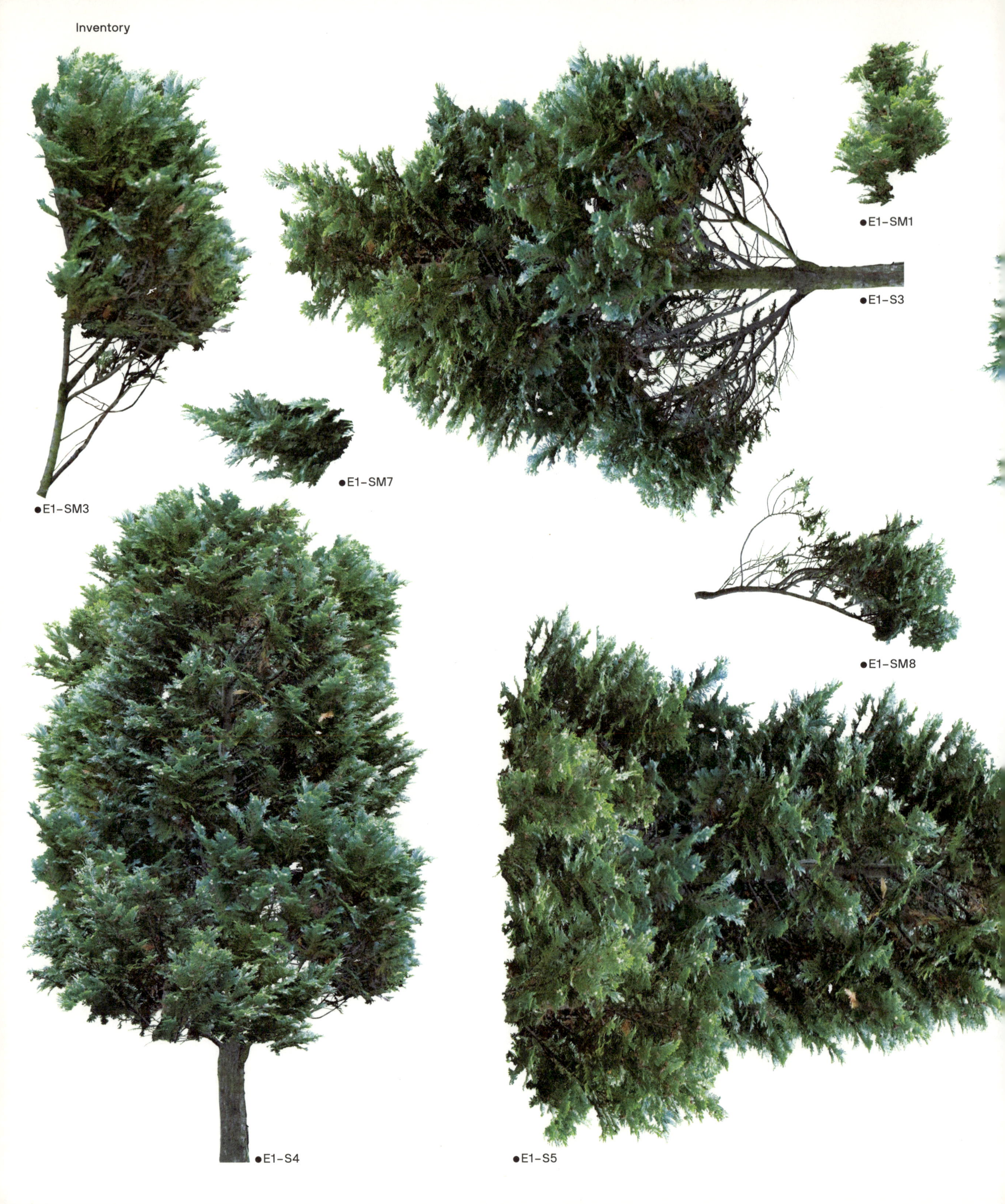
●E1–SM1
●E1–S3
●E1–SM3
●E1–SM7
●E1–SM8
●E1–S4
●E1–S5

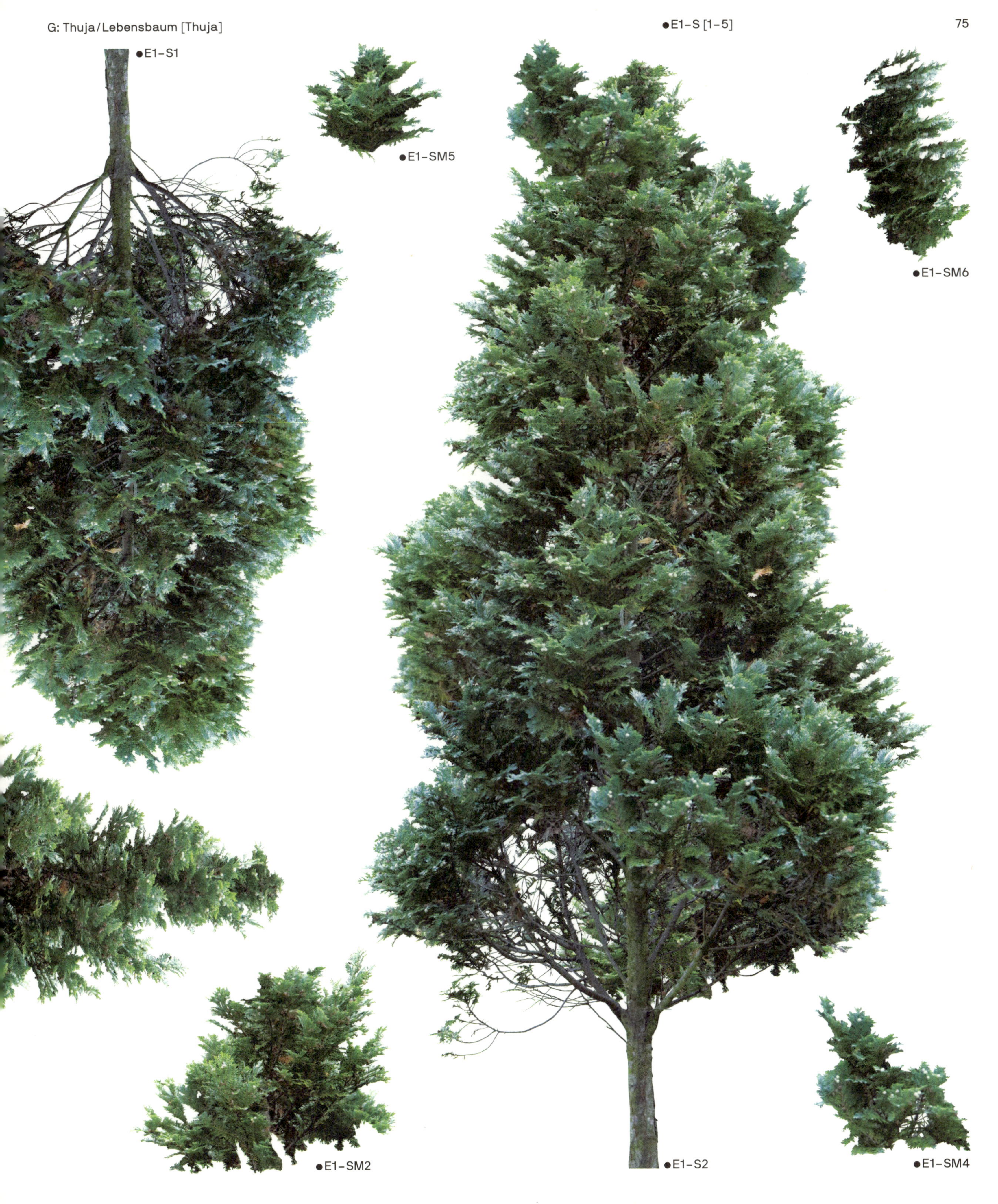
●E1–S1
●E1–SM5
●E1–SM6
●E1–SM2
●E1–S2
●E1–SM4

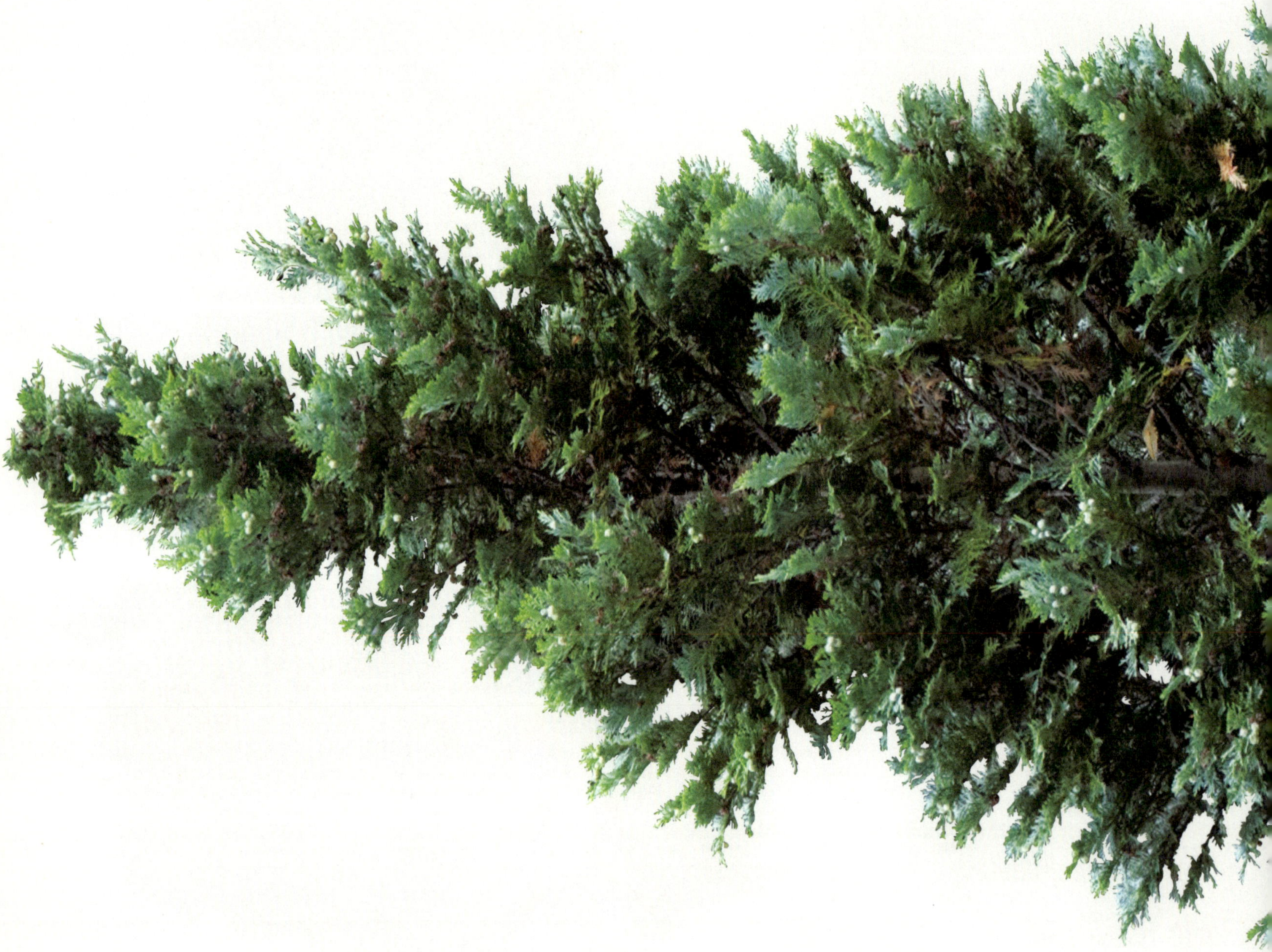

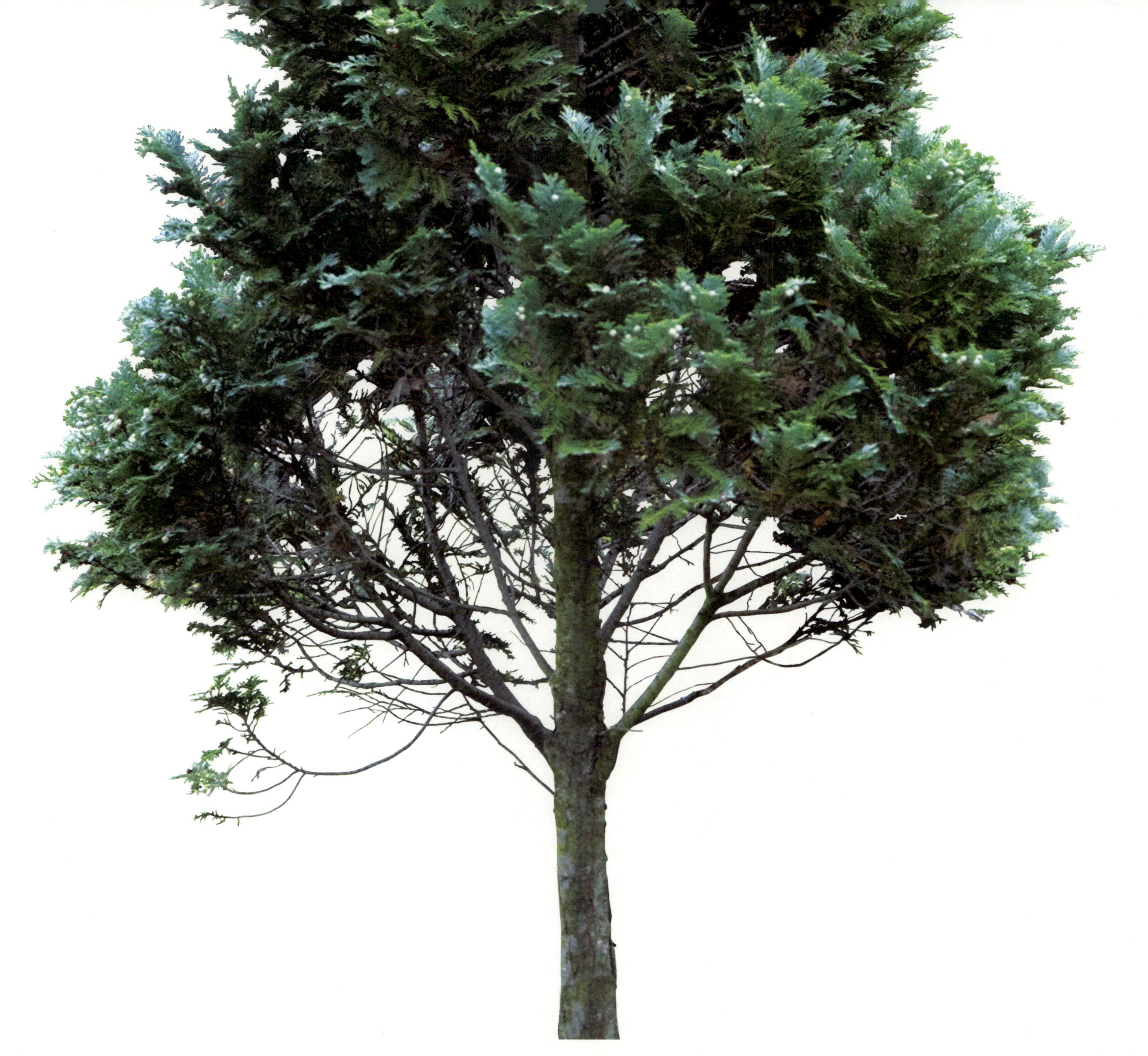

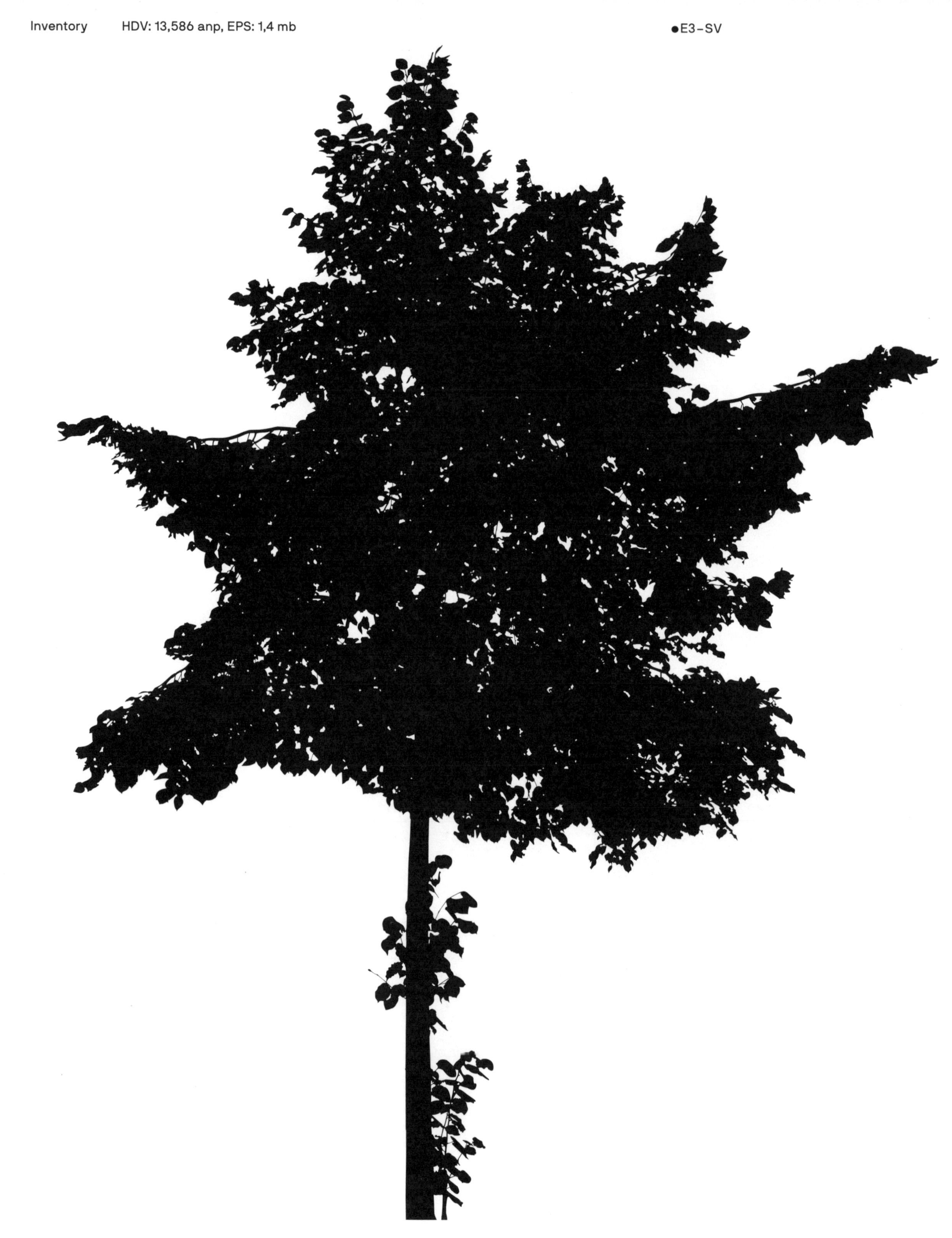

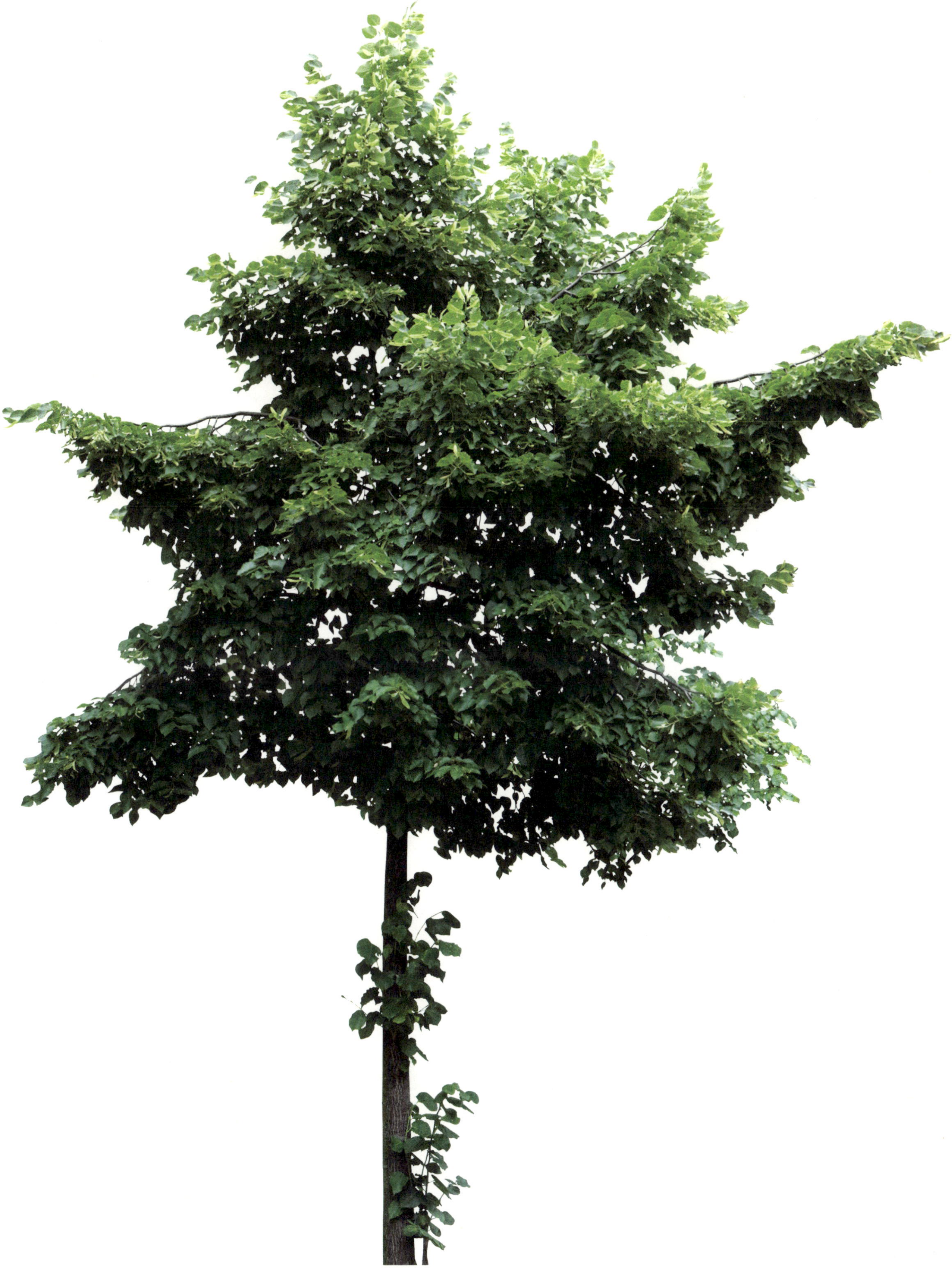

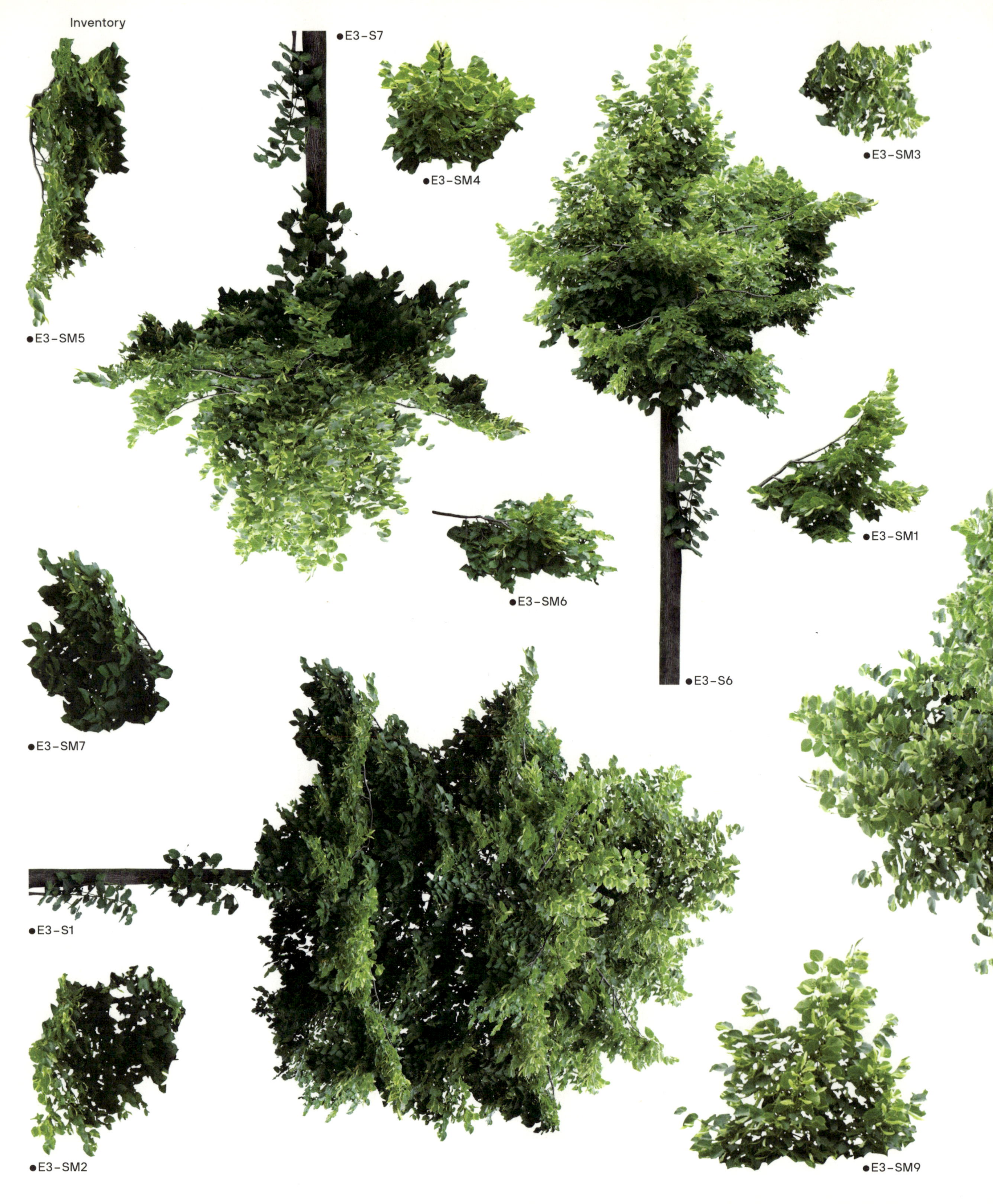

Inventory
E3-S7
E3-SM4
E3-SM3
E3-SM5
E3-SM1
E3-SM6
E3-S6
E3-SM7
E3-S1
E3-SM2
E3-SM9

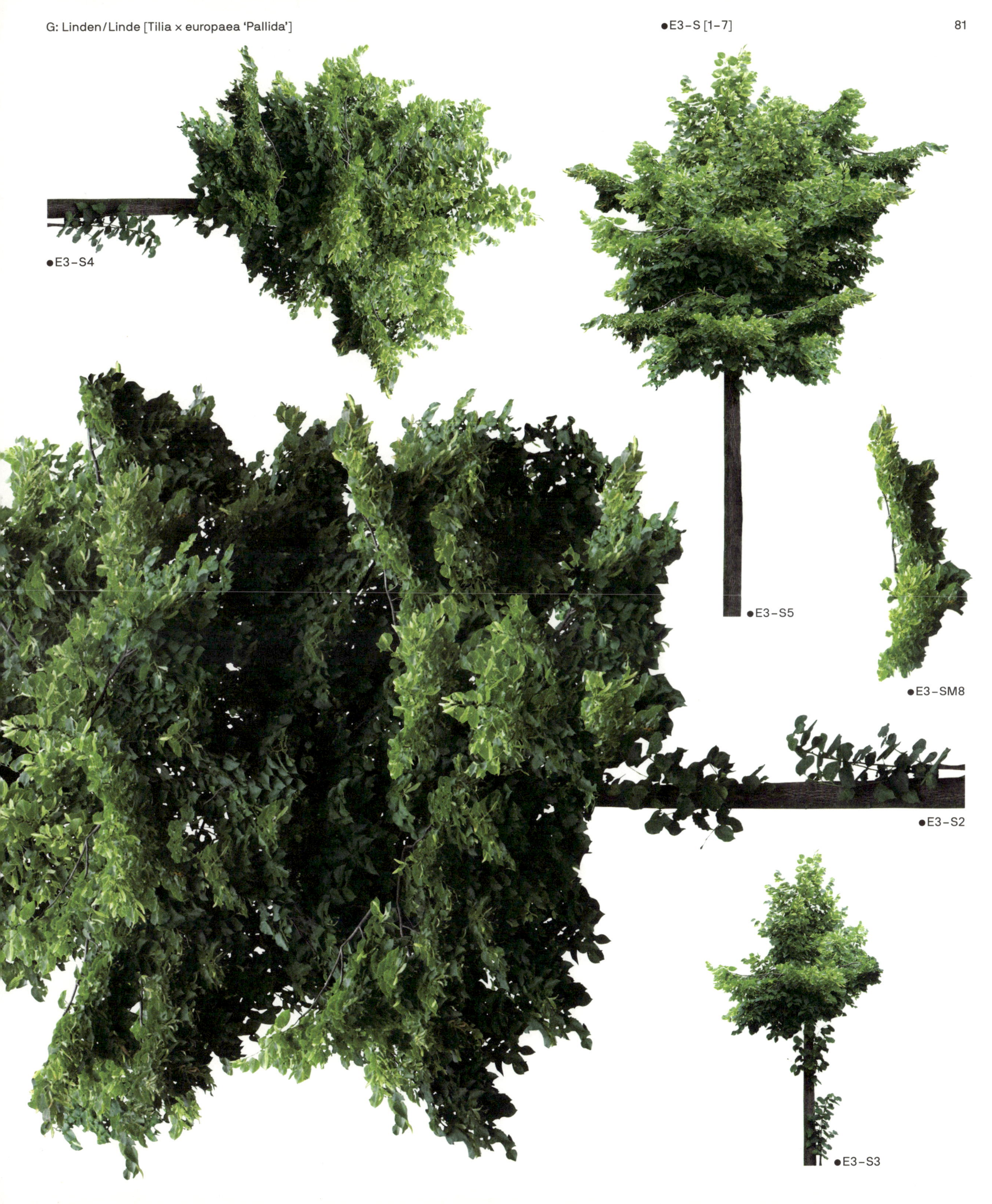
●E3–S4
●E3–S5
●E3–SM8
●E3–S2
●E3–S3

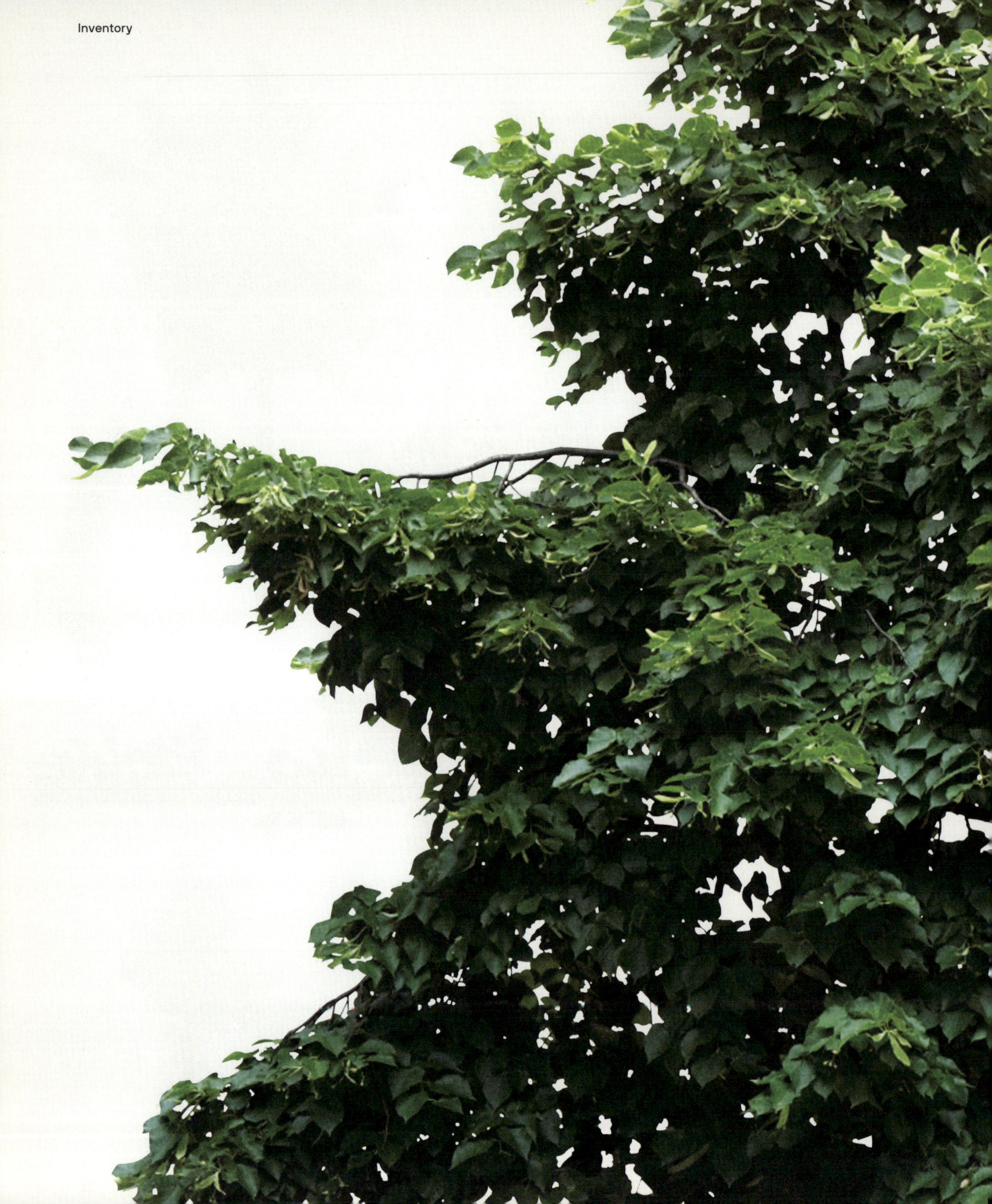

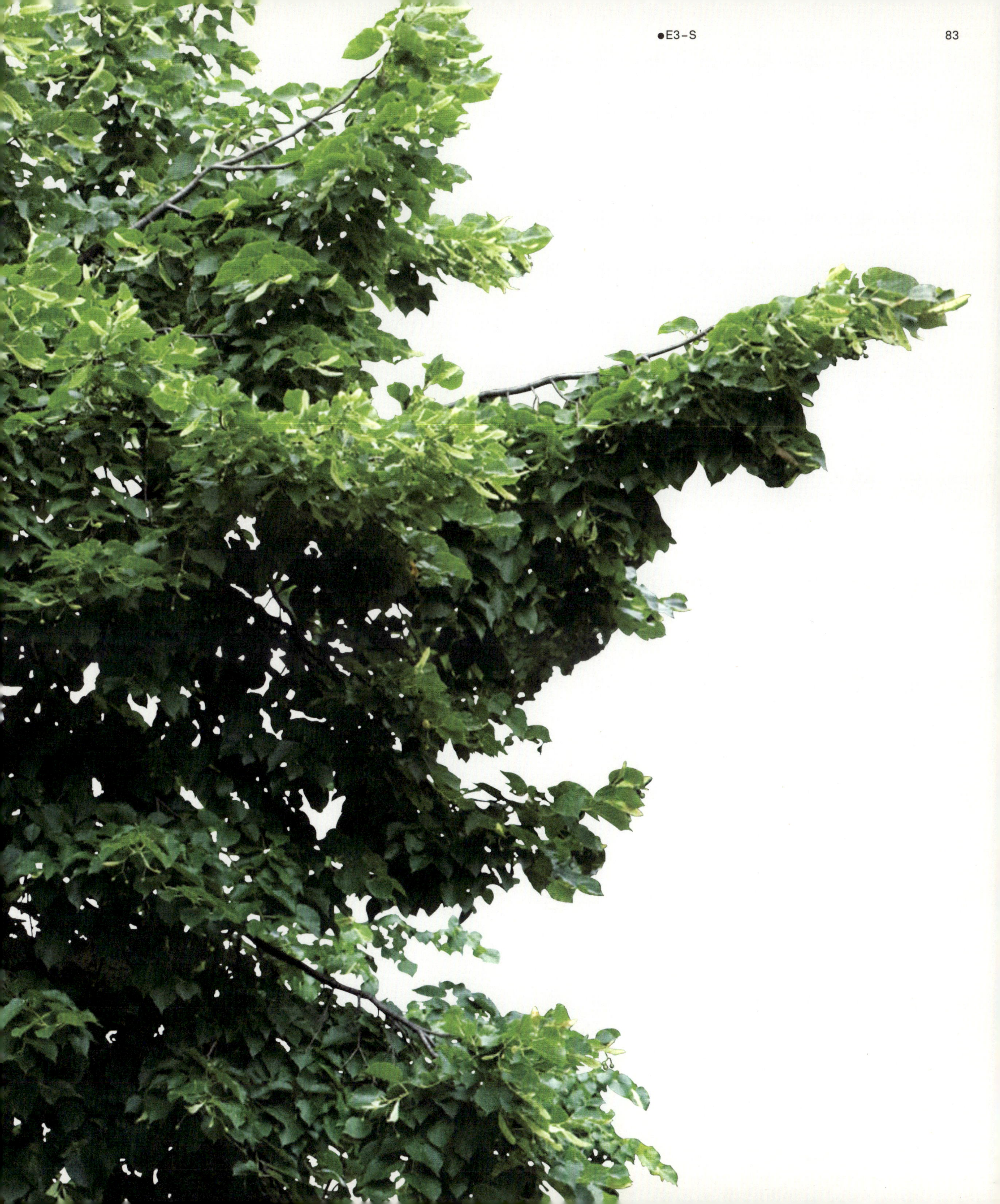

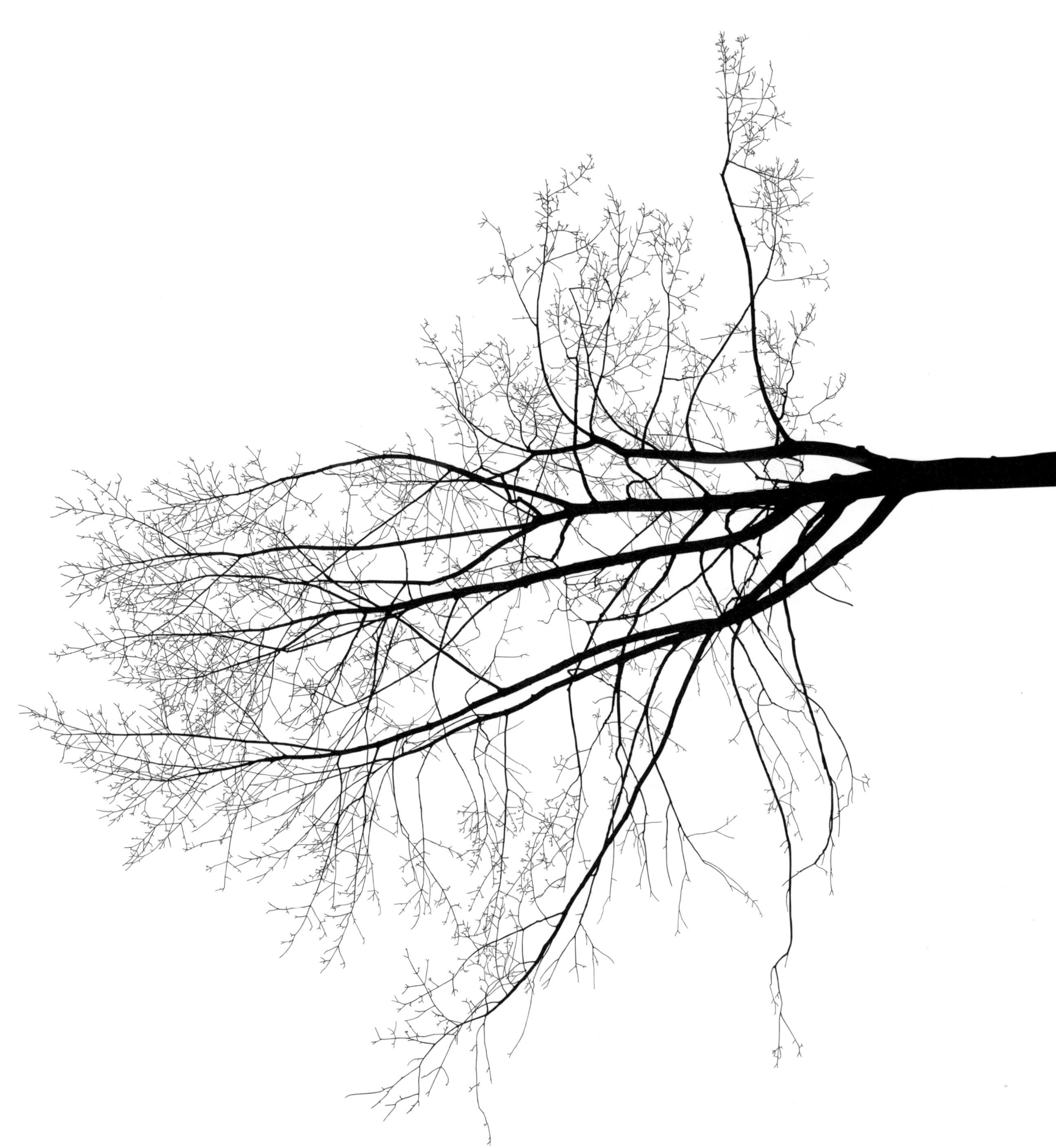

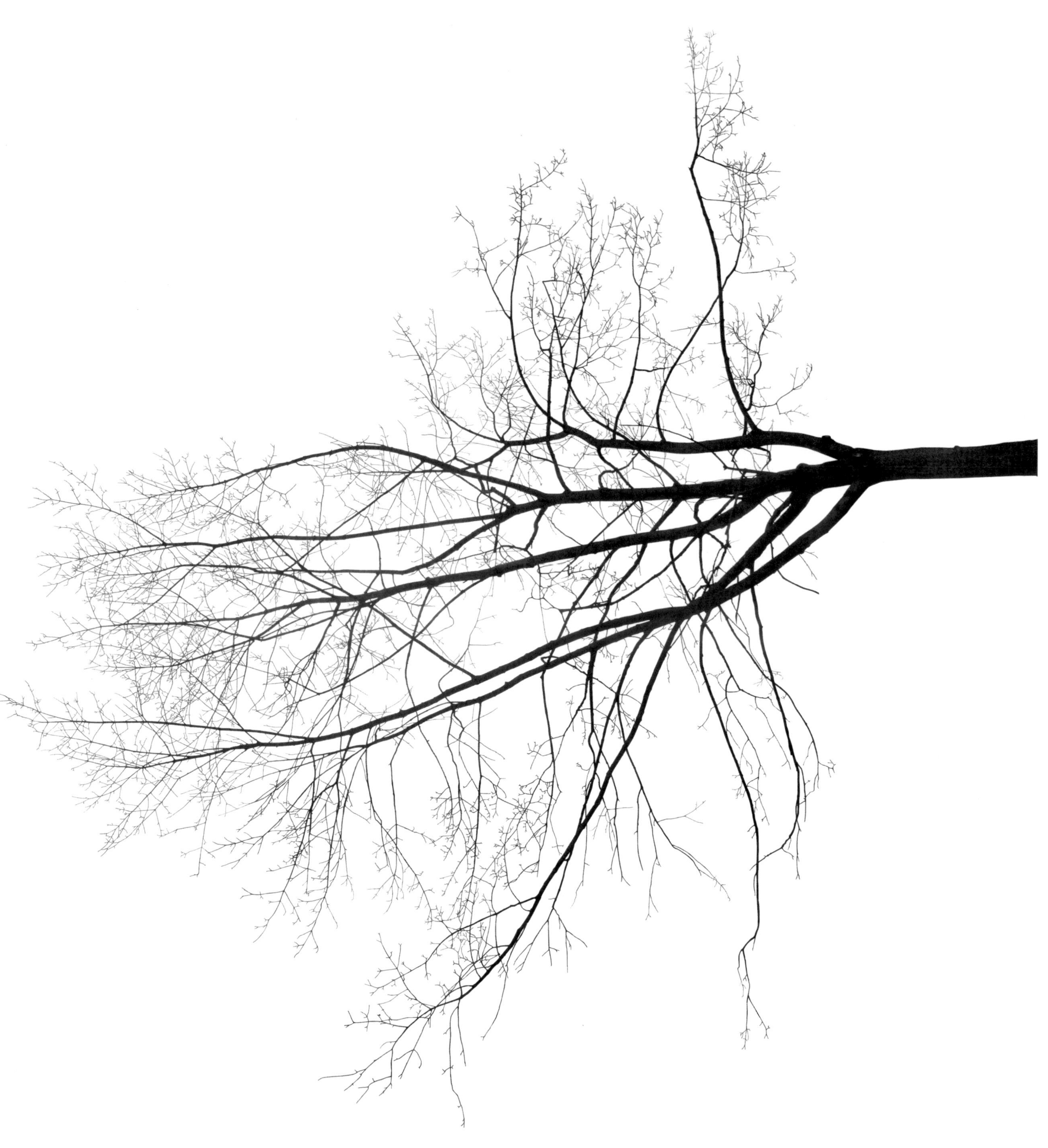

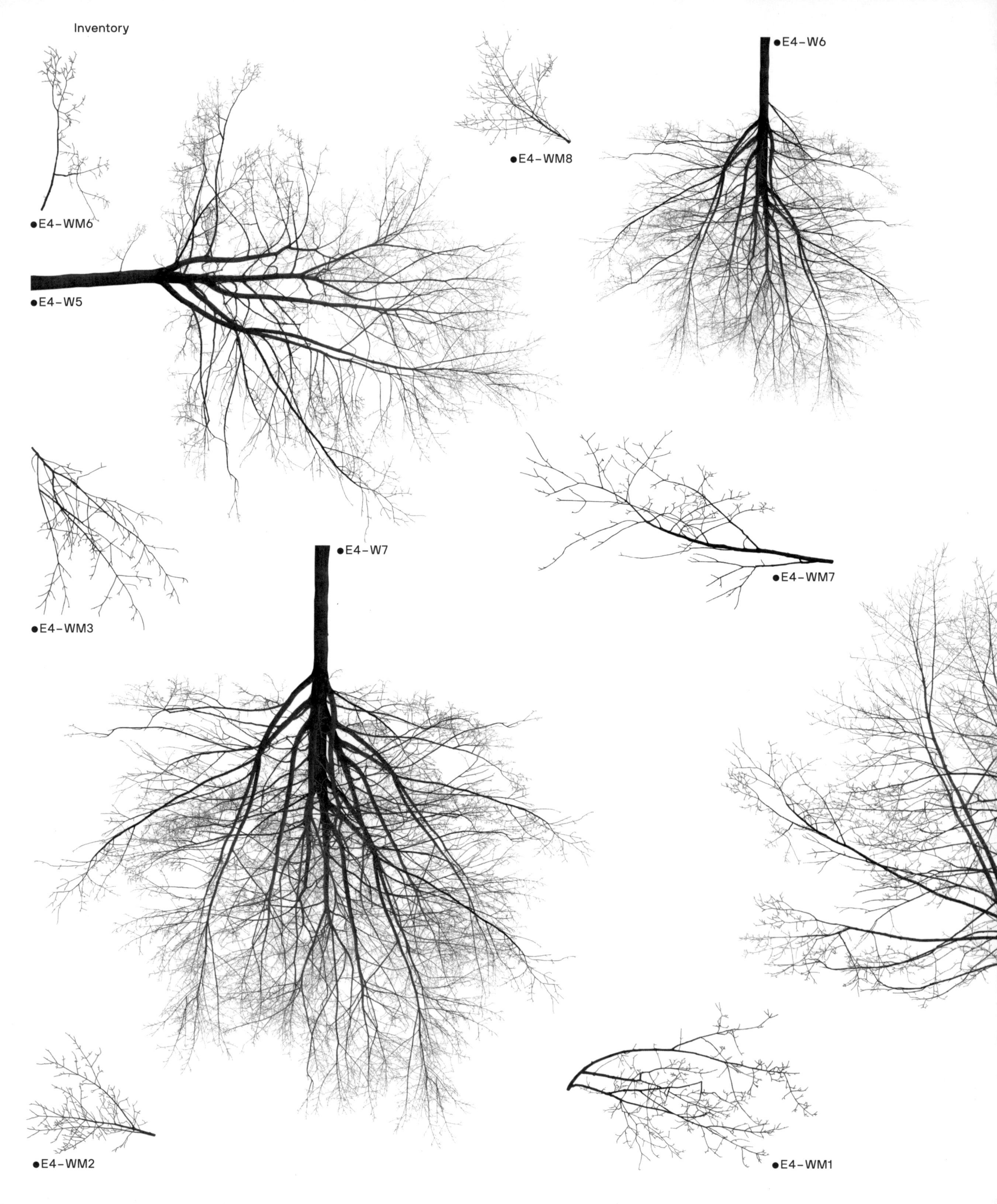

Inventory
E4–WM6
E4–W5
E4–WM8
E4–W6
E4–WM3
E4–W7
E4–WM7
E4–WM2
E4–WM1

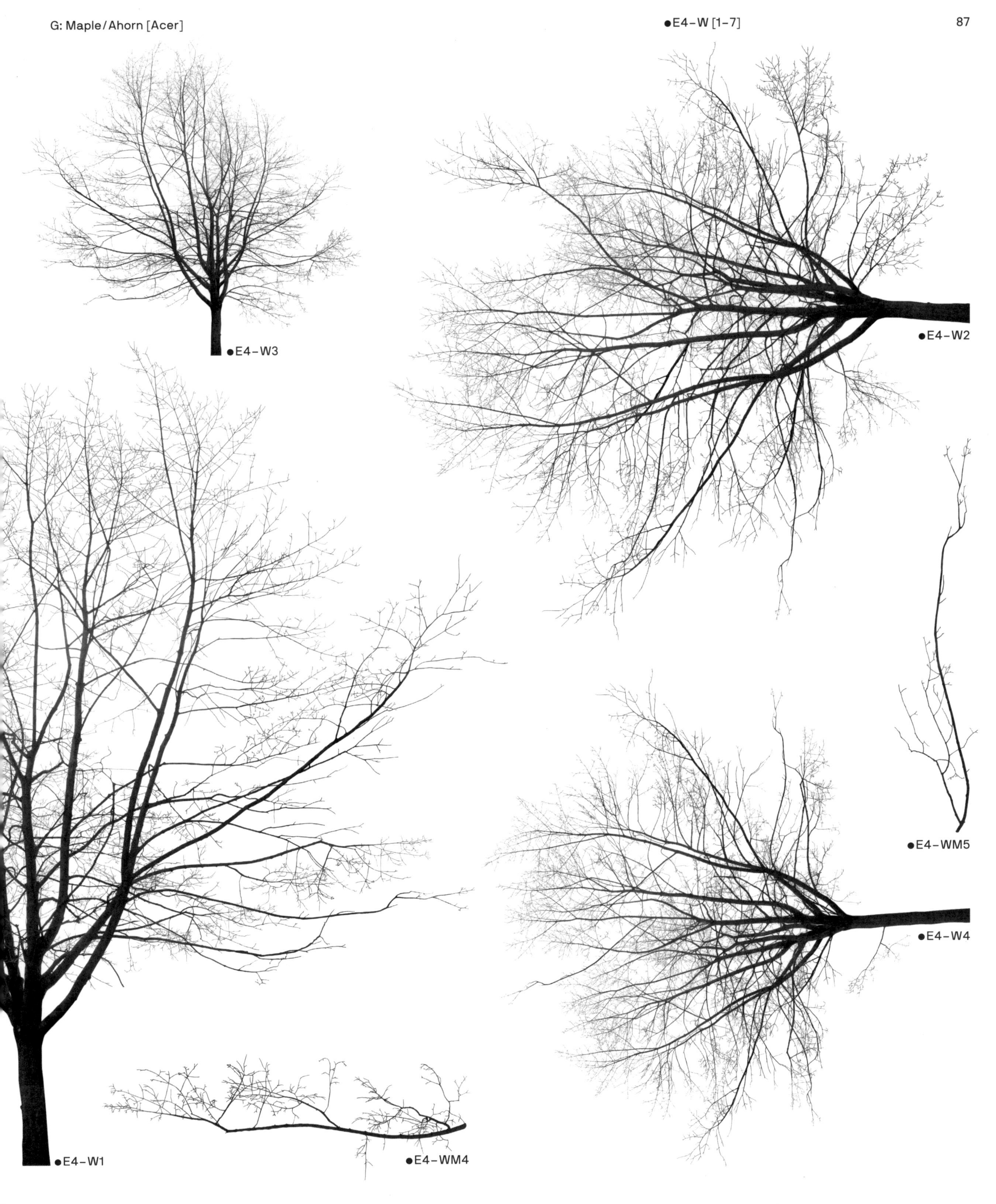

●E4–W3
●E4–W2
●E4–WM5
●E4–W4
●E4–W1
●E4–WM4

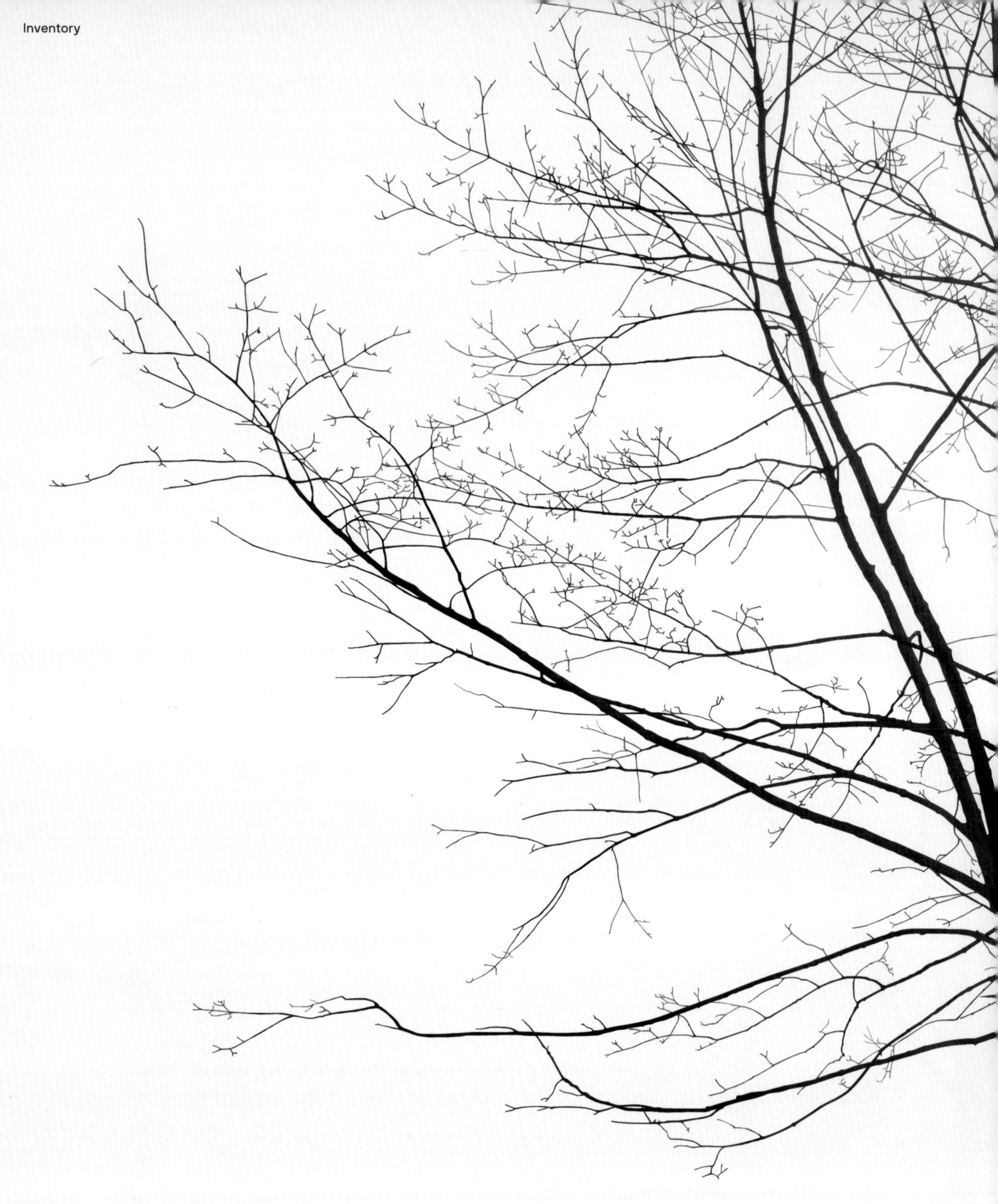

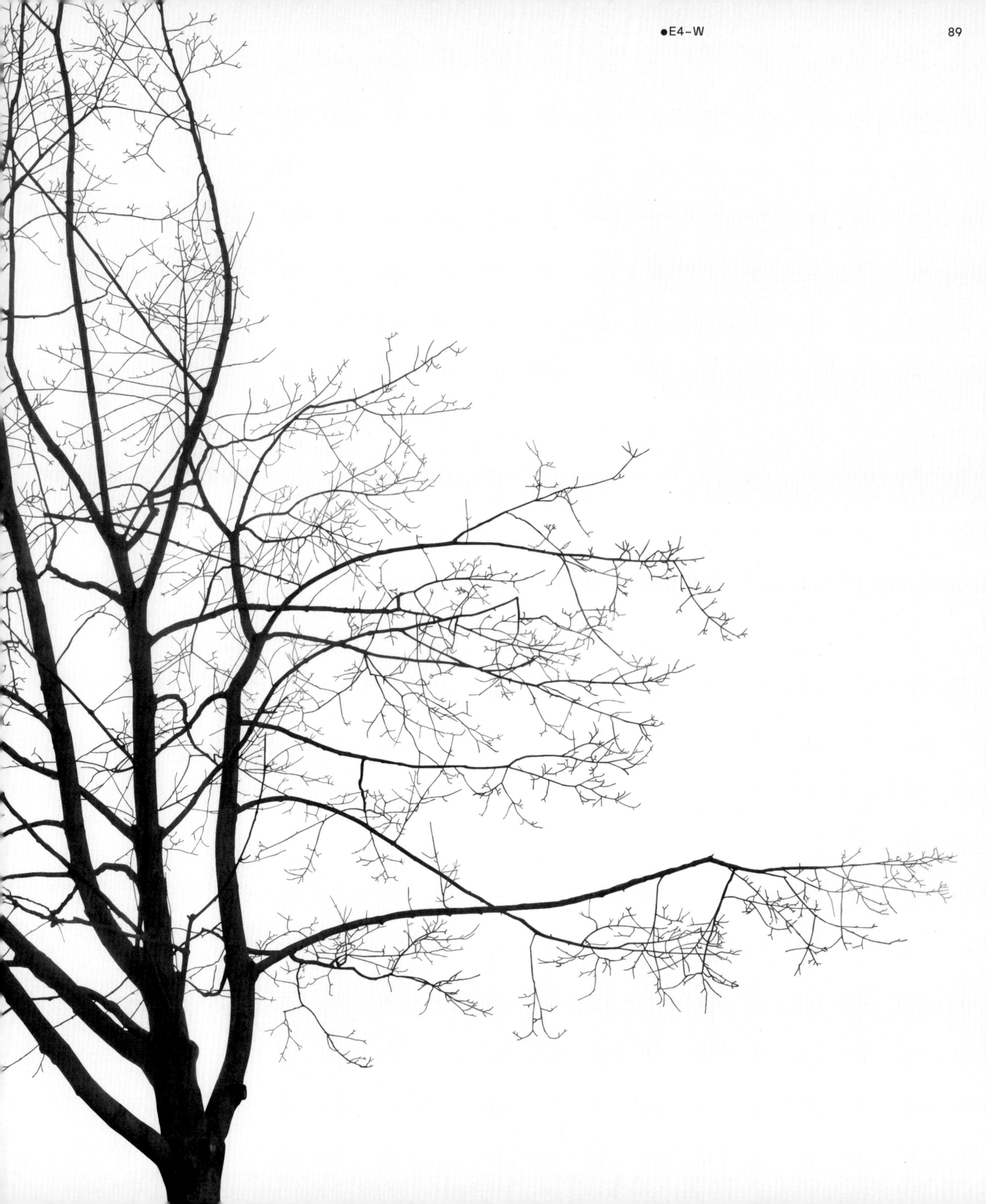
●E4-W

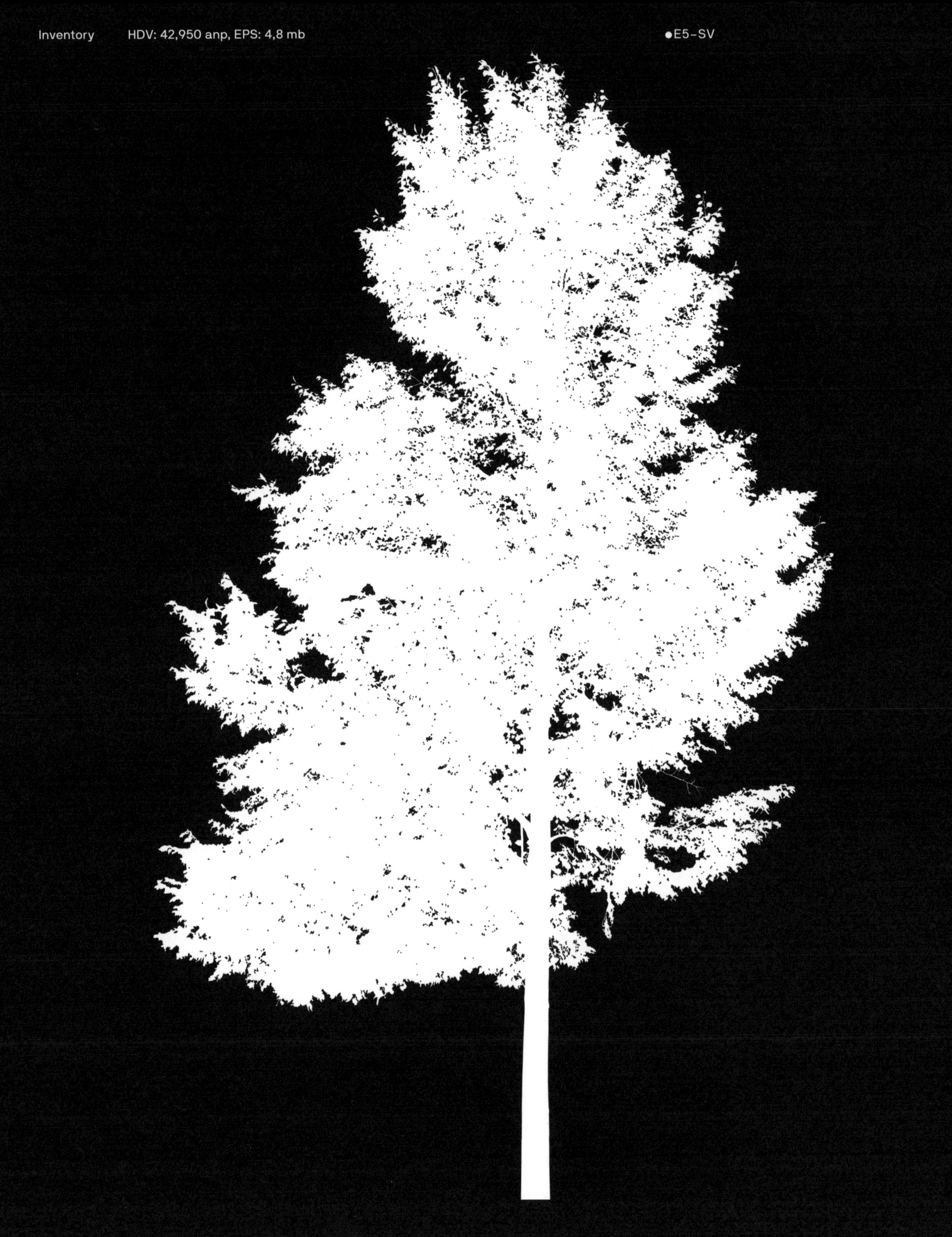

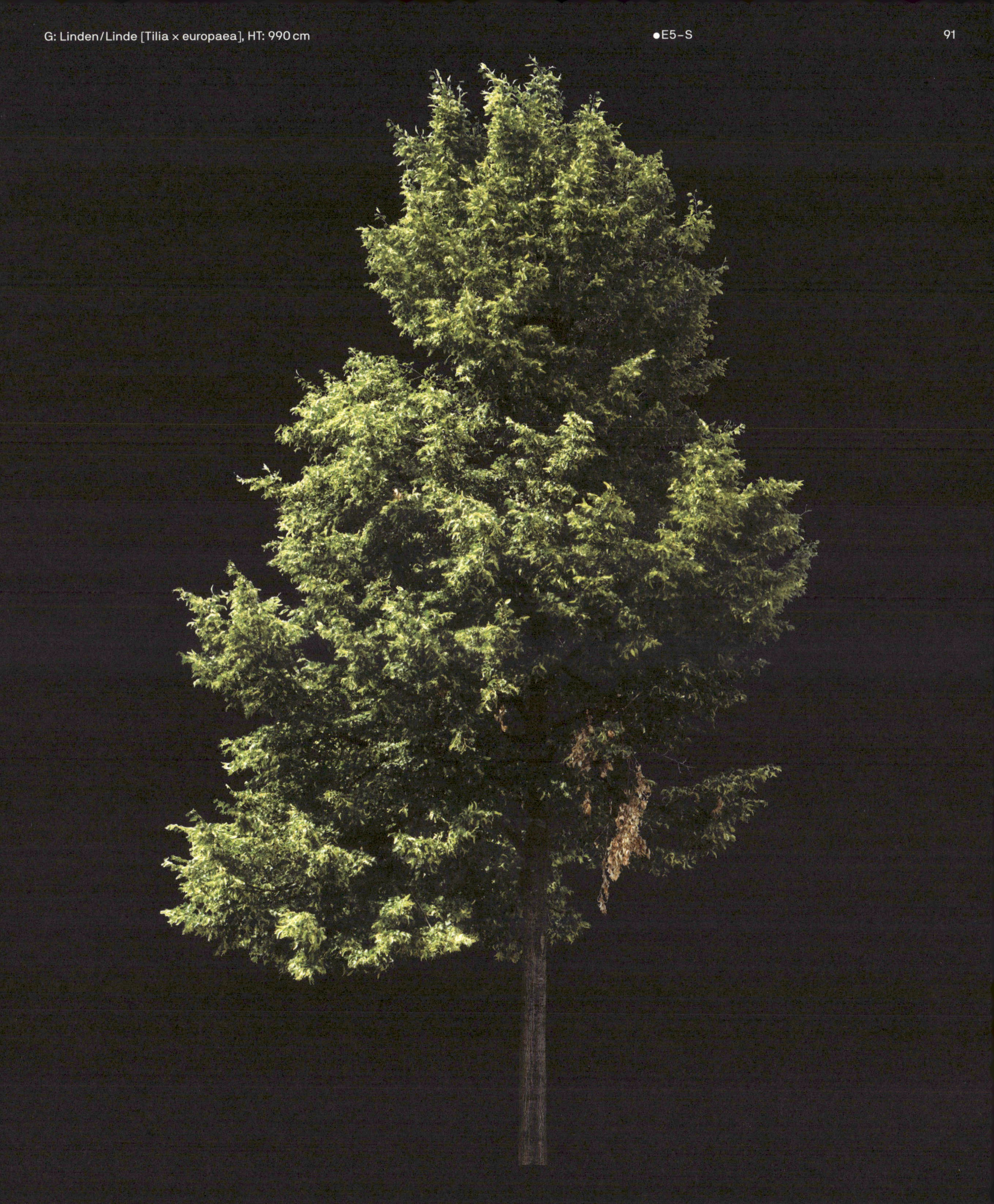

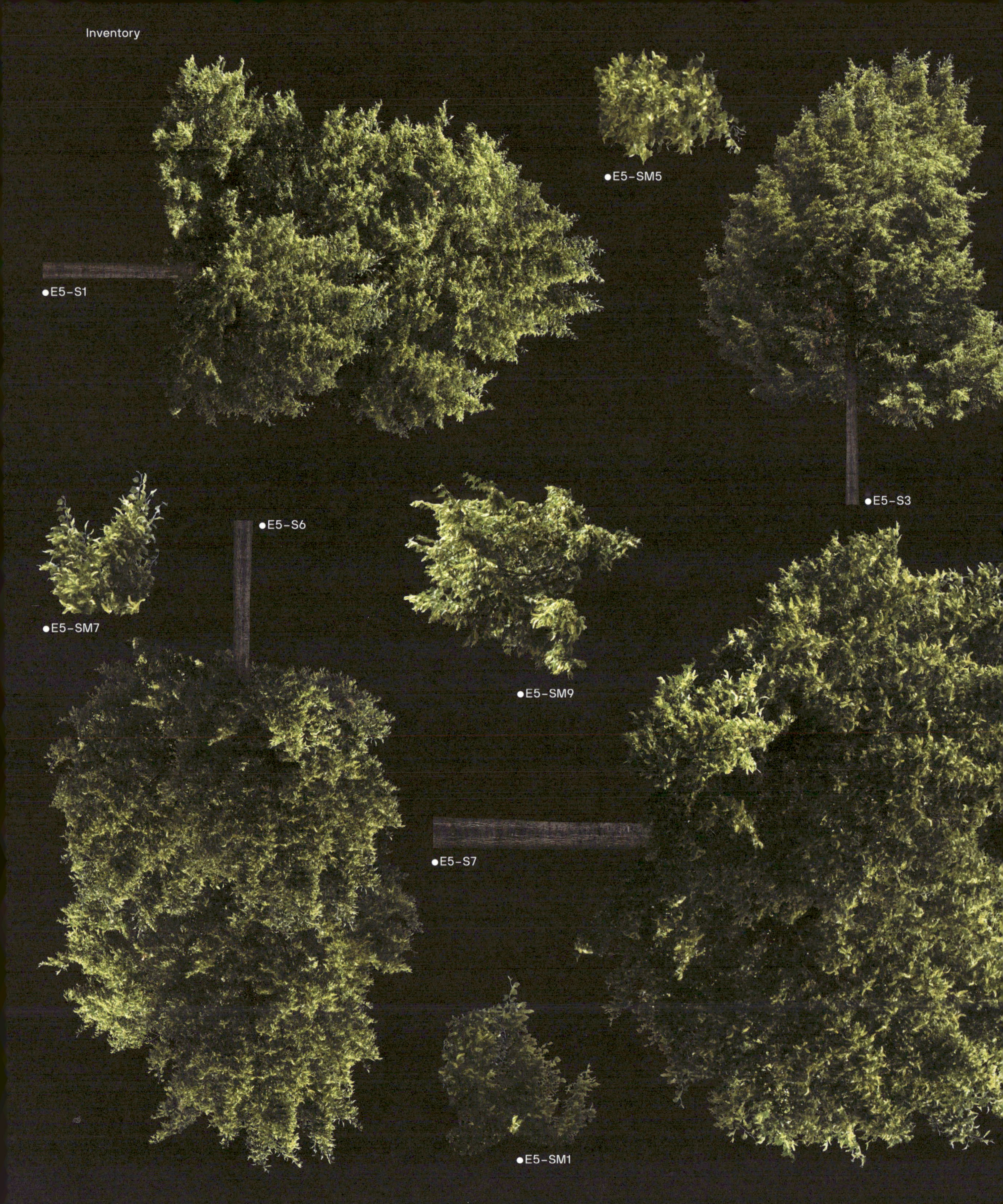

Inventory
E5-SM5
E5-S1
E5-S3
E5-S6
E5-SM7
E5-SM9
E5-S7
E5-SM1

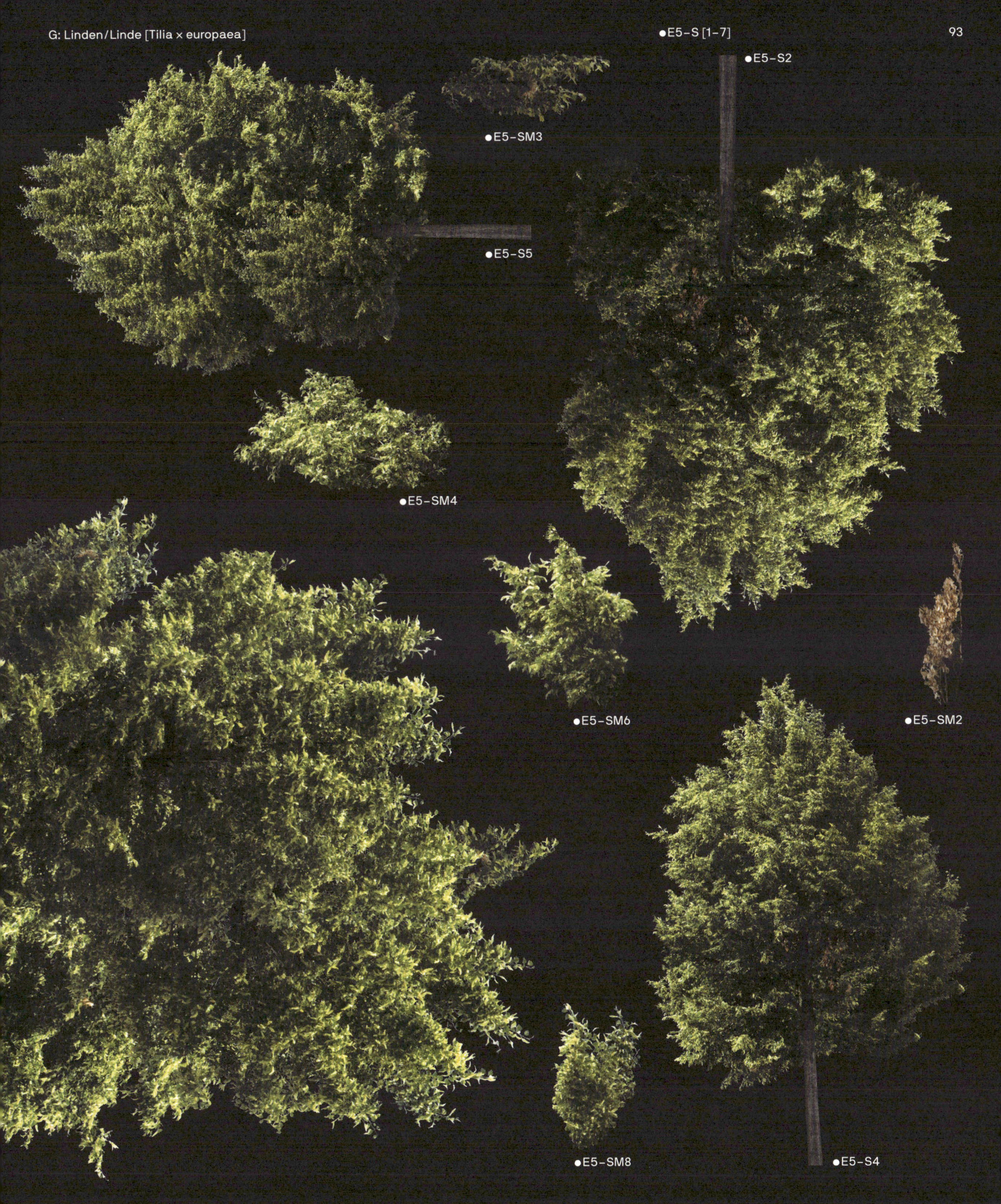
●E5–S [1–7]
●E5–S2
●E5–SM3
●E5–S5
●E5–SM4
●E5–SM6
●E5–SM2
●E5–SM8
●E5–S4

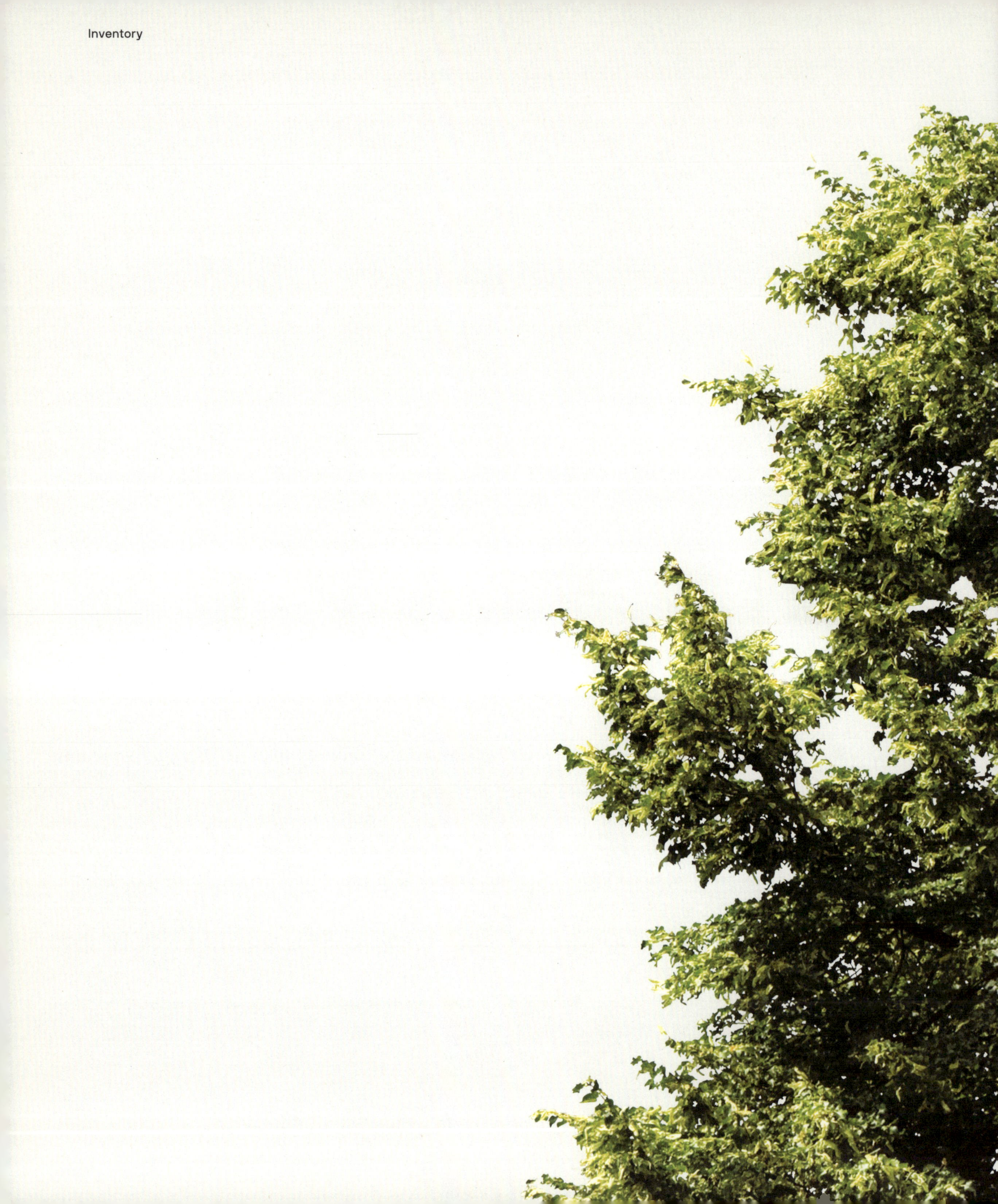

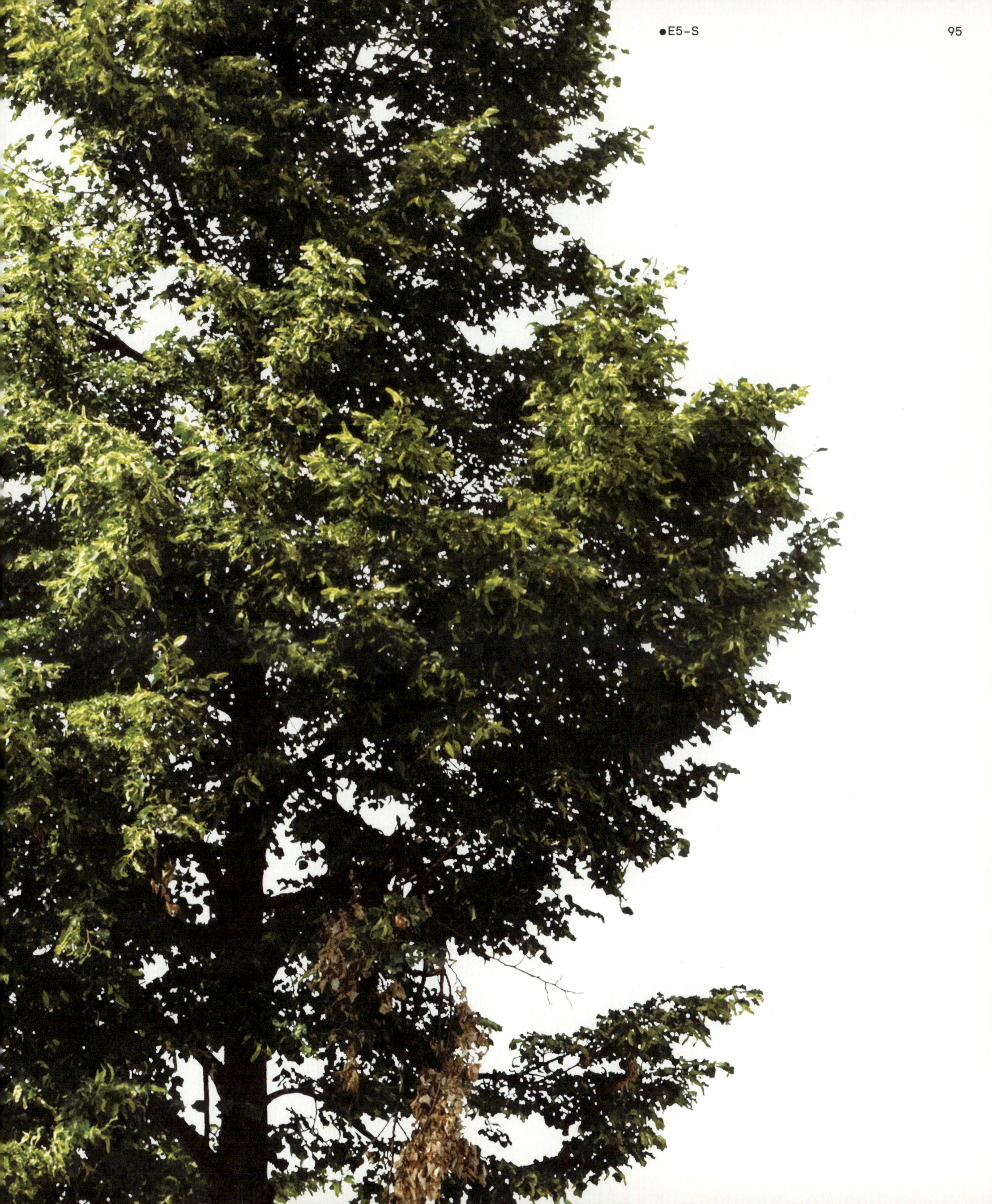

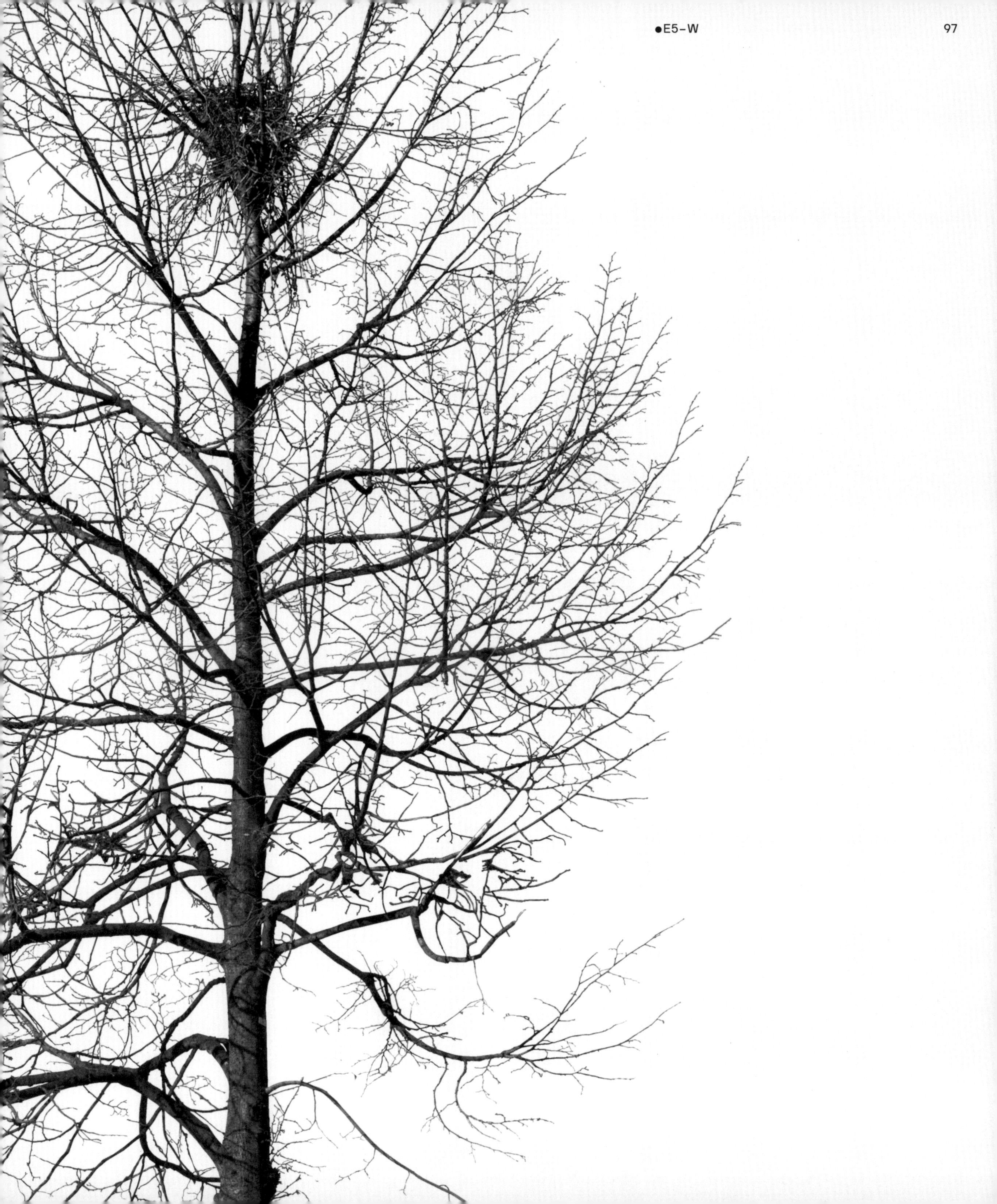

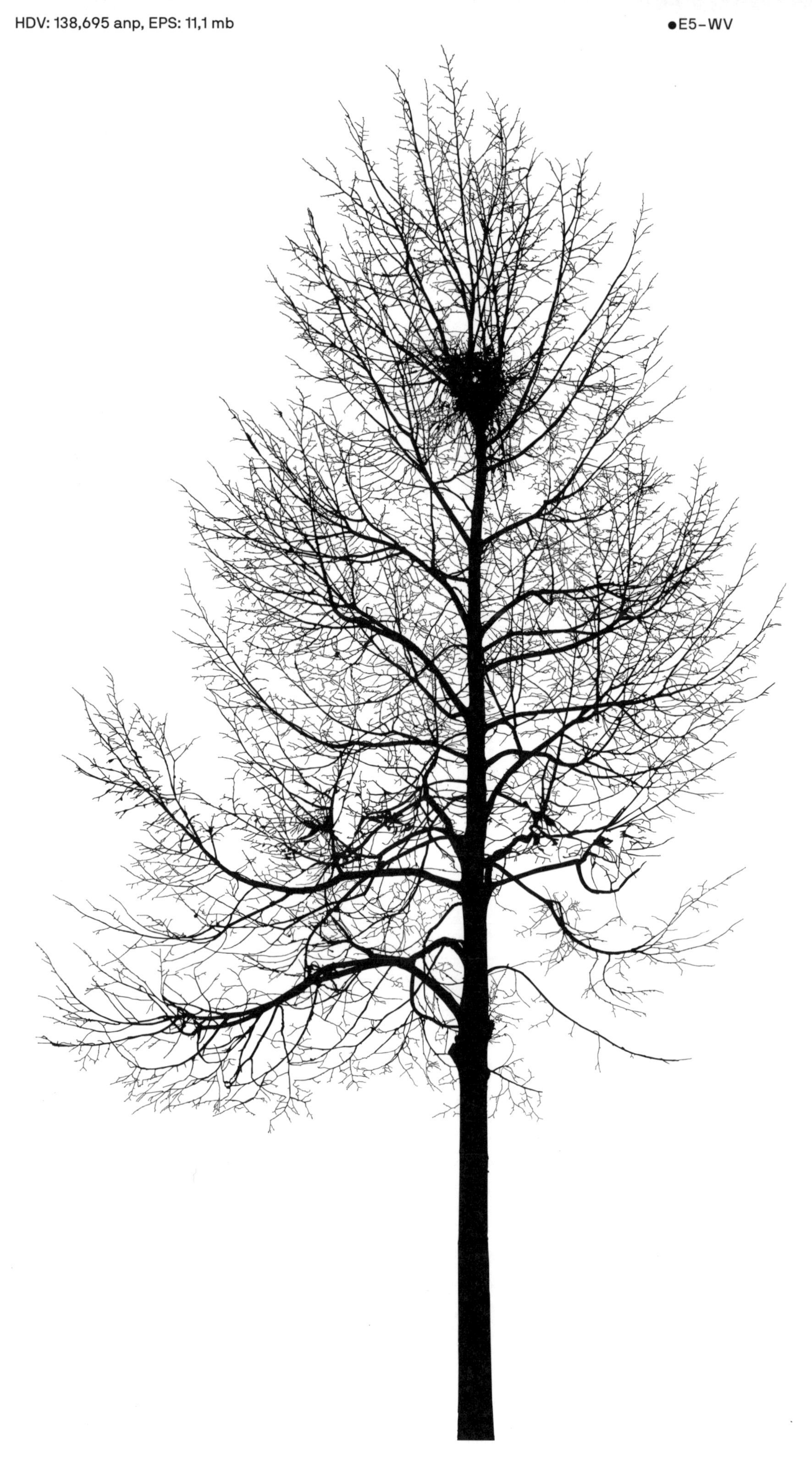

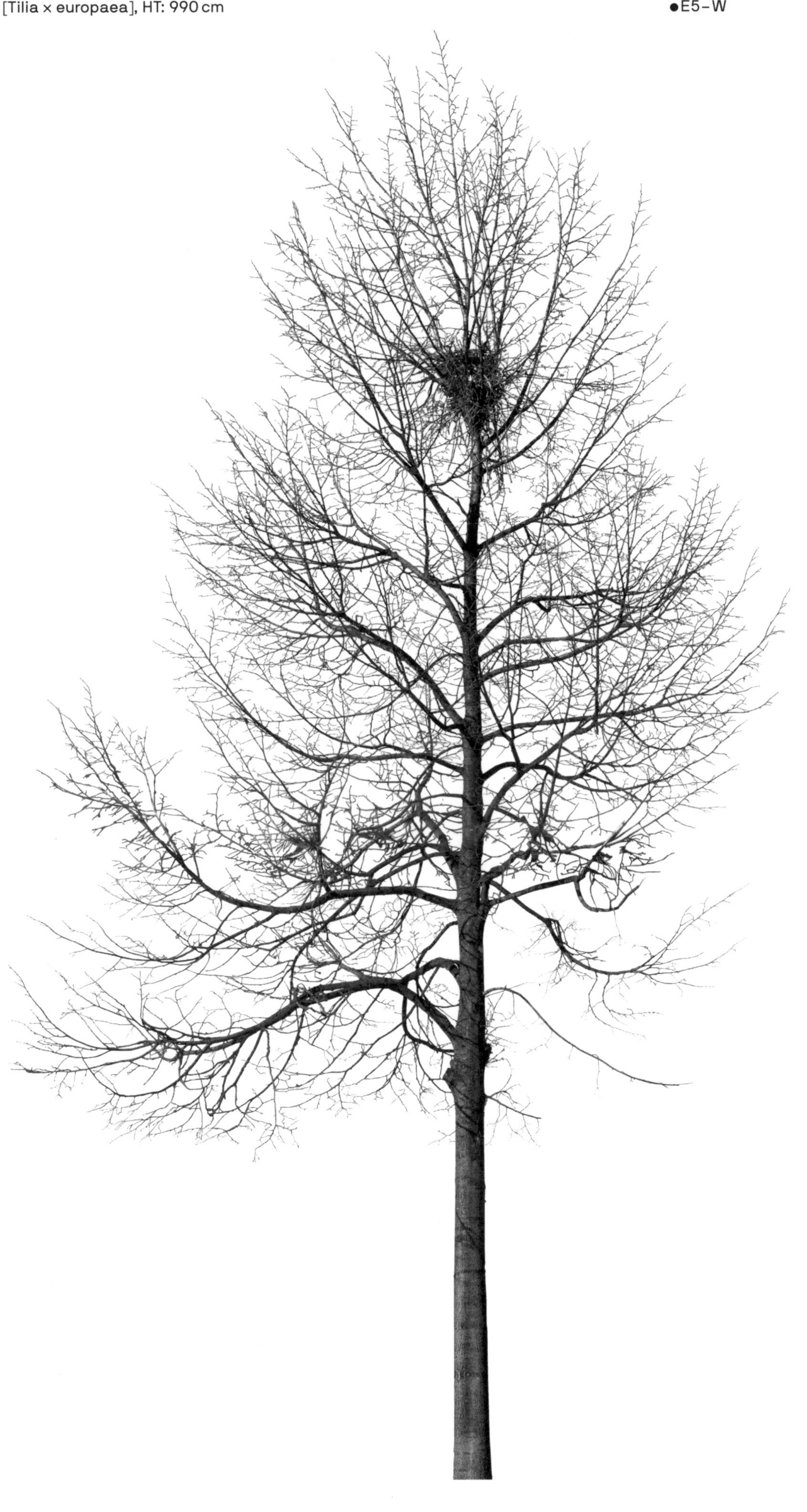

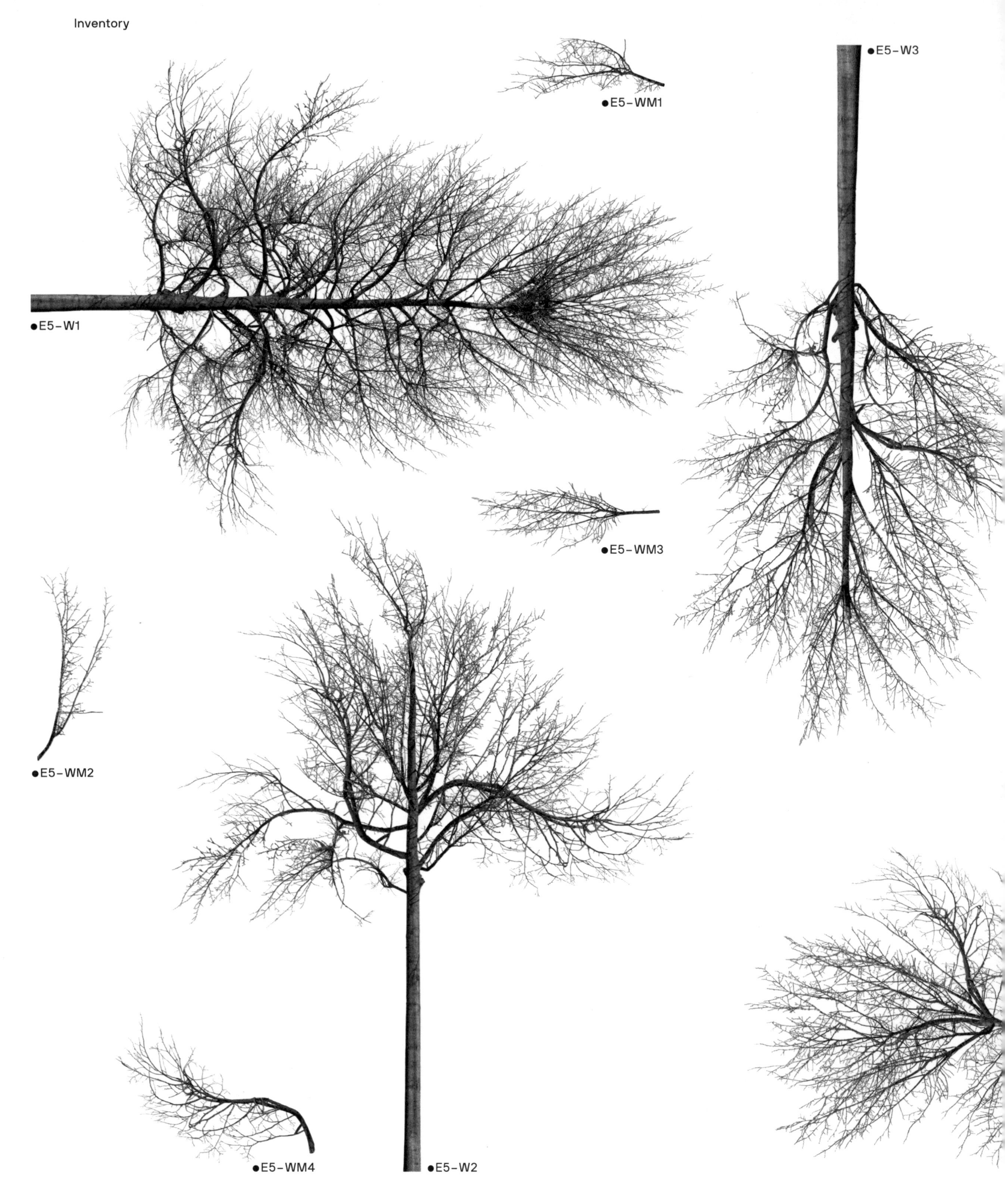

E5-WM1
E5-W3
E5-W1
E5-WM3
E5-WM2
E5-WM4
E5-W2

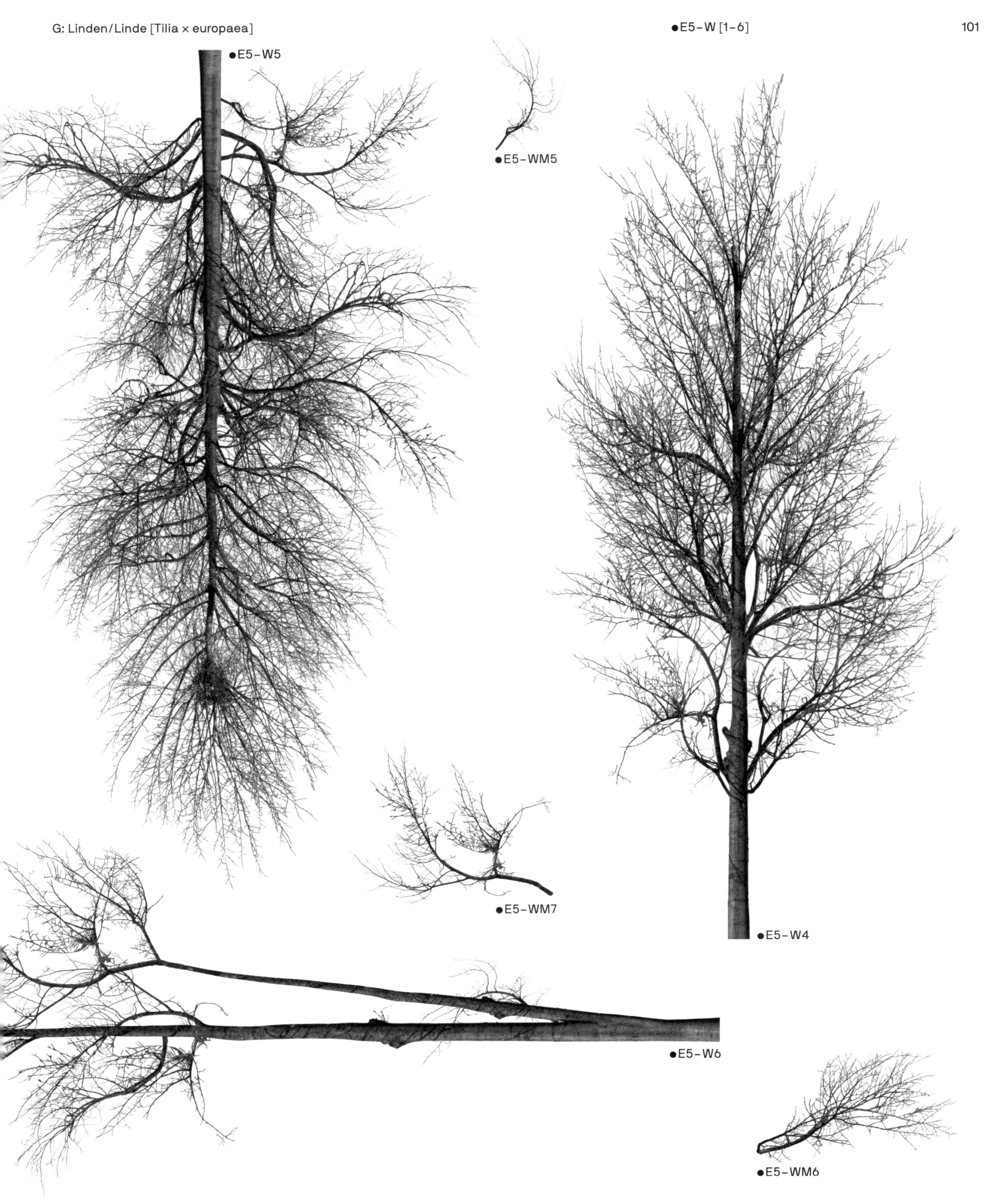
●E5–W5
●E5–WM5
●E5–WM7
●E5–W4
●E5–W6
●E5–WM6

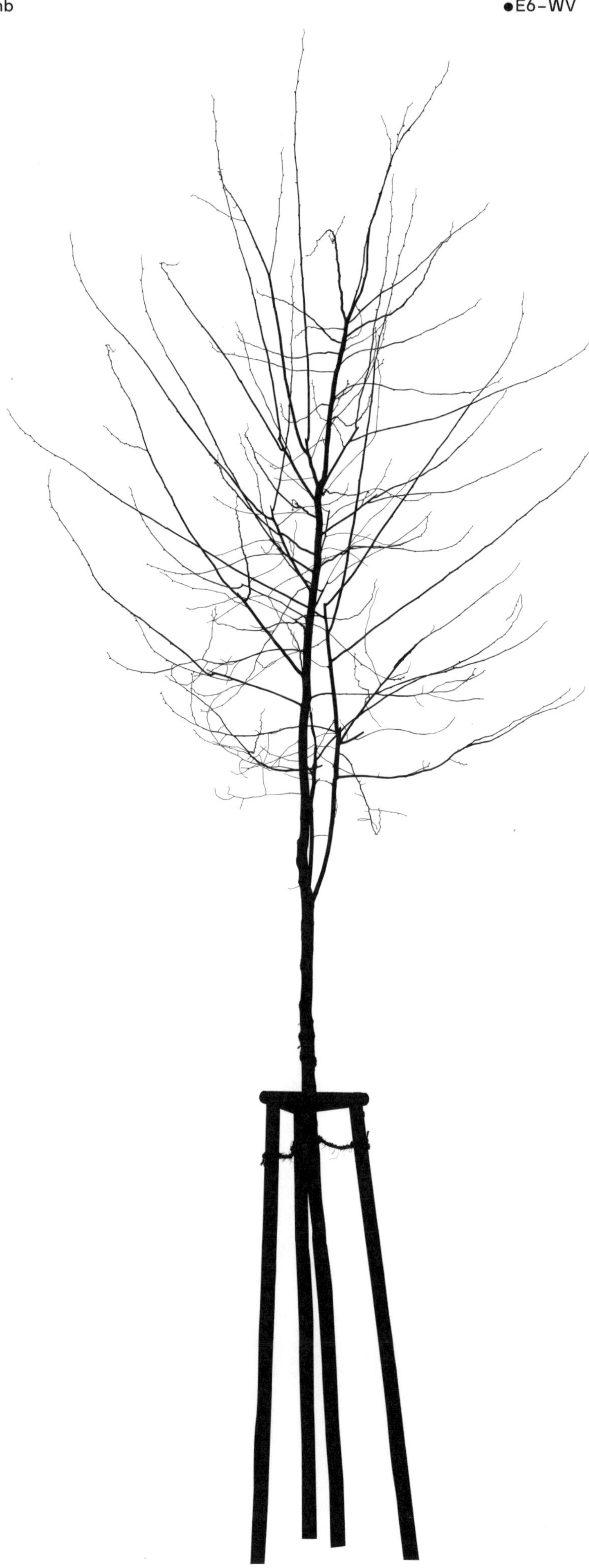

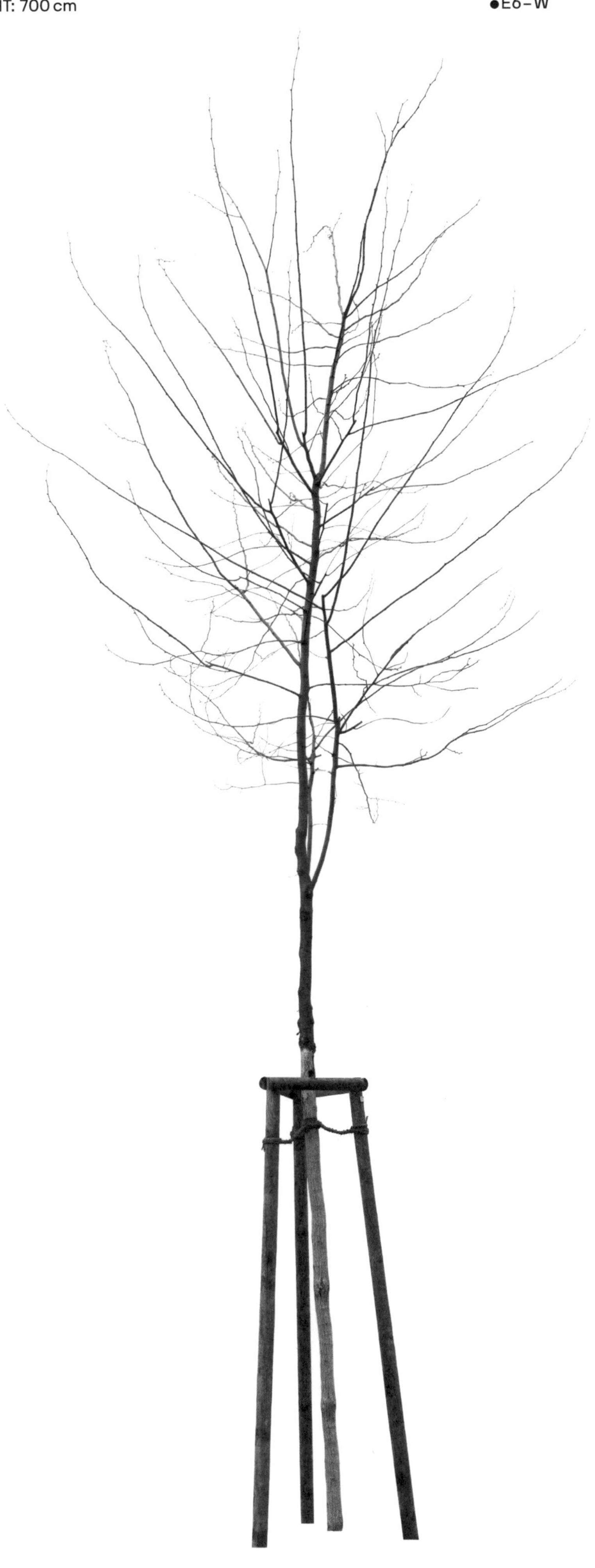

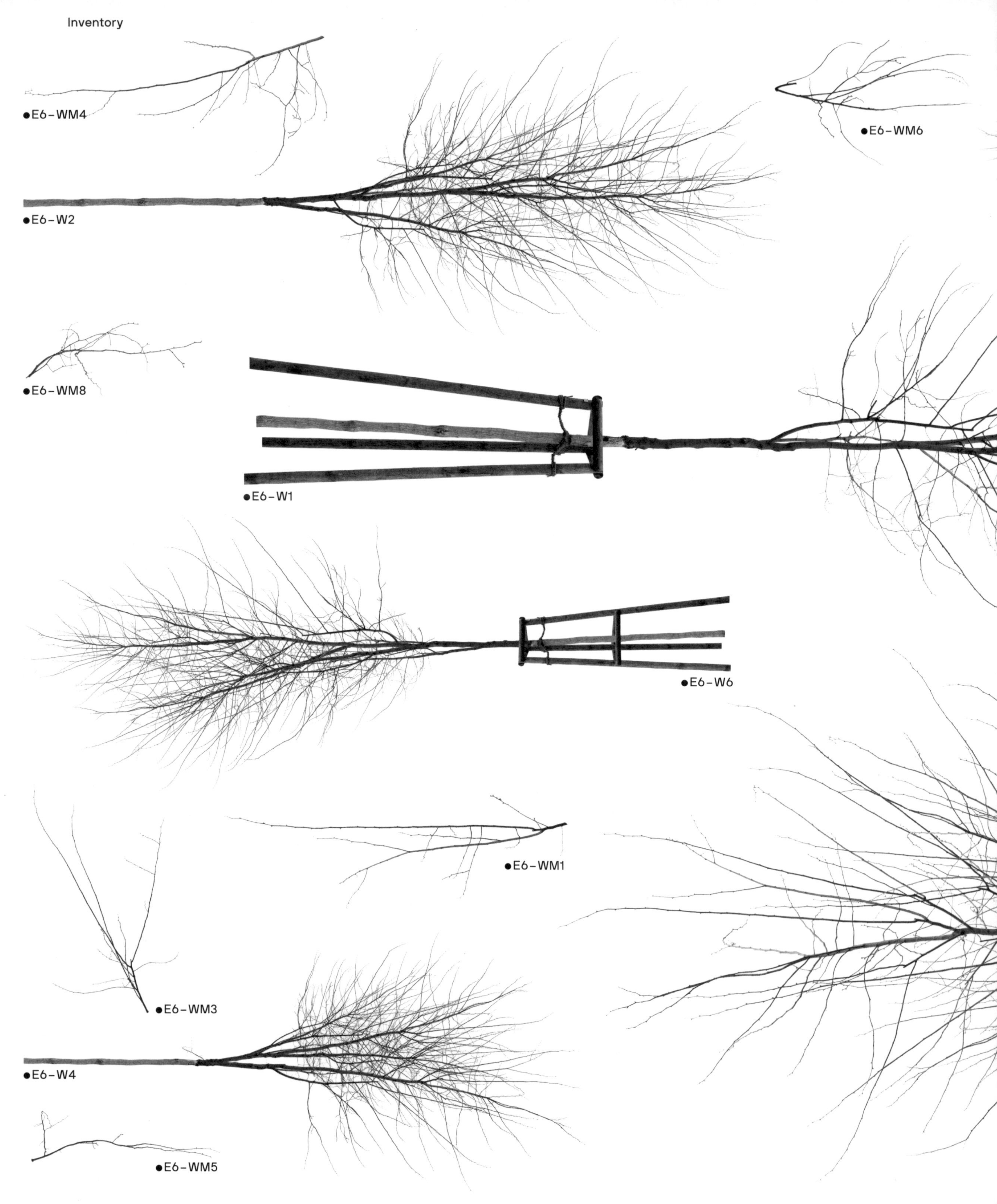

Inventory
●E6-WM4
●E6-WM6
●E6-W2
●E6-WM8
●E6-W1
●E6-W6
●E6-WM1
●E6-WM3
●E6-W4
●E6-WM5

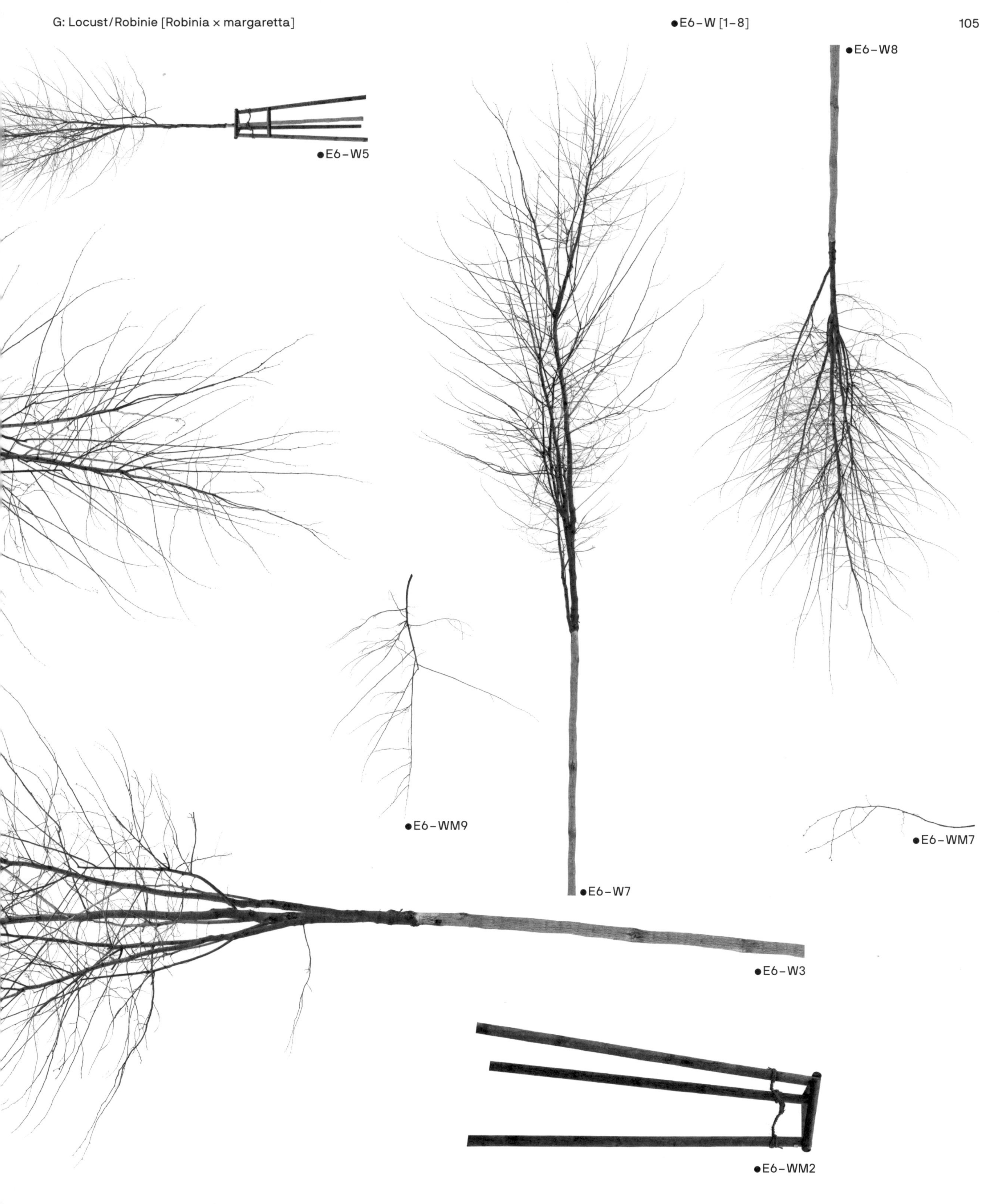
●E6-W8
●E6-W5
●E6-WM9
●E6-WM7
●E6-W7
●E6-W3
●E6-WM2

Inventory

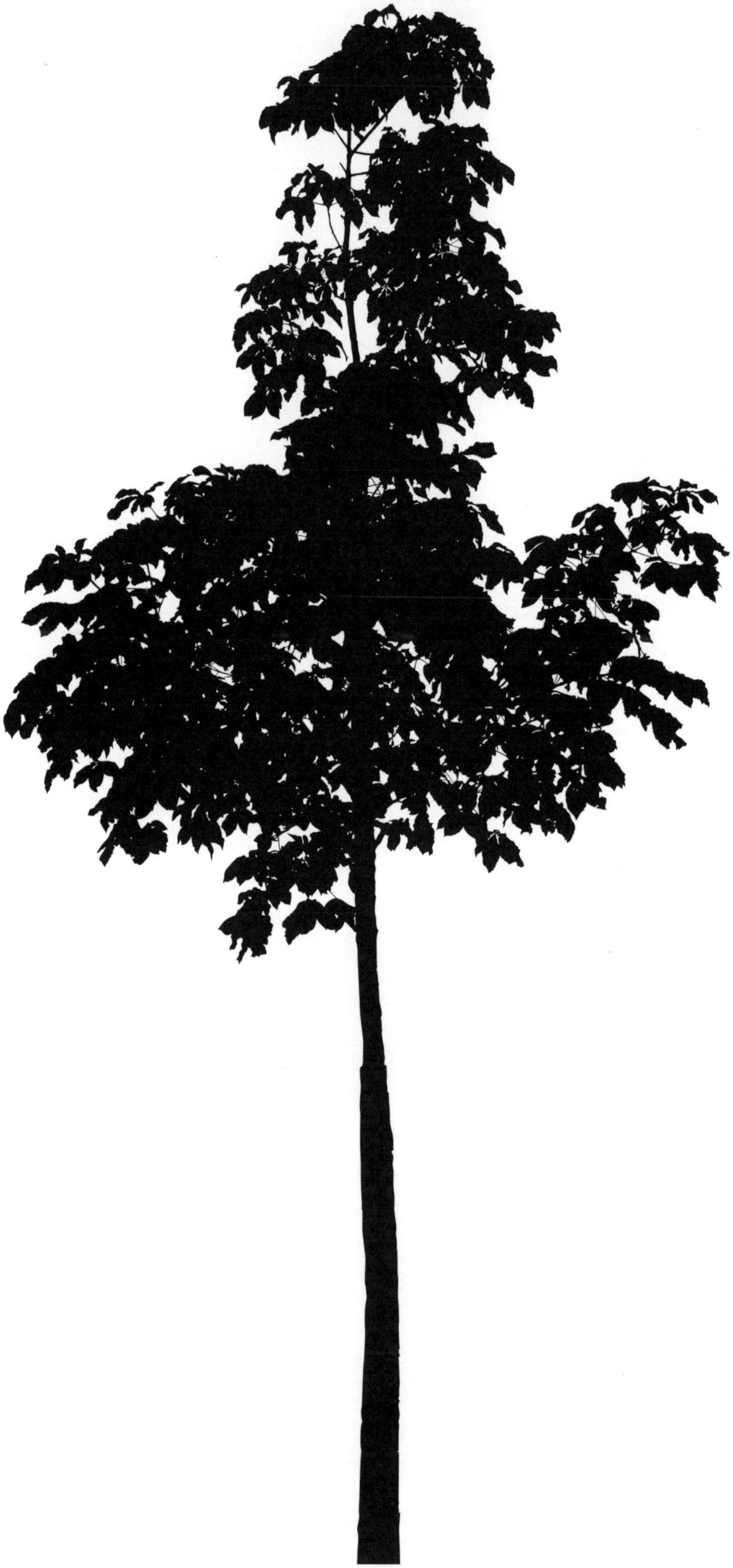

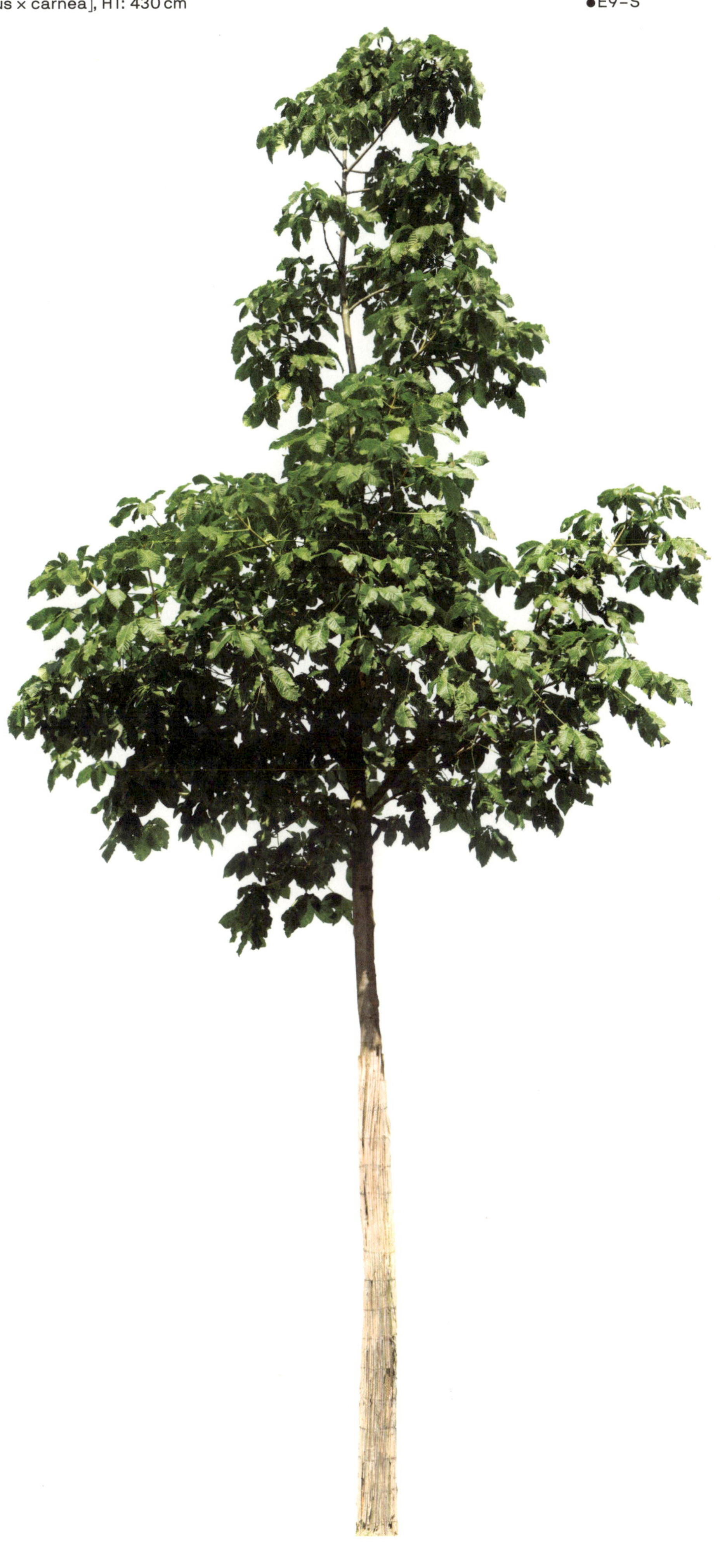

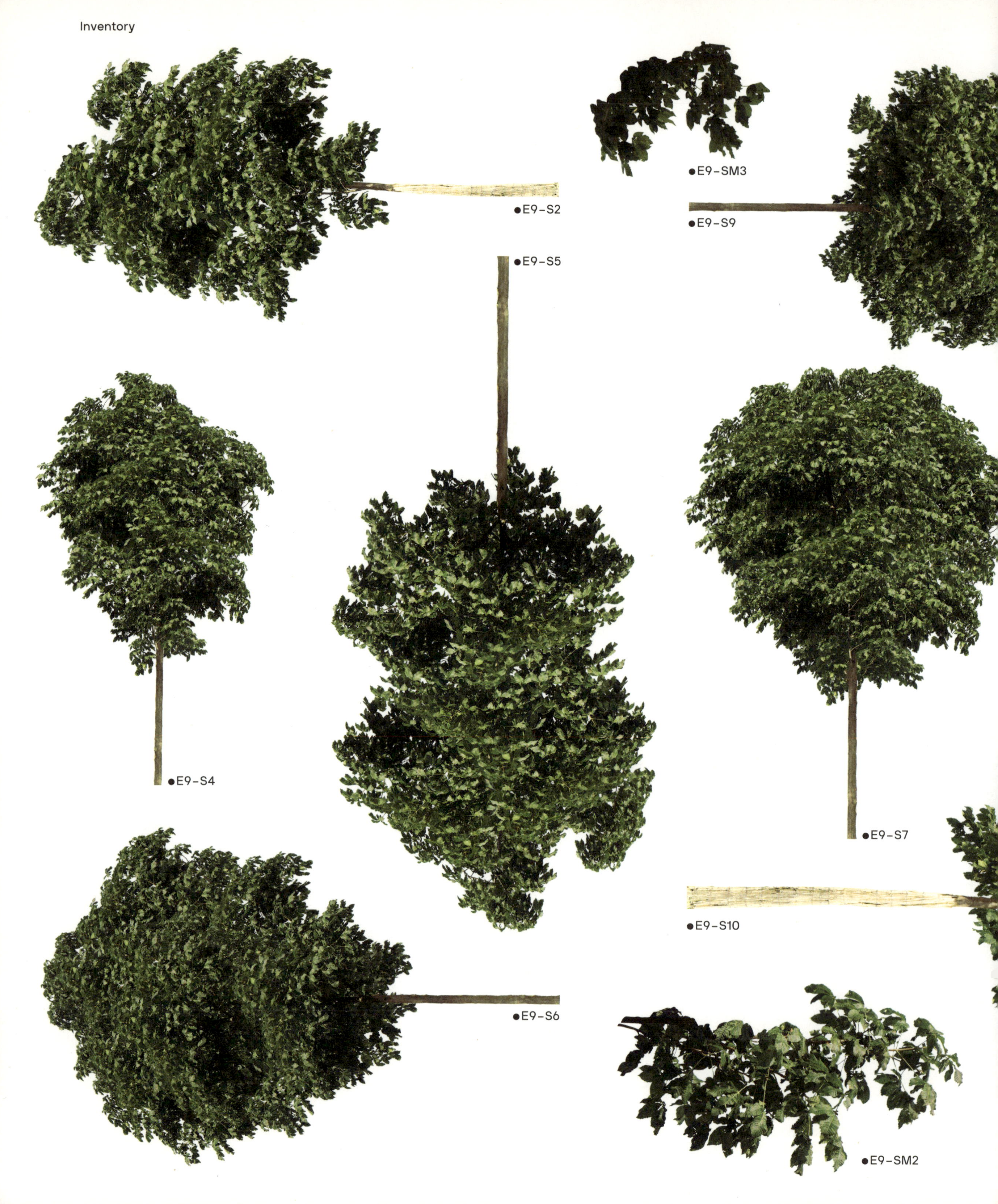
●E9–S2
●E9–SM3
●E9–S9
●E9–S5
●E9–S4
●E9–S7
●E9–S10
●E9–S6
●E9–SM2

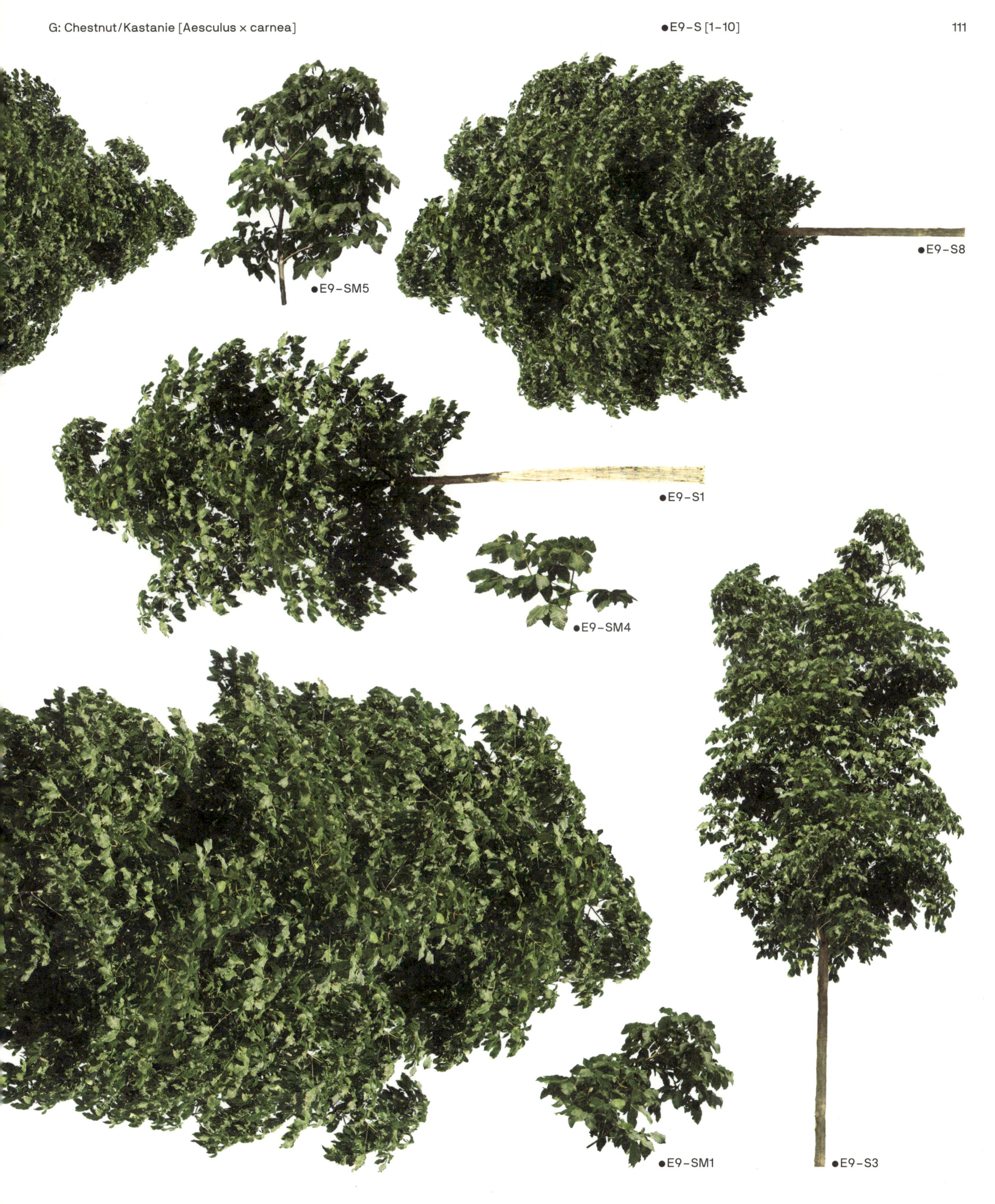
●E9–SM5
●E9–S8
●E9–S1
●E9–SM4
●E9–SM1
●E9–S3

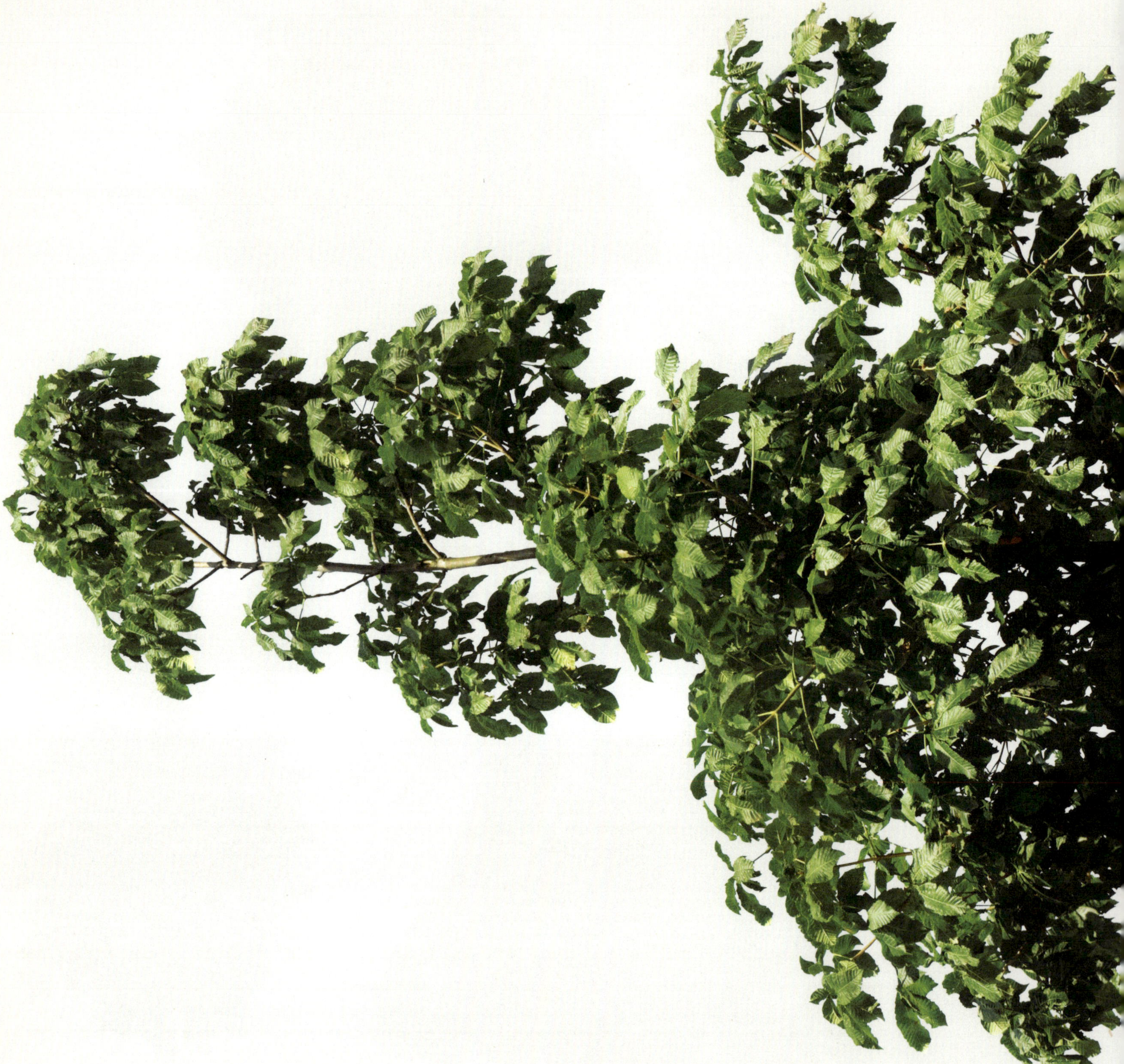

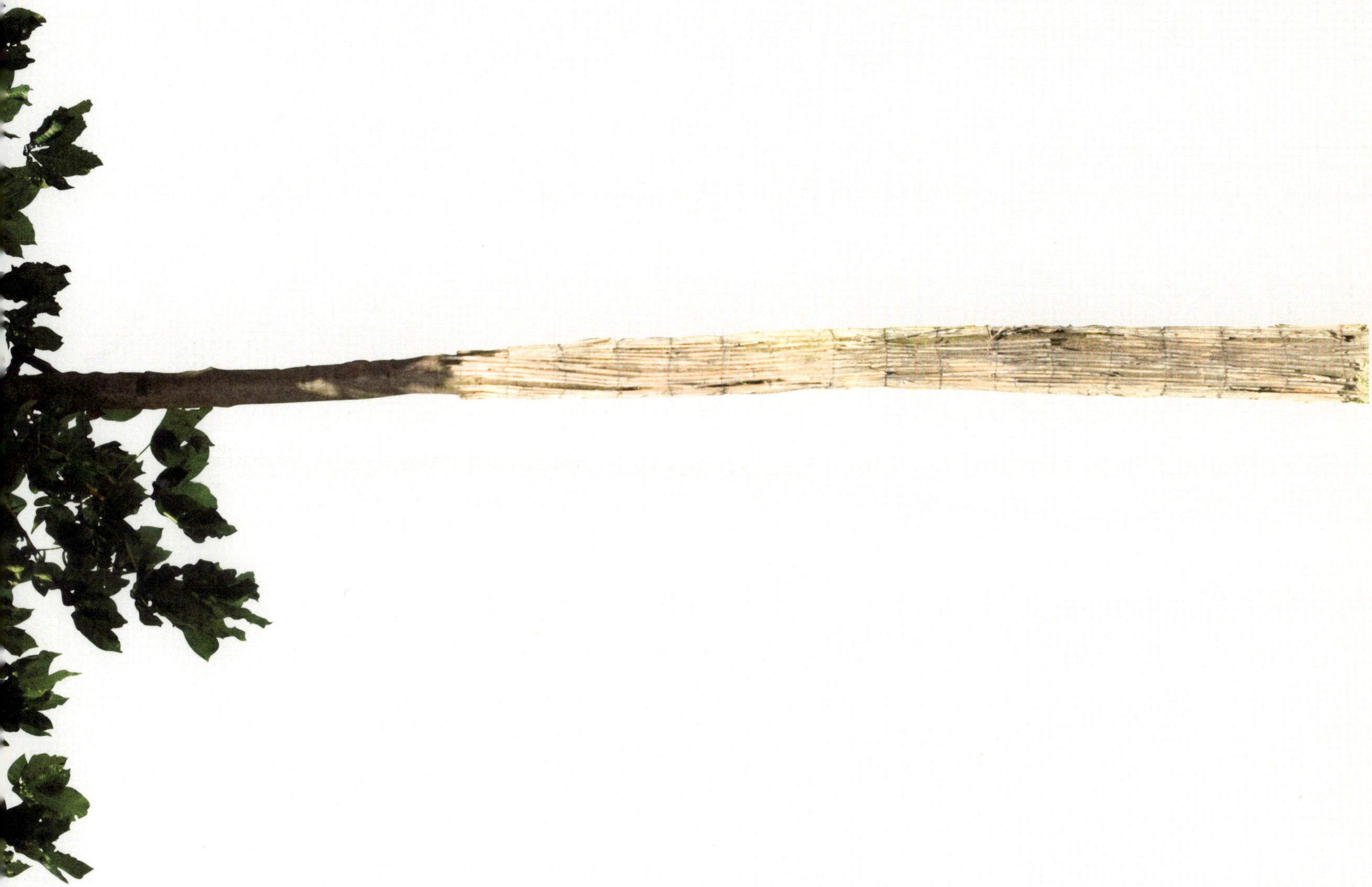

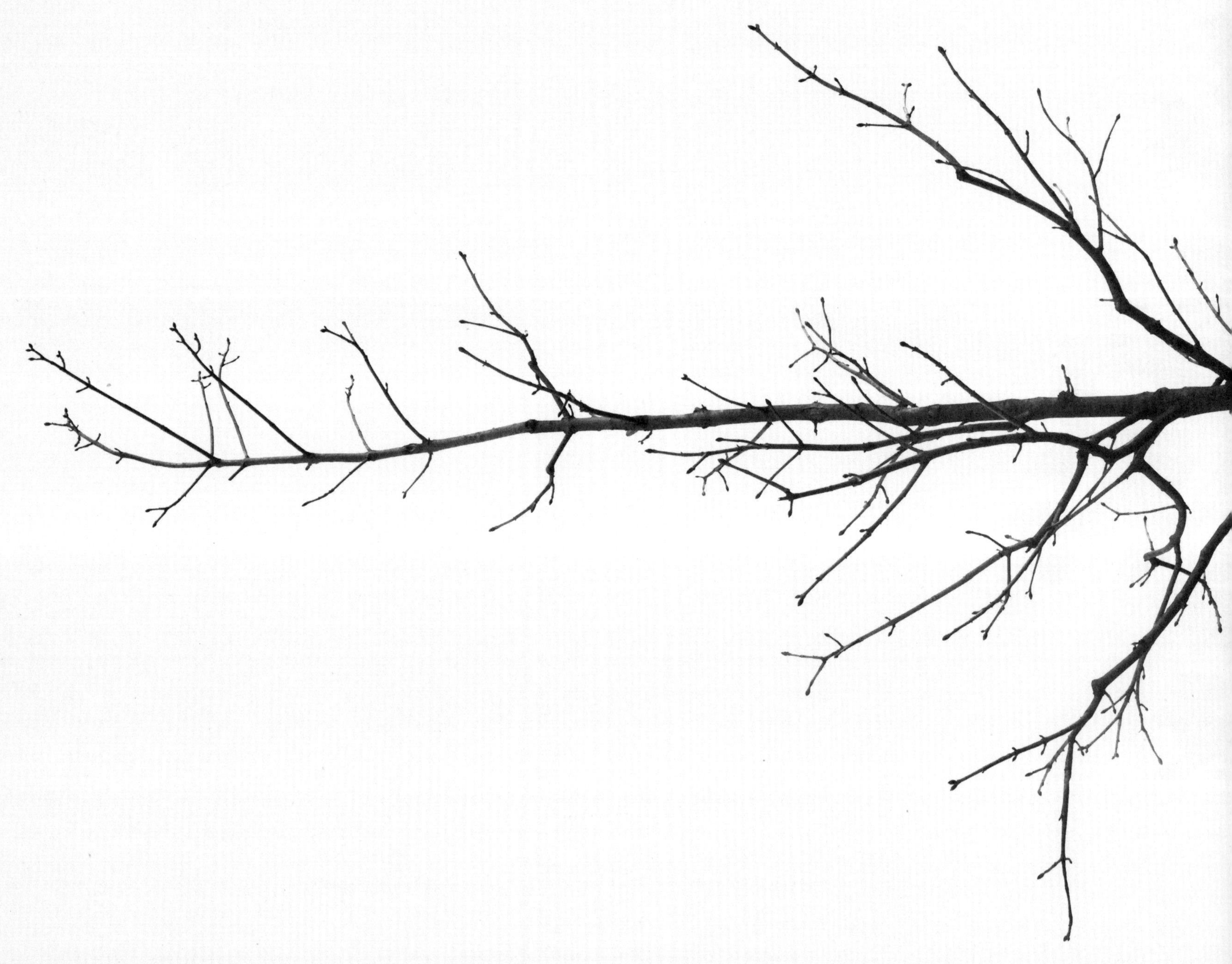

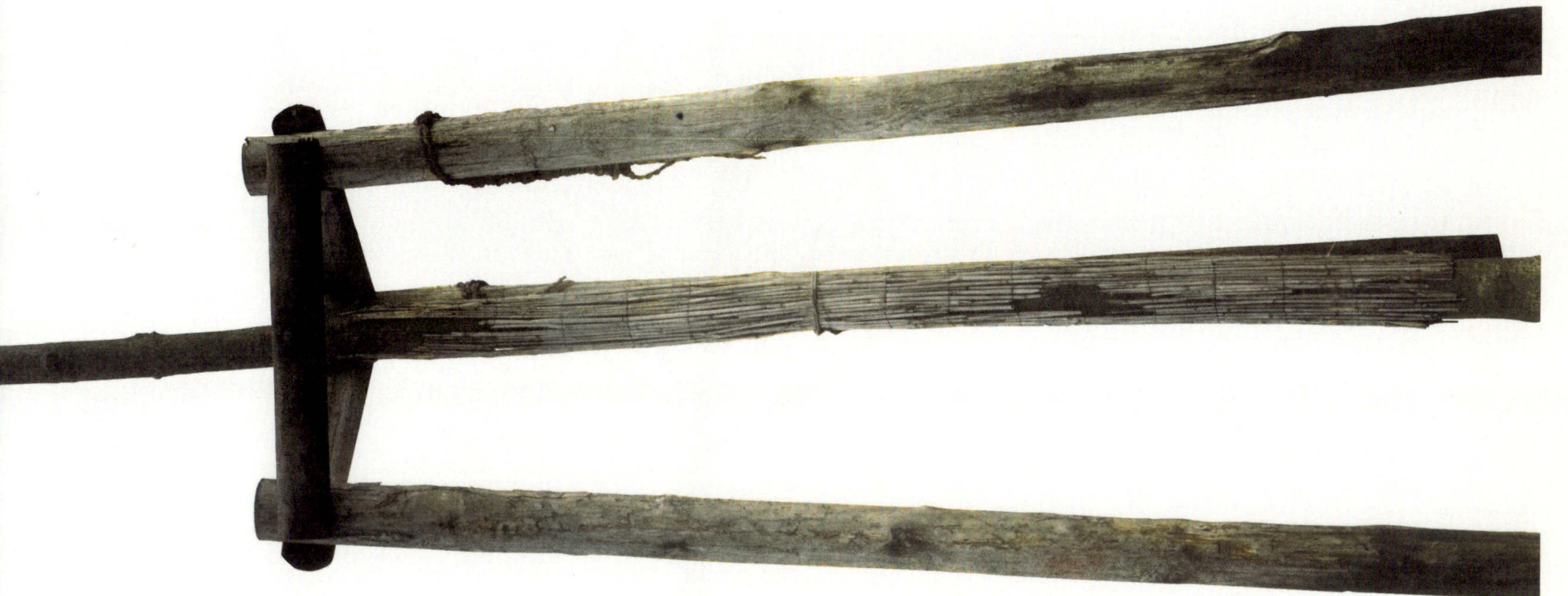

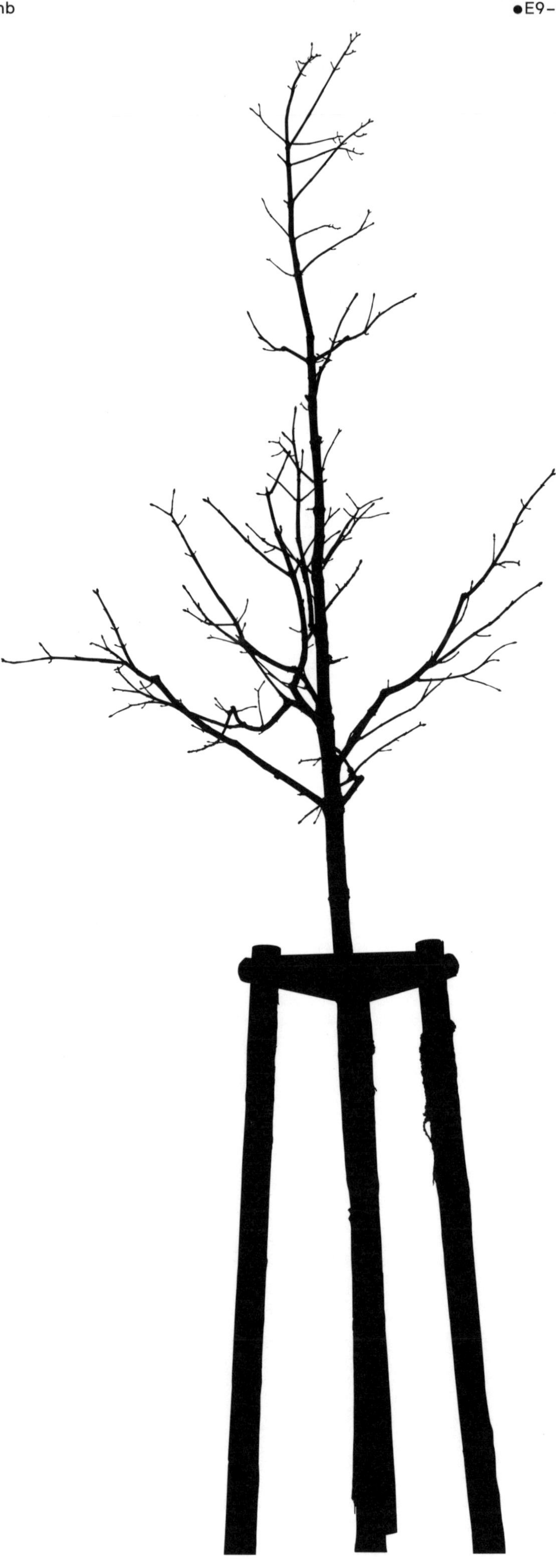

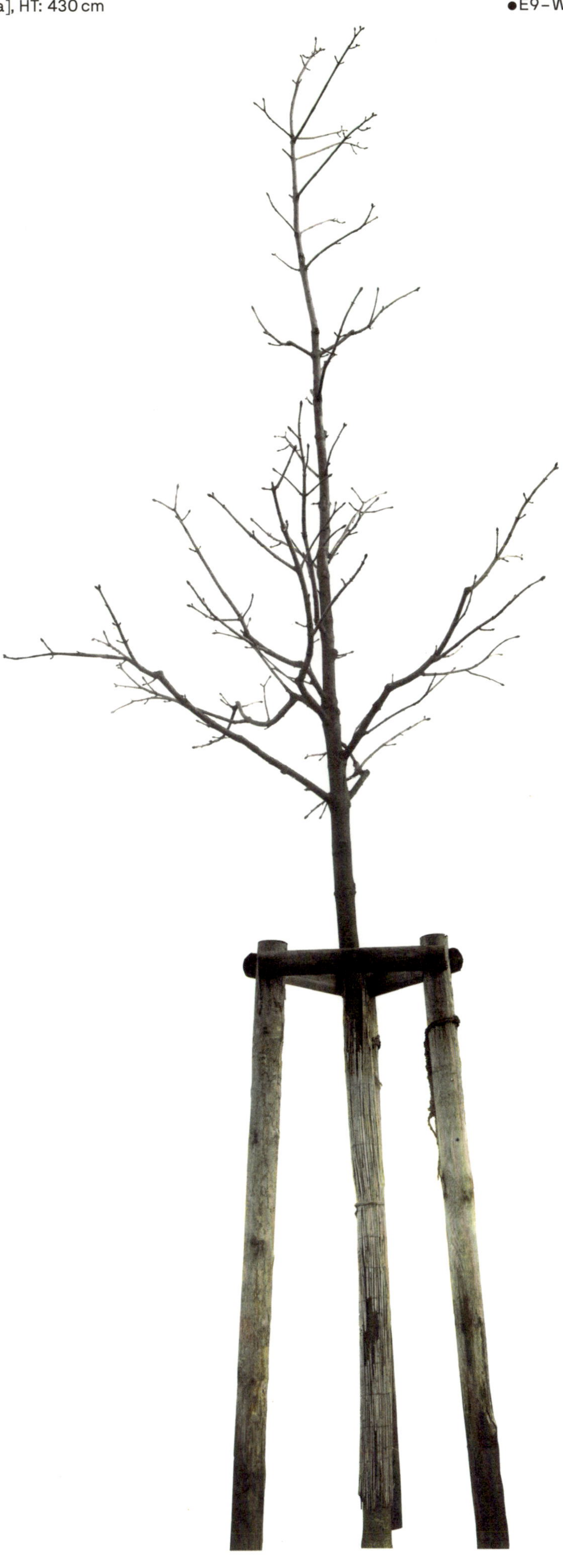

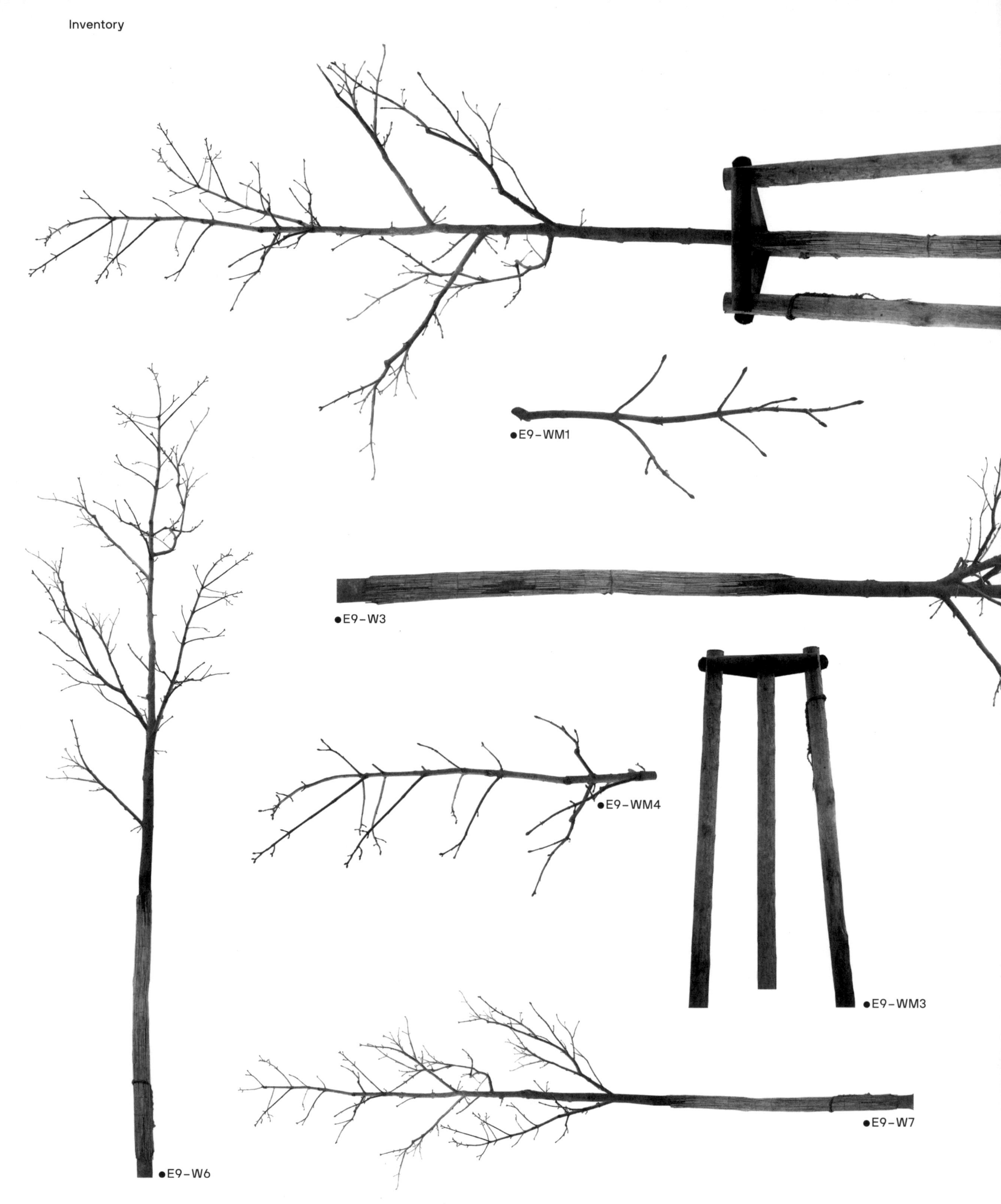

●E9–WM1
●E9–W3
●E9–WM4
●E9–WM3
●E9–W6
●E9–W7

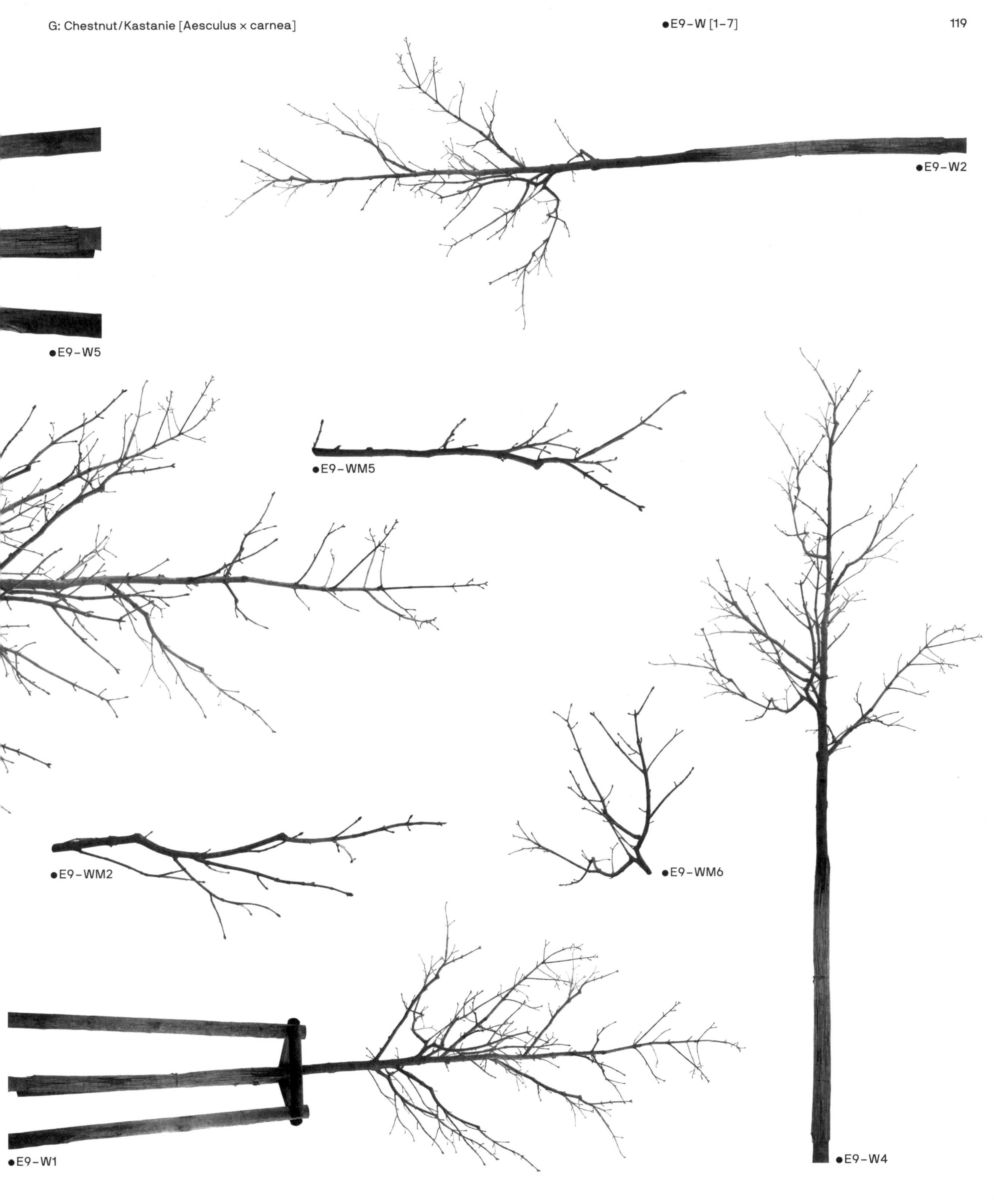
●E9−W2
●E9−W5
●E9−WM5
●E9−WM2
●E9−WM6
●E9−W1
●E9−W4

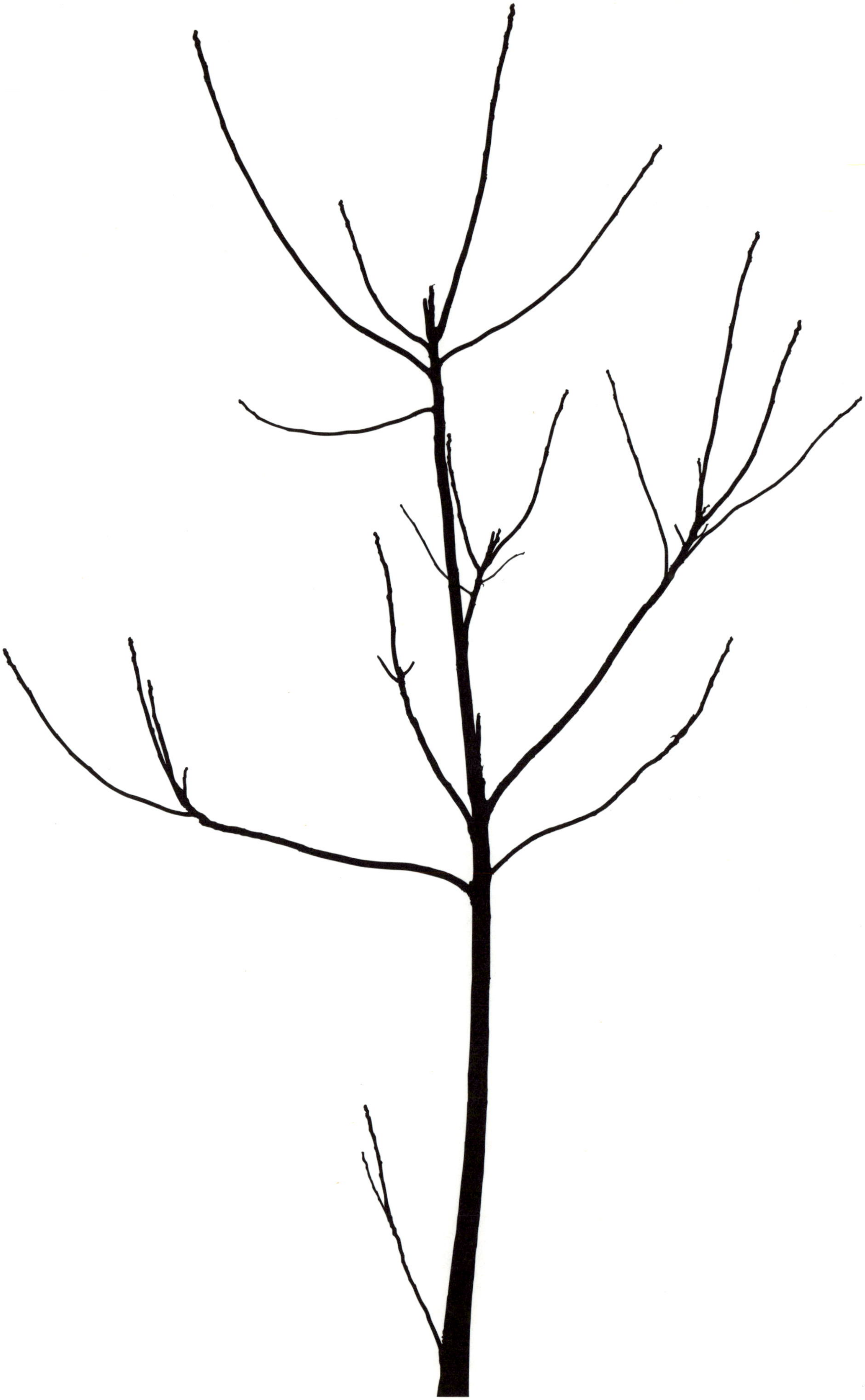

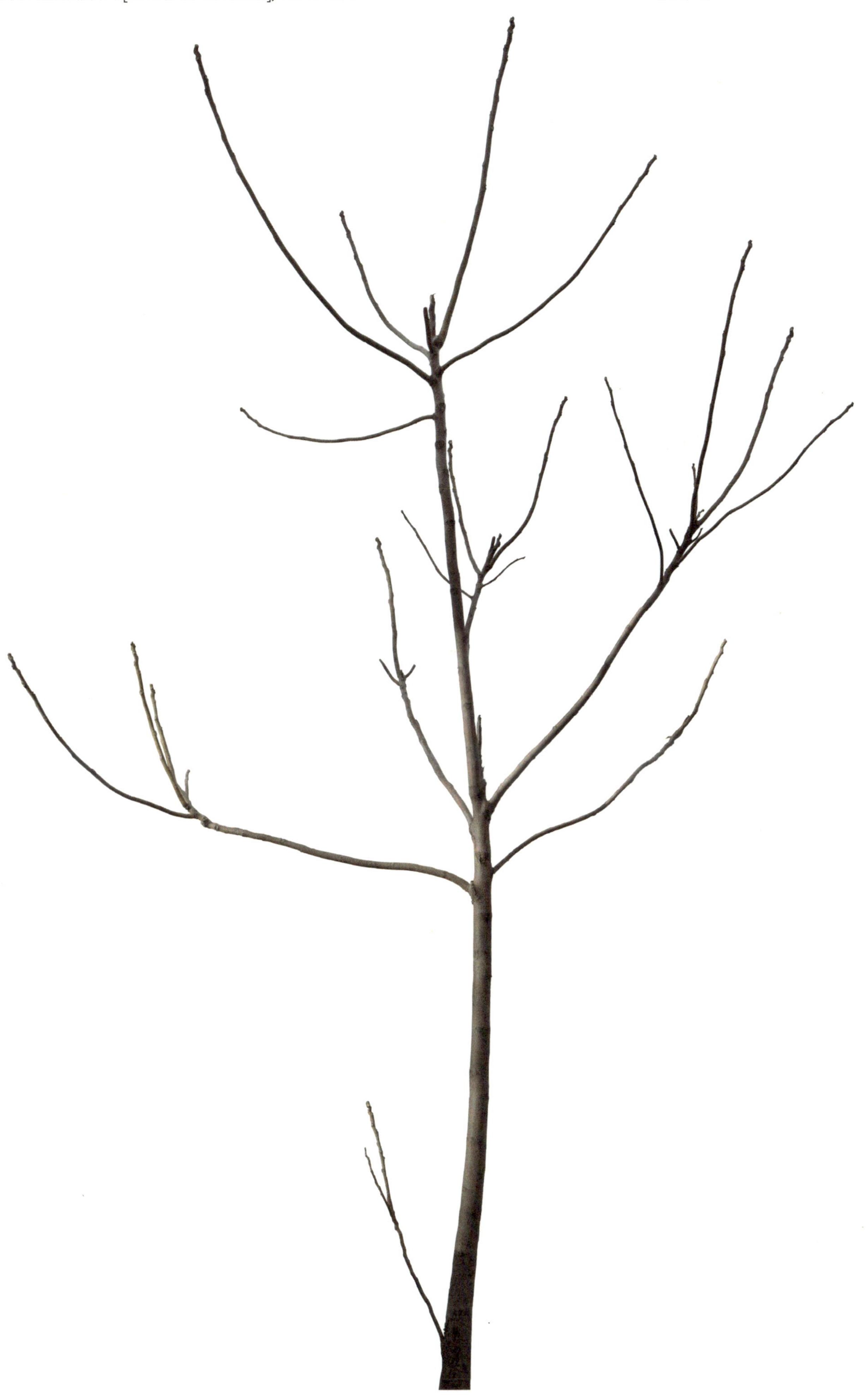

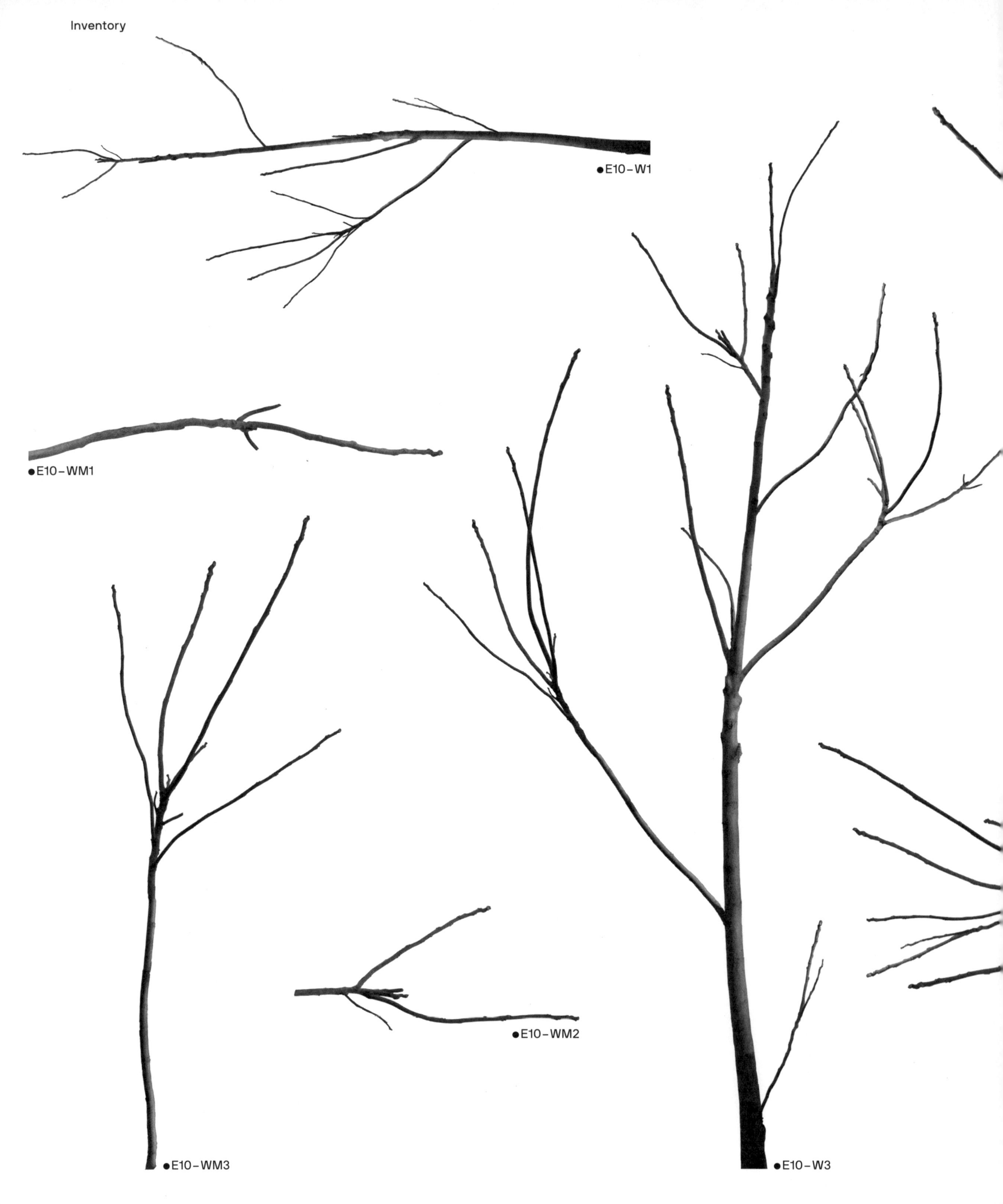

Inventory
E10–W1
E10–WM1
E10–WM2
E10–WM3
E10–W3

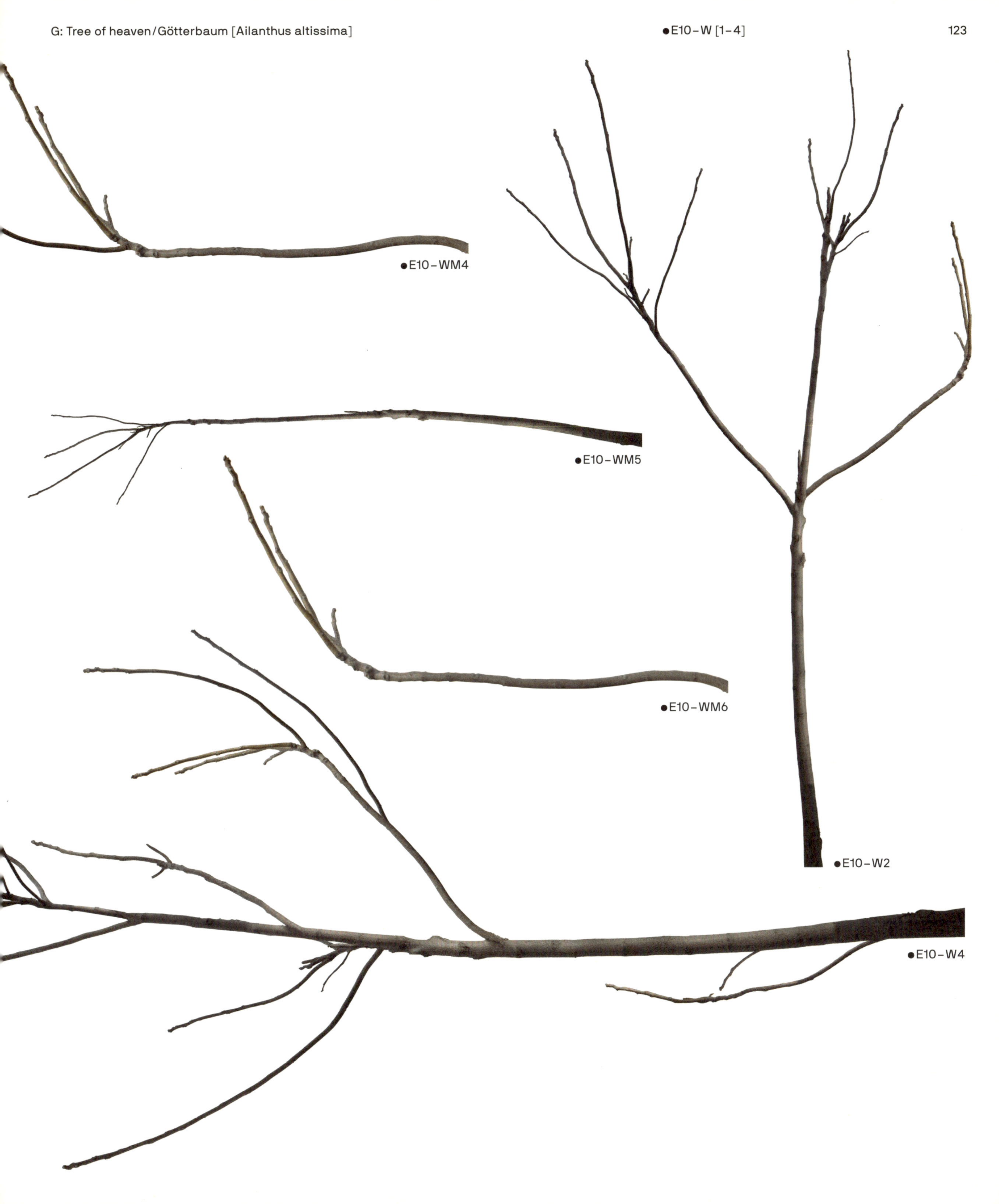
●E10–WM4
●E10–WM5
●E10–WM6
●E10–W2
●E10–W4

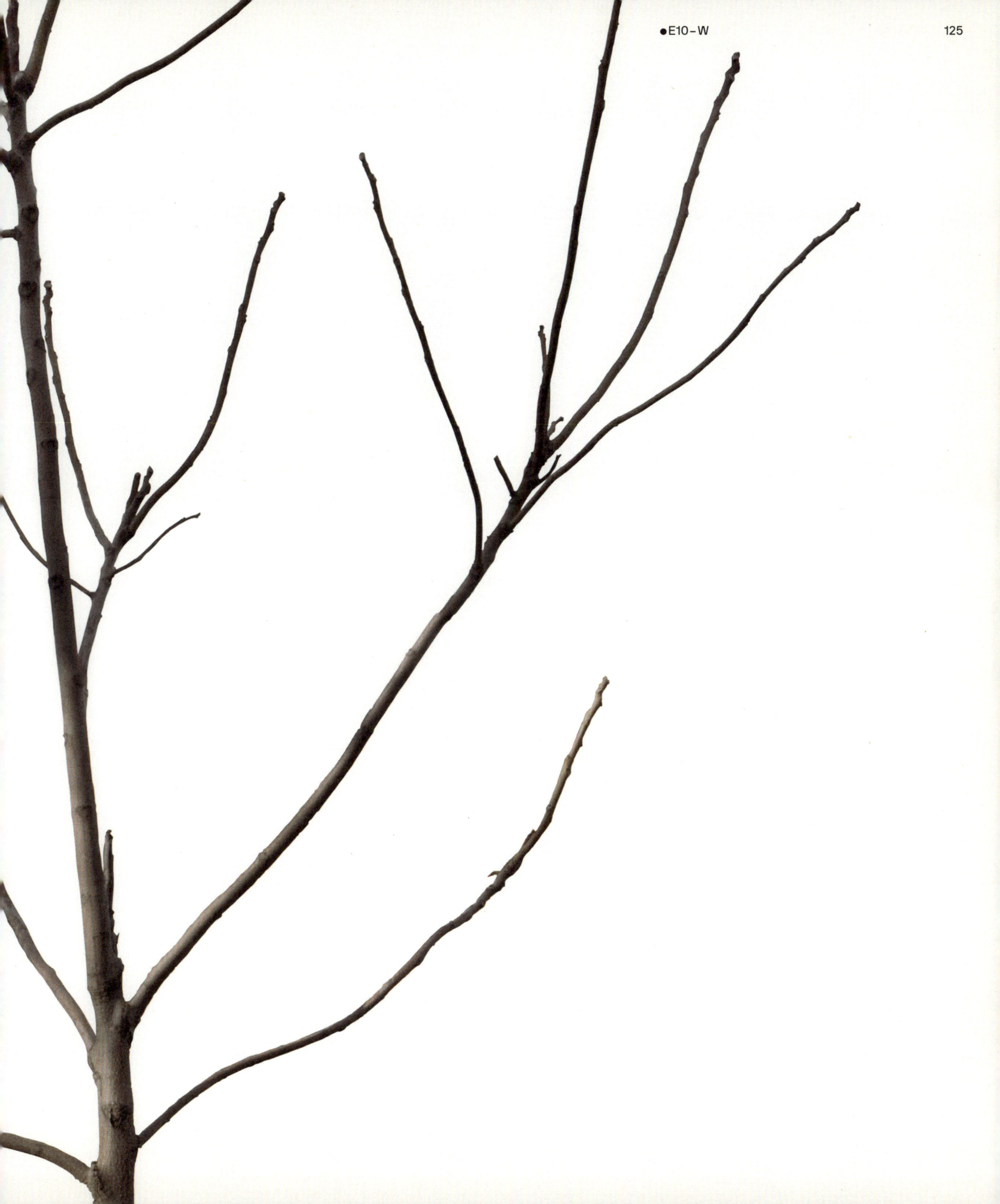

```
U4   S  W    Linden       [Tilia]
U6      W    Lilac        [Syringa]
```



```
U4   S  W    Linden       [Tilia]
U6      W    Lilac        [Syringa]
```

U4–U6

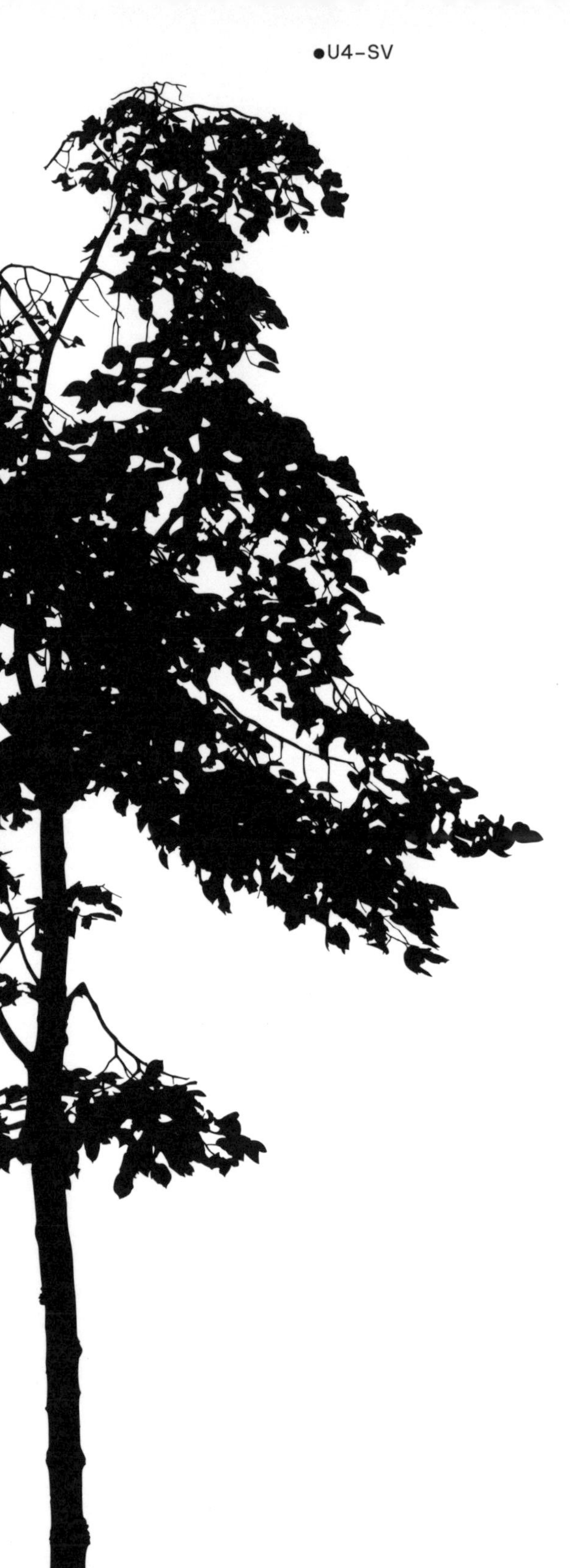

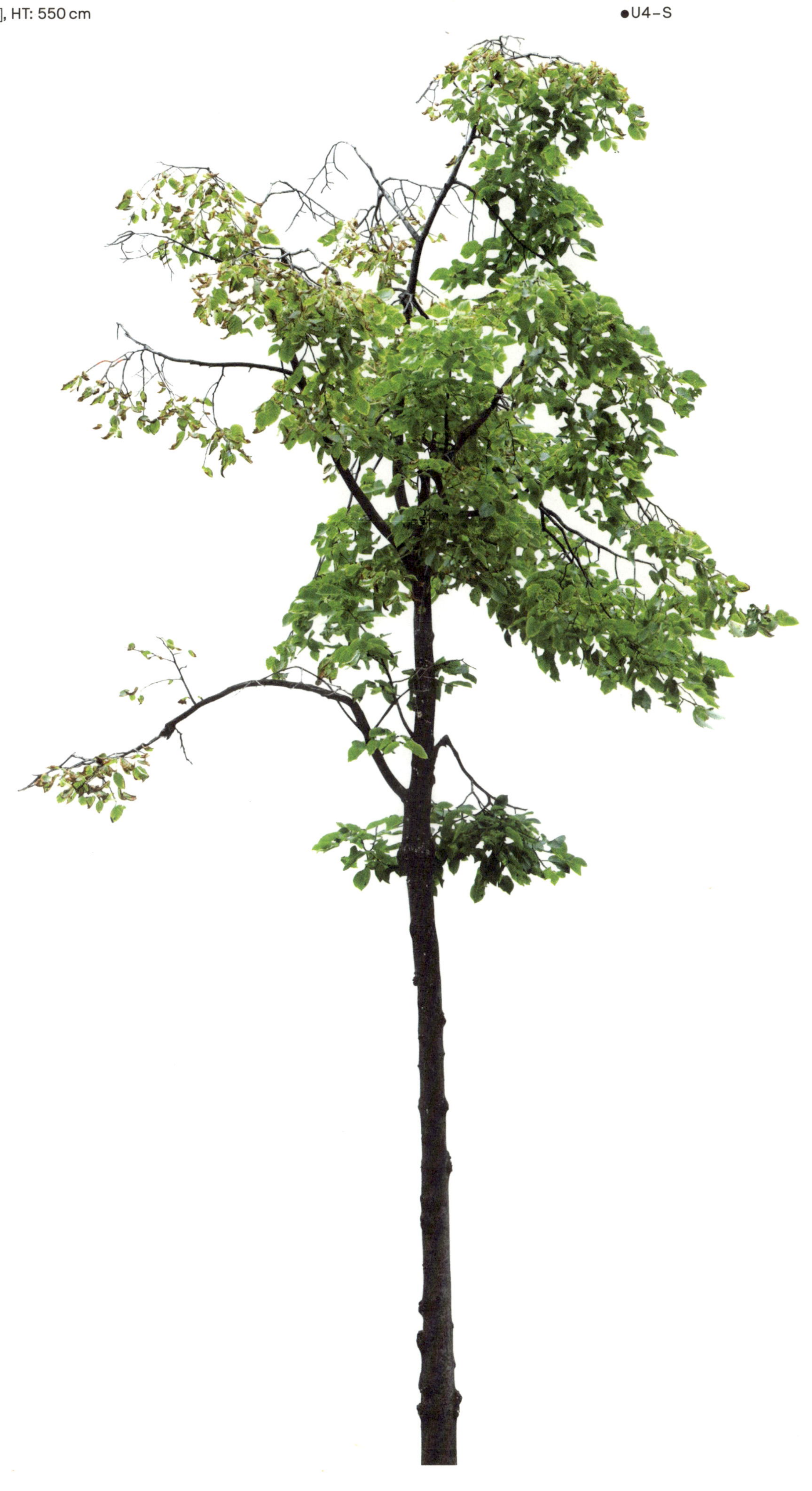

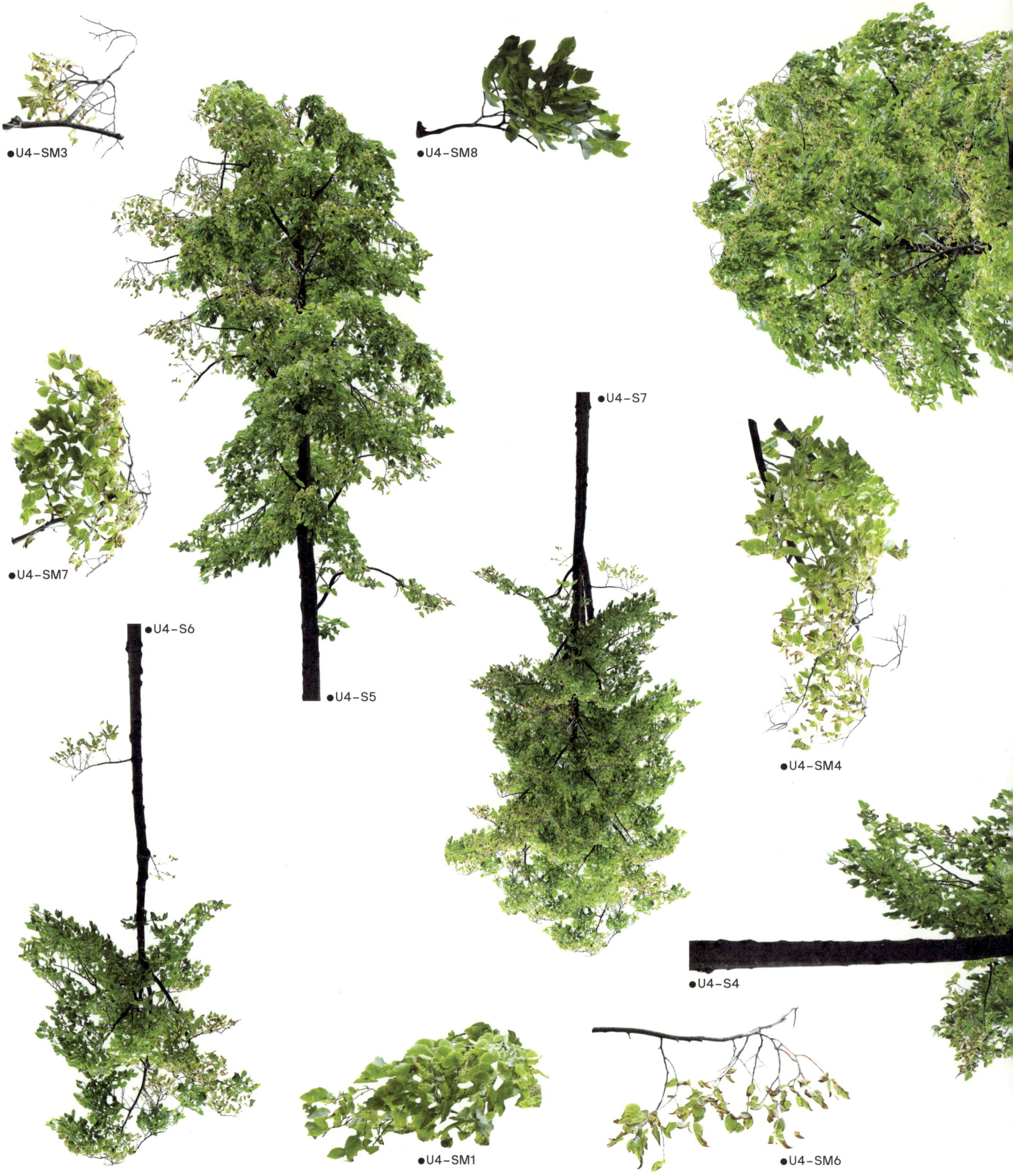

Inventory

●U4–SM3

●U4–SM8

●U4–SM7

●U4–S6

●U4–S5

●U4–S7

●U4–SM4

●U4–S4

●U4–SM1

●U4–SM6

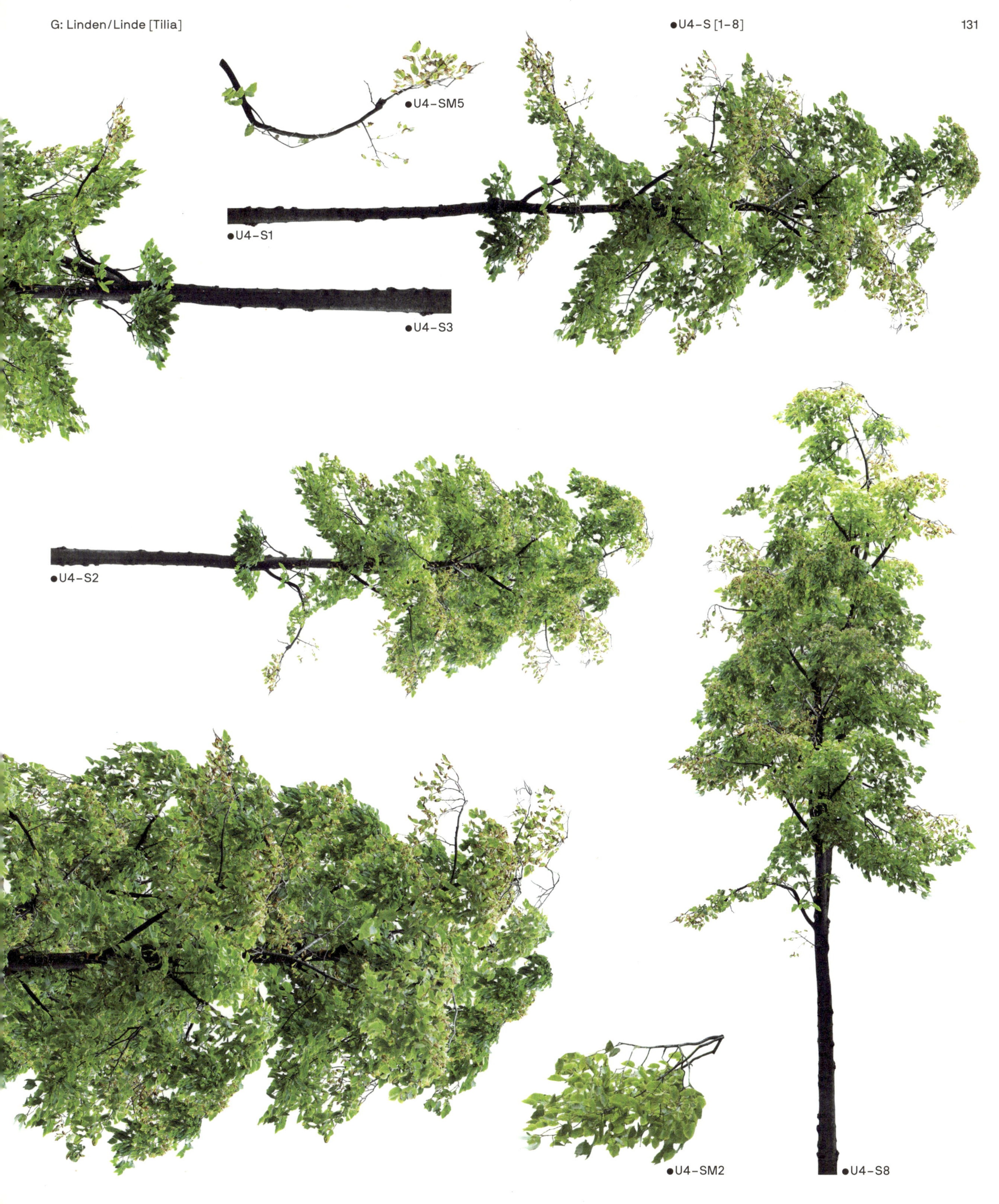
●U4–SM5
●U4–S1
●U4–S3
●U4–S2
●U4–SM2
●U4–S8

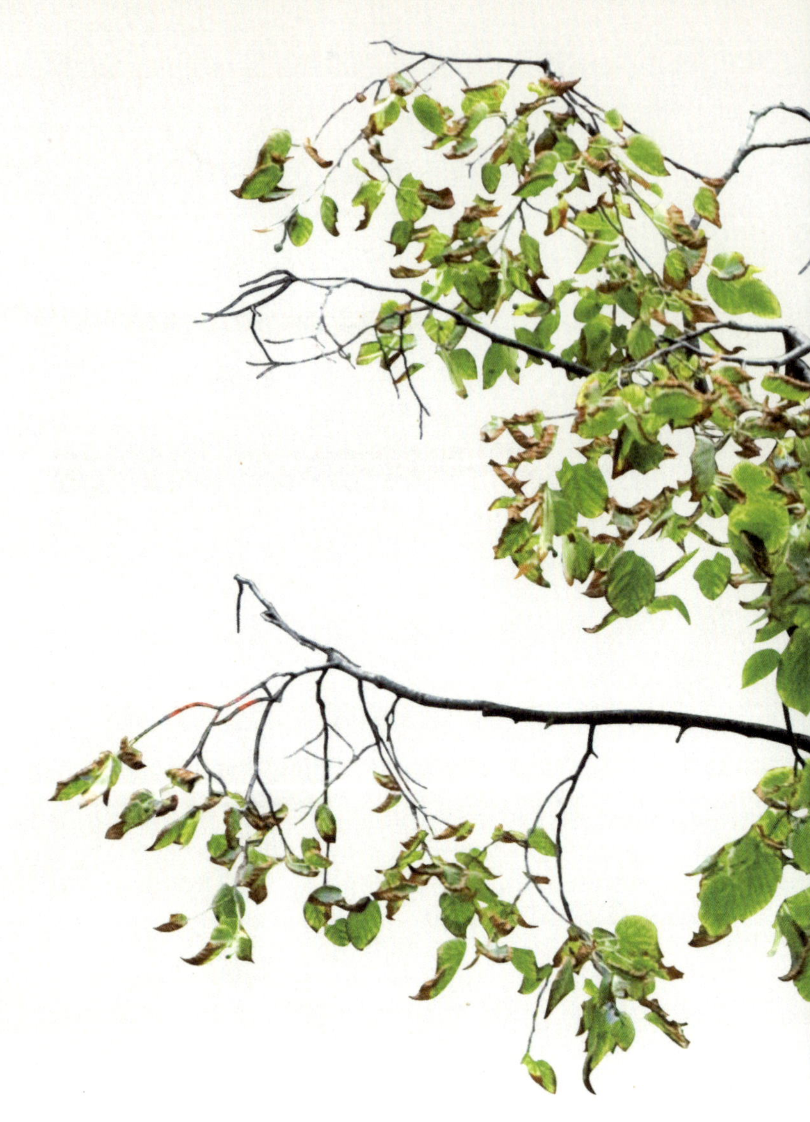
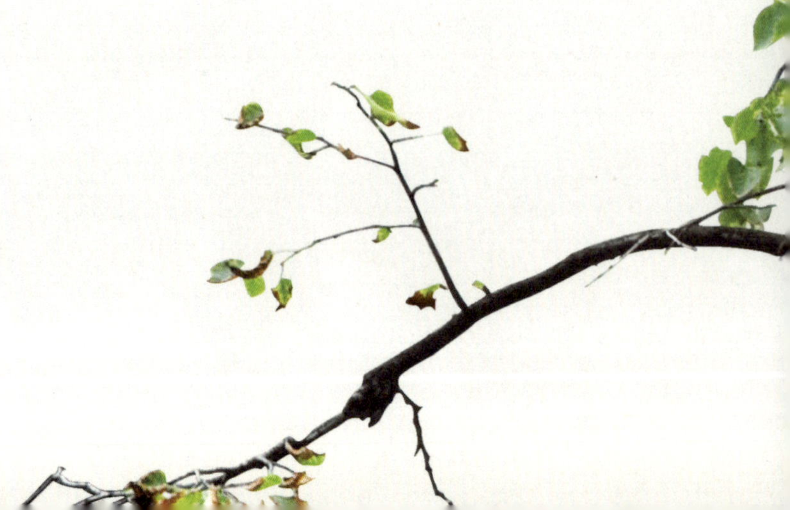

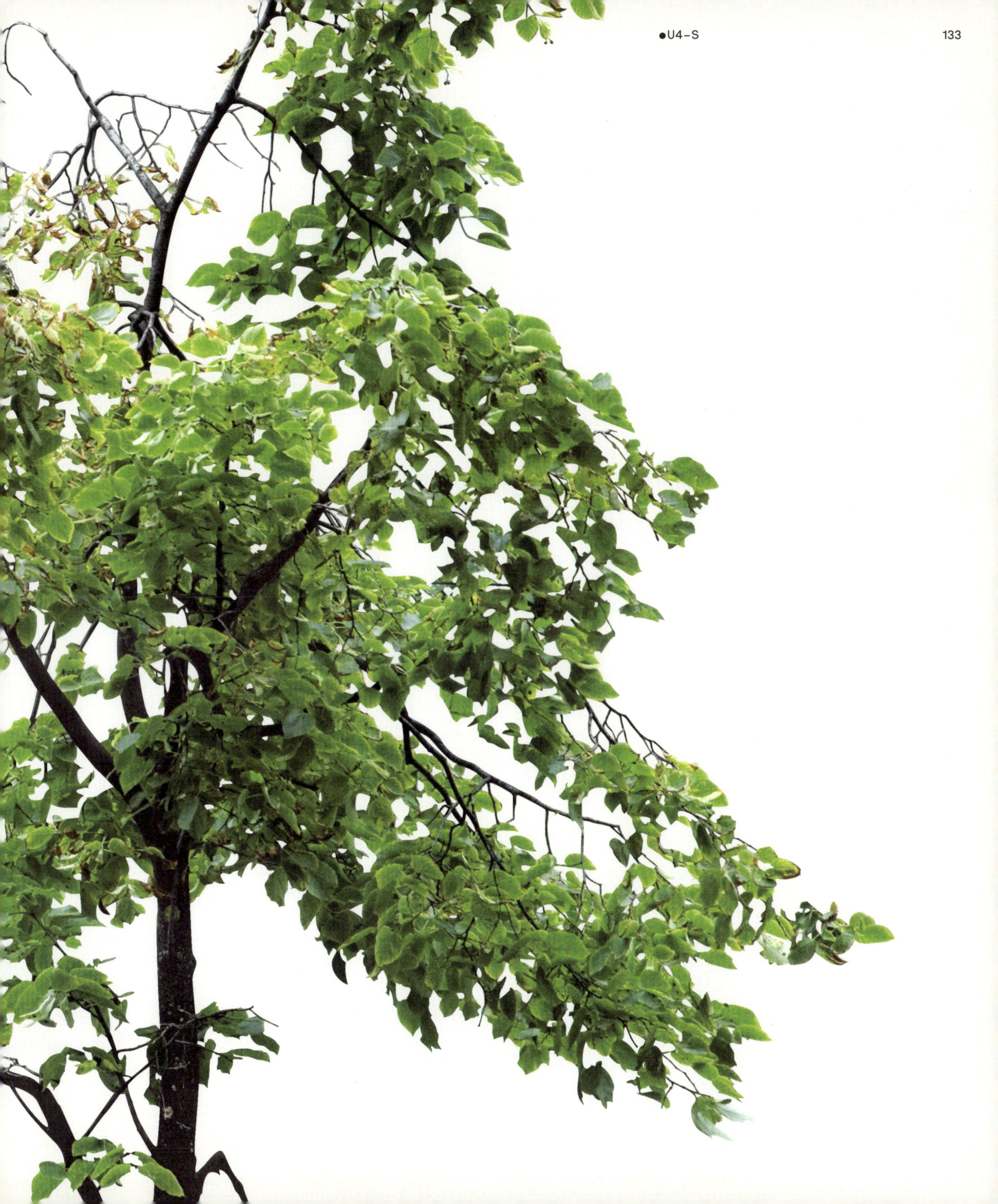

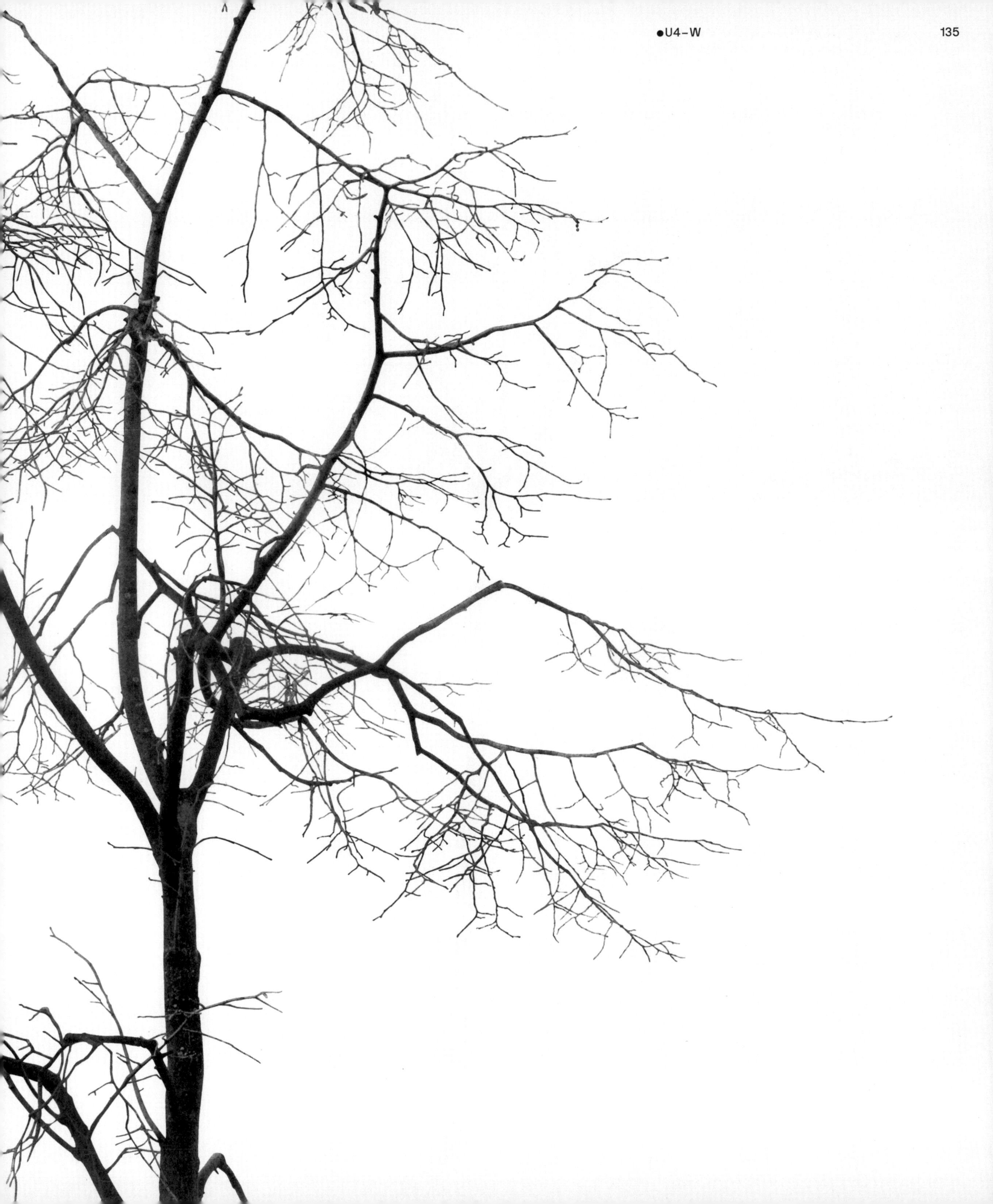

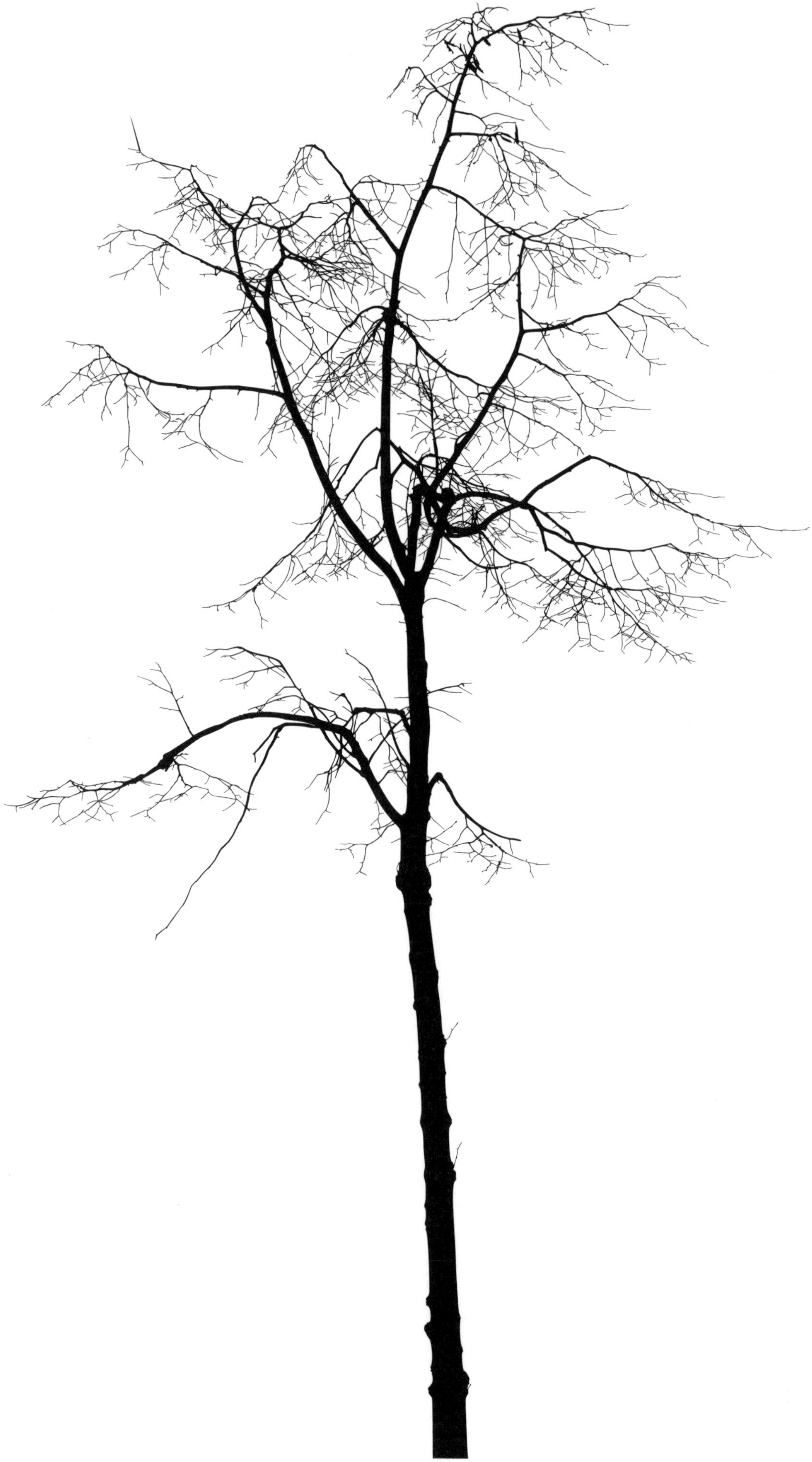

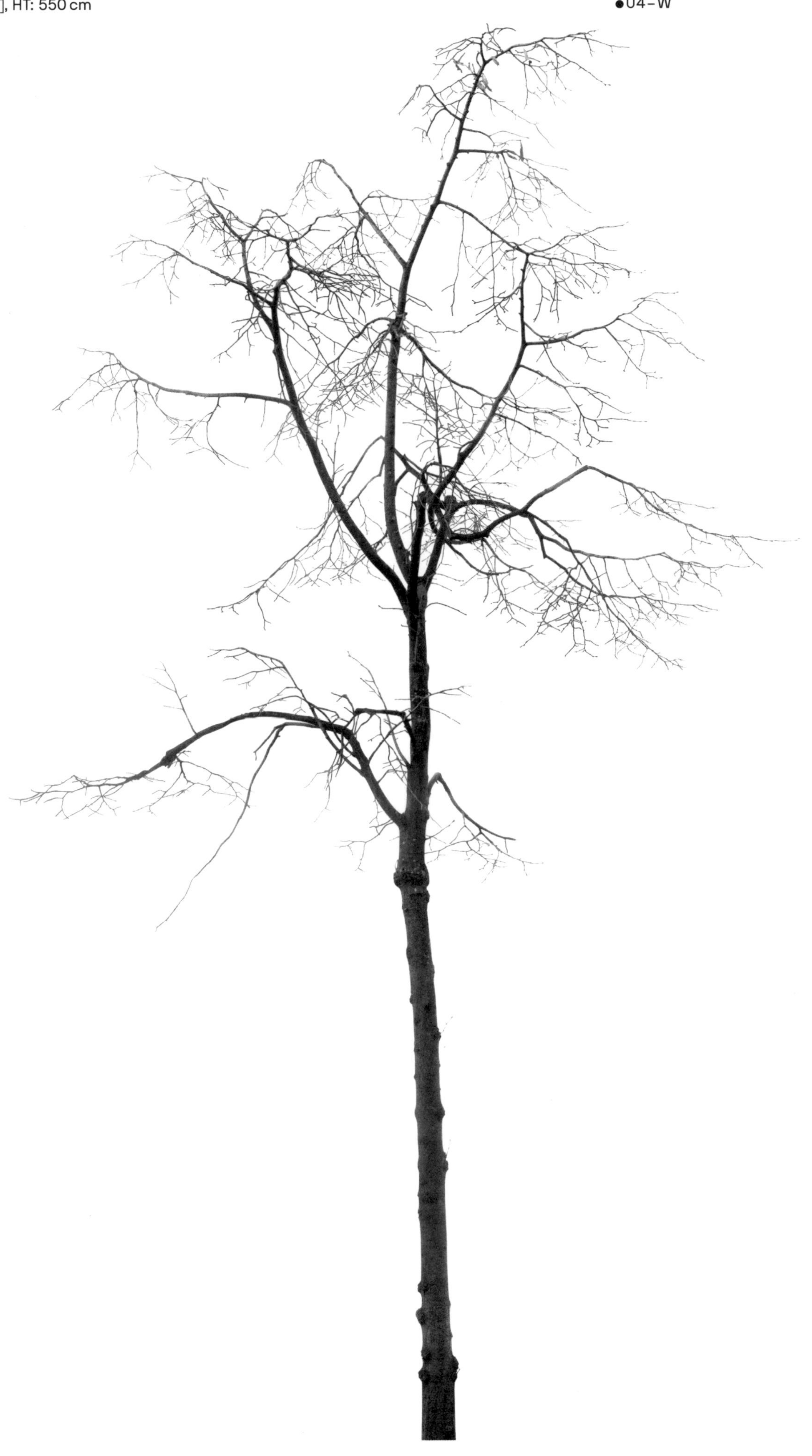

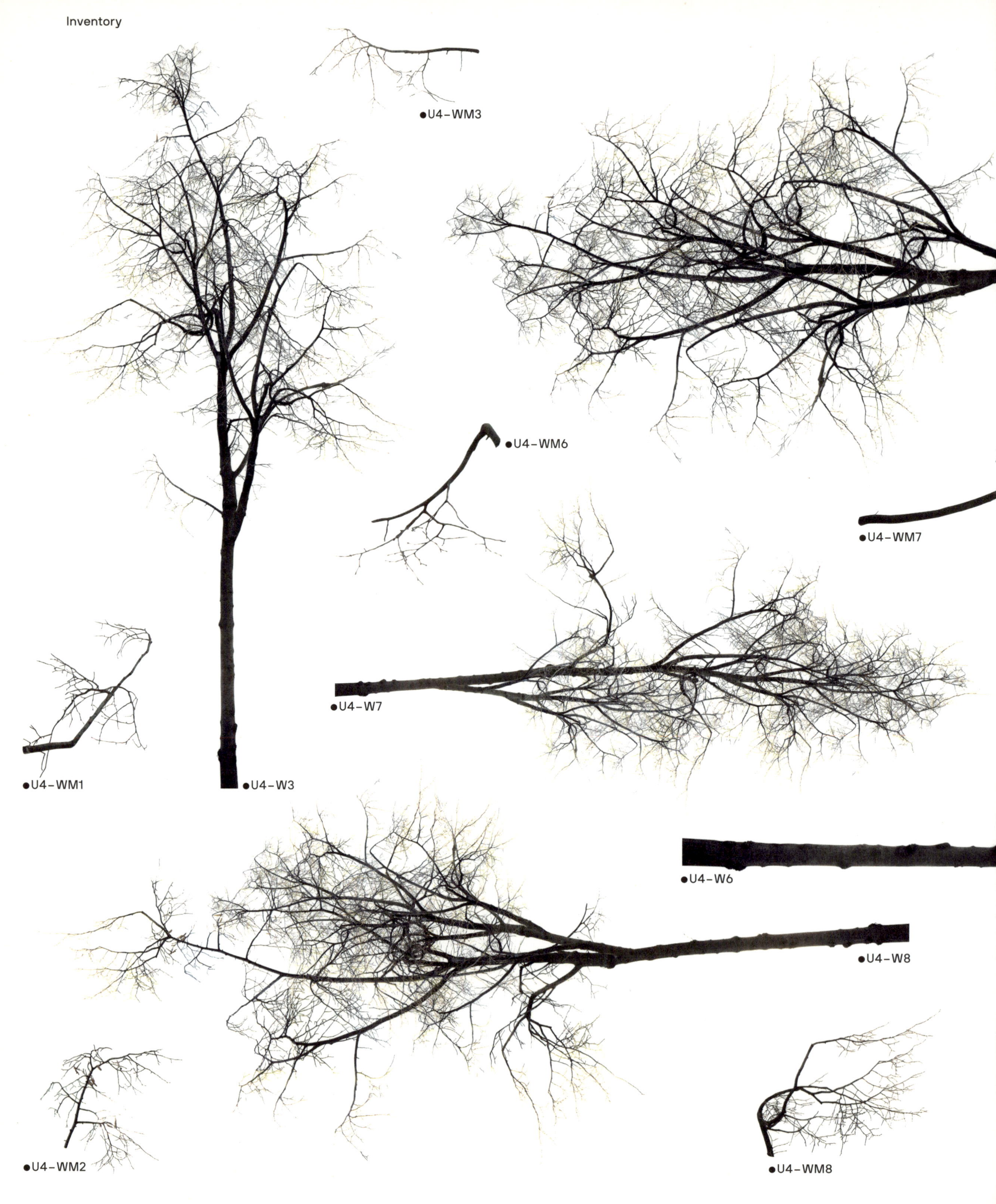

●U4–WM3
●U4–WM6
●U4–WM7
●U4–WM1
●U4–W3
●U4–W7
●U4–W6
●U4–W8
●U4–WM2
●U4–WM8

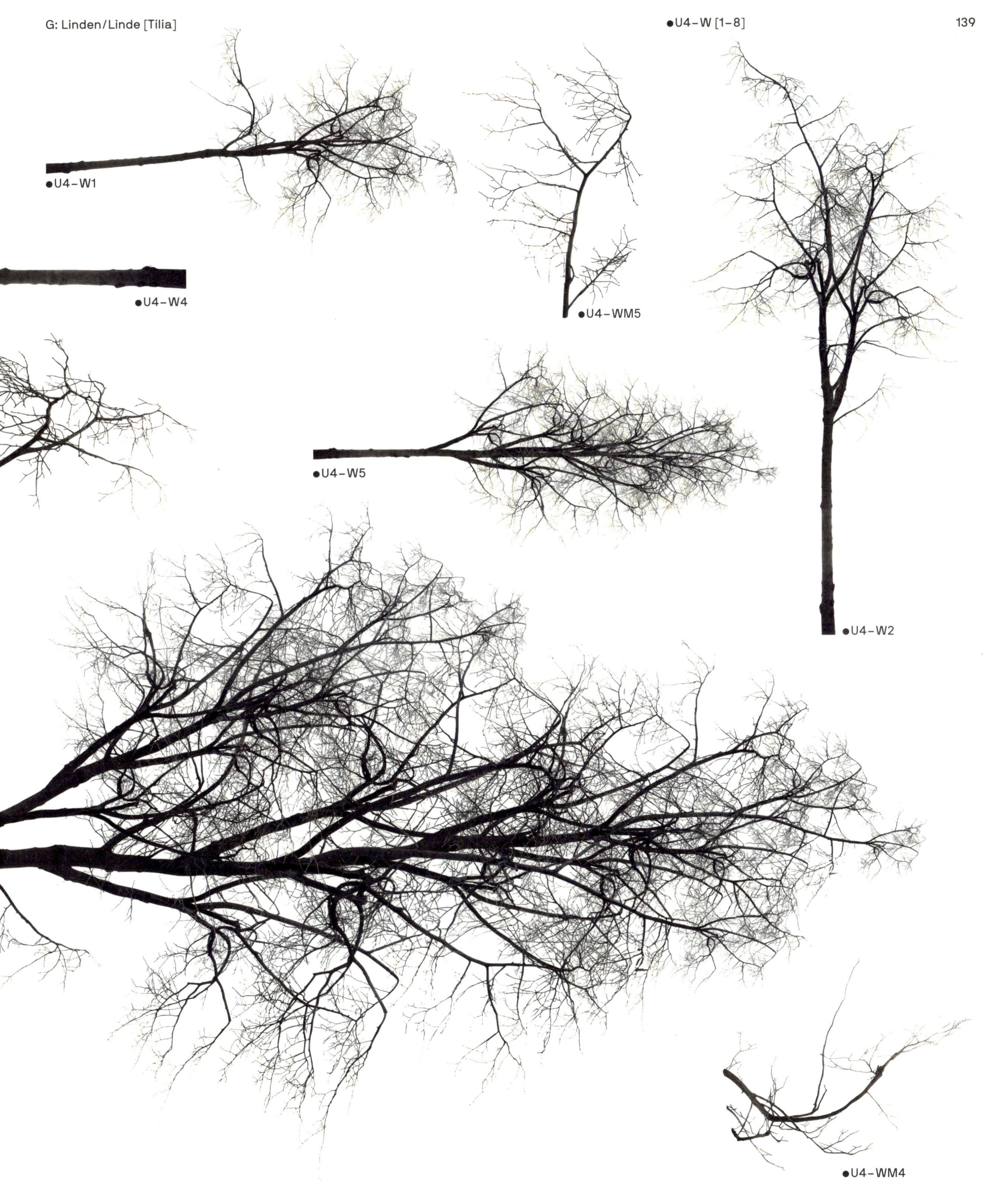

●U4–W1
●U4–W4
●U4–WM5
●U4–W5
●U4–W2
●U4–WM4

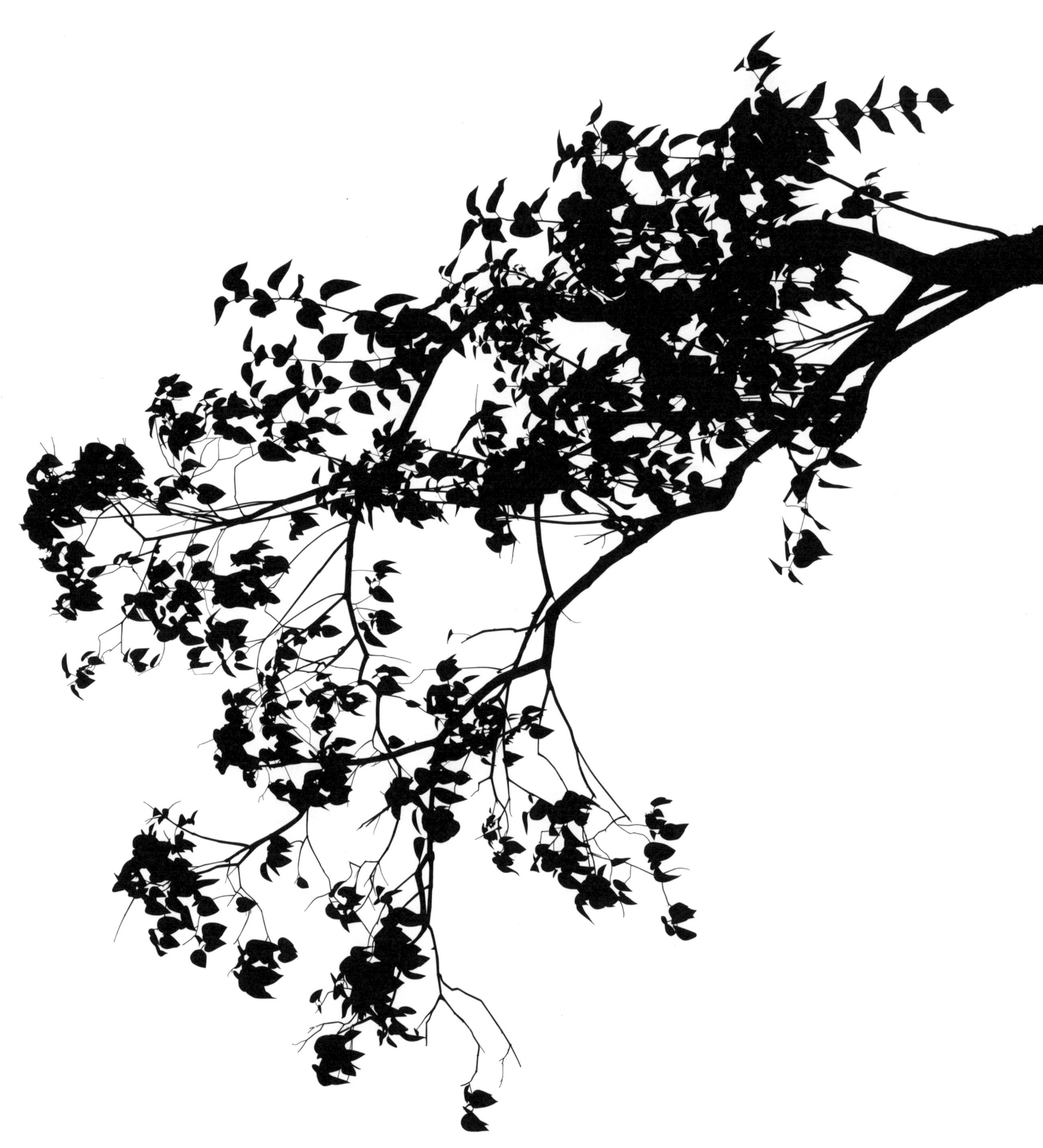

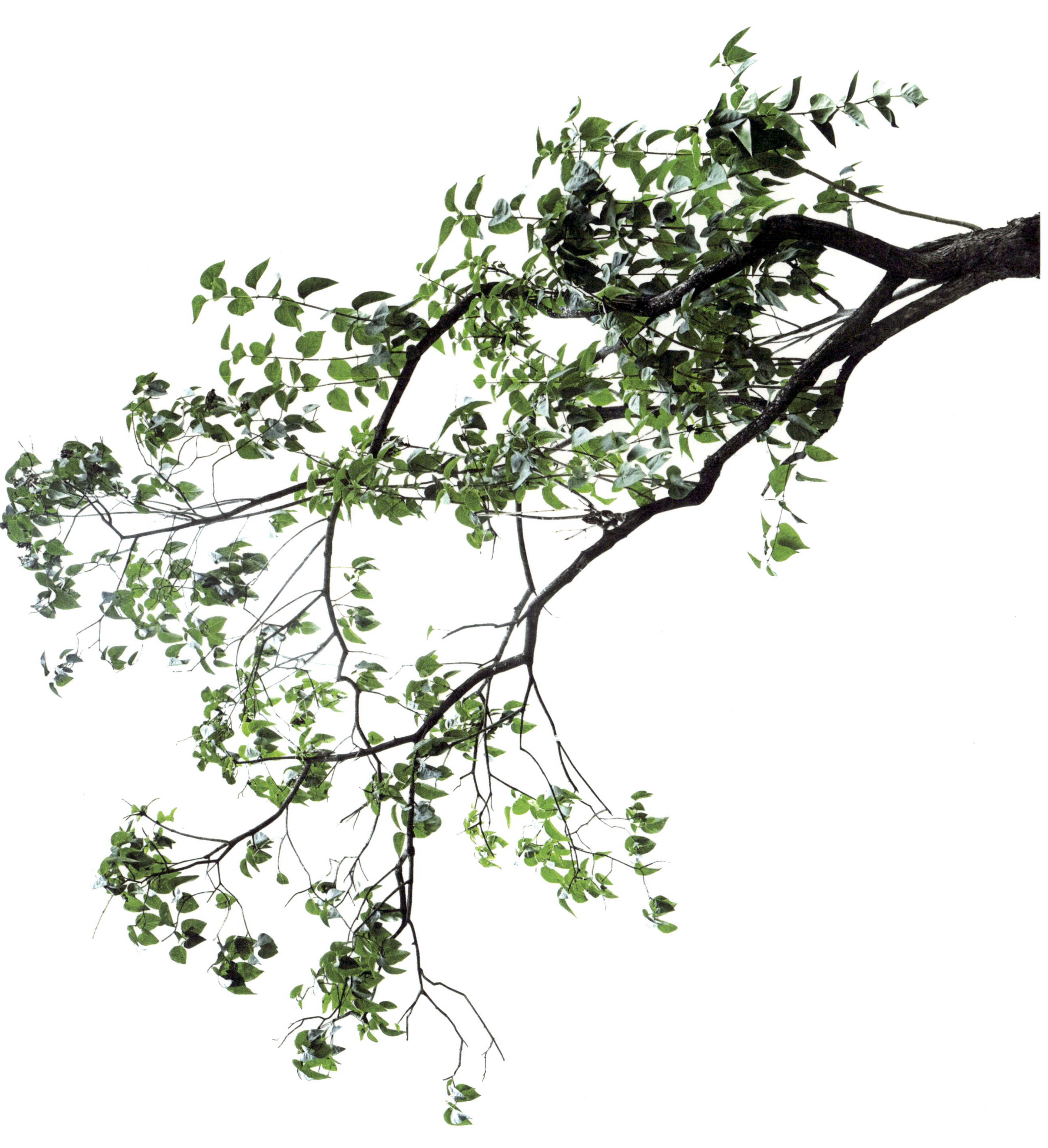

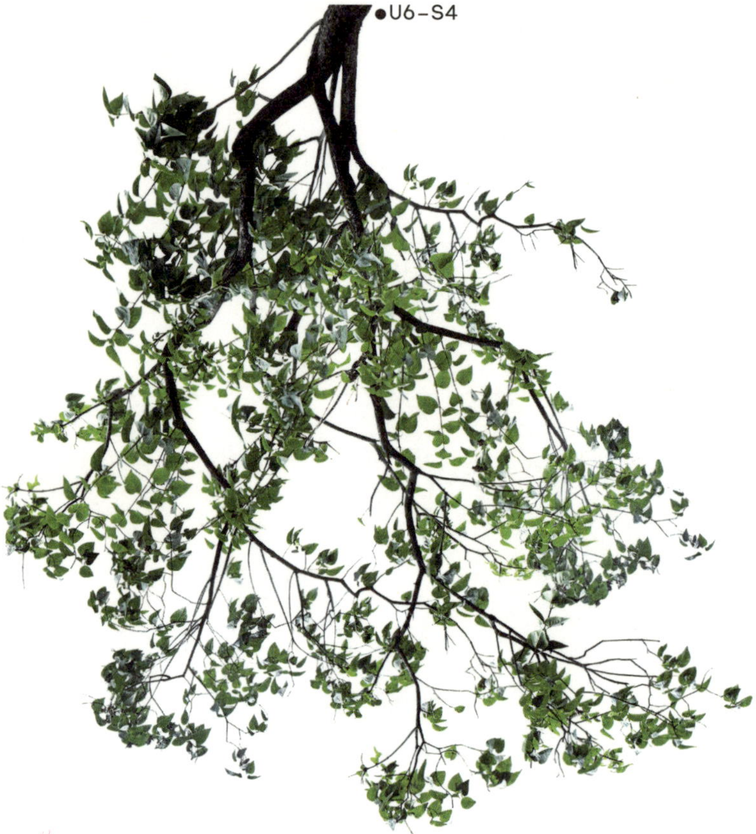

●U6–S4
●U6–SM2 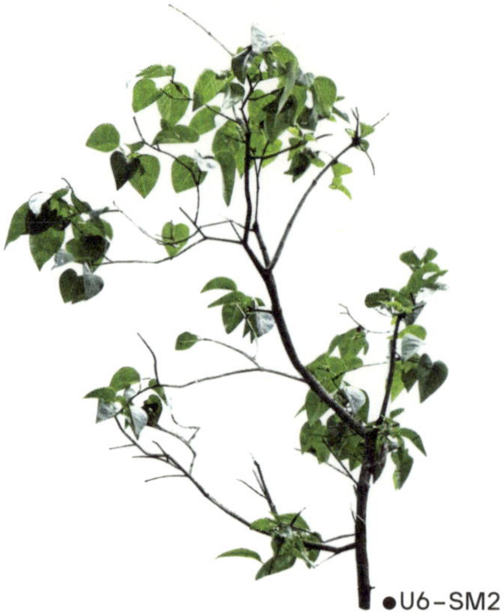
●U6–S1 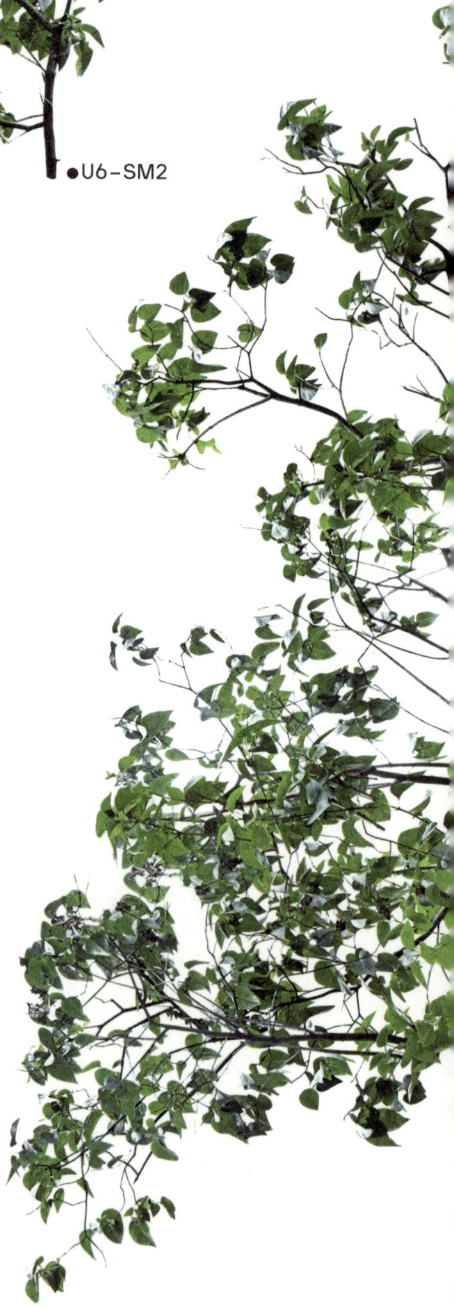 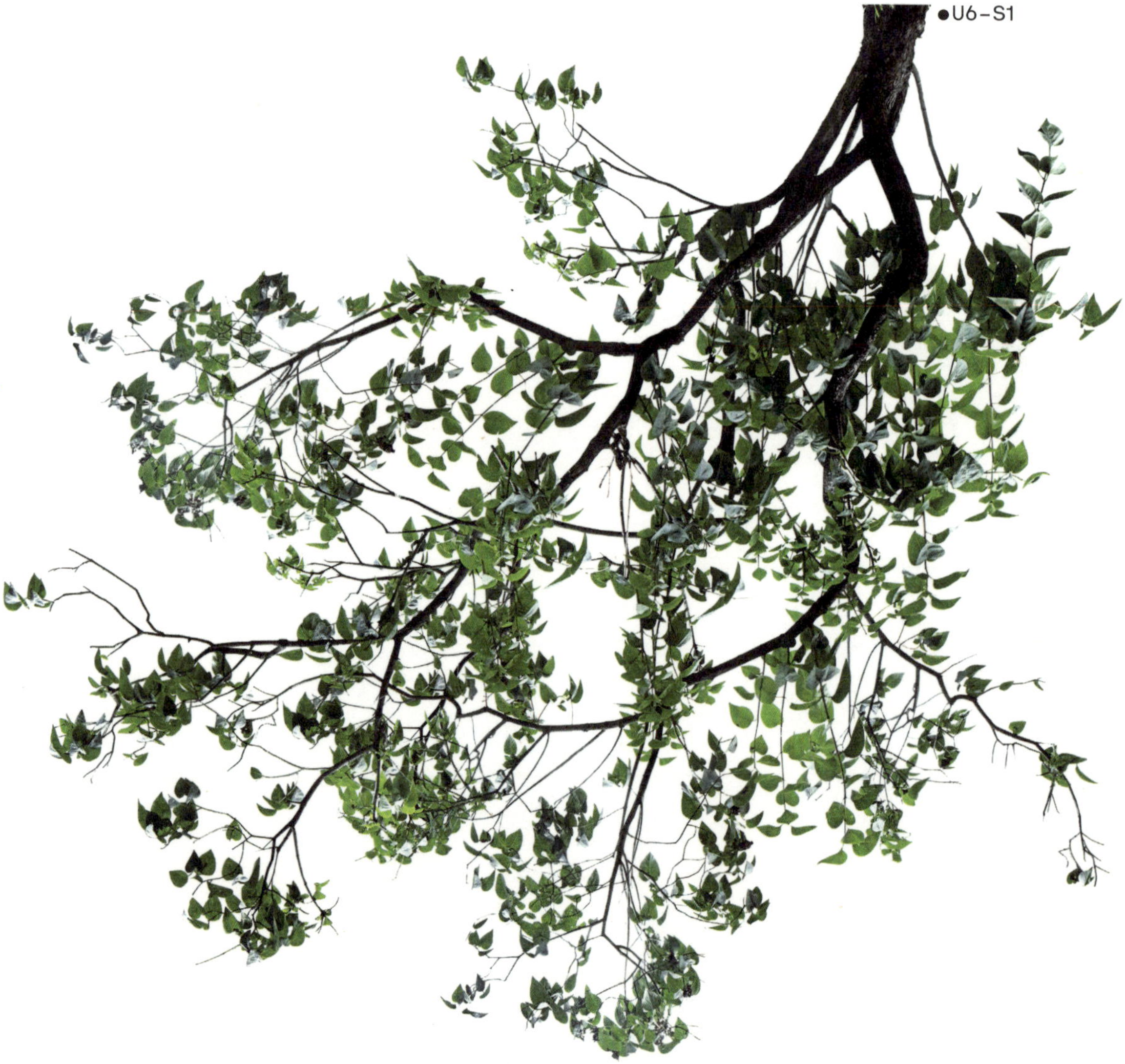
●U6–S4

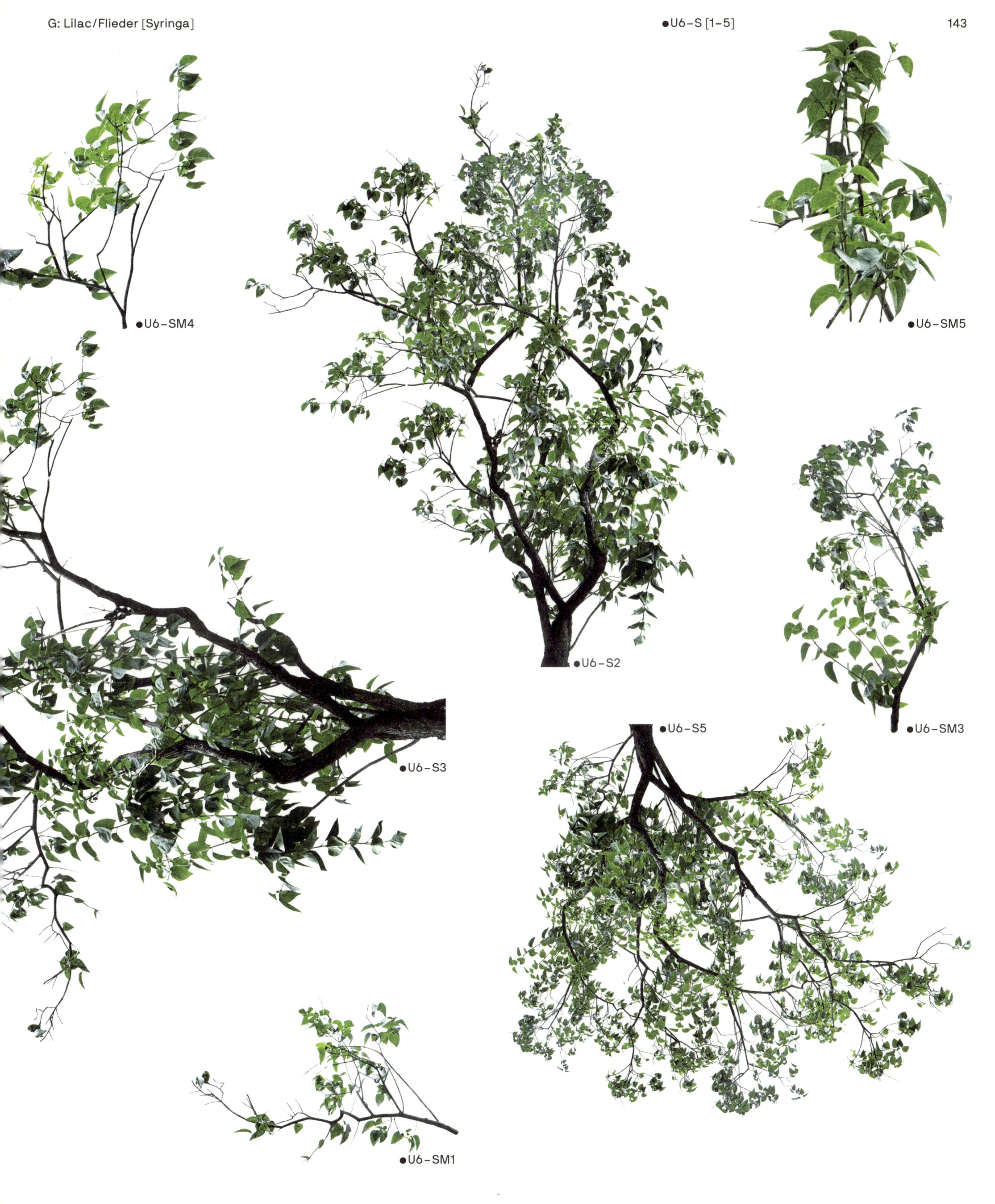

●U6-SM4
●U6-SM5
●U6-S2
●U6-S3
●U6-S5
●U6-SM3
●U6-SM1

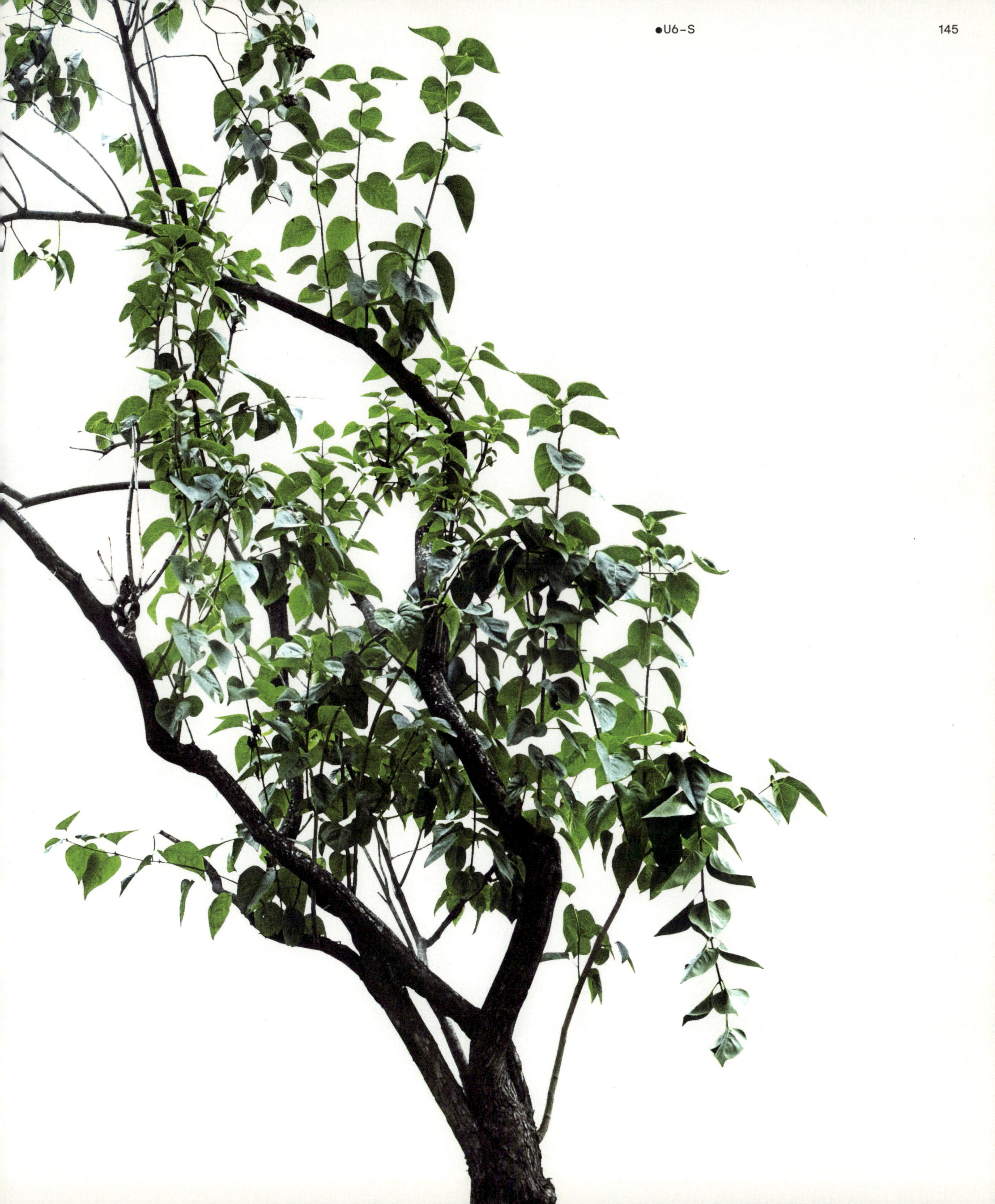

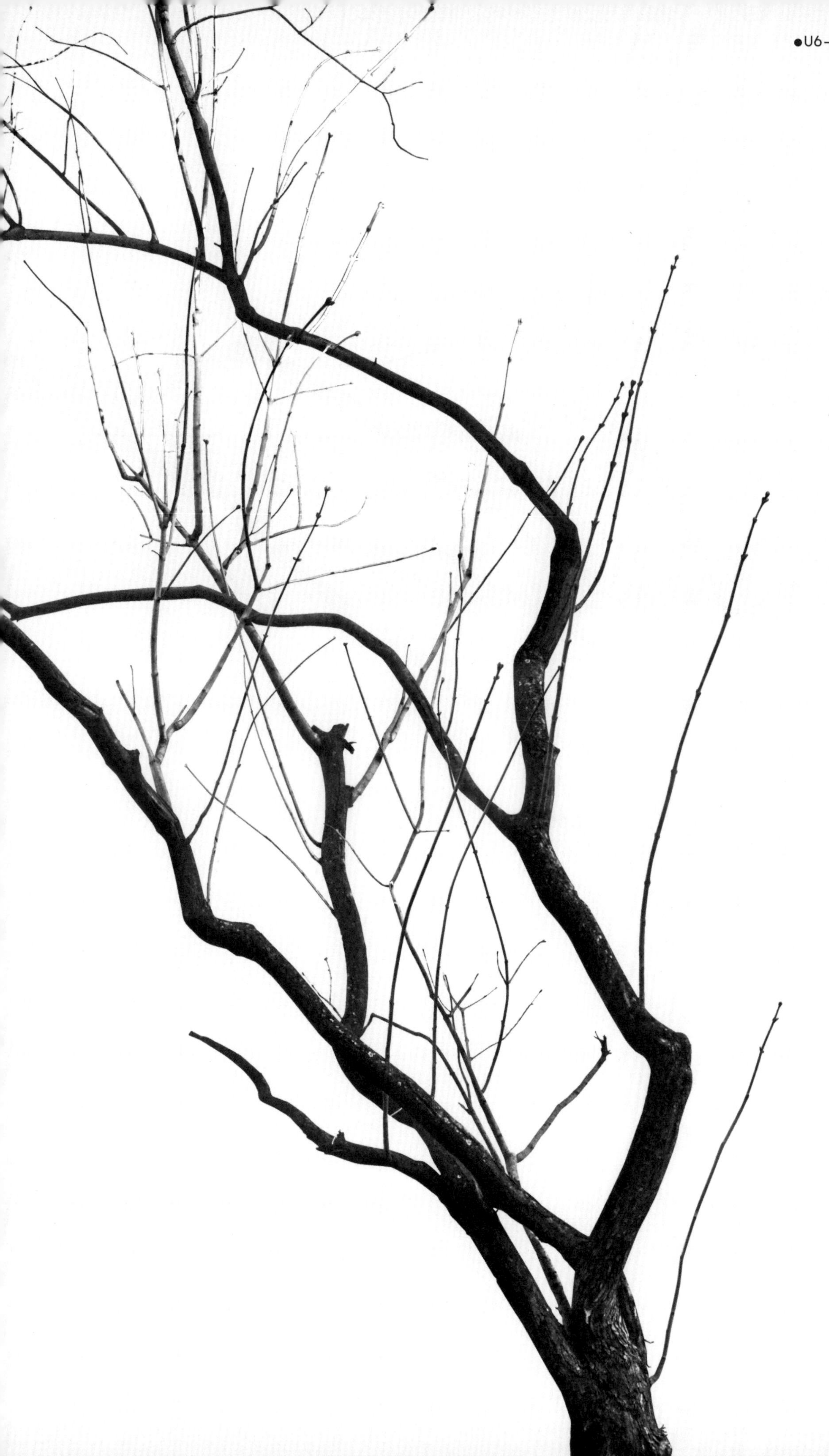

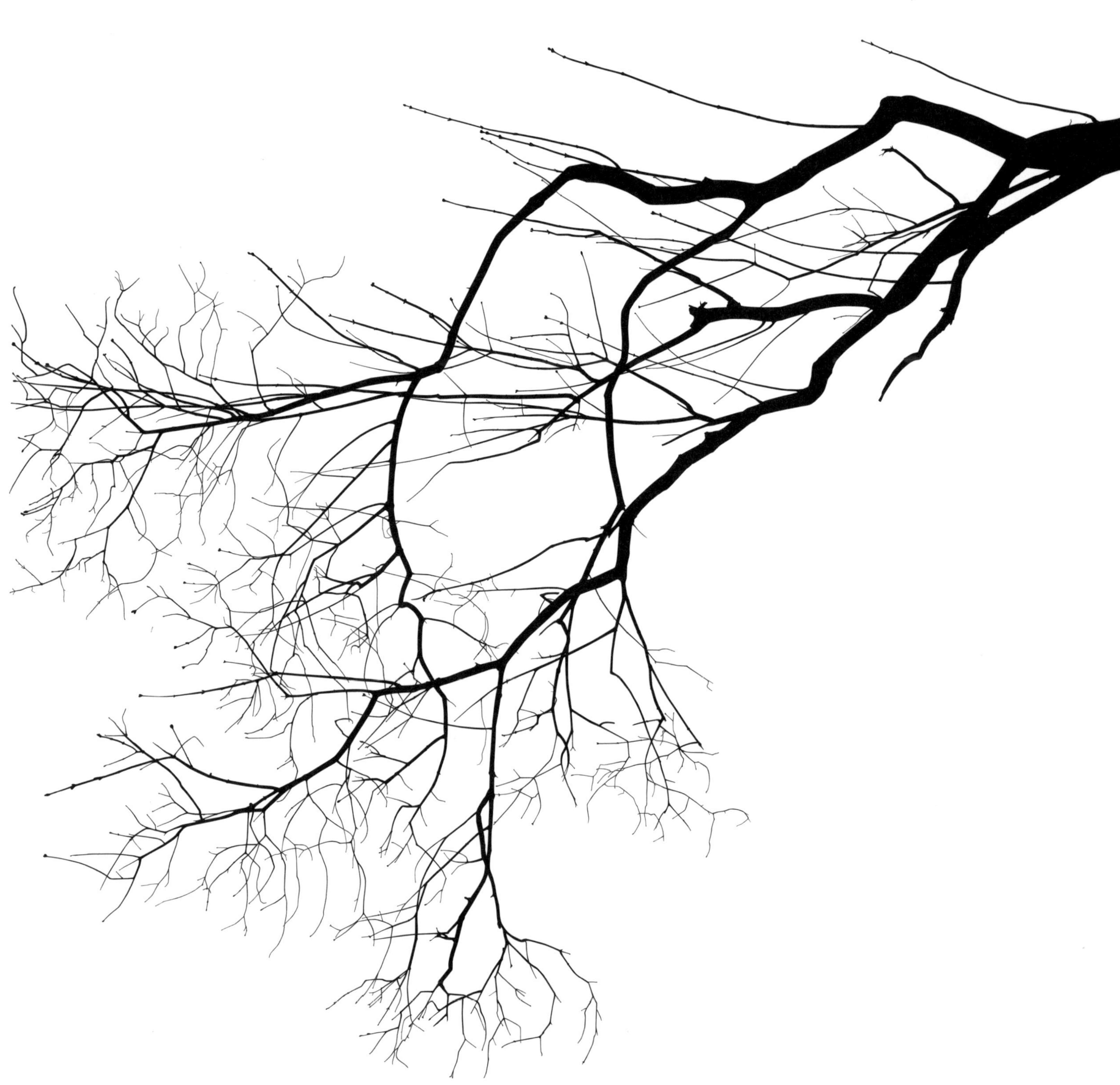

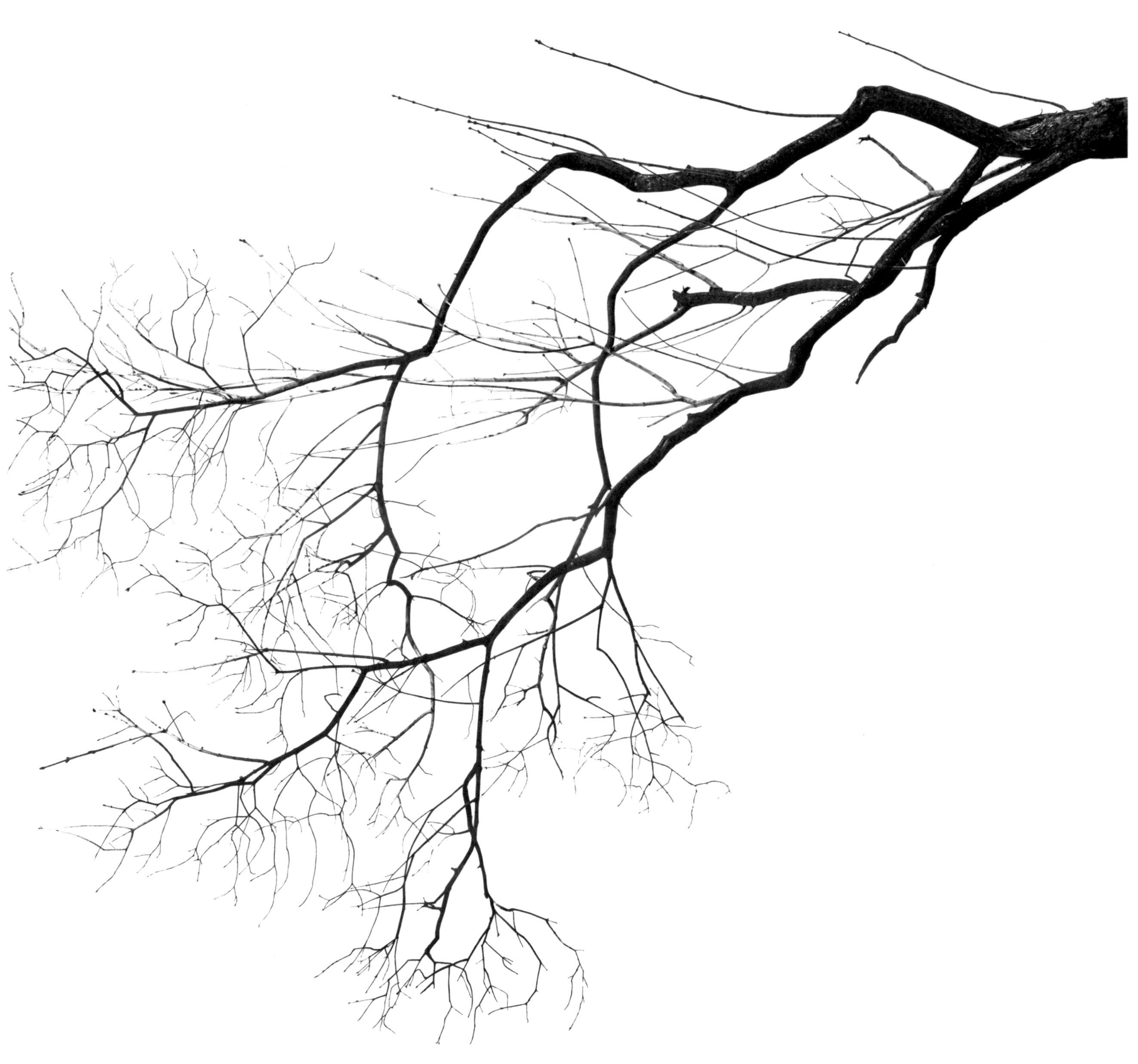

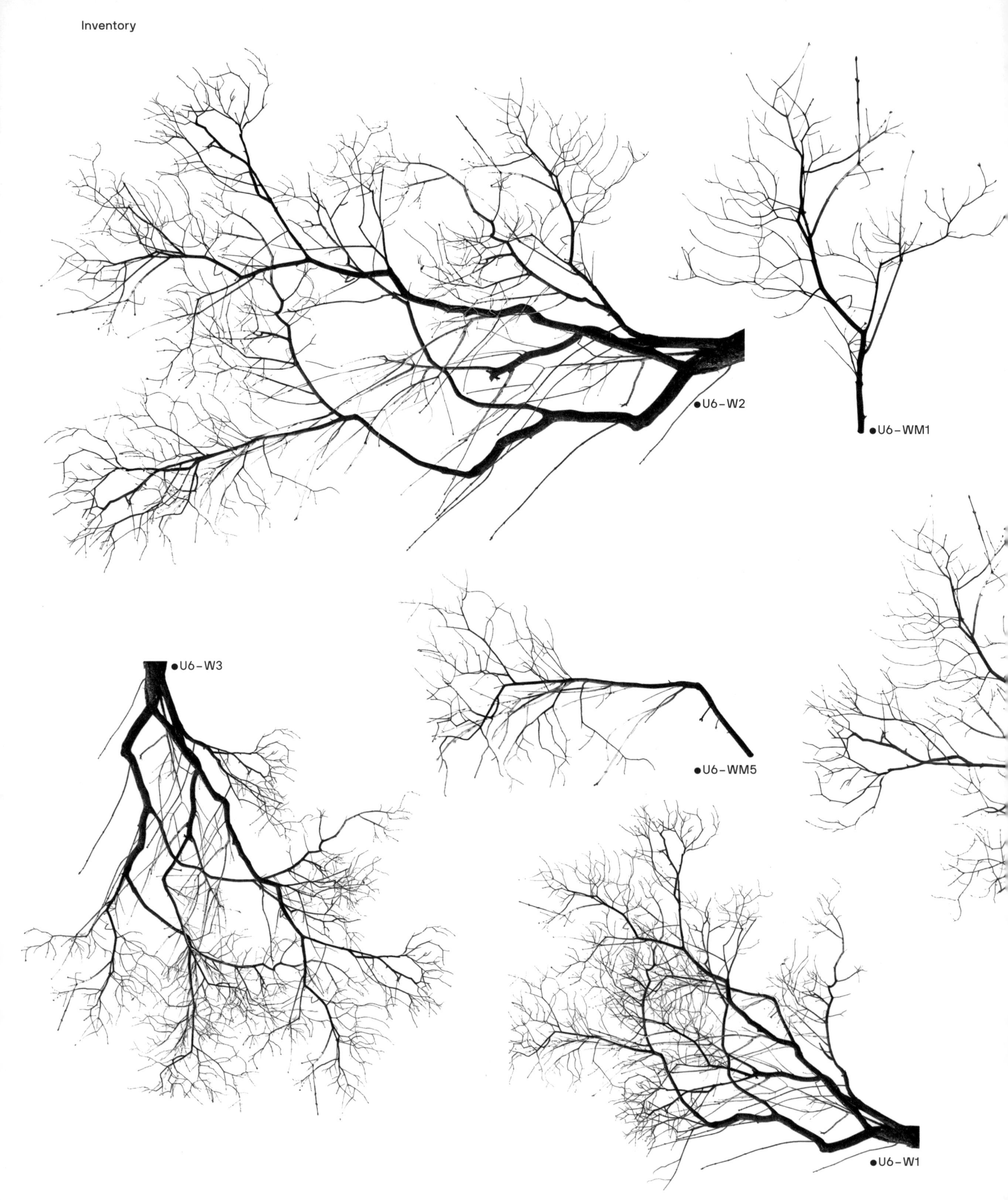
●U6–W2
●U6–WM1
●U6–W3
●U6–WM5
●U6–W1

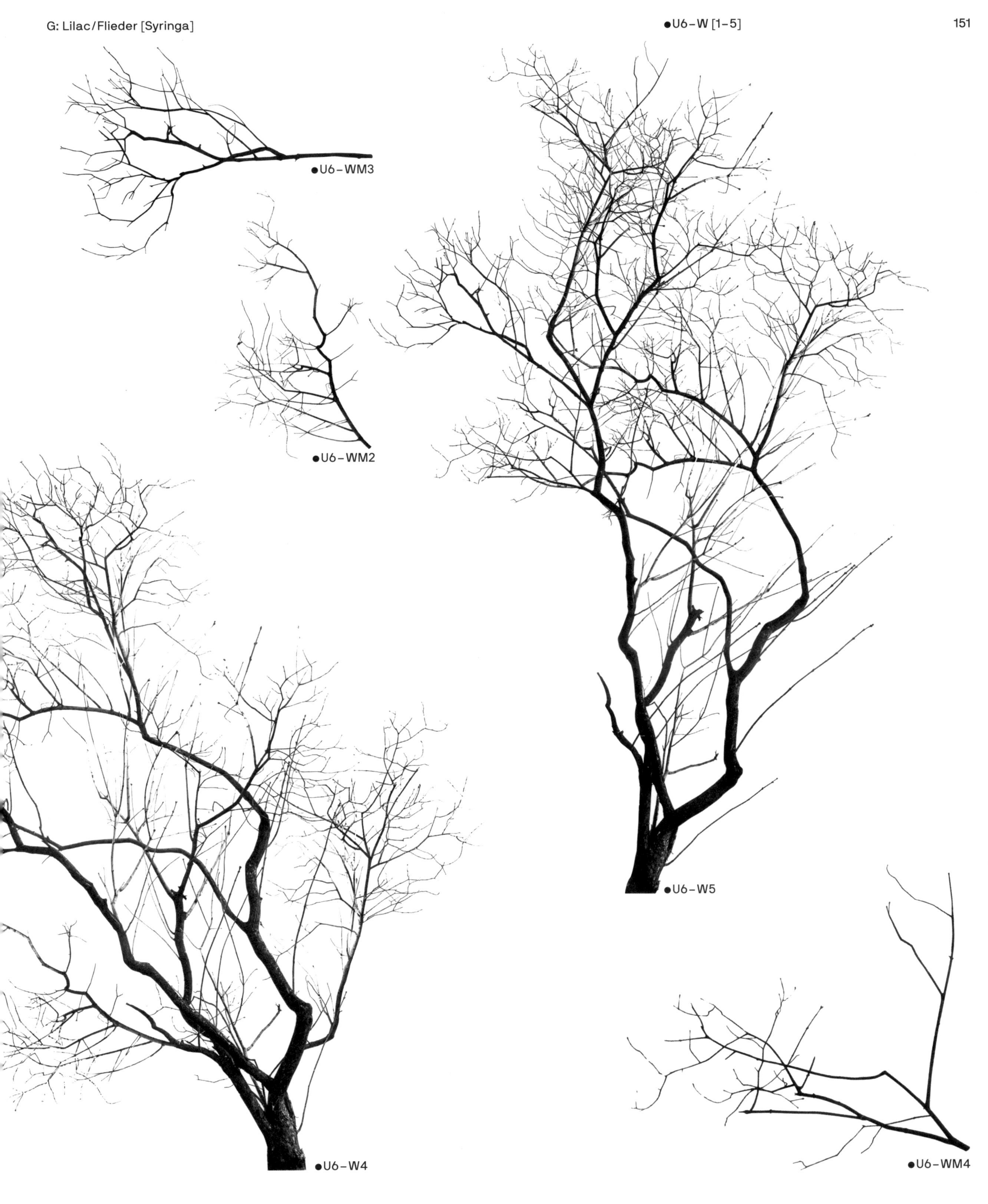
●U6–WM3
●U6–WM2
●U6–W5
●U6–W4
●U6–WM4

```
B3    S  W      Linden         [Tilia cordata]
B9    S         Chestnut       [Aesculus x carnea]
B10      W      Hazel          [Corylus colurna]
B13   S  W      Linden         [Tilia cordata]
B14      W      Silver maple   [Acer saccharinum]
B15   S  W      Linden         [Tilia tomentosa]
B16      W      Linden         [Tilia cordata]
```

B3–B16

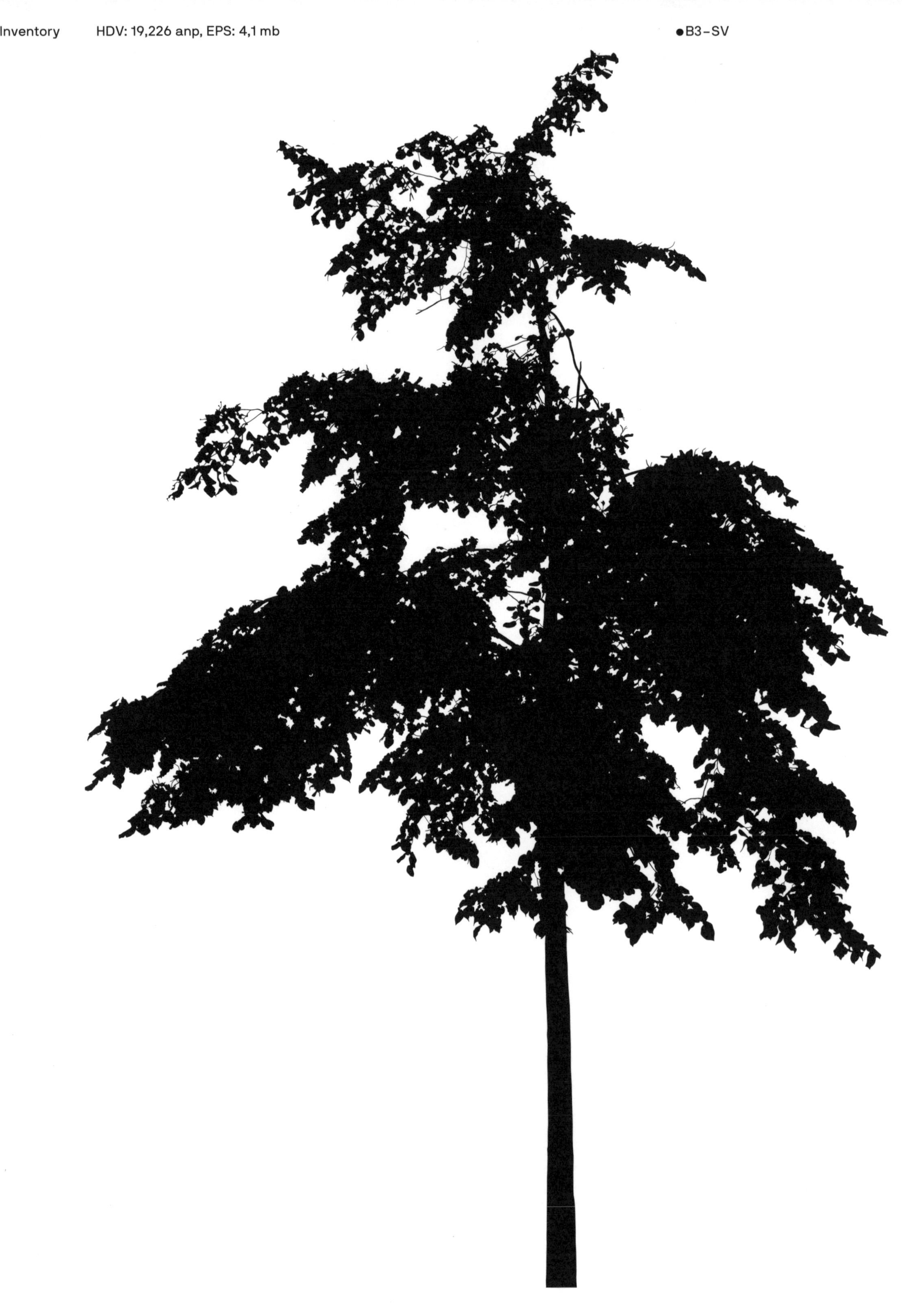

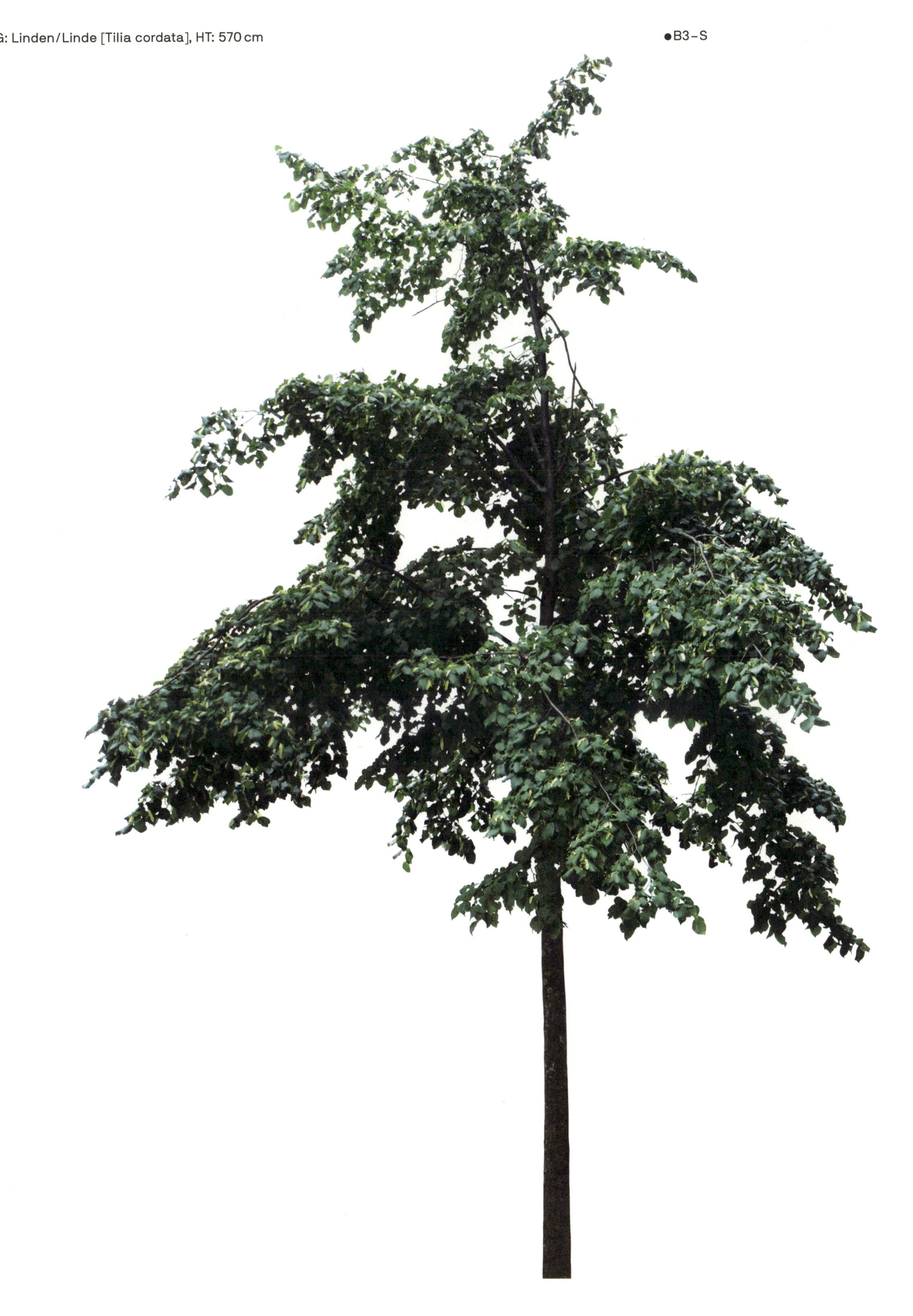

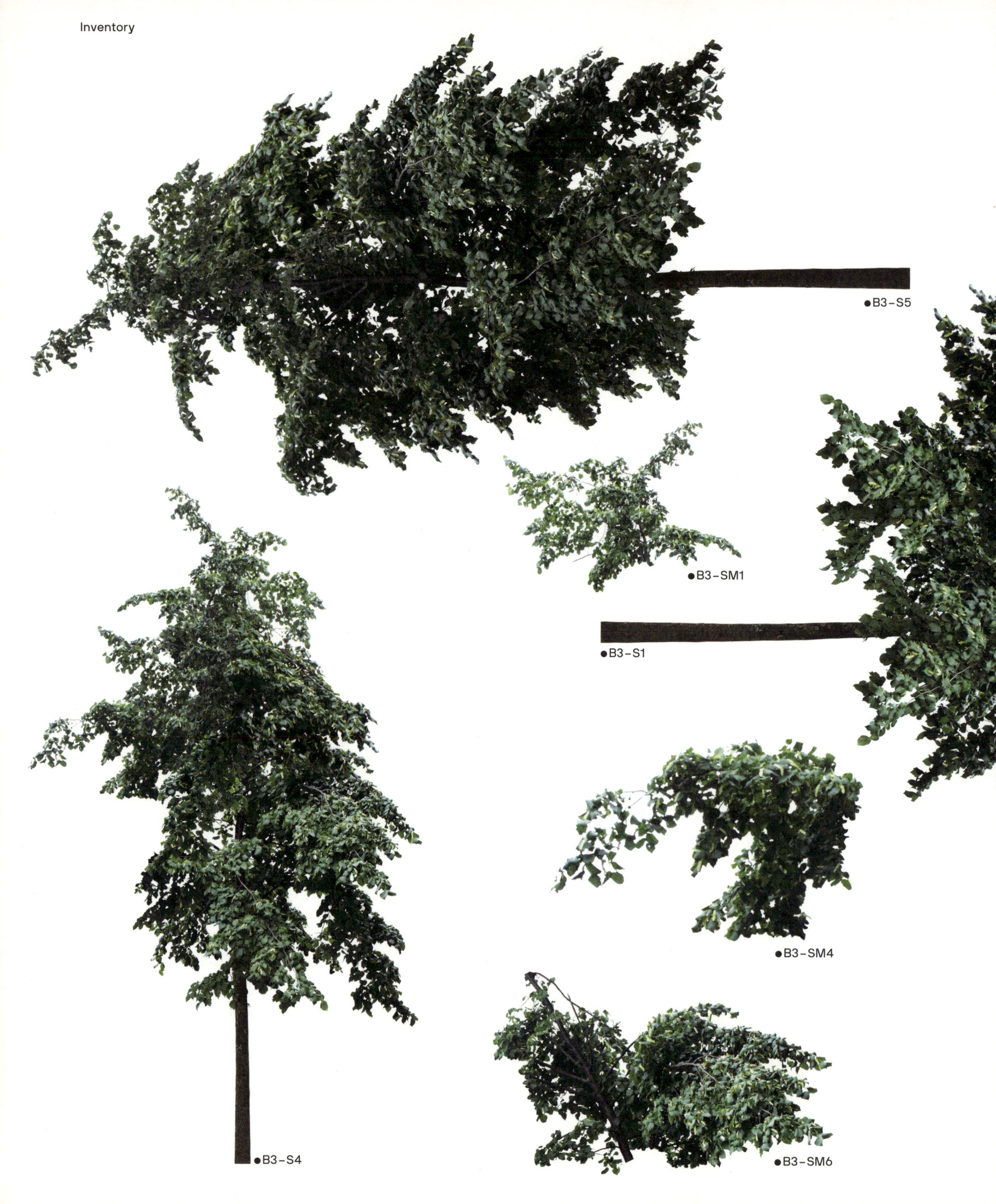
●B3–S5
●B3–SM1
●B3–S1
●B3–SM4
●B3–S4
●B3–SM6

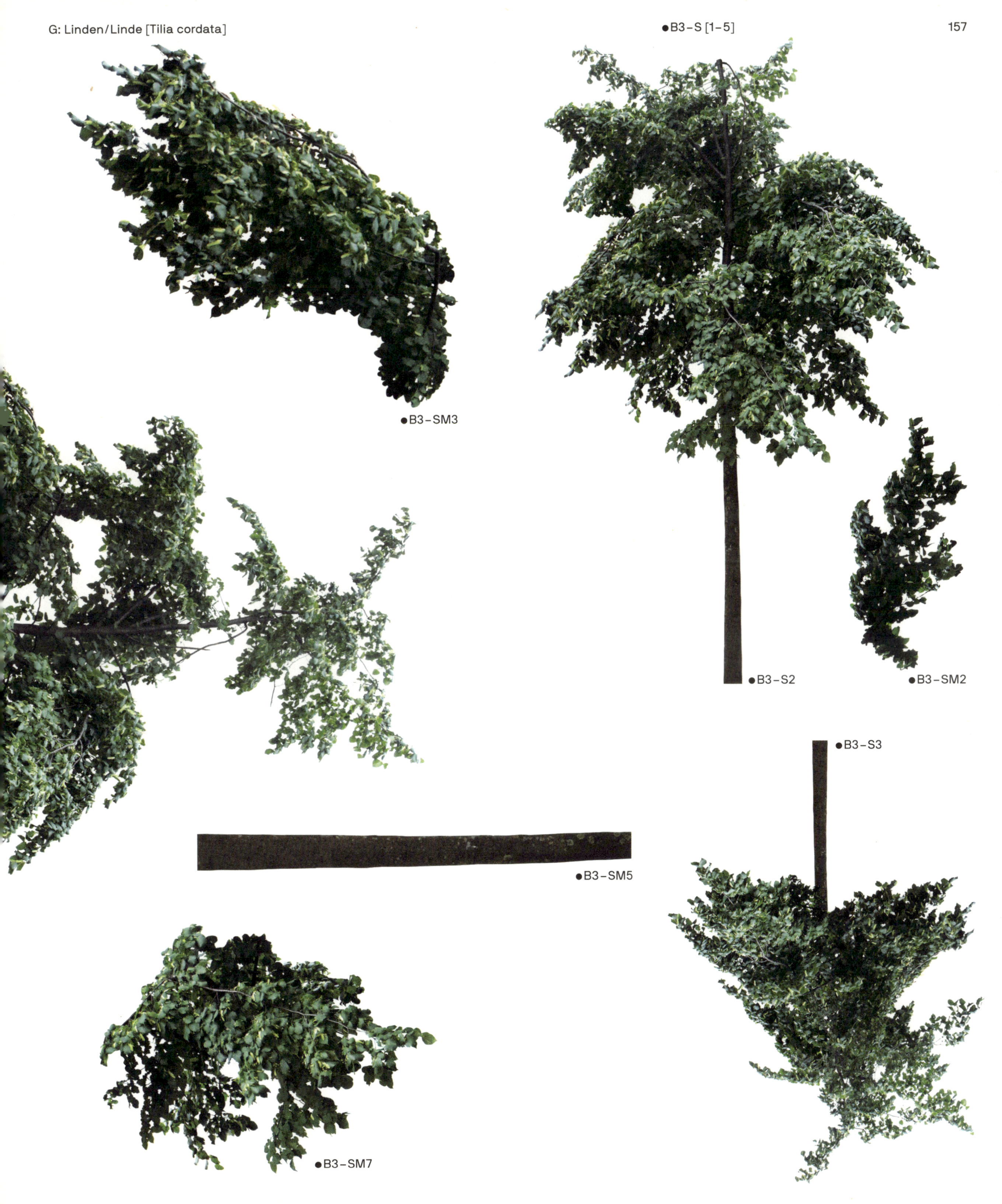
●B3–SM3
●B3–S2
●B3–SM2
●B3–S3
●B3–SM5
●B3–SM7

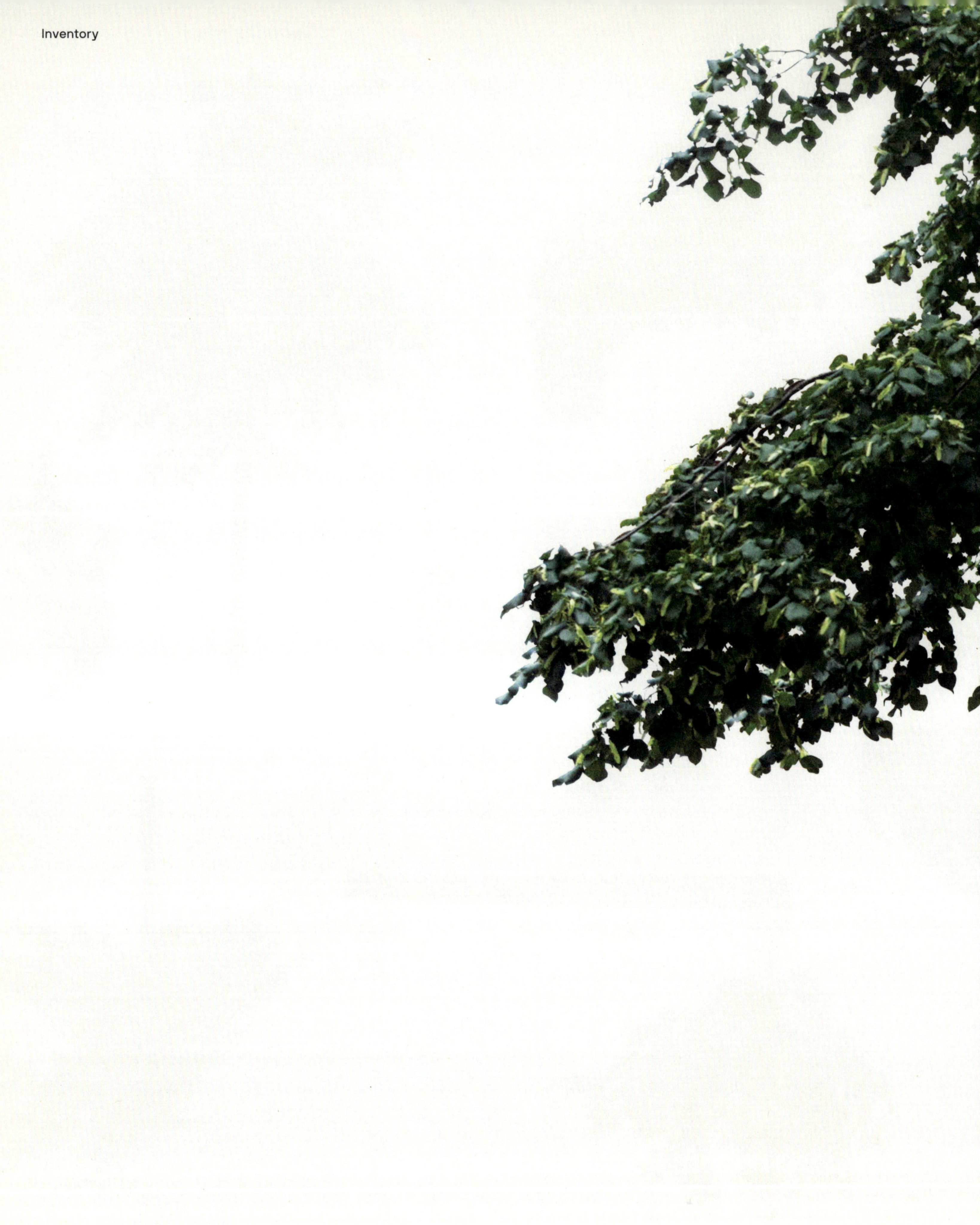

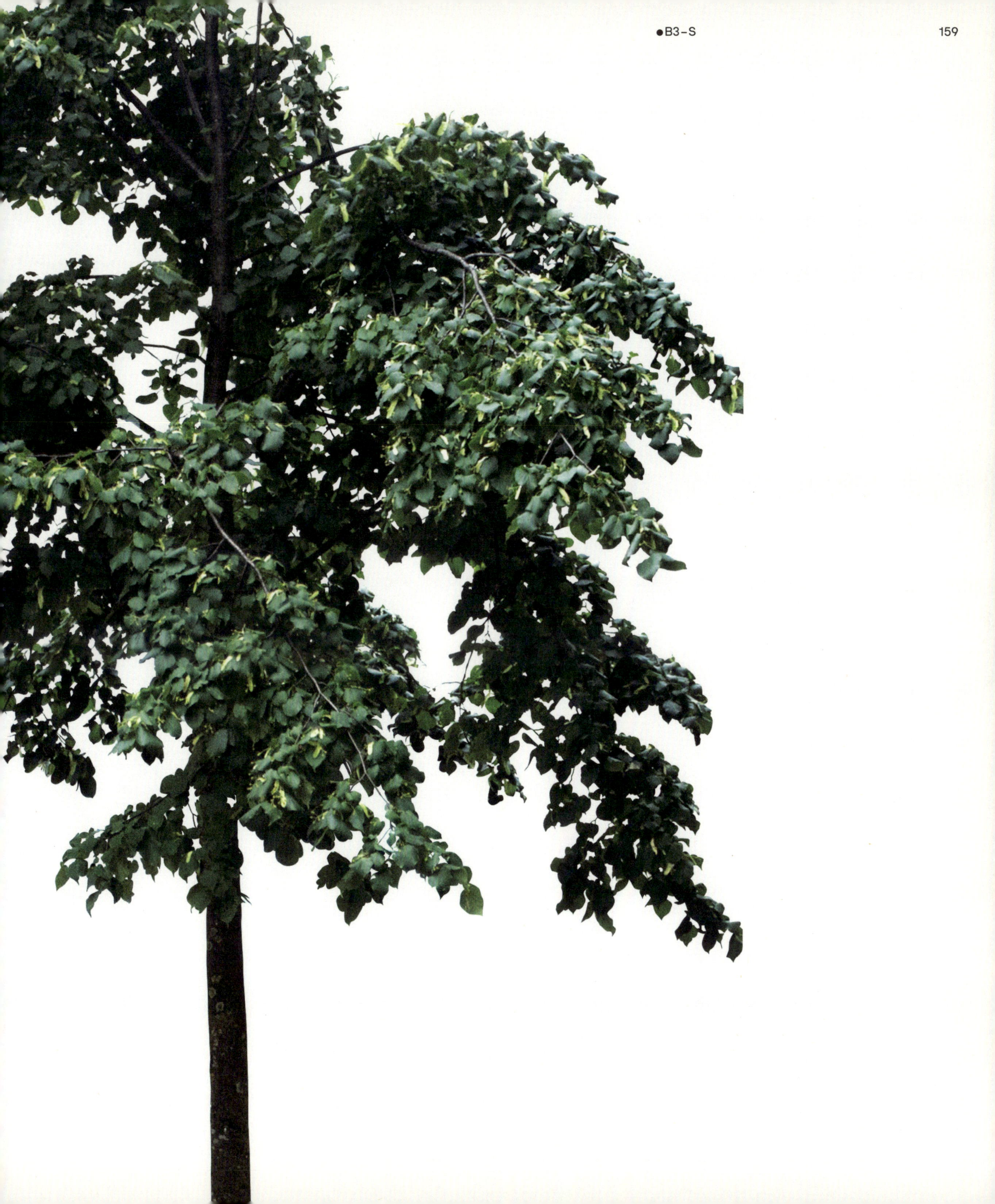

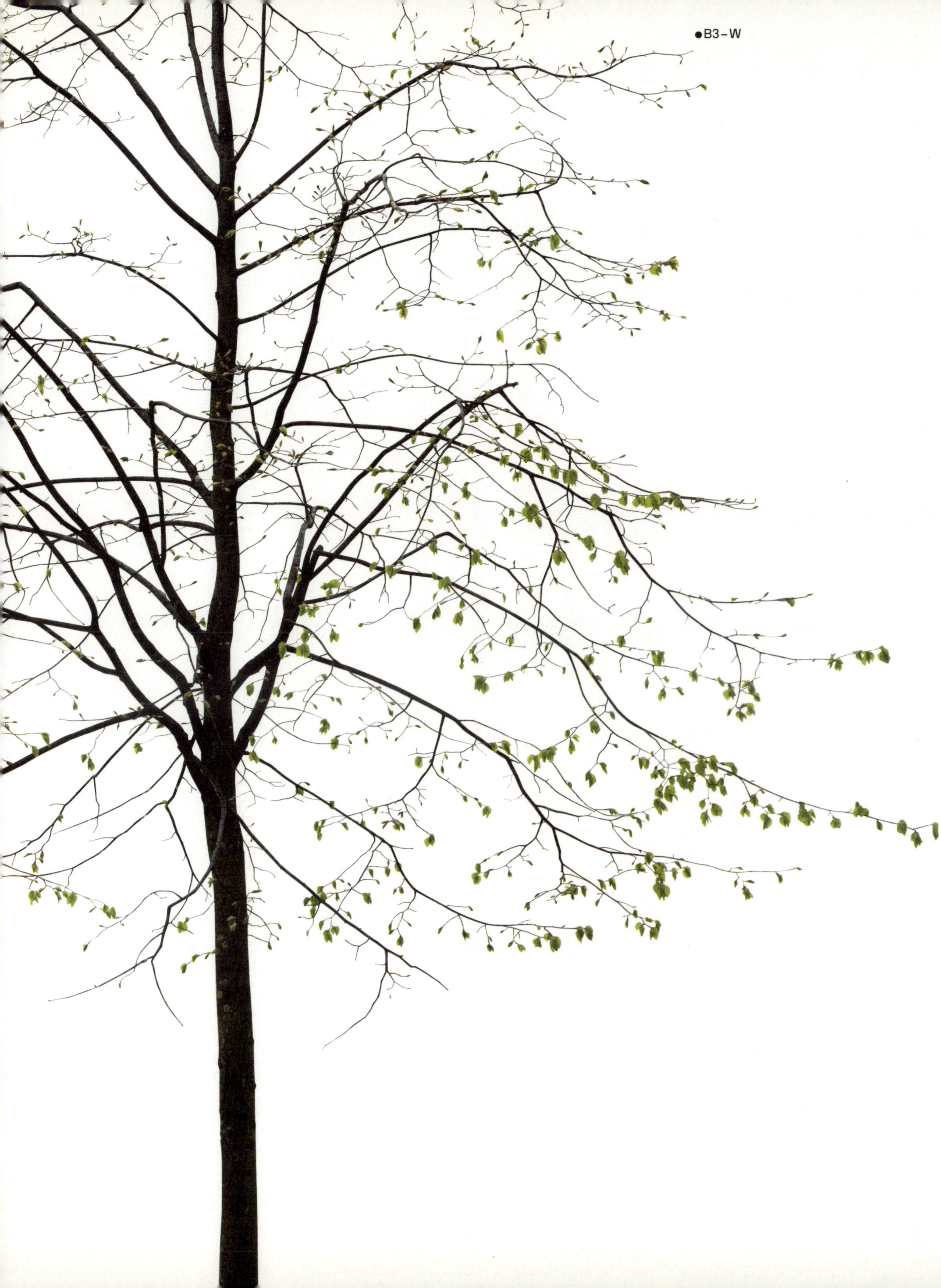

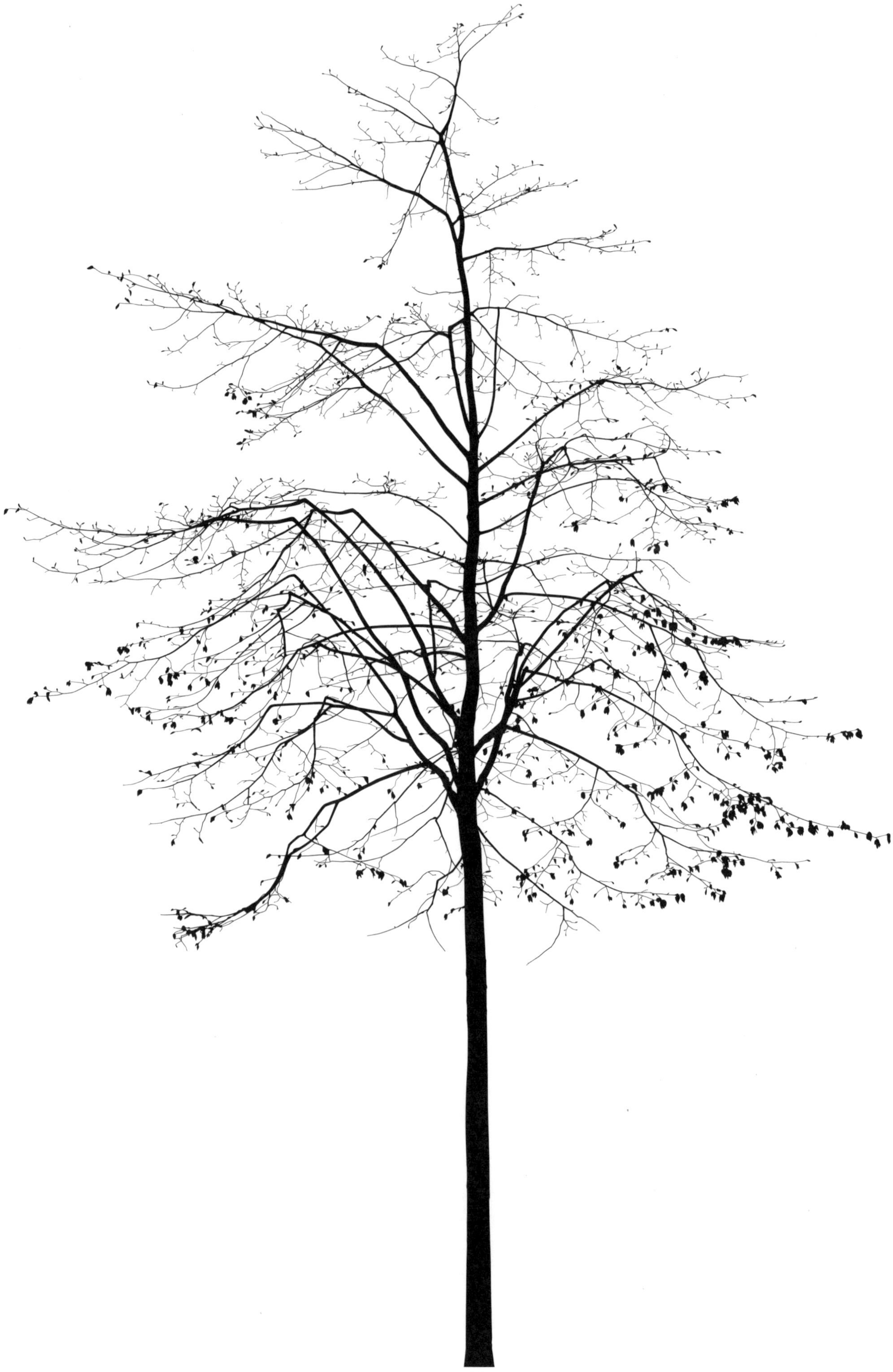

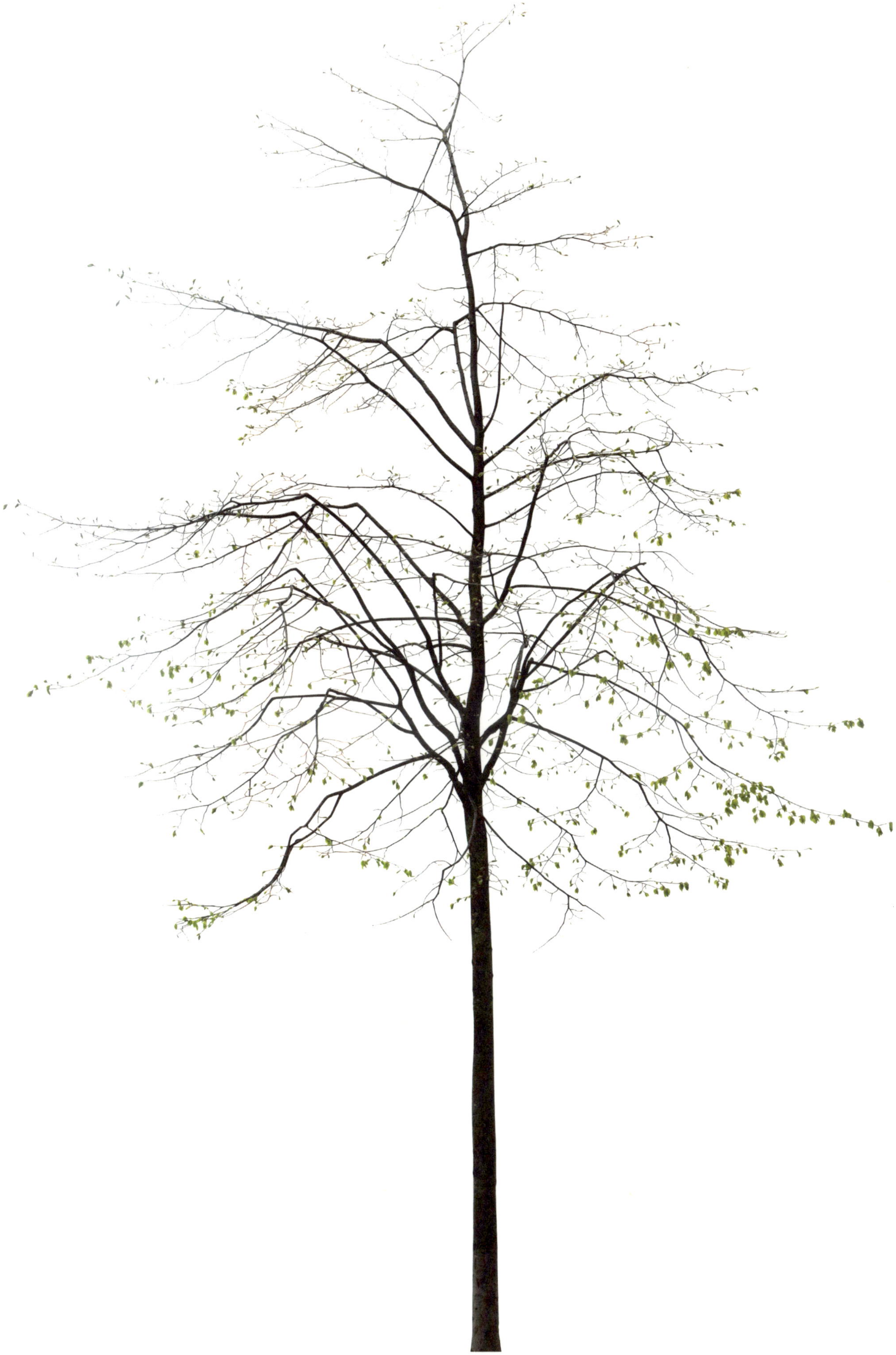

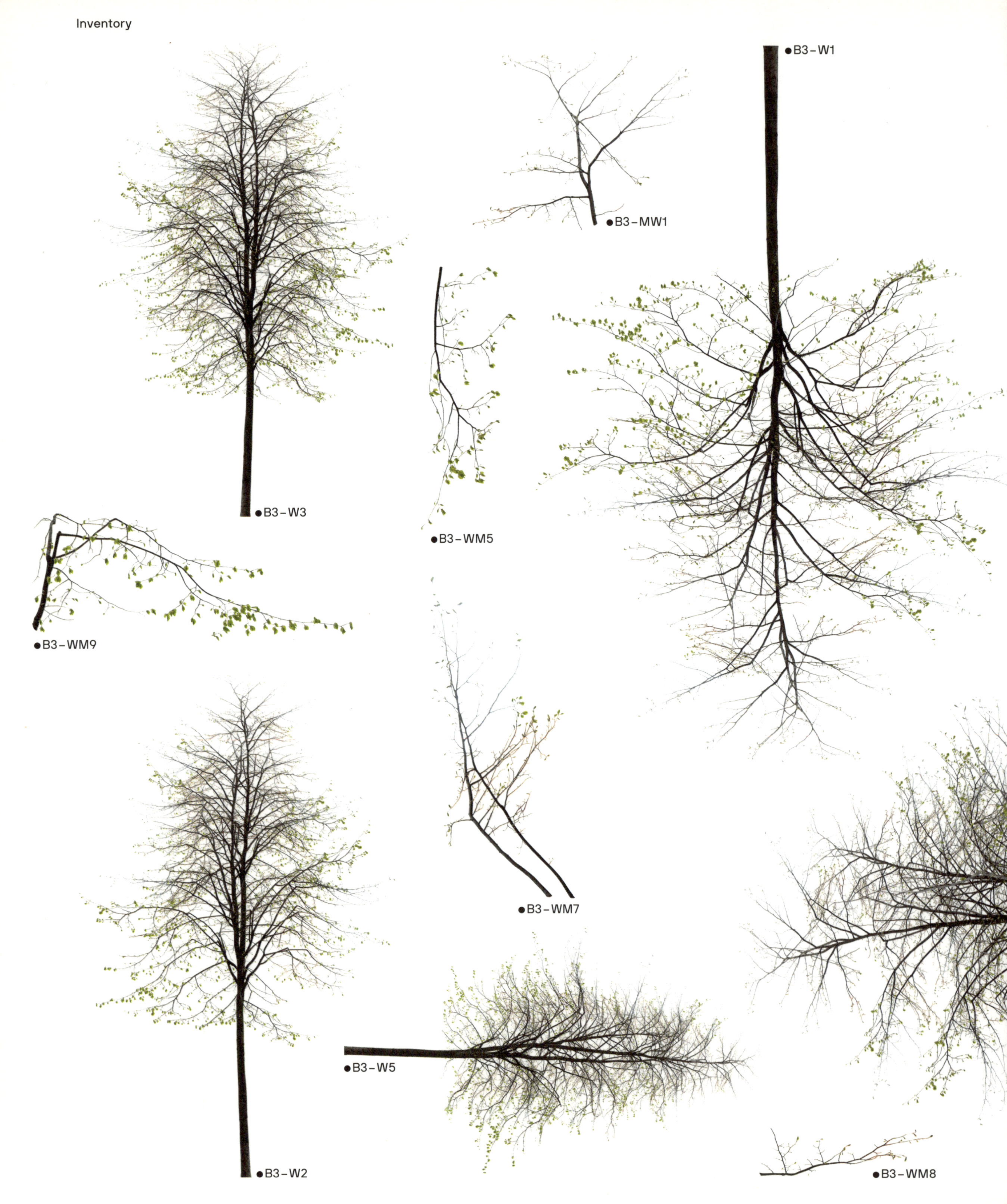

●B3–W1
●B3–MW1
●B3–W3
●B3–WM5
●B3–WM9
●B3–WM7
●B3–W2
●B3–W5
●B3–WM8

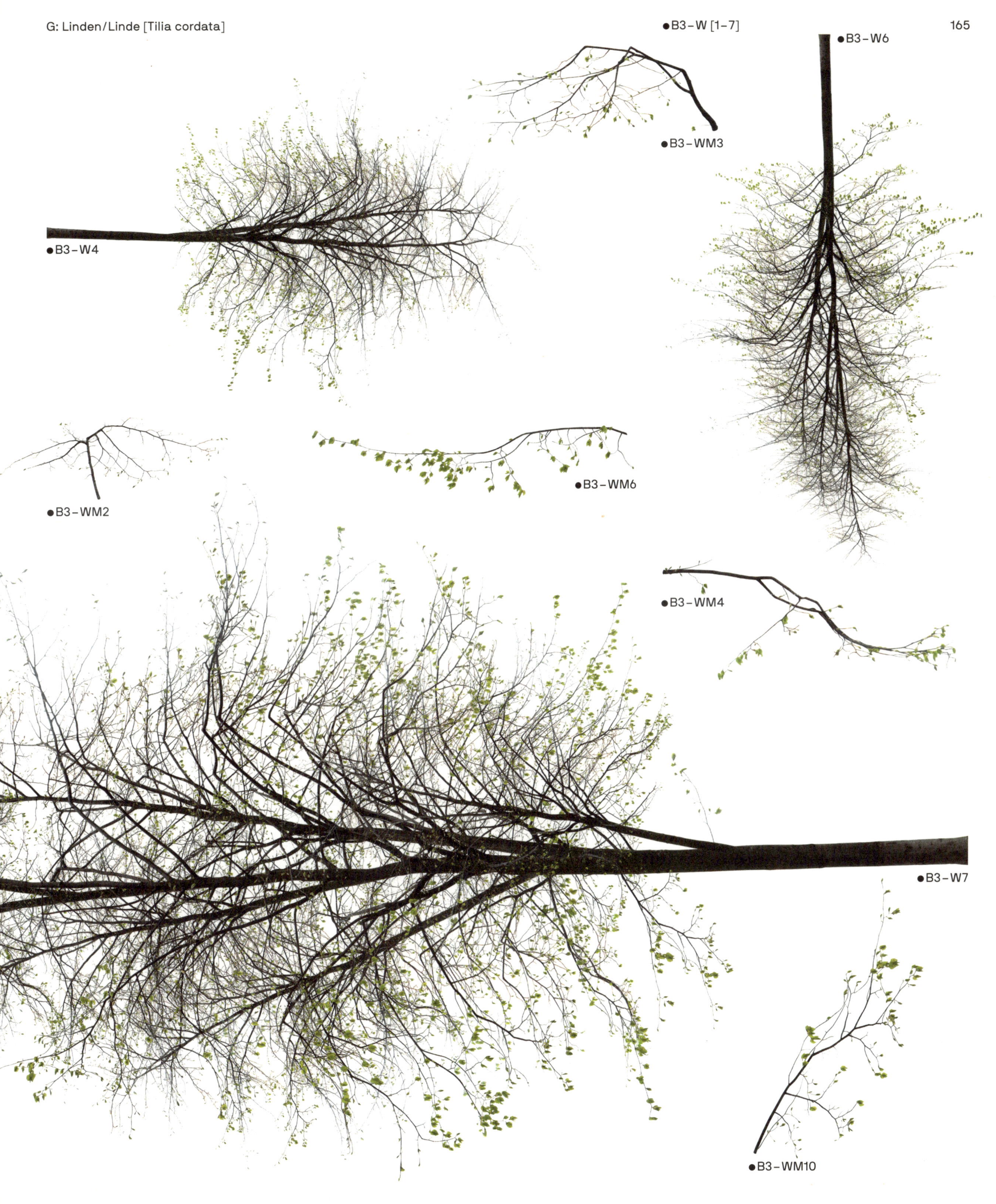
●B3–W [1–7]
●B3–WM3
●B3–W6
●B3–W4
●B3–WM2
●B3–WM6
●B3–WM4
●B3–W7
●B3–WM10

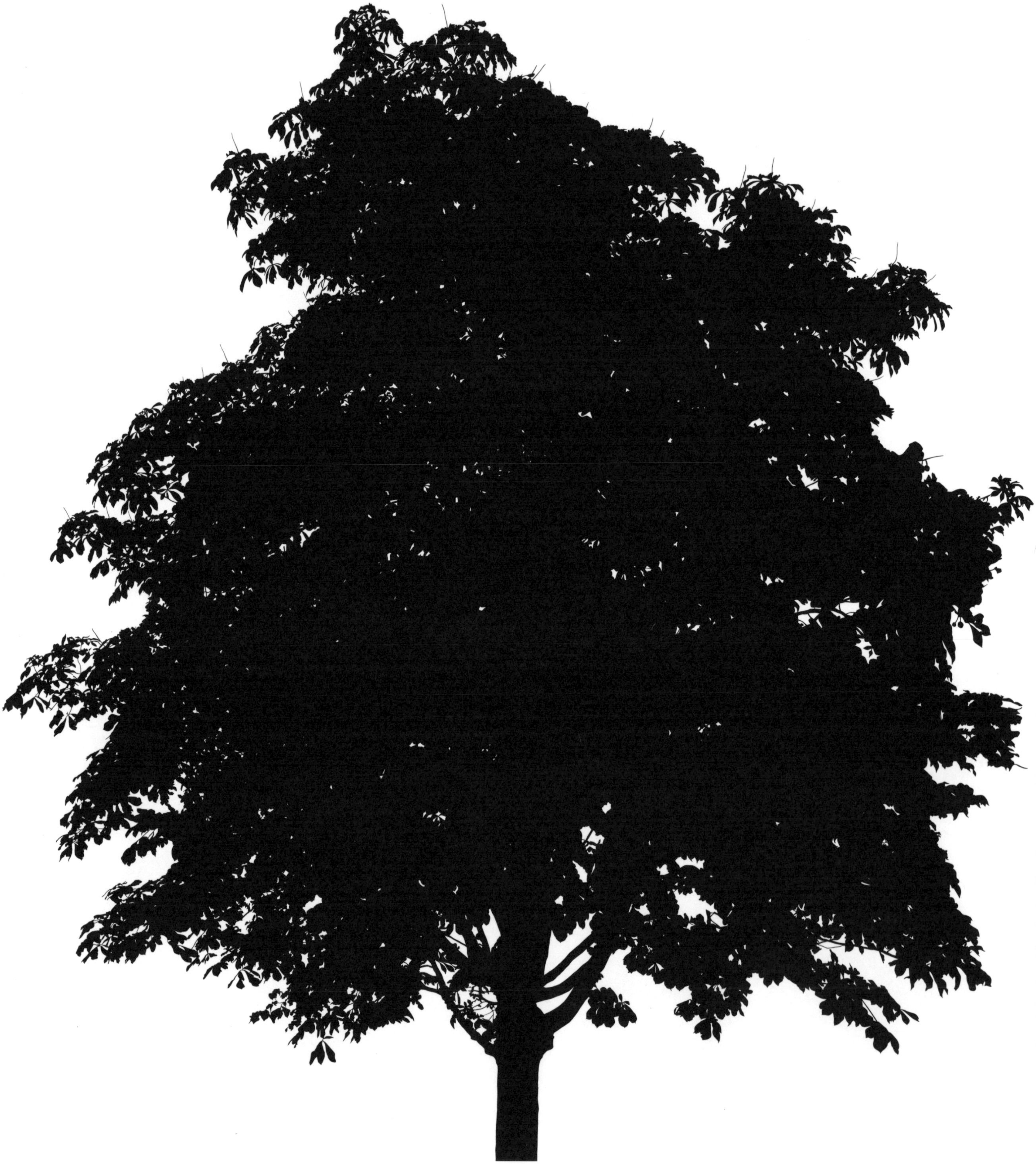

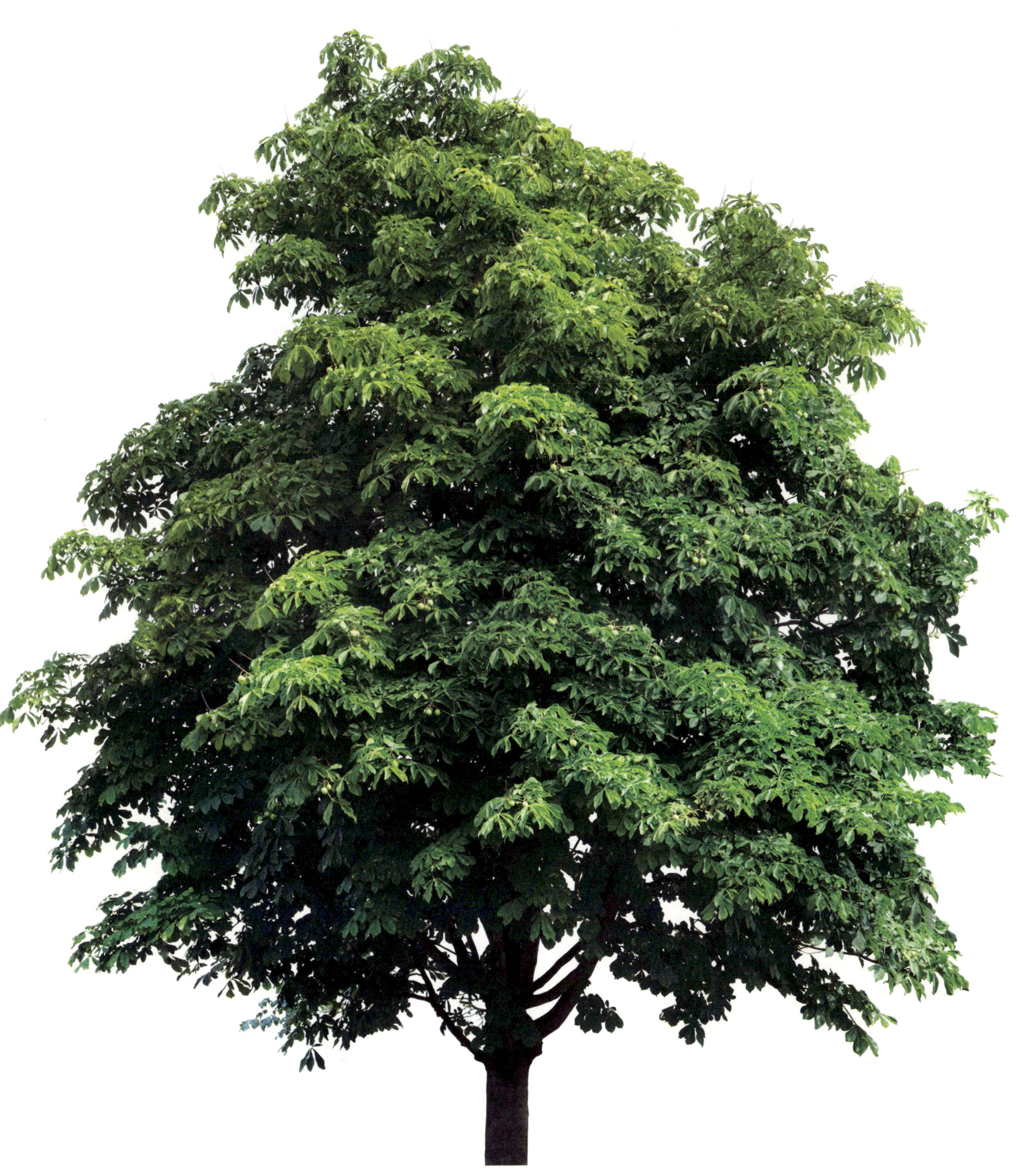

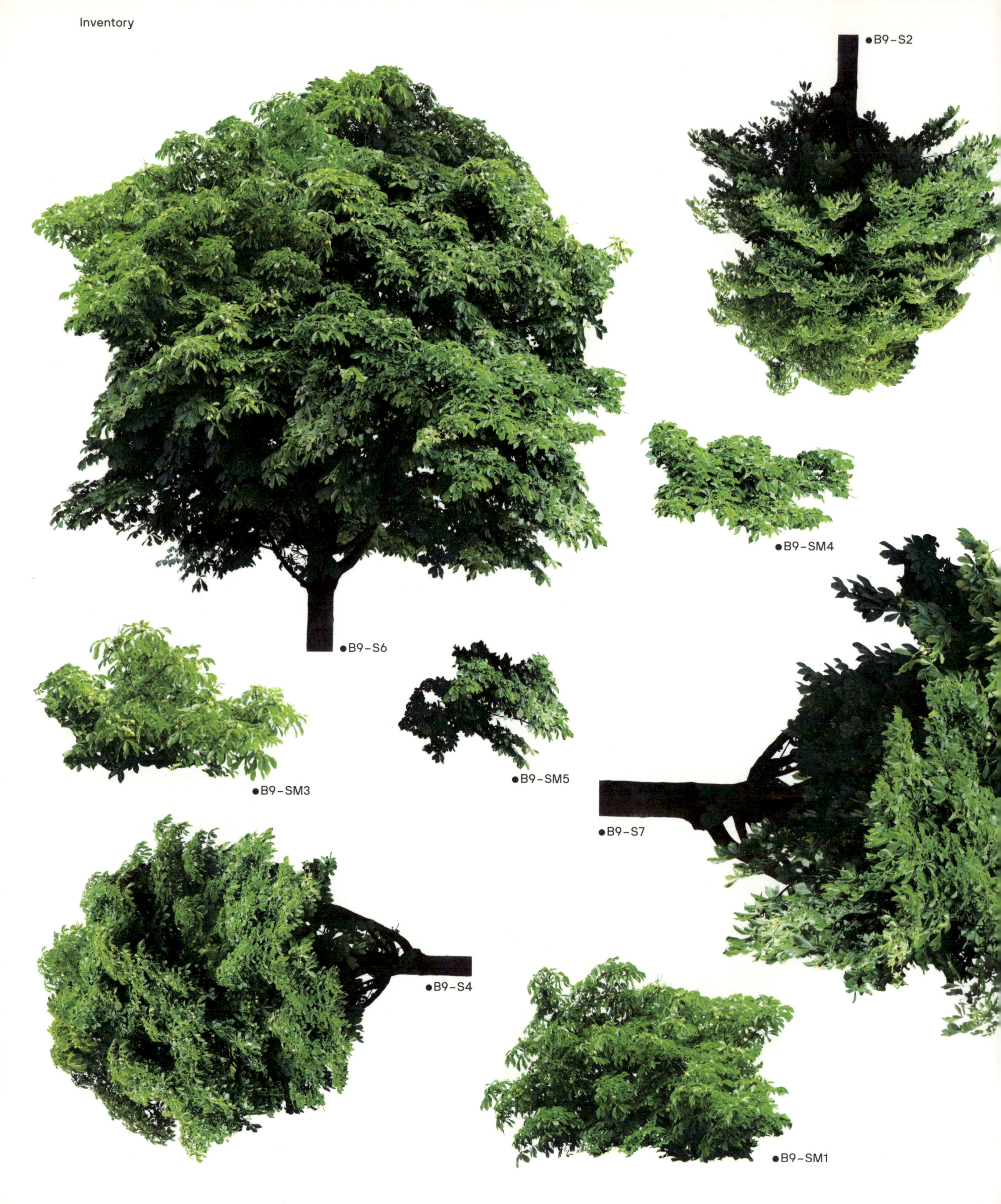
●B9-S2
●B9-SM4
●B9-S6
●B9-SM3
●B9-SM5
●B9-S7
●B9-S4
●B9-SM1

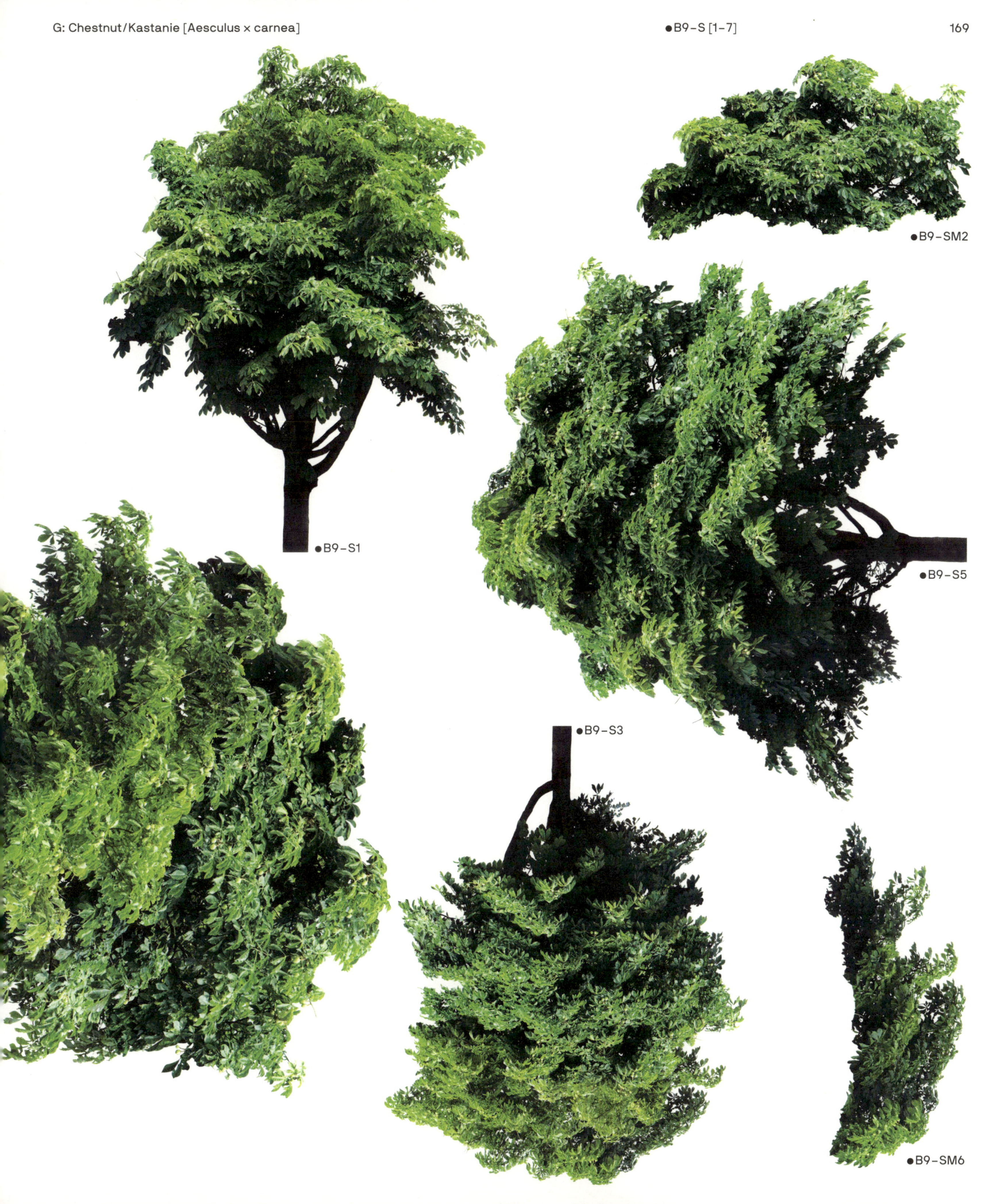
●B9–S1
●B9–SM2
●B9–S5
●B9–S3
●B9–SM6

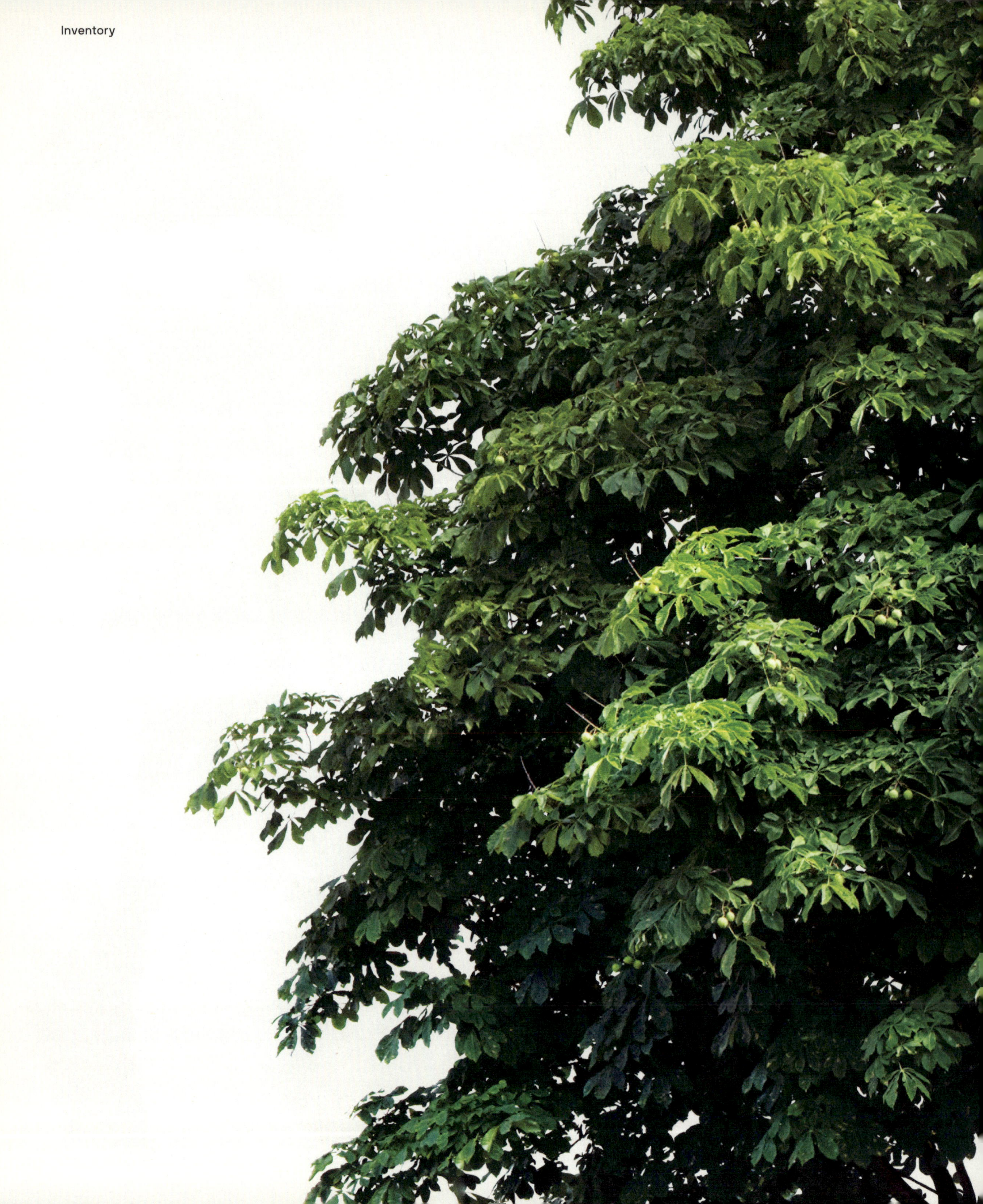

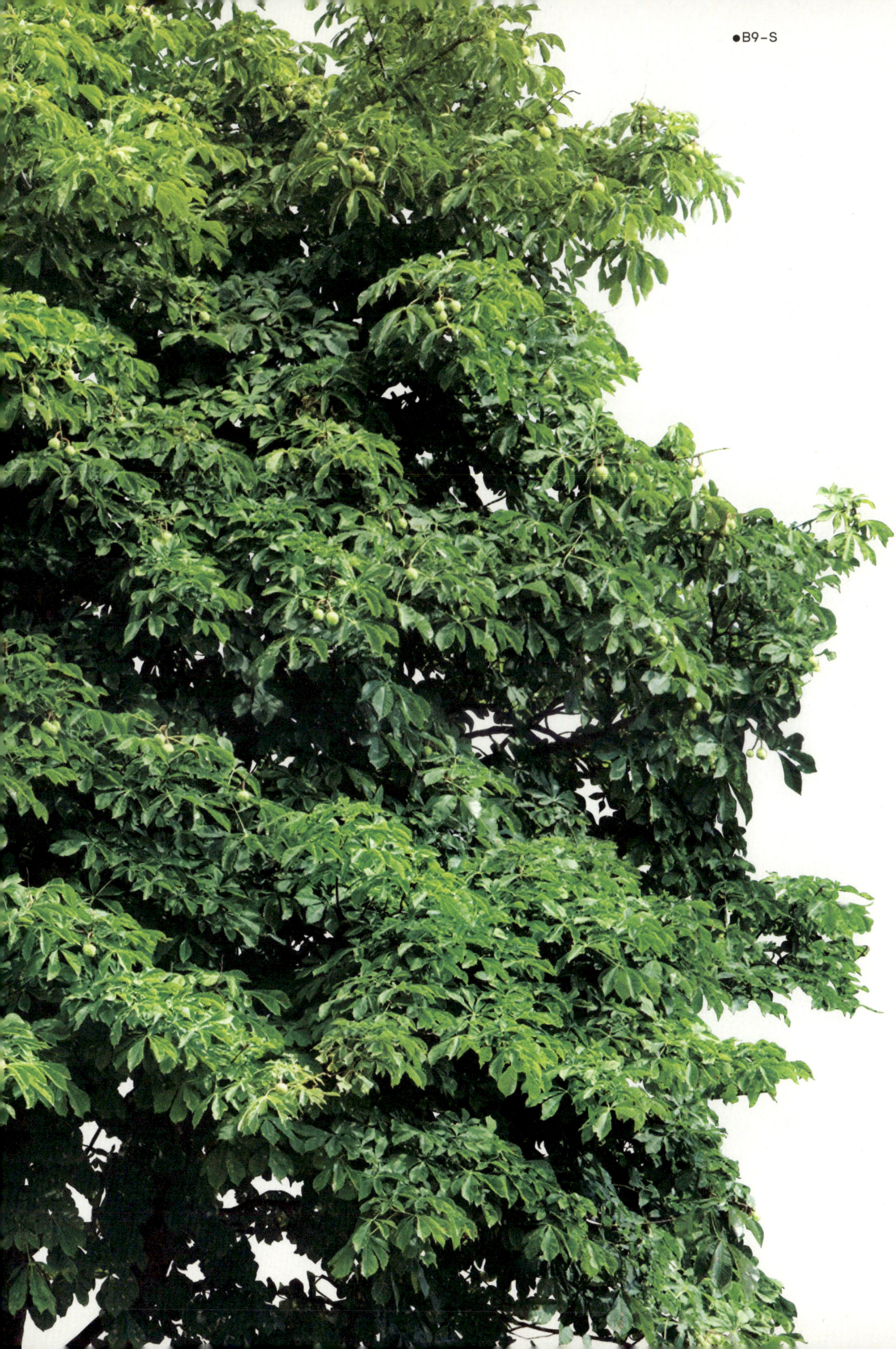

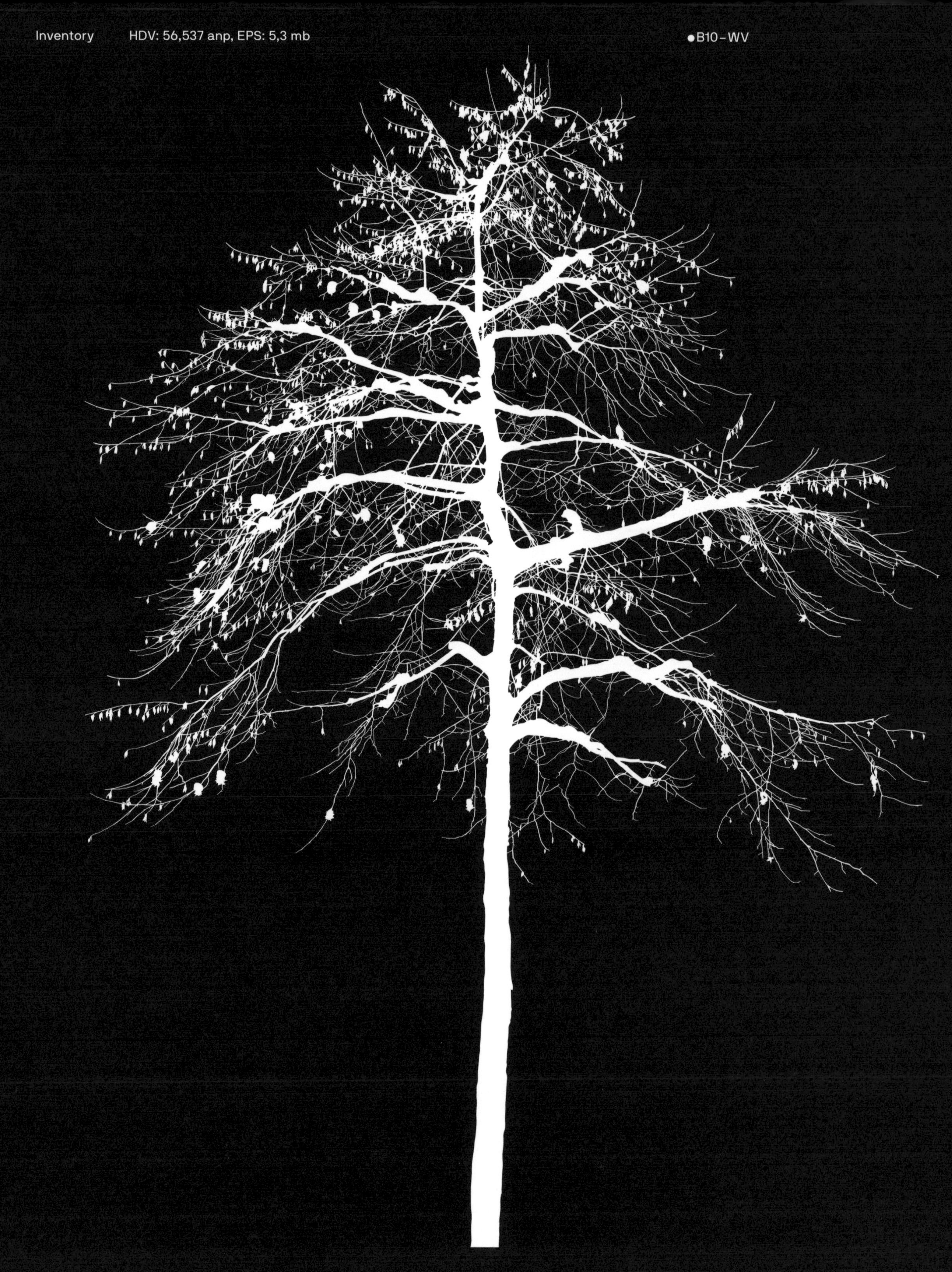

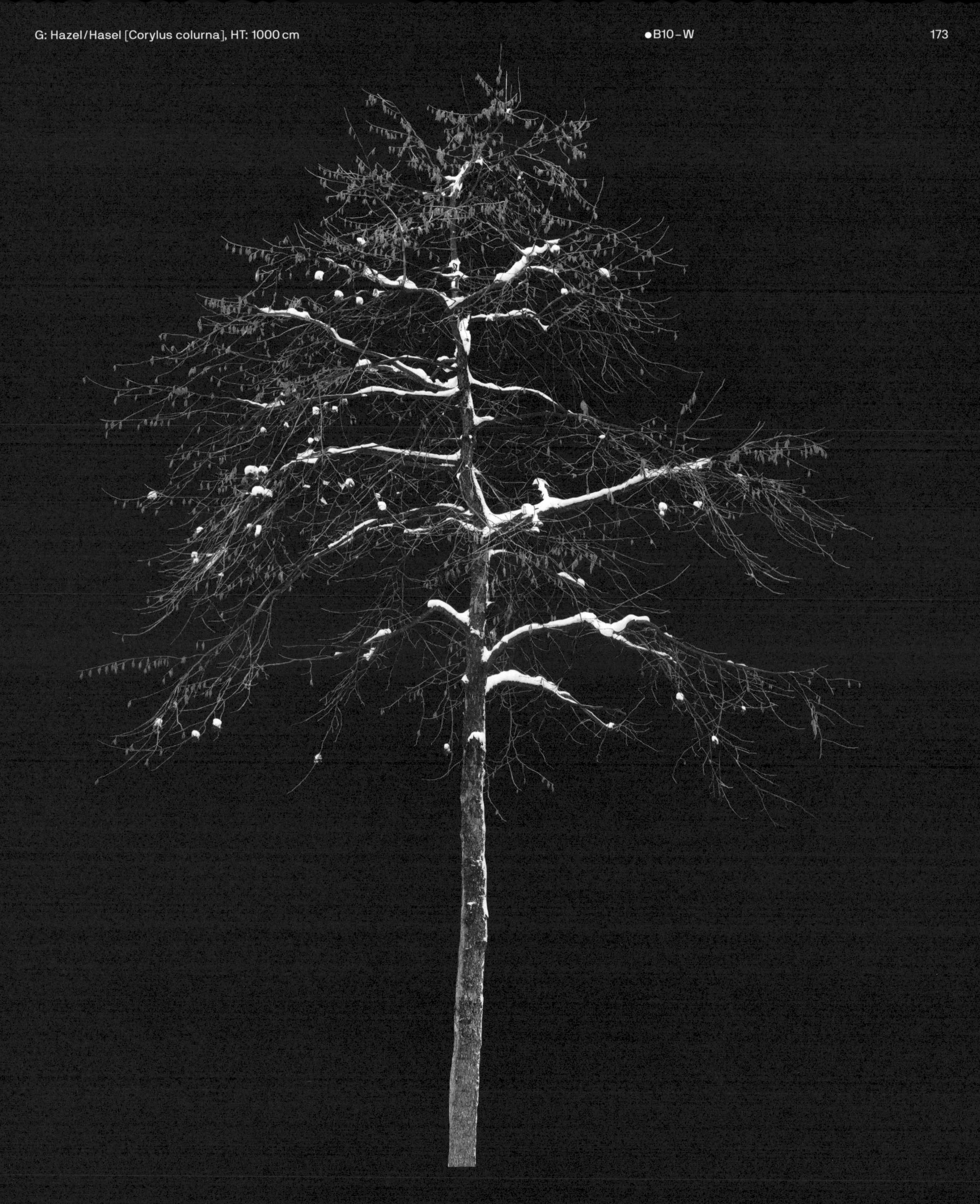

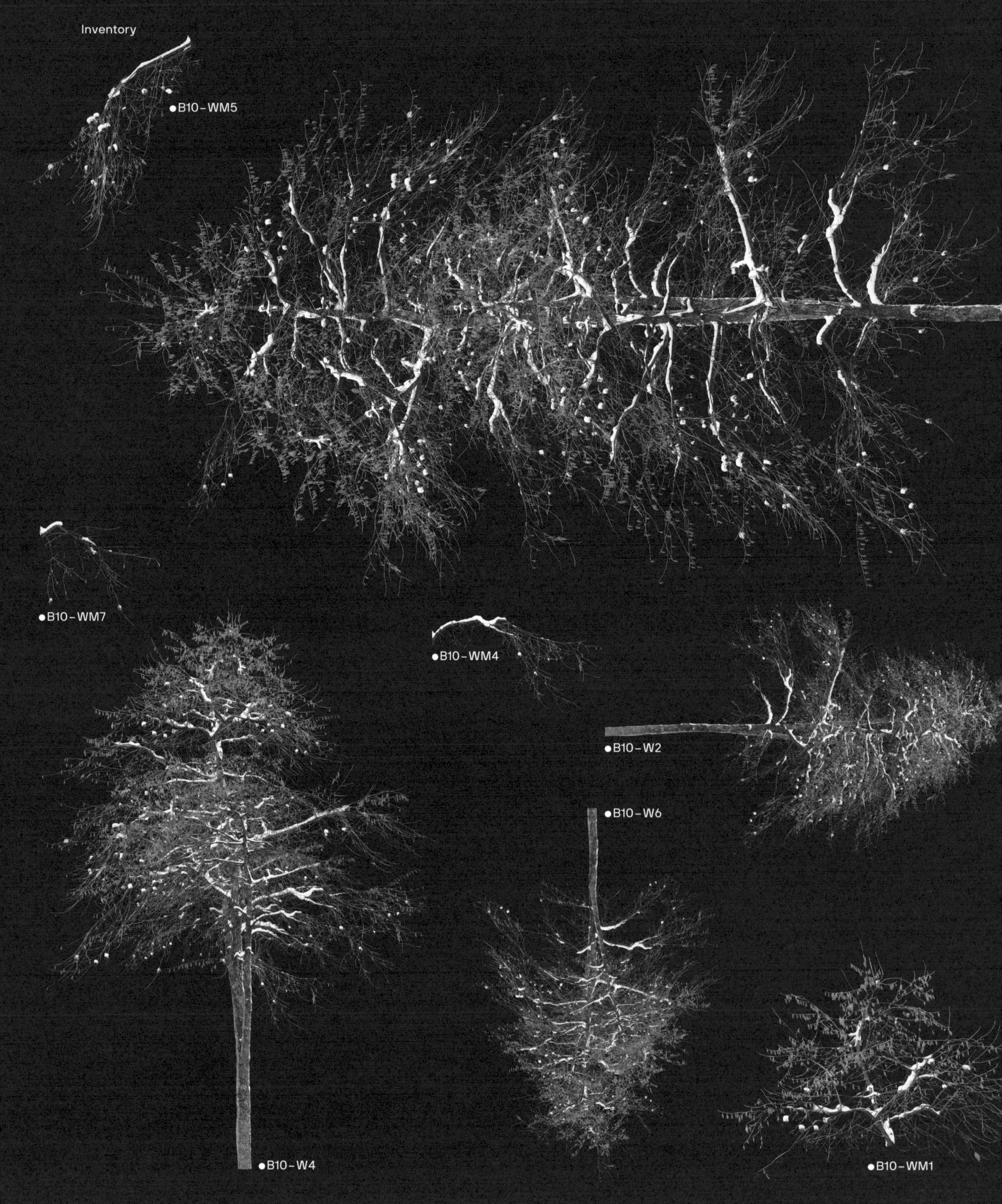

Inventory
B10-WM5
B10-WM7
B10-WM4
B10-W2
B10-W6
B10-W4
B10-WM1

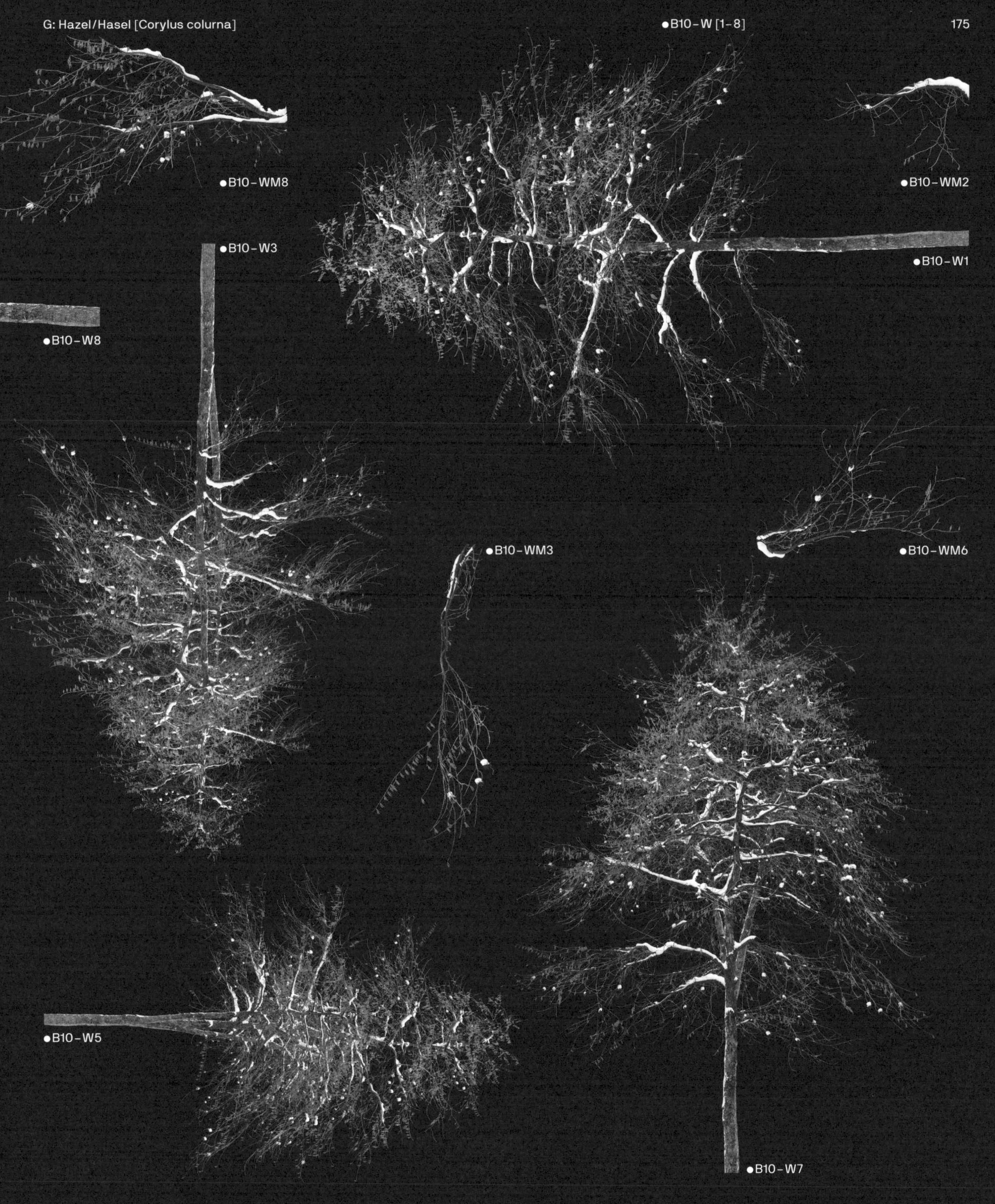

●B10−WM8
●B10−WM2
●B10−W3
●B10−W1
●B10−W8
●B10−WM3
●B10−WM6
●B10−W5
●B10−W7

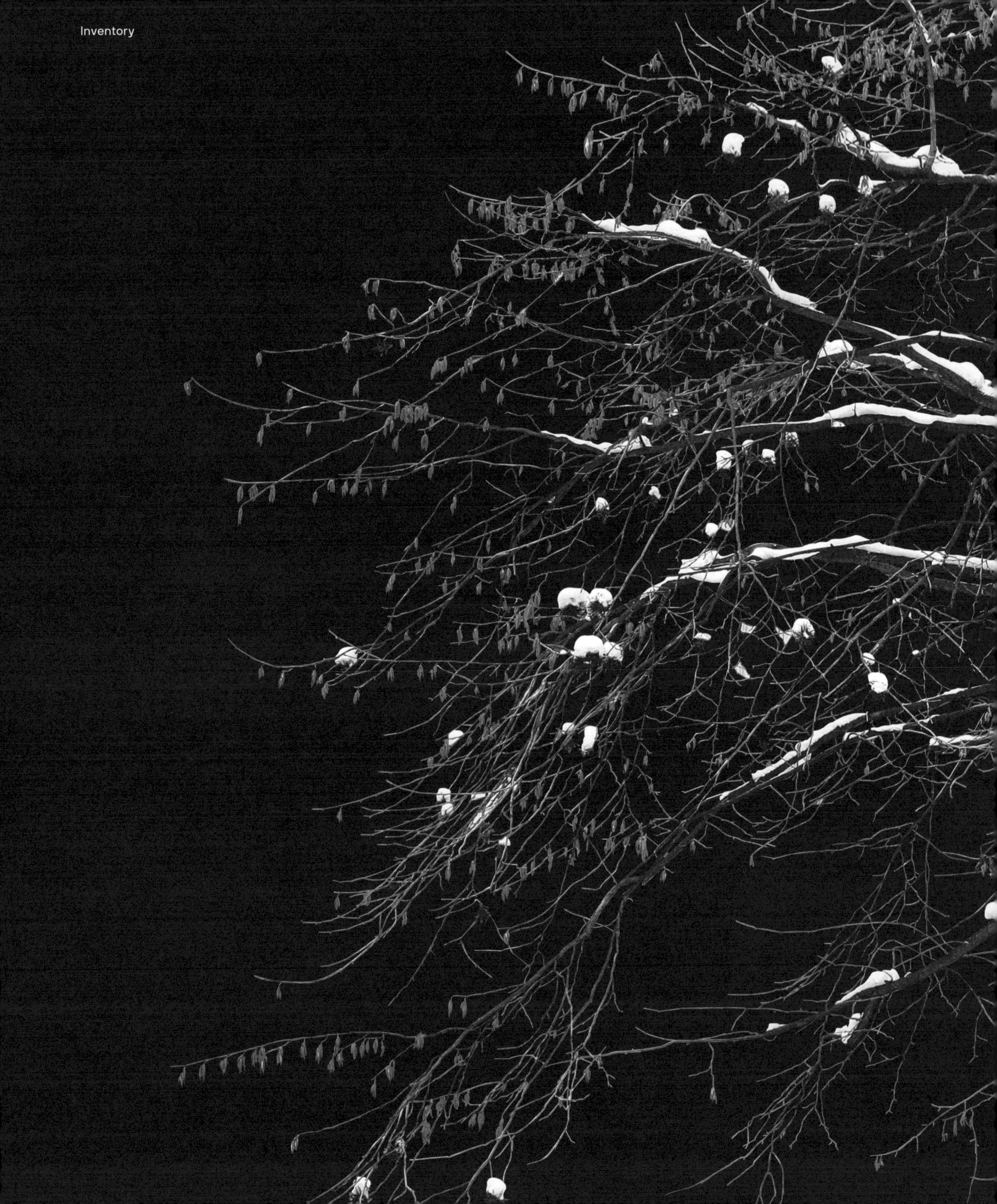

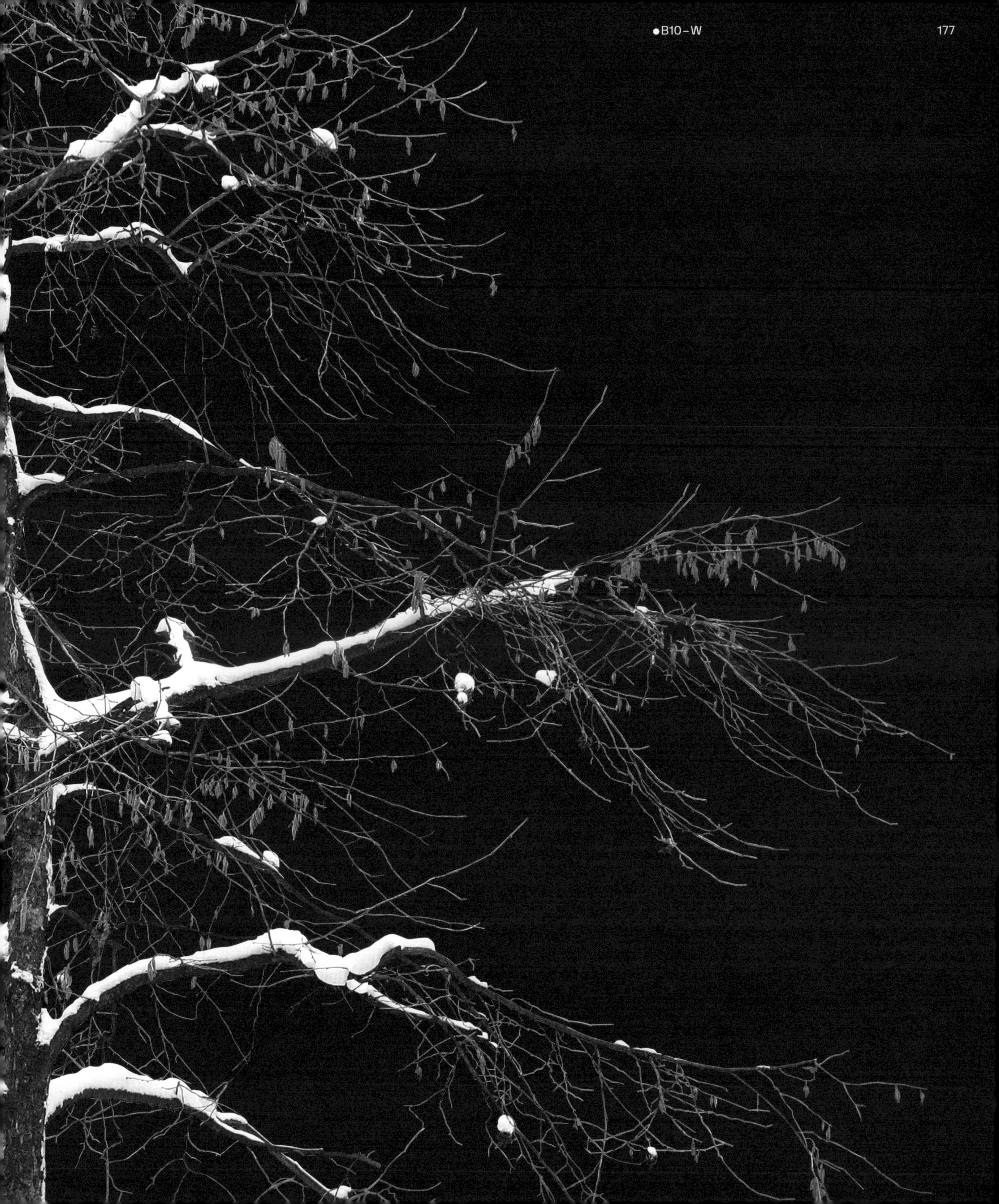

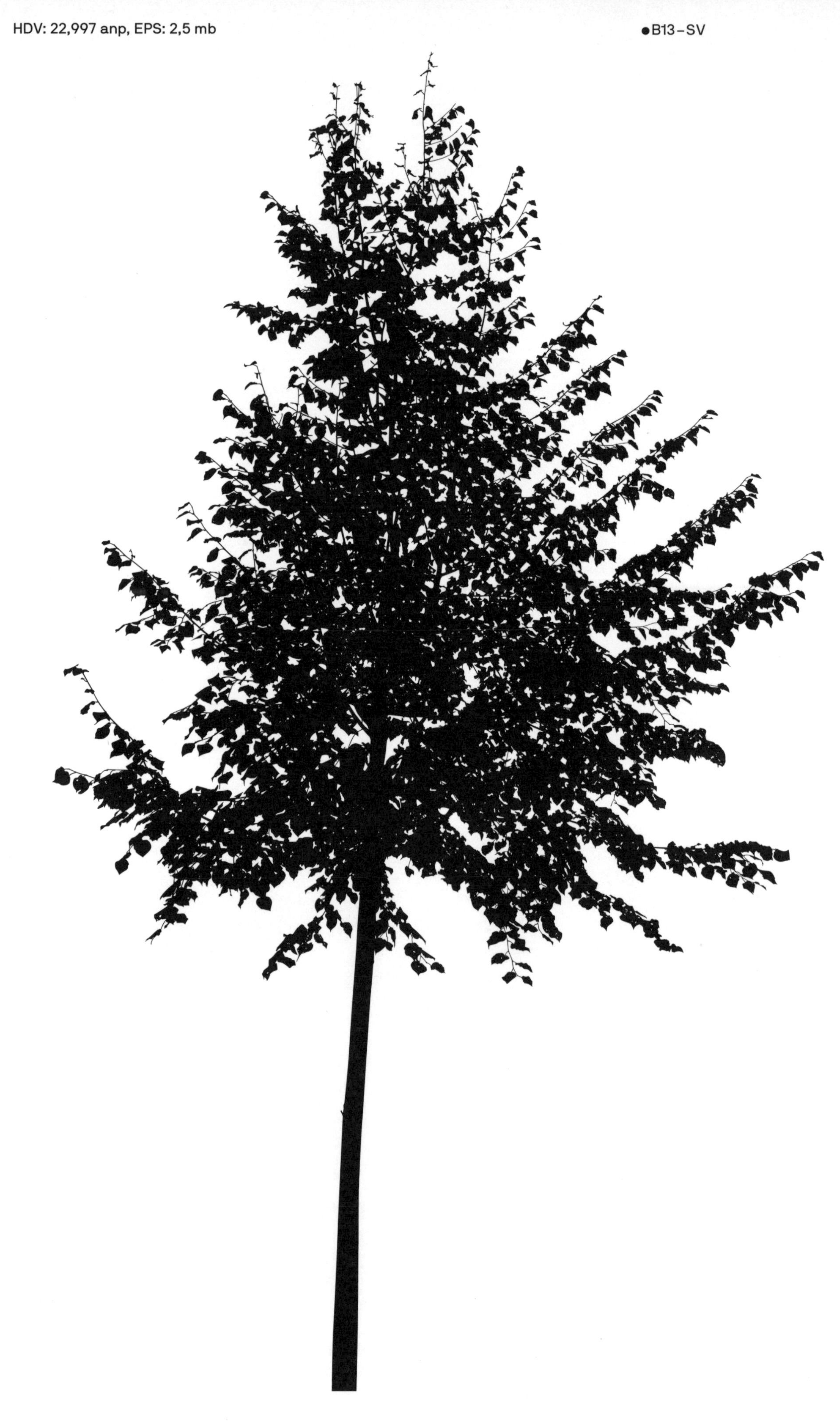

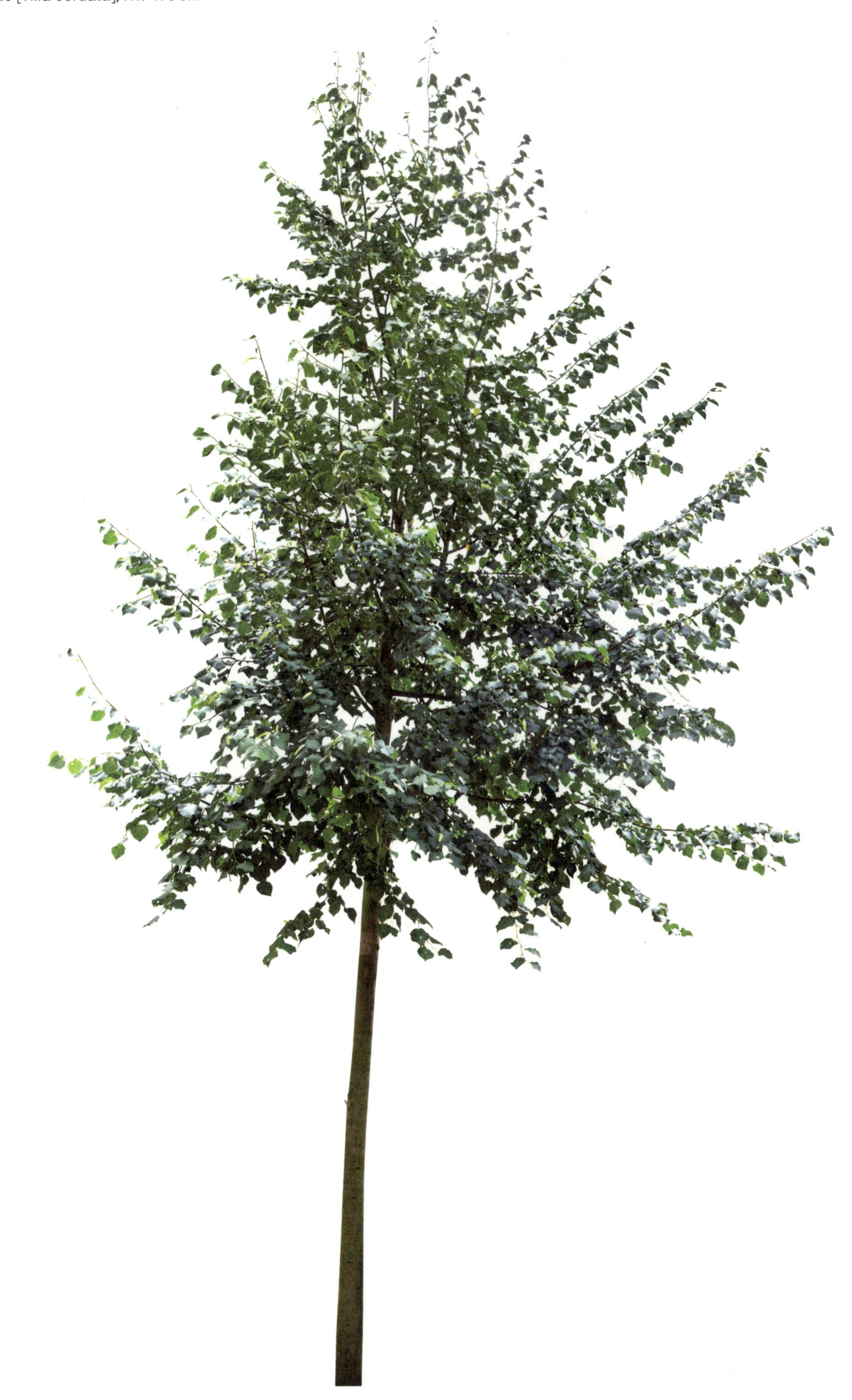

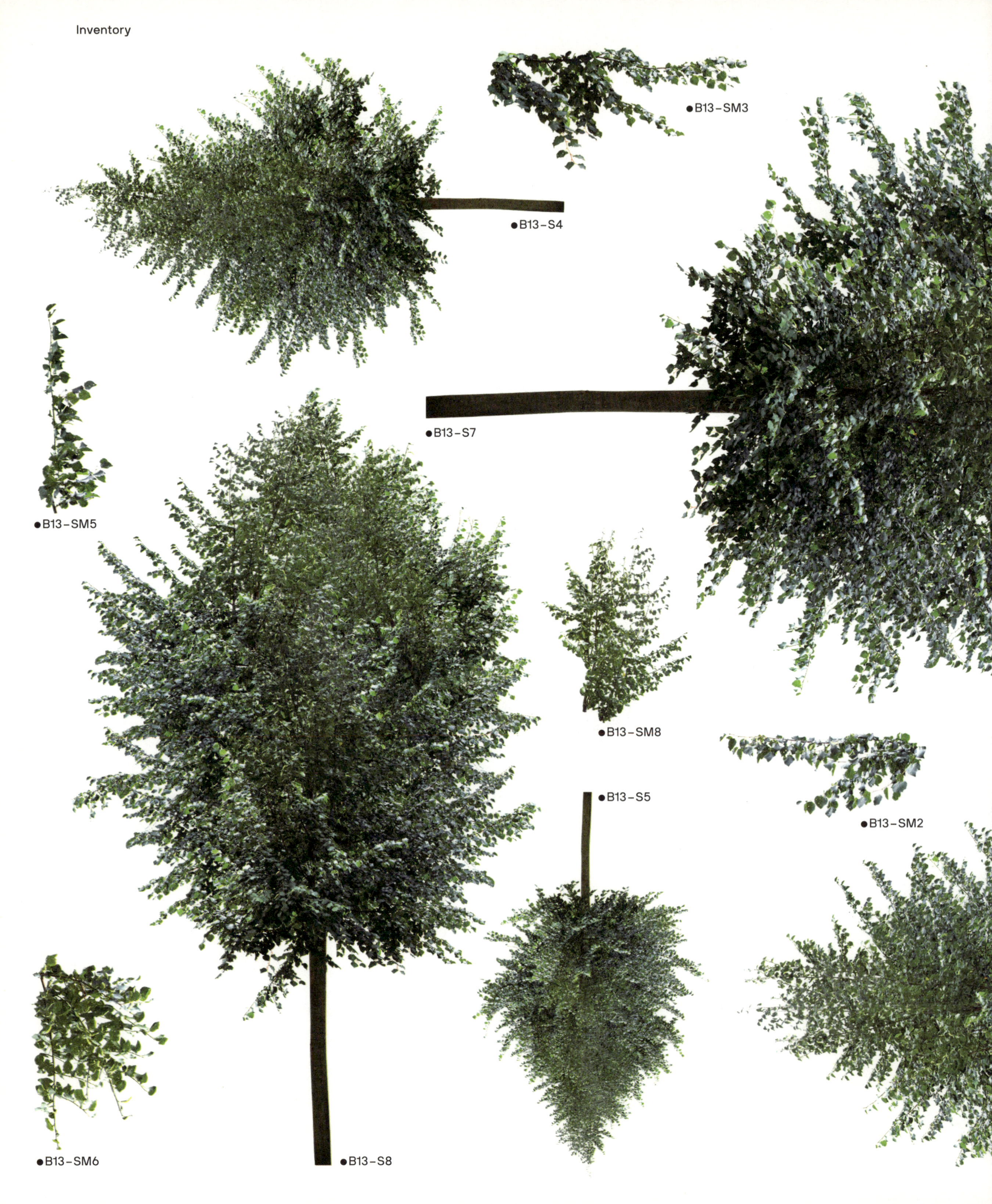
●B13–SM3
●B13–S4
●B13–S7
●B13–SM5
●B13–SM8
●B13–S5
●B13–SM2
●B13–SM6
●B13–S8

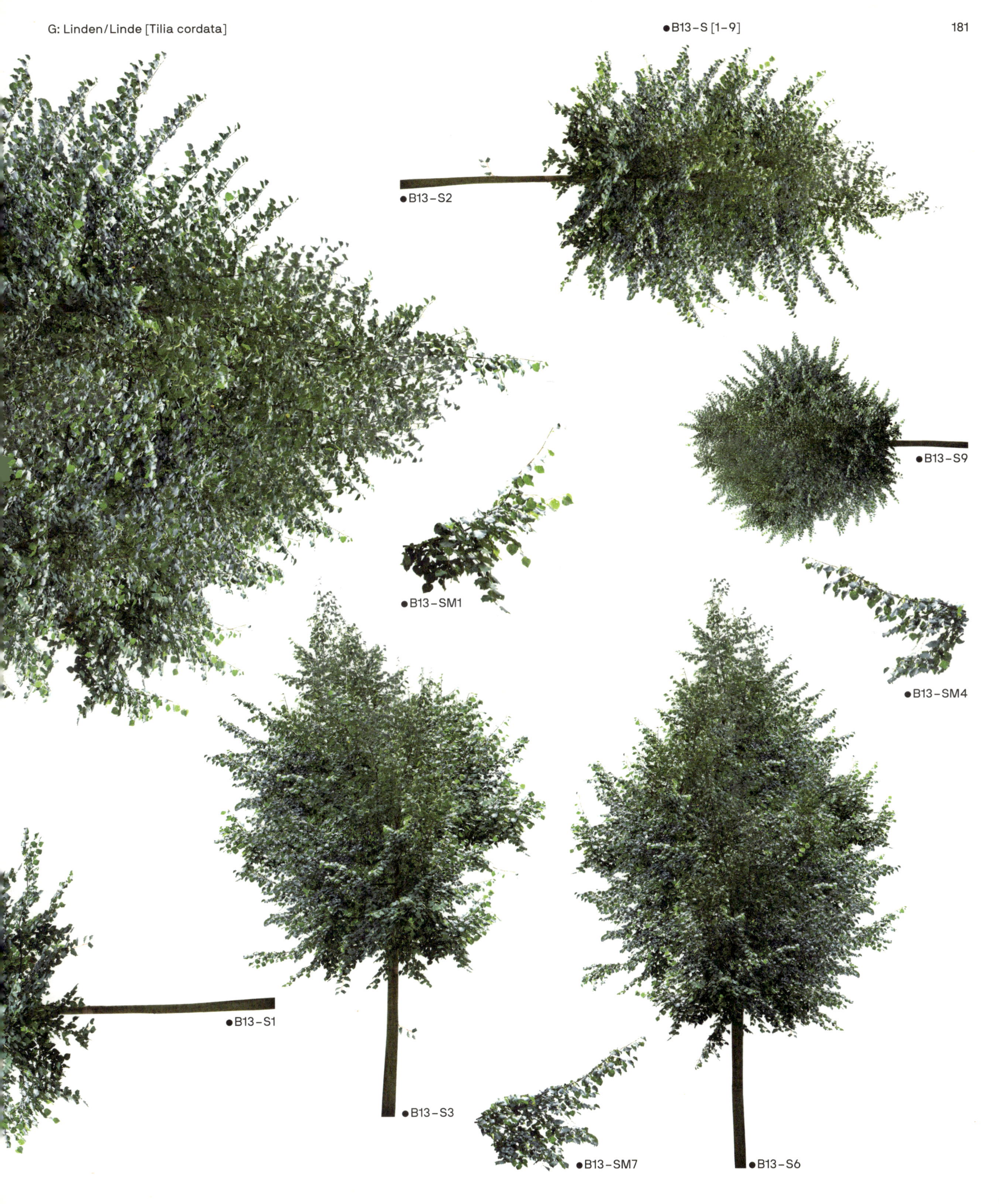
●B13–S [1–9]
●B13–S2
●B13–S9
●B13–SM1
●B13–SM4
●B13–S1
●B13–S3
●B13–SM7
●B13–S6

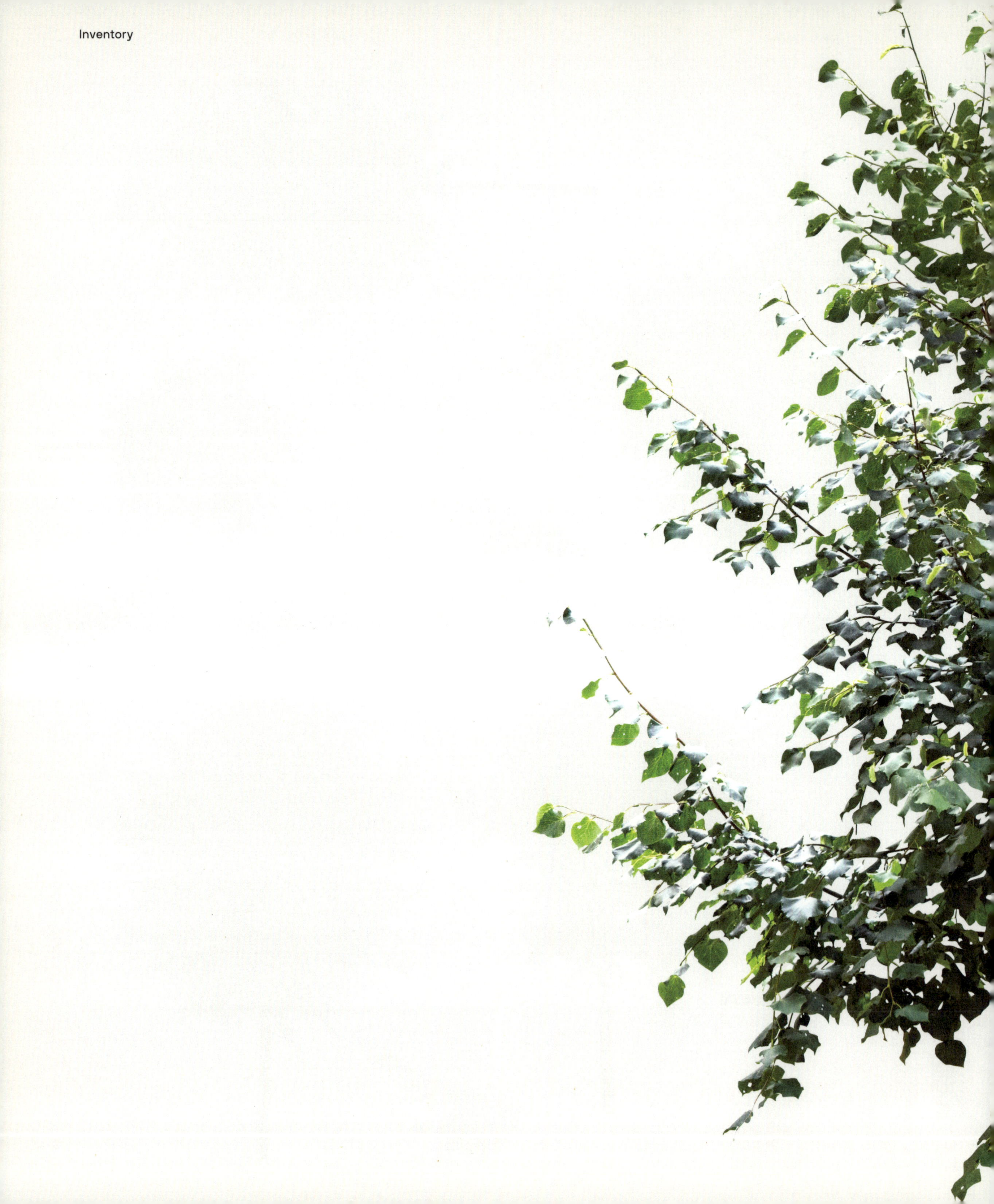

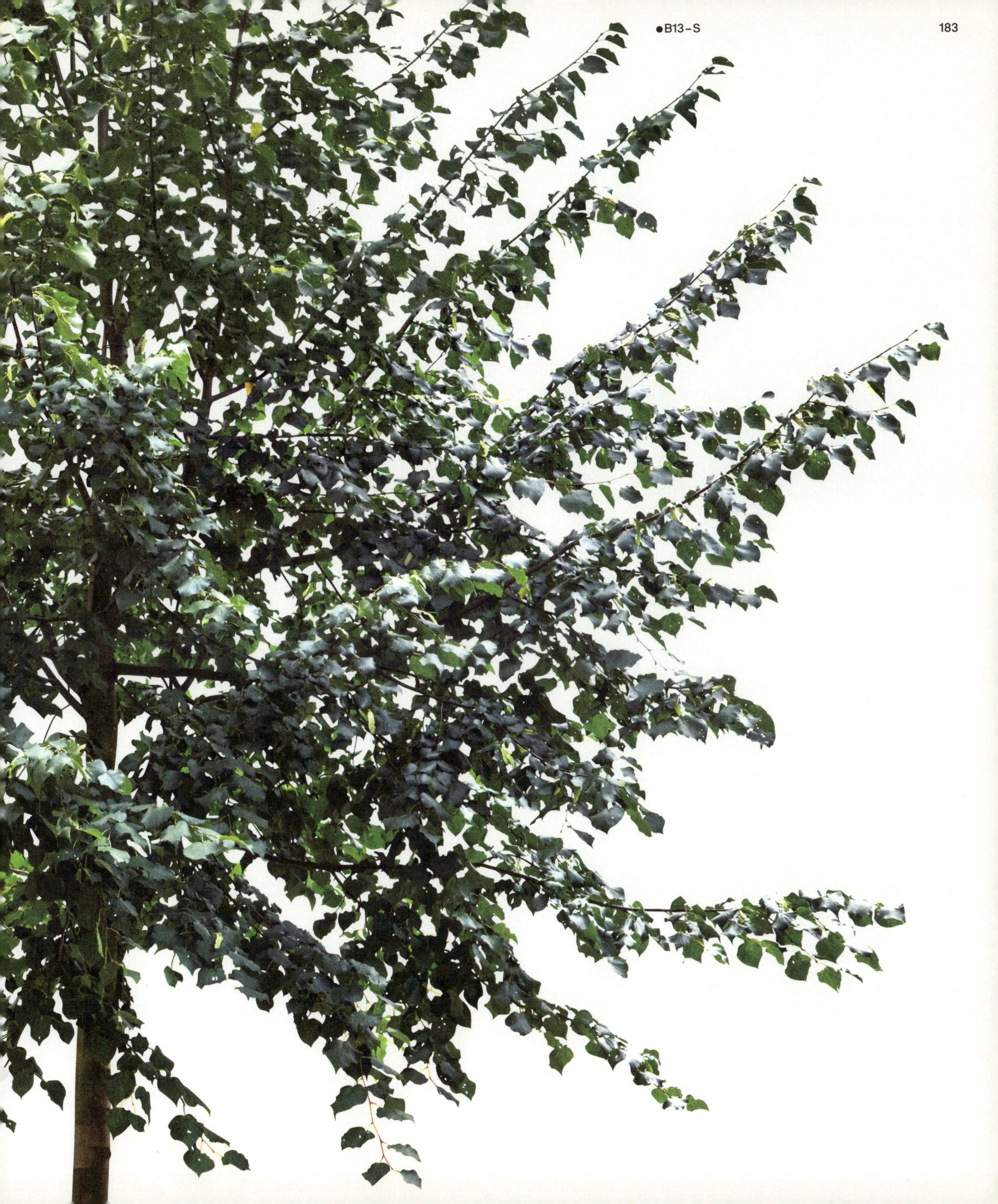

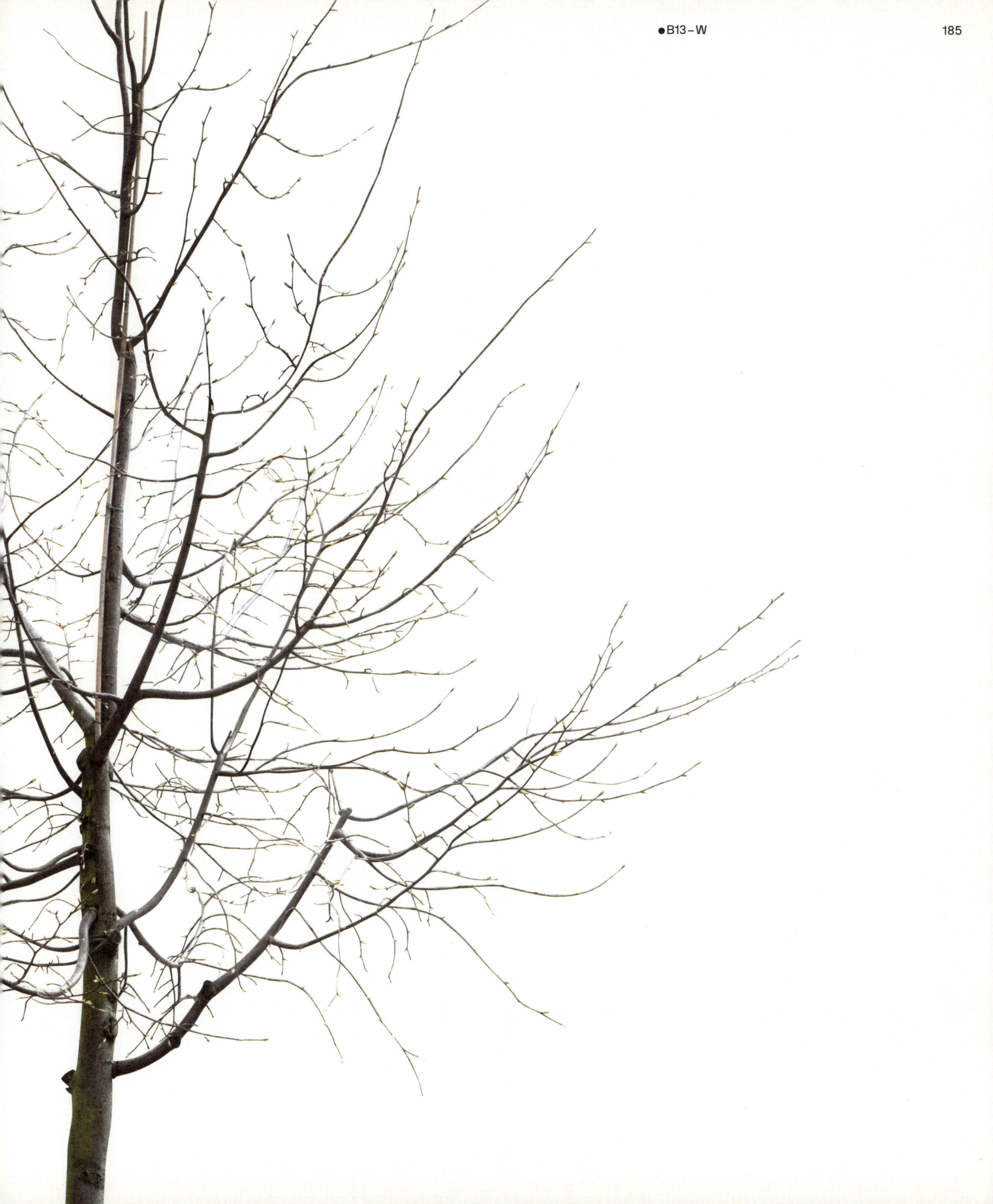

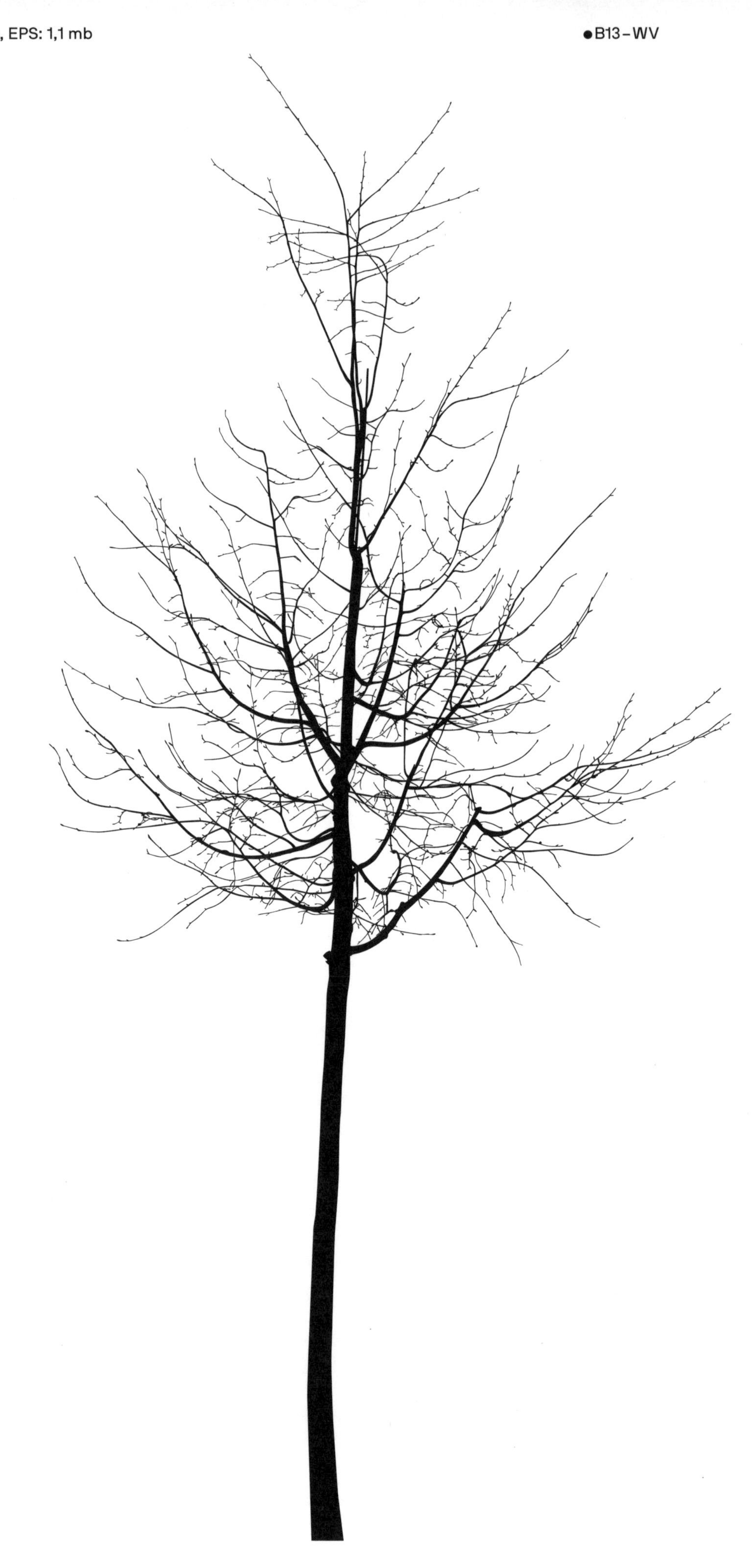

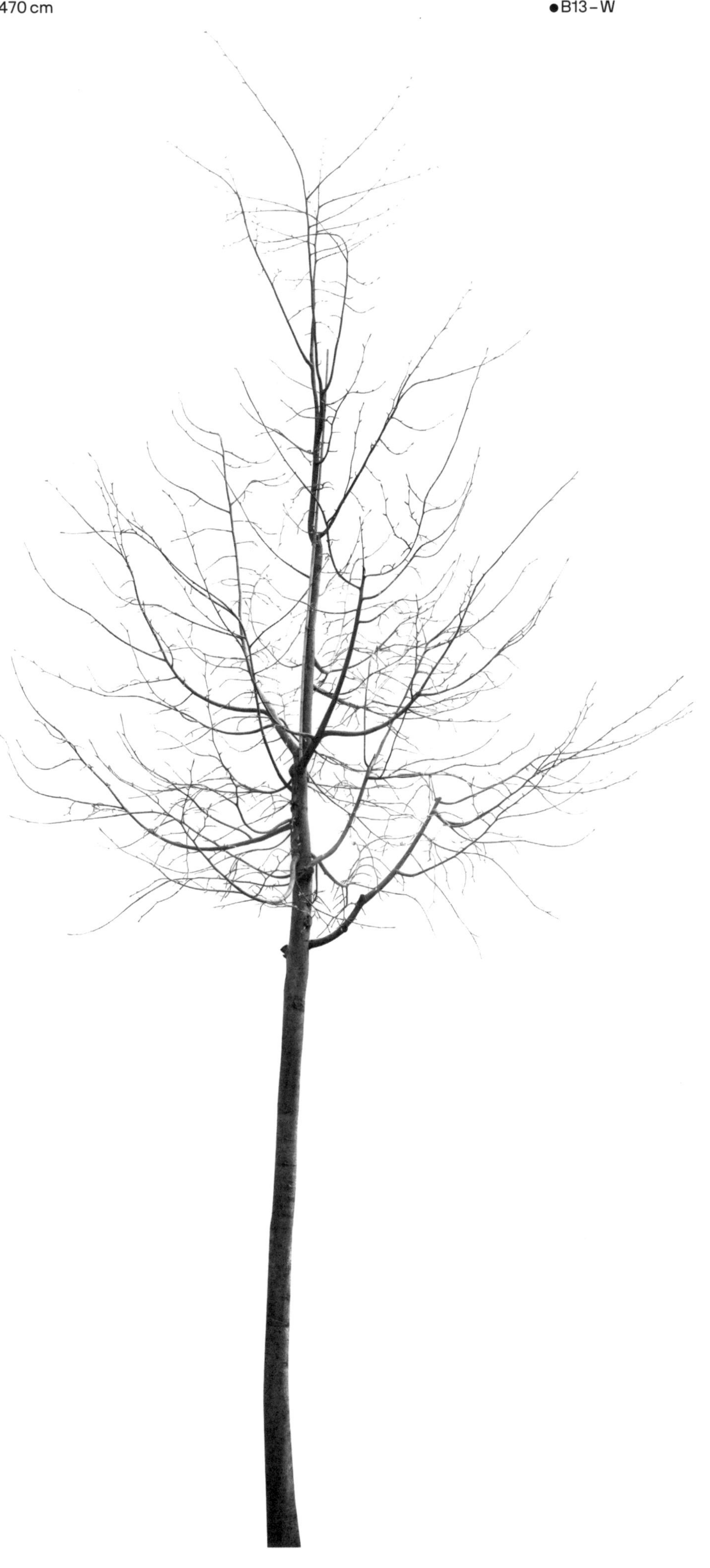

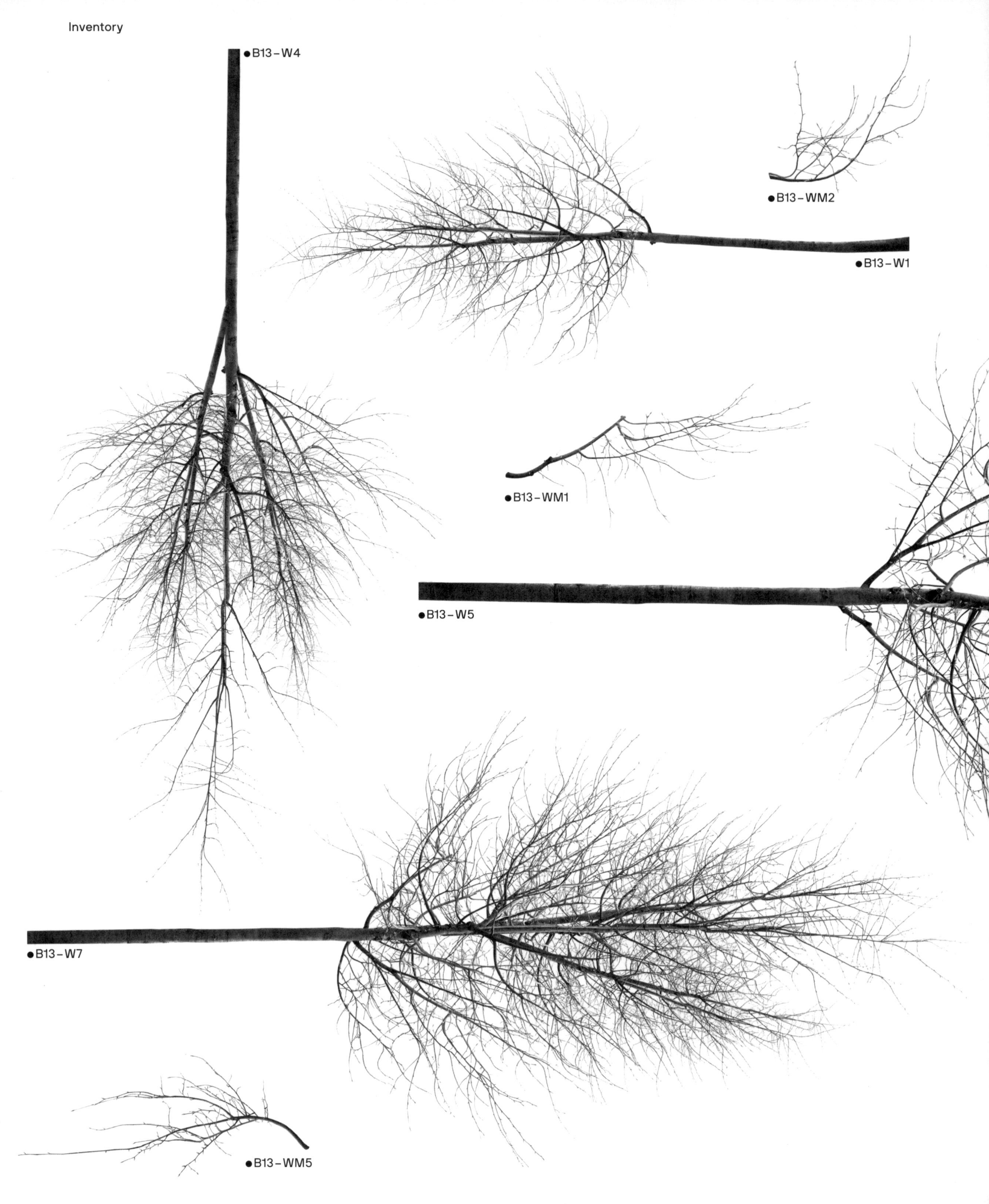

B13–W4
B13–WM2
B13–W1
B13–WM1
B13–W5
B13–W7
B13–WM5

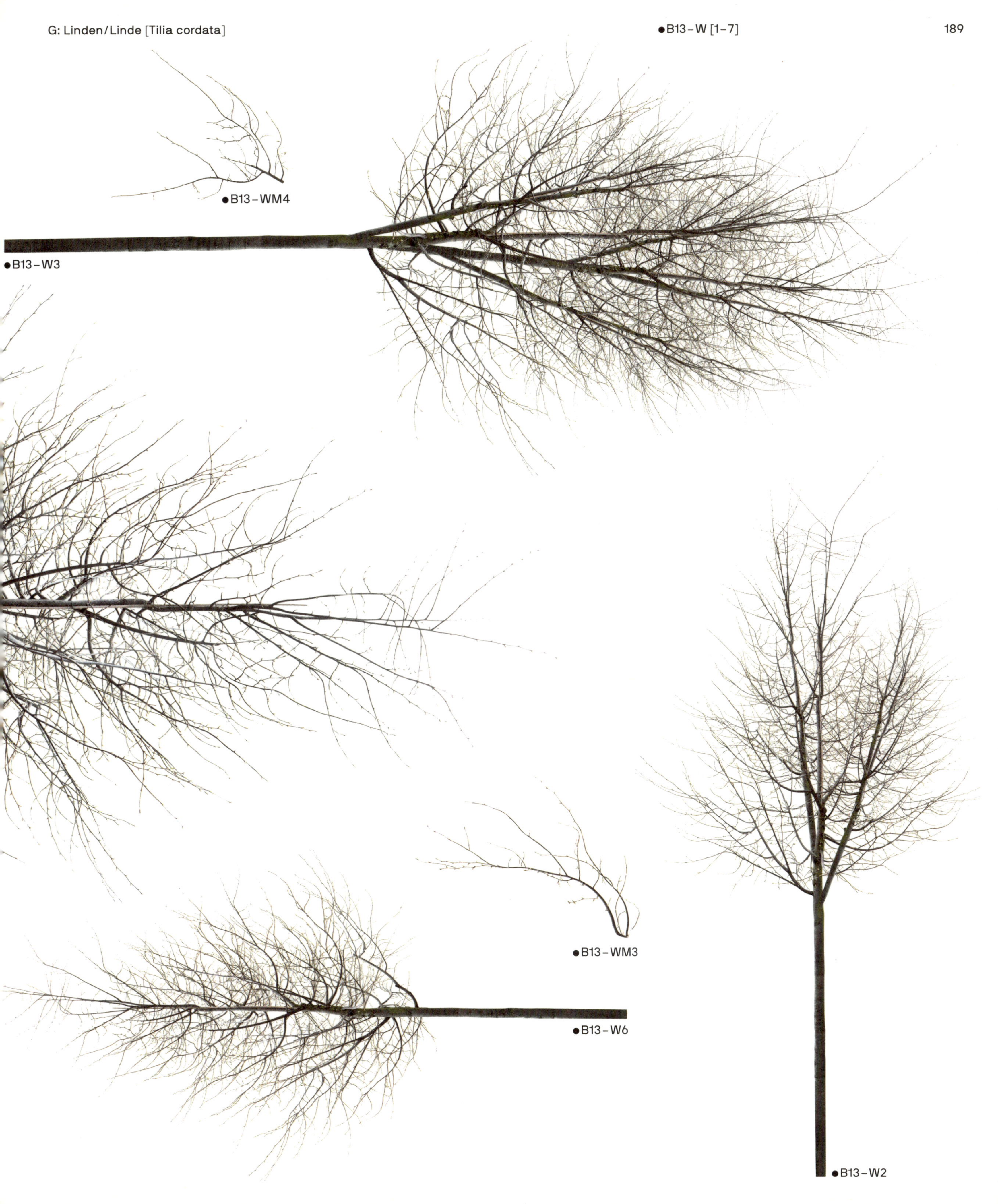
●B13–WM4
●B13–W3
●B13–WM3
●B13–W6
●B13–W2

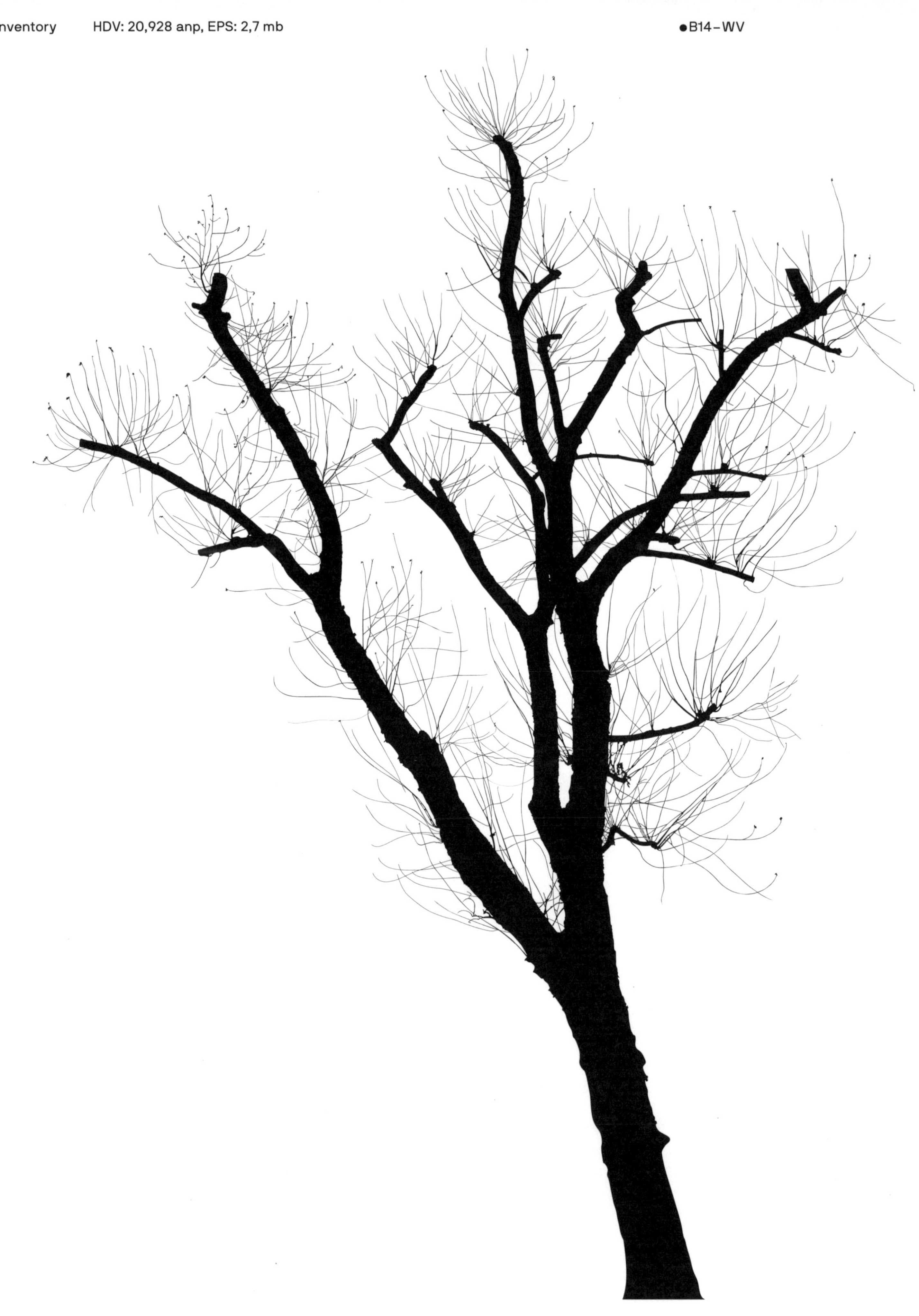

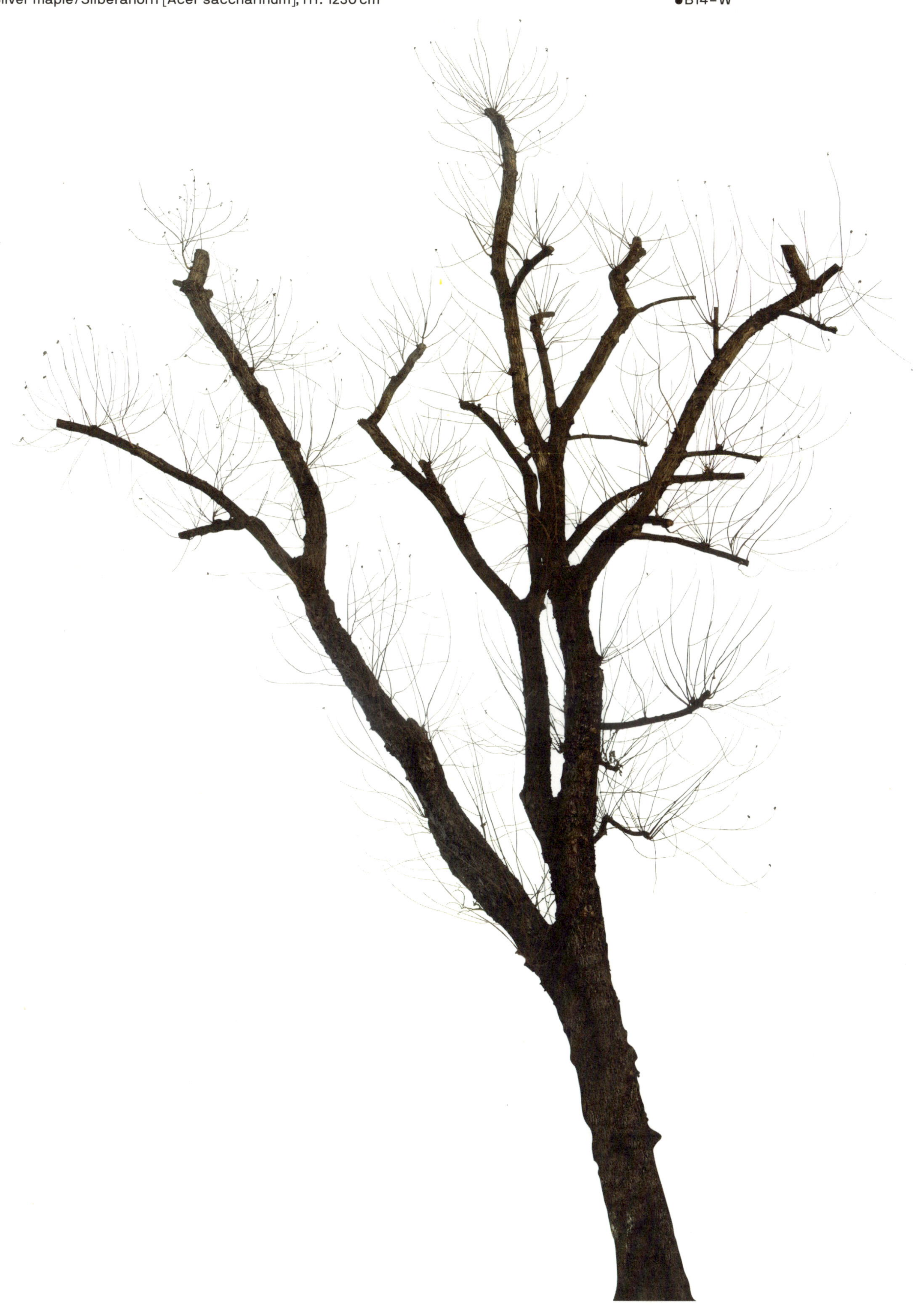

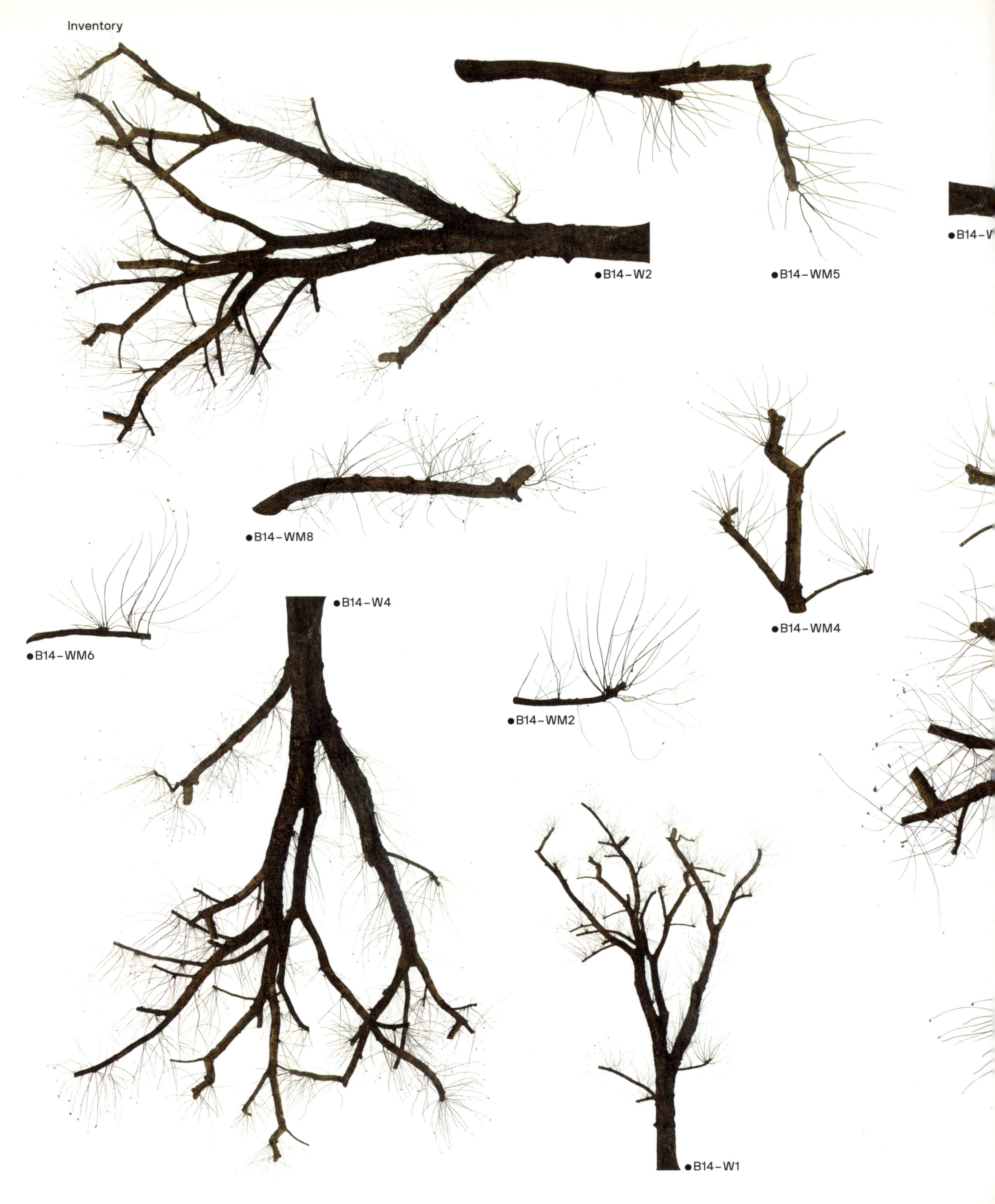

Inventory
●B14–W2
●B14–WM5
●B14–W
●B14–WM8
●B14–W4
●B14–WM4
●B14–WM6
●B14–WM2
●B14–W1

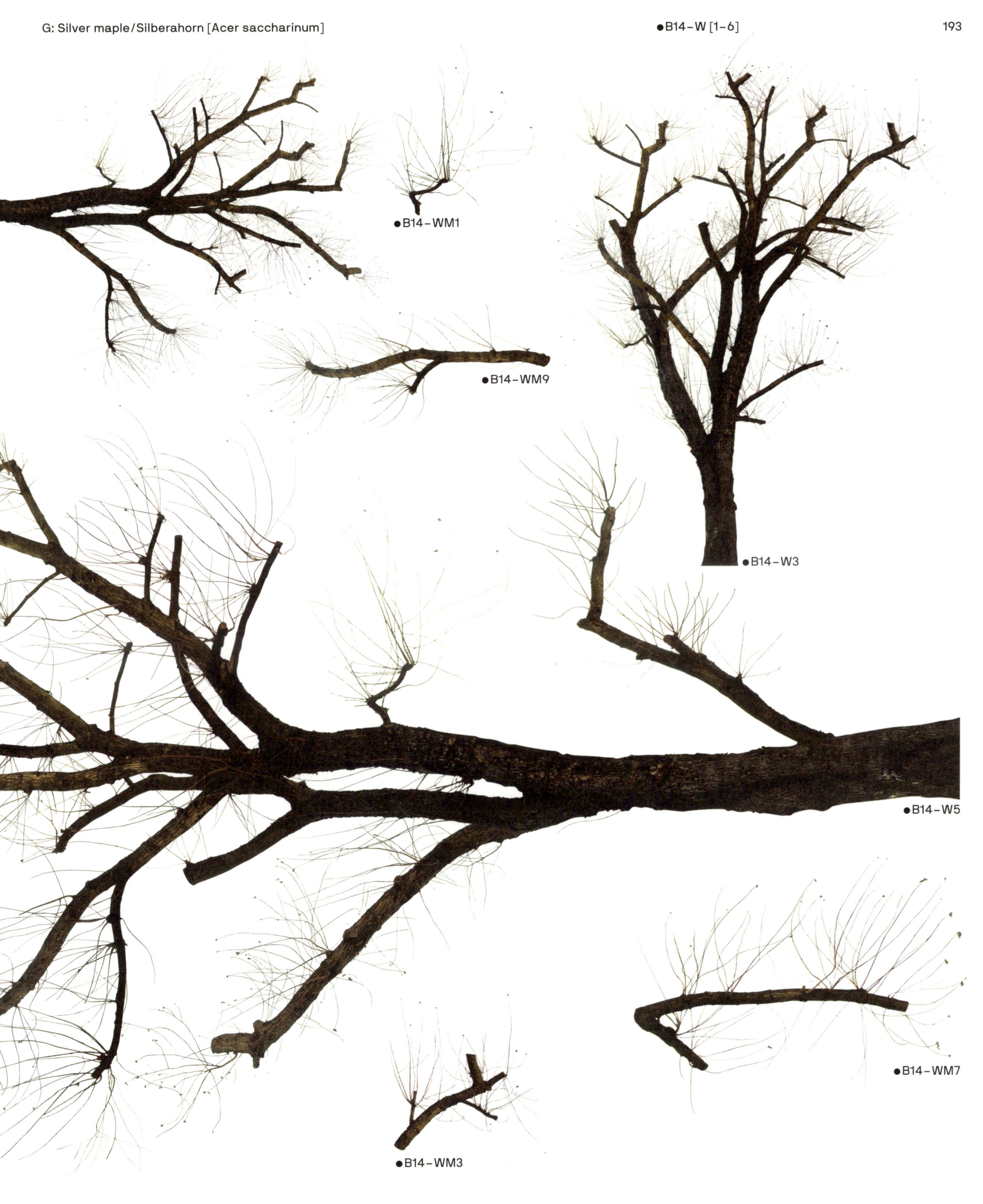
●B14–WM1
●B14–WM9
●B14–W3
●B14–W5
●B14–WM7
●B14–WM3

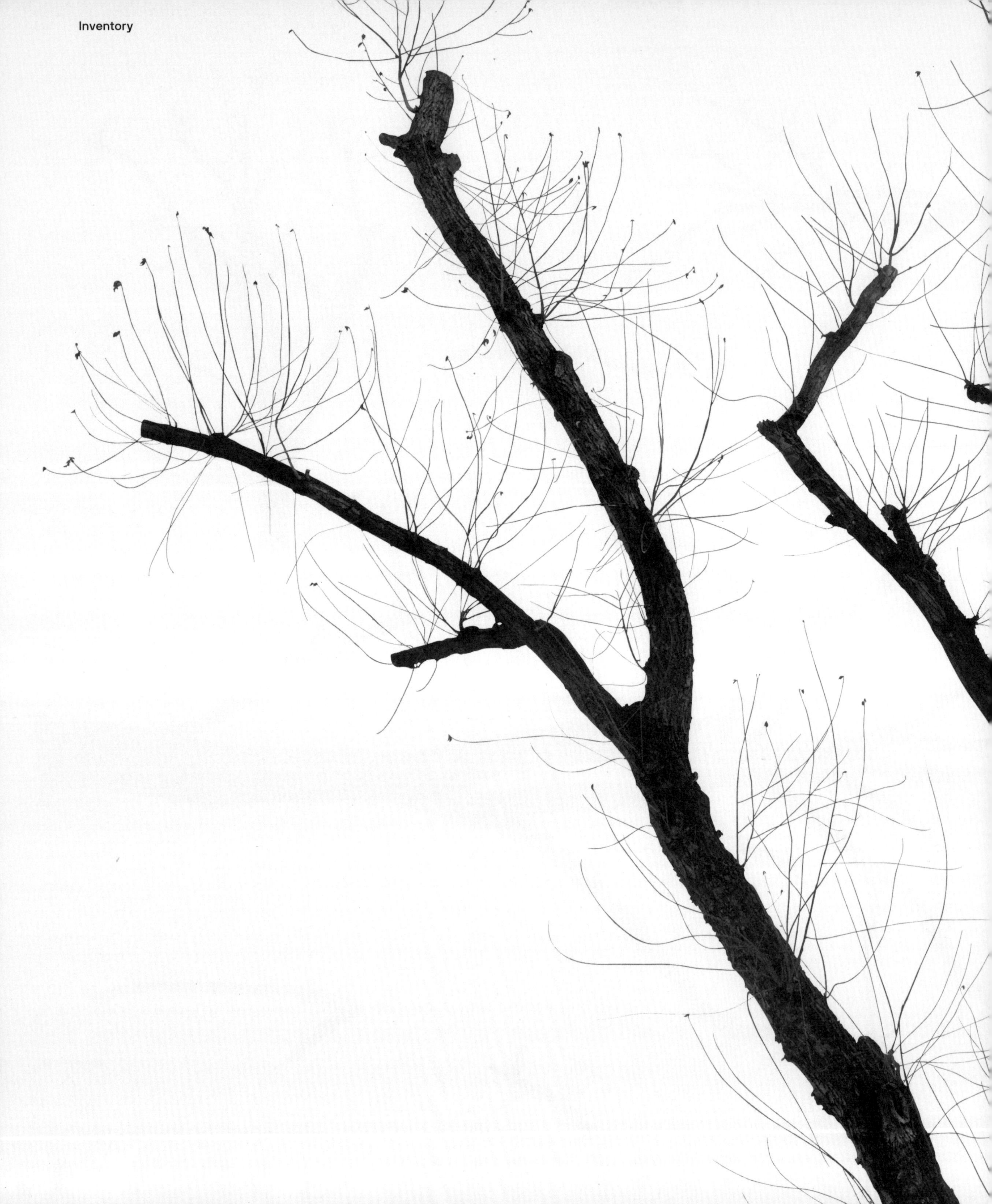

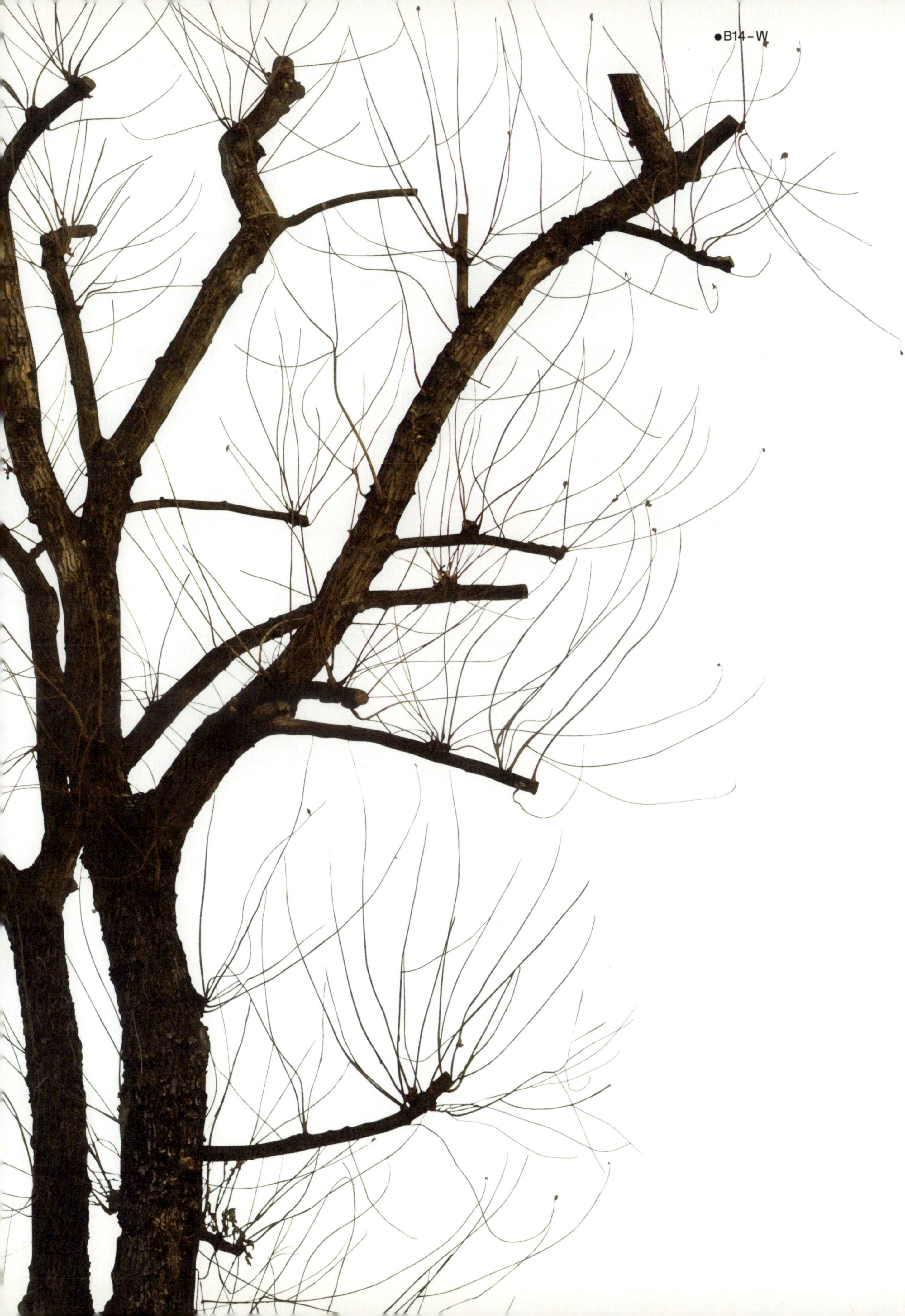

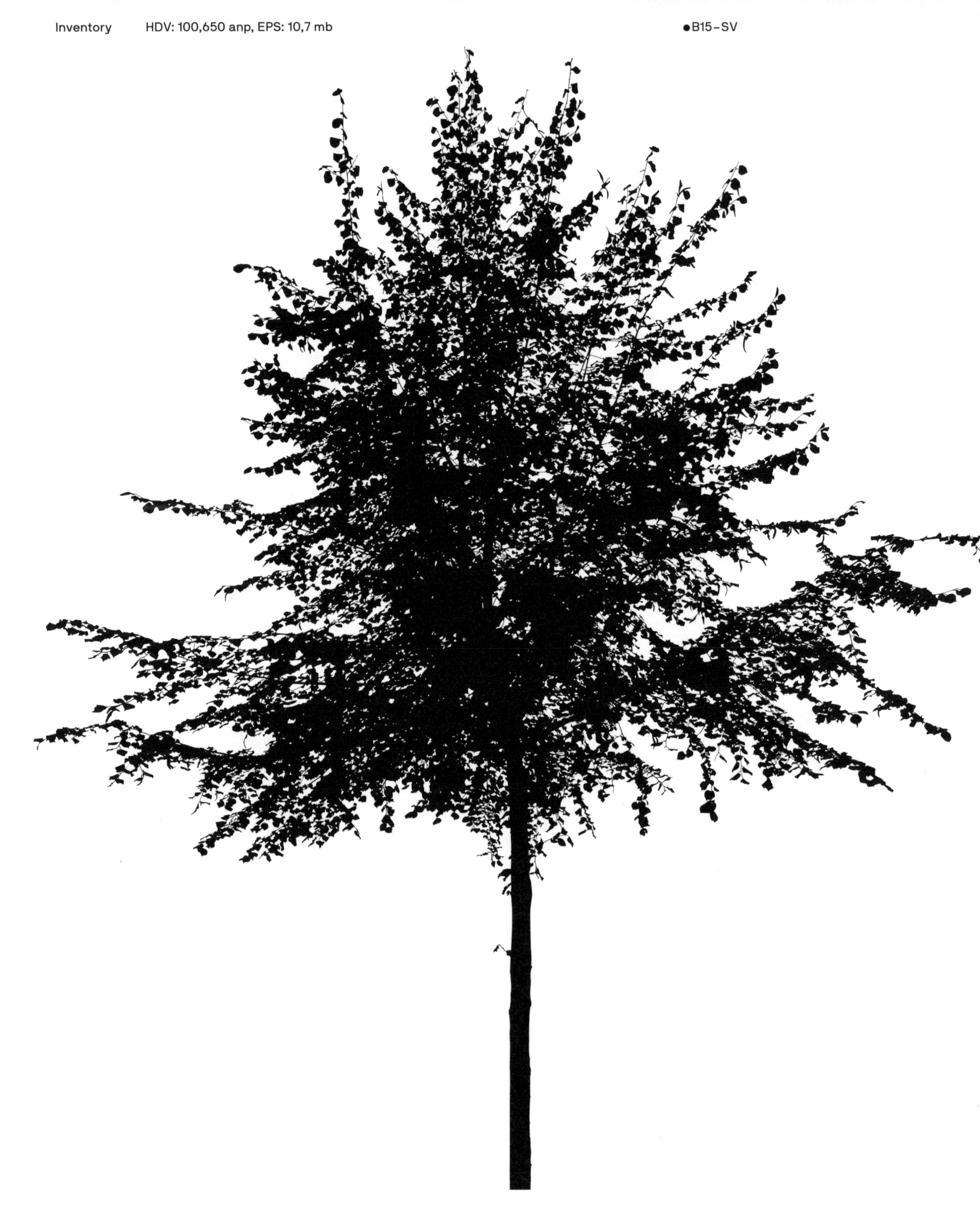

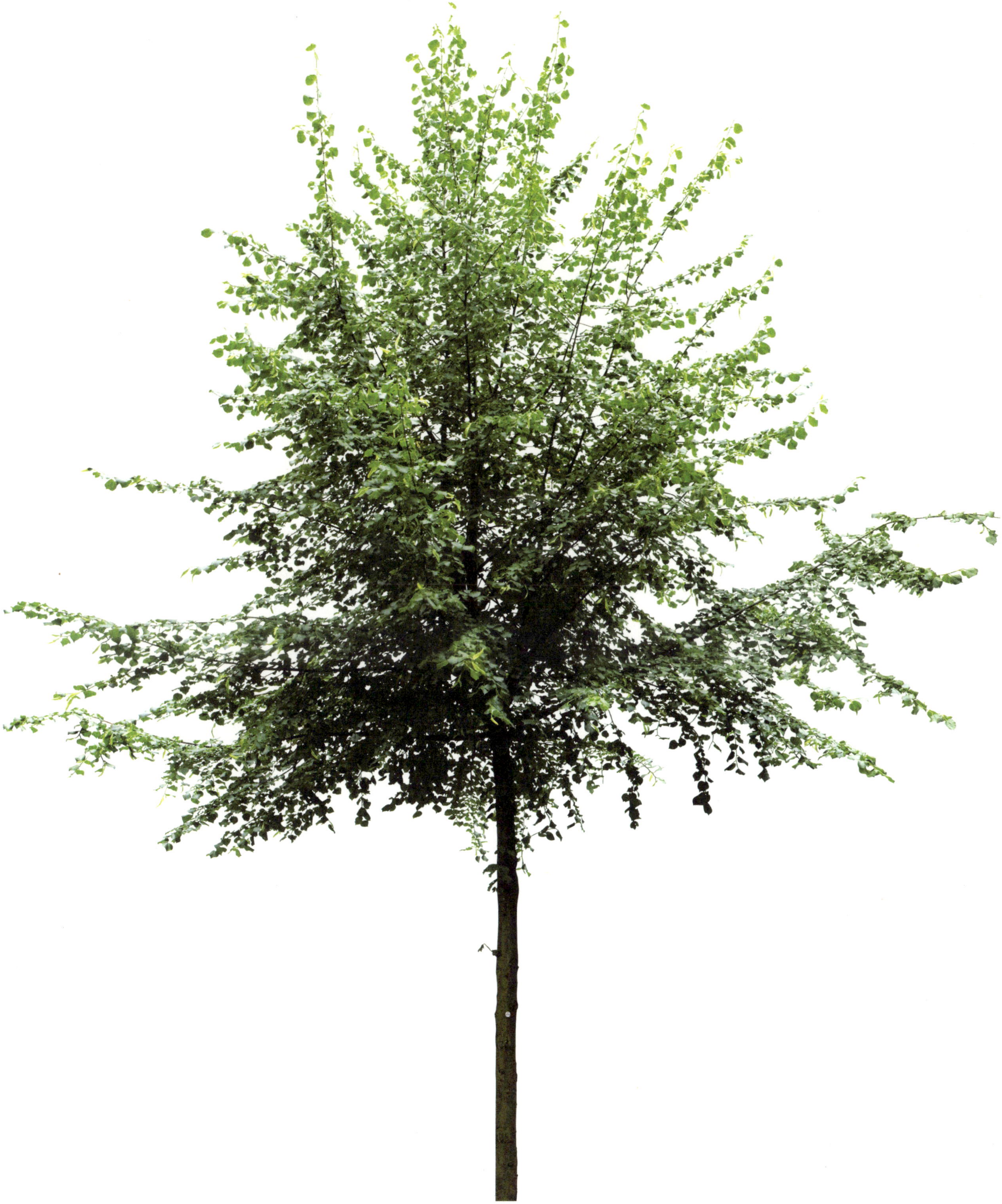

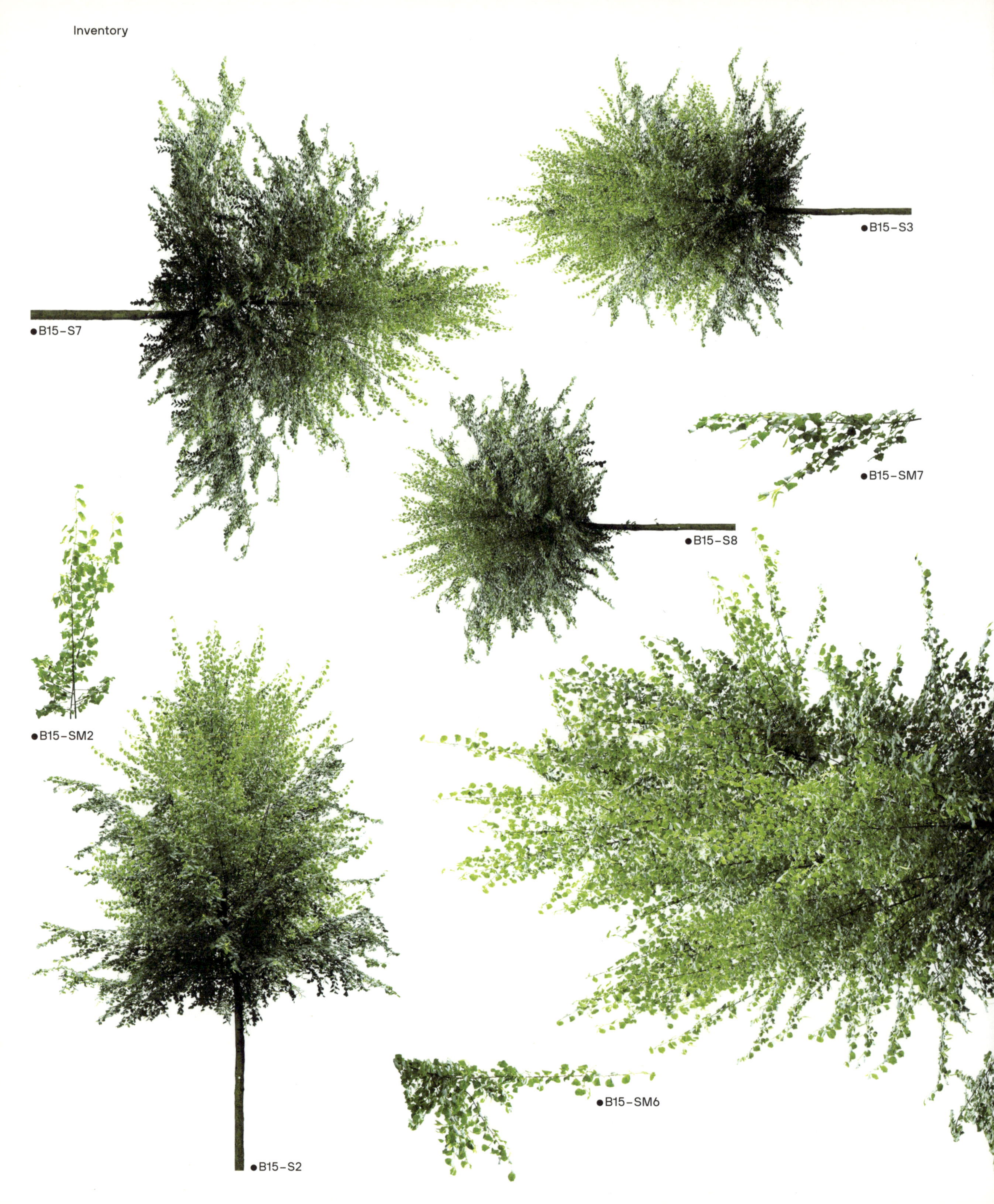
●B15–S3
●B15–S7
●B15–SM7
●B15–S8
●B15–SM2
●B15–S2
●B15–SM6

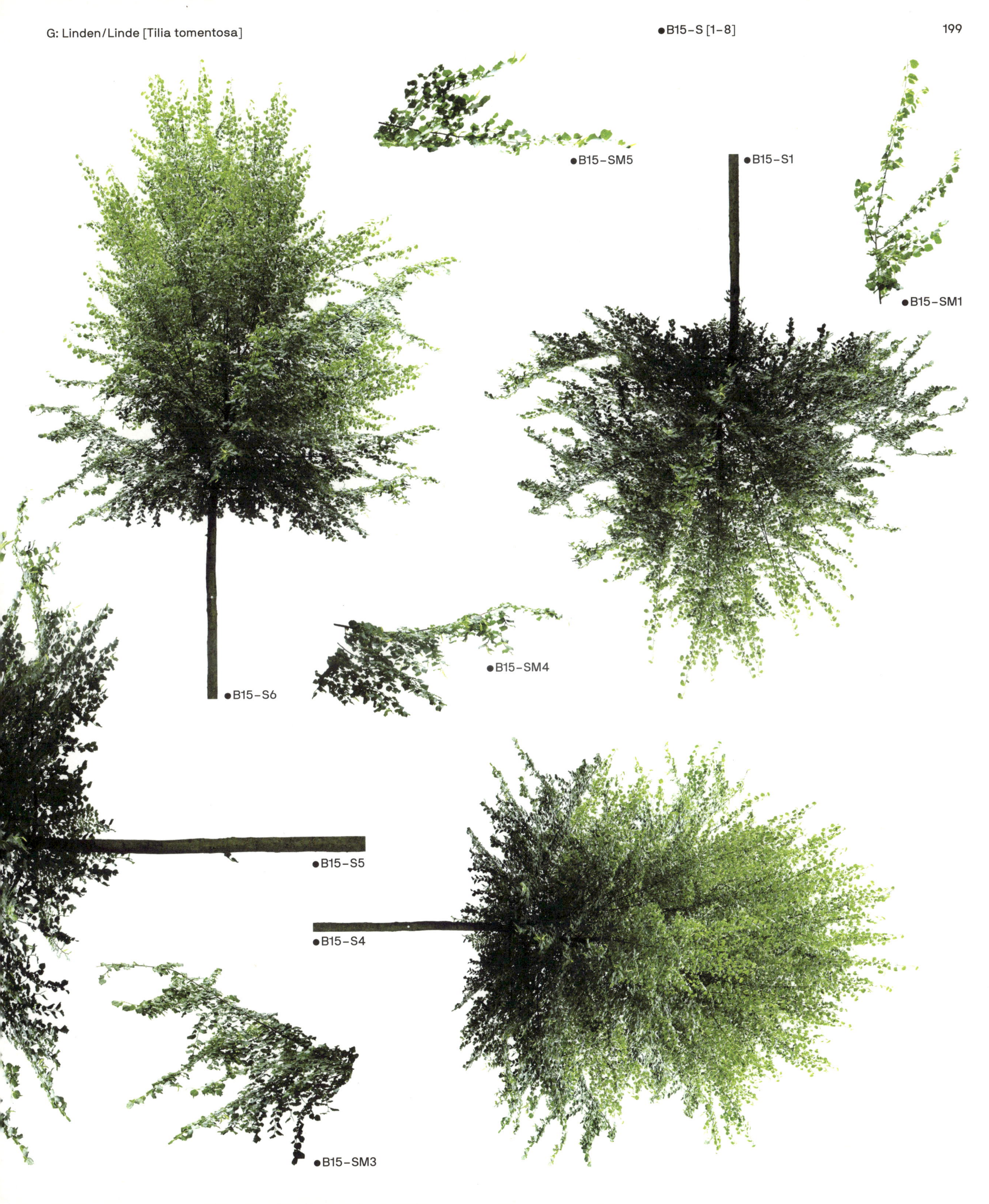
●B15–SM5
●B15–S1
●B15–SM1
●B15–S6
●B15–SM4
●B15–S5
●B15–S4
●B15–SM3

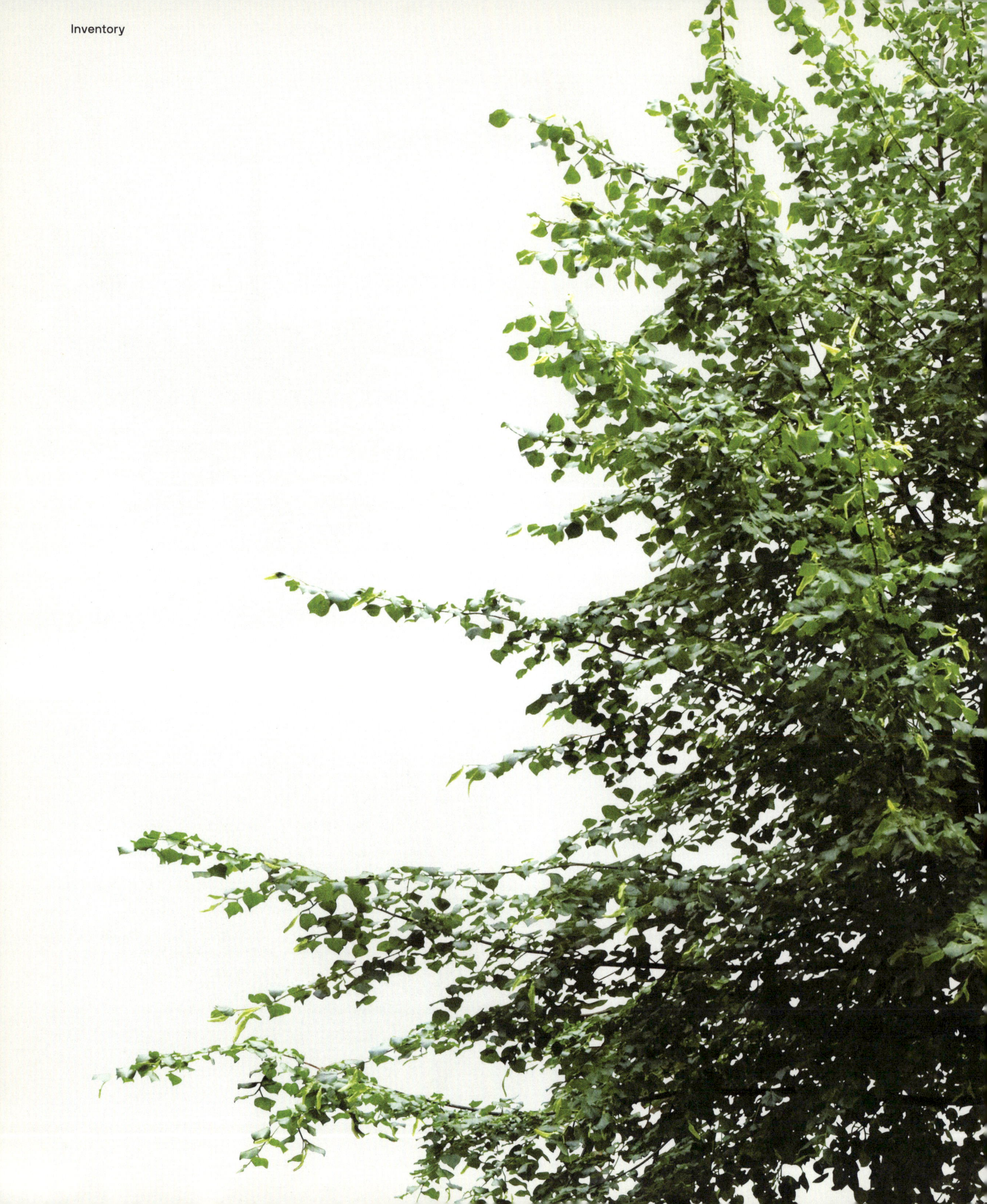

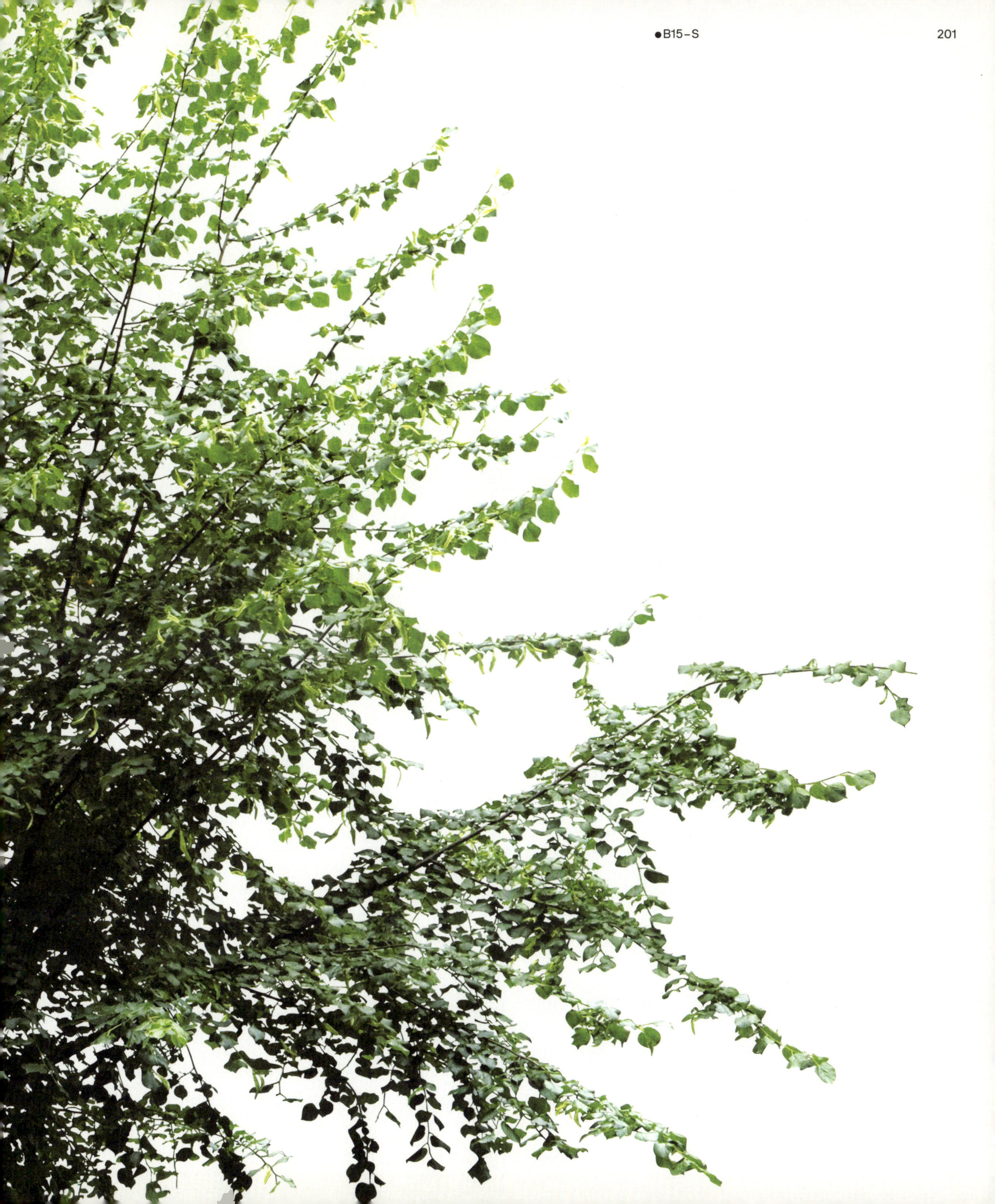

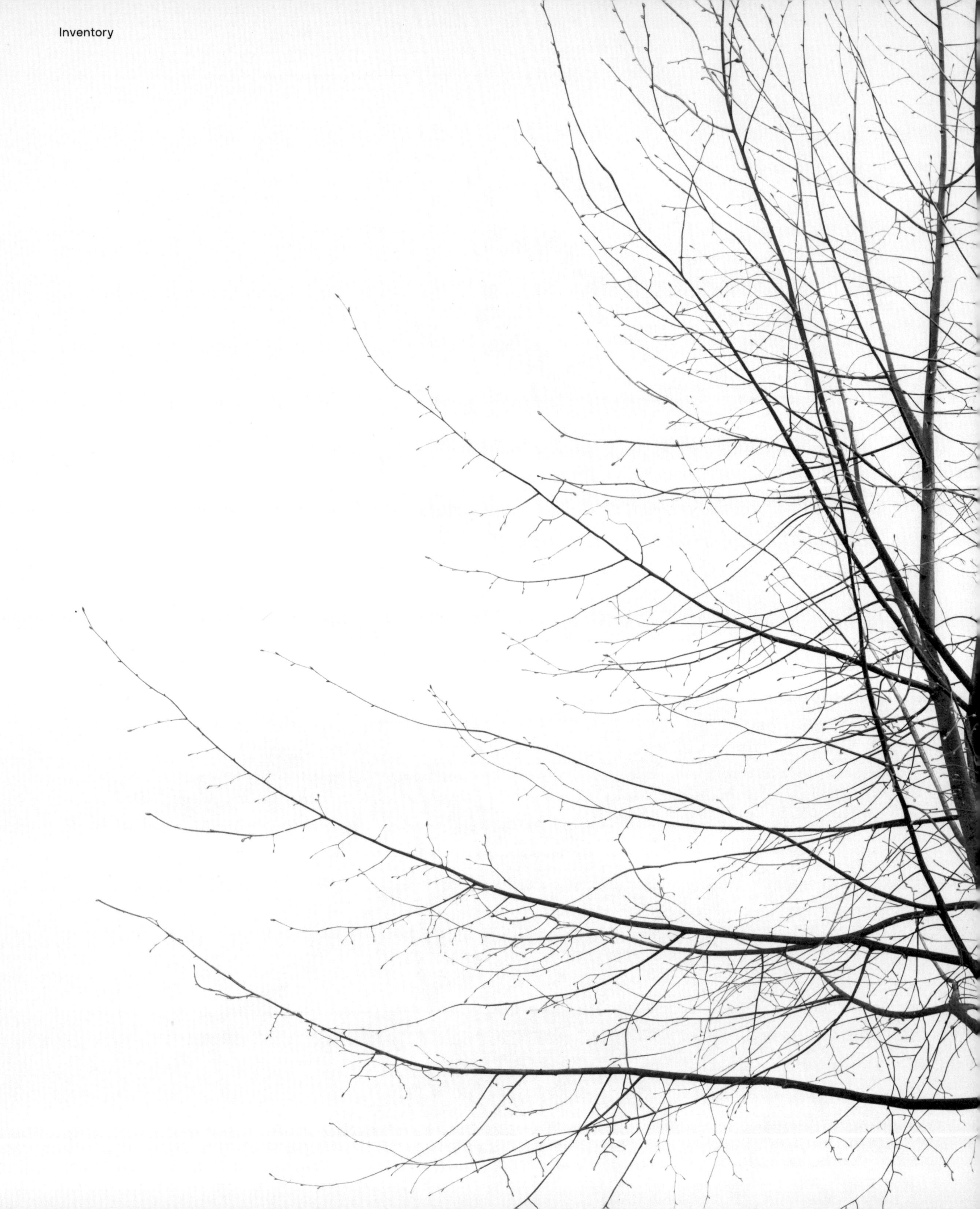

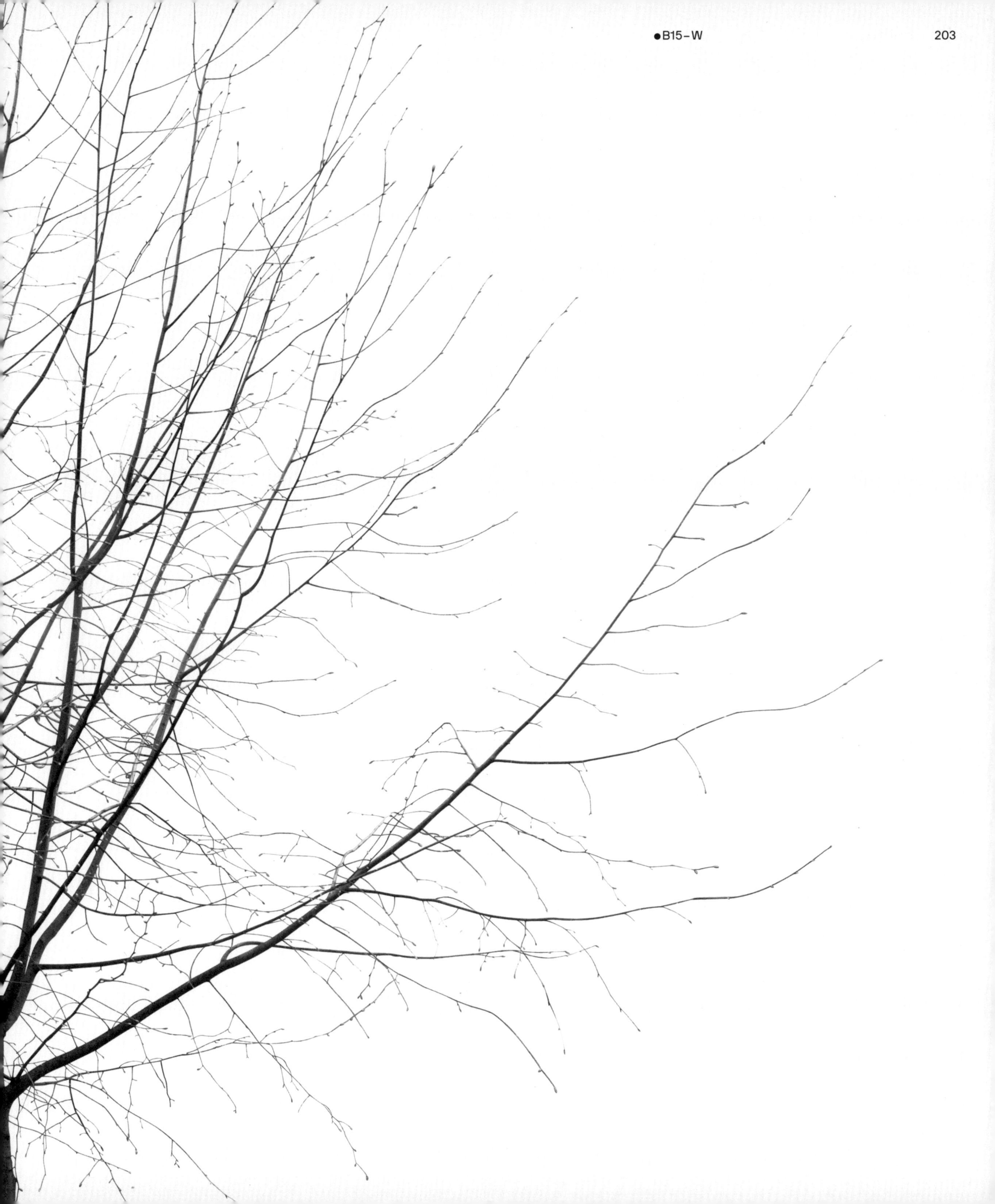

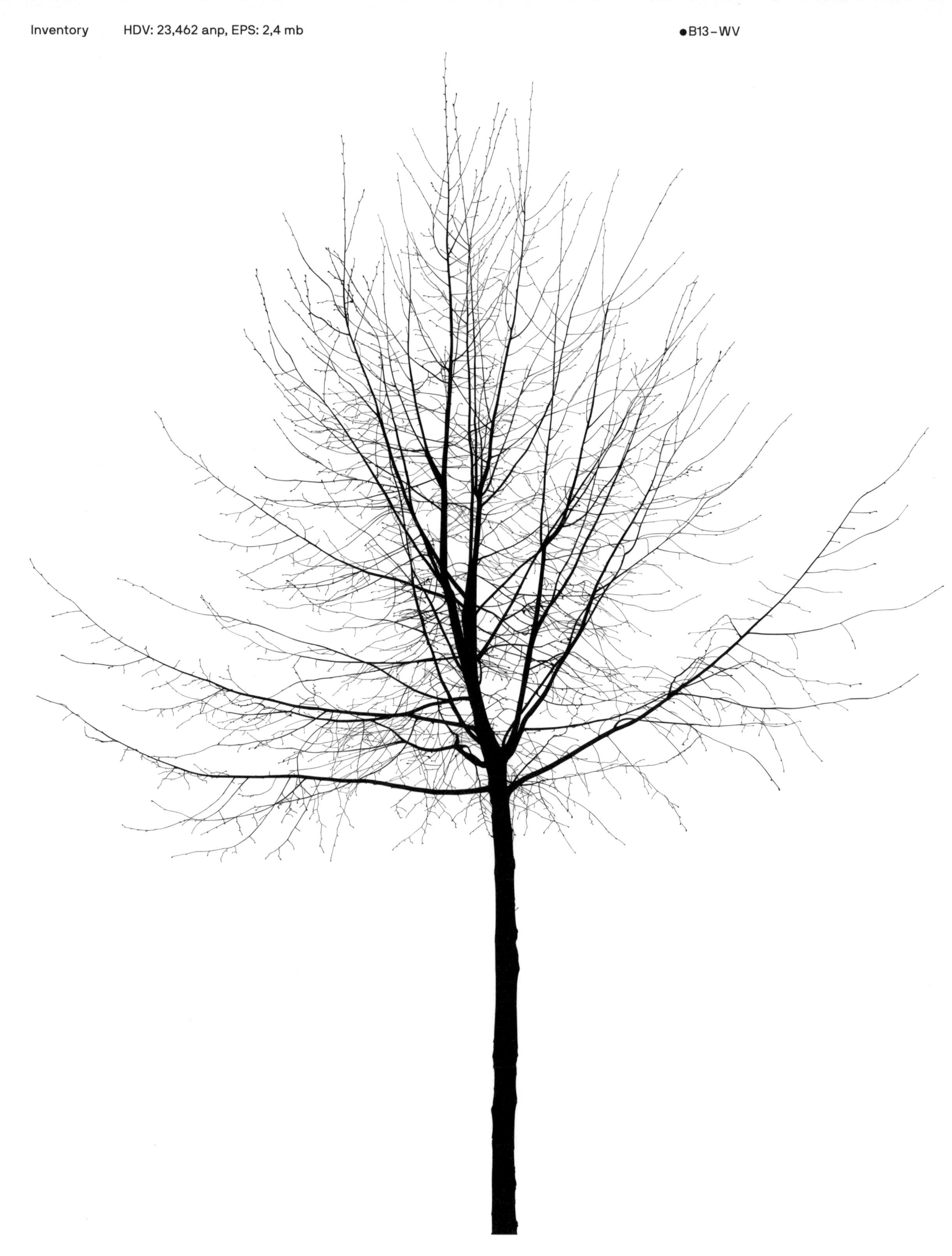

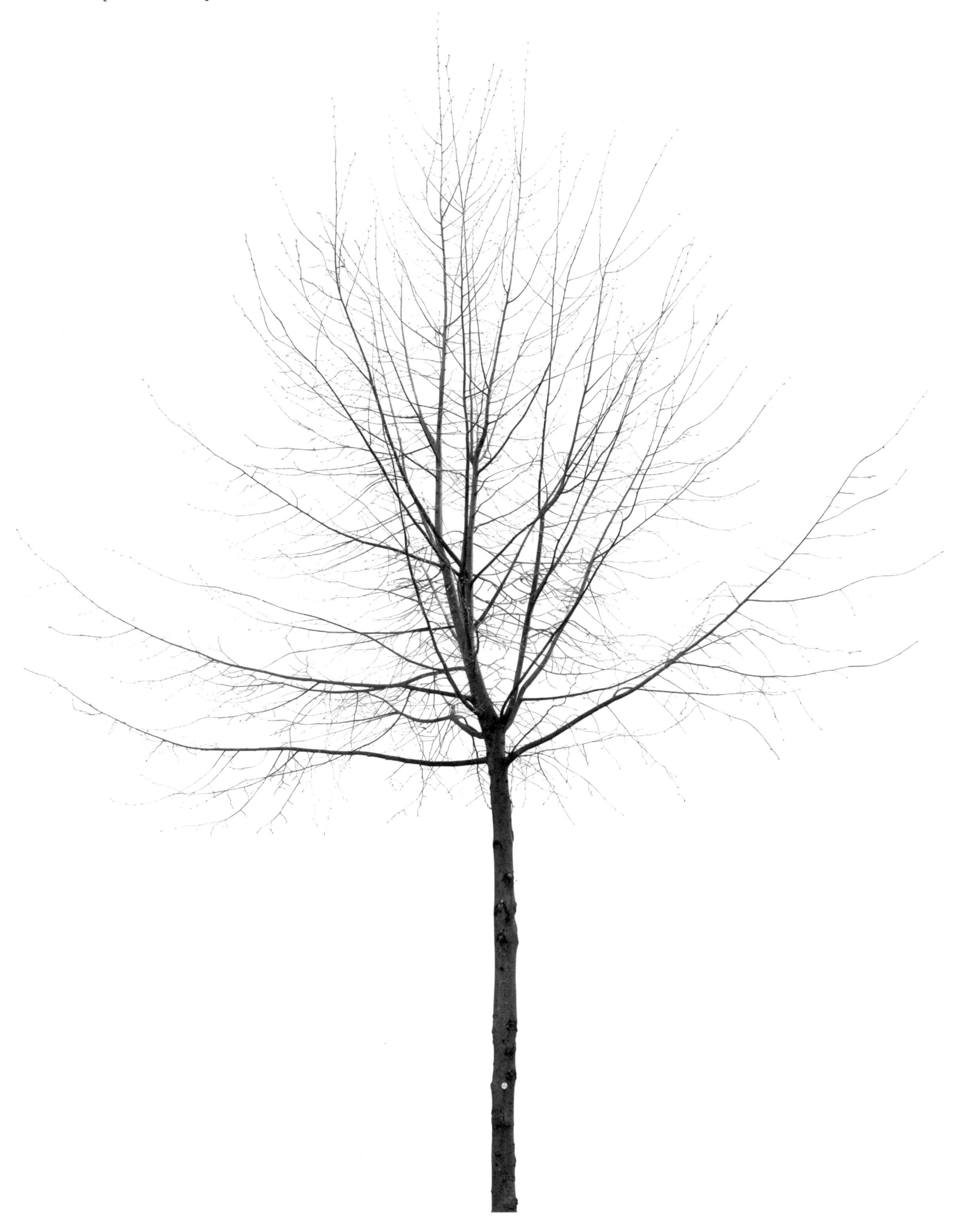

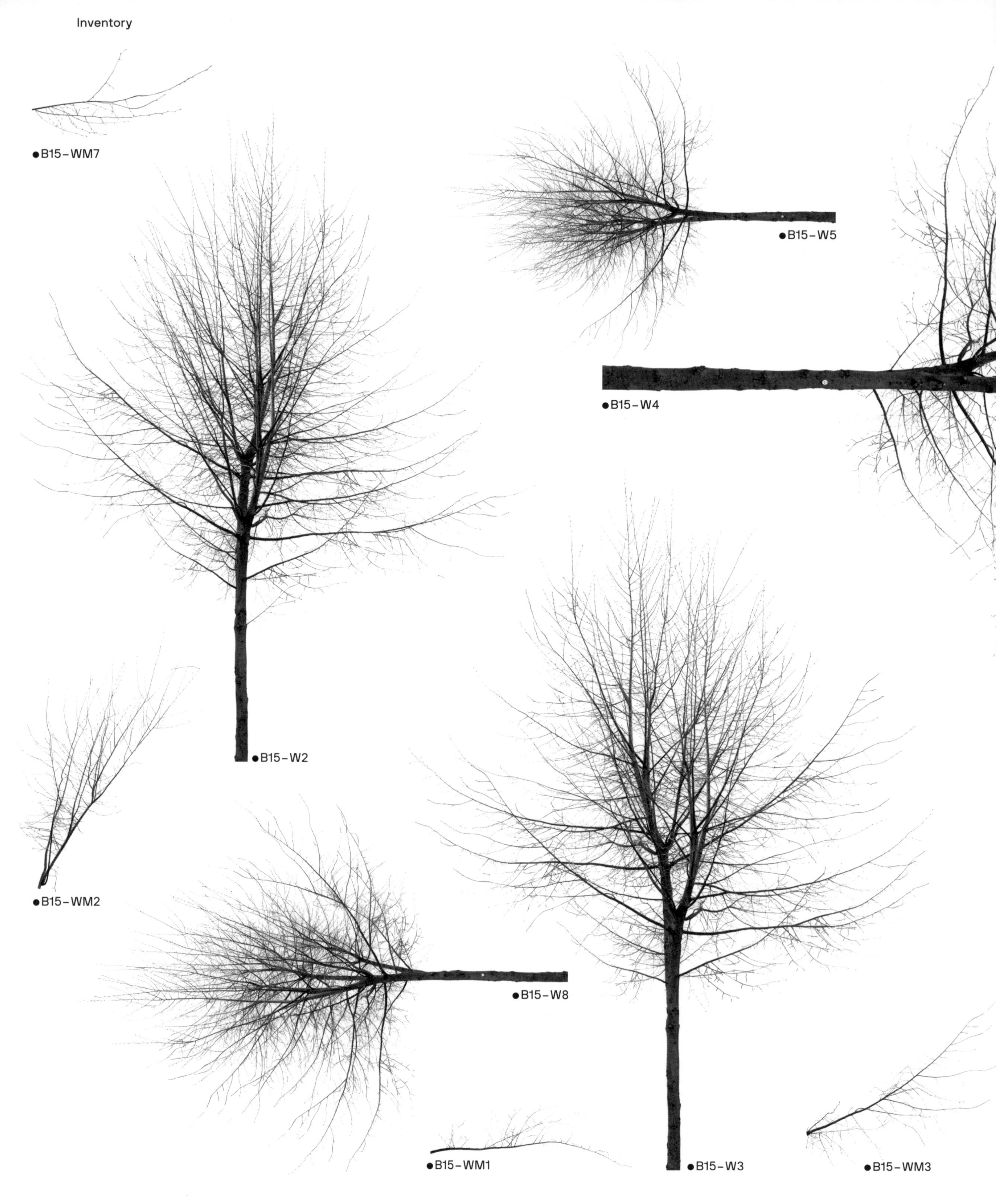

●B15–WM7
●B15–W5
●B15–W4
●B15–W2
●B15–WM2
●B15–W8
●B15–WM1
●B15–W3
●B15–WM3

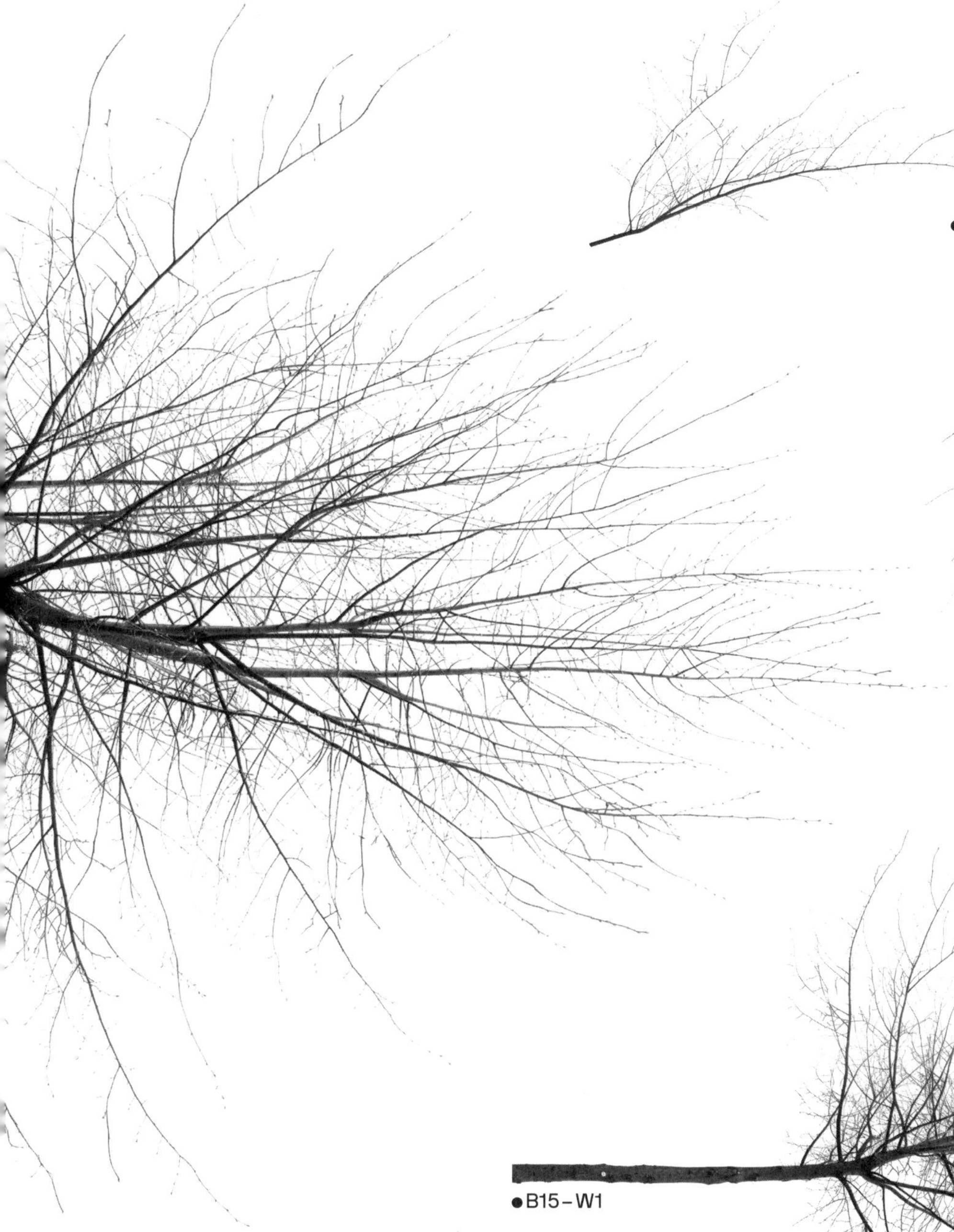

●B15–W [1–8]
●B15–W7 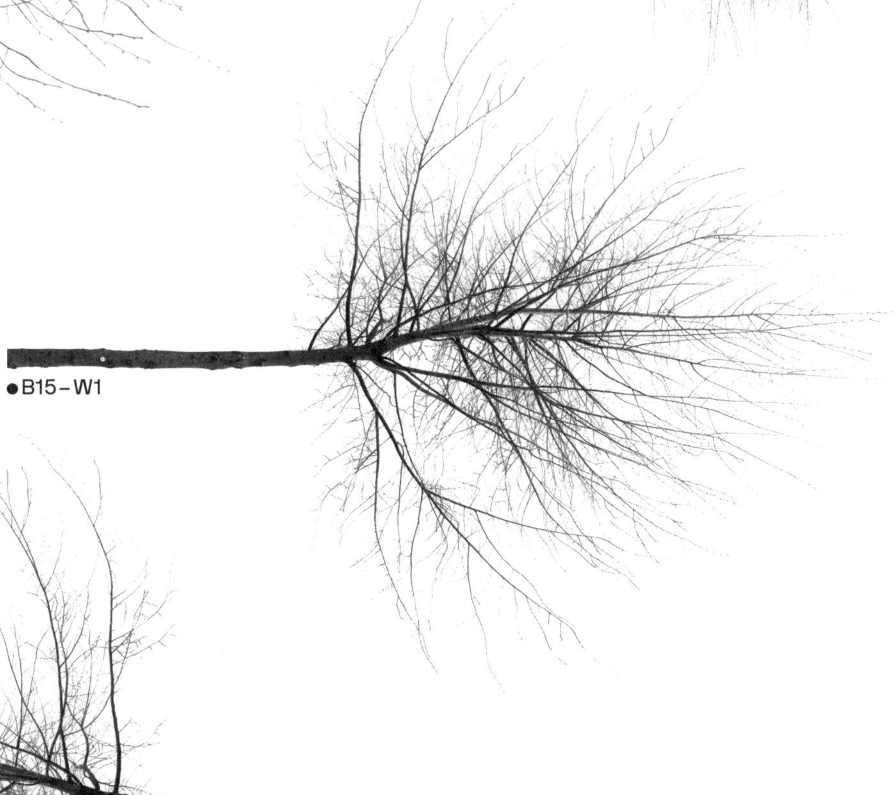
●B15–WM5
●B15–W1
●B15–WM6 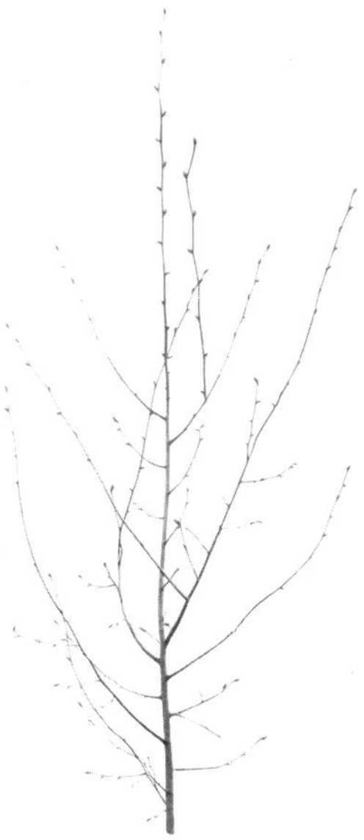
●B15–W6 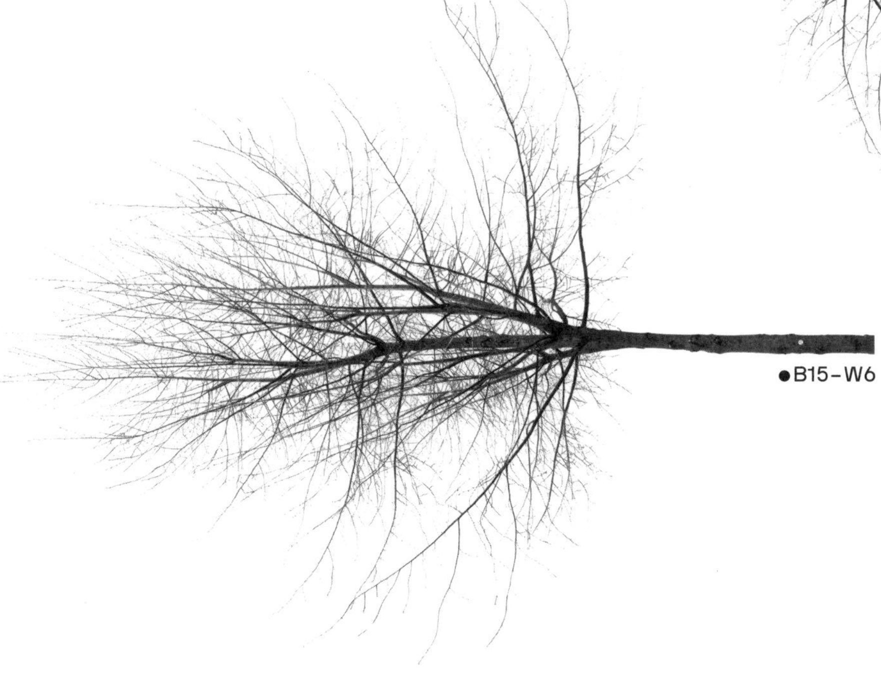
●B15–WM4

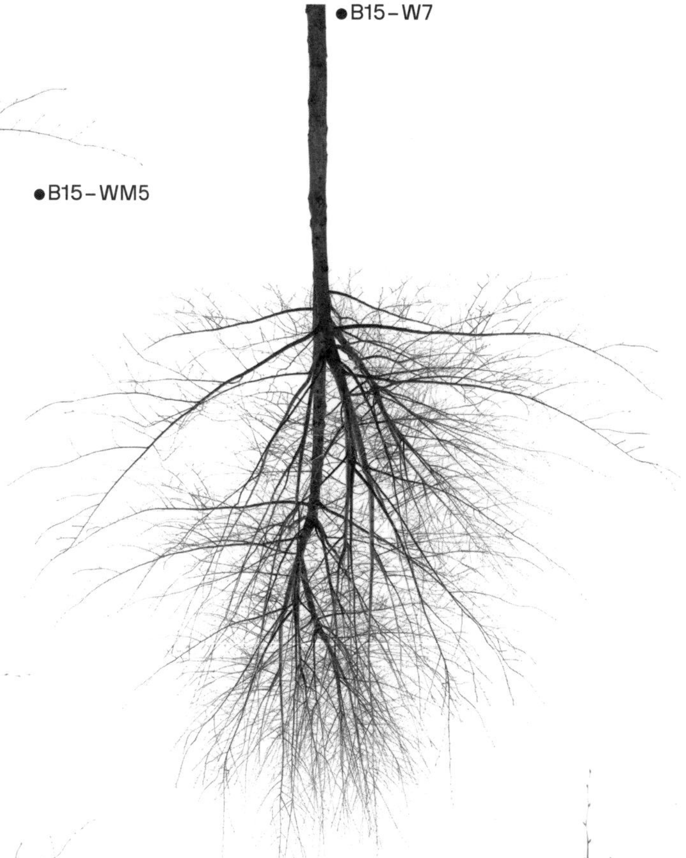

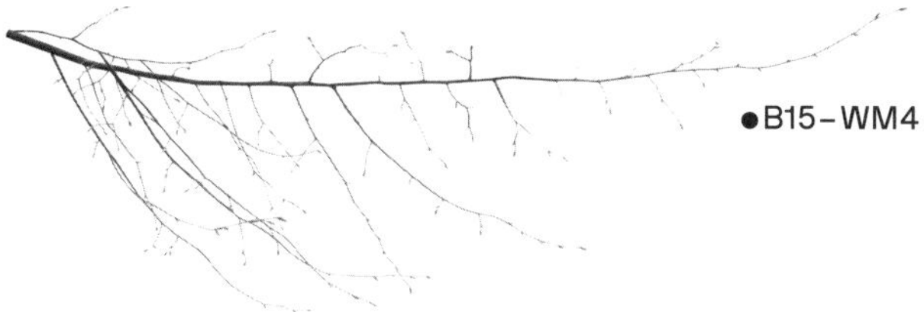

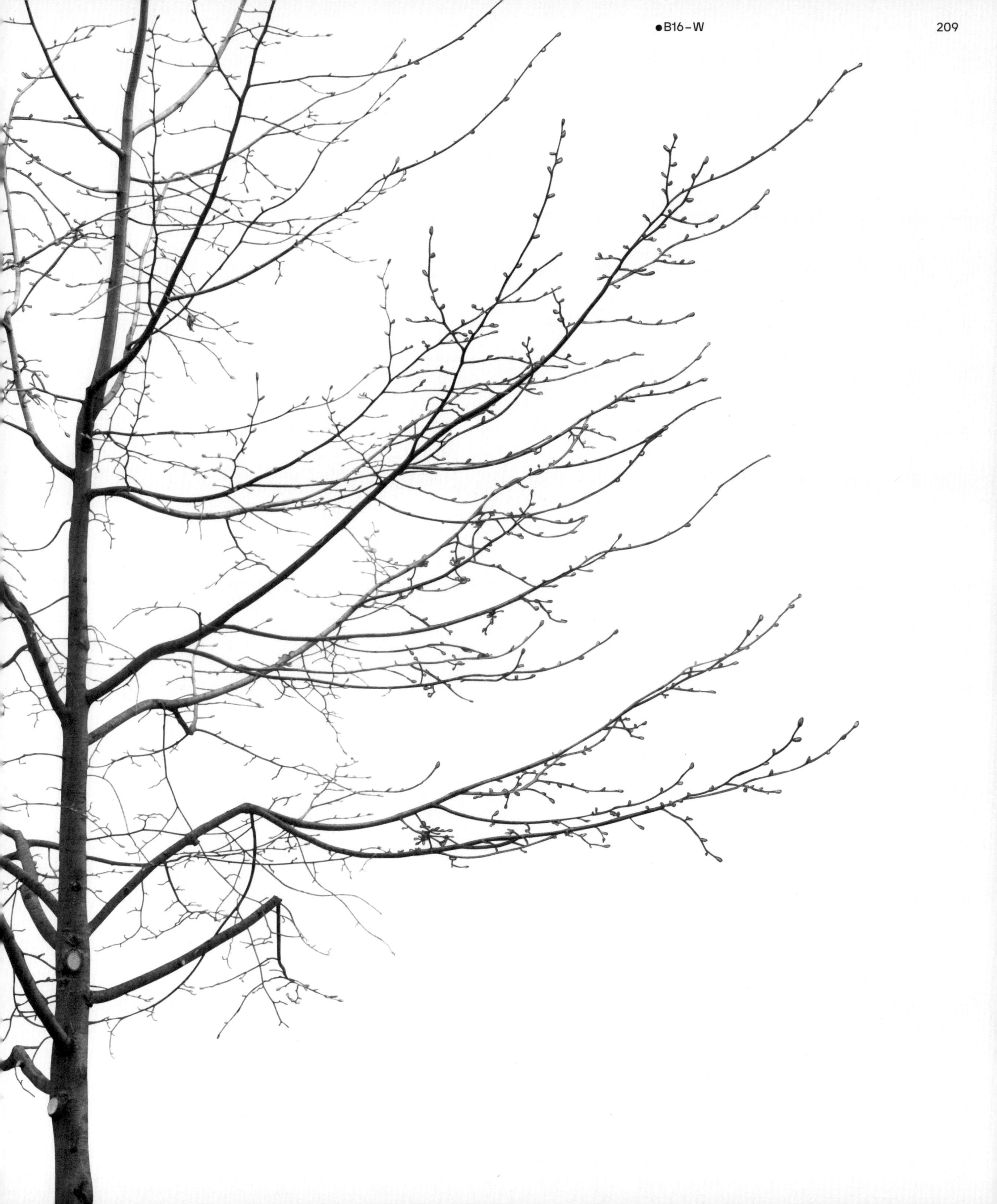

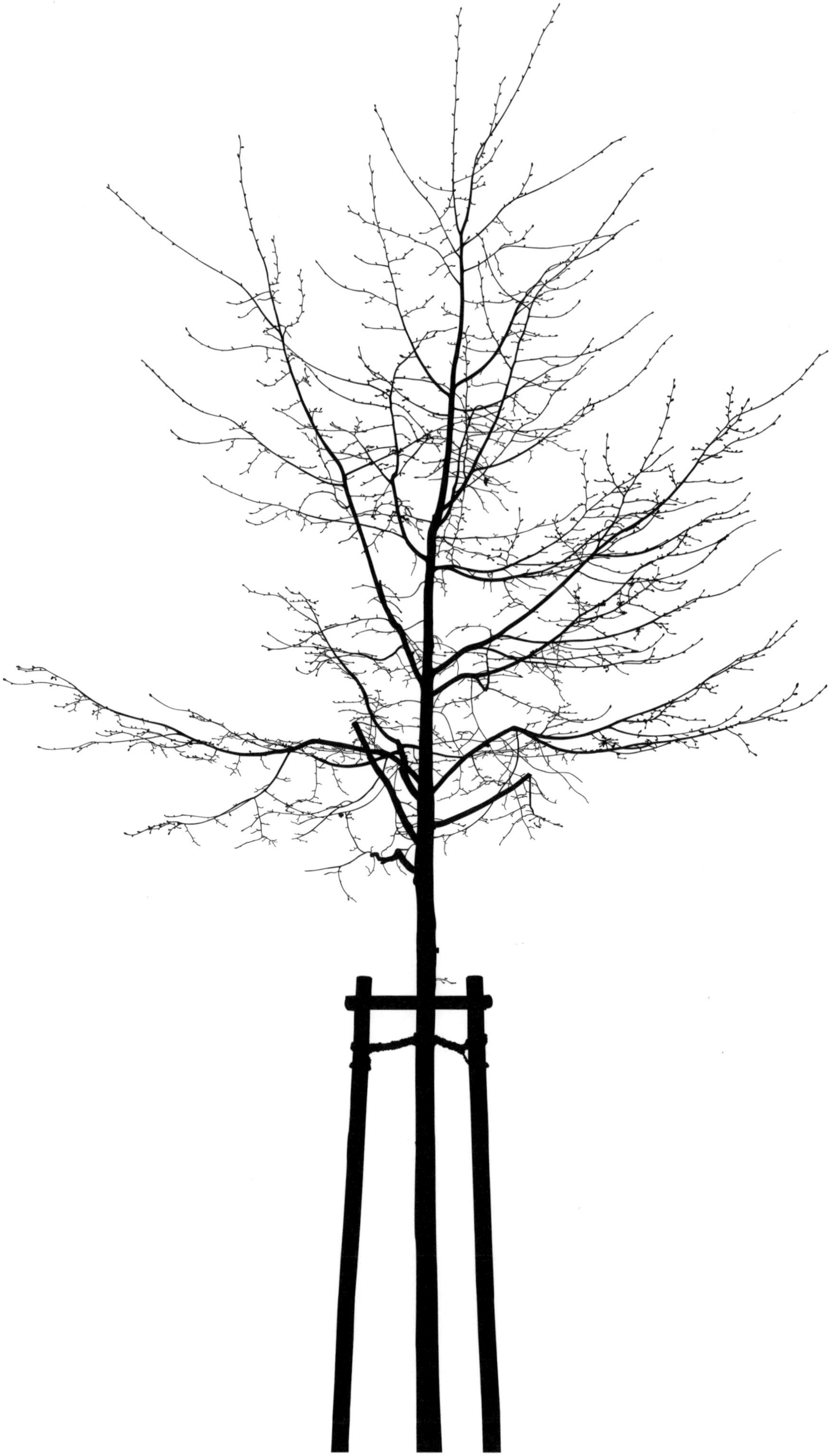

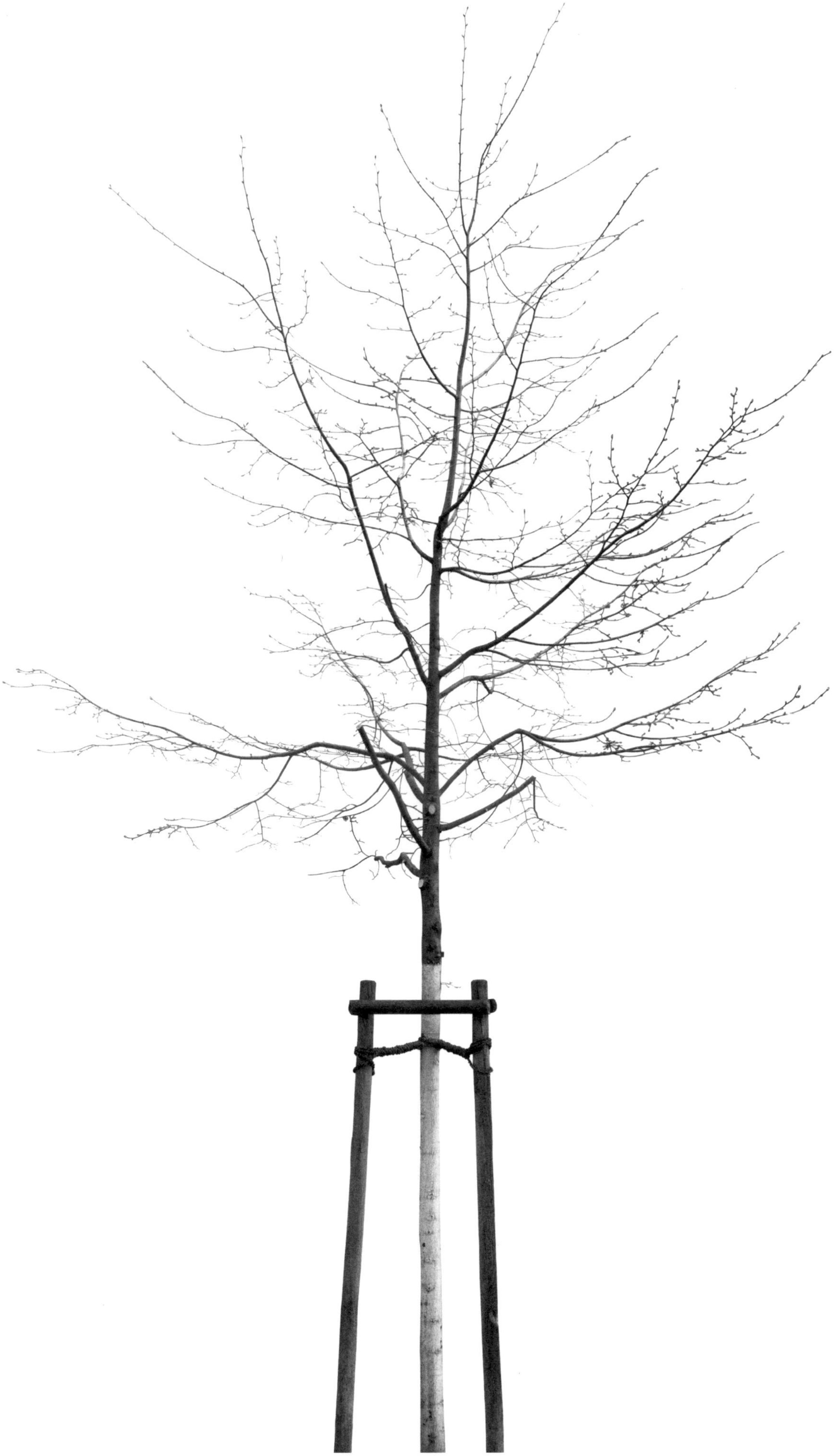

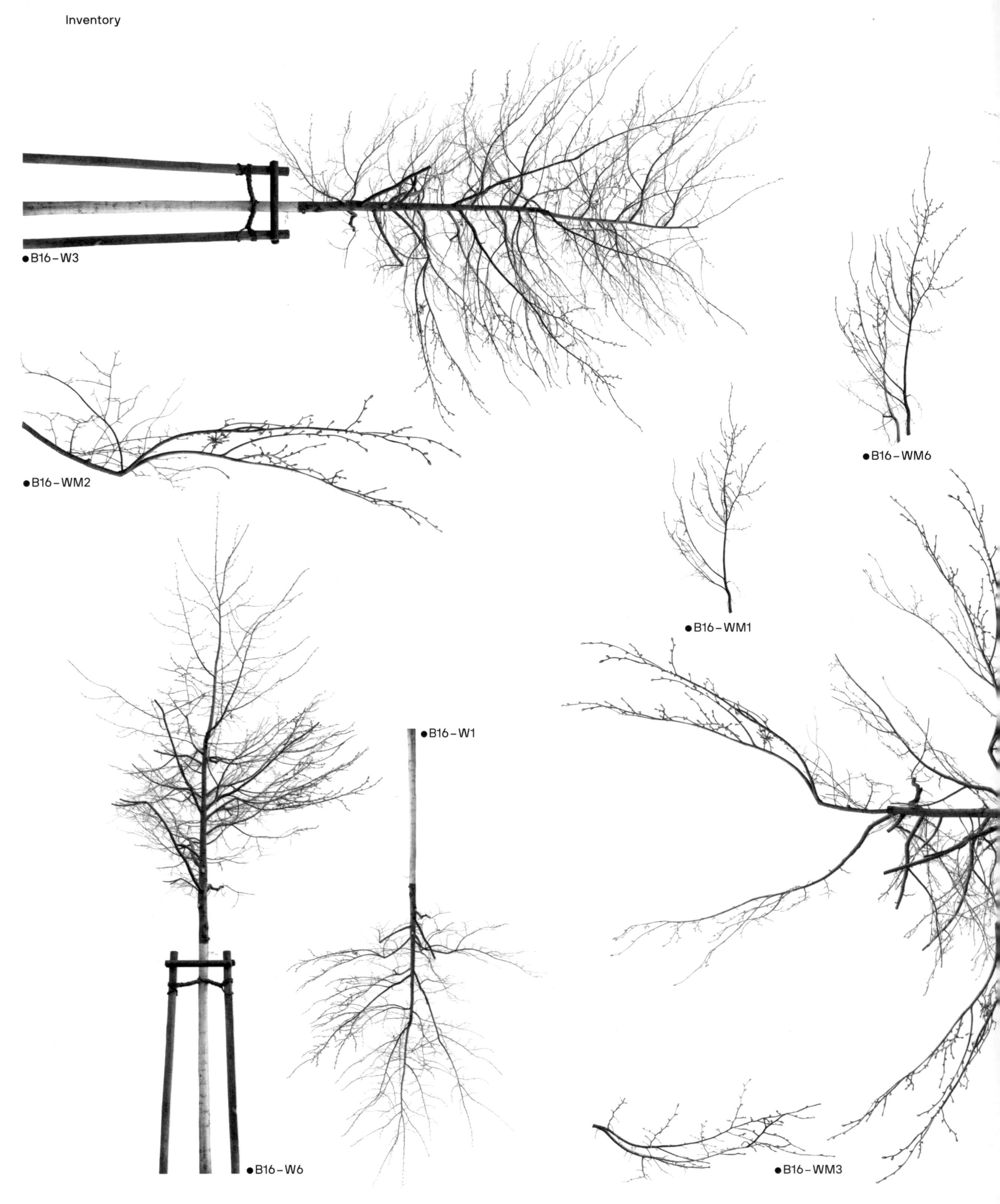
●B16–W3
●B16–WM2
●B16–WM6
●B16–WM1
●B16–W1
●B16–W6
●B16–WM3

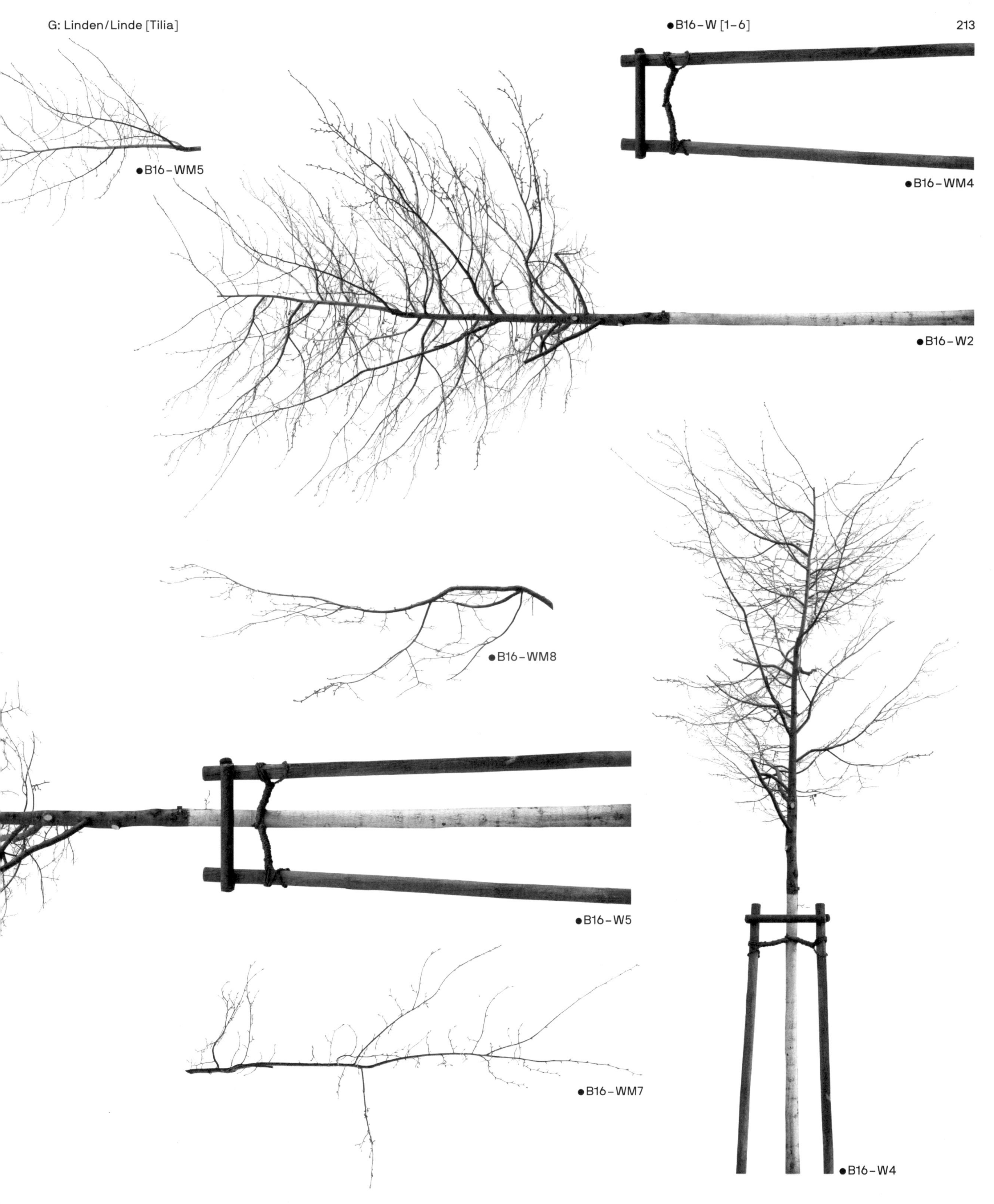
●B16-W [1-6]
●B16-WM5
●B16-WM4
●B16-W2
●B16-WM8
●B16-W5
●B16-WM7
●B16-W4

```
A2   S      Maple           [Acer platanoides]
A9   S  W   Maple           [Acer platanoides]
A10  S      Maple           [Acer]
A12  S      Poplar          [Populus nigra 'Italica']
A14  S  W   Linden          [Tilia americana]
A16     W   Tree of heaven  [Ailanthus altissima]
A18  S      Linden          [Tilia × intermedia]
```

A2–A18

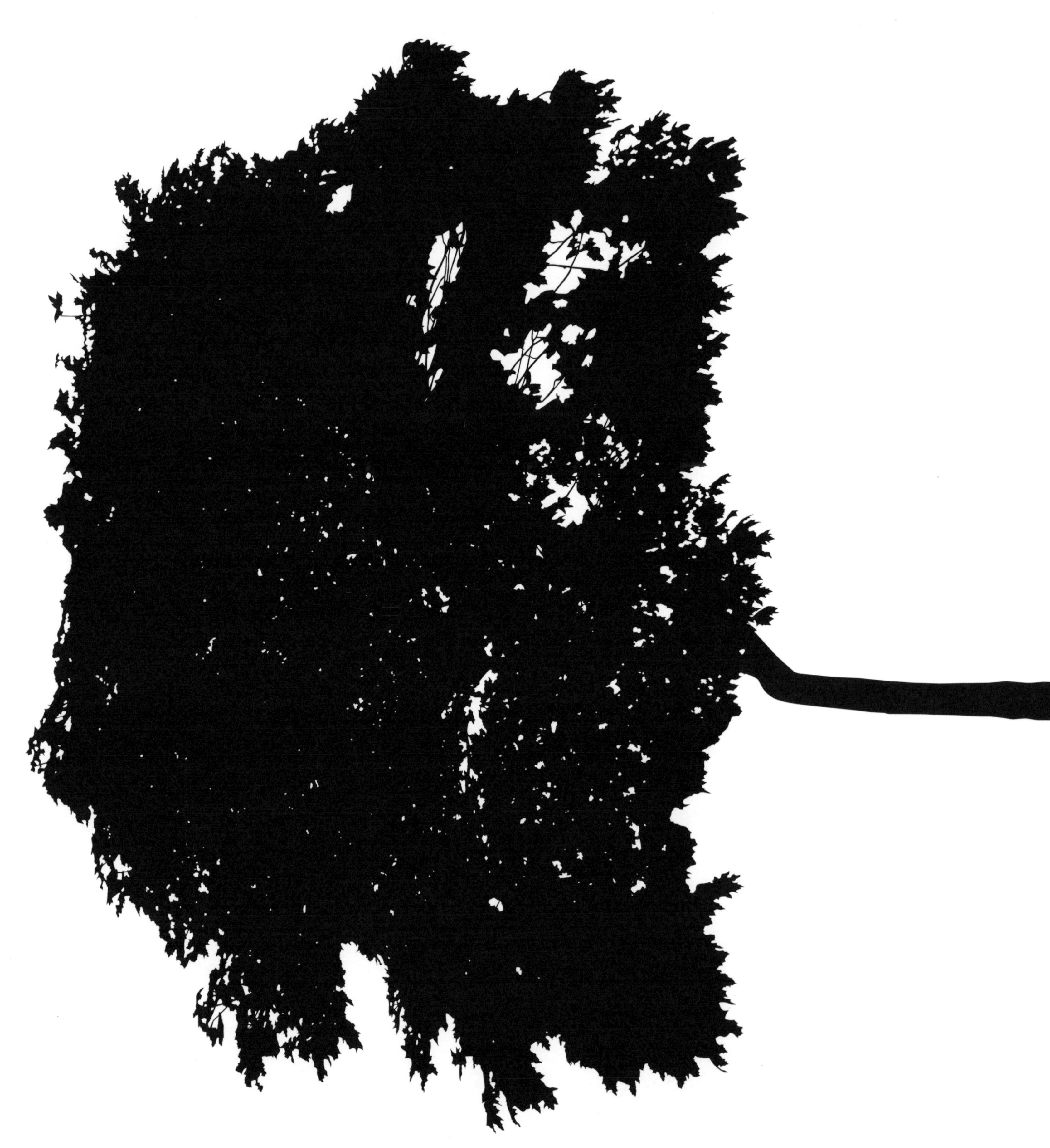

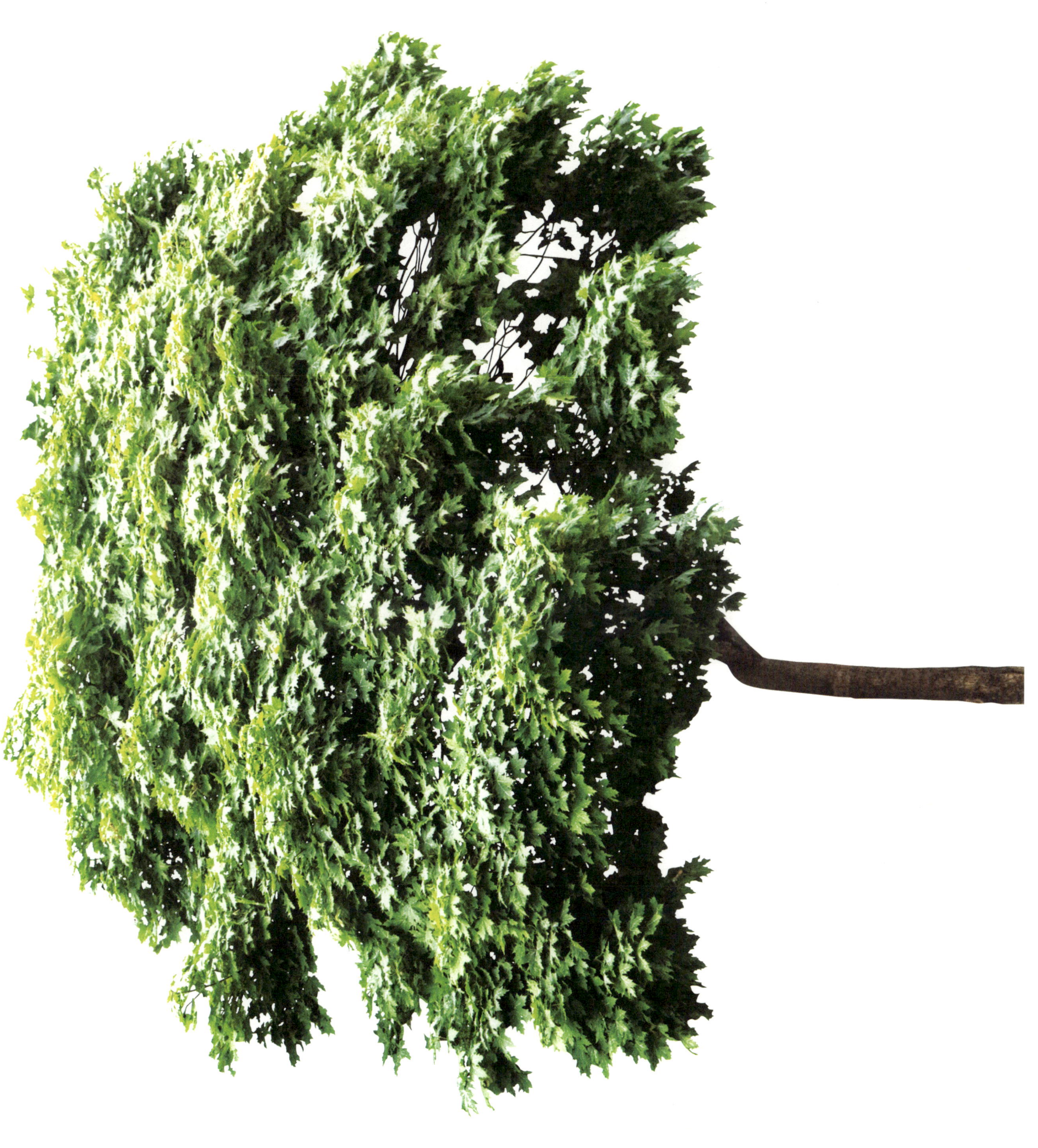

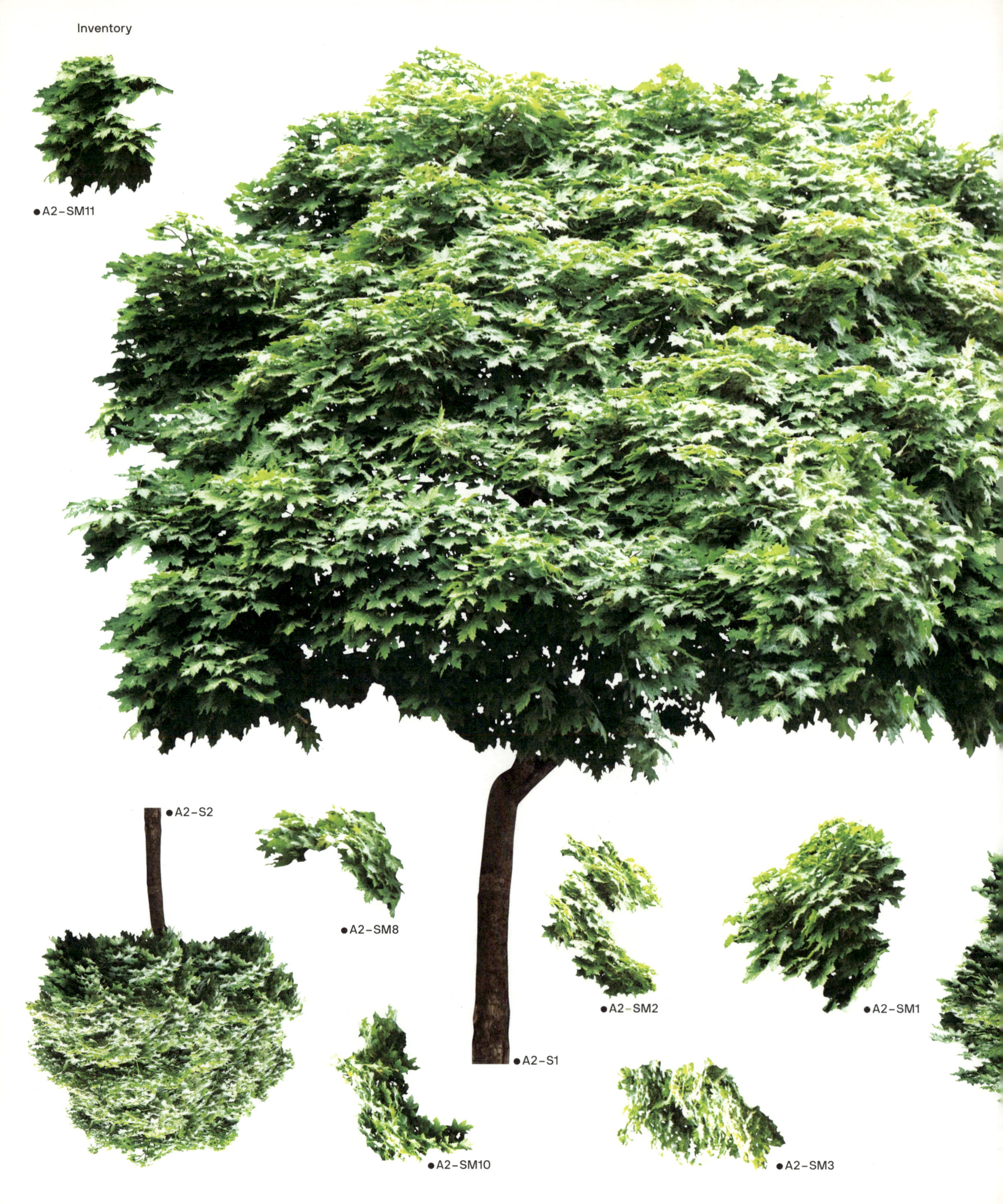
Inventory
●A2–SM11
●A2–S2
●A2–SM8
●A2–SM2
●A2–SM1
●A2–S1
●A2–SM10
●A2–SM3

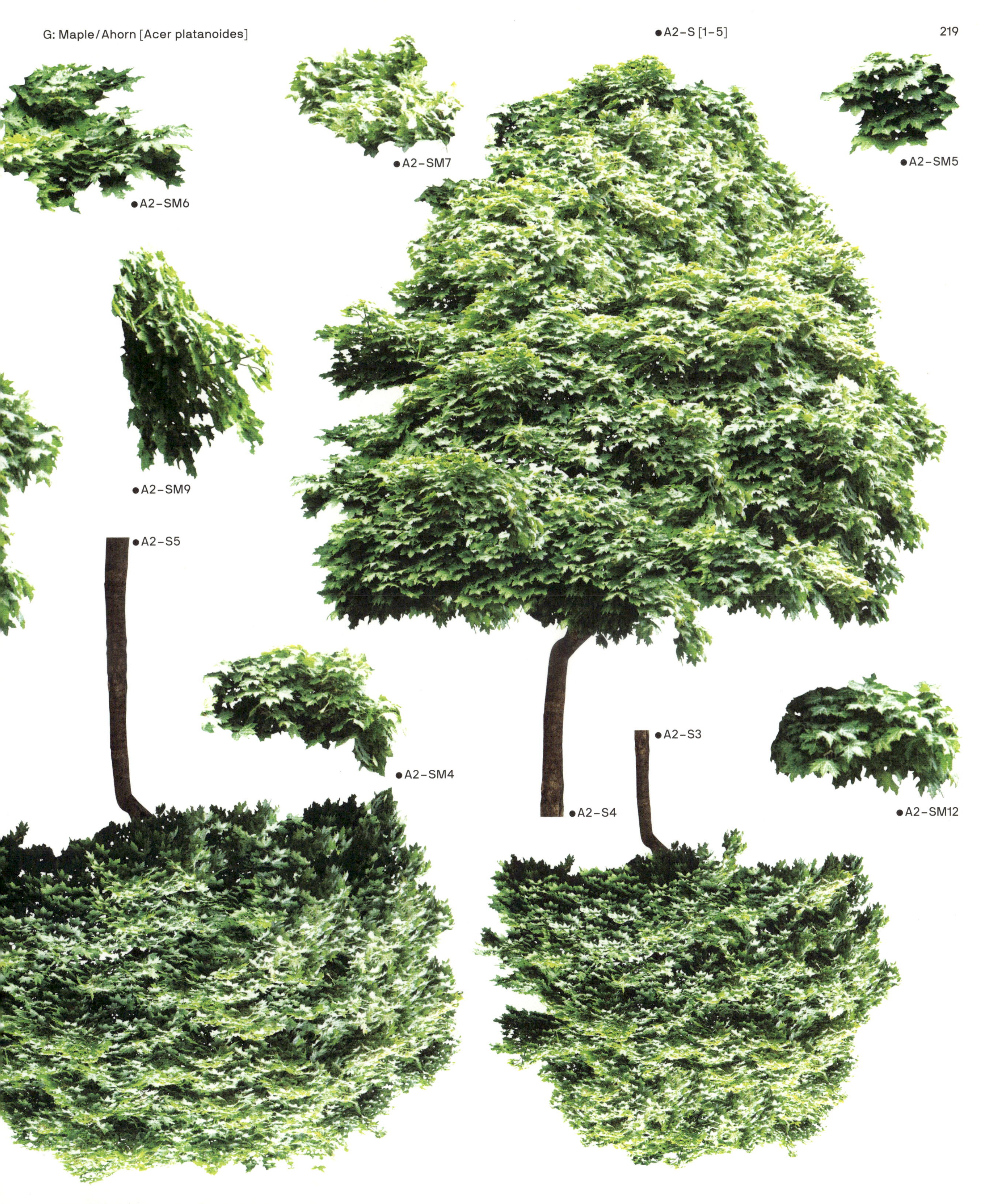
●A2–S [1–5]
●A2–SM7
●A2–SM5
●A2–SM6
●A2–SM9
●A2–S5
●A2–SM4
●A2–S3
●A2–S4
●A2–SM12

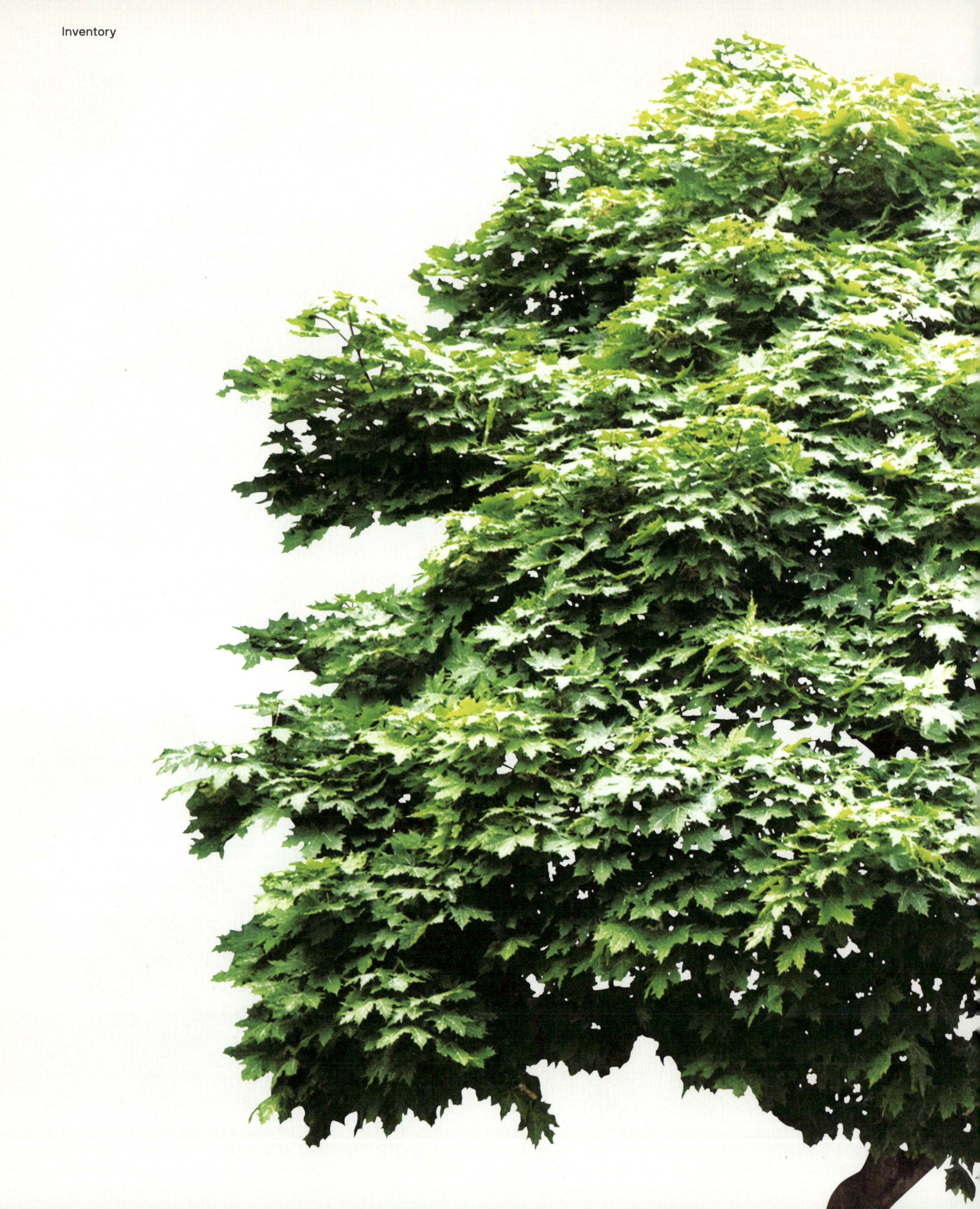

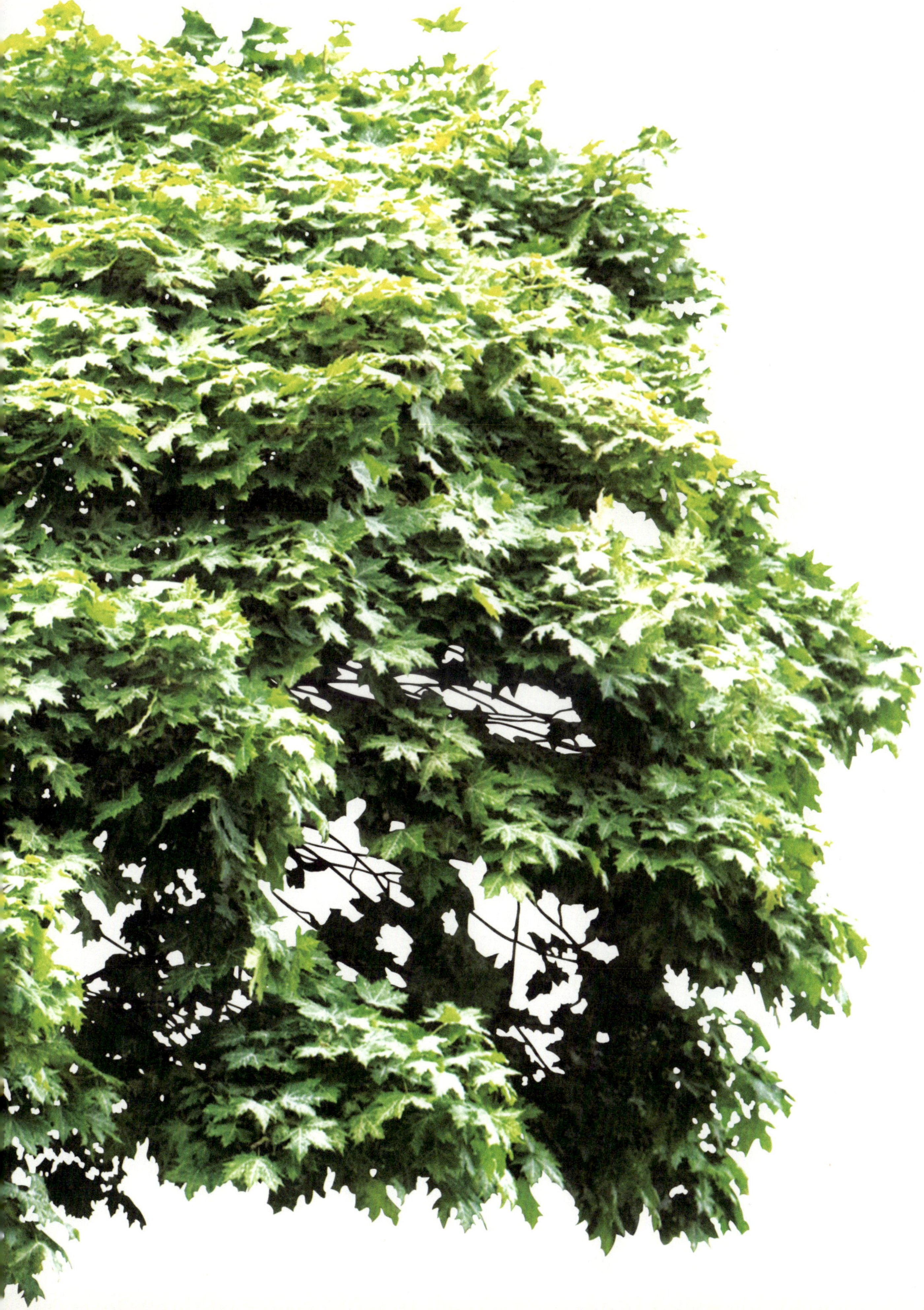

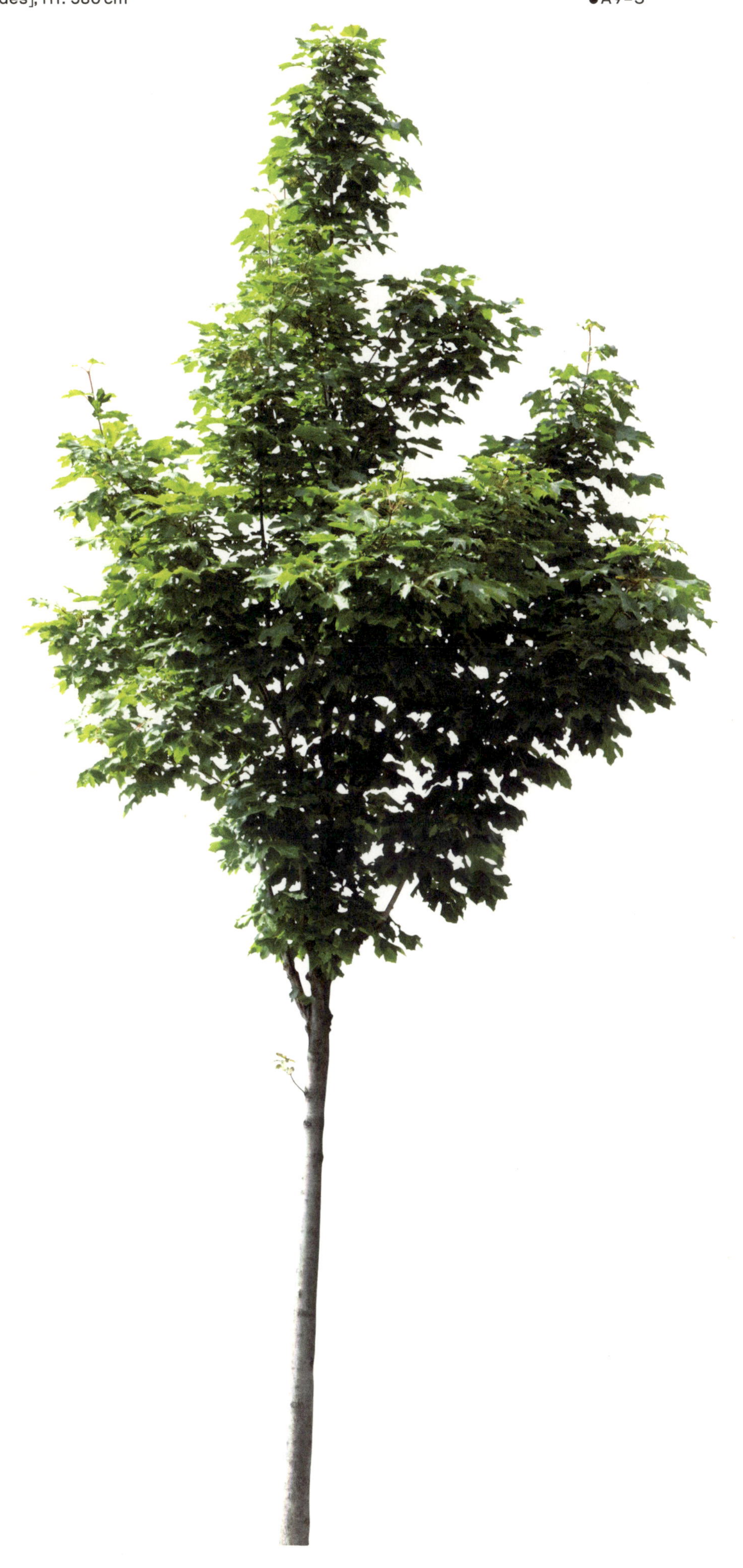

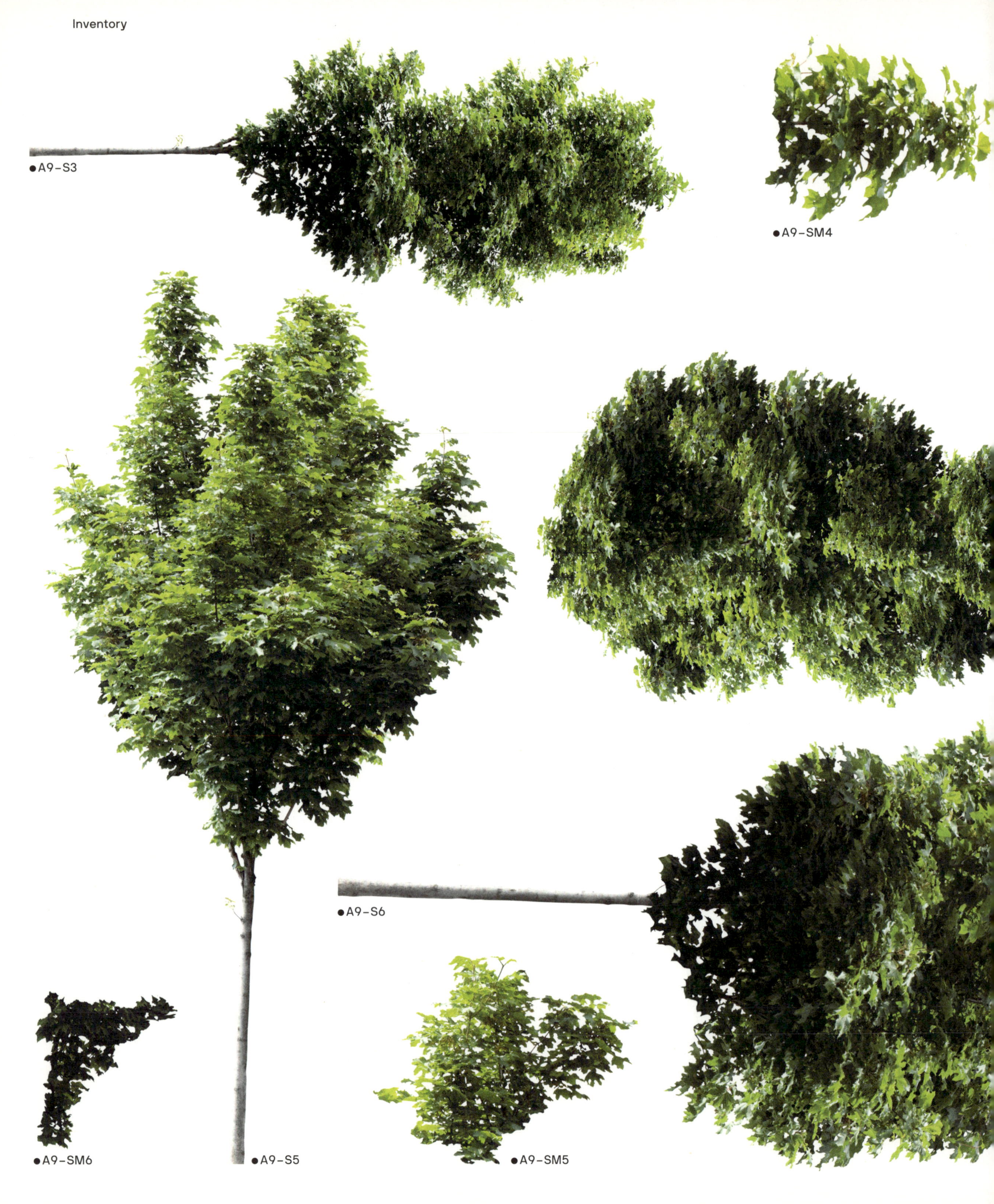
●A9–S3
●A9–SM4
●A9–S6
●A9–SM6
●A9–S5
●A9–SM5

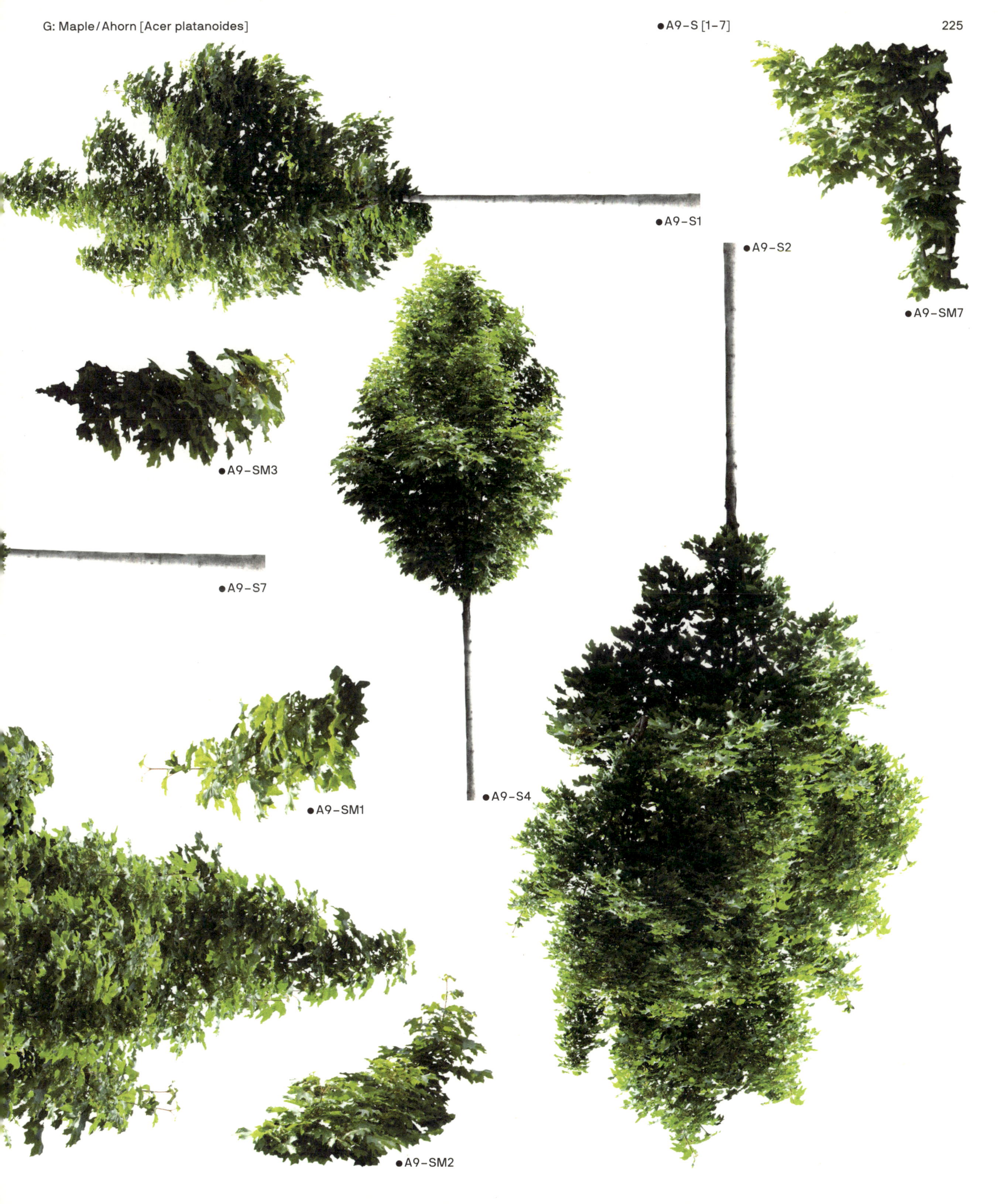

●A9–S1
●A9–S2
●A9–SM7
●A9–SM3
●A9–S7
●A9–SM1
●A9–S4
●A9–SM2

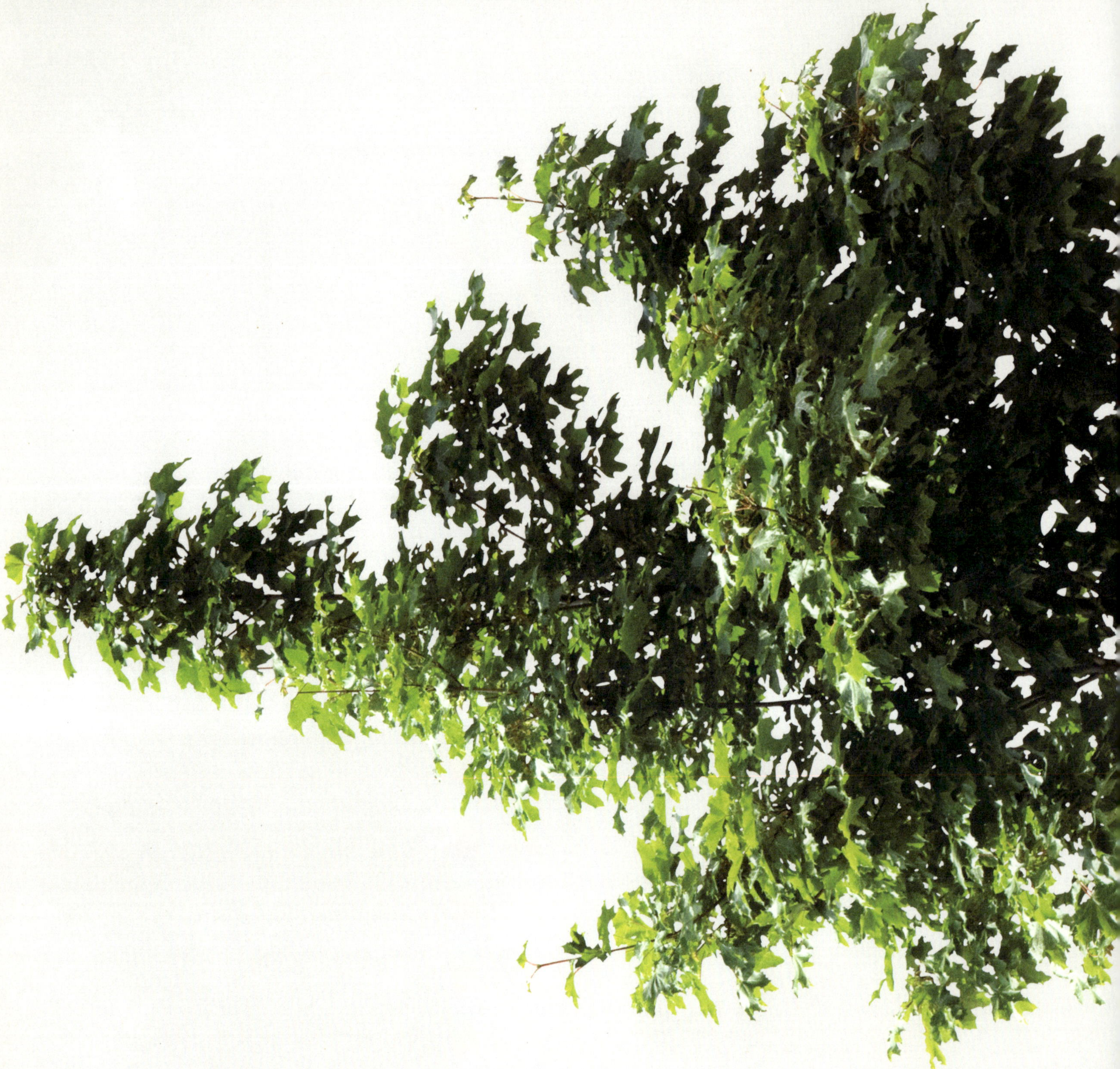

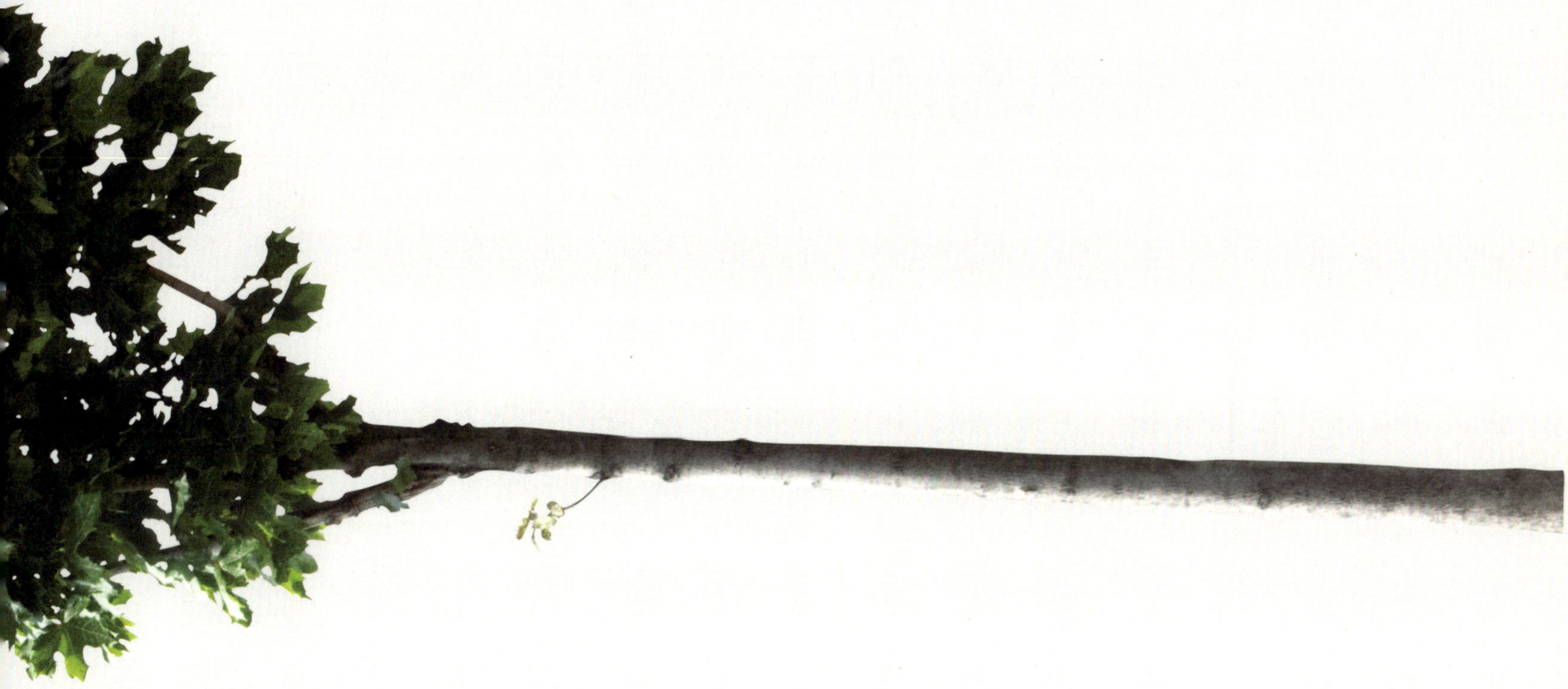

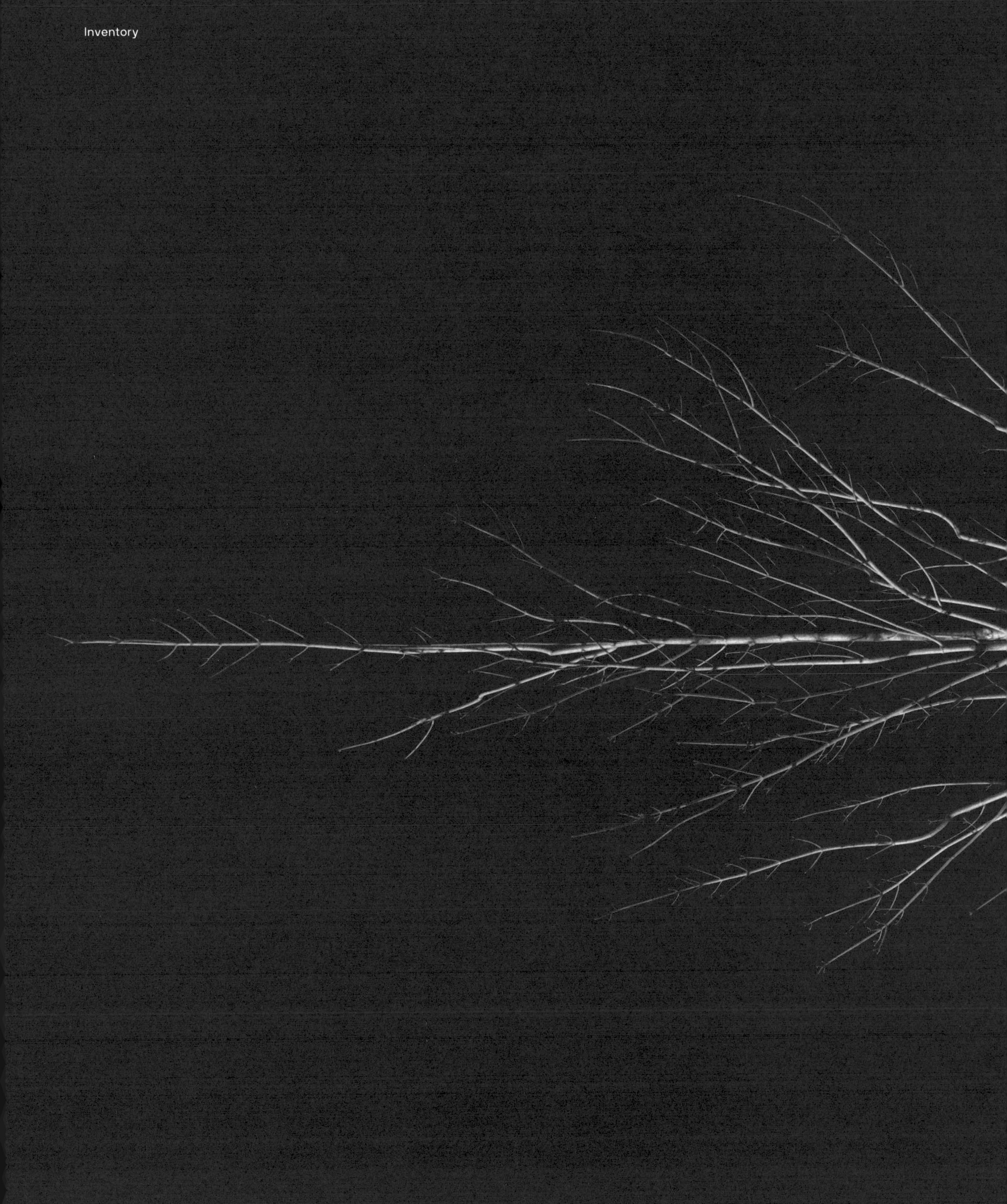

Inventory

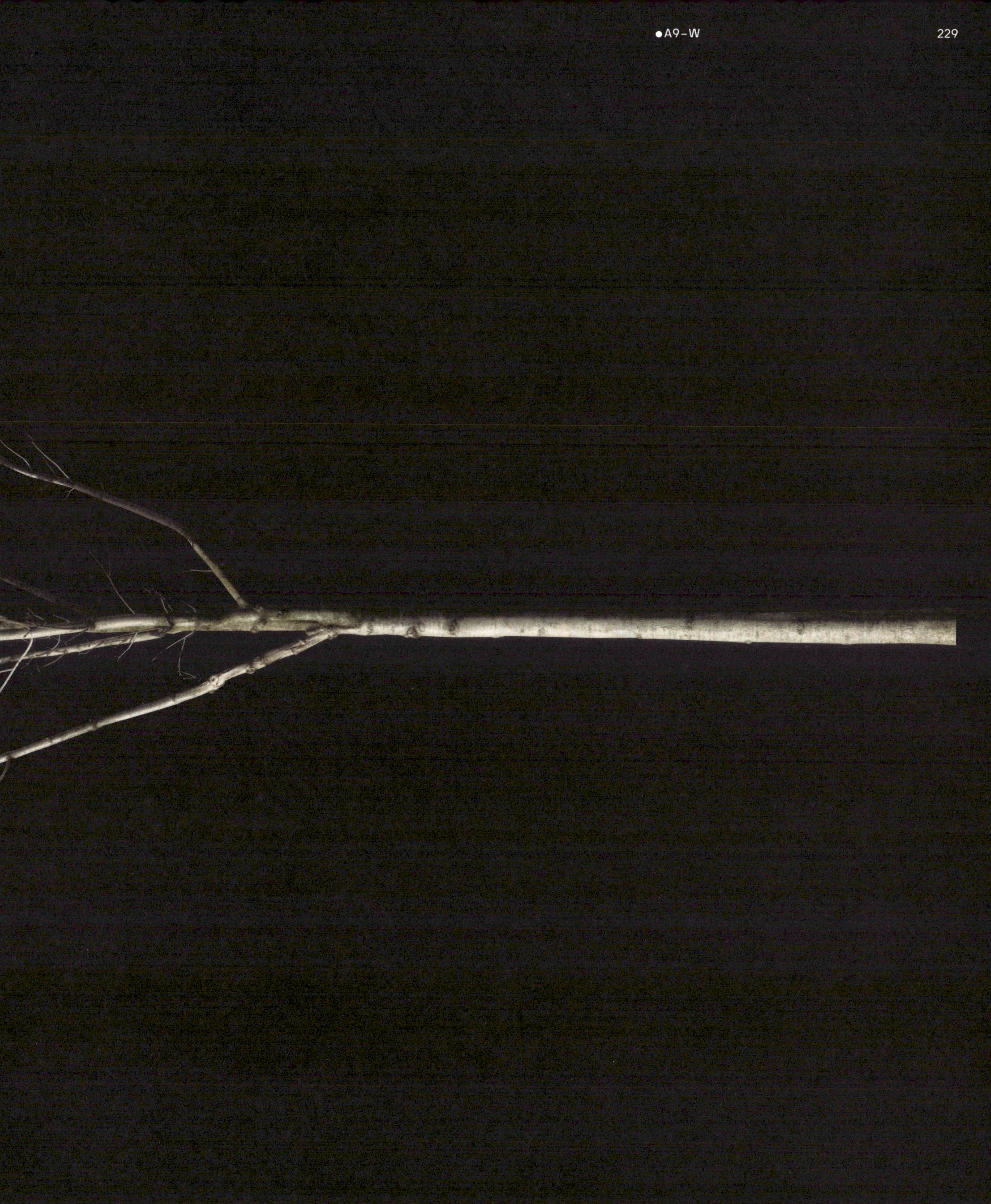

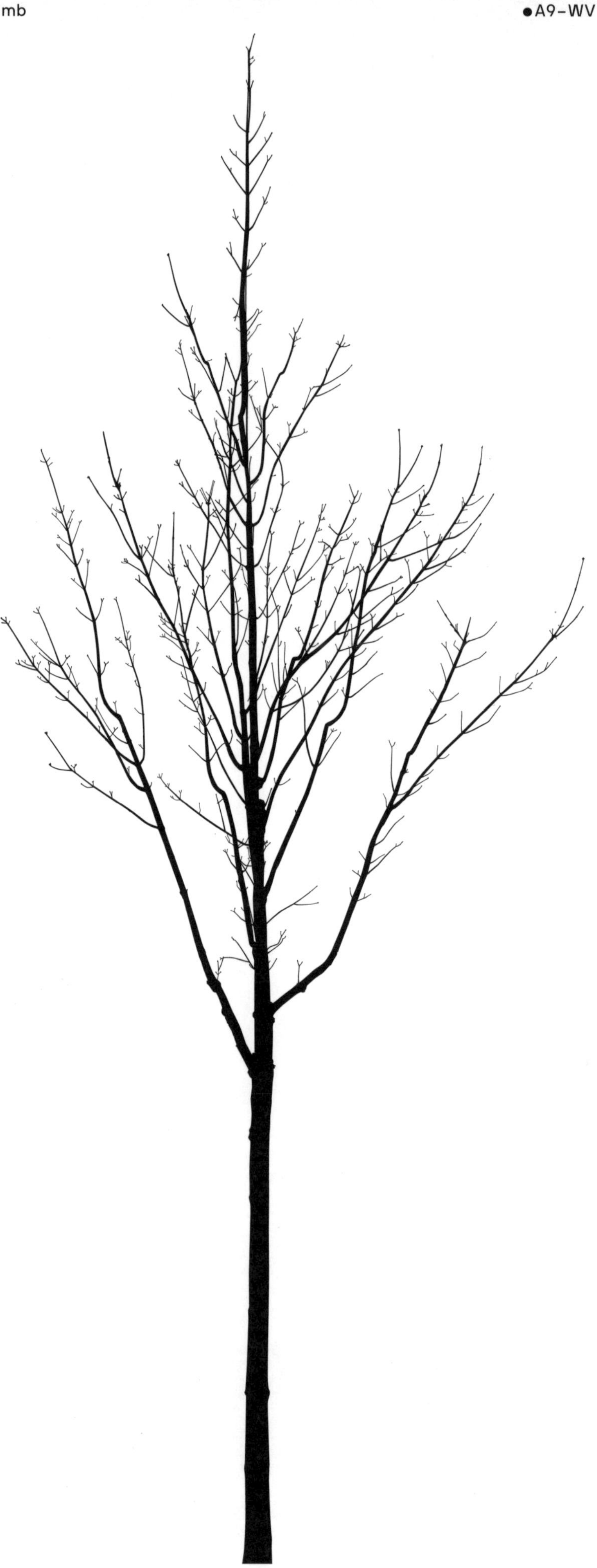

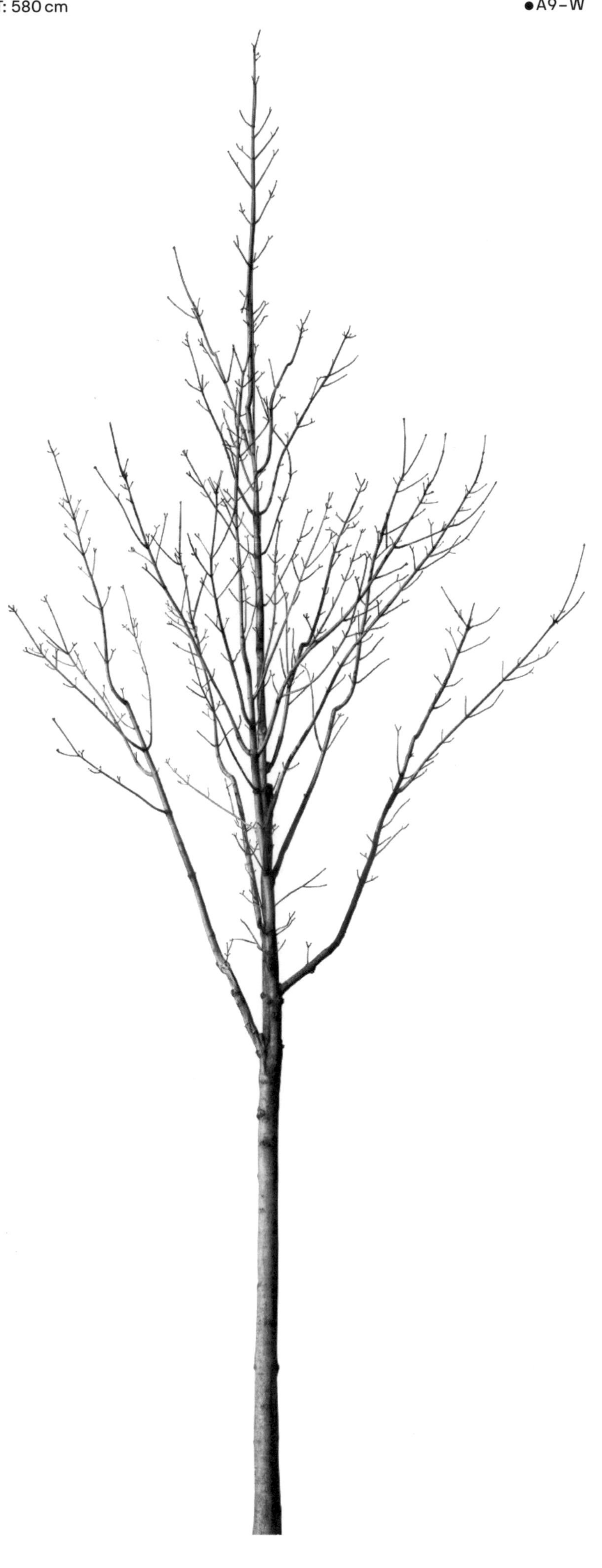

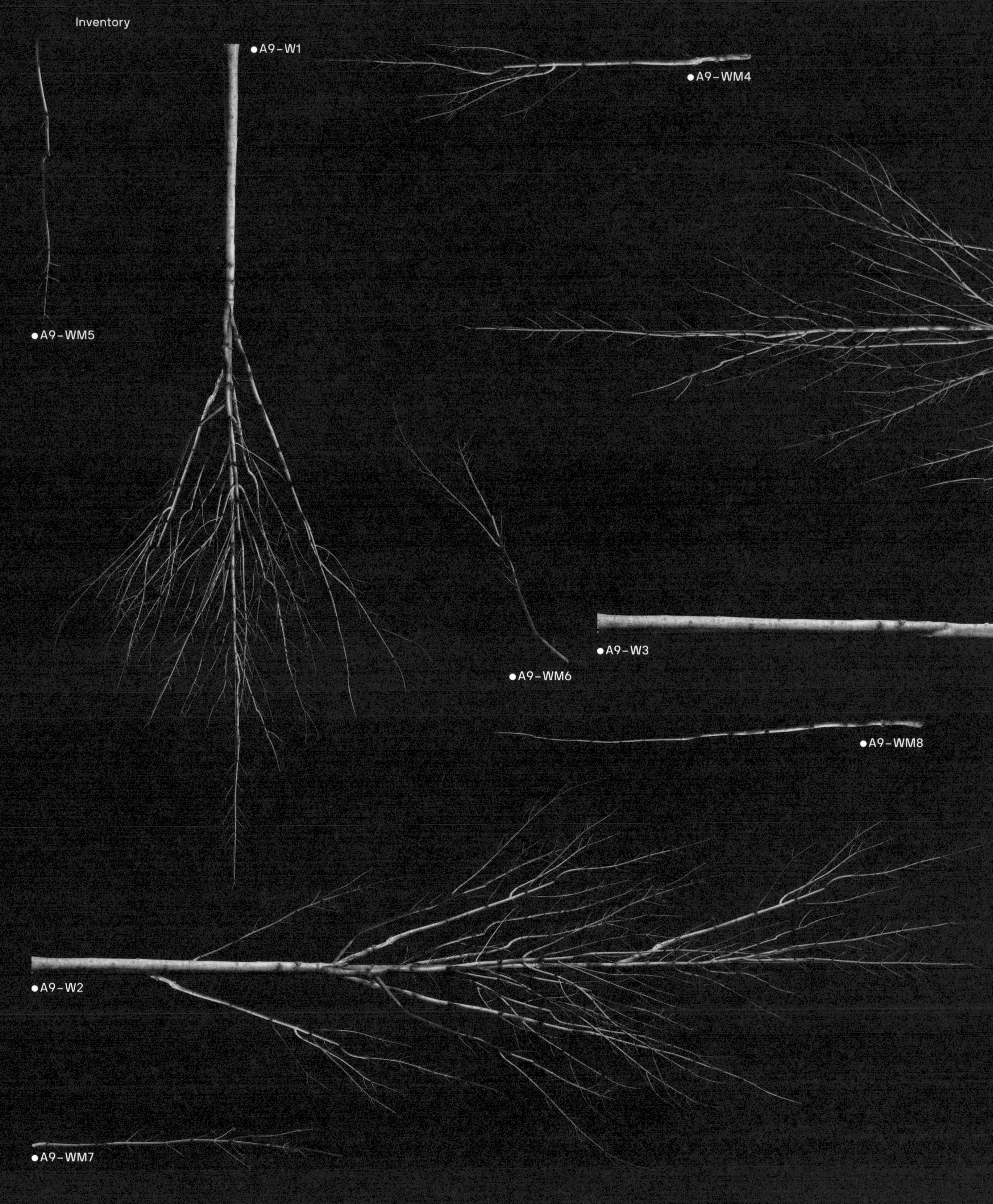

Inventory
A9-W1
A9-WM4
A9-WM5
A9-W3
A9-WM6
A9-WM8
A9-W2
A9-WM7

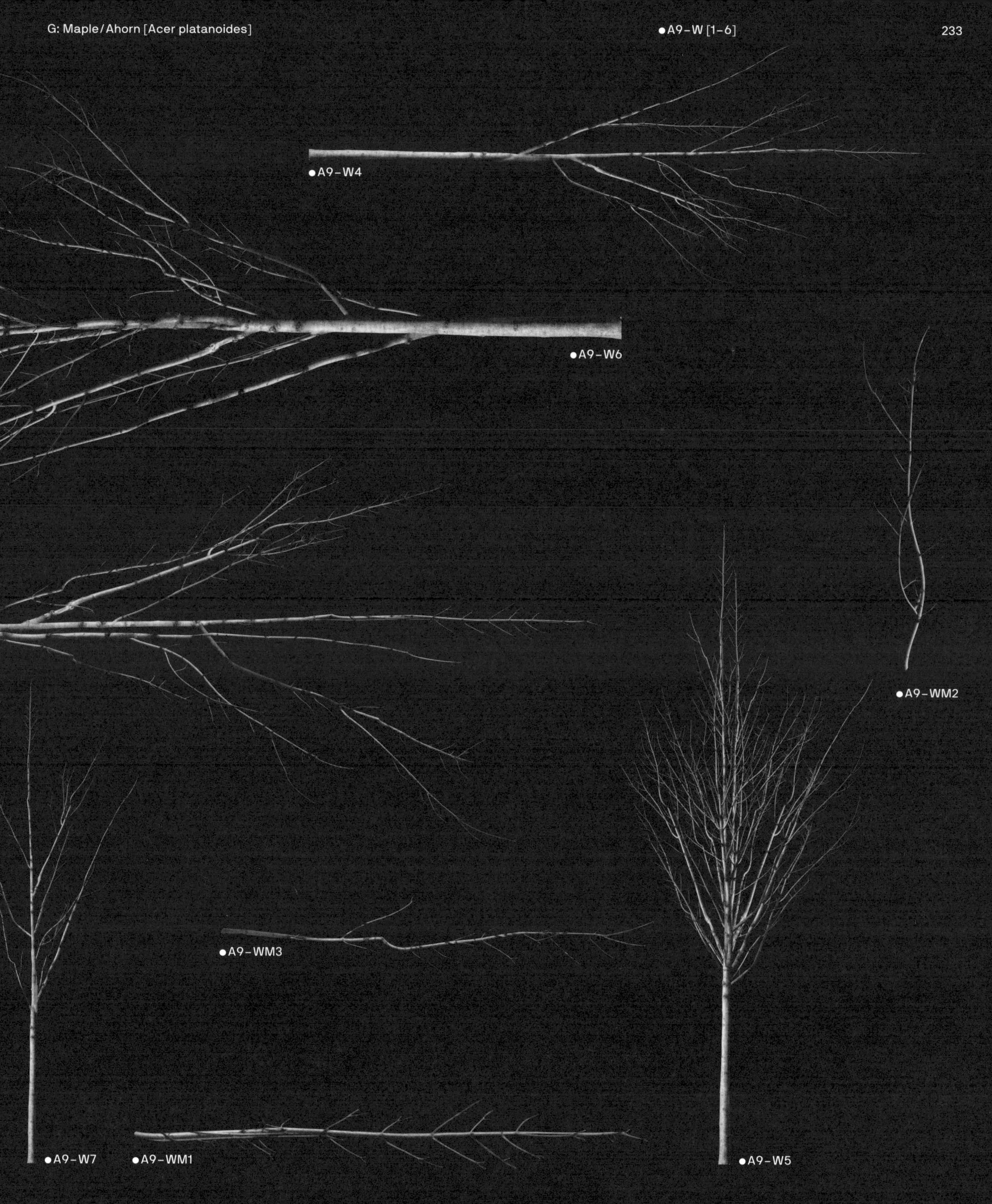

●A9–W4
●A9–W6
●A9–WM2
●A9–WM3
●A9–W7
●A9–WM1
●A9–W5

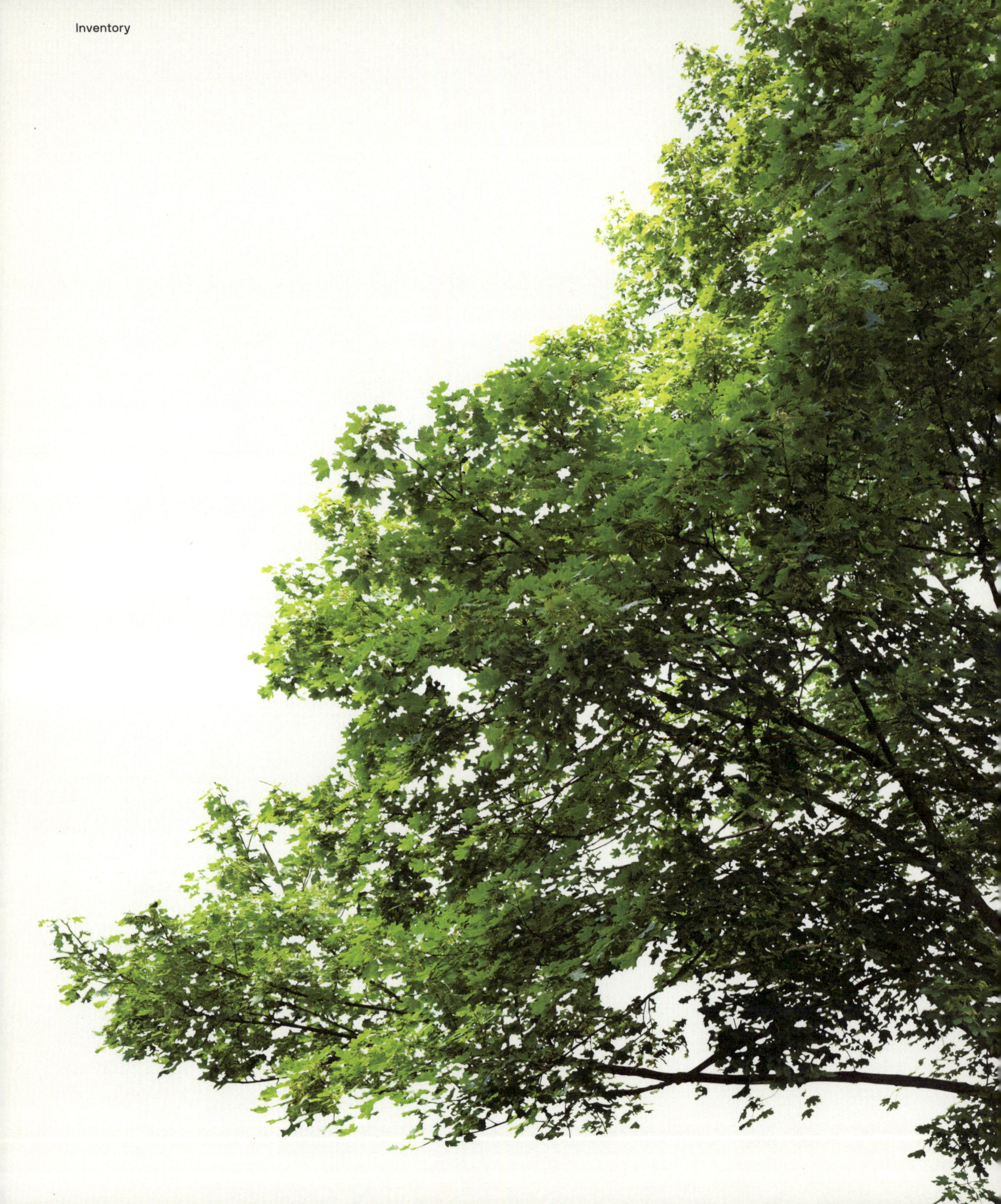

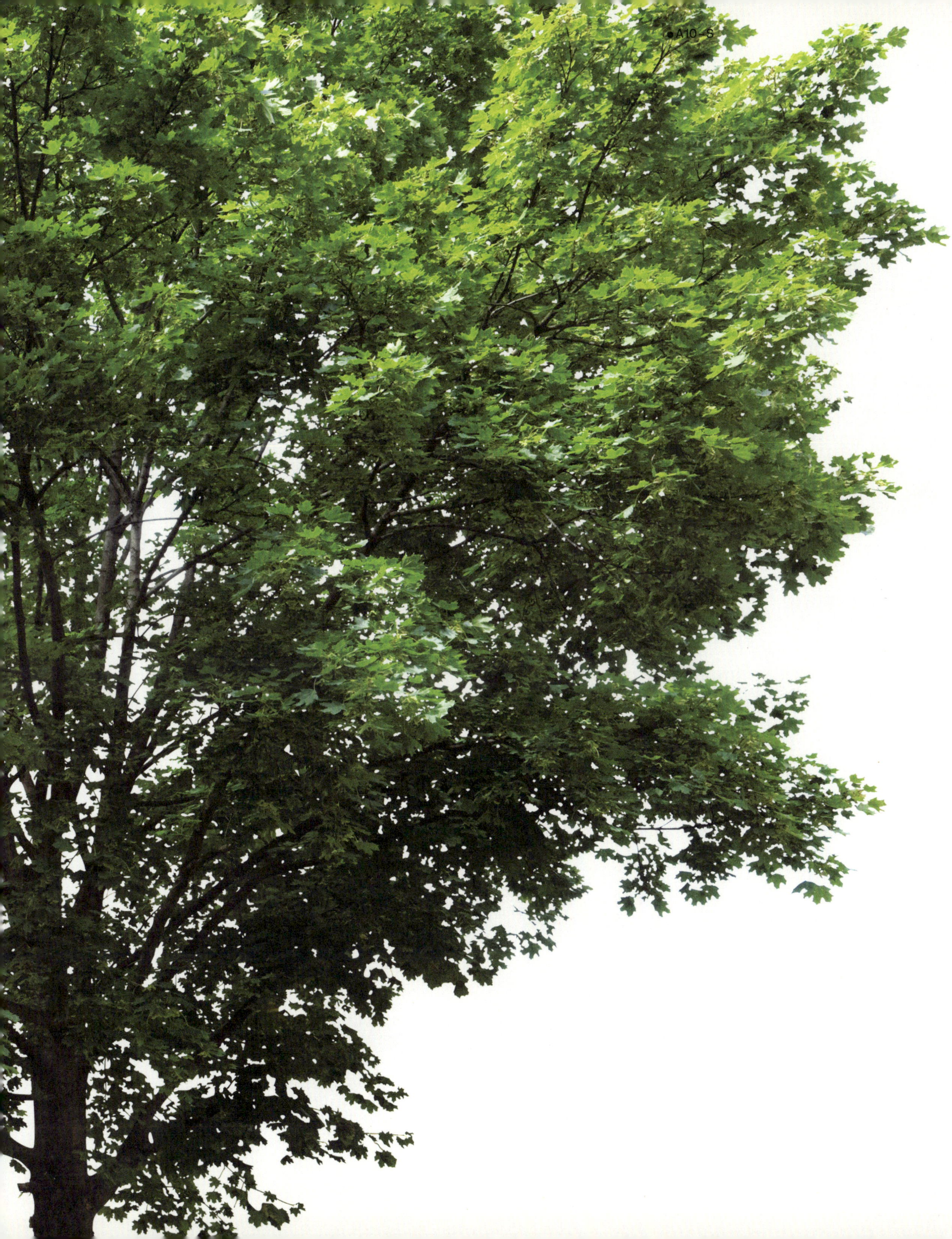

A10-S

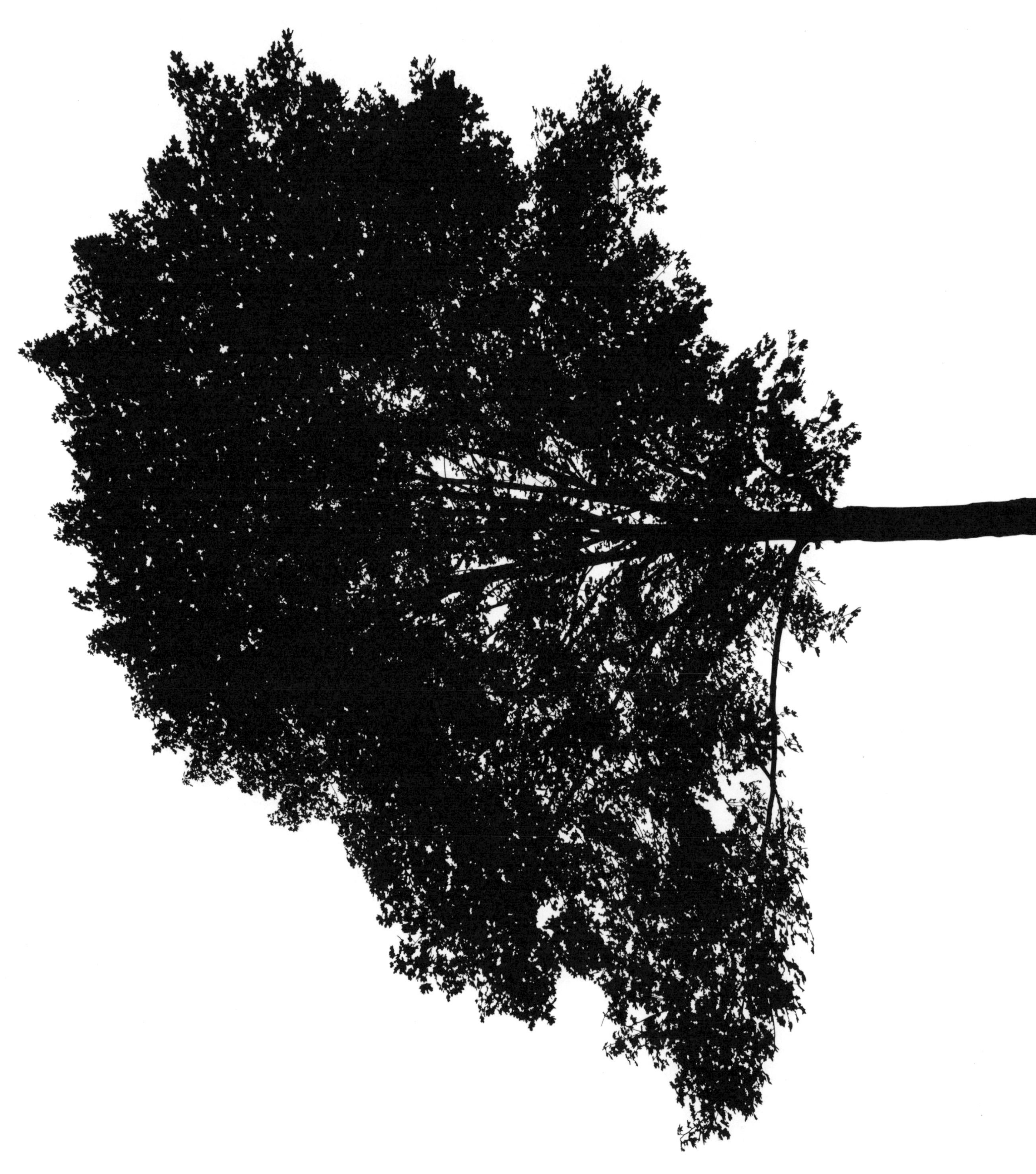

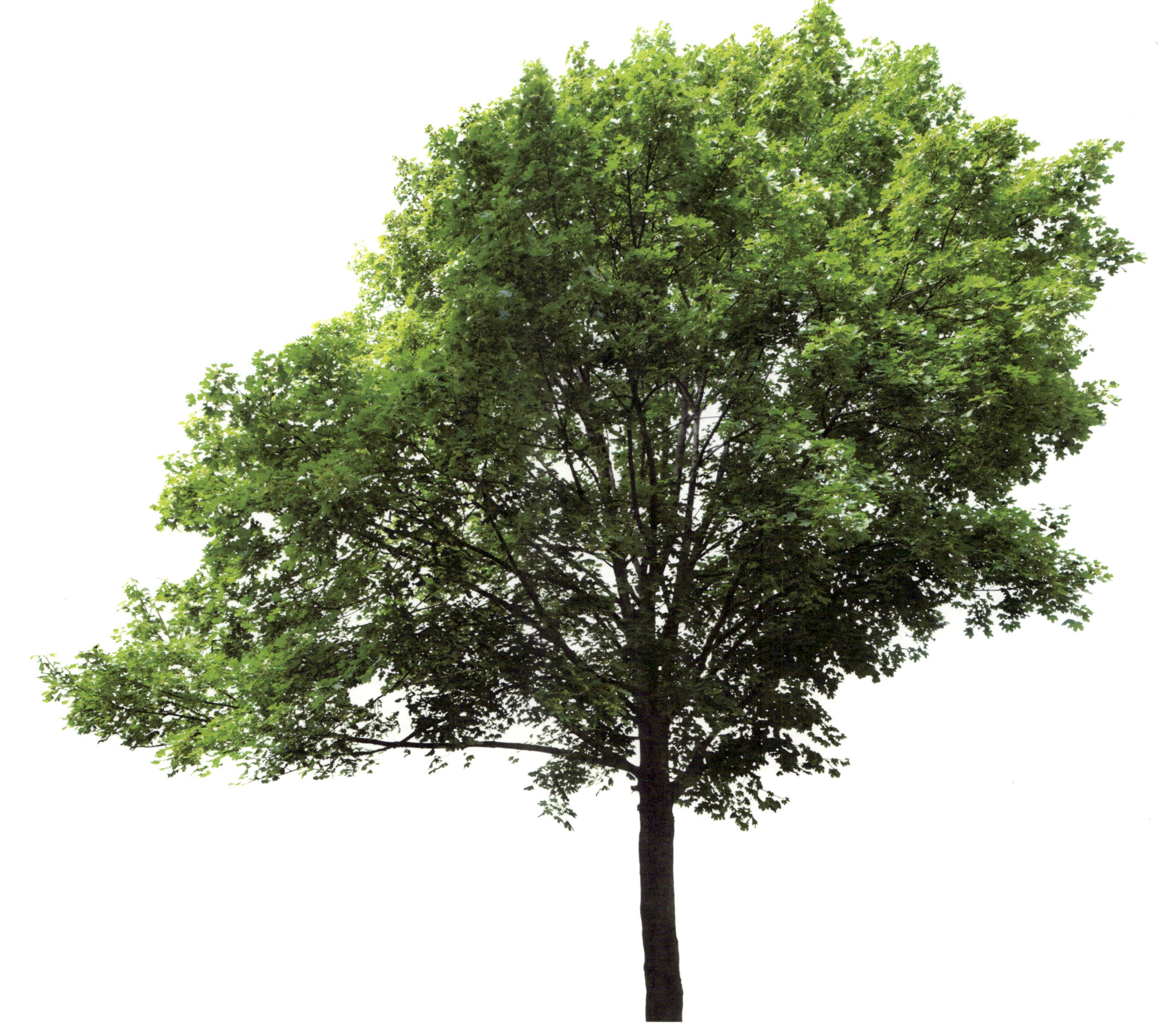

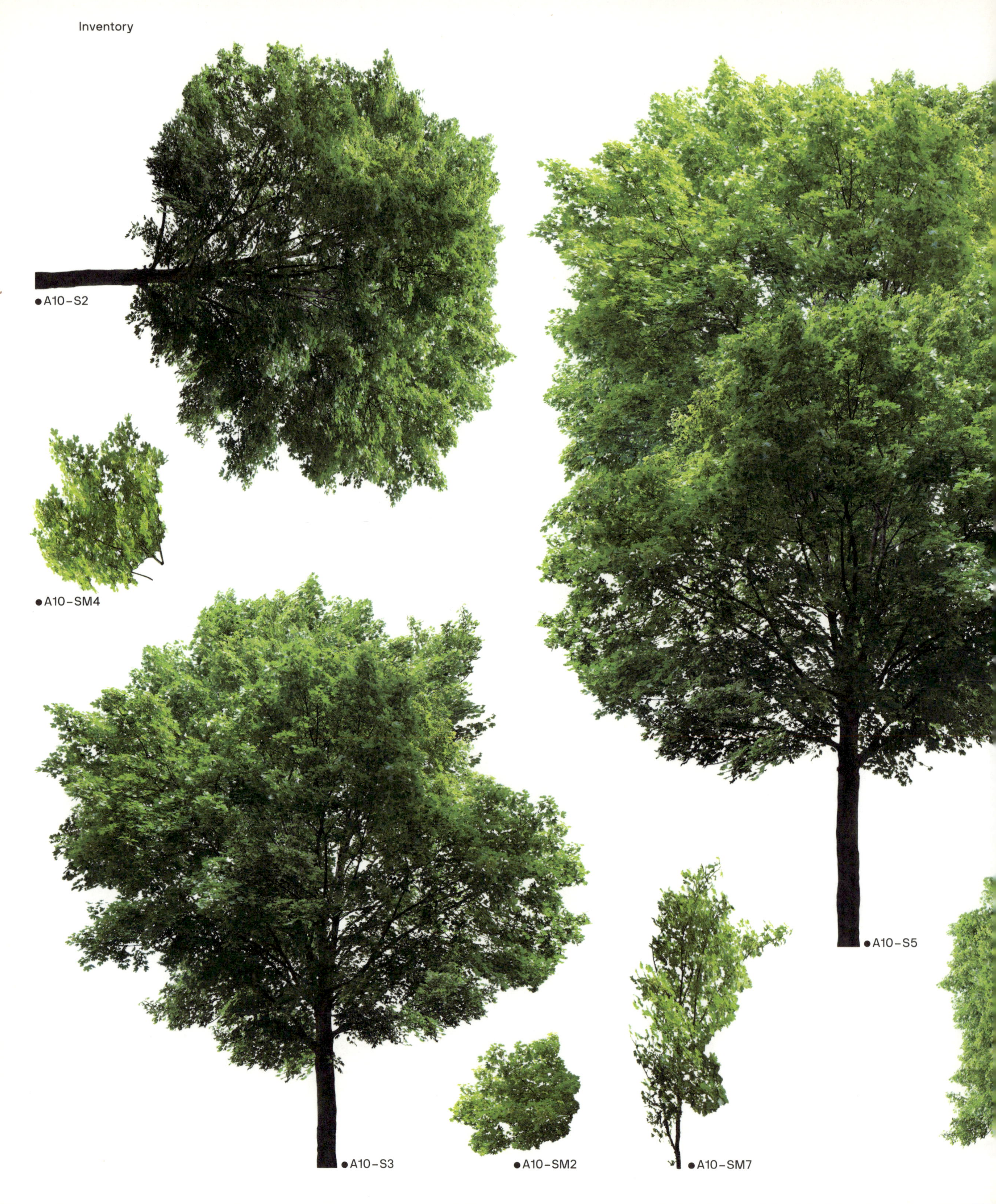
● A10–S2
● A10–SM4
● A10–S3
● A10–SM2
● A10–SM7
● A10–S5

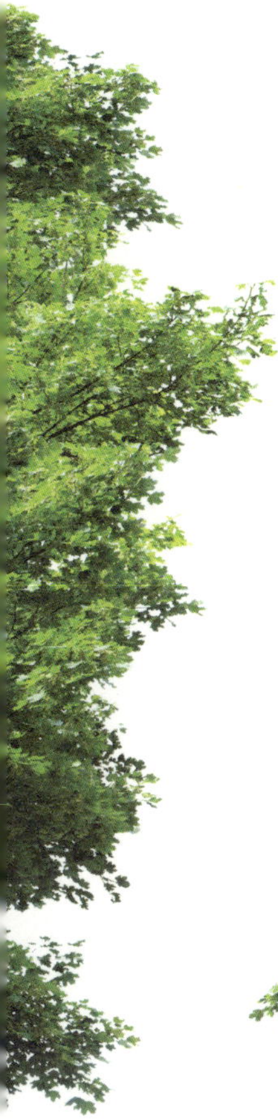

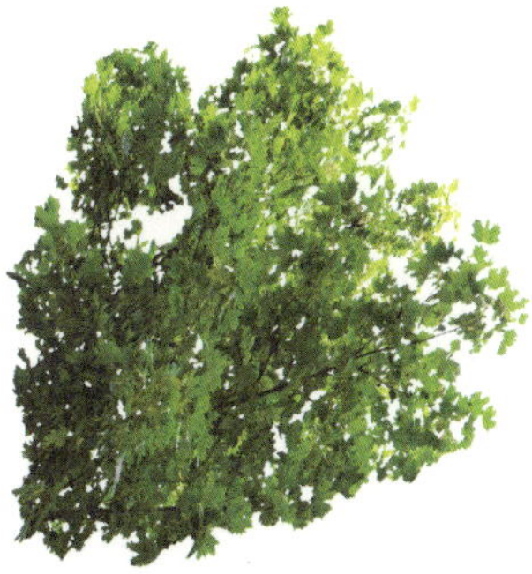

●A10–SM5

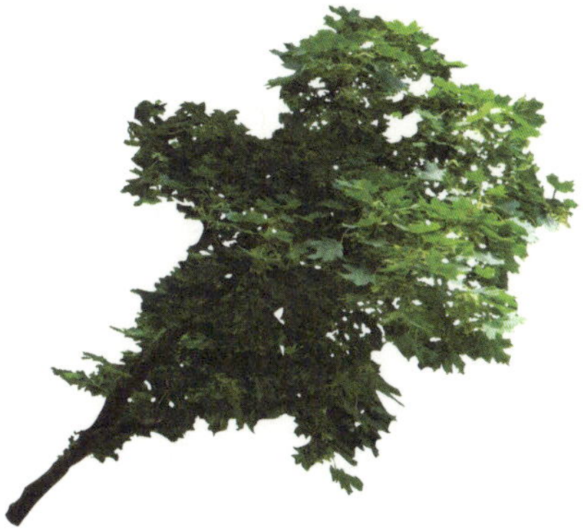

●A10–SM3

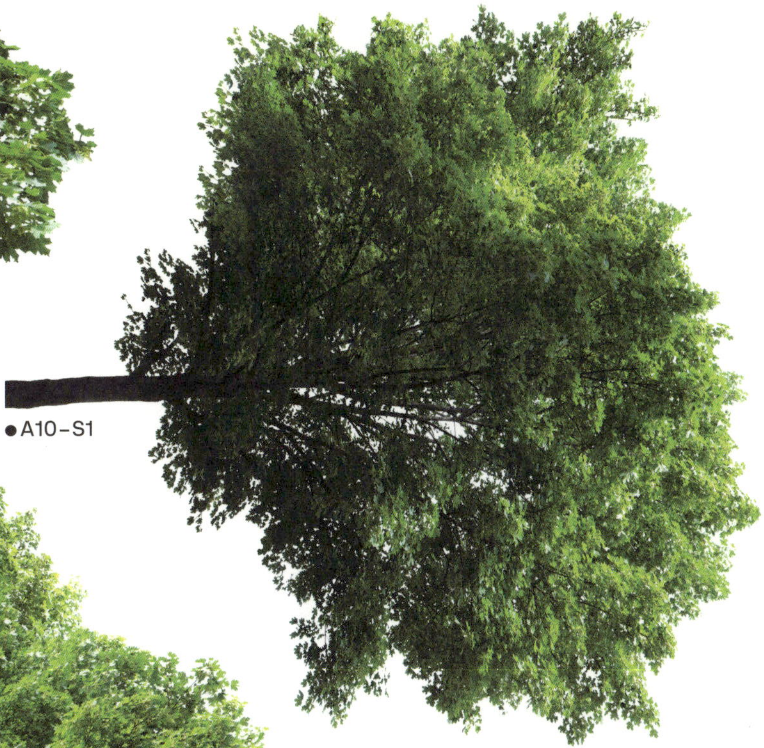

●A10–S1

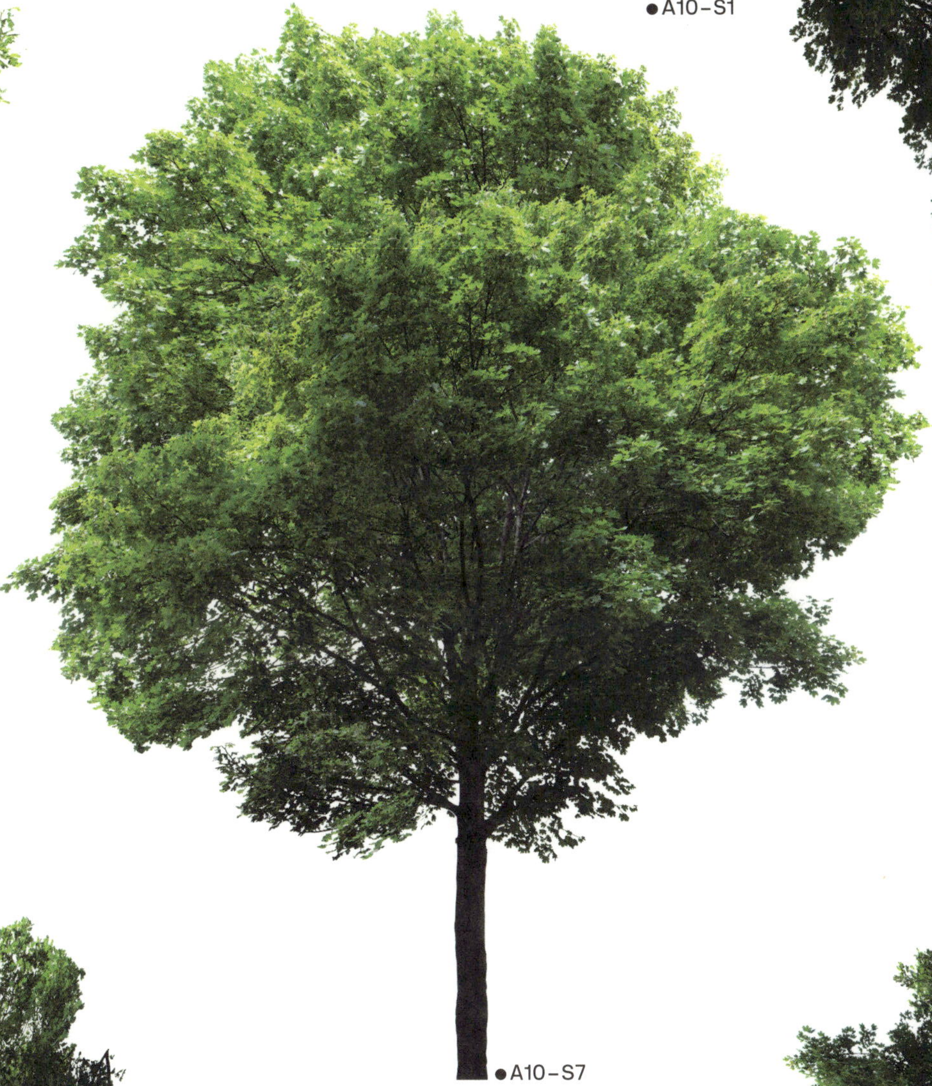

●A10–S6

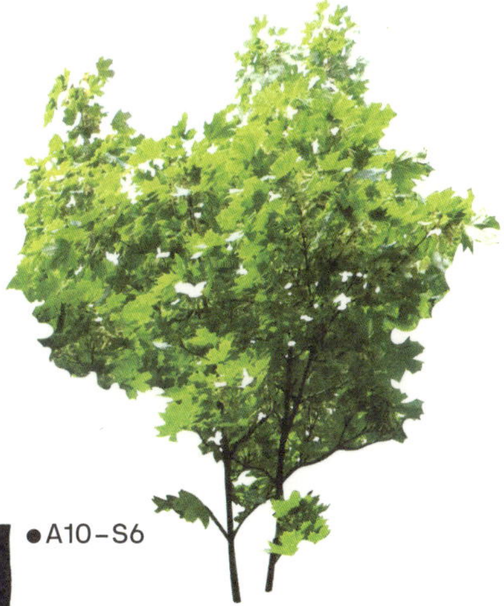

●A10–SM1

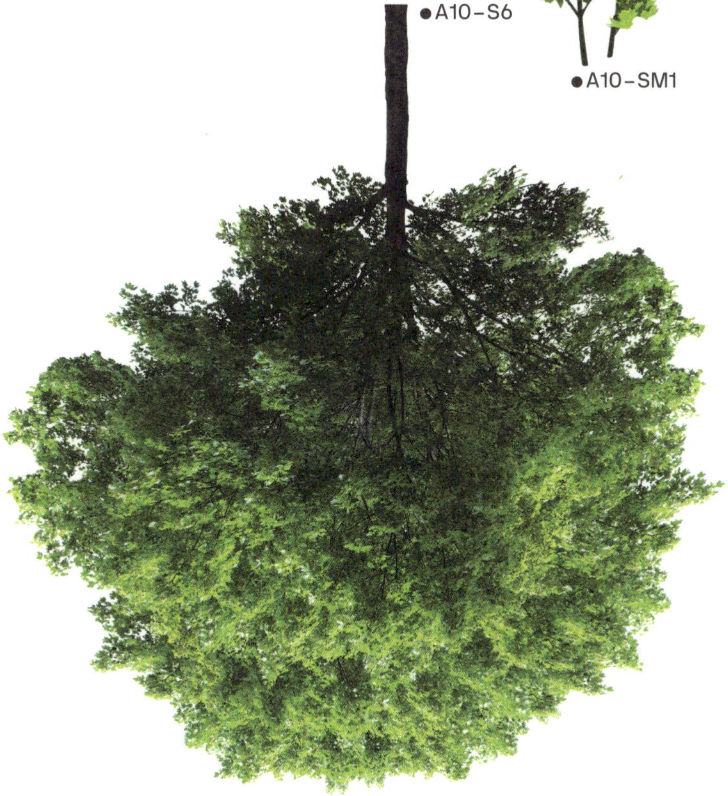

●A10–S7

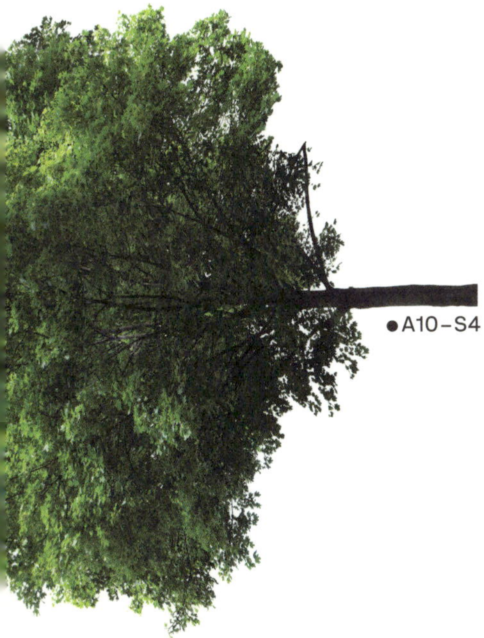

●A10–S4

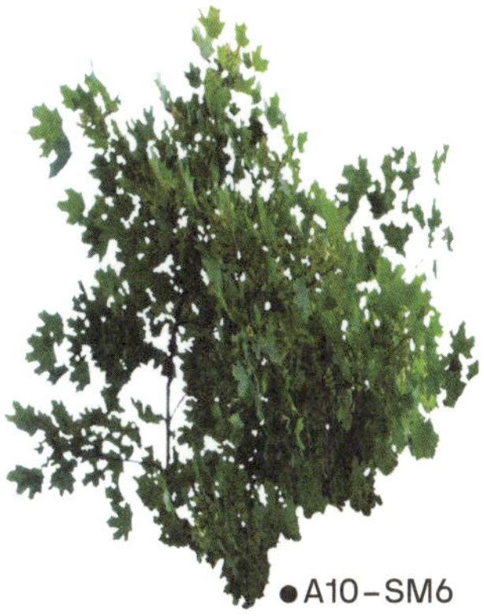

●A10–SM6

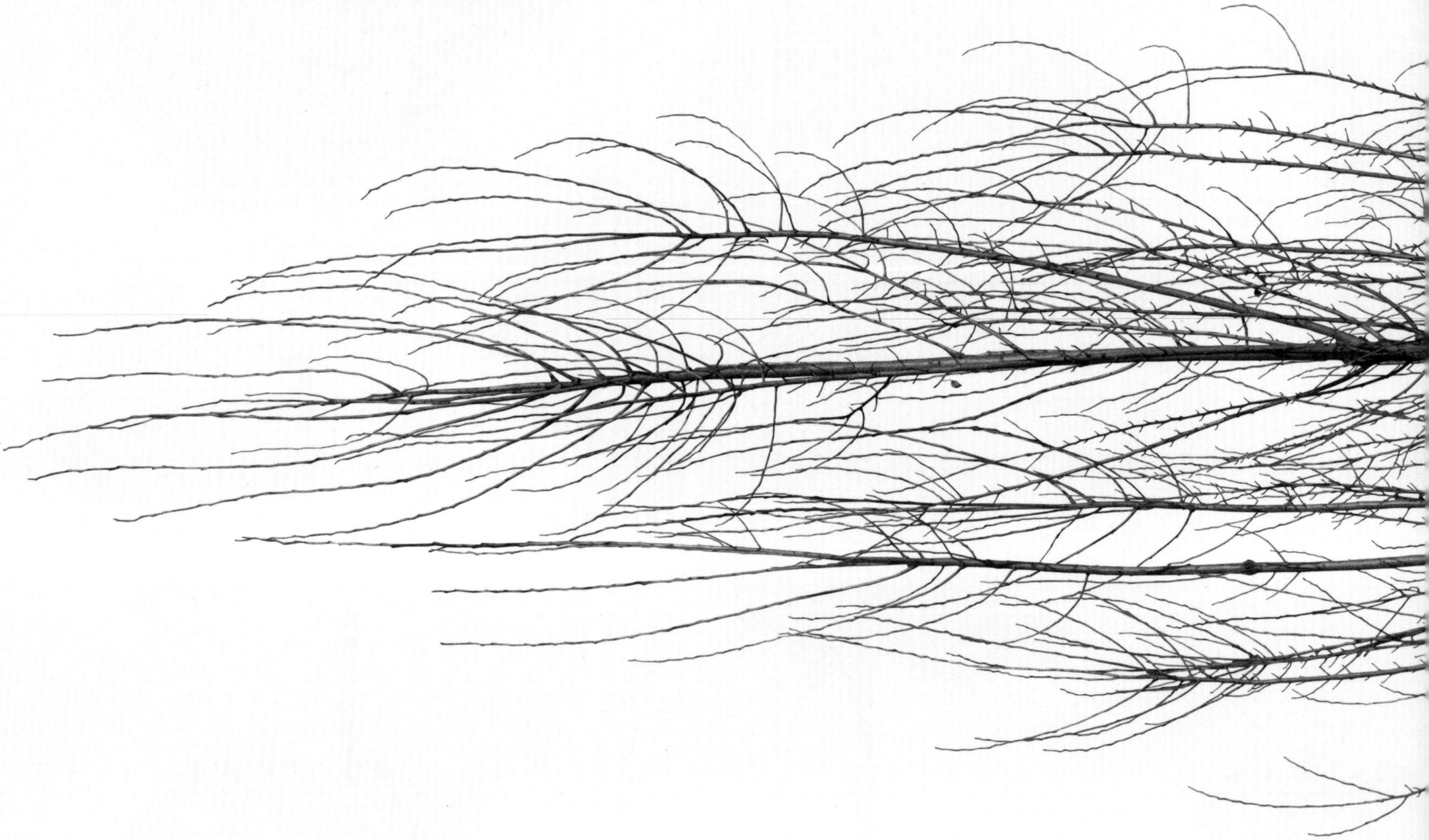

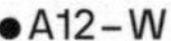

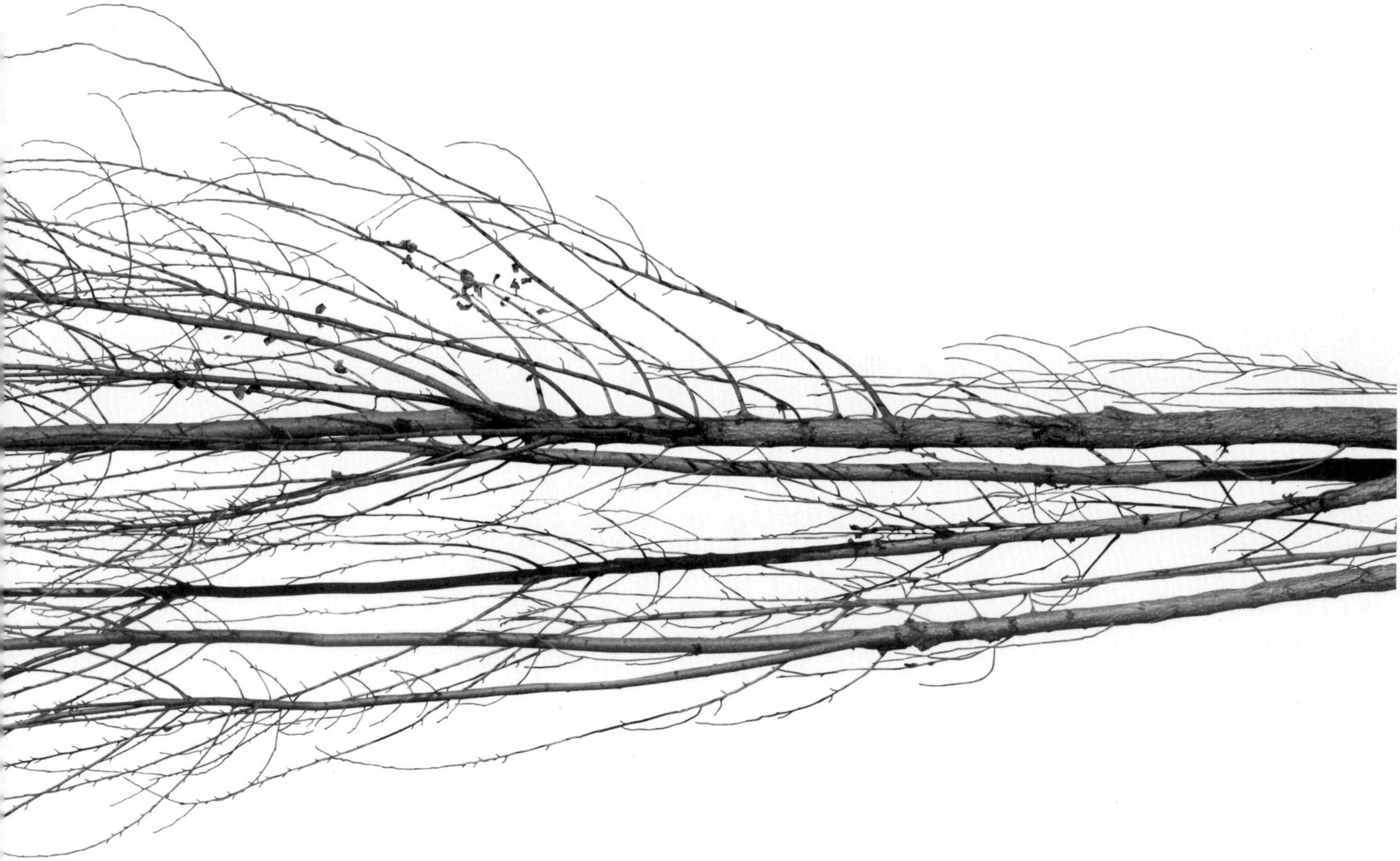

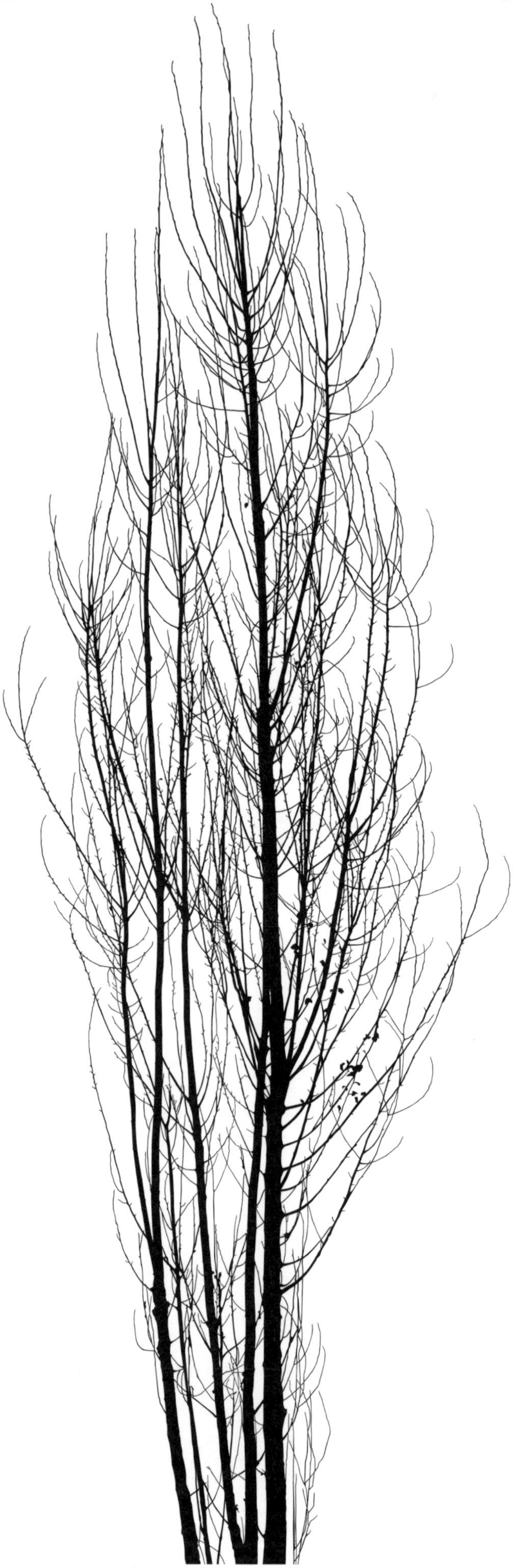

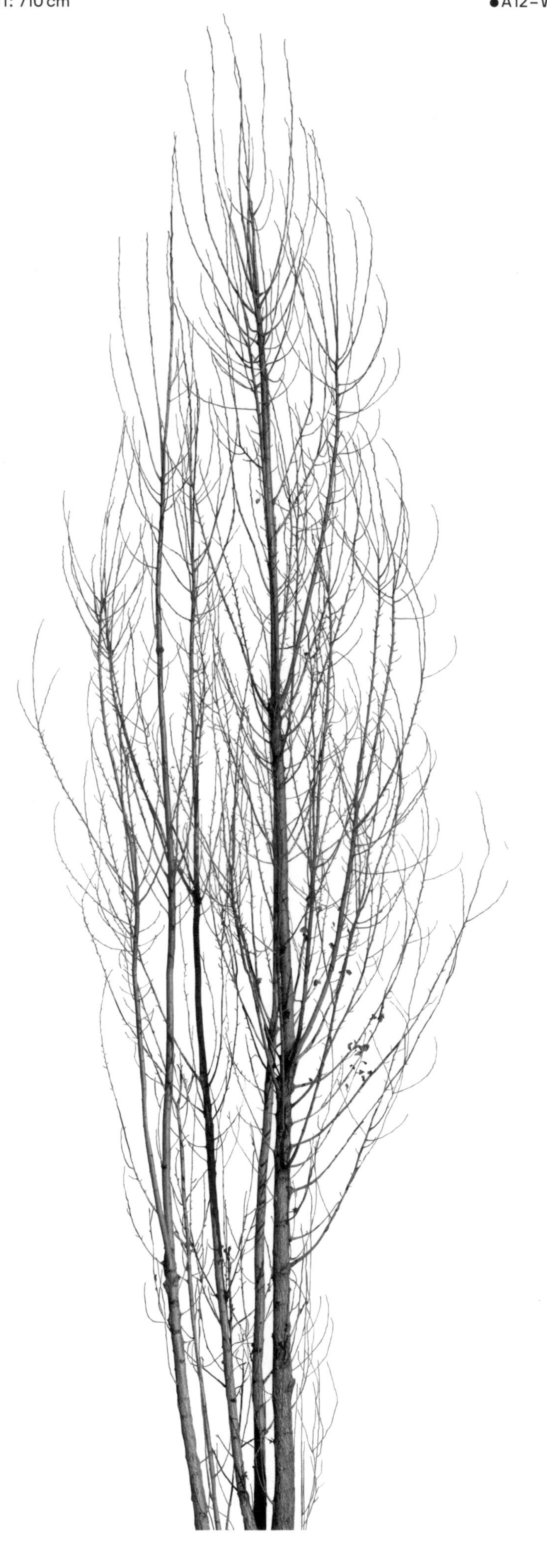

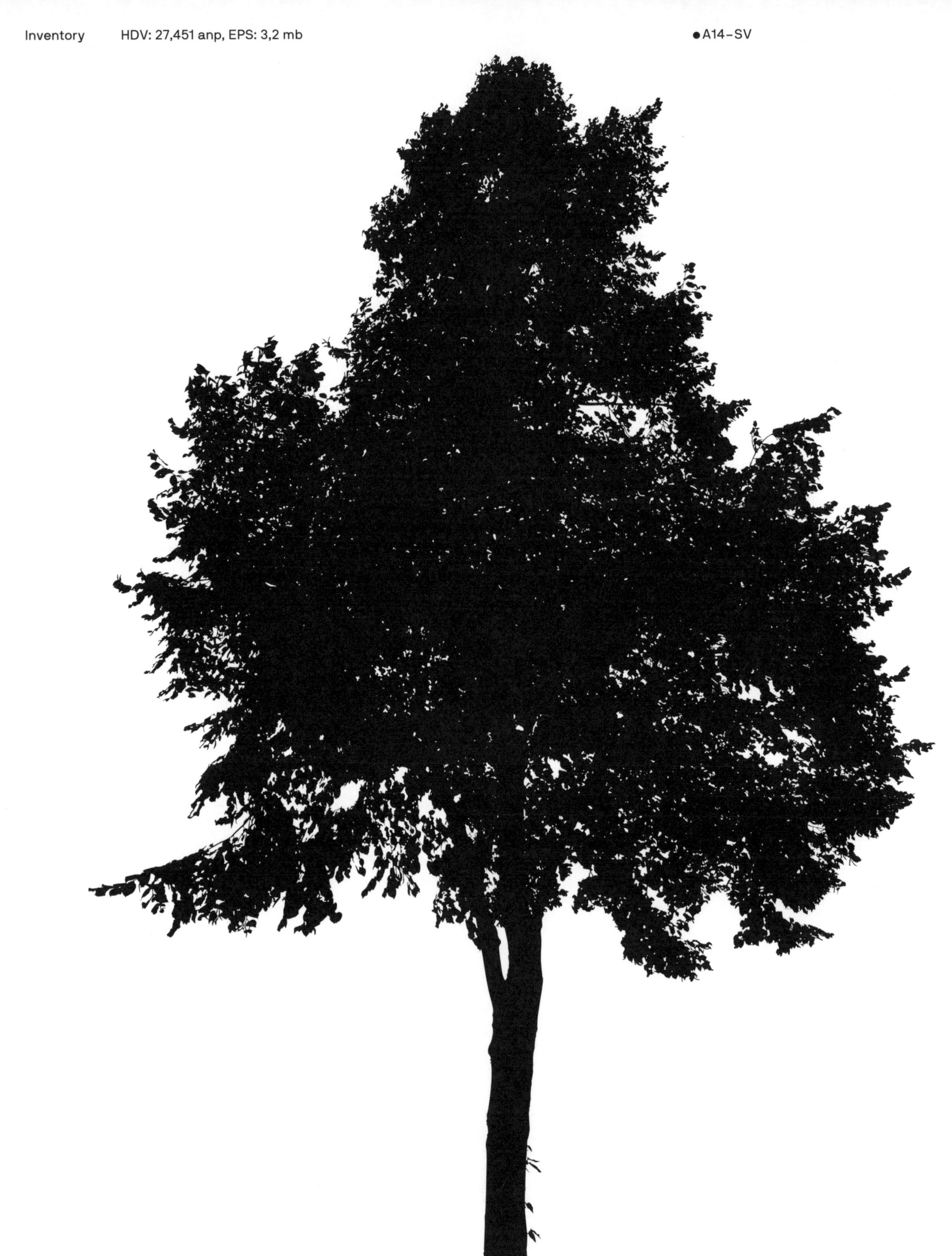

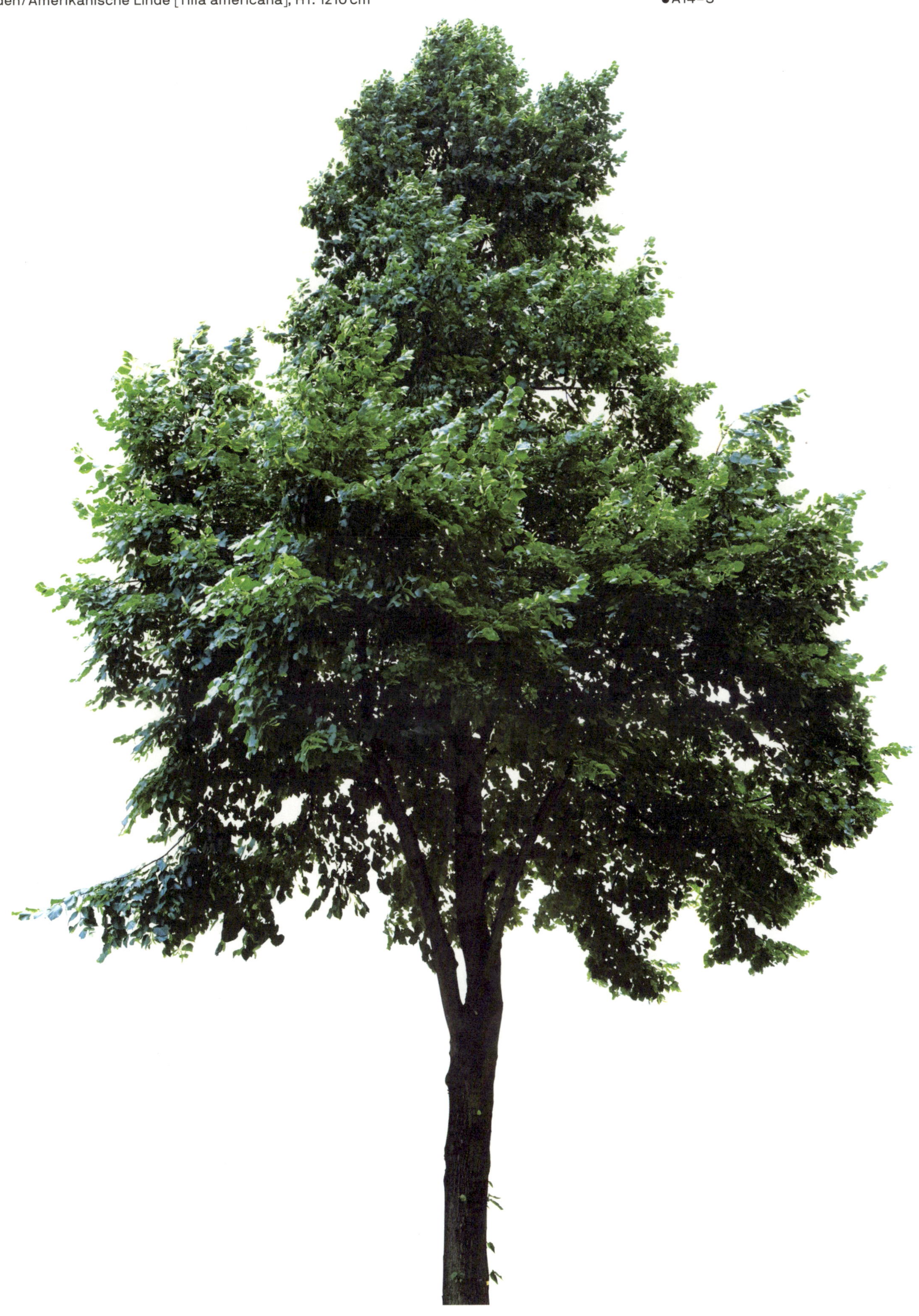

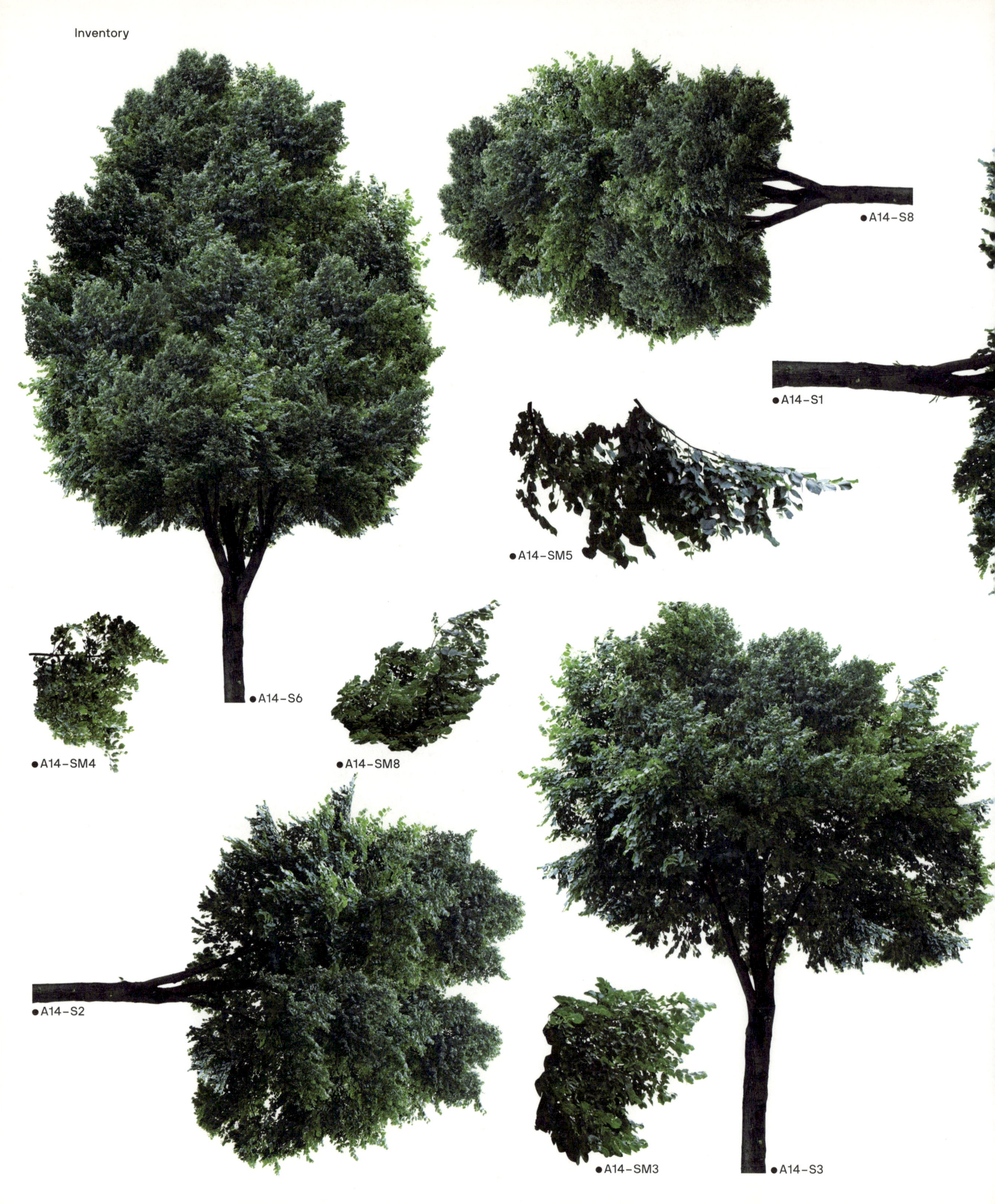
●A14–S8
●A14–S1
●A14–SM5
●A14–S6
●A14–SM4
●A14–SM8
●A14–S2
●A14–SM3
●A14–S3

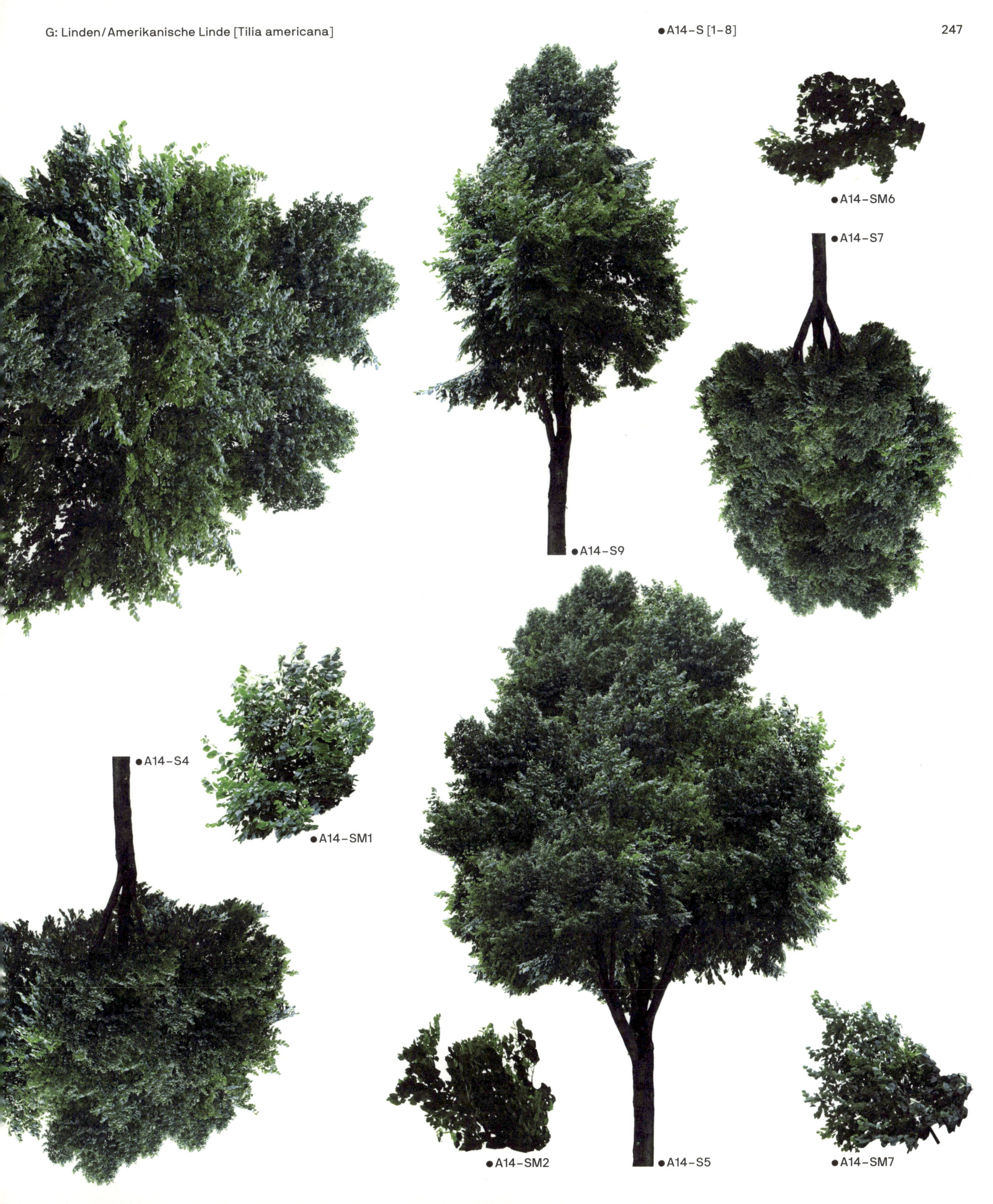

●A14–SM6
●A14–S7
●A14–S9
●A14–S4
●A14–SM1
●A14–SM2
●A14–S5
●A14–SM7

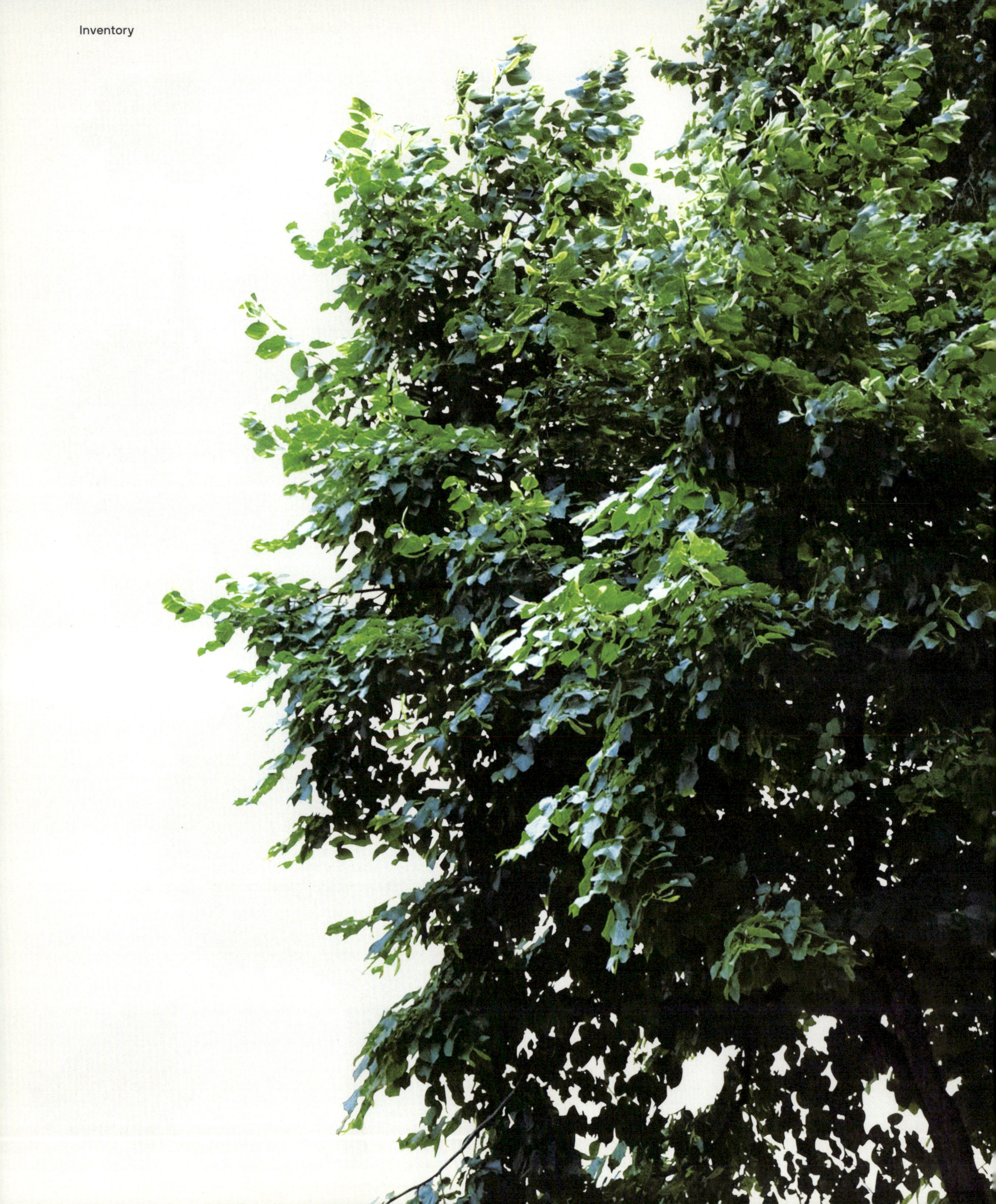

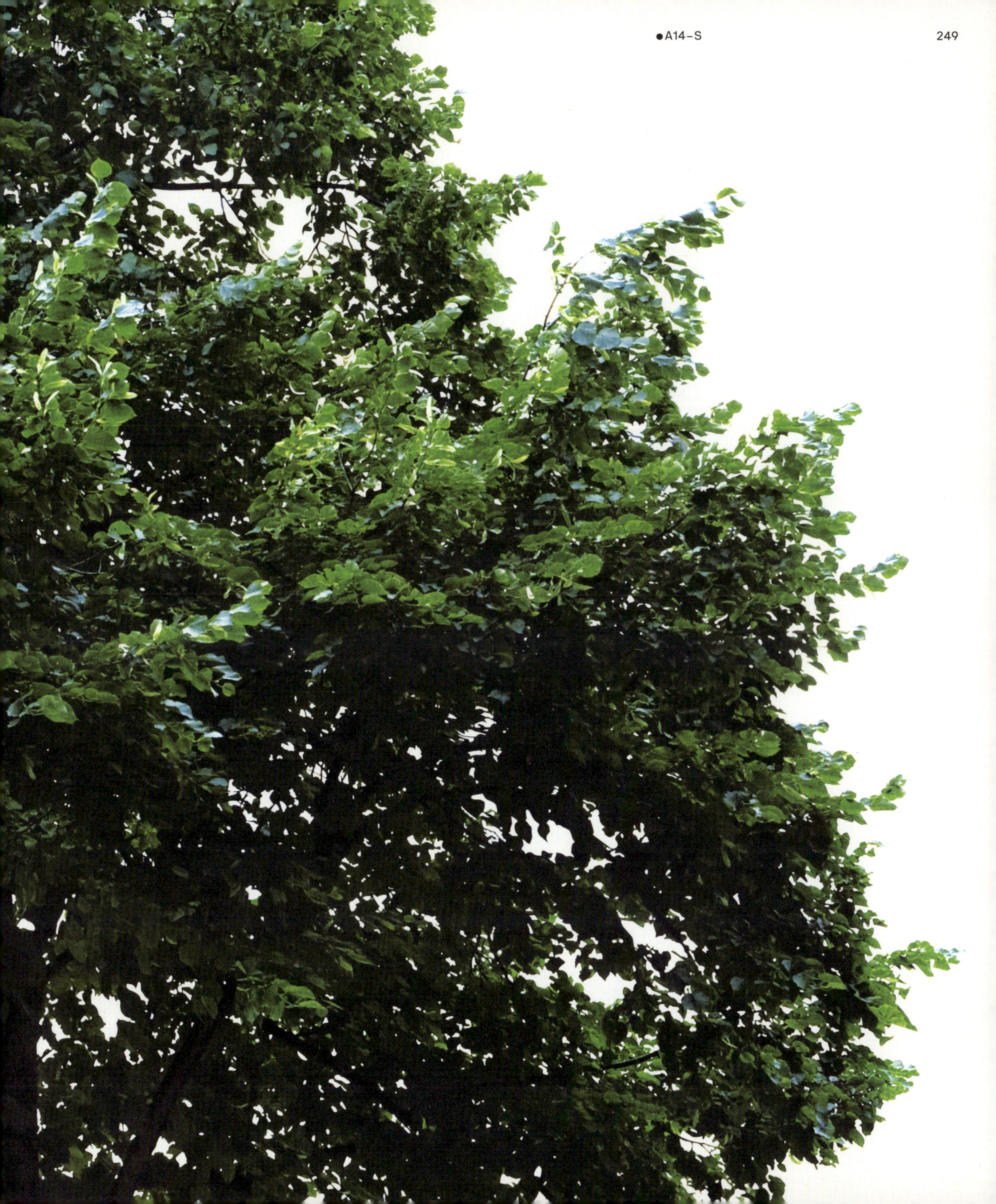

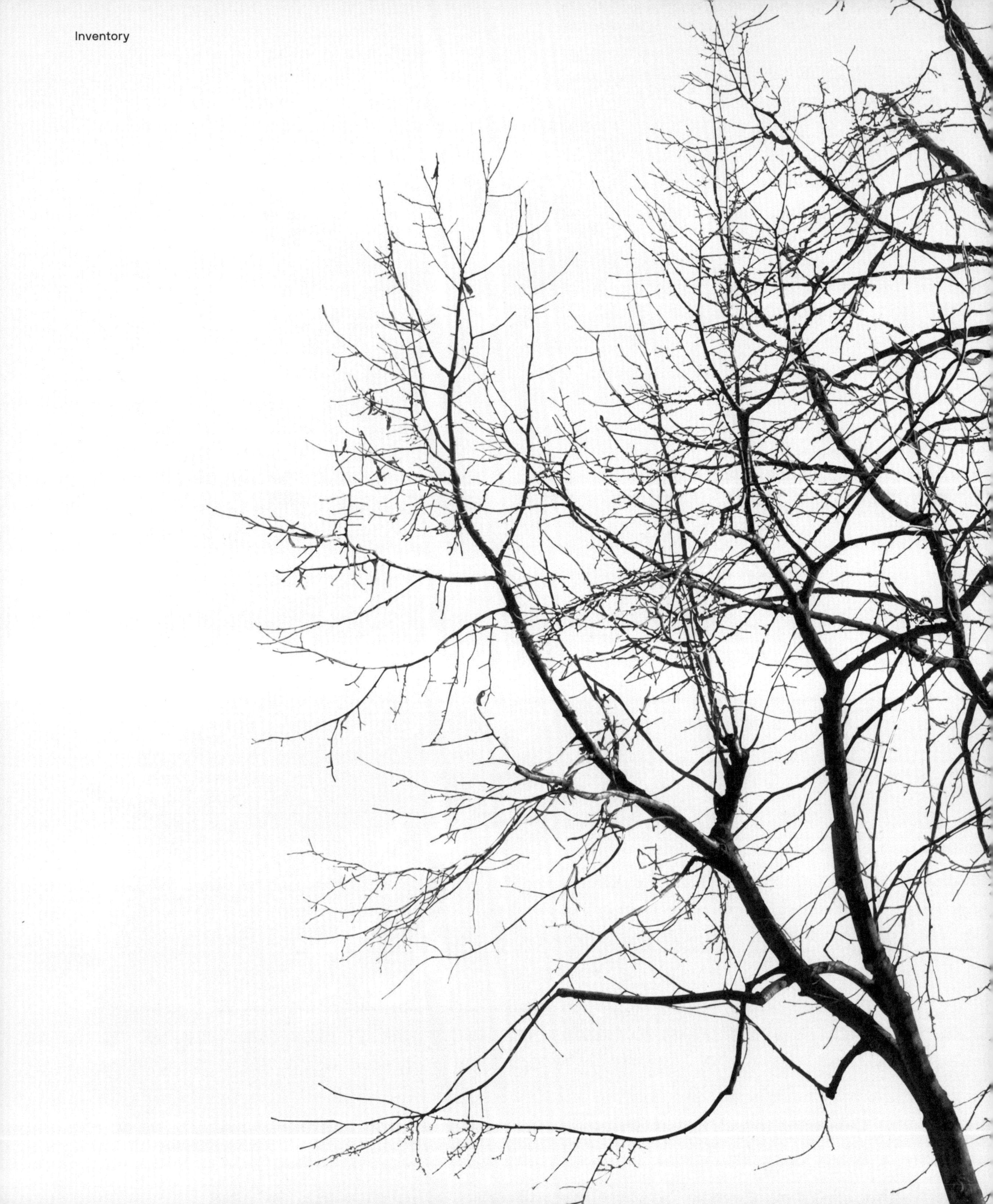

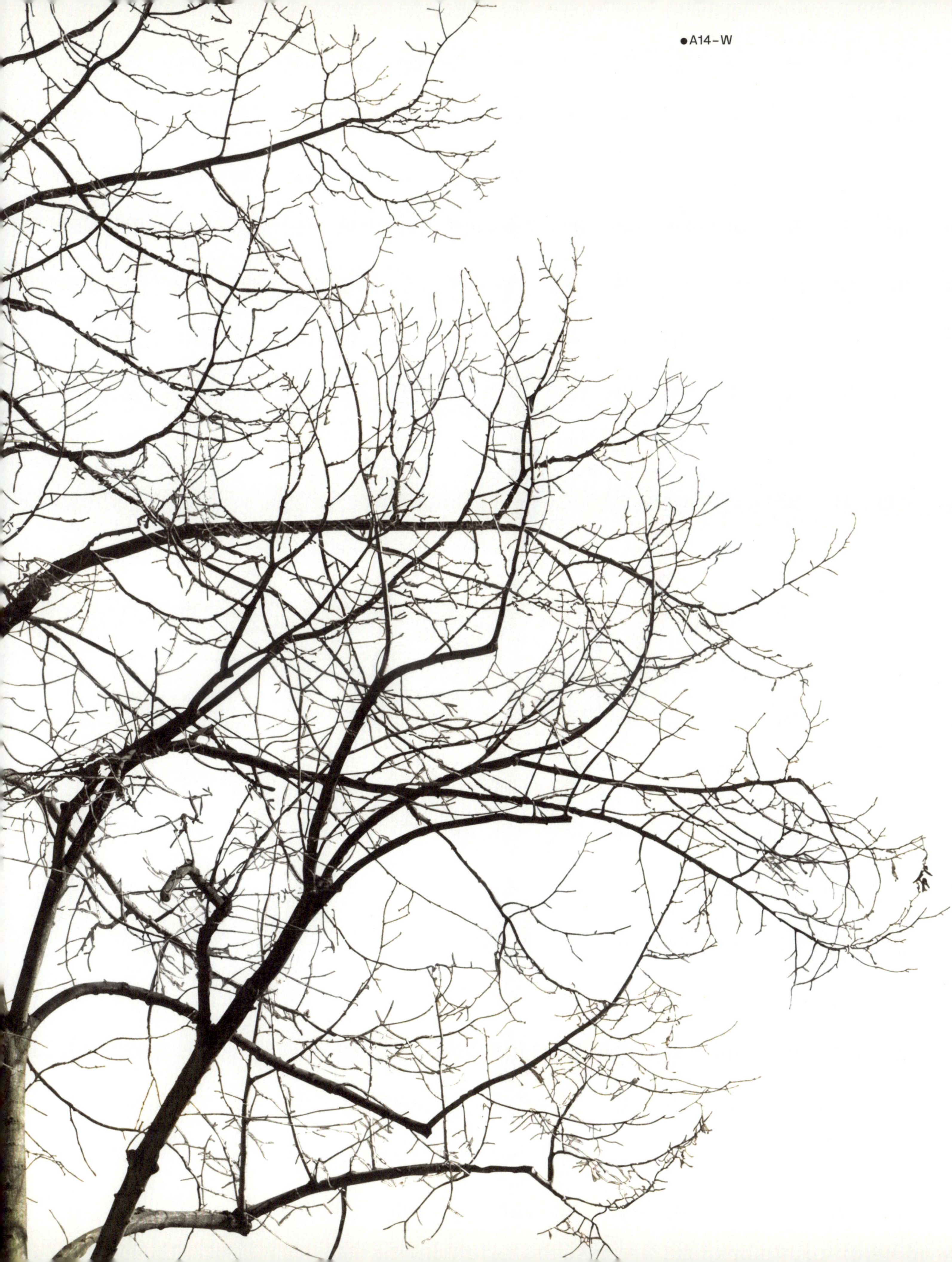

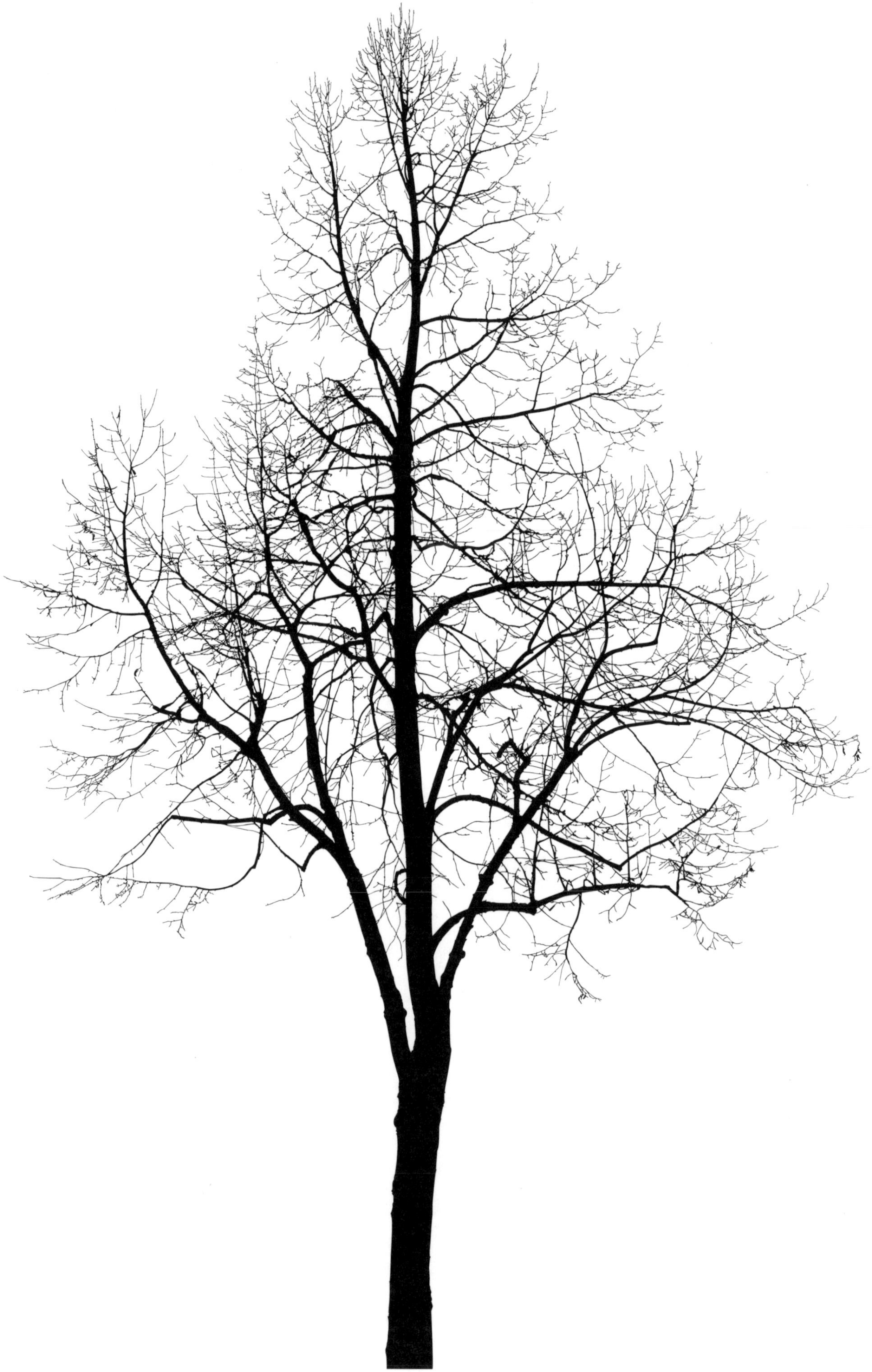

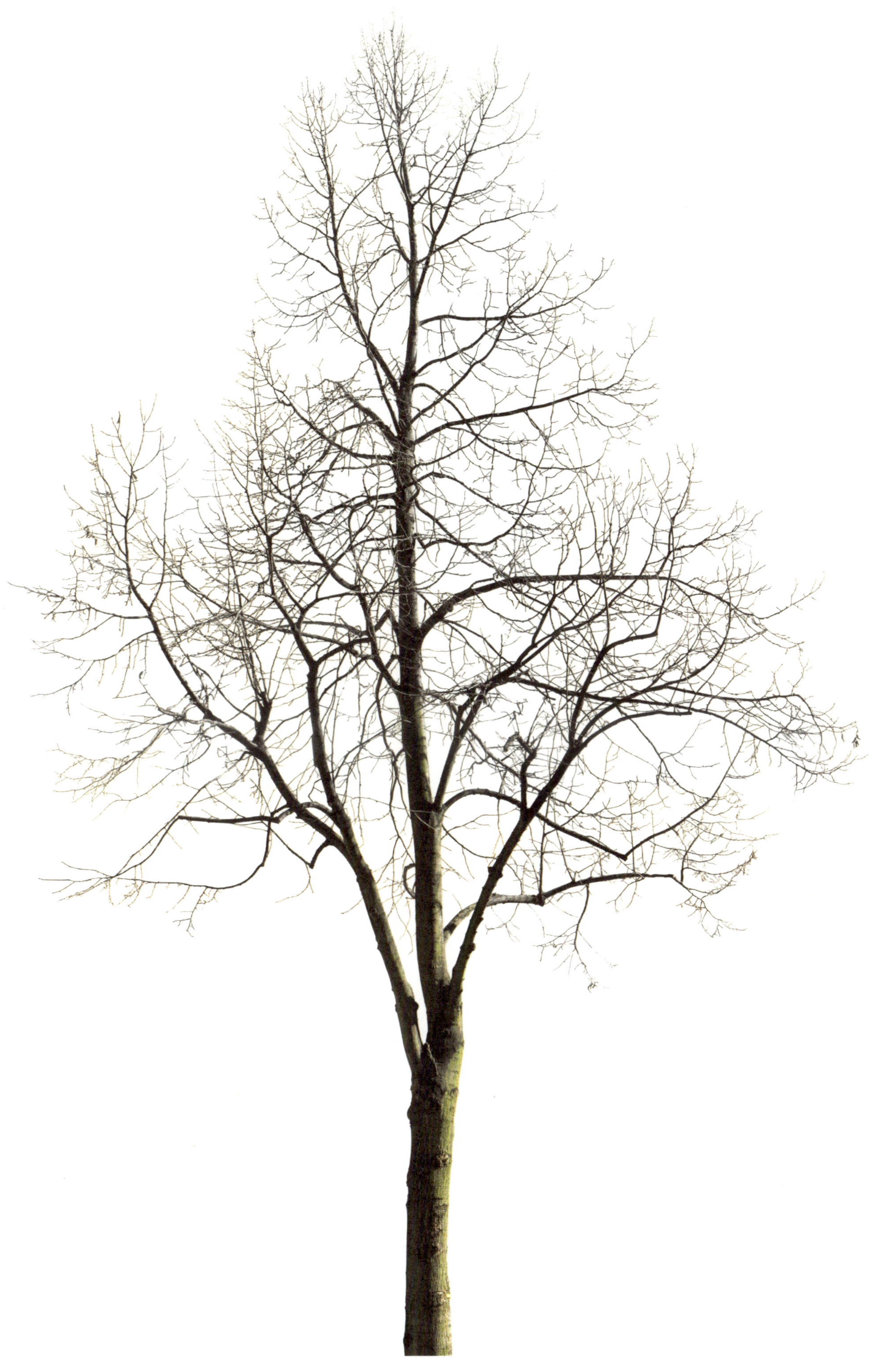

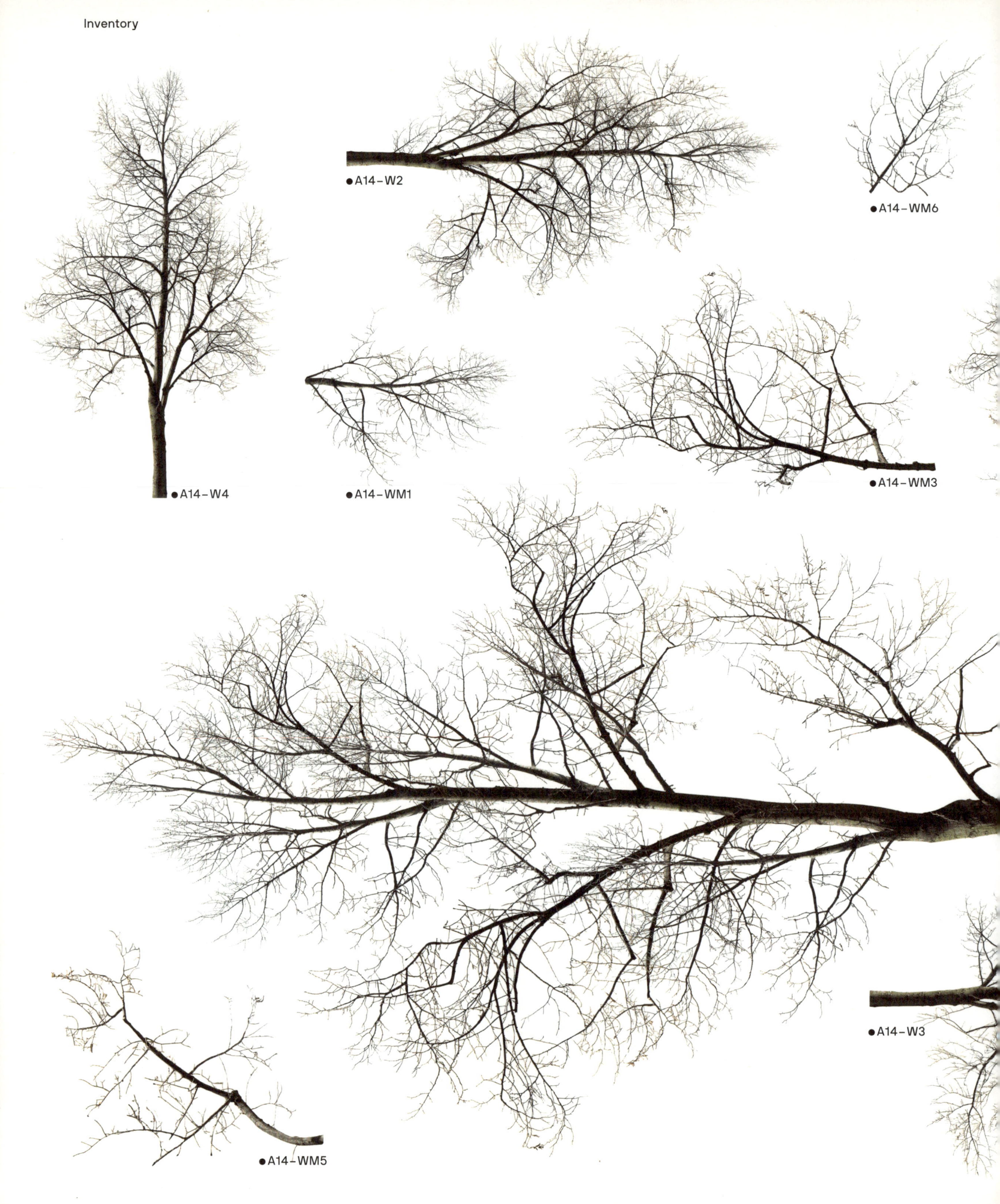

●A14–W2
●A14–WM6
●A14–W4
●A14–WM1
●A14–WM3
●A14–WM5
●A14–W3

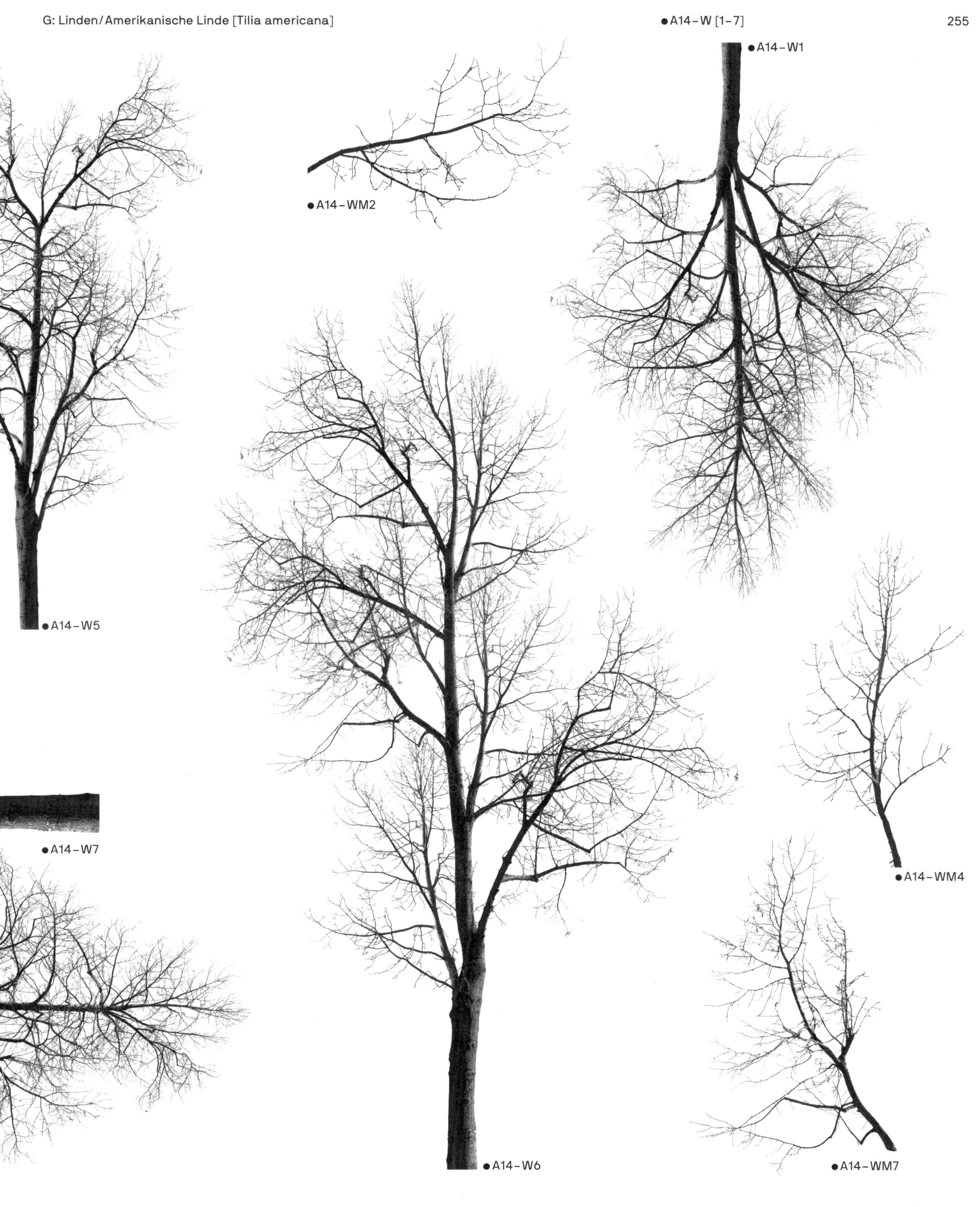
●A14–W [1–7]
●A14–W1
●A14–WM2
●A14–W5
●A14–W7
●A14–WM4
●A14–W6
●A14–WM7

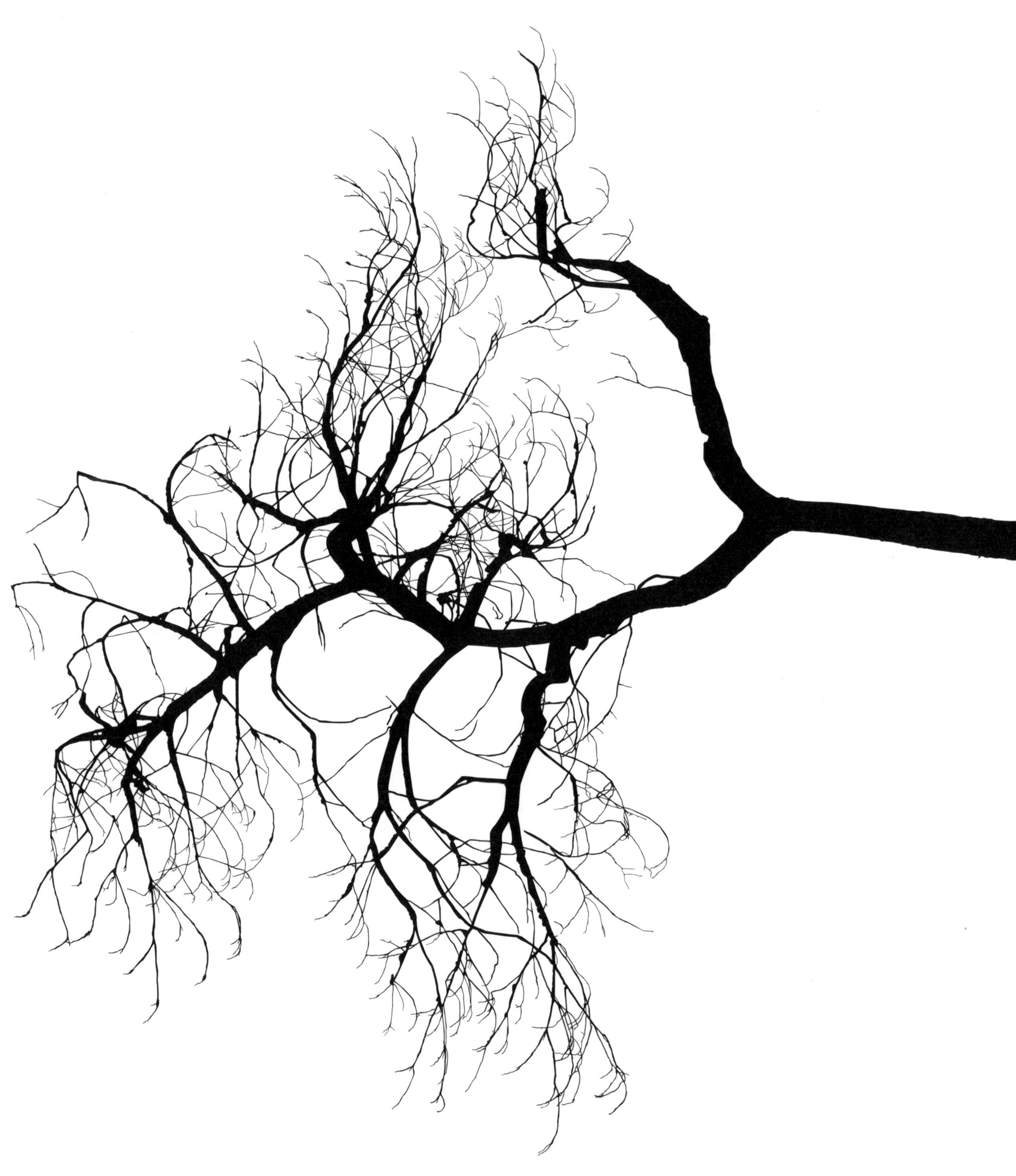

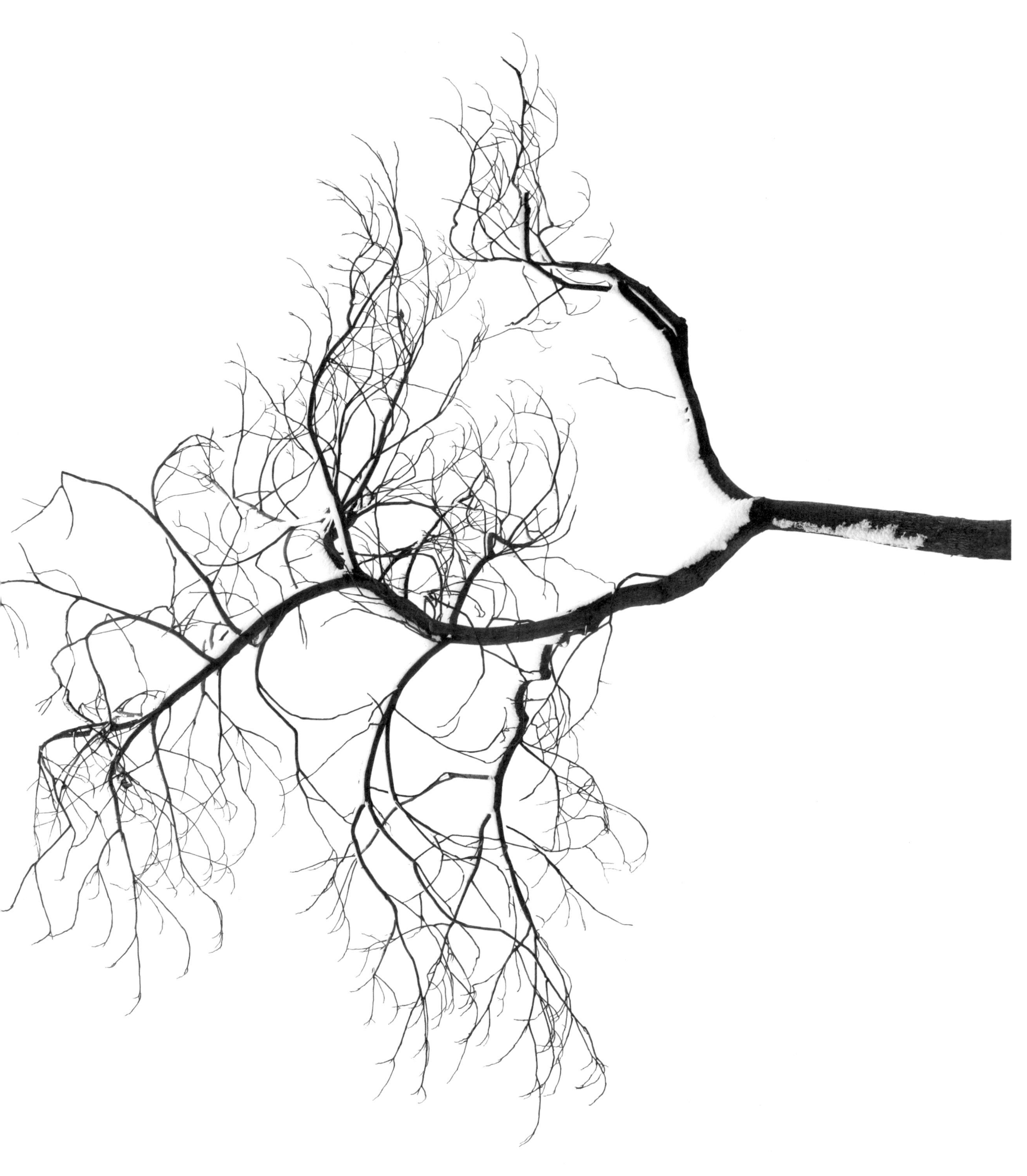

Inventory

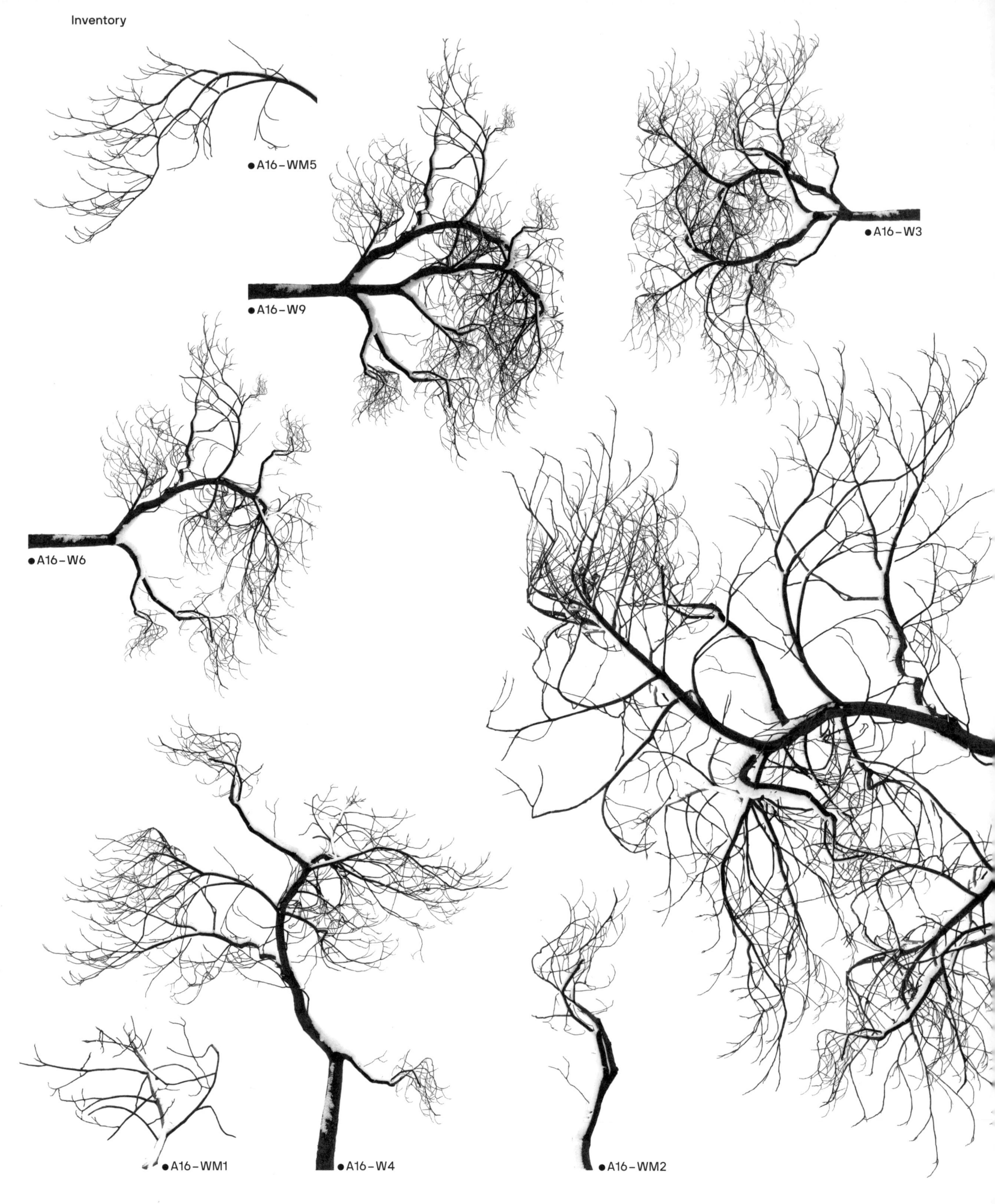

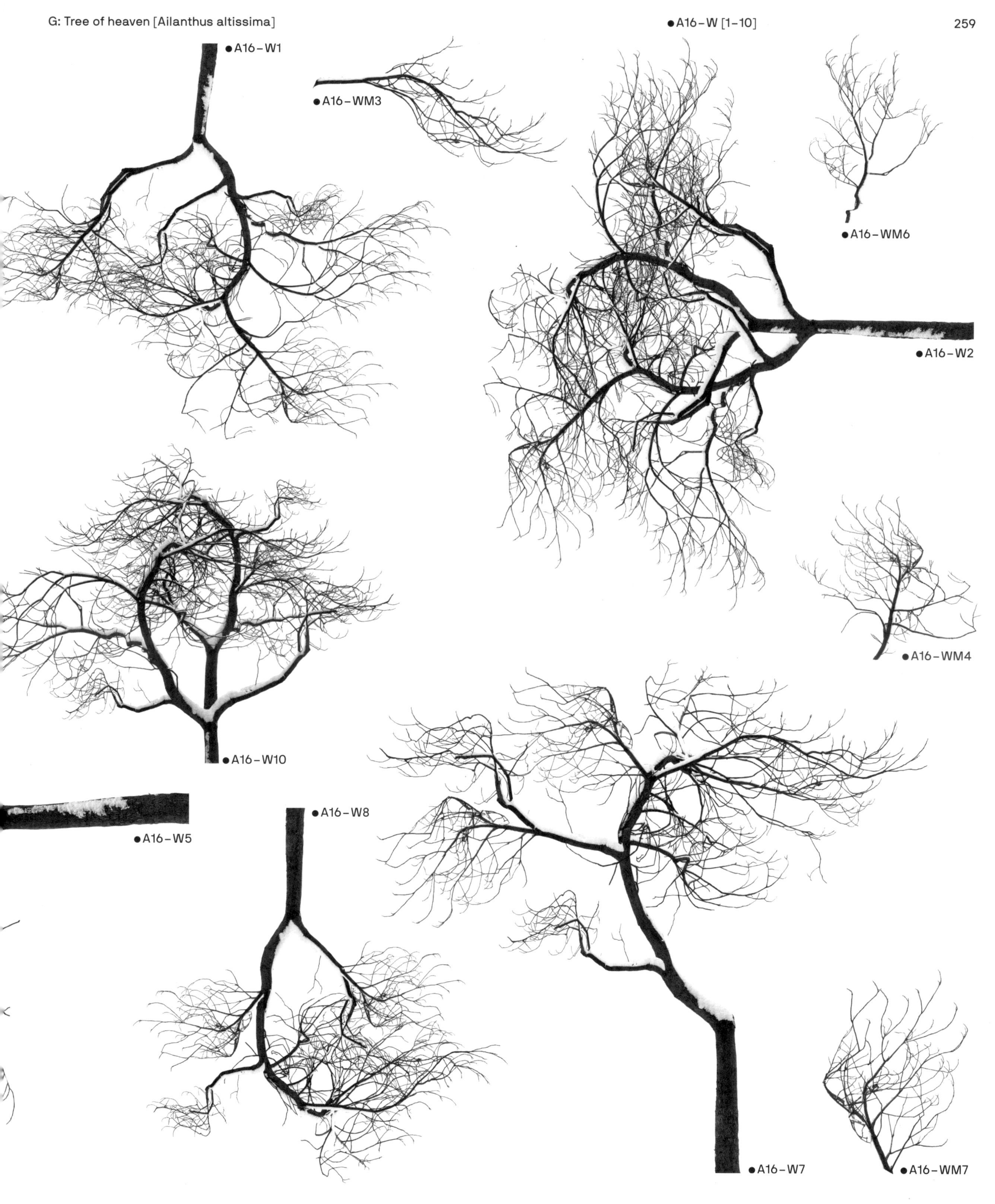
●A16–W1
●A16–WM3
●A16–WM6
●A16–W2
●A16–WM4
●A16–W10
●A16–W5
●A16–W8
●A16–W7
●A16–WM7

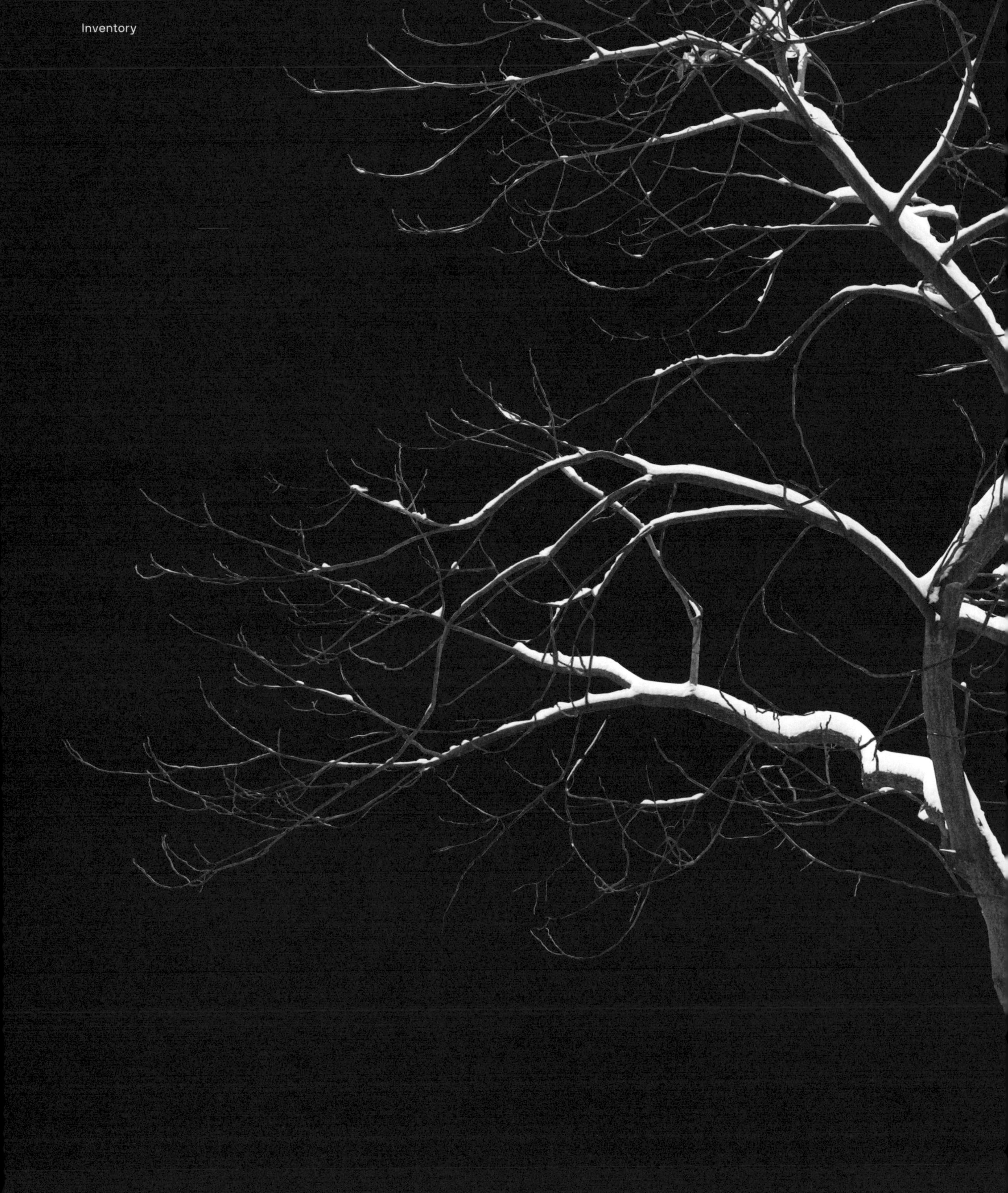

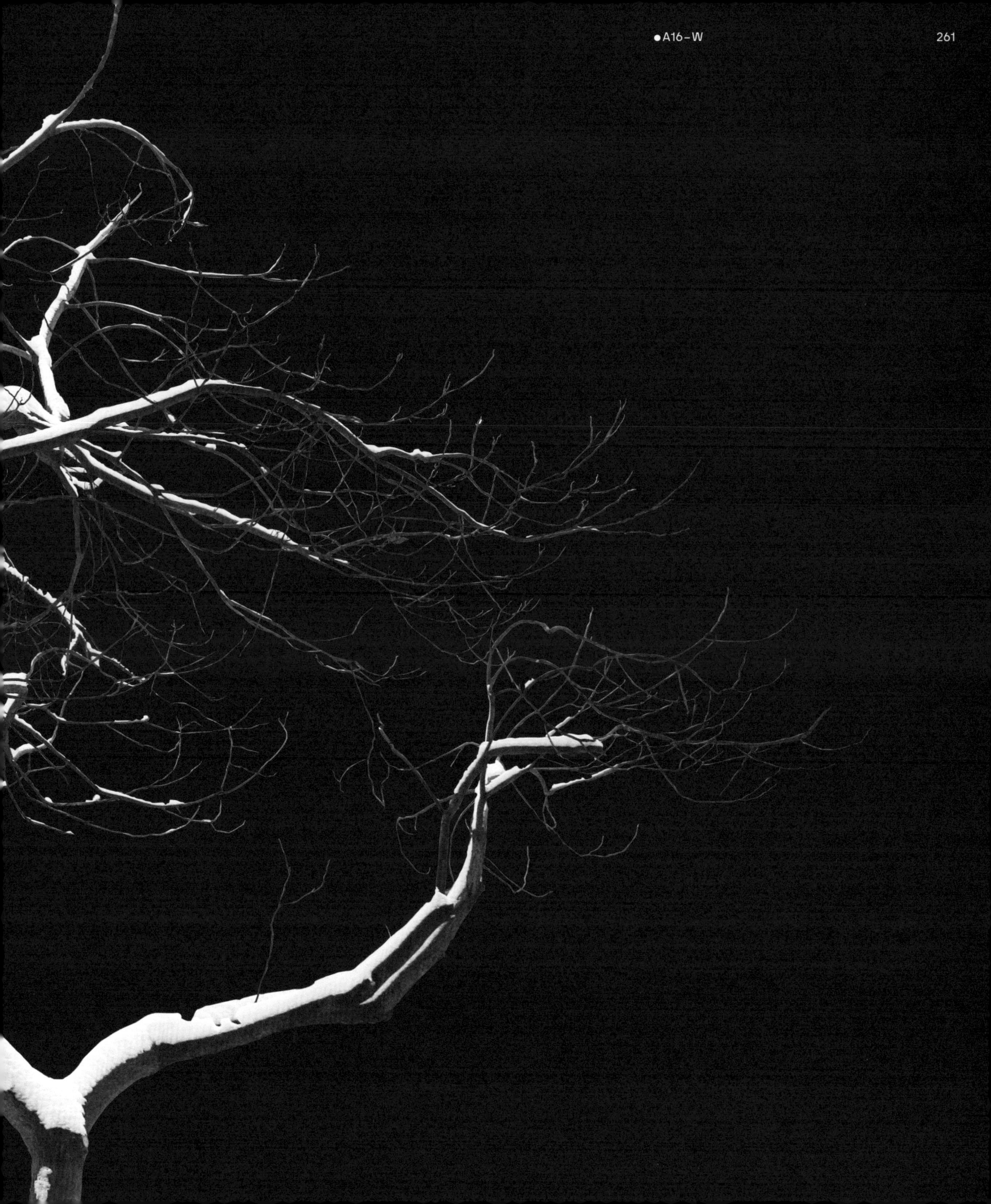

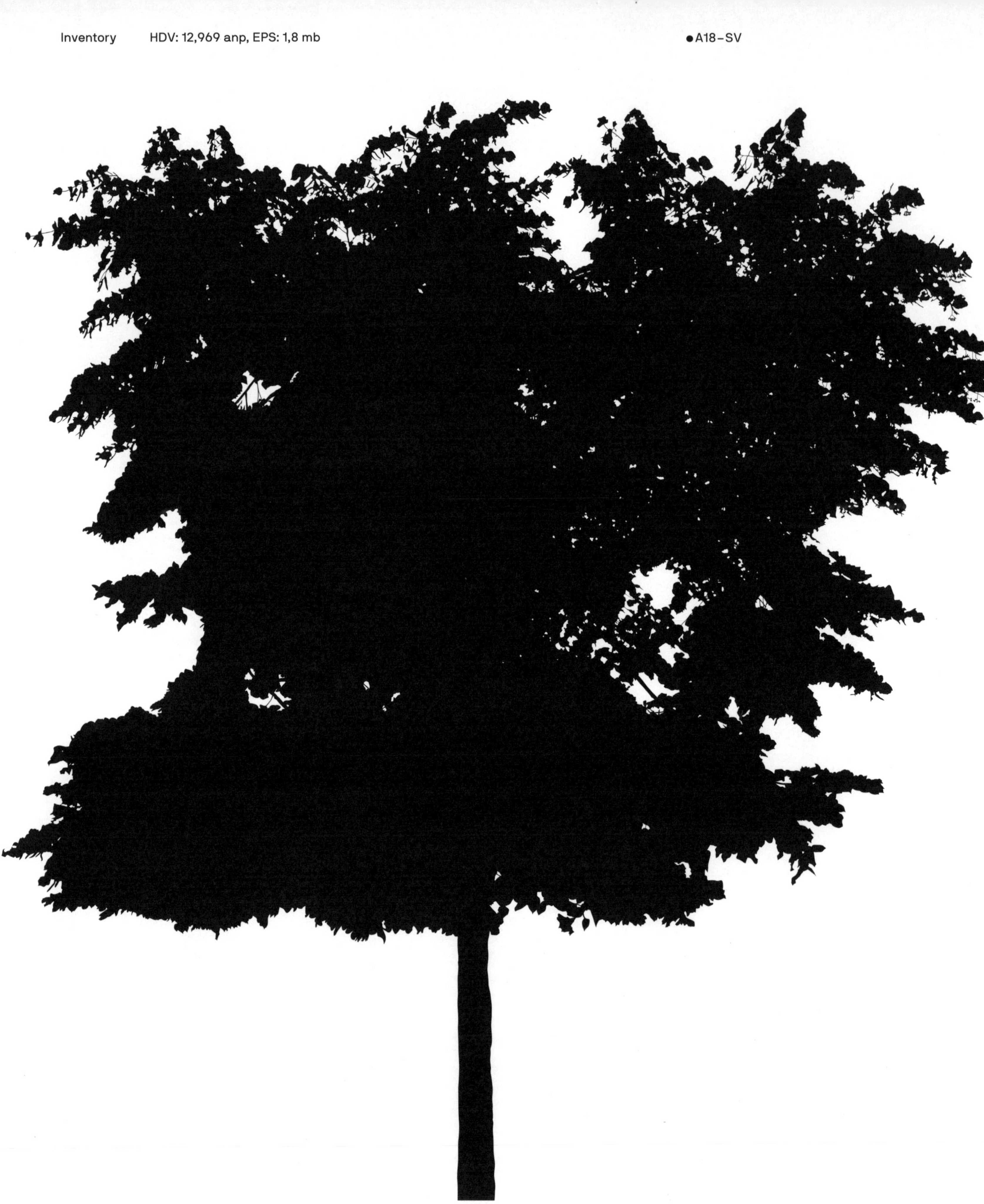

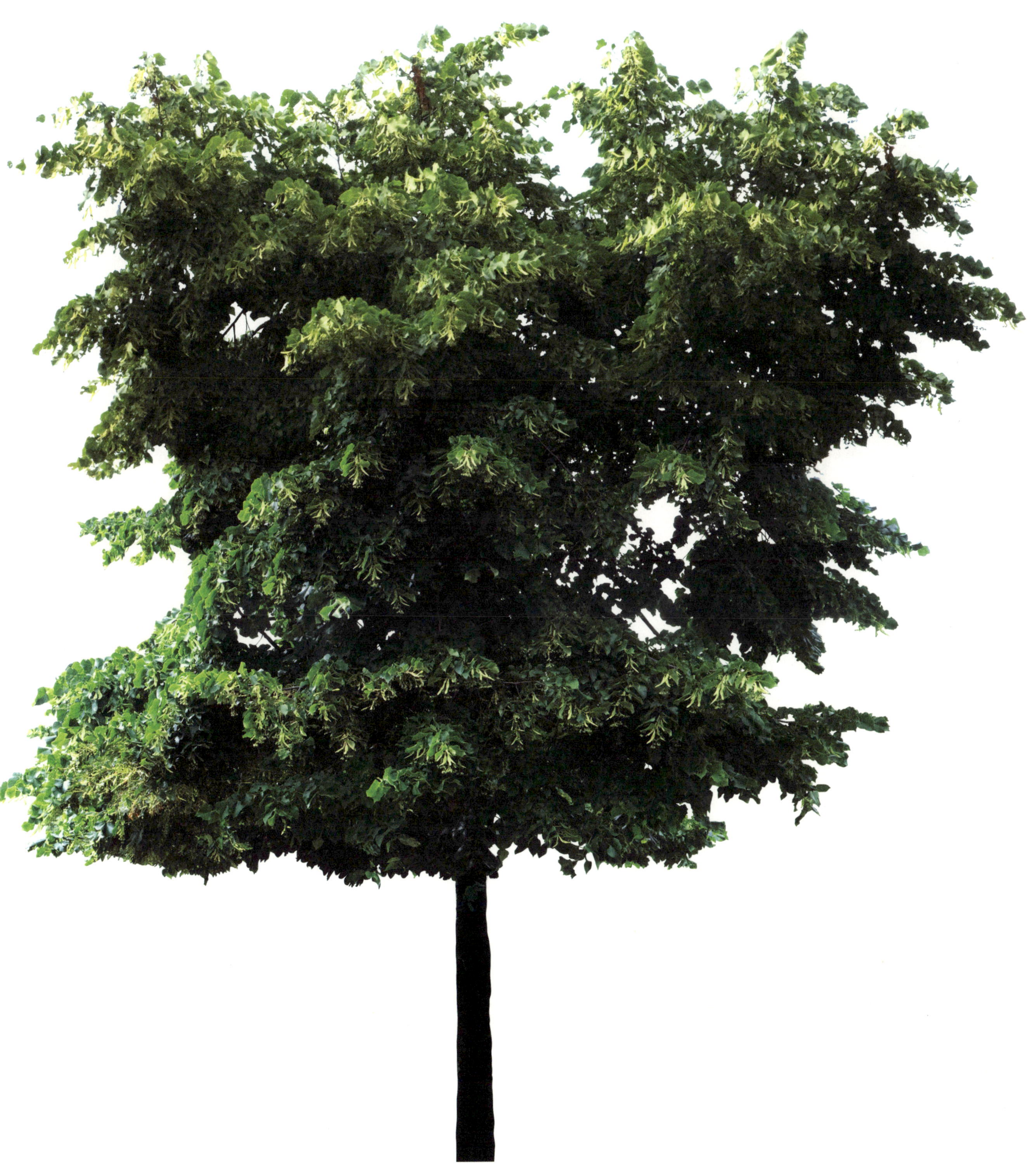

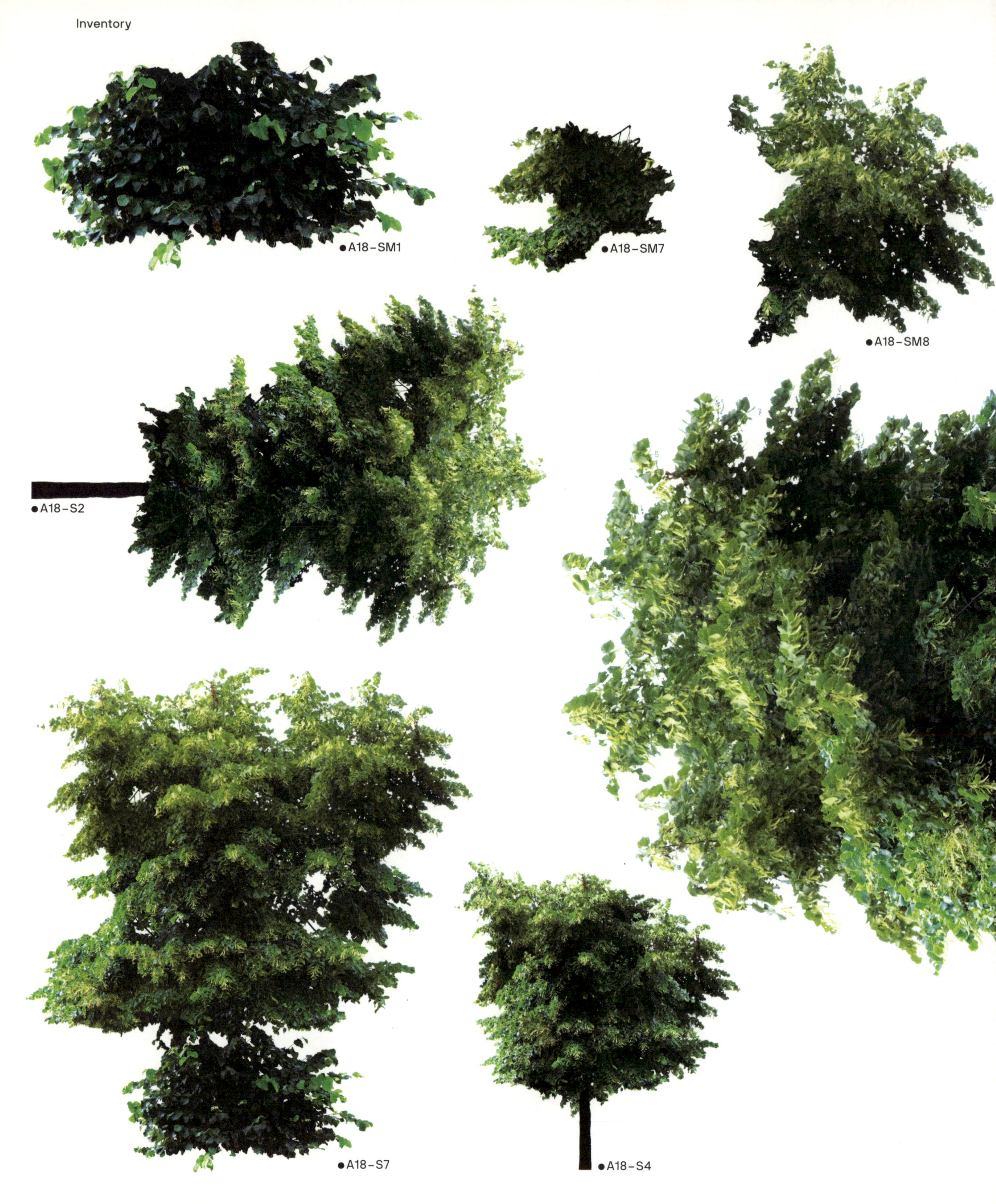

●A18−SM1
●A18−SM7
●A18−SM8
●A18−S2
●A18−S7
●A18−S4

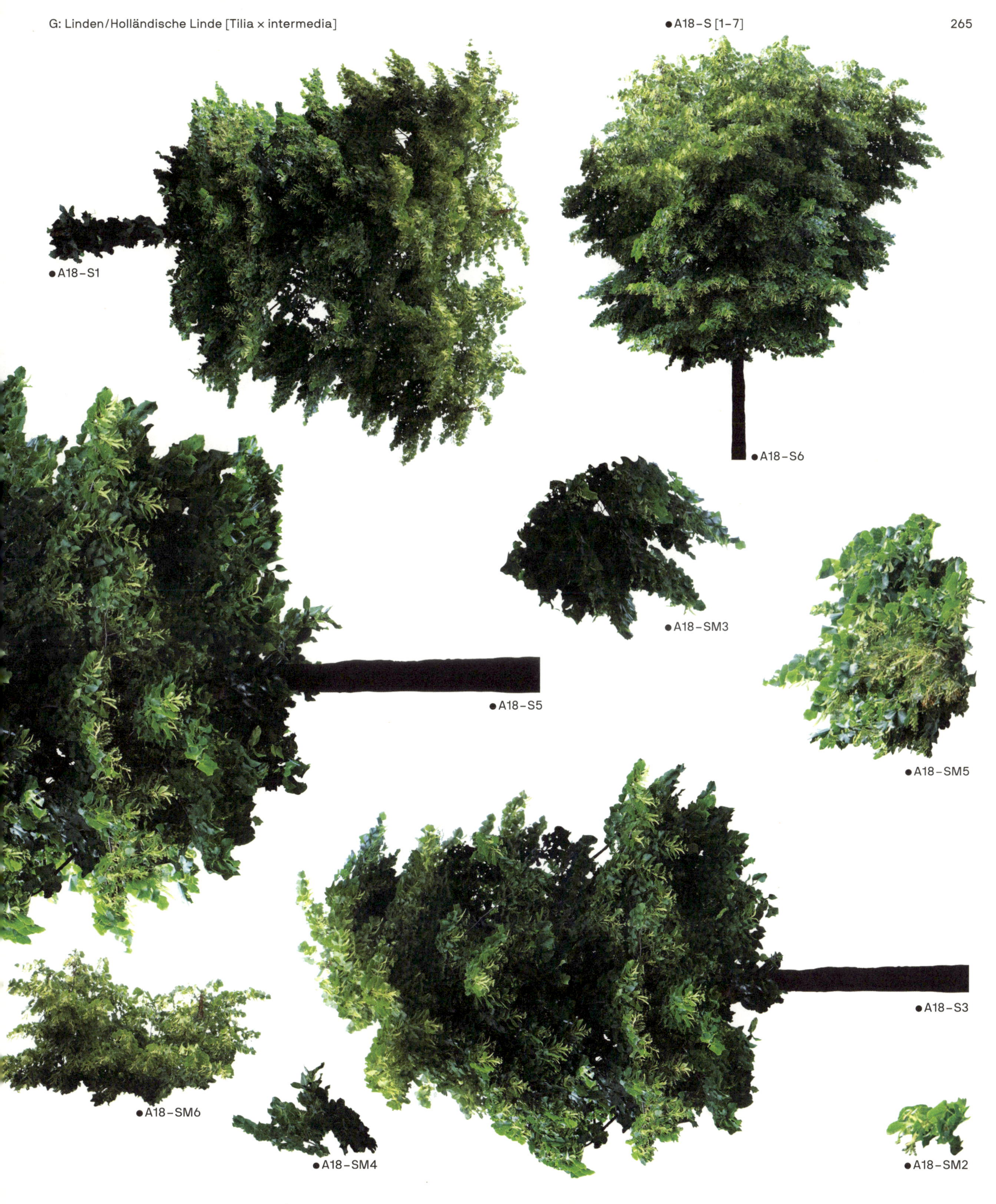
●A18–S1
●A18–S6
●A18–SM3
●A18–S5
●A18–SM5
●A18–S3
●A18–SM6
●A18–SM4
●A18–SM2

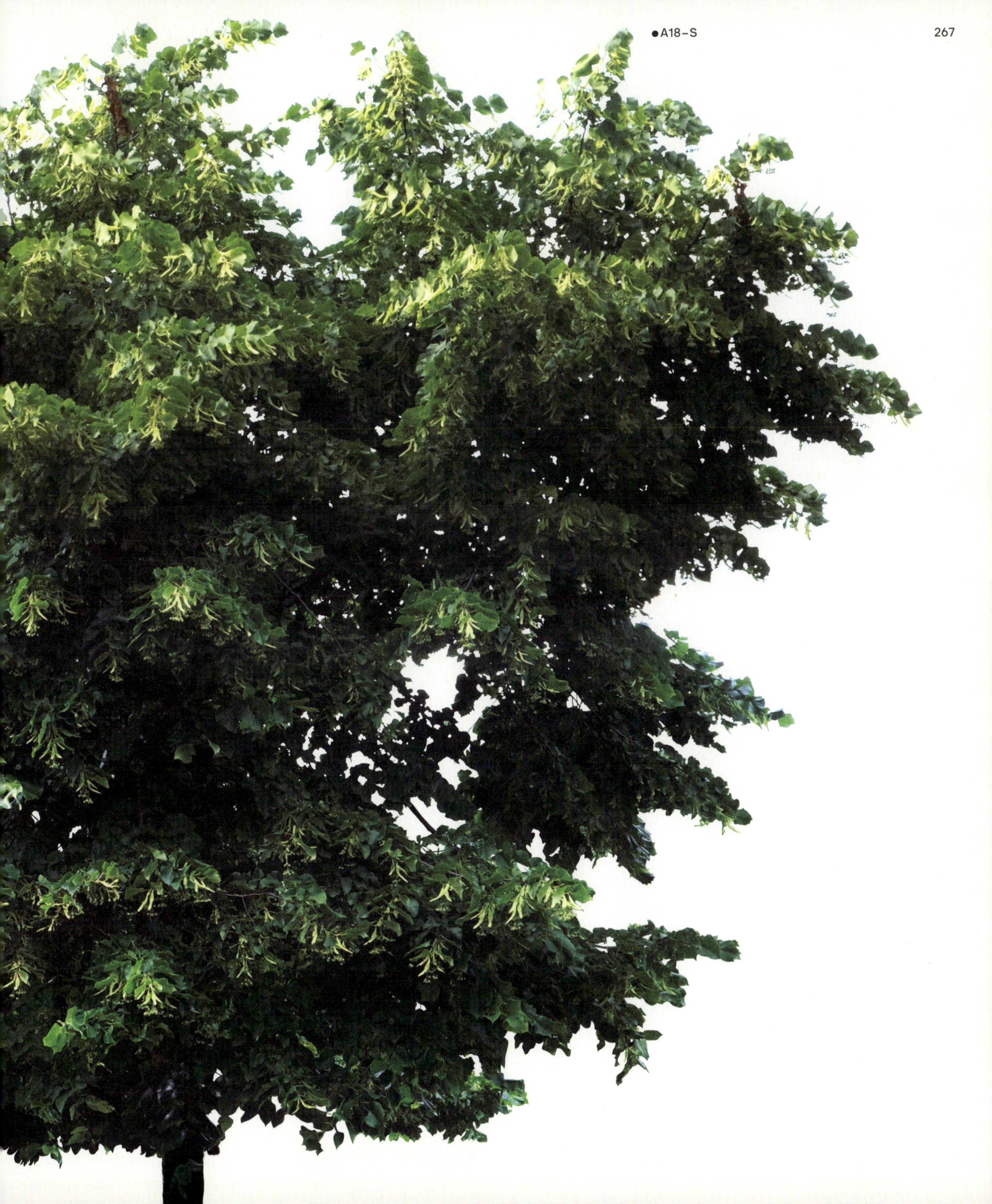

| U7 | W | Locust | [Robinia pseudoacacia] |
| U9 | W | Morello Cherry | [Prunus] |

U7–U9

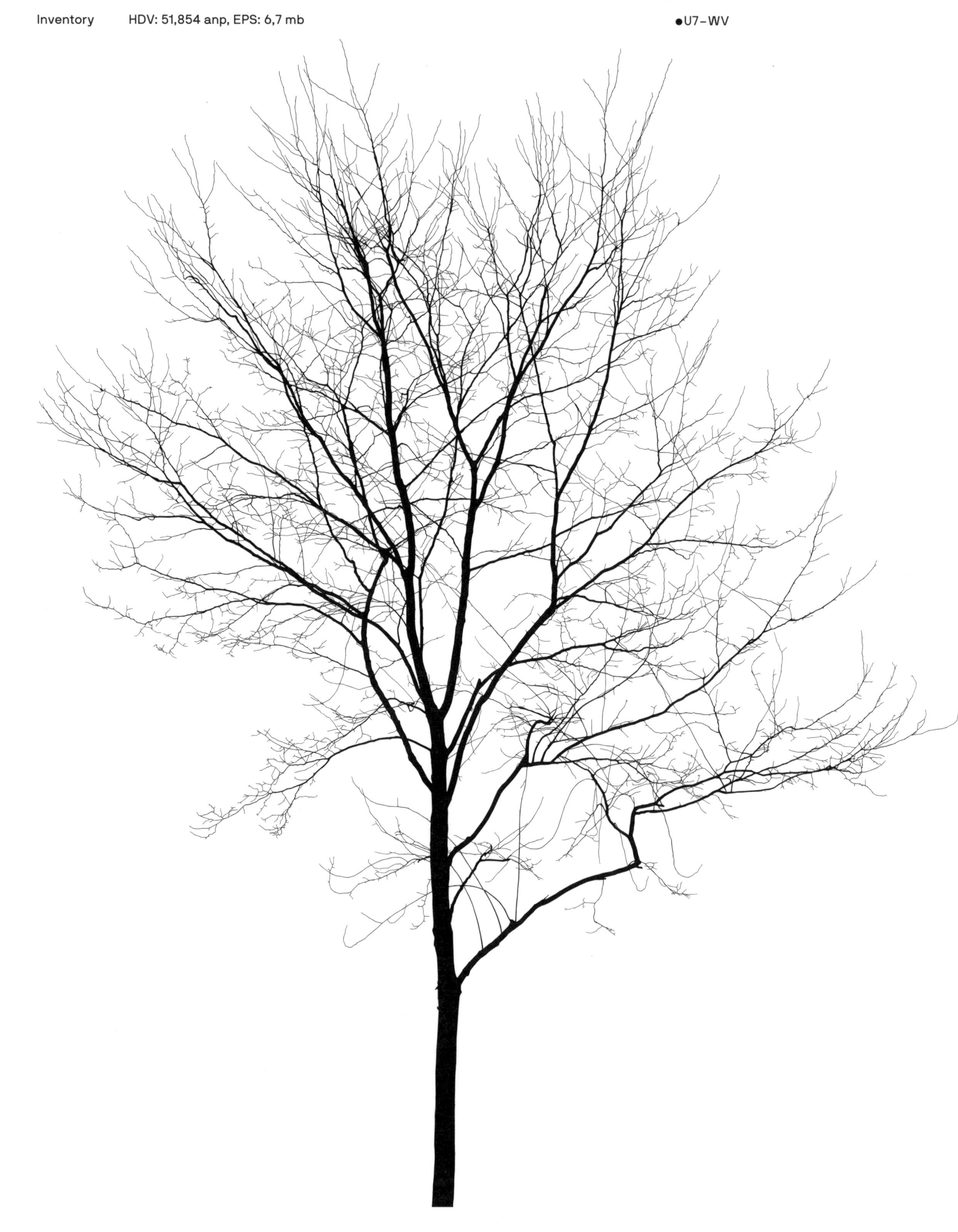

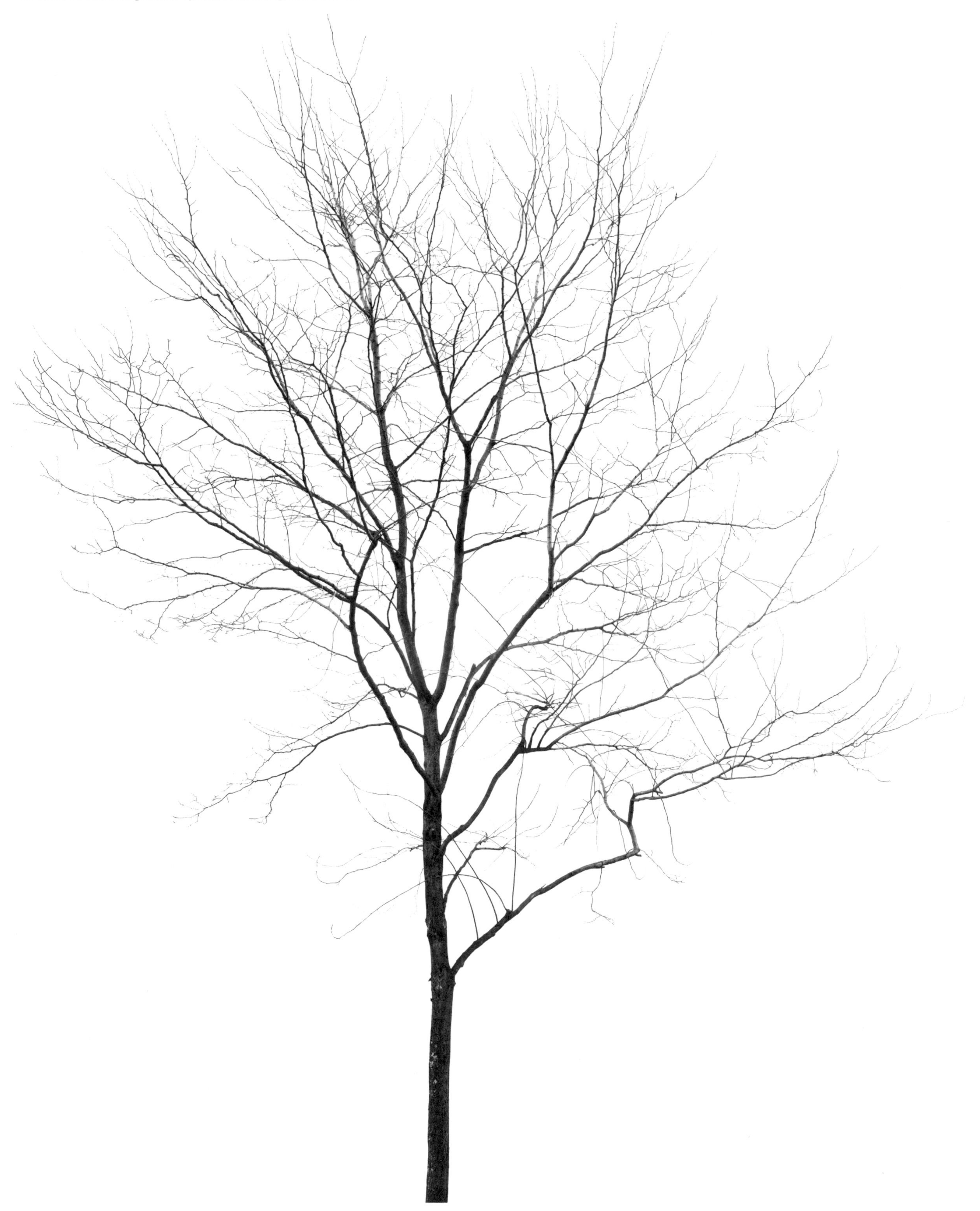

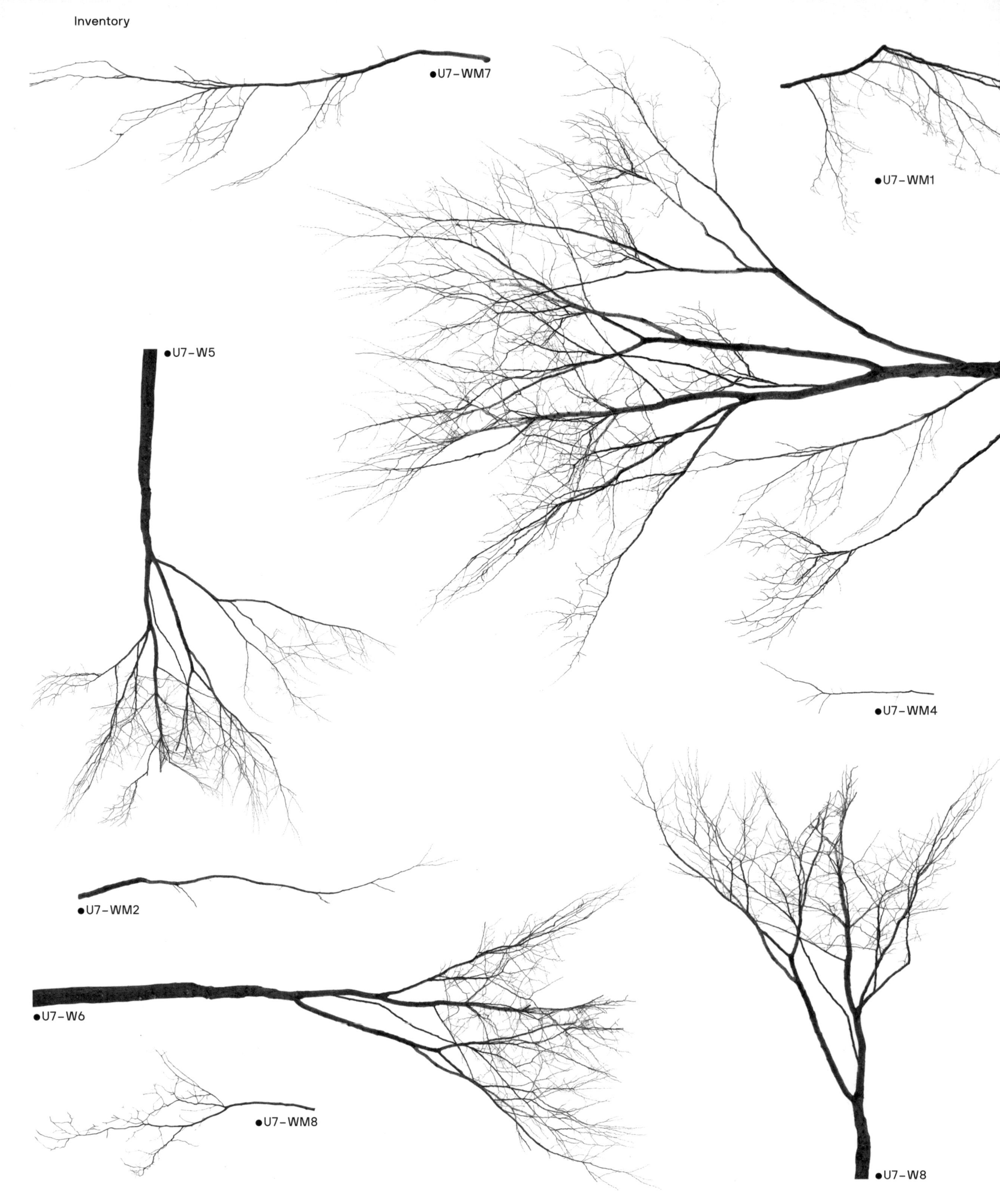

Inventory
U7–WM7
U7–WM1
U7–W5
U7–WM4
U7–WM2
U7–W6
U7–WM8
U7–W8

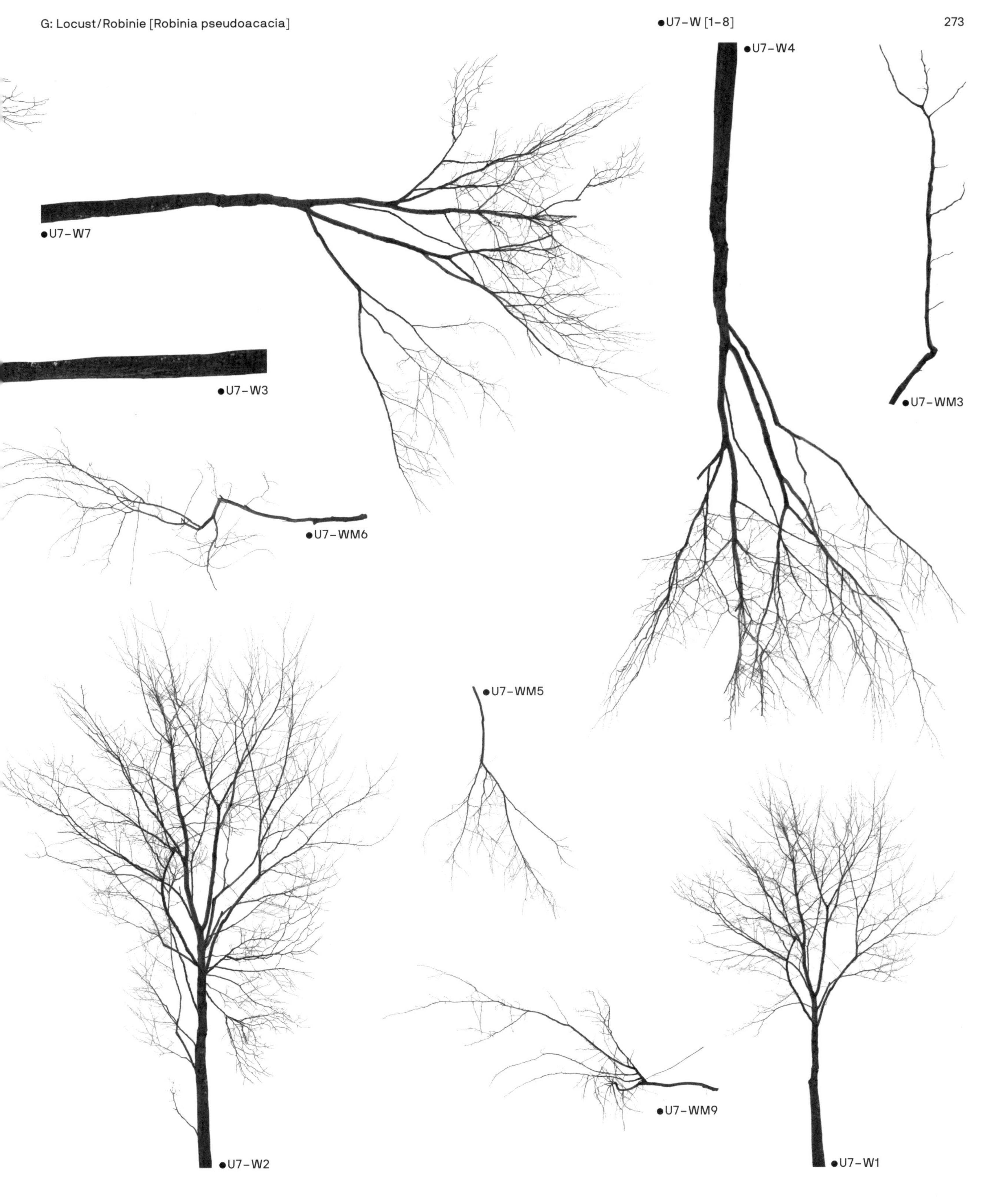
●U7–W [1–8]
●U7–W4
●U7–W7
●U7–W3
●U7–WM3
●U7–WM6
●U7–WM5
●U7–W2
●U7–WM9
●U7–W1

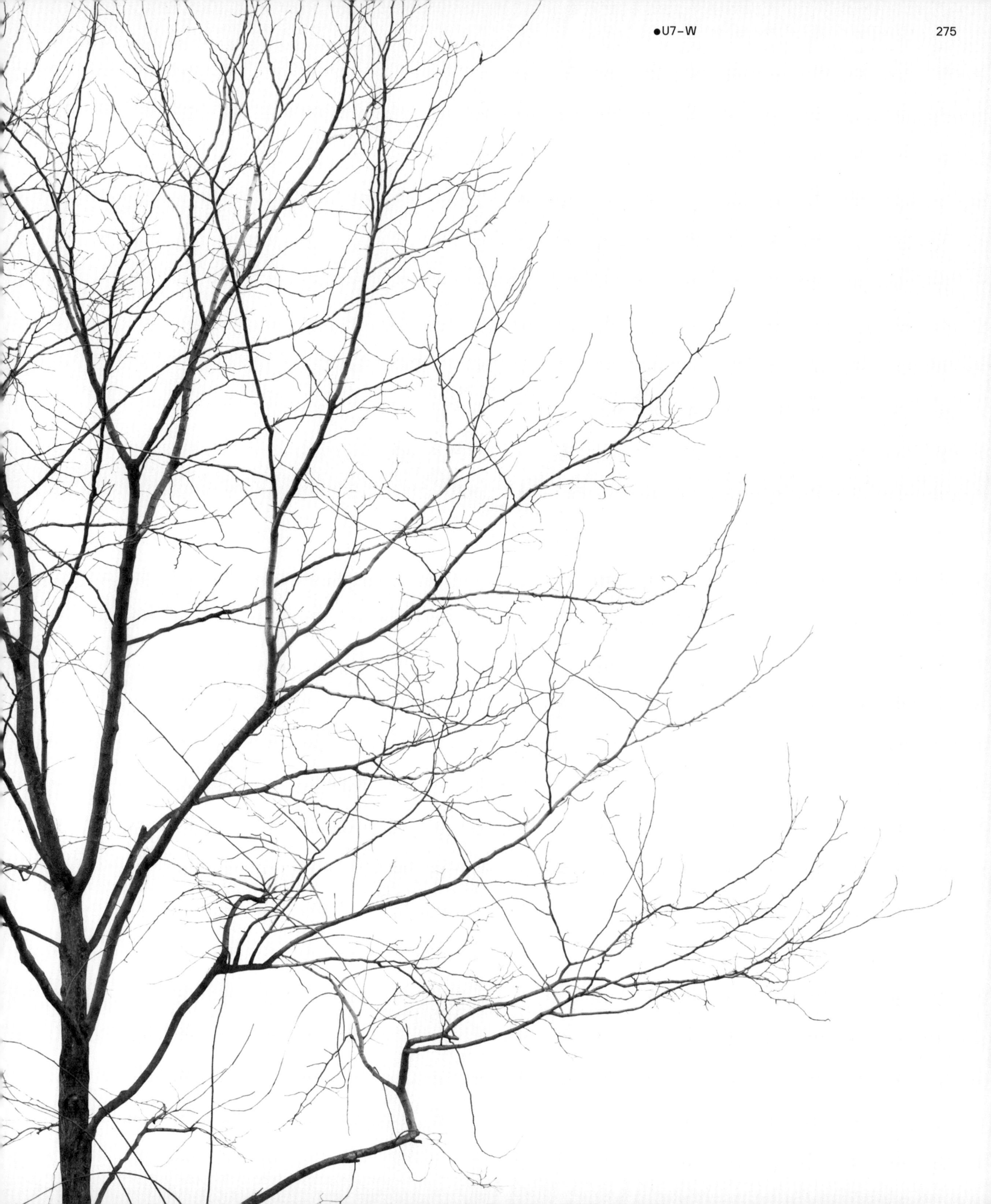

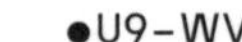

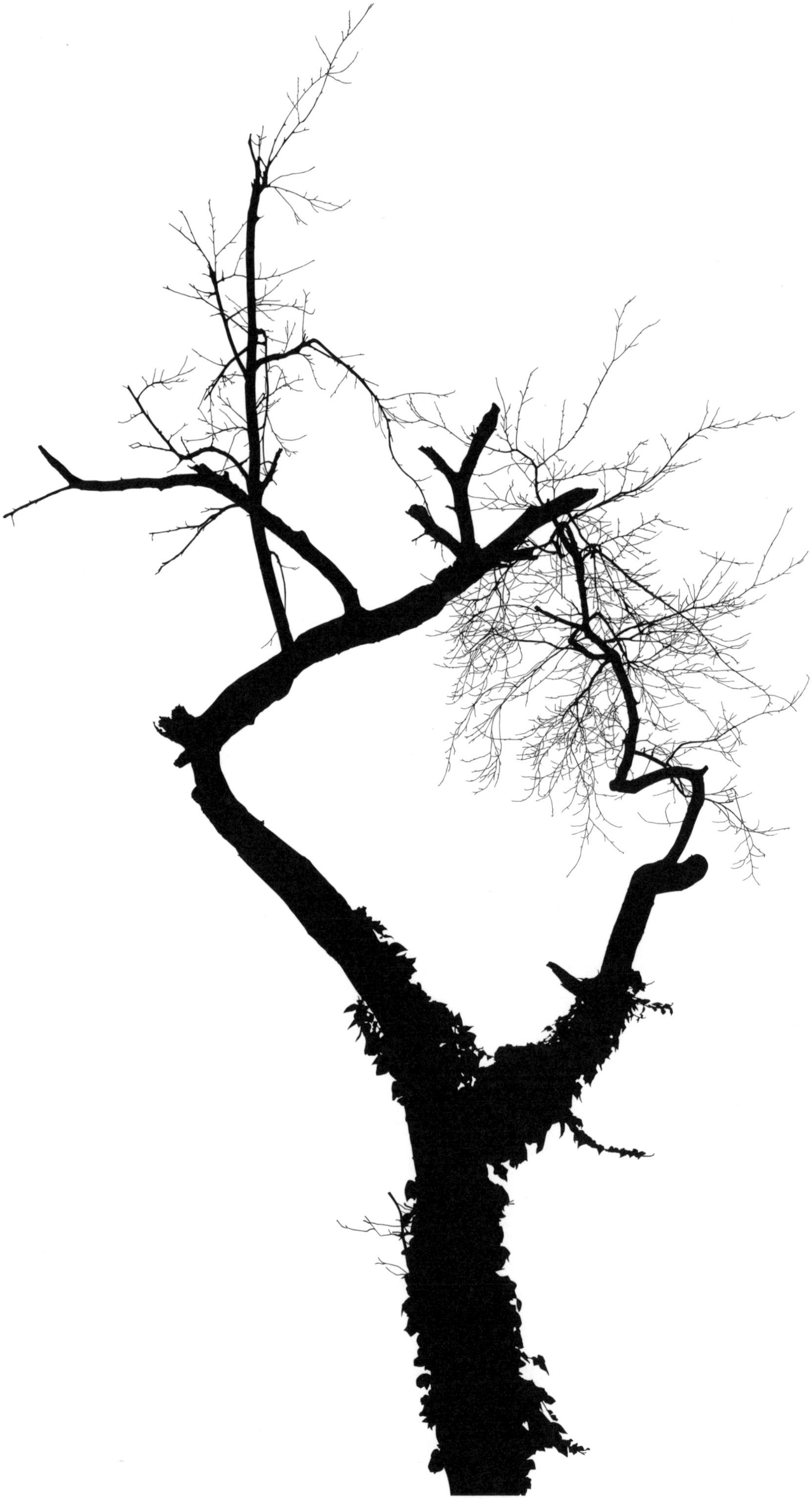

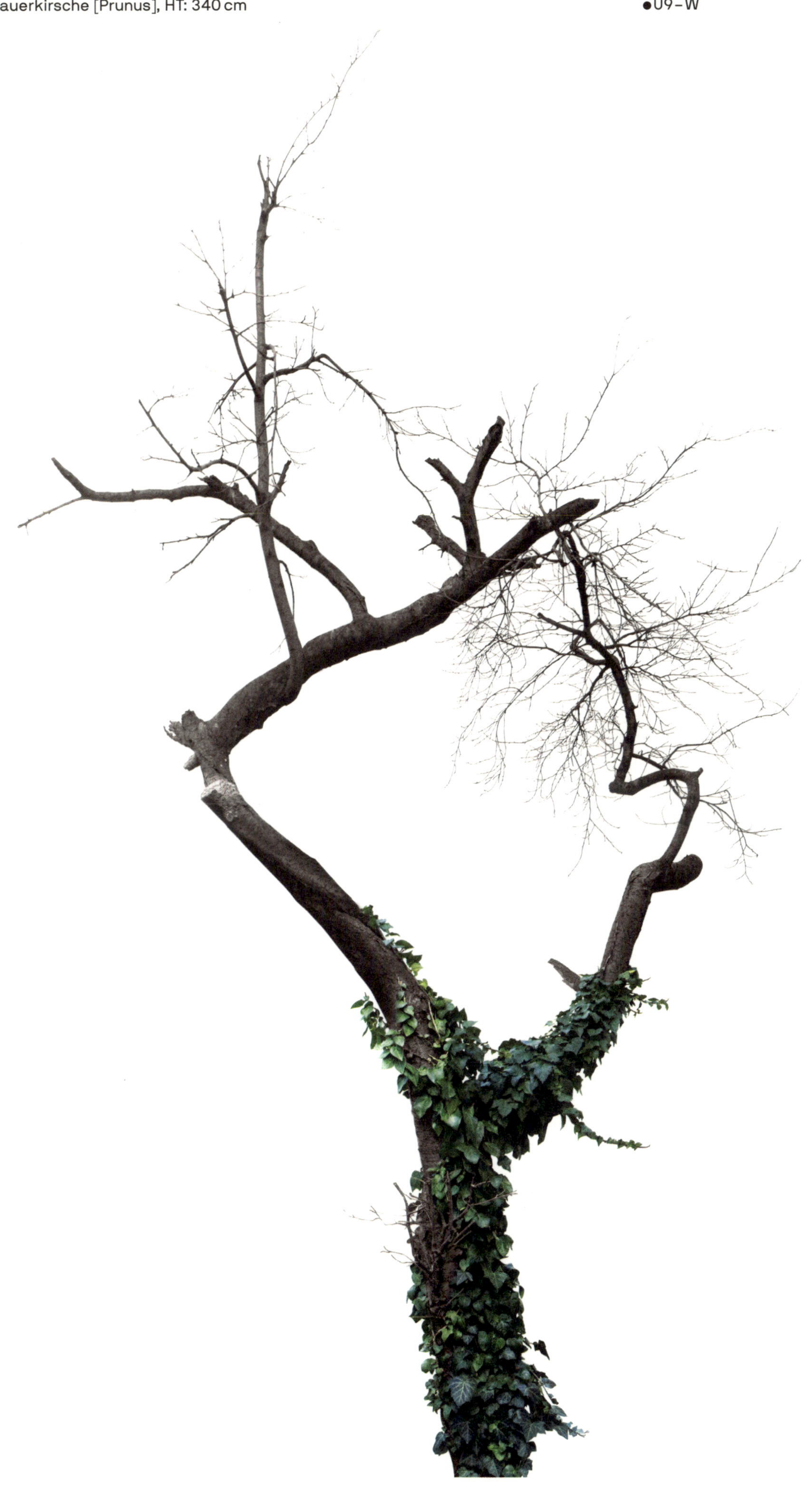

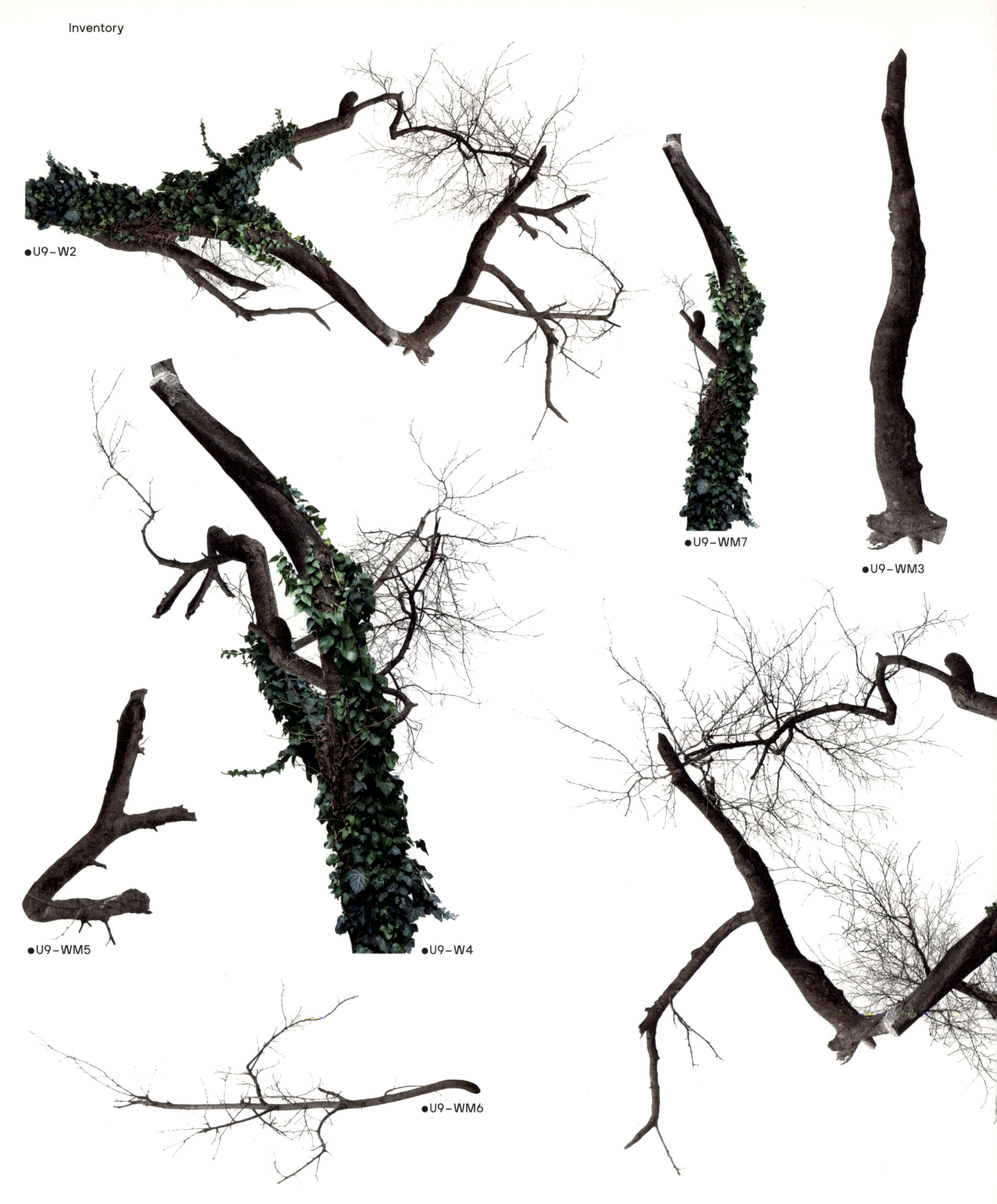
●U9–W2
●U9–WM7
●U9–WM3
●U9–WM5
●U9–W4
●U9–WM6

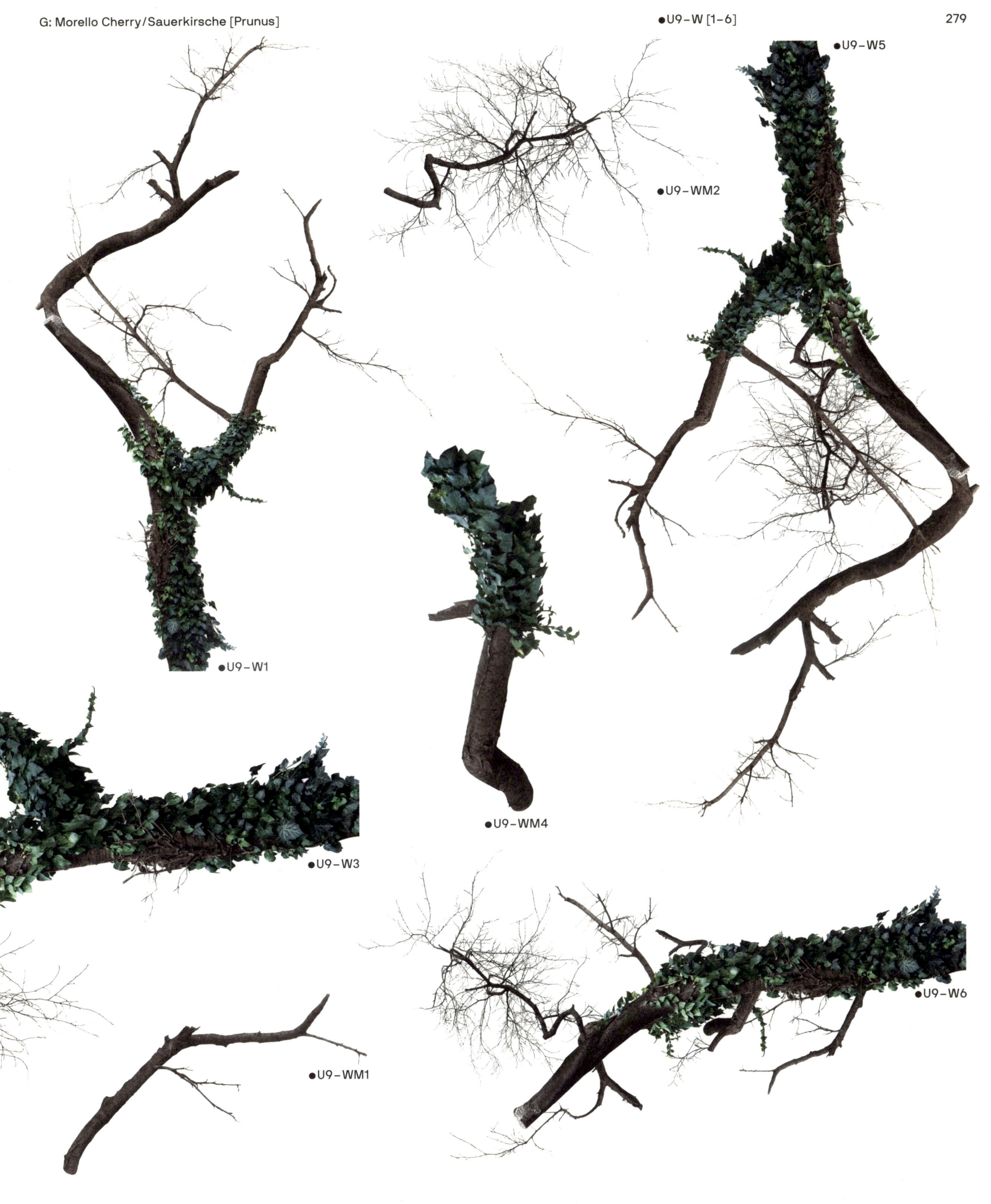
●U9–W [1–6]
●U9–W5
●U9–WM2
●U9–W1
●U9–W3
●U9–WM4
●U9–WM1
●U9–W6

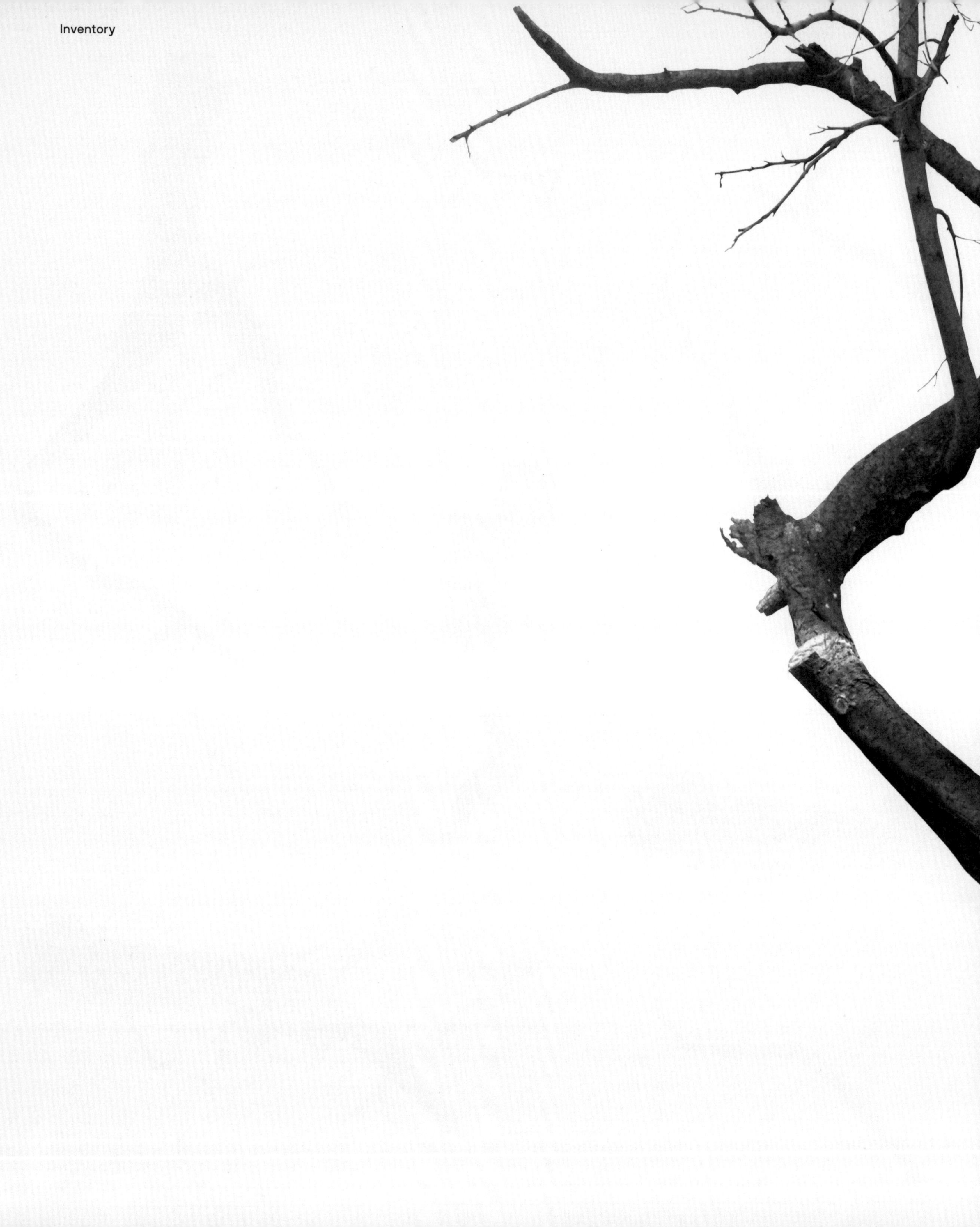

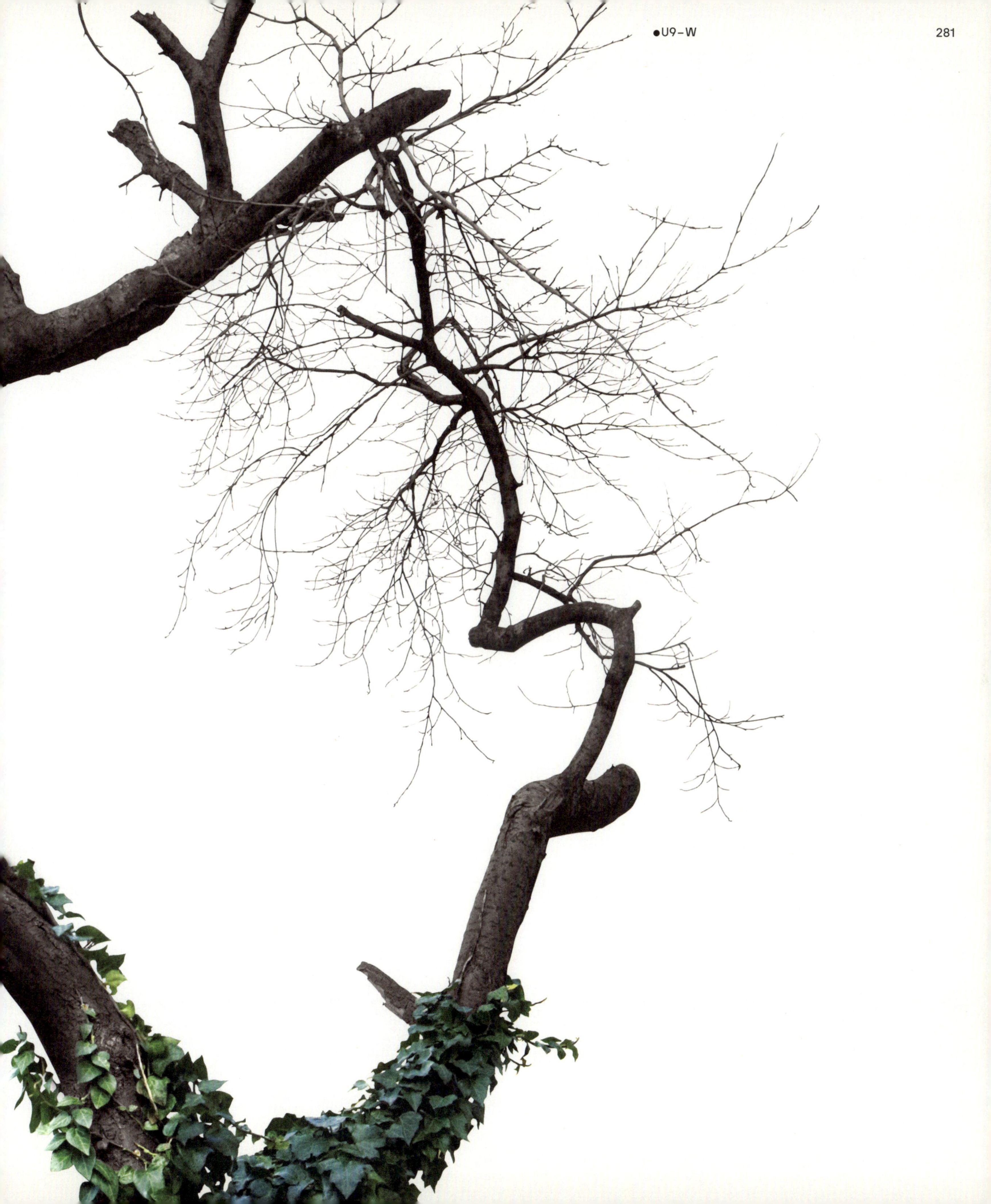

Inside Forst

Lars Müller in conversation with Stefan Gandl and Benjamin Ganz

LM: Before we talk in depth about the collaboration between Lars Müller Publishers and Neubau, and the product of this collaboration, the 'Neubau Forst Catalogue', let's go back in time. In September 2008 Wim Crouwel opened the 'Neubauism' exhibition at the renowned MU Eindhoven in the Netherlands. 'Neubauism' was the title of the first comprehensive survey and the museum installation of your two archival publications, 'Neubau Welt' (2005) and 'Neubau Modul' (2007).

What motivated Neubau to spend the next five years in the 'forest', assembling an archive of trees – why trees in the first place? Was that planned from the start?

SG: We didn't plan to spend five years on 'Forst'. I based the plans on the approximate time frame of the other two publications, reckoning on two to three years, and this was a complete miscalculation. But we were entering new territory again and a project lasts as long as it takes to finish it.

As to the situation at the beginning: at the time of the 'Neubauism' exhibition, both of our books, 'Neubau Welt' and 'Neubau Modul' had just sold out again. We bought up the remainders and made them available as part of the 'Neubauism' box set published in conjunction with the exhibition.

One of our personal heroes, Wim Crouwel, opened our show with an introduction he wrote for our exhibition publication. The archives we developed were used by our design contemporaries worldwide, finding their way into newspapers, magazines, websites, textbooks, into global advertising, TV adverts, music videos, into fashion and art; they found entry into museums, were used in architecture, appeared in product designs, corporate branding, etc. And on the side these two books also brought Neubau many exciting new clients. To sum it

up: 'Neubauism' took us to a new apex, both personally and professionally. At that point in time Christoph Grünberger and I had actually achieved everything on our wish list. It was the right time to retreat, think things over, and spend some time in the forest, metaphorically speaking.

BG: Two bestsellers published within just two years, containing a total of more than 3,000 objects, the 'Neubauism' exhibition opened by Crouwel – at that point, pausing the expansion of the Neubau archive would certainly have been justified.

We could have spent all of our time simply taking care of our clients' projects. After all, over the past decade Neubau has set the bar higher with every project – certain things were expected of us. So, if we were going to continue, it would have to be with a project that would overshadow everything else, including the two previous books. And, as Stefan has already said, 'retreating to the forest' is meant metaphorically; it has nothing at all to do with rest and relaxation … because we didn't relax one bit, on the contrary.

SG: And to return to the question of why trees in the first place – I would like to see this answered on two levels: ostensibly, practical use and the existing market niche, then the ideal value and the symbolic effect of making something apparently impossible possible. After all, we could have spent five years messing about with cars, or publishing the obligatory studio monograph ('10 Years of Neubau') – but that would have been too easy and stereotypical.

One of the things that led to the 'Forst' project was the archive of tools that the two other books had already established. There was no comparable work, no manually developed

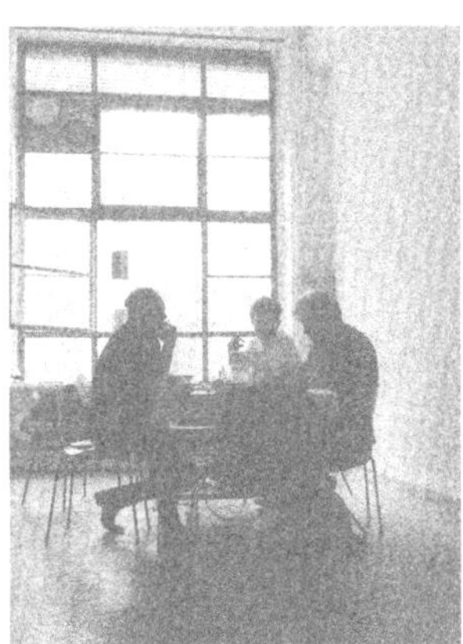

SG, BG, LM
Neubau, Studio / Berlin
July, 2014

library of trees that came close to covering the print quality, number, and attention to detail now offered in 'Neubau Forst Catalogue'. Today's market offers badly isolated trees by lacking knowledge of editing tools instead of proper vector masks or poorly rendered trees that relate too closely to tracing techniques in popular software applications that looks accordingly computer-generated. To get isolated tree sculptures, various species, in summer – as well as in wintertime, shot from the same angle and perspective, and additional tree modules to create an endless number of new trees is a novelty which wasn't available to architects and visualisation studios prior to 'Neubau Forst'. Thanks to 'Neubau Welt' and the reactions to the vector objects used around the world, we already had a good idea of which themes from our archive were popular and should be expanded. Also, we had already had some successful commercial experiences with vector trees in particular. In 2007, when we received a significant commission to create a vector forest silhouette, we were the only ones who were capable of solving such a difficult task, and of providing the necessary quality and details within the given time period. This opened up another market niche for us, and confirmed that our appropriated vector craftsmanship was not just a mad idea.

BG: After all, every graphic designer thinks that he can easily vectorise a tree by hand. Most of those who try it give it up two days afterwards, at the latest. It's amazing. You need a good deal of patience and conviction to do it. From this perspective, 'Neubau Forst' is also a consequential response to the two previous publications. You take what is by far the most complicated theme as far as vector illustrations are concerned – the tree – and add another degree of difficulty by departing from the pure black-and-white illustration and including the real image. With the source photo integrated into the final artwork, there's no room for cheating or deception.

For 'Forst', we not only explored our own limitations but, above all, the limitations of the available software. In 2002, when Stefan began using Macromedia® Freehand® to make the vector trees for 'Neubau Welt', he realised that even though the software had saved a set of data containing 32,000 hand-set vector points, it was, surprisingly enough, no longer able to open it. Of course, no handbook mentions this anchor point limit. Apparently, nobody else dealt with those kinds of problems as we did. That was very frustrating, because the data, which took days to create, were lost. It wasn't until Neubau started using Adobe® Illustrator® that we were able to create more complicated paths. A winter vector tree in 'Neubau Welt' already has up to 82,000 anchor points set by hand, which took four days of work. In comparison, a single vector tree in 'Neubau Forst' has up to 120,000 manually set anchor points, and some of them took up to three months to create.

LM: During our work together I visited your studio here in Berlin several times; we've had many intense conversations and excited discussions. This has also given me a very different perspective of the project and the work methods. I now know that software limitations were not the only hurdles that had to be overcome during this protracted project.

SG: In 2009, in order to integrate both the studio commissions, as well as such a complicated project as the 'Neubau Forst Catalogue' into the everyday work process, I had to first of all gather the right team together in Berlin. Although relatively small teams of up to eight people completed the other two books within periods of two to three years, 'Forst' was a completely different undertaking, an entirely new experience. Ultimately, there were twenty designers involved in 'Neubau Forst' during the years 2009 to 2014. Christoph Grünberger and Paul Heys supported the project from the beginning, albeit from afar. I began working on 'Forst' in Berlin in 2009 with a small team consisting of myself, Jörg Petri, and later, Marius Hanf. In 2010 we were joined by Miriam Busch, Margarida Castel Branco, and Cezanne Noordhoek. In 2011 the project really took off, and François Leherissier, Benjamin Ganz, Akane Sakai, David Pope, Daniel Cottis, Bhav Mistry, Tom Holmes, Will Smith, Oriol Salles, and Moritz Otten were added to the team. Marine Stephane, Maximilian Voormann, and Robert Loeber followed in 2012. The final 'Neubau Forst' team was an international troupe, welded together by motivation and not least by the fact that everyone involved knew that this was a once-in-a-lifetime opportunity – no other studio at the time was doing anything remotely similar. This made us a committed, unique club.

When the project began, it wasn't clear to us how we would be able to photograph the trees in high resolution; did we want to work with photographers, or do it ourselves? In order to remain spontaneous and flexible, we decided upon the latter. We assumed that we would have to photograph the trees in front of a monochrome background, do something along the lines of the fascinating works of art by the South Korean photographer Myoung Ho Lee.[01] Ho Lee took photographs of trees outdoors, using an oversized white canvas as a background. The idea of running about the countryside lugging a twenty-five-square-metre roll of fabric had a touch of DIY, craftsmanship, and back-to-the-roots about it, but it was entirely unsuited to 'Forst'. We decided to do a test series using solitary trees in the Hartz Forest (Germany). The advantage of these freestanding trees was that we would have a mostly monochromatic sky for a background. Pictures of the first trees were actually quite impressive. In order to get high-resolution photographic data, we took several individual photos of the tree and then later assembled them like a puzzle [02] to recreate the tree. To avoid the trying process of assembling photo puzzles by hand, we first used a special panorama software to create the mega-data. Later, Adobe® Photoshop® took care of that for us. Even though we still had to do some corrections afterwards, it nevertheless saved us a great deal of time.

LM: But how did you bring the tree theme to the city, to Berlin? You did ask some photographer friends about obtaining a 'white background without a roll of fabric'. You mentioned that suggestions such as artificial fog, or even infrared photography, were not particularly encouraging or practical. Why did you originally believe that you had to have a monochrome background?

SG: You could also say, 'If you're too close, you can't see the forest for the trees'. The advantage of having a monochrome background for trees is that it reduces the surrounding noise of branches and leaves. But that was a classic error in thought; we thought: 'perfect background, perfect photo-illustration'. At the time it simply wasn't clear to us that we had already tested the solution and could use this technique to take real trees, as we did in 'Neubau Welt', out of the urban environment and isolated them from the background. It wasn't until I was on the train, watching out of the windows as the blurry trees sped past, that it dawned on me: if Neubau is known for its perfect, faithfully detailed vector illustrations, then the quality of the background wouldn't matter at all as long as the photographs were of sufficient quality.

BG: And, in fact, this method of distillation worked. So we were able to realise the photographs in Berlin, leave the country and go back to our urban space. Then, in order to do

01.
Myong Ho Lee
Photographer (*1975)
Yossi Milo Gallery (NY)
yossimilo.com

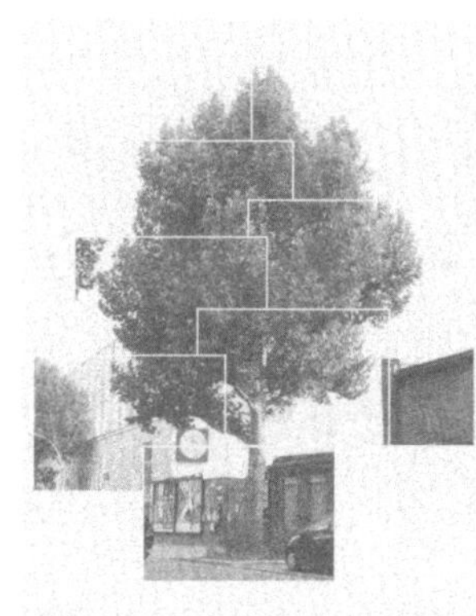

02.
Large-scale compositions of trees created from puzzles of photographs which were then merged to obtain a sufficient image resolution

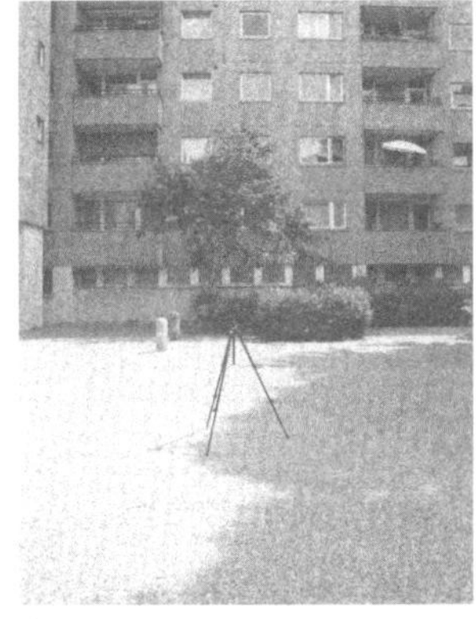

03.
NBF-Manual
Neubau (2009)
(Hanf, M., Gandl, S.)

04.
Position documentation in order to shoot the tree sculptures from the same perspective and angle in different seasons

justice to the name of the studio, Neubau Berlin, the theme of the next work had to have something to do directly with the studio and Berlin. Only then would the printed book be authentic. So the first attempts at photographing trees in the city were successful, and by then it was time to solve the next problem – the continous homogeneity of the archive – so we had to achieve a unified style of drawing. If you are illustrating as a collective, then it's quite possible for each and every illustration to be in a different style. We absolutely had to avoid this, just as we had to for 'Neubau Welt'. This problem arose not only because we were working within a big team, but also because we had already documented so many different types of trees. The solution for this problem came from the 'NBF Tree Manual'[03].

SG: Yes, it was Marius who made the breakthrough, solving it by establishing guidelines for illustrating a tree for 'Neubau Forst'. In the manual 'NBF: How to draw a tree', we established how to match up the sizes of the photographs, how large a drawing of a tree should be in comparison to other species, as well as how far you can zoom in on details when the vectors of the outlines are being done manually. All of that decisively influenced the homogeneity of our forest archive.

BG: Yet another milestone in the development of the project was the 'Forst' matrix, which, among other things, appears in the form of a dot matrix on the cover, while on the first pages of the book different data help to decode the individual points. After all, it actually deals with 72 sites around the city of Berlin. And, except for the area around 'Tempelhofer Feld' – Berlin's former city airport – there is a tree at each one of these points.

SG: We developed the 'Forst' matrix in the Cezanne/ Margarida team. With it, we were at last able to select the trees for the archive. Since the studio is located in Berlin, we had already decided that the trees for 'Neubau Forst' had to be derived from the city of Berlin's image. Yet another component linked to Neubau is typography.

Ultimately, we were easily able to connect the two factors by superimposing the individual letters of the studio name, 'N' 'e' 'u' 'b' 'a' 'u', set in NB–Grotesk 55R™, onto the Berlin city map. The studio's address is the fixed centre of our matrix. The font construction points define the locations of the trees in the archive. So, in fact, the information 'Neubau', written with trees from the city of Berlin, is concealed in the abstract dot matrix on the cover.

BG: Once we had figured out the principle for selecting the trees, then we had to start documenting the locations. Since we wanted to document summer and winter trees from the same perspective, we usually went in teams of two to the individual sites, where we chose a suitable angle for the photograph. The location of the photograph was also documented, so that six months later, we could shoot the summer or winter version from the same perspective. In order to do this, we looked for a notable element at the site where the picture was taken, or else photographed the position of the tripod on site[04]. Interestingly enough, some of the trees had either been swallowed up by construction sites, and were thus difficult to access, or else had been eliminated entirely from the street scene. Not only did the appearance of the city change over the course of the five years that it took to produce the pictures, but so did the quality of the camera's photographs, and thus, in the end, we had to go to the sites more than once.

LM: As designers you mainly always emphasise the utility value of the products you generate – and in the case of

'Neubau Forst', it is indisputably useful for architectural visualisations, as well as for illustration and visual composing. Besides their practical use, you also spent some of your research time exploring the tree as a motif, and how it is used in art. It went from Martin Kippenberger, Gerhard Richter, and Yoko Ono to Joseph Beuys, you said. But what does 'Neubau Forst' have to do with the Neukölln Landscape Planning Office in Berlin and Joseph Beuys?

SG: There is actually a surprising anecdote about that. In the summer of 2012, after we had already isolated the trees, we still had to define the species of trees and coordinate with the Landscape Planning Office in Berlin.

The Landscape Planning Office marks every officially planted tree in the city with a number, which is also imprinted on a little plate and attached to each tree. Fortunately, while doing the NBF cataloguing, we also documented these little plates. I then sent all of the information we had available to the Neukölln branch, requesting help in determining the species of the trees and the dates they were planted, as well as the circumferences of their trunks. A few weeks later Guido Fellhölter rang me. The Landscape Planning Office was very astonished at this unusual request. The office was also accordingly sceptical and did not want to share any information at first. They were worried that we would actually cut down the trees. I tried to explain to him that we only did digital 'sawing', and that the actual trees would not be damaged in any way. We were simply documenting the city of Berlin's trees in our book project; they would be 'distilled' out of the urban context and later be made available as digital tree sculptures. Somewhat in the same way that Joseph Beuys' '7000 Oaks for Kassel' was made available as a so-called social sculpture – only we would send the 315 Berlin tree sculptures as ambassadors all over the world. To my great astonishment, this rather presumptuous comparison broke the ice. Guido Fellhölter was suddenly very excited, and cried, 'Beuys, Beuys, Beuys' into the telephone. Finally, he said that, in his eyes, Beuys was the greatest. Now, I had certainly not counted on that. I was thrilled to hear that somebody in the administration of the parks commission in Neukölln had heard the name Joseph Beuys. But the best was yet to come – Guido was not only familiar with the name, but he had actually done some planting for Beuys! It turned out that when Guido was a student, he had worked on the '7000 Oaks' project, and planted some of Beuys' oaks in Kassel. A mere hour later Guido was sitting in our studio, helping us to deteminethe species of all of the trees, even those that weren't officially in the register. He spent weeks gathering all of the information, and he followed our project as far as the printing stage. We are infinitely grateful to him for all of that. Without Beuys, and Guido's support, we would never have been able to realise 'Neubau Forst' in this form. Thirty years later it gives a completely new meaning to Beuys's slogan, 'Stadtverwaldung statt Stadtverwaltung', or 'reforest the city, don't control it'.

BG: At the beginning of this conversation Stefan mentioned a wish list. For us and for the 'Neubau Forst Catalogue', Lars Müller Publishers was number one on our list of publishers. There is no better publisher for this project – both the attitude and the publisher's programme are a perfect match for the content of our book. Still, with its duality of analogue and digital, the 'Neubau Forst Catalogue' is not actually a typical project for Lars Müller Publishers. Nevertheless, today we can state that this product in particular is indicative of the future in many ways, also for the publisher. What is it about the 'Neubau Forst Catalogue' that is of especial interest to Lars Müller Publishers, and what finally induced the company to realise this publication and include it in its programme?

LM: Duality of analogue and digital – that is actually the point for me. I find that when I'm talking to book distributors that this is my exact argument. I don't go overboard every time, but I do say that I myself do not want to go digital, to switch to digital. I can't, and I don't want to. Don't demand it of me. I know how to make books. But I enter into partnerships with people who bring with them as much understanding for my role as I bring for theirs. And together we are the future – the future is both analogue and digital. And it's only in the adolescence of the digital age that there is this apparent exclusivity. The digital stories today – it's not simply older people who are saying, 'yes, analogue still exists' – the kids themselves come and realise, 'hey, check it out, this is incredible'. It's the rediscovery of analogue. The pendulum is not simply moving in one direction, as it did before; instead, three times a day it swings in both directions. Analogue and digital.

SG: There is, by the way, a strong parallel to today's music market – the rediscovered, tactile experience of vinyl, with its incomparable 12-inch format for artwork, versus the insubstantial/weightless, but popular MP3 format. Even though the digital audio format does actually improve the quality of the music and helps to popularise its content, because it seems to be available universally, separating the music from its place of origin, it still hasn't achieved the visual stimulus found in the tactile aspect of the 12-inch cover. After all, there's a good reason why it's called 'cover artwork' – it's a 'work of art', and as such it can stand on its own, distinct from the music. As contradictory as it may sound, when I really want to have the ultimate audio experience, I still can't avoid buying the black disc packed inside of a 12-inch cover art. At least, that's the way that I see it, personally, and in that, I recognise a clear analogy to our analogue-digital product. The complete 'Forst' experience lies in the collaboration of both sorts of media – the physical book and the non-physical download.

LM: That's true. Still, the vinyl niche is just a bit too narrow for me – I don't want to see our book there. I think that the vinyl niche is narrower. It's going to stay narrow, because, for those who have this affinity, its allure lies in its exclusivity. There will never again be a mass market for the vinyl record. But the book market is still a mass market. Here, we should remind people of the advantages of the book, as opposed to the digital. And the advantage of the book over digital media is that you interact with a real object. So you always have the whole and the representation – visibility – what is sufficient for content. In our case, with 'Neubau Forst', it's very special. We're talking about a physical, a corporeal reality – the tree. The usage is digital, but then, logically, we break it down to what comes closest to the digital tree – and that's the book. And we enjoy each moment, as it were, of this process of representation, of creating, of making. The book celebrates content that is digitally available, first in a useful way, and then to everyone's great good fortune. So with 'Neubau Forst', it's a sea change. This point of intersection has not yet been exhausted. And I'm saying – this is where our conversation began – that I'm so glad that the CD and DVD have been outgrown.

SG: And the USB stick, too. You were the one who actually opened our eyes and separated the 'Neubau Forst Catalogue' – the printed work – from the digital product.

LM: Yes, exactly, but after all, we originally planned to distribute it separately from the book. But we also outgrew the USB stick and with that, we actually re-established the radicalism of the book, as well as the radicalism of the digital product at the same time. What will change is that, in ten years,

the digital product will be far more elegant, and that will, I hope, make the intersection even more attractive.

I imagine that this is the beginning of a development that will contribute to the preservation of the book – that it won't require any more compromises. The book as such can remain a book. Because it's fine the way it is – it's been fine for a long time. And the new thing doesn't come at the cost of the book, but in addition to the book. And that means that, in principle, we're not doing anything new at all. We're simply adhering to the differences between the media. A book doesn't want to be the same as digital media, and the digital doesn't try to do what a book does; instead, you distinguish what each side can do well. And that's what's new about 'Neubau Forst'. So, basically, we're radicalising the worlds of both media.

SG: In book form we also once again muster evidence of the extraordinary love of detail and the print quality of the isolated and masked trees without white gaps. The possible applications demonstrated sharpen the intersection and the possibilities of both media, while highlighting the differences.

LM: Yes, we're honing that, and we're actually requiring consumers to act responsibly, in expecting that they will take advantage of what the book is capable of doing – there will always be those who scan things from the book, that's clear, okay, go ahead and do it – but we assume that people will realise what they can do with the book, and what they can do with the data. And that's also important, because the data have more material applications, while the book has more conceptual applications. The price model (book to digital content) creates a sense of fairness. The user actually has to pay for your efforts. And the book price can be a bit higher, as it has to pay for itself. And with that, we're also up-to-date economically – that's simply the situation today.

SG: With 'Forst', we experience the intersection, as well as the immediate, exemplary symbiosis of hardware and software, book and download. With the catalogue and its contents, we do what we can't do digitally, and vice versa. Anyone who buys the book is also investing in the digital product. You receive a price reduction equal to the value of the book, if you also decide to download the digital product as well. This is another benefit of buying the book. And anyone who decides not to buy the book, but simply wants the digital tool, receives the download at the regular price.

LM: Frankly, we also have to say that there is no price transparency for the book. We hope that there will be no overhead for the digital product. All of the overhead – and this is a development over the last thirty years – which makes a book so difficult to manage today – well, there are no storage and shipping costs. And those are the two factors that have contributed the most to cost increases over the last three decades. At the same time the notion 'greed is good' has developed, putting an enormous amount of pressure on the product price – although that also applies to the digital product, as well – but far more abstractly. At some point you'll reach your break-even threshold, and then you can be happy. I haven't had that pleasure in the last fifteen years. I am simply pleased if we reach this threshold at all. In this respect you can say that the book has lost. And in this respect, it's the vinyl story, where the book is forced into an elitist niche, where you say that the digital popularises content, while the book has to find a niche for itself and appeal to the elite – here, you're going to see the masses. I still see this as a grey area for the book. Unless we succeed at maintaining this type of intersection, where people say, oh, I want both. And hopefully we can communicate this – if we say on the last page that we, the editors and publishers, Neubau and Lars Müller Publishers, are proud to be able to offer this package that deals with this encounter of the two media worlds with extraordinary precision and keenness.

SG: For me, this principle is very clearly aligned with the Letraset tradition from the 1960s. An established model is revived, transferred to the present day in the form of an unusual book experience and supplemental digital content, a download-able work tool. The 'Neubau Forst Catalogue' not only provides oversight, but also shows the digital content and its applications in print. We make use of the possible effects that can be achieved by, for instance, printing on different paper stock. The book offers additional context, while the digital product offers additional functions. The book remains a stand-alone work, which has a supplemental, useful dimension in the way that it relates to the digital content. Something entirely new emerges out of this convergence.

LM: Still, the publisher asserts the claim that this sensible symbiosis between the analogue and the digital may remain the exception. Naturally, I assert the claim that the book is complete unto itself. There must be books that continue to be sufficient in and of themselves. As well as those that have no disadvantage when compared to the digital, but are an independent, true medium on their own. And that's perhaps an idealised hope of mine, that the people who understand our intersection or this symbiosis will also think about it a bit and recognise the book's autonomous value. I'm somewhat egotistical about that, and think – I don't give a damn how things go for you. I assert the claim that the book is complete unto itself. 'Neubau Forst Catalogue' does have the function of a teaser, but it is exclusively the function. Obviously, Neubau Forst's trailblazing achievement is certainly on the digital level.

SG: When you spend five years working with a team of twenty designers on a self-initiated project, investing a total of more than 37,900 work hours, that's way more than a statement. For me, the actual standard, the crucial criterion by which I judge a project, is my own level of enthusiasm. If I personally see the potential in an idea, its usefulness, then I know that there are plenty of people who will see it the same way. But, after all of that work, after sixty months, when you can open up in just a fraction of a second a single piece of vector tree data containing thousands of manually set anchor points, which took three months to make, then it's impossible to explain to anyone the enormous amount of work that went into this document. It's absolutely ridiculous. Three months of doing nothing but clicking and correcting a pixel image enlarged to the point of abstraction, and in less time than it takes to wave your hand, the thing has been opened, and possibly copied. Of course, a few of the trees were developed in just a few days, while most were finished in two to three weeks. It's difficult to explain the uniqueness of this achievement, even to the professional user of our digital product, someone who would have the most understanding of our work. As a counterpart to the digital product, the 'Neubau Forst Catalogue' also has the advantage of being fully functional in CO_2-neutral space. Even if you don't recognise the CO_2 neutrality of the digital product at first, the digital form of 'Forst' is also sustainable. Because the 'Neubau Forst Archive' developed on the computer left behind a carbon footprint of about 450 kg of CO_2. But this half a ton of CO_2 created while working on the digital trees can be saved in the future, since nobody will have to spend months going to the trouble of removing the background from photographs of these

trees. So both parts of the 'Neubau Forst Catalogue' – the analogue book and its FSC® certified paper, and most especially the digital project, the 'Neubau Forst Archive', the data collection – comprise a sustainable product.

LM: It's also much simpler if there is a book that explains to the reader what has to be done to achieve all of this. When I'm watching a film, for example, I really love to see how something that I think of as a product was made. That's why I like to watch cooking shows, too. Because I see the processes.

SG: In the 'Neubau Forst Catalogue' the 'Ambience' chapter is the 'making-of'. Here you can see the 72 sites of the trees being captured in their original environment over a period of five years, during different seasons of the year. You can see the unique 'colour' of Berlin, which was deliberately removed from the photographs in the "tree-distilling-process" in order to have all-purpose, universally applicable tree sculptures. Seen as a whole, the 'Ambience' chapter documents a study of space and time. Because of the changes in Berlin caused by construction, some of these trees don't exist anymore. One tree' – B14 – which was planted in 1870 right here, in front of our studio on Paul-Lincke-Ufer, and survived two world wars, was cut down during the last winter of the NBF project, because it was in poor health. We were able to capture this silent historical witness in photo-graphs. And even though we weren't able to take both summer and winter versions of all 72 trees and put them all into vector format during the five-year production period, at least this part of the process of cataloguing is completely documented and captured in book form. Looking at the 'Neubau Forst' project as a whole, it seems to me to be extremely relevant and worth pointing out. This chapter also lends the necessary gravity to the entire project and its digital distillate.

LM: It's like a live concert – it's about the audience having enough knowledge, regardless of whether you play or not – that the audience has enough respect to realise: they've been practising! It needs this immediacy. It needs participation, some foreknowledge; otherwise even a book is nothing. You have to create this context. And we're slowly generating context for the digital. And what we're doing here – we're offering context, we take you back to the image of Berlin. The everyday situations, the most ordinary façades – no spectacular architecture – it's reality. And in this reality there is a tree. And now we take this tree and turn it into a star. That's what this book is about. And if you want to, you can take this tree and plant it wherever you will.

SG: The principle developed for 'Neubau Forst' is applicable to every city. The 'Neubau Forst Catalogues' manifest an aspect of these vibrant city sculptures, and Lars Müller Publishers will distribute them around the world. Thanks to the digital archive available for downloading, the Berlin trees will have a new life in virtual form, and can be planted in every city in the world, or slightly modified, thanks to the tree modules and digital image-processing software. Hopefully, they will spread, perhaps even run rampant and 'reforest' cities in the future. I'm already looking forward to seeing where we will reencounter or rediscover them.

Neubau Forest

Forest includes forestscapes generated entirely from the 'Neubau Forst' inventory. Tree sculptures and modules are combined to simulate a virtual forest and to exhibit initial explorations into the potential of the 'Neubau Forst' inventory – Neubau Forest.

— Printed on Multi Art Gloss 150 gsm

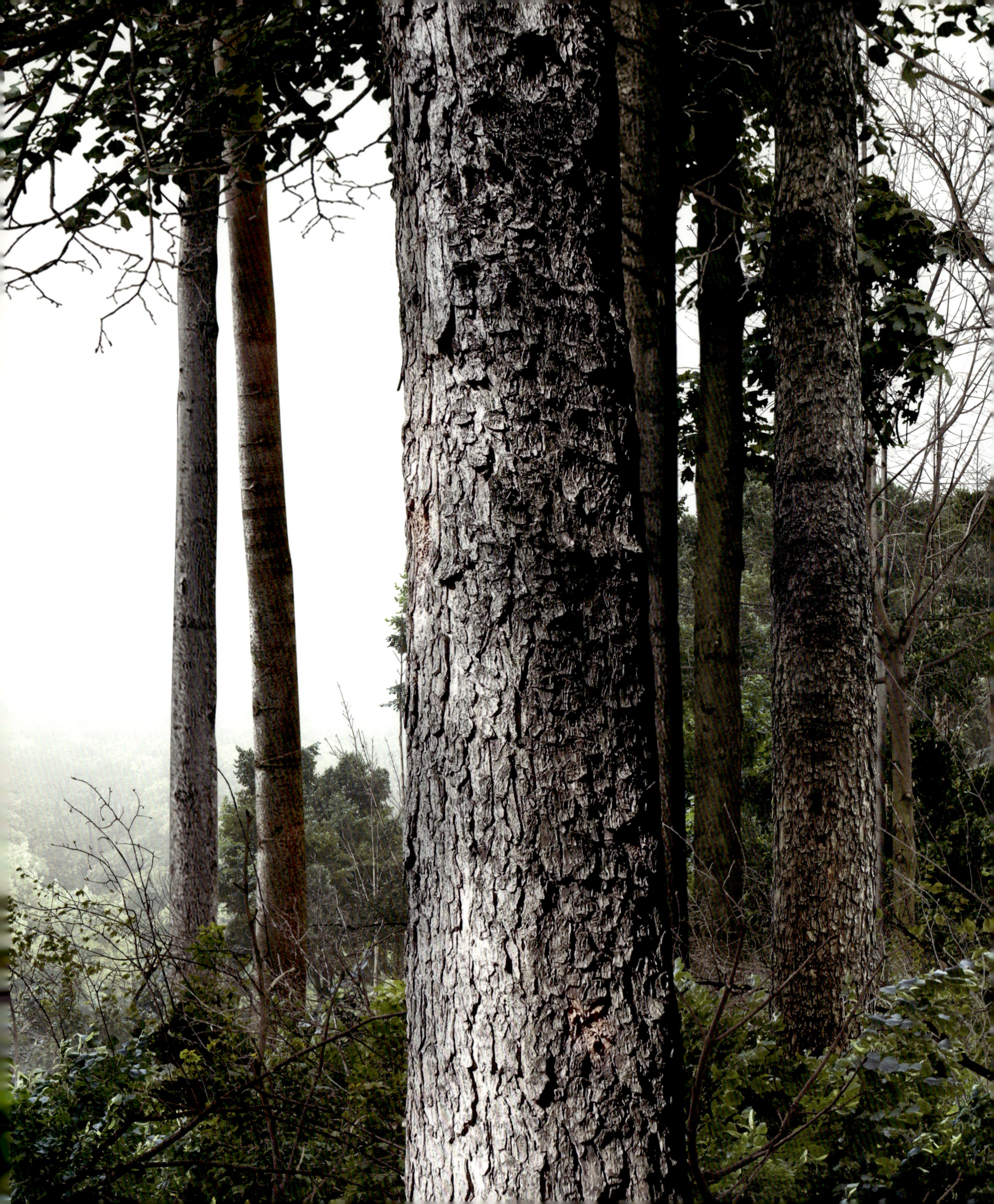

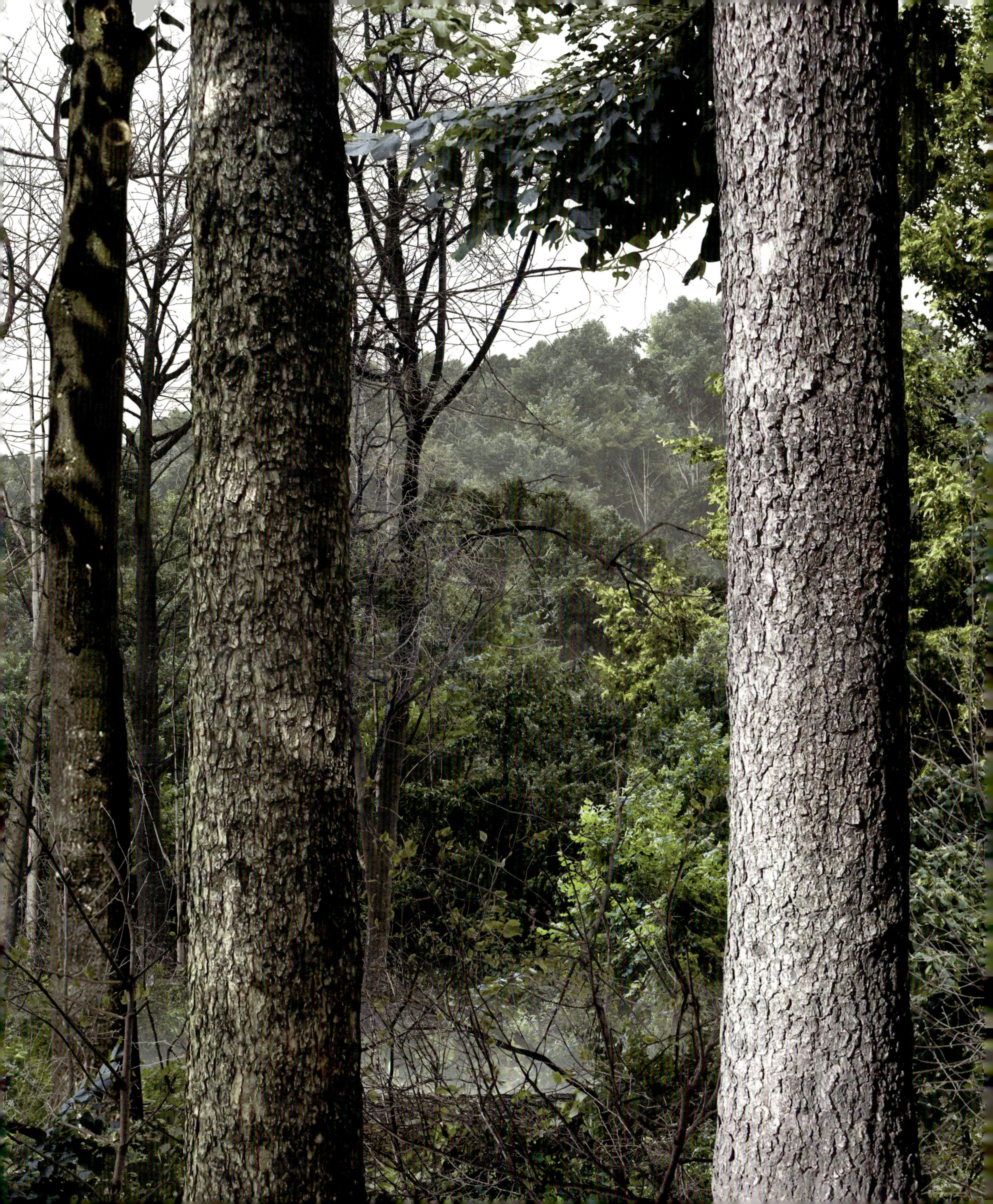

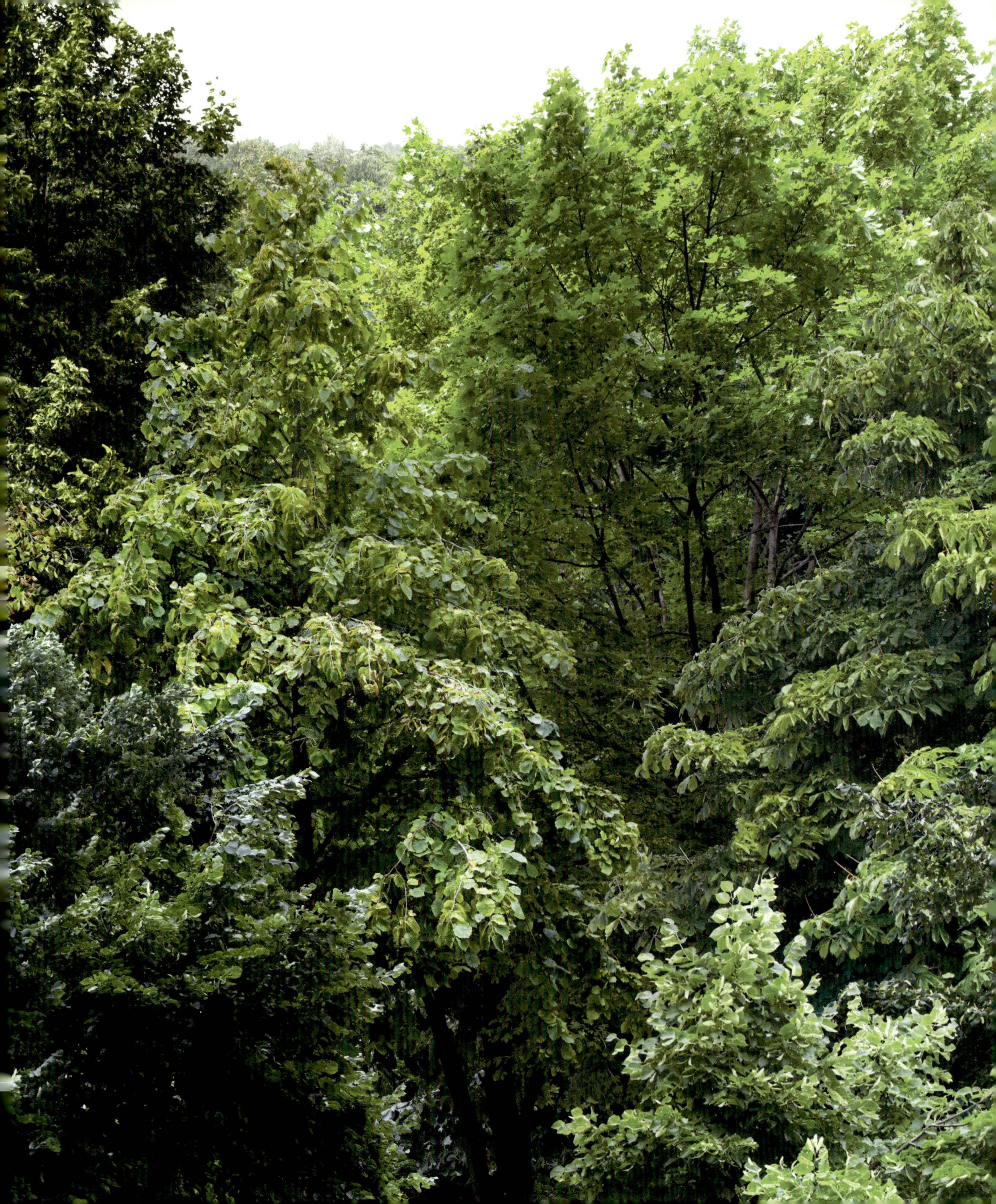

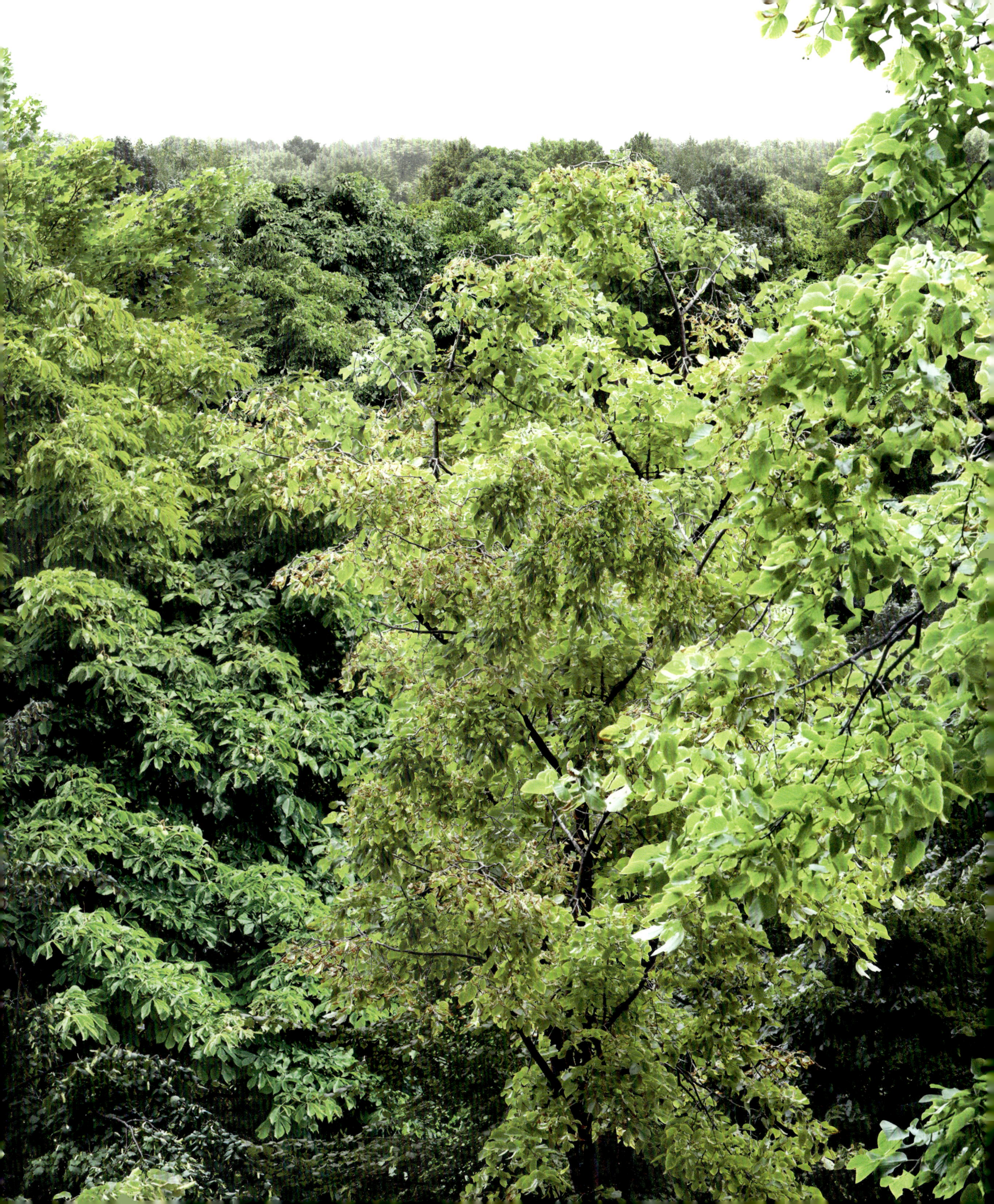

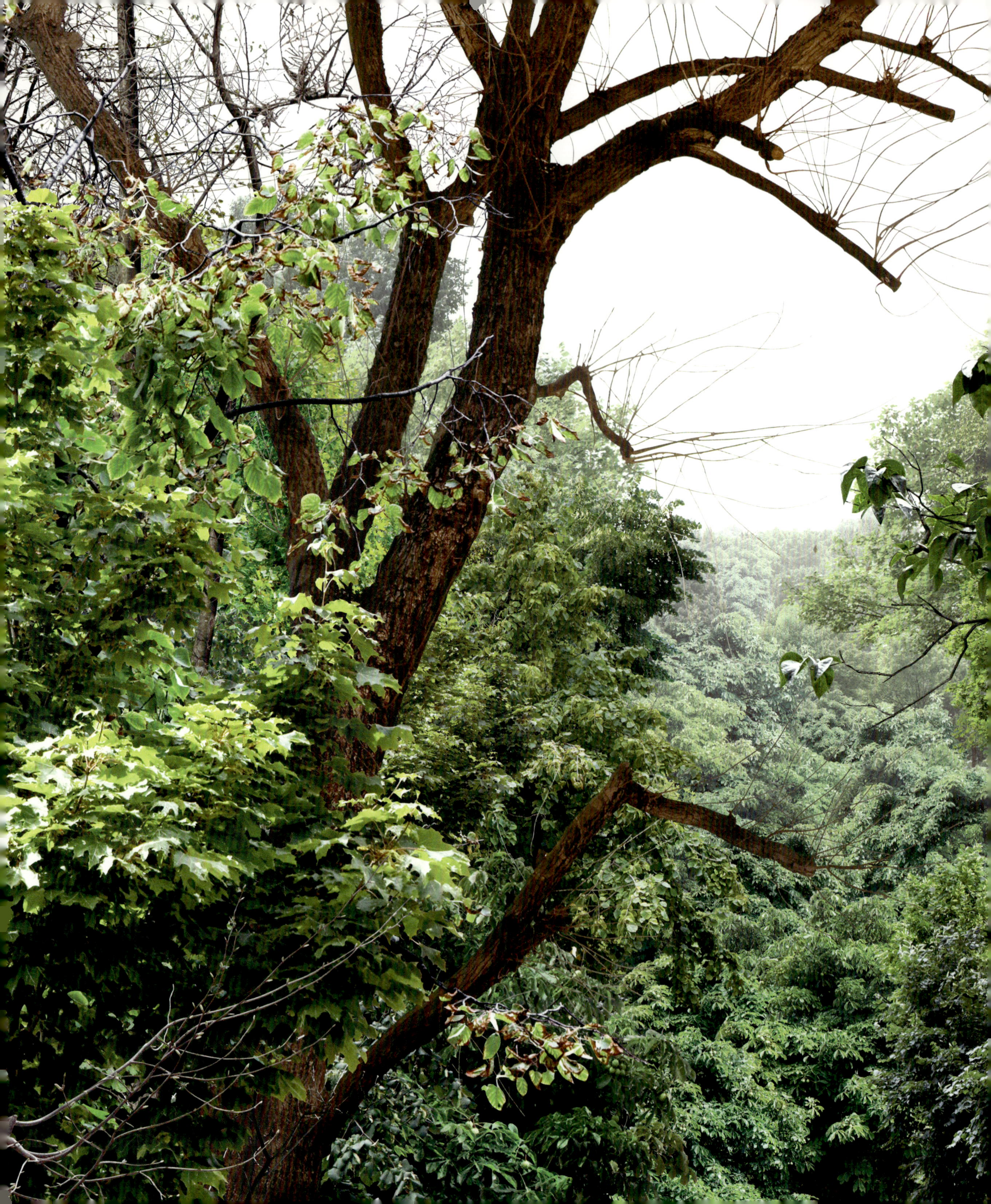

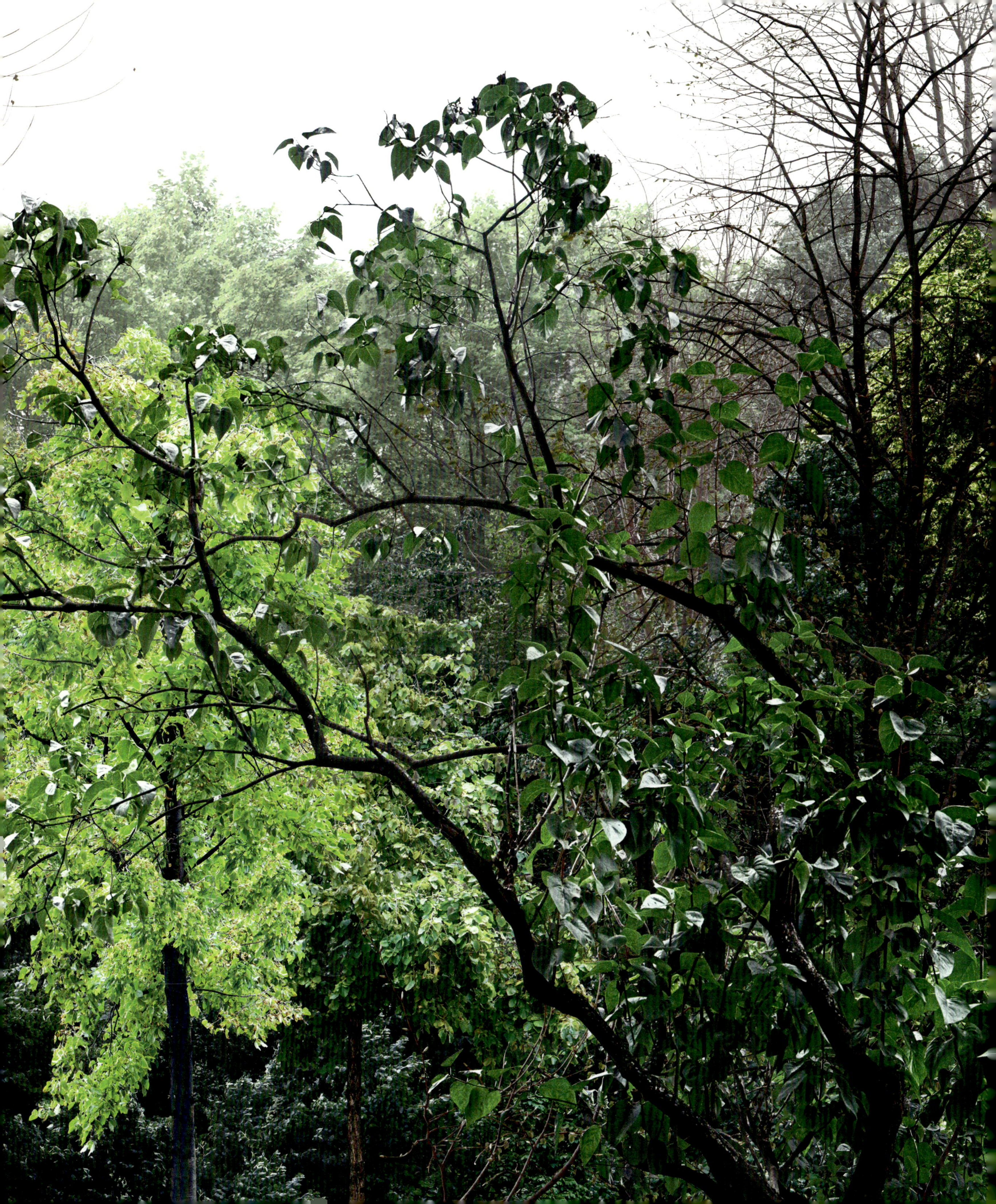

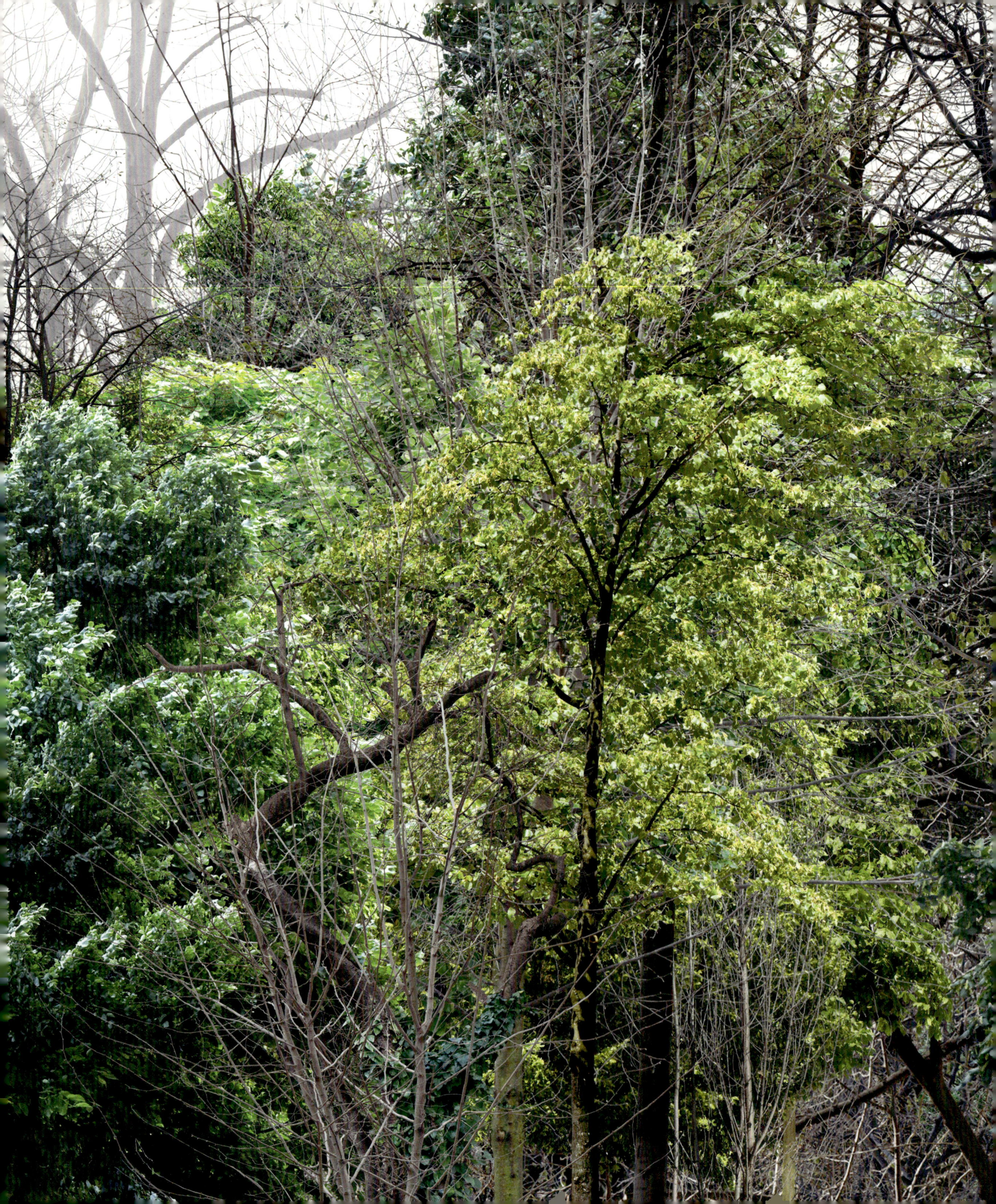

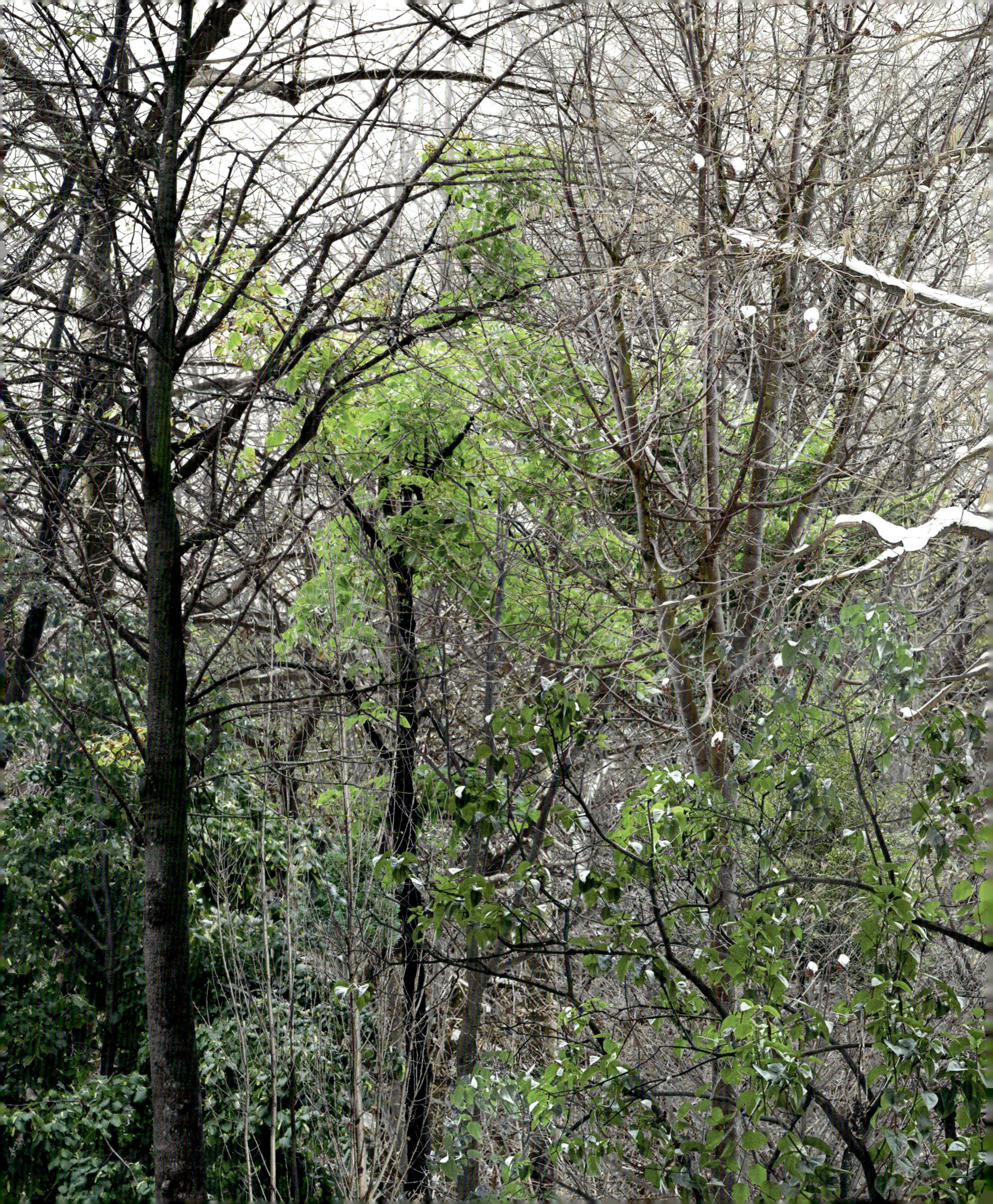

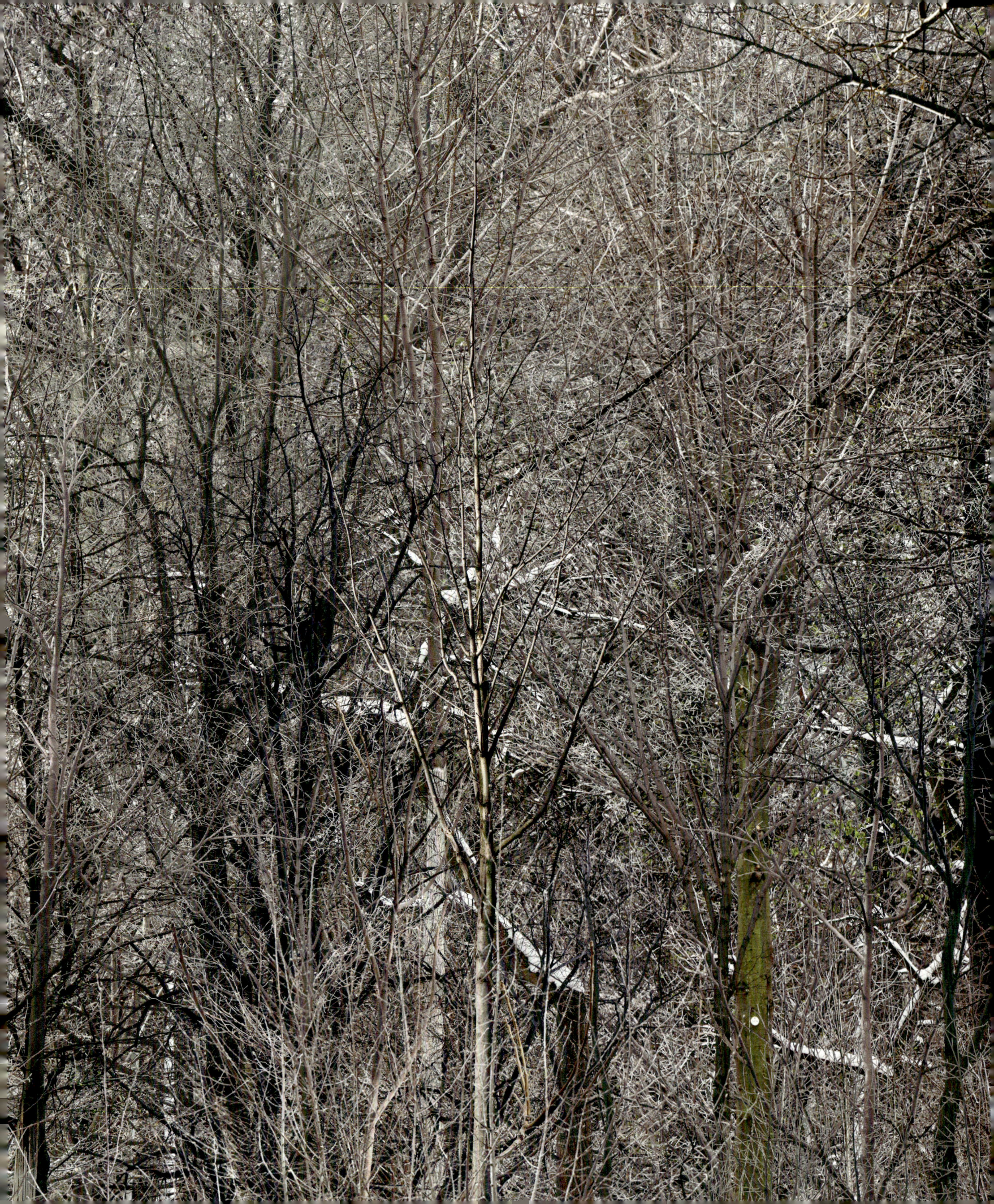

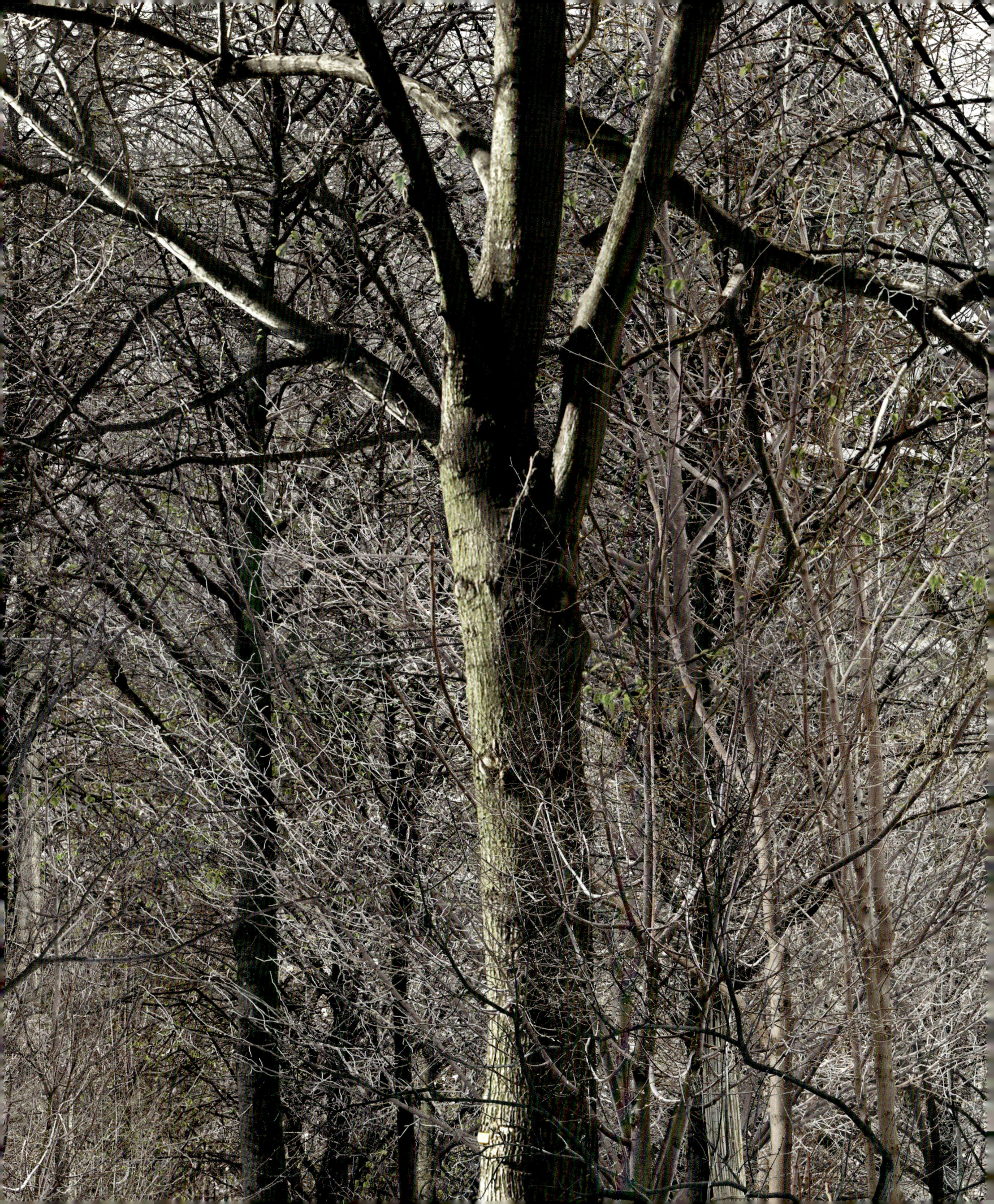

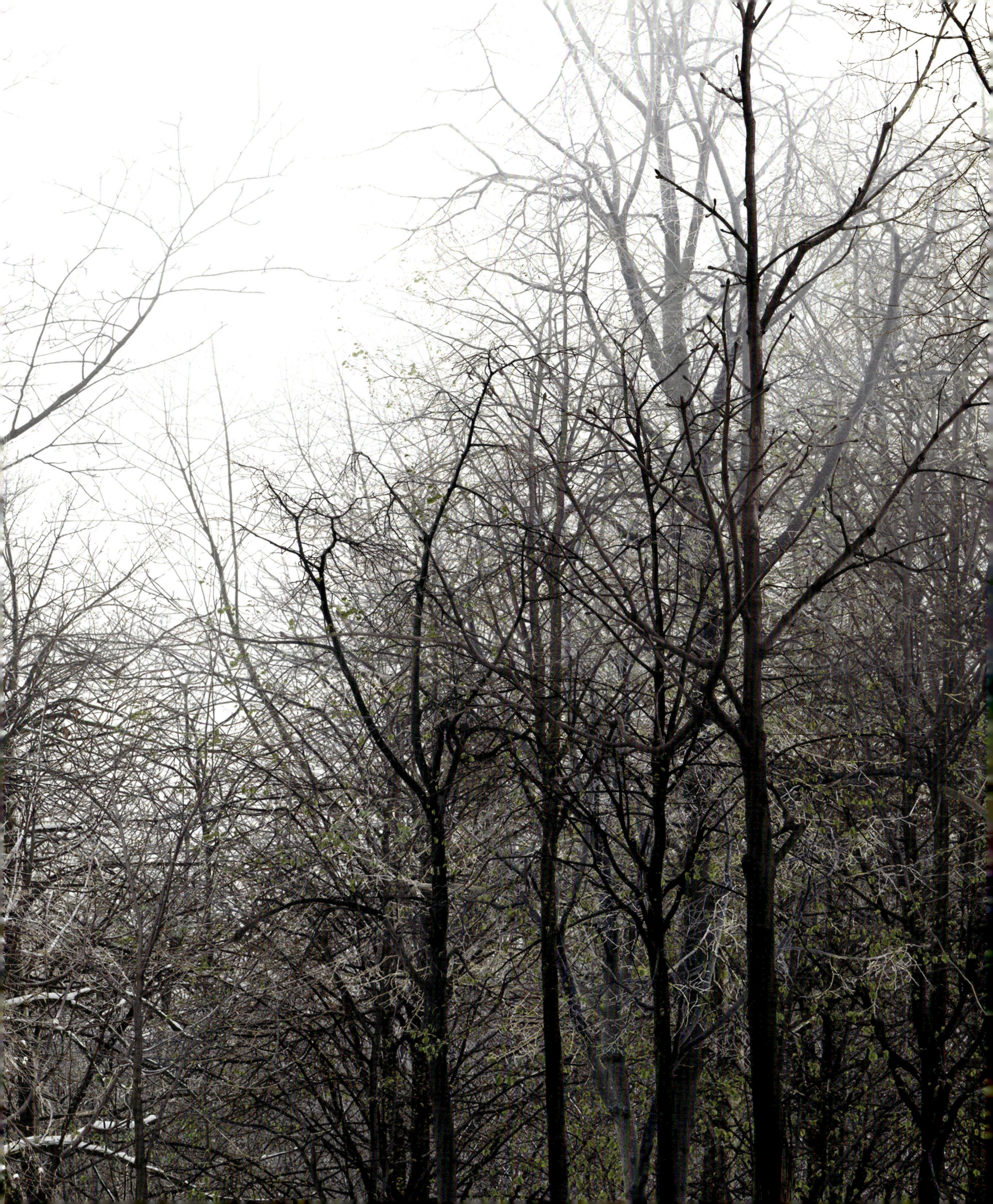

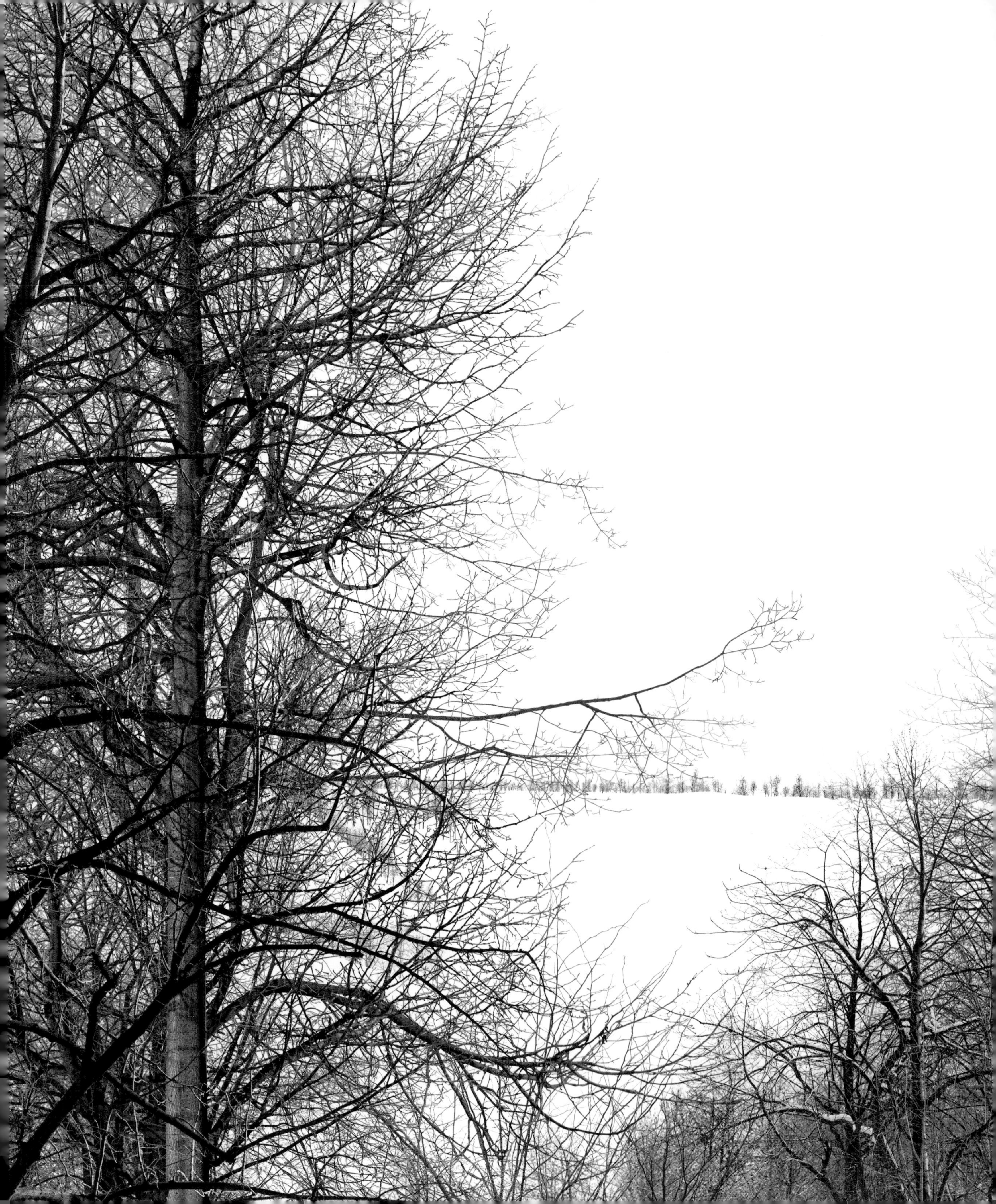

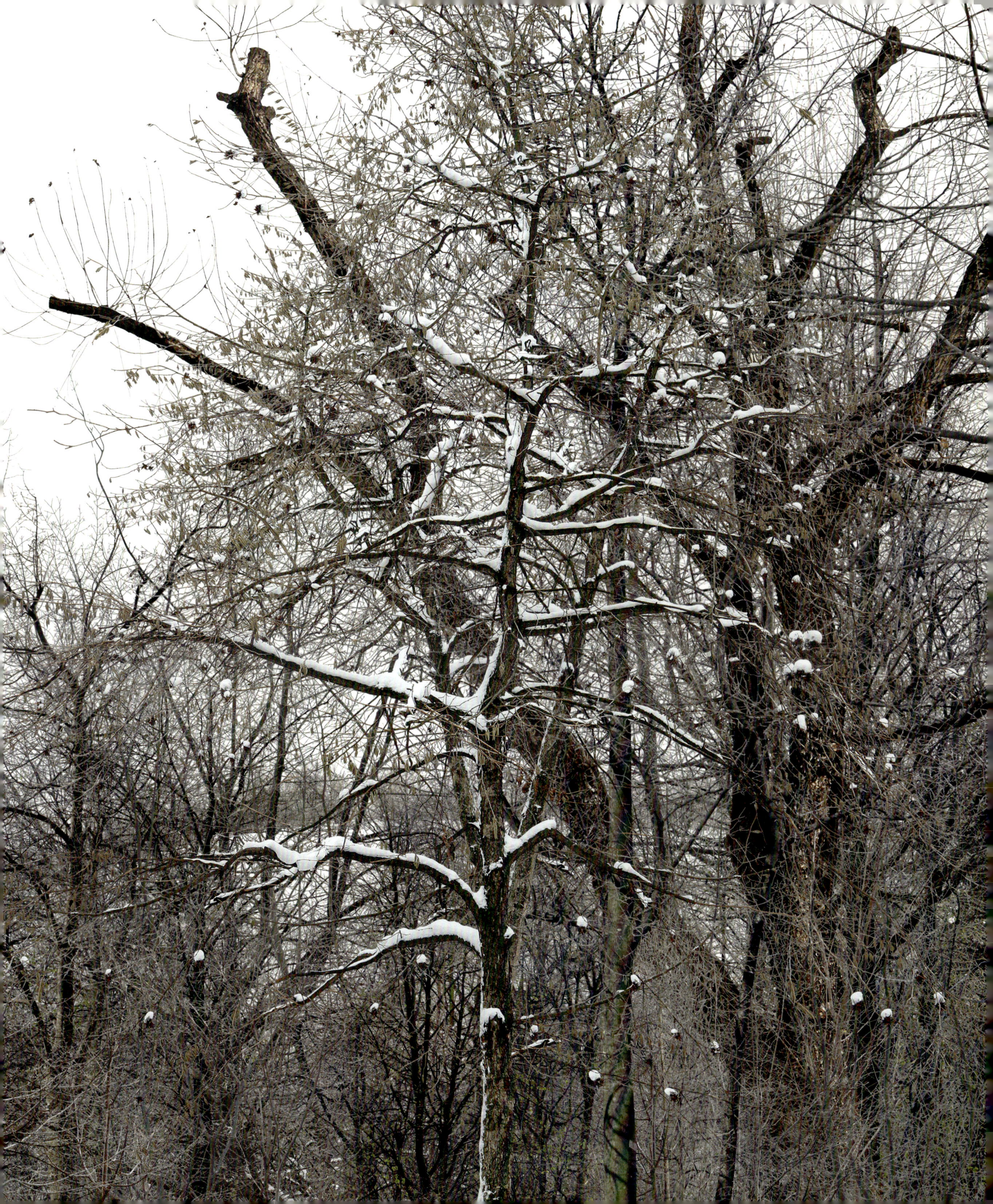

```
N1      Linden                  [Tilia cordata]
N5      Hop-Hornbeam            [Ostrya carpinifolia]
N8      Plane                   [Platanus x acerifolia]

E4      Maple                   [Acer]

U3      Maple                   [Acer]

B11     Linden                  [Tilia]
B14     Silver maple            [Acer saccharinum]

A3      Honey locust            [Gleditsia triacanthos]
A5      Cornelian cherry        [Cornus mas]
A7      Elm                     [Ulmus Resista]
A11     Locust                  [Robinia]
A14     Linden                  [Tilia americana]
A17     Linden                  [Tilia]

U7      Locust                  [Robinia pseudoacacia]
```

Texture
N1–U10

Texture includes a selection of bark close-ups exploring the 'Neubau Forst' inventory in micro/macro scale. The tree barks documented during 2009–2013 capture the seasonally variable appearance of all specimens included in the 'Neubau Forst' Locator Matrix.

— Printed in duotone (Black + PMS Cool Grey 5) on Munken Print White 115 gsm

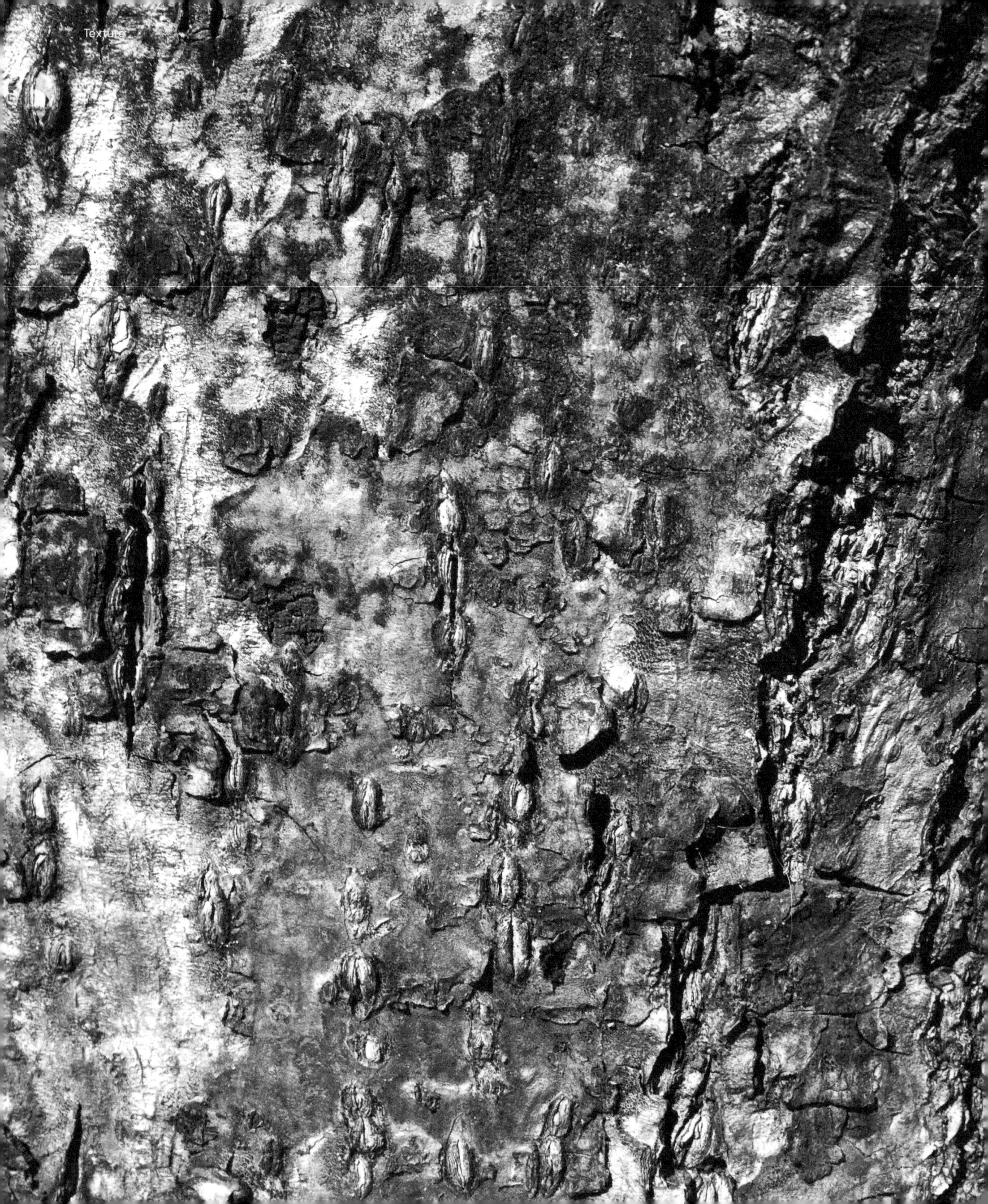
Texture

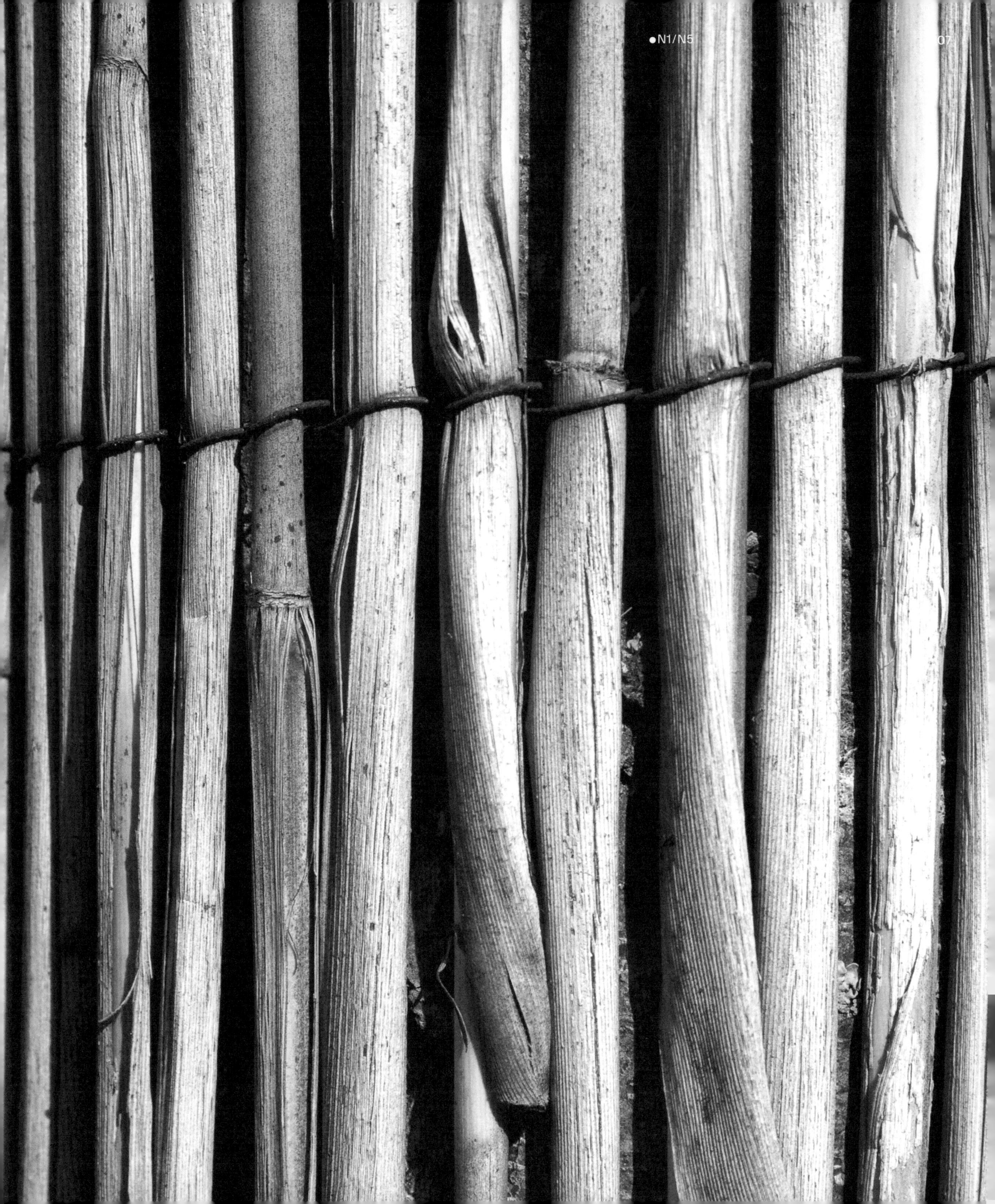

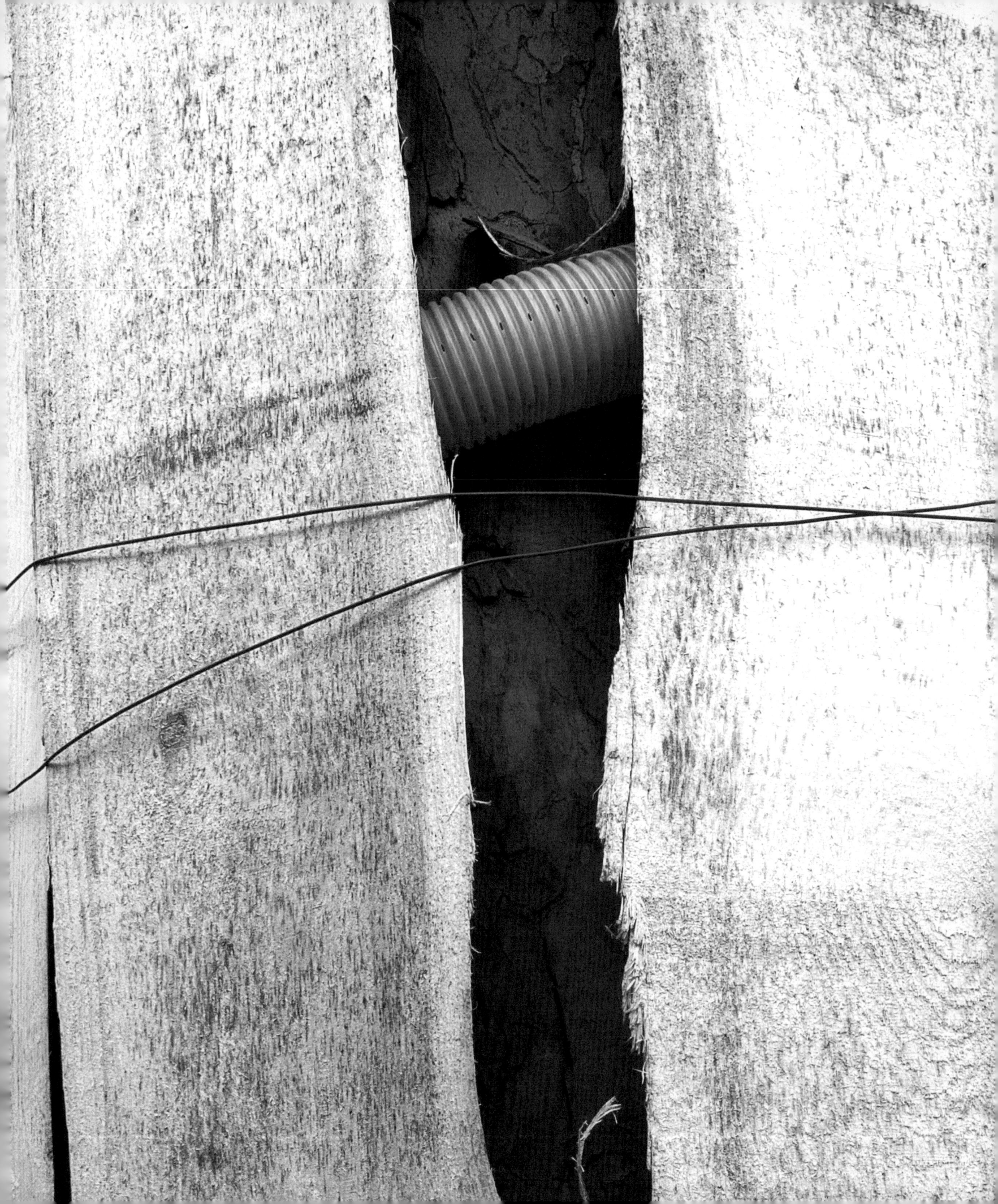

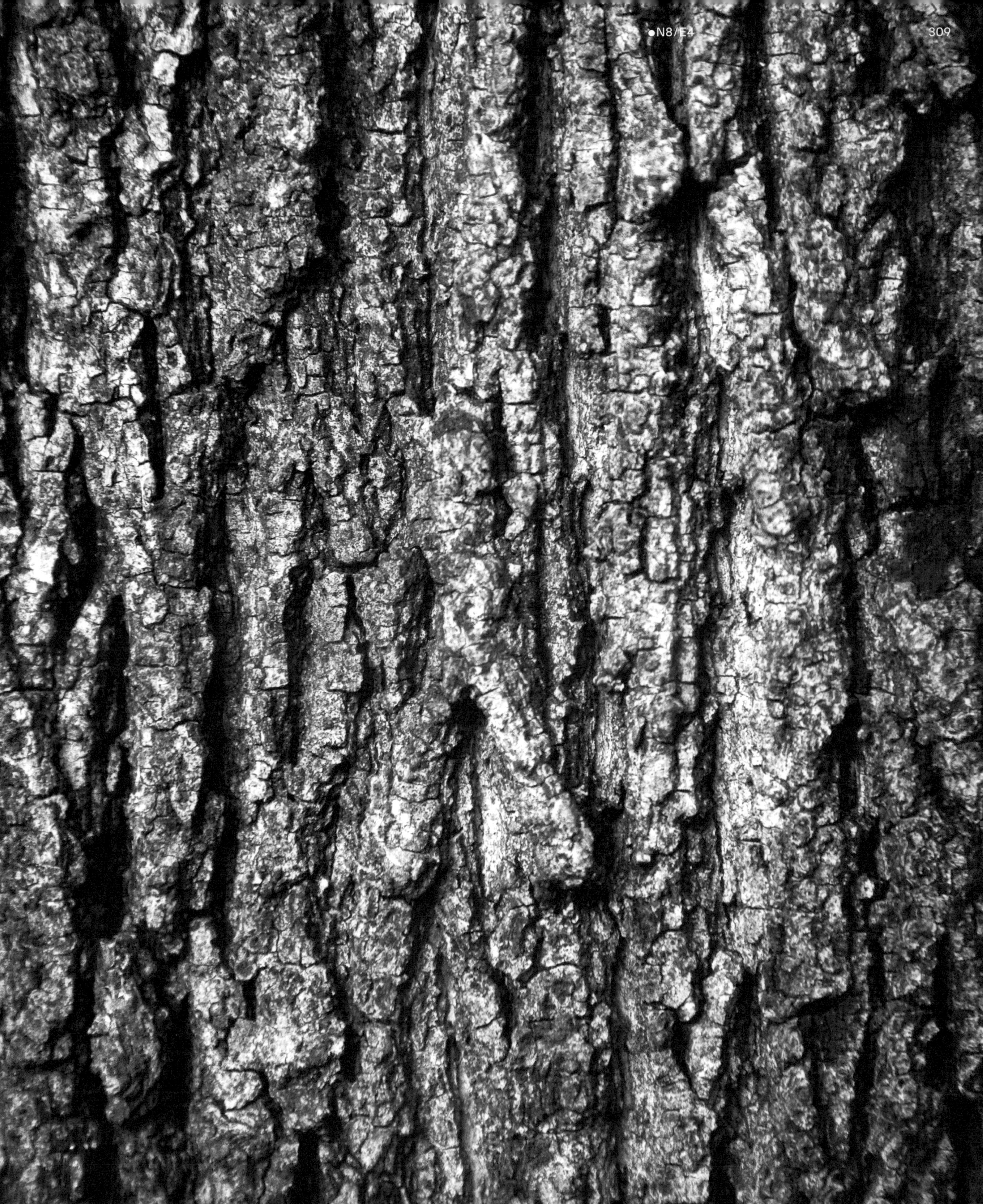

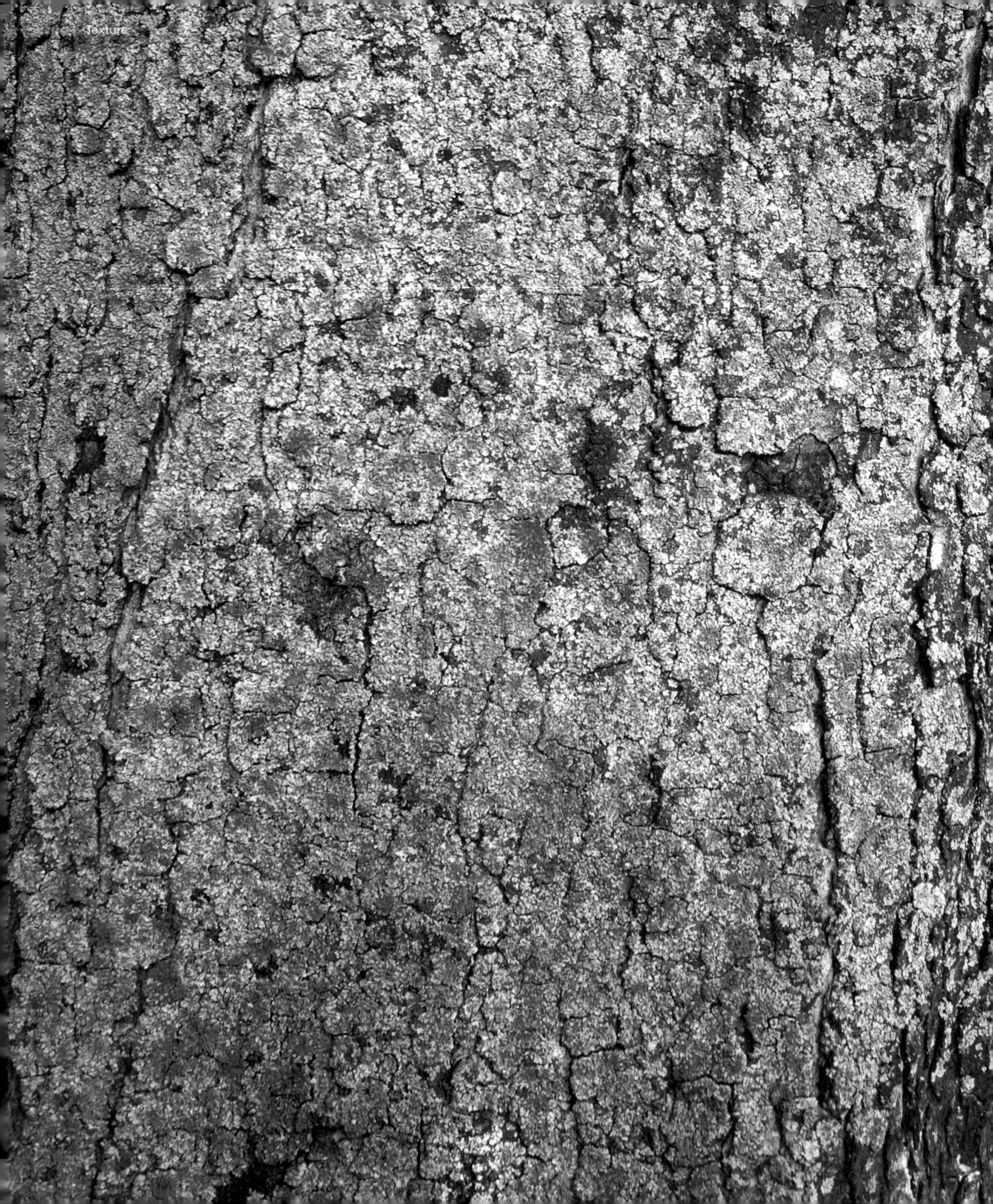
Texture

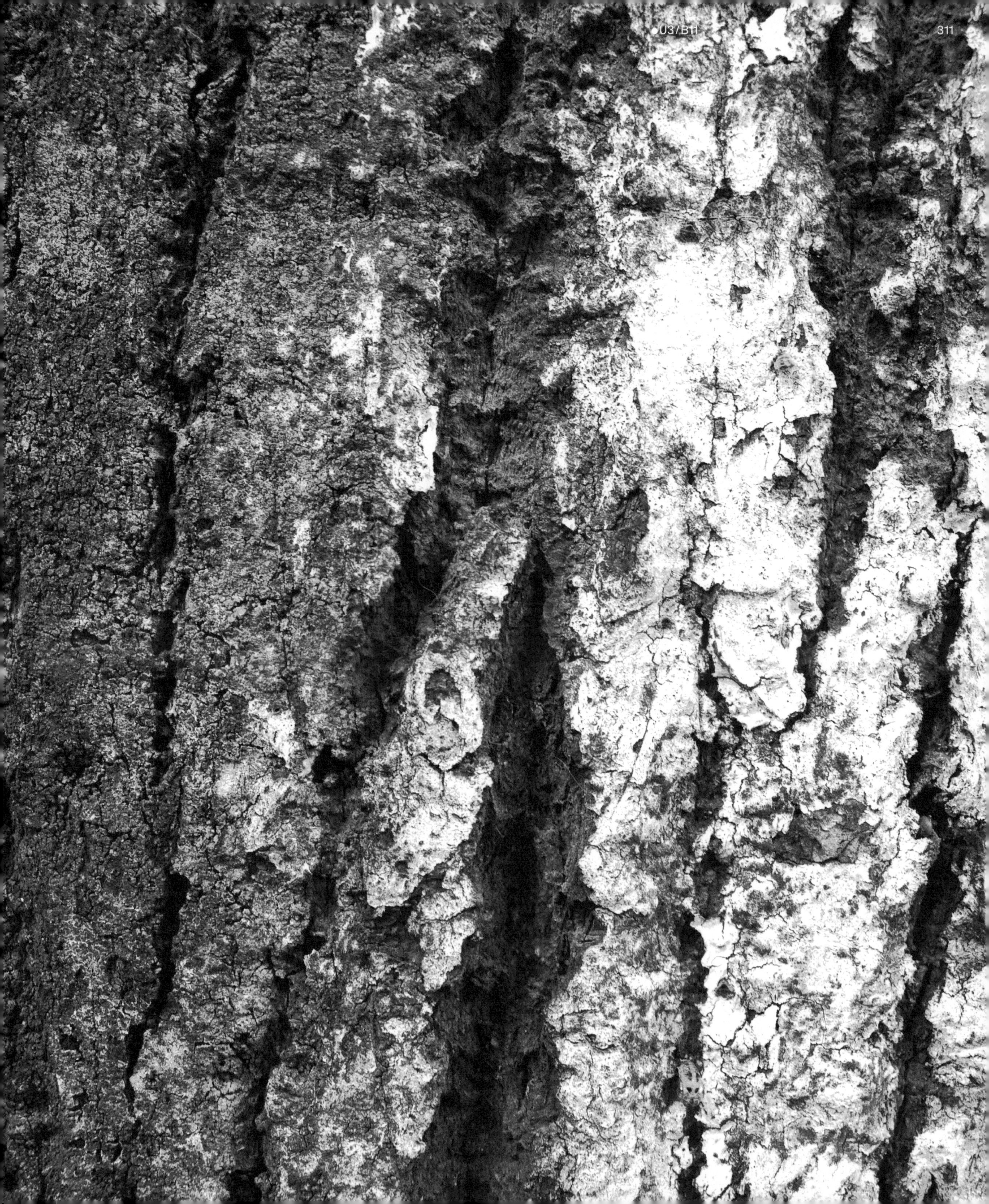

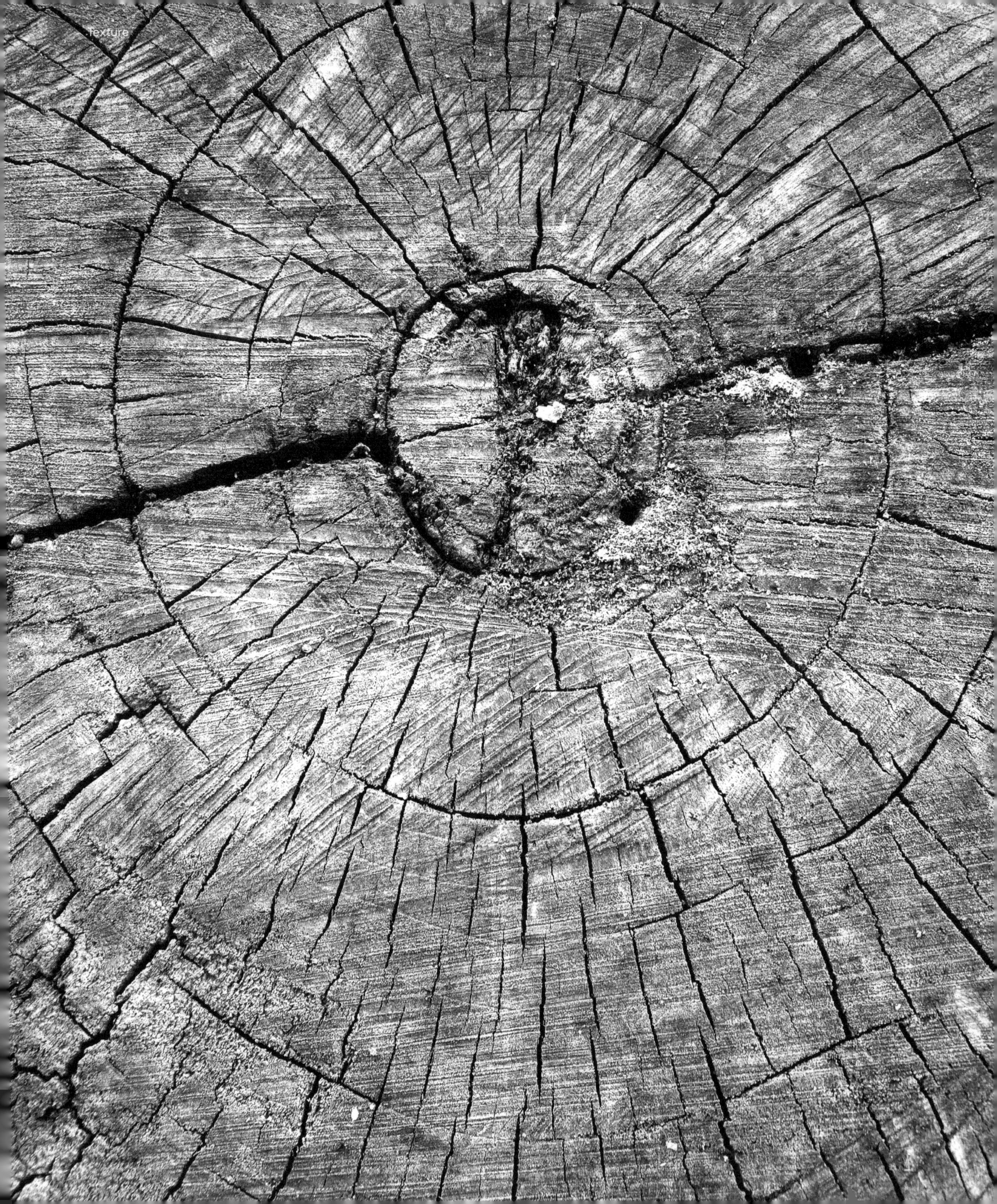

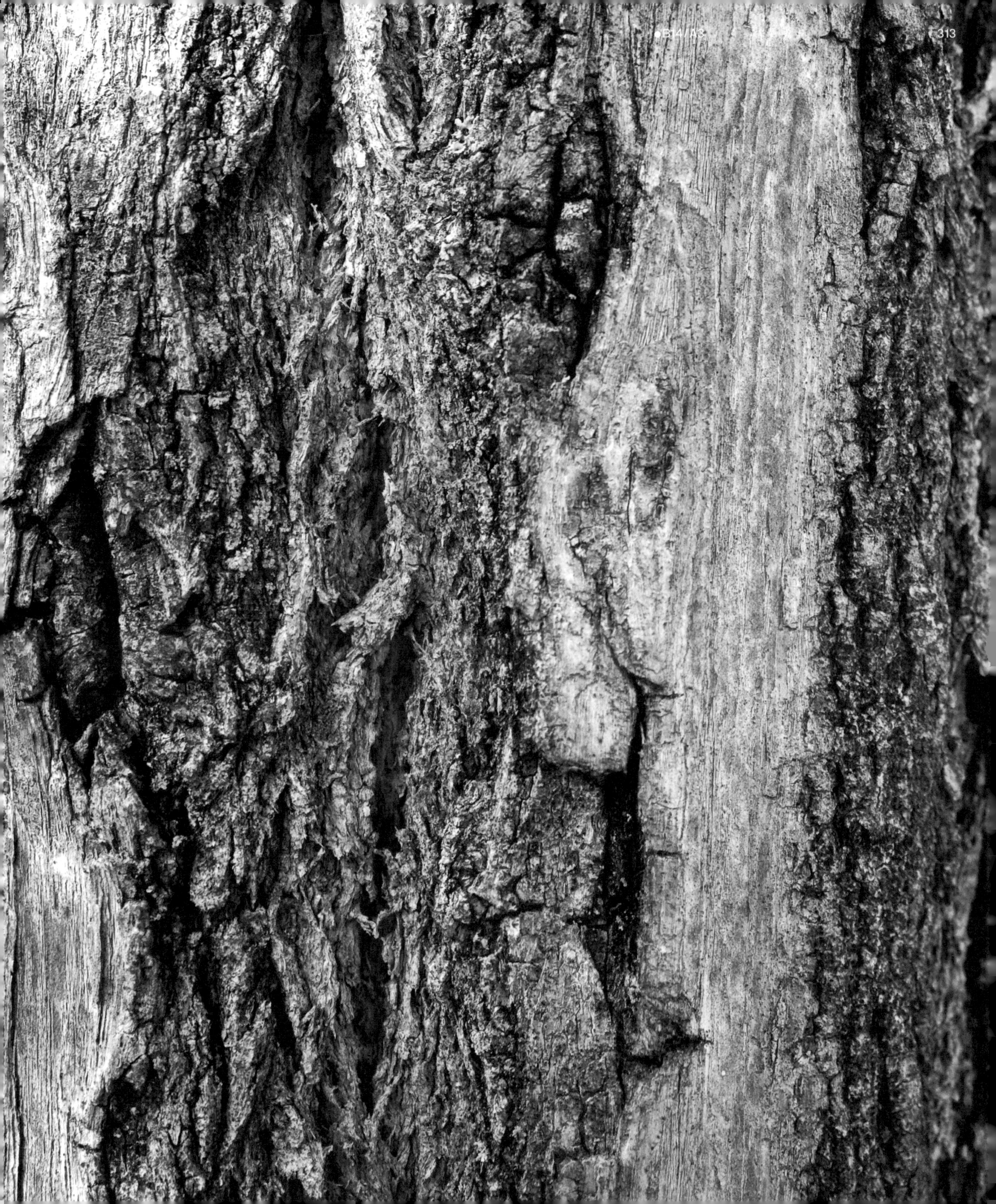

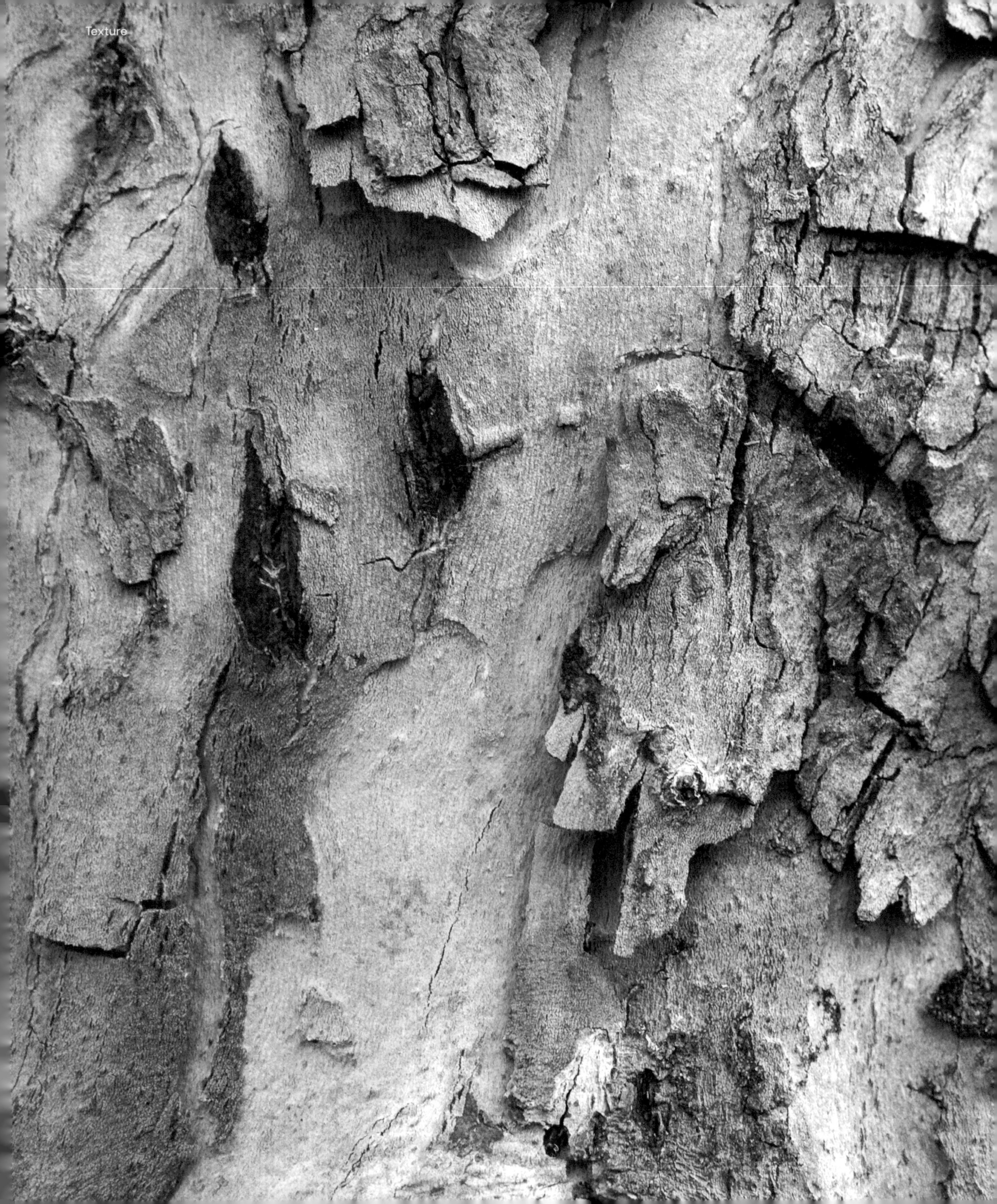
Texture

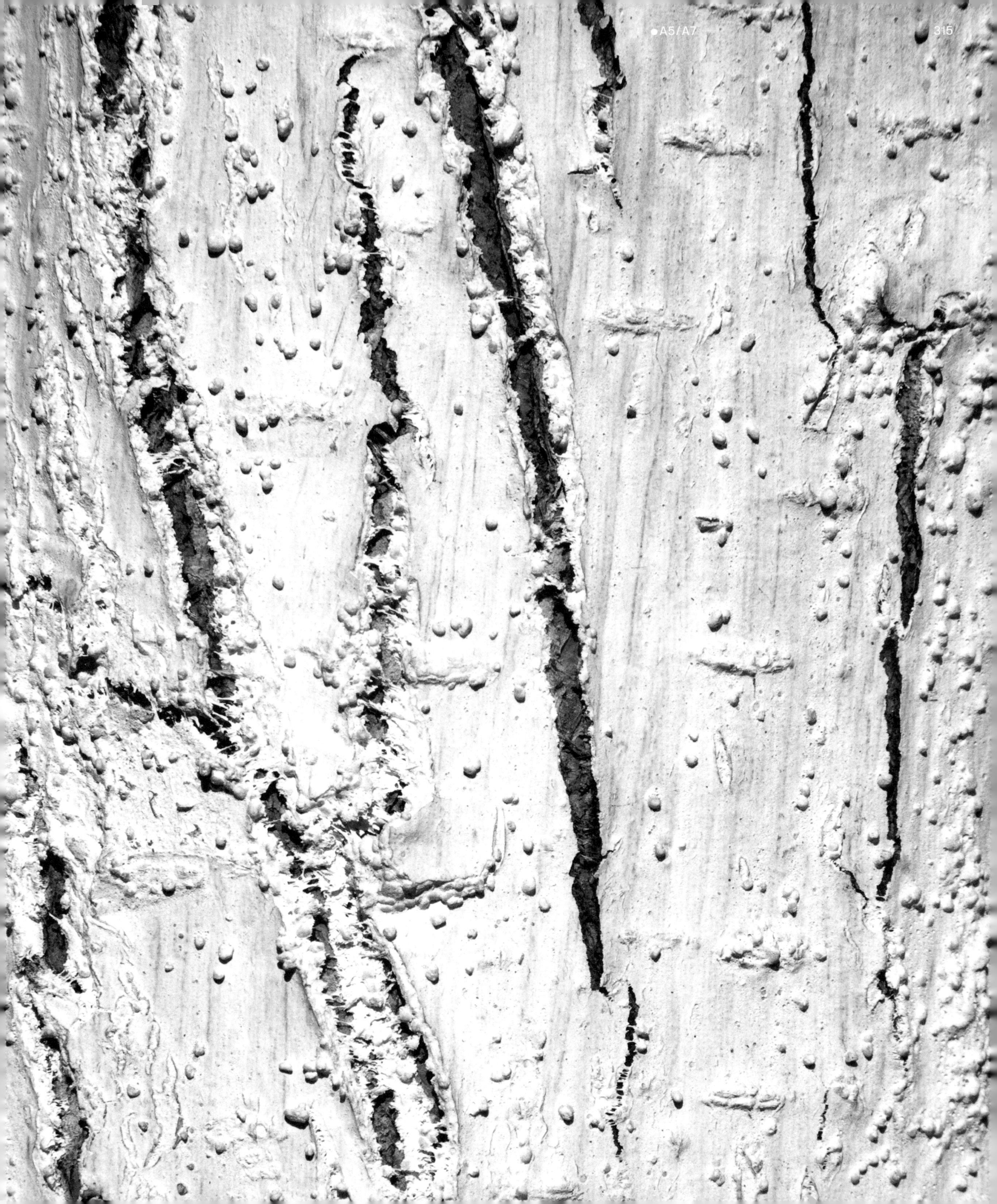

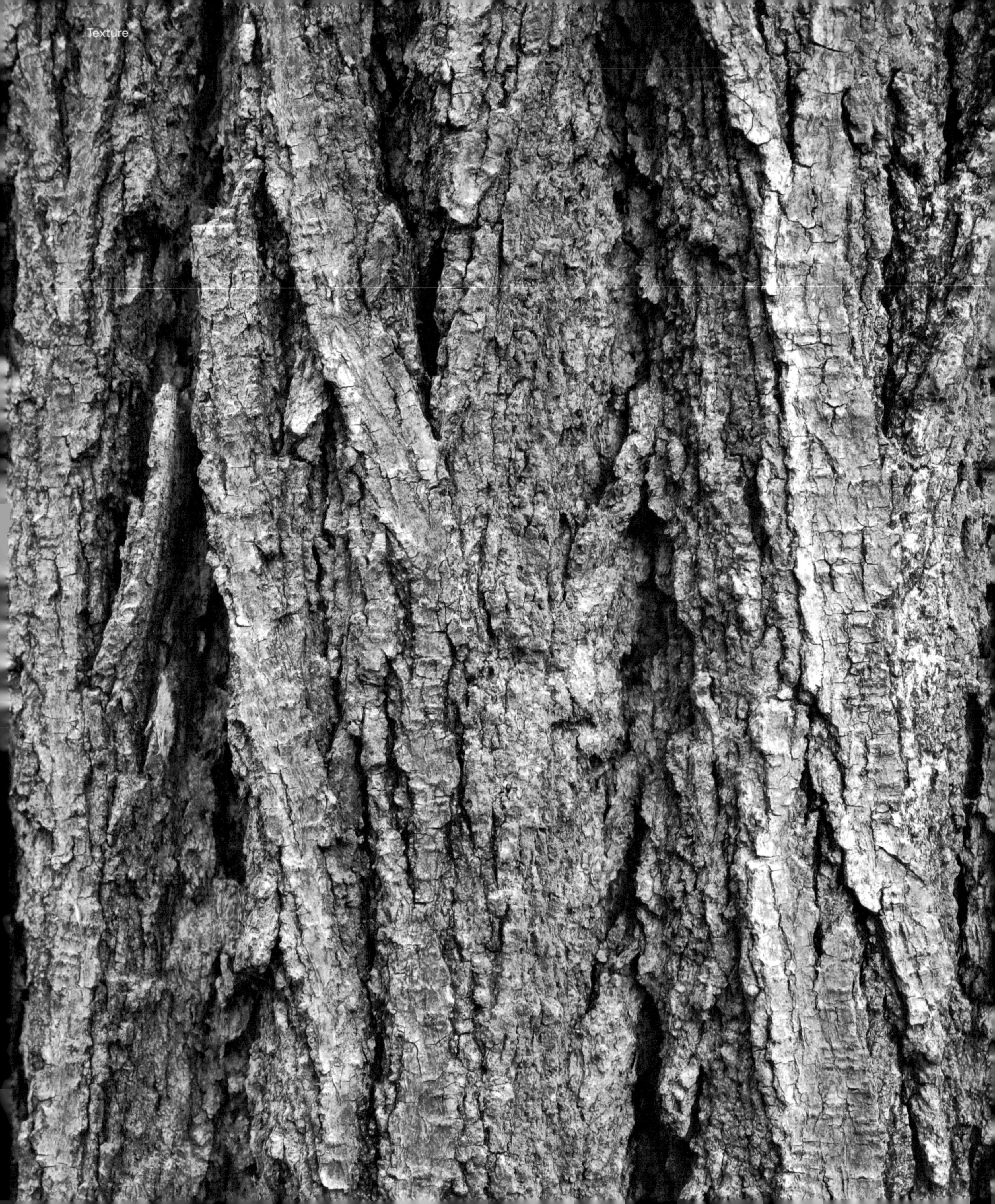
Texture

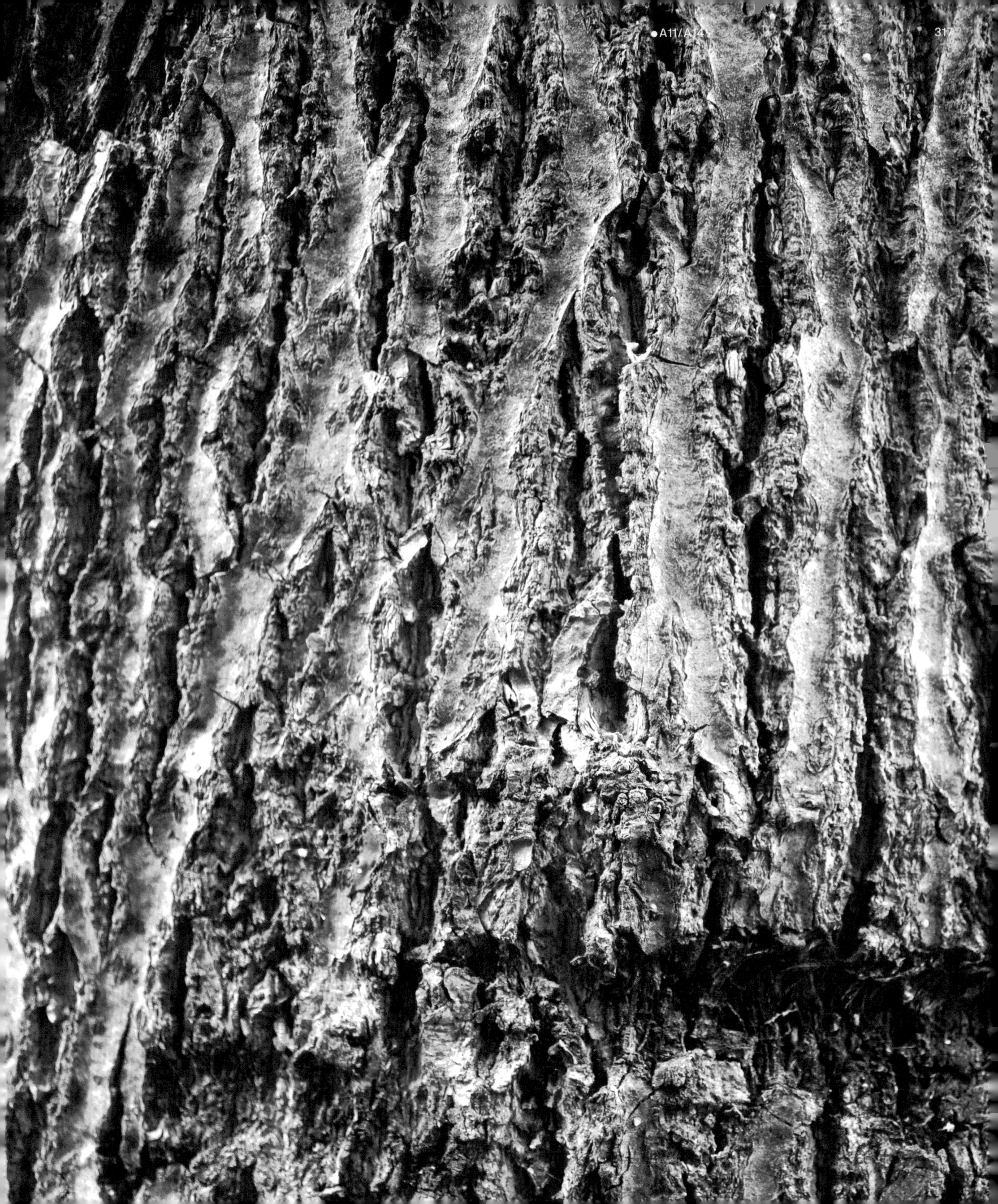
A11/A14

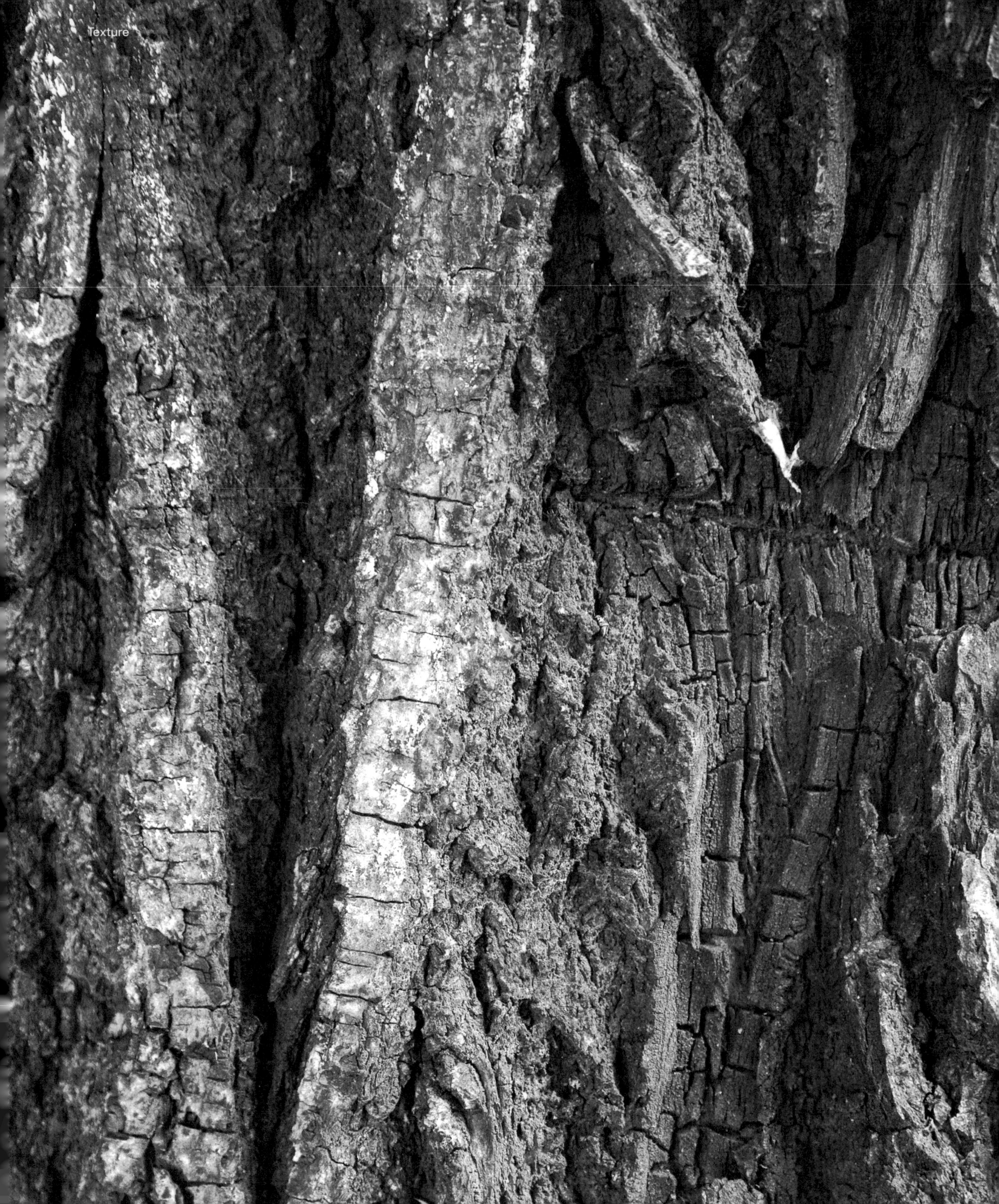

Texture

N1   Linden   [Tilia cordata]
N2   Tempelhofer Feld
N3   Linden   [Tilia x europaea]
N4   Linden   [Tilia cordata]
N5   Hop-Hornbeam   [Ostrya carpinifolia]
N6   Tempelhofer Feld
N7   Locust   [Robinia]
N8   Plane   [Platanus x acerifolia]
N9   Alder   [Alnus]
N10 Linden   [Tilia]
N11 Maple   [Acer plat. 'Columnare']
N12 Hazel   [Corylus colurna]

E1   Thuja   [Thuja]
E2   Hornbeam   [Carpinus betulus]
E3   Linden   [Tilia x europaea]
E4   Maple   [Acer]
E5   Linden   [Tilia x europaea]
E6   Locust   [Robinia x margaretta]
E7   Chestnut   [Aesculus x carnea]
E8   English yew   [Taxus baccata]
E9   Chestnut   [Aesculus x carnea]
E10 Tree of heaven   [Ailanthus altissima]
E11 British oak   [Quercus robur]

U1   Maple   [Acer platanoides 'Globosum']
U2   Locust   [Robinia pseudoacacia]
U3   Maple   [Acer]
U4   Linden   [Tilia]
U5   Plane   [Platanus x acerifolia]
U6   Lilac   [Syringa]

B1   Plane   [Platanus x acerifolia]
B2   Tempelhofer Feld
B3   Linden   [Tilia cordata]
B4   Silver birch   [Betula pendula]
B5   Hazel   [Corylus colurna]
B6   Blue spruce   [Picea Pungens]
B7   Tempelhofer Feld
B8   Tempelhofer Feld
B9   Chestnut   [Aesculus x carnea]
B10 Hazel   [Corylus colurna]
B11 Linden   [Tilia]
B12 Linden   [Tilia]
B13 Linden   [Tilia cordata]
B14 Silver maple   [Acer saccharinum]
B15 Linden   [Tilia tomentosa]
B16 Linden   [Tilia]

A1   Maple   [Acer platanoides]
A2   Maple   [Acer platanoides]
A3   Honey locust   [Gleditsia triacanthos]
A4   Mistletoe   [Viscum minimum]
A5   Cornelian cherry [Cornus mas]
A6   Oak   [Quercus robur]
A7   Elm   [Ulmus Resista]
A8   Tempelhofer Feld
A9   Maple   [Acer platanoides]
A10 Maple   [Acer]
A11 Locust   [Robinia]
A12 Poplar   [Populus nigra 'Italica']
A13 Linden   [Tilia]
A14 Linden   [Tilia americana]
A15 Silver lime   [Tilia tomentosa]
A16 Tree of heaven   [Ailanthus altissima]
A17 Linden   [Tilia]
A18 Linden   [Tilia x intermedia]
A19 Pine   [Pinus]
A20 Hawthorn   [Crataegus prunifolia]
A21 Linden   [Tilia]
A22 Hawthorn   [Crataegus laevigata]
A23 Spruce   [Picea]

U7   Locust   [Robinia pseudoacacia]
U8   Maple   [Acer platanoides]
U9   Morello Cherry   [Prunus]
U10 Maple   [Acer]

Ambience
N1–U10

Ambience consists of all 'Neubau Forst' trees. Variable in season, all trees are assigned to their original location within Central Berlin. Ambience documents the tree and its original environment and location as a means of re-relocation. Presenting the trees in their original habitat demonstrates the 'true colour' of the tree, the city, and its shared surroundings. Circumstances of which have been erased through the 'Neubau Forst' distilling process.

— Printed on Hello Fat Matt 150 gsm

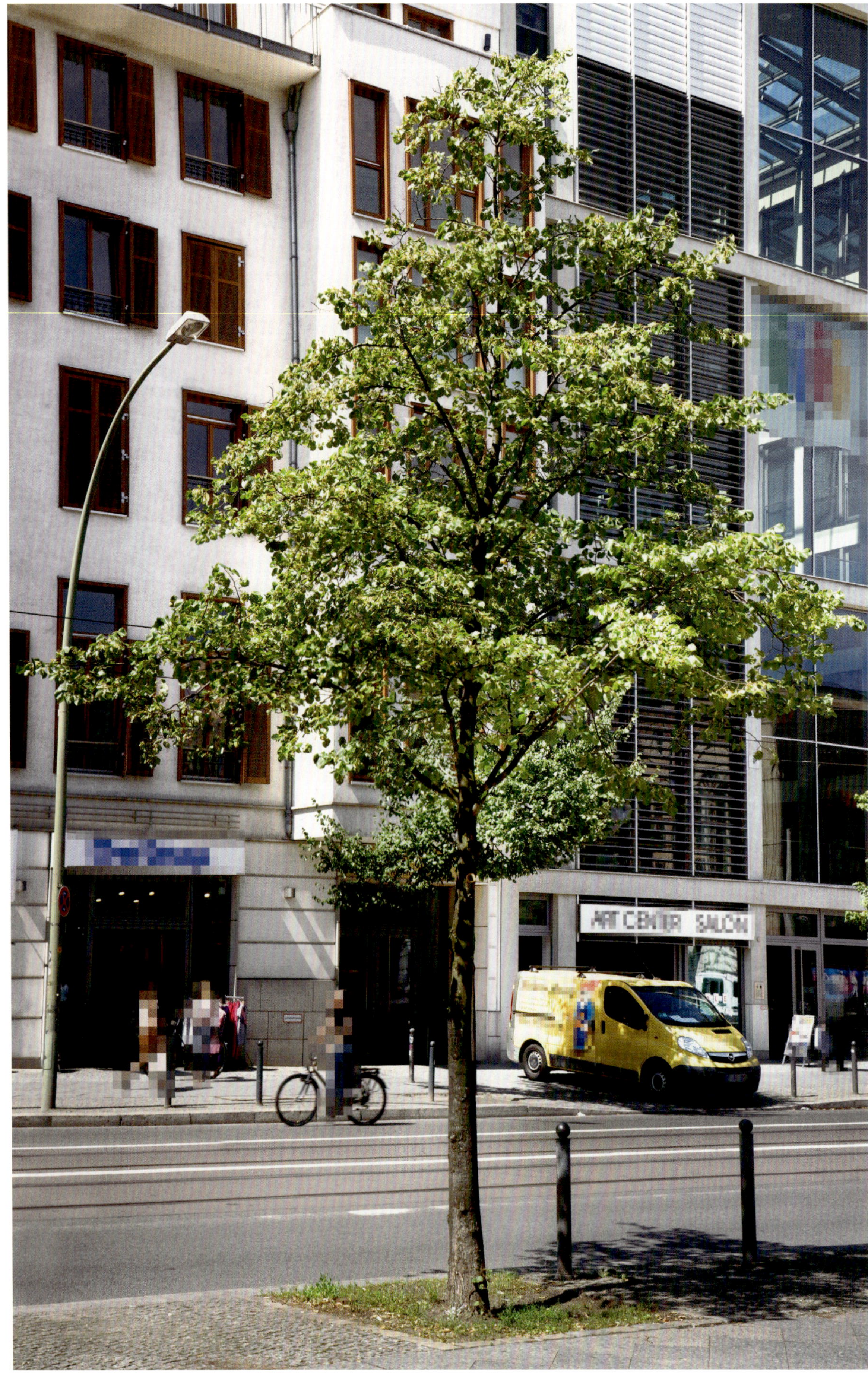

N1–S   N1–W   G: Linden/Linde [Tilia cordata]
o   o   ADR: Friedrichstrasse 105, 10117 Mitte Berlin
                GPS: 52.523118, 13.387895, HT: 520 cm, YR: 1990

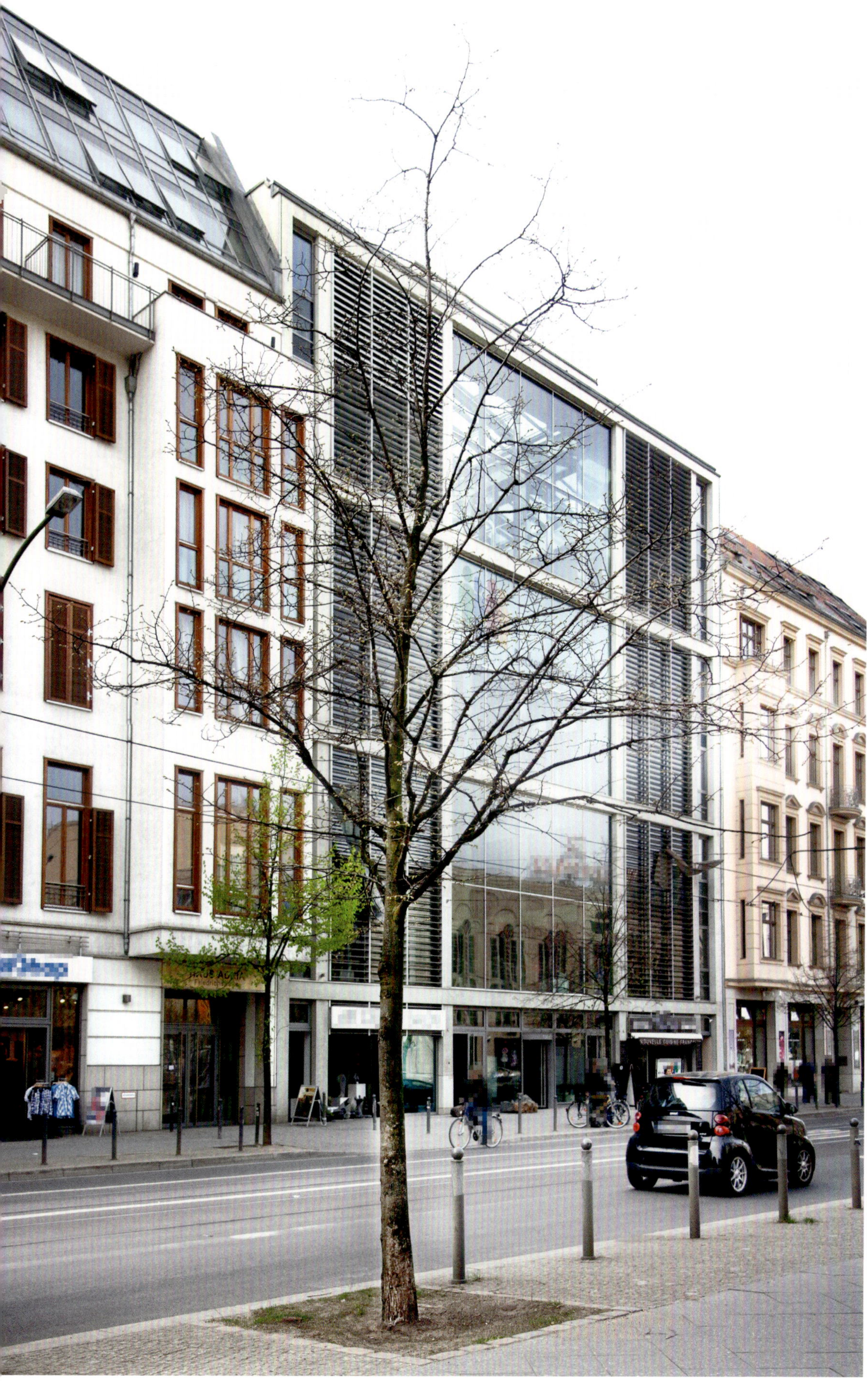

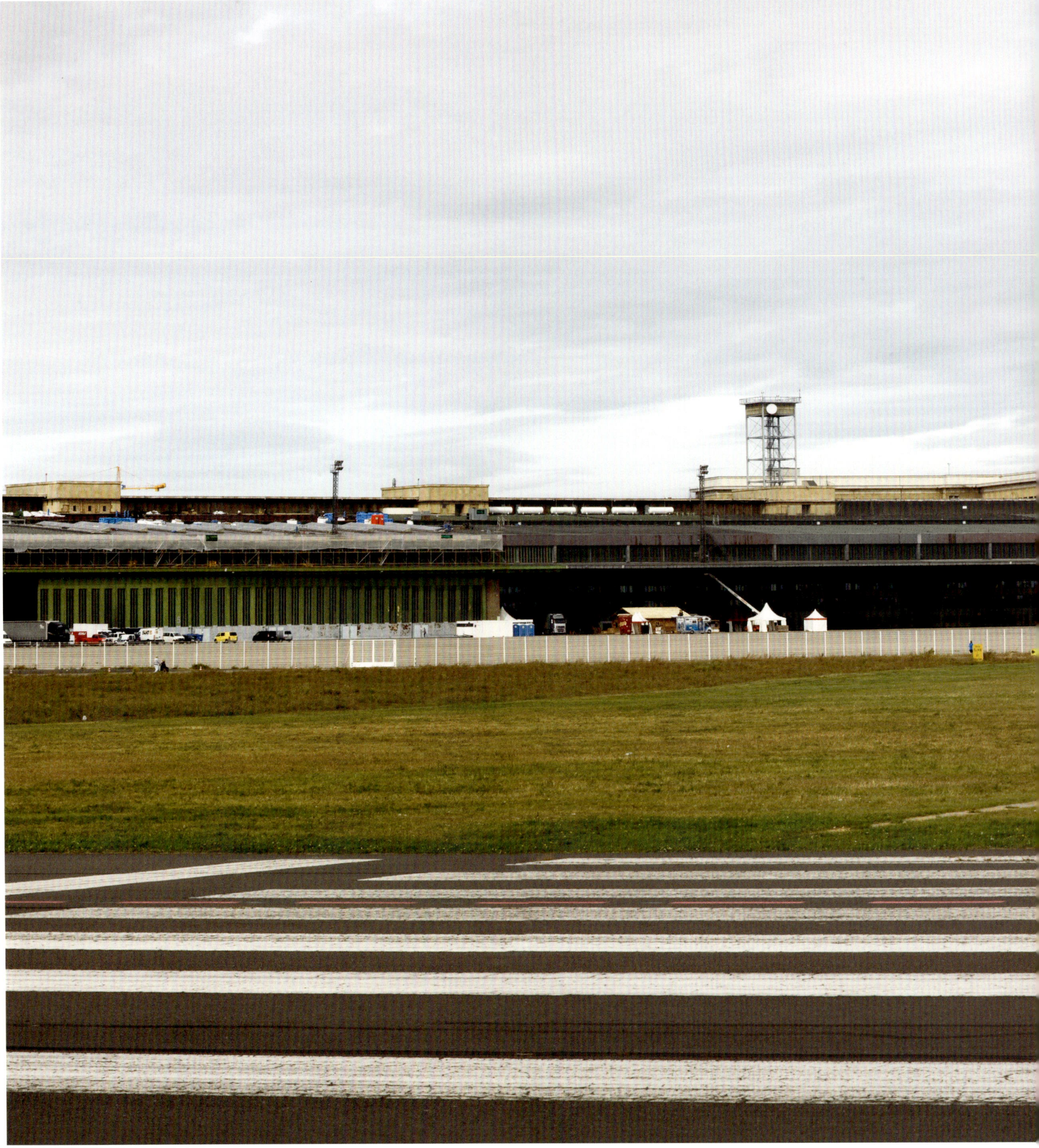

Tempelhofer Feld
GPS: 52.47083, 13.38851

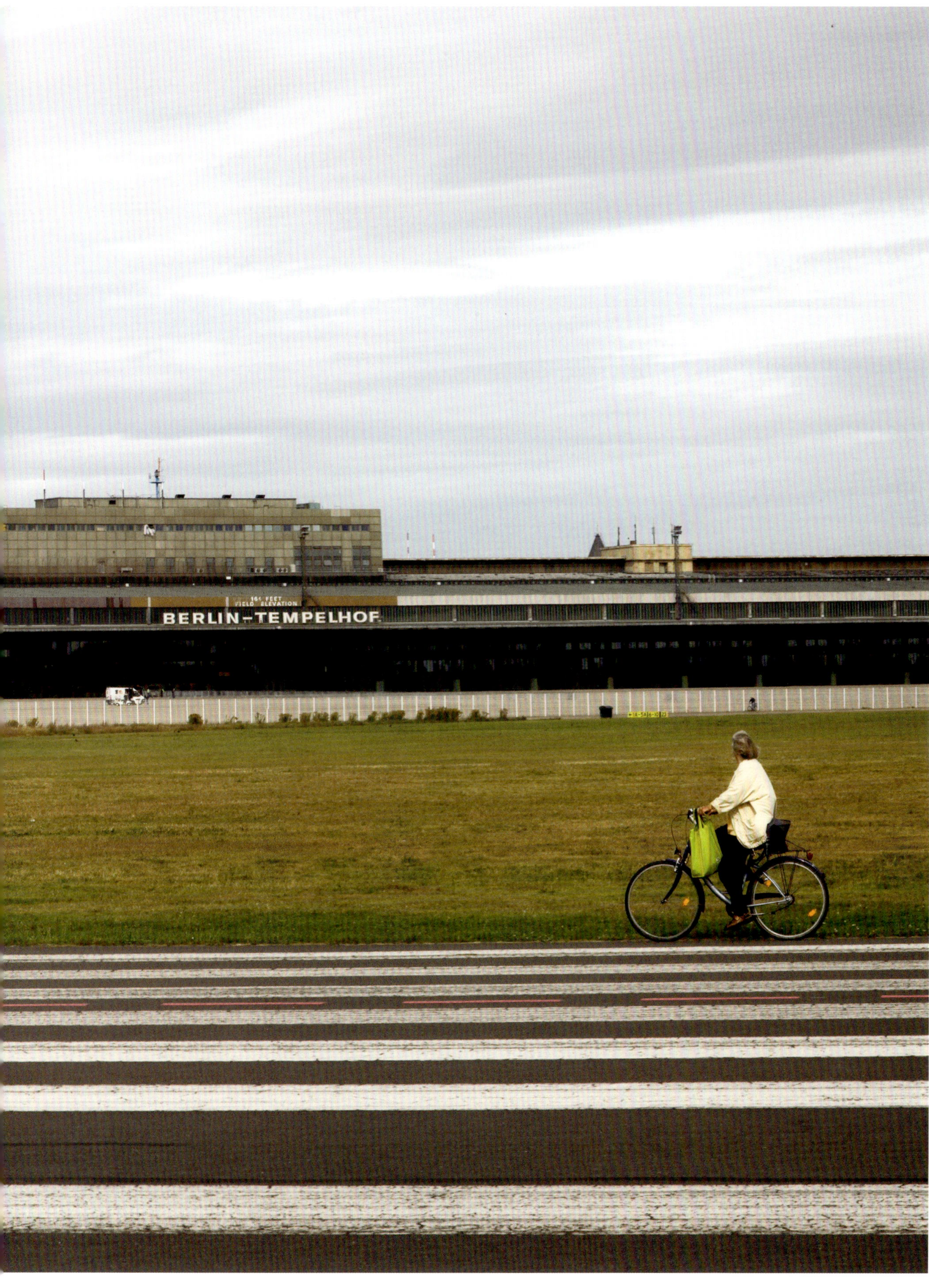
466 FEET
FIELD ELEVATION
BERLIN-TEMPELHOF

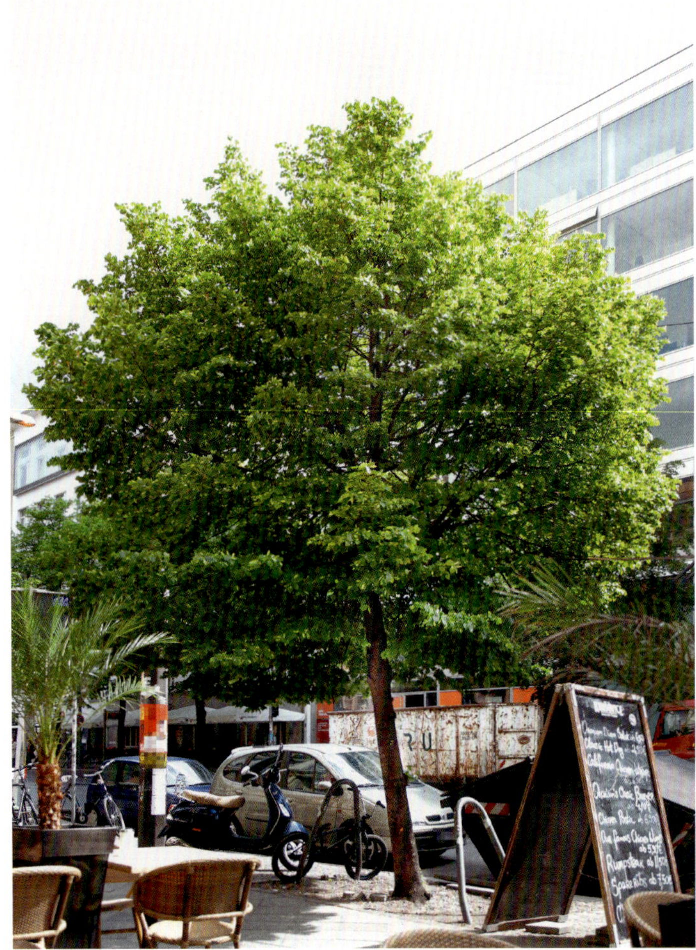 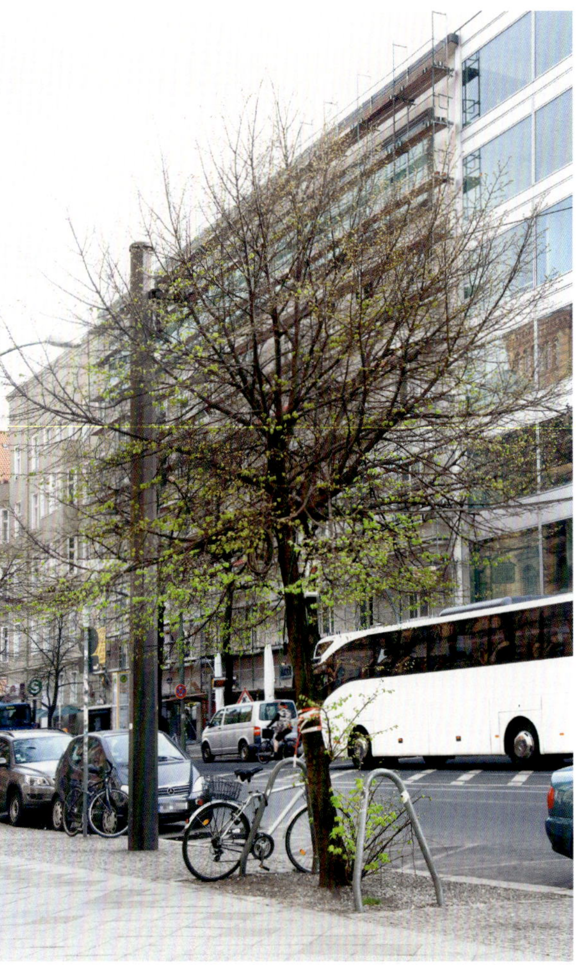

N3–S   N3–W   G: Linden/Linde [Tilia × europaea]
                            ADR: Oranienburger Strasse 38, 10117 Mitte Berlin
                            GPS: 52.525423, 13.391413, HT: 570 cm, YR: 1988

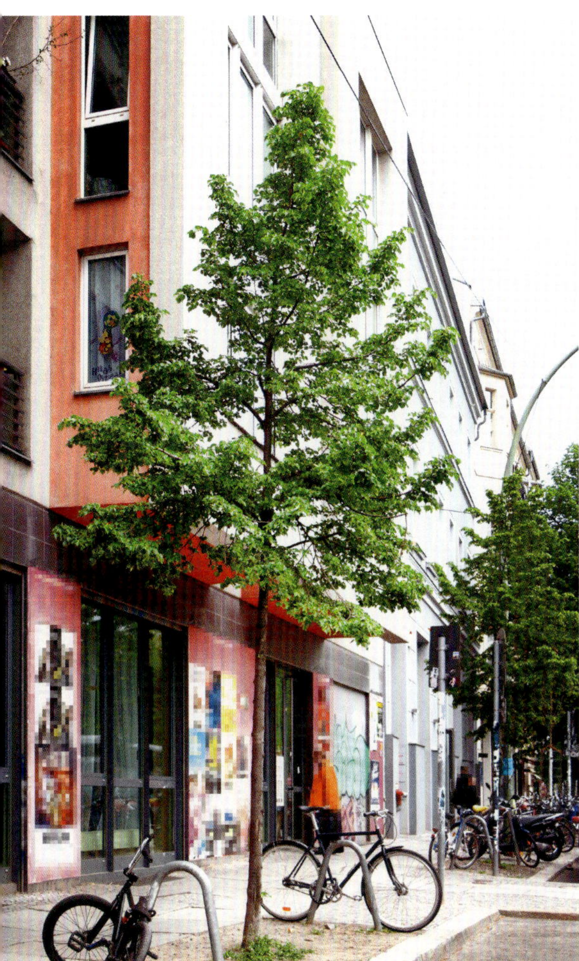
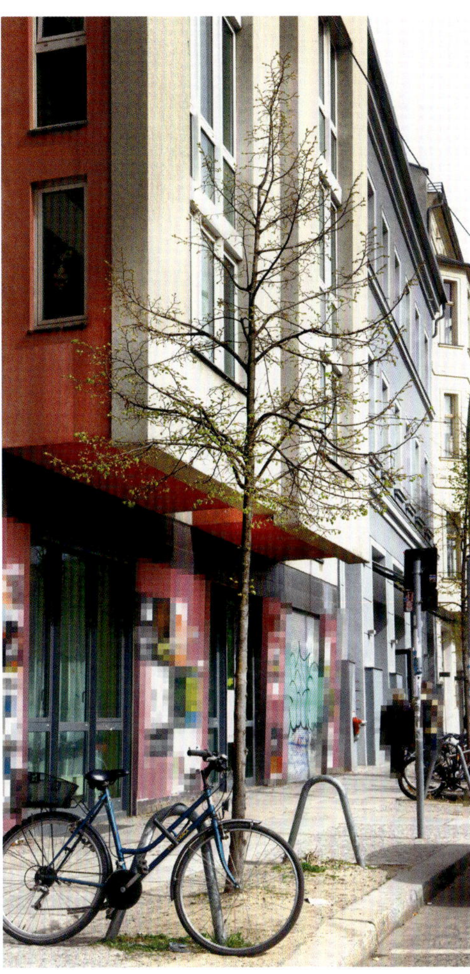

N4–S   N4–W   G: Linden/Linde [Tilia cordata]
ADR: Oranienburger Strasse 20, 10178 Mitte Berlin
GPS: 52.524101, 13.396542, HT: 650 cm, YR: 2005

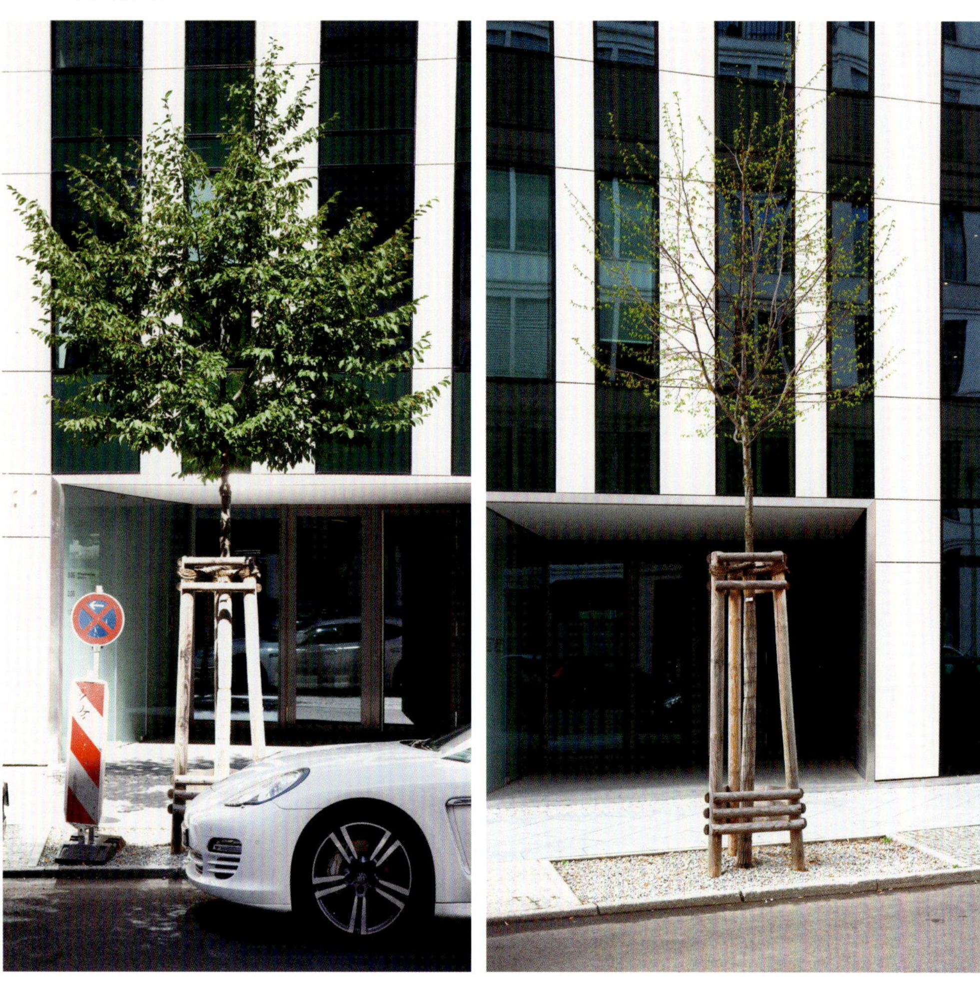

N5–S   N5–W   G: Hop-Hornbeam / Hopfenbuche [Ostrya carpinifolia]
ADR: Jägerstrasse 41, 10117 Mitte Berlin
GPS: 52.514481, 13.397191, HT: 570 cm, YR: 2009

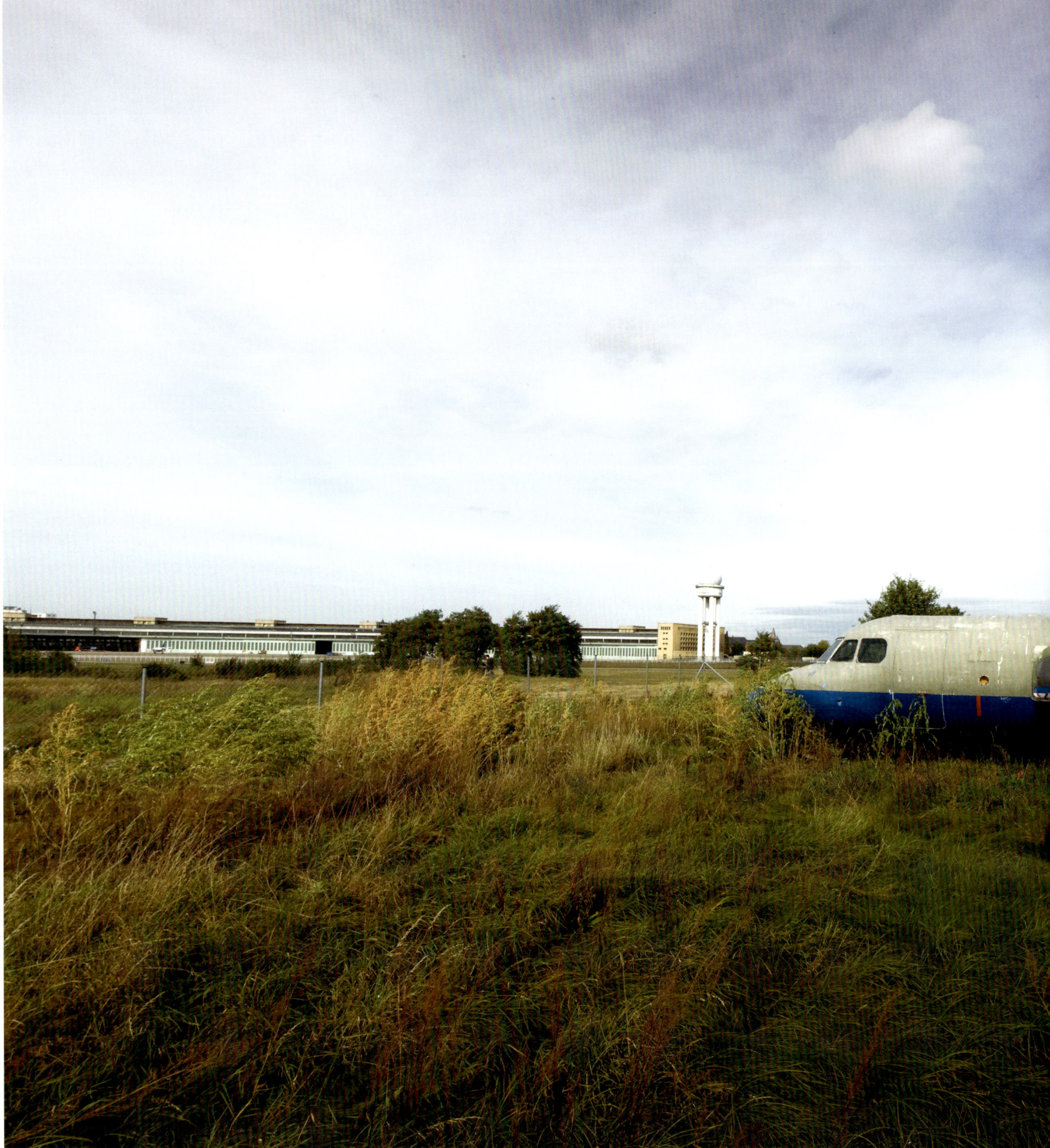

Tempelhofer Feld
GPS: 52.47085, 13.39734

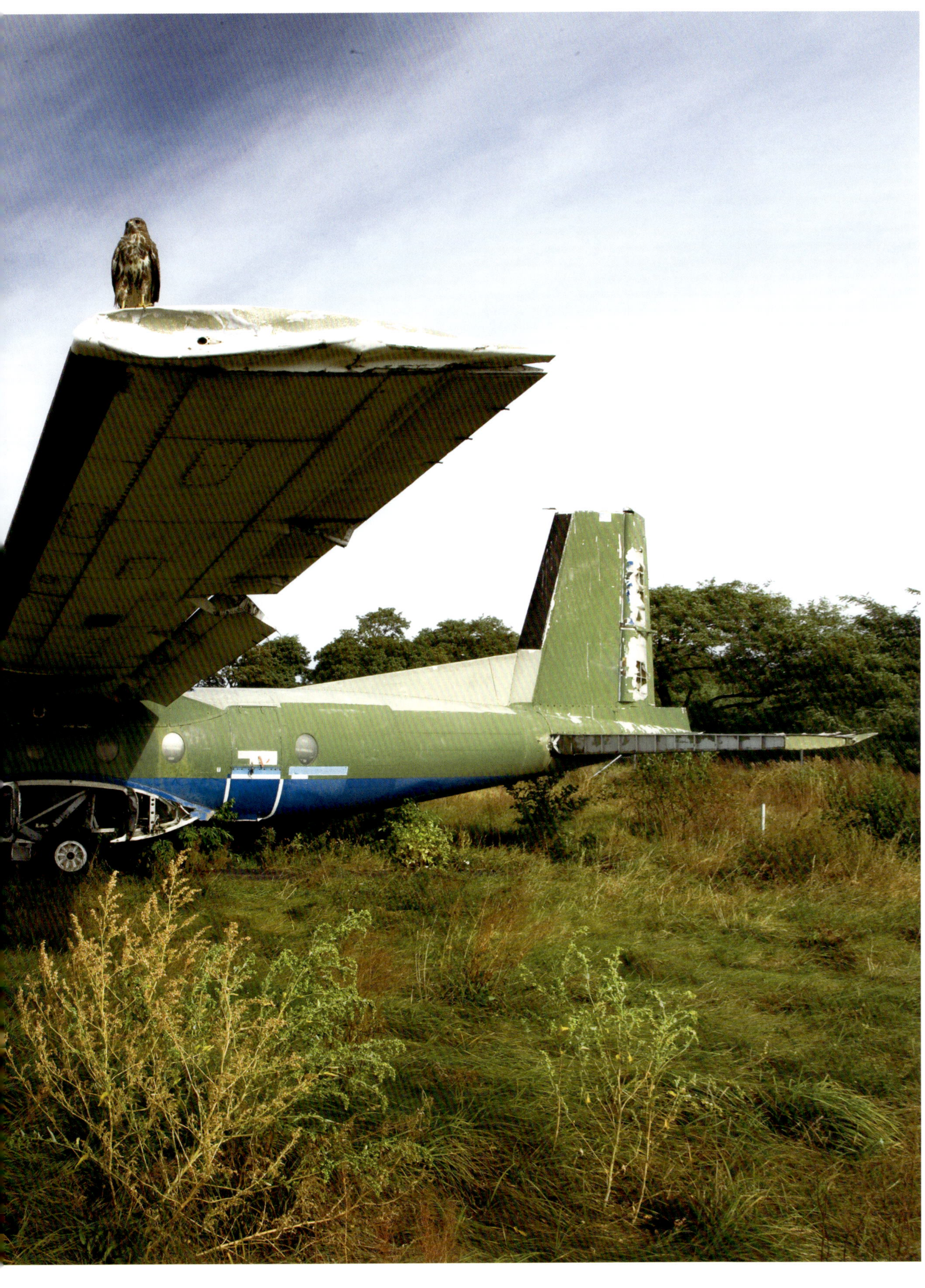

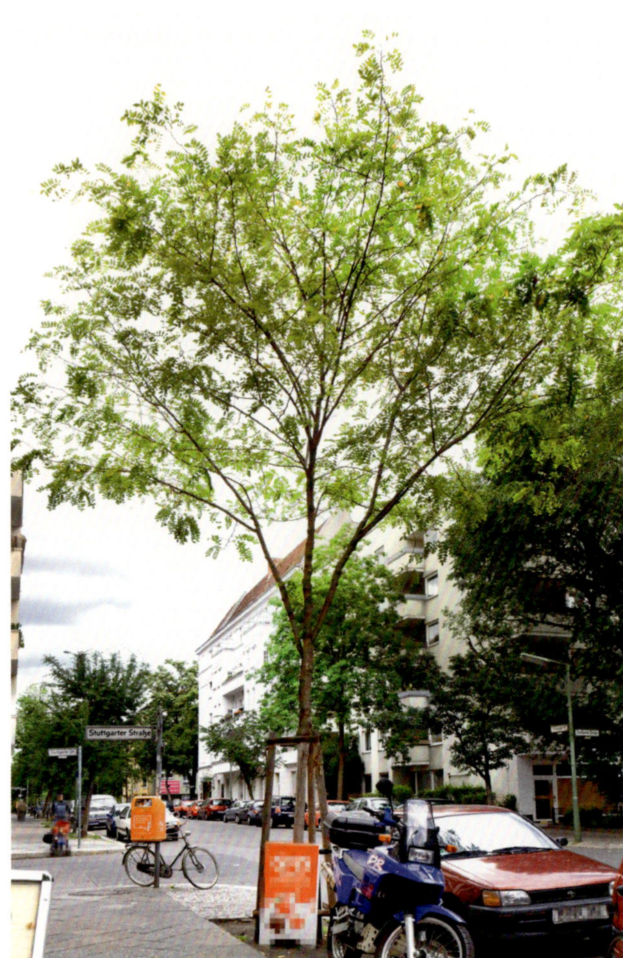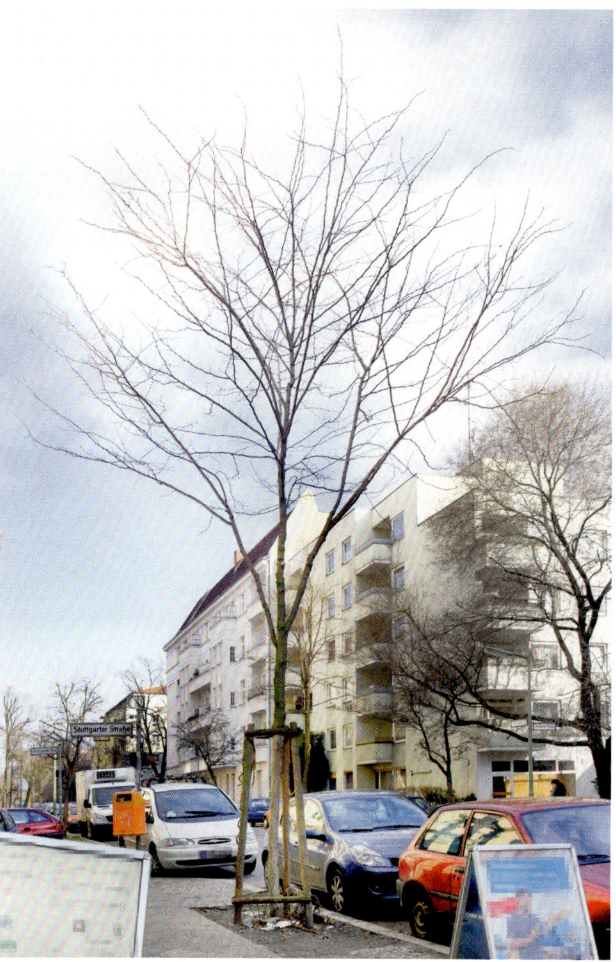

N7–S   N7–W   G: Locust / Robinie [Robinia]
              o   ADR: Roseggerstrasse 40, 12059 Neukölln Berlin
                           GPS: 52.479798, 13.445954, HT: 750 cm, YR: 1982

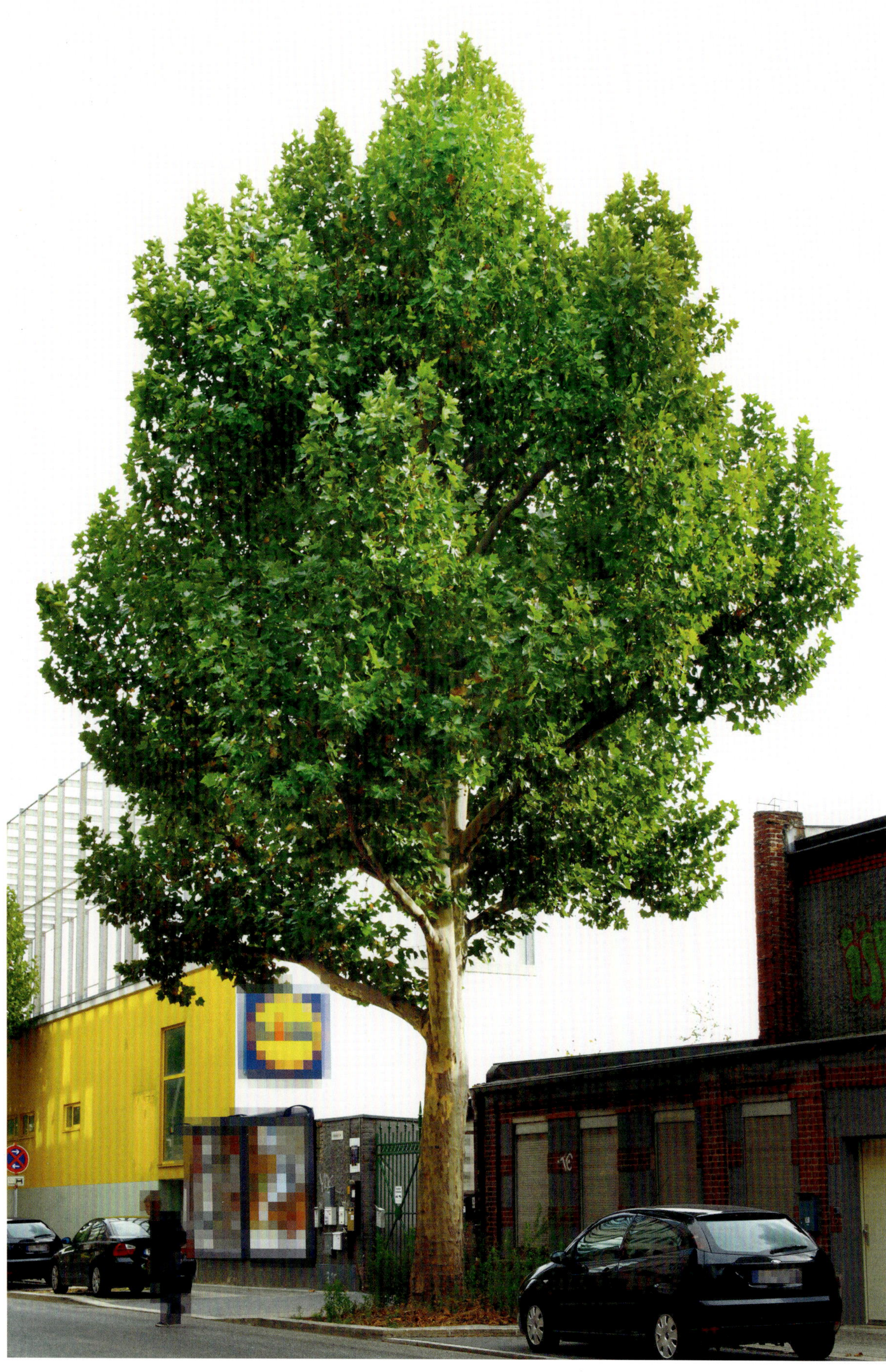

N8–S   N8–W   G: Plane / Platane [Platanus × acerifolia]
○   ○   ADR: Lahnstrasse 75, 12055 Neukölln Berlin
                        GPS: 52.468046, 13.445585, HT: 1700 cm, YR: 1890

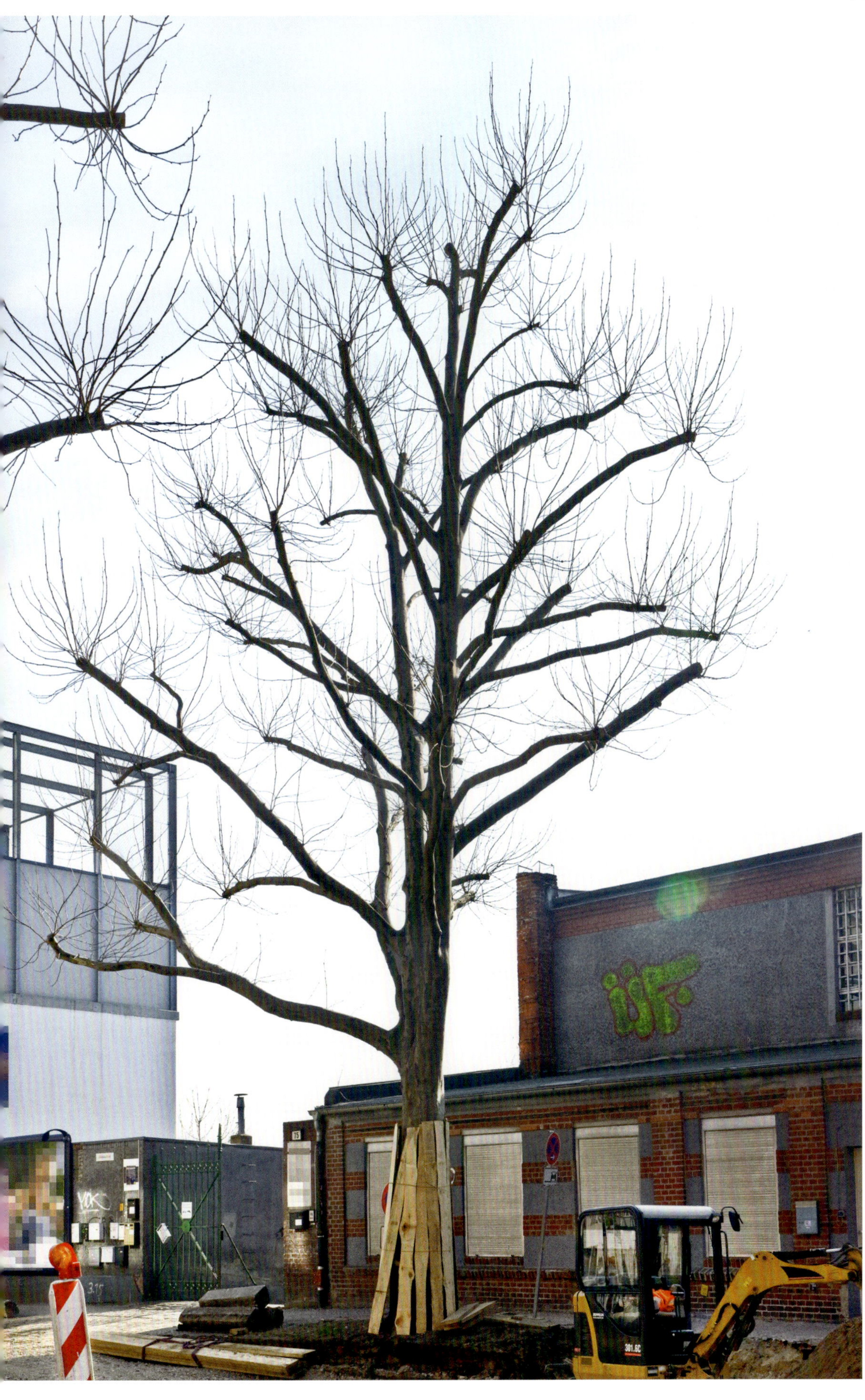

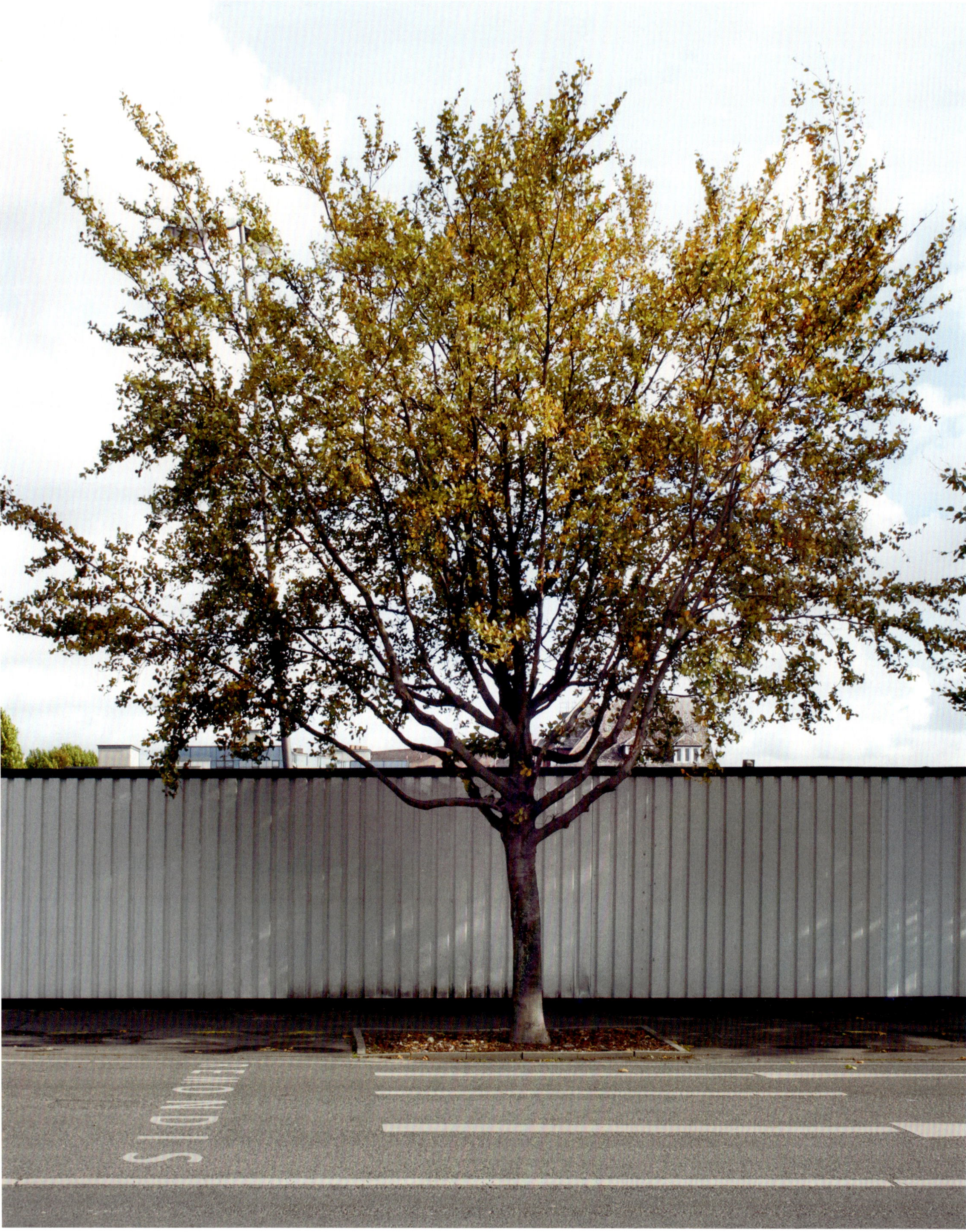

N9–S   N9–W   G: Alder / Erle [Alnus]
                            ADR: Lahnstrasse 39, 12055 Neukölln Berlin
                            GPS: 52.468150, 13.450510, HT: 1100 cm, YR: 1992

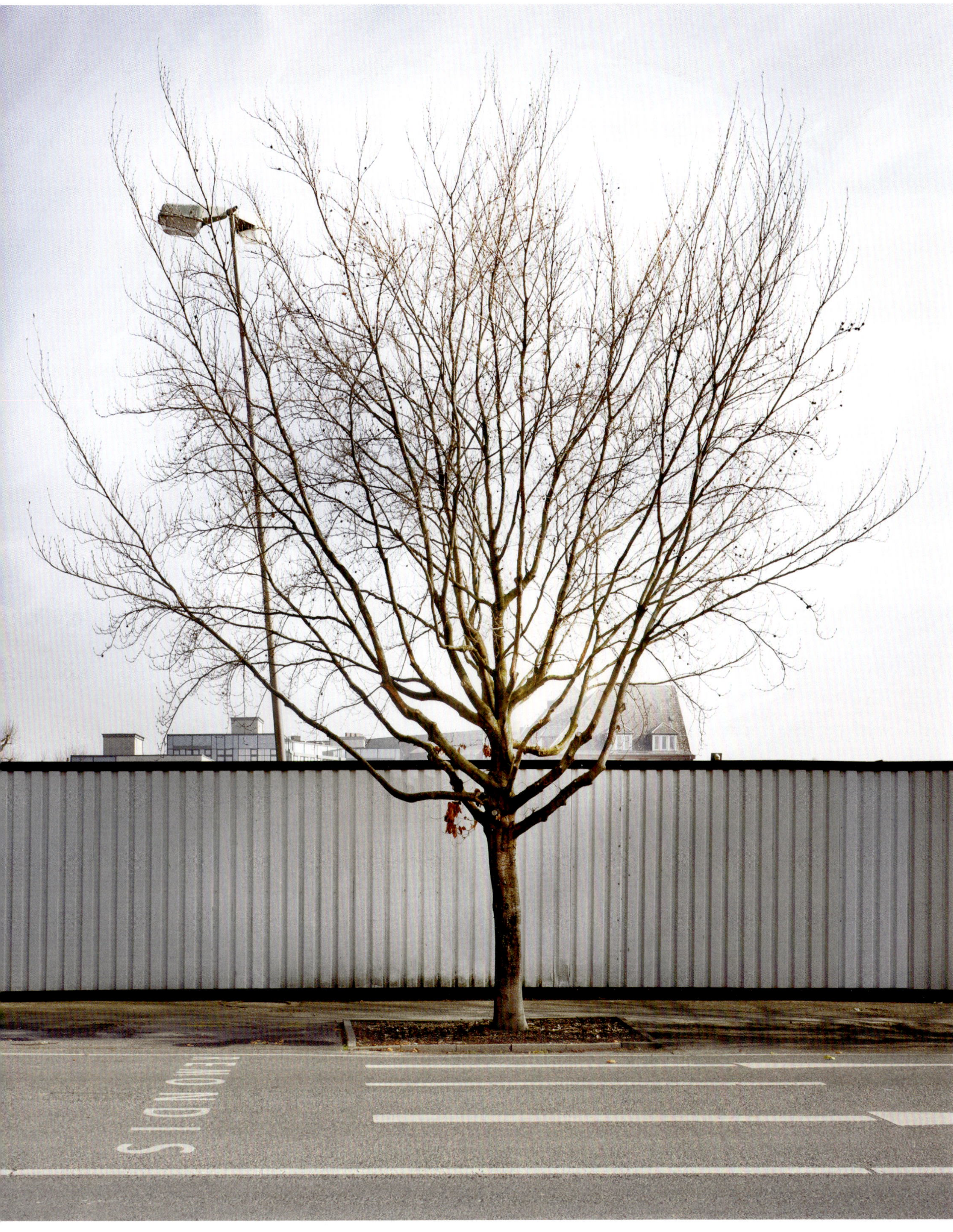

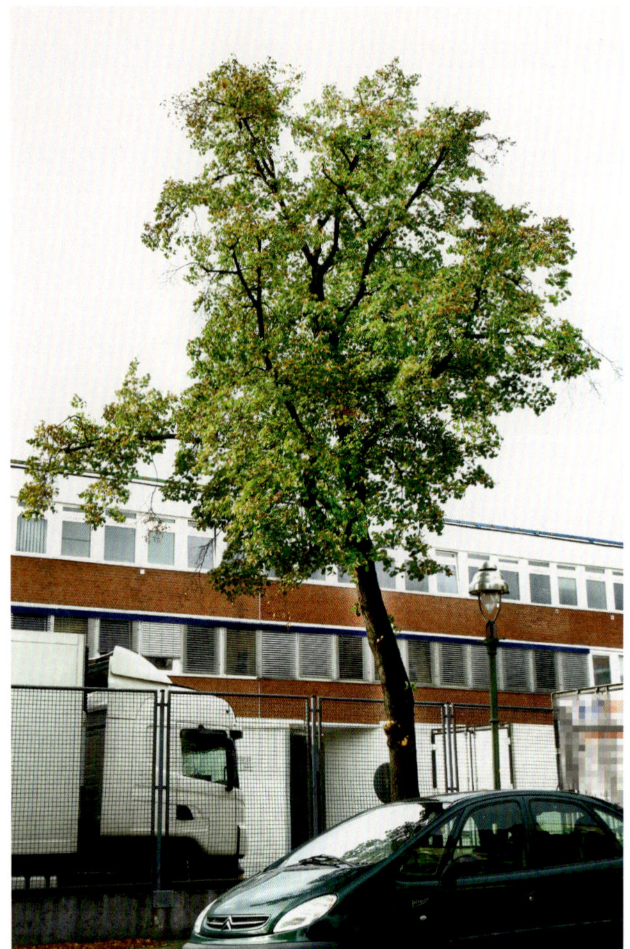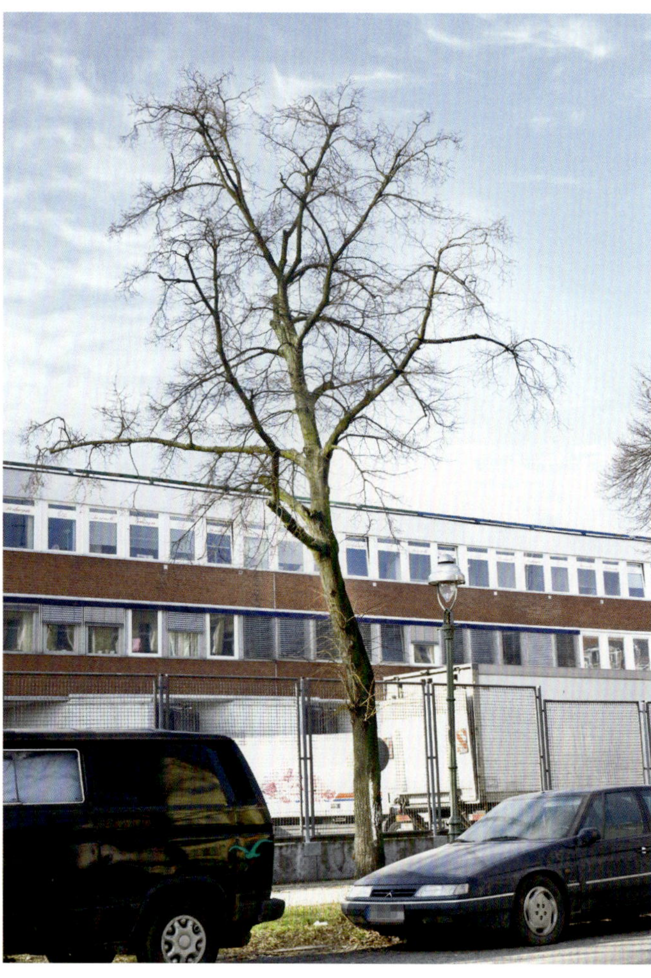

N10–S   N10–W   G: Linden/Linde [Tilia]
                              ADR: Niemetzstrasse 40, 12055 Neukölln Berlin
                              GPS: 52.469870, 13.453207, HT: 1070 cm, YR: 1950

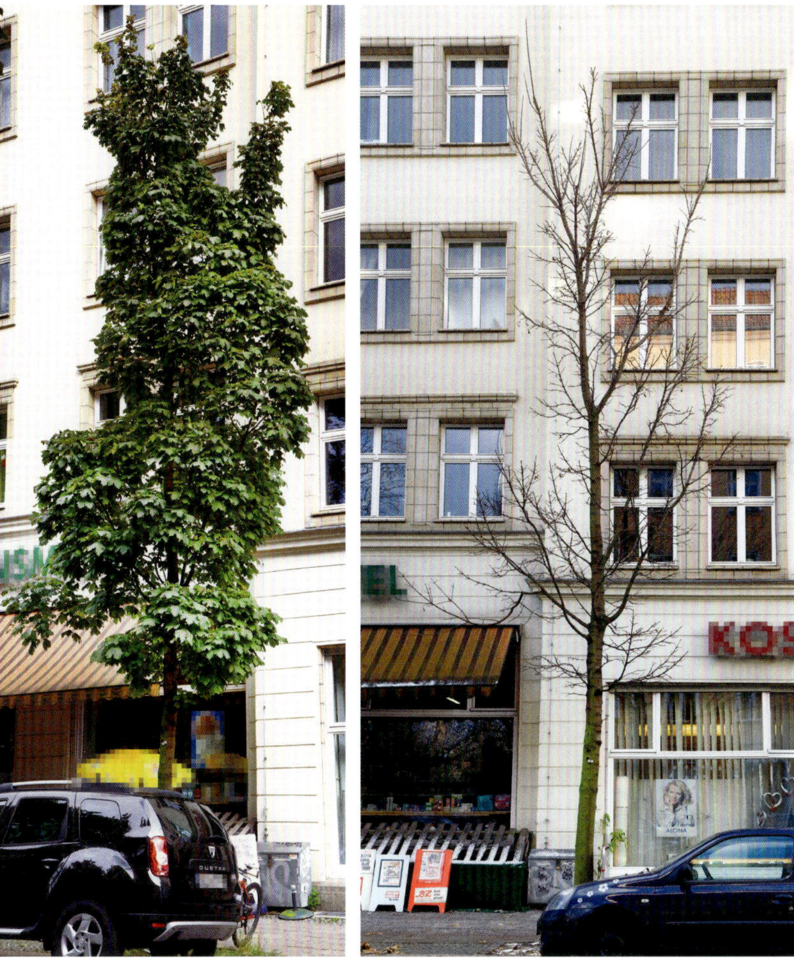

N11–S   N11–W   G: Maple/Ahorn [Acer plat. 'Columnare']
○   ADR: Auerstrasse 10, 10249 Friedrichshain Berlin
                                 GPS: 52.518839, 13.443873, HT: 1030 cm, YR: 2002

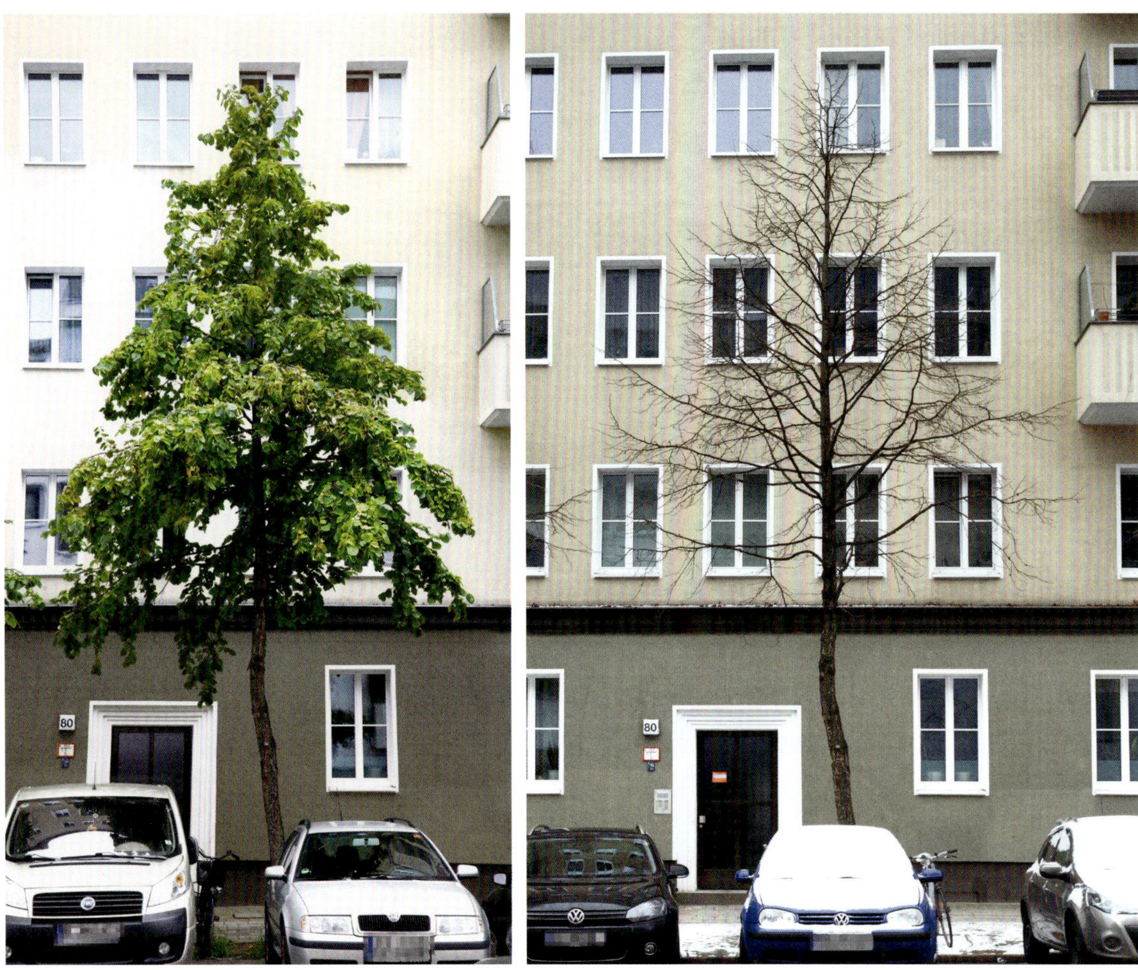

N12–S   N12–W   G: Hazel/Hasel [Corylus colurna]
o   ADR: Richard-Sorge-Strasse 80, 10249 Friedrichshain Berlin
                                    GPS: 52.518663, 13.448439, HT: 1100 cm, YR: 1988

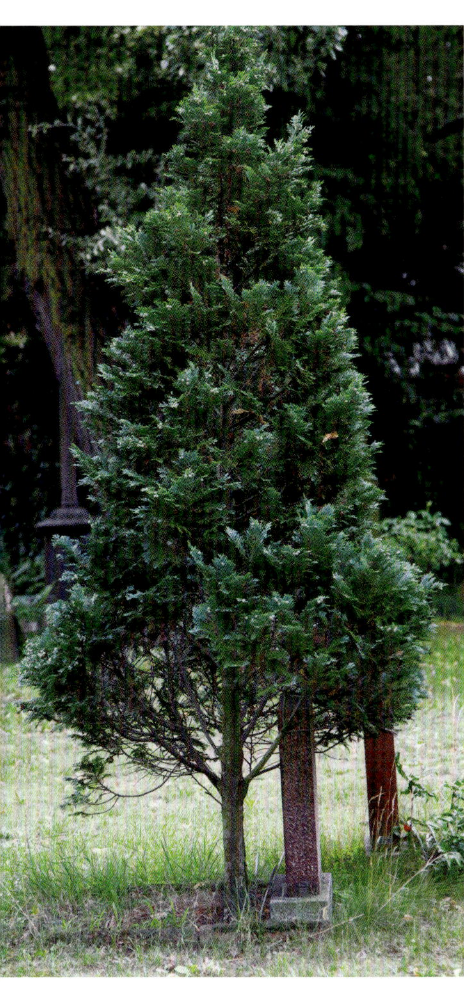
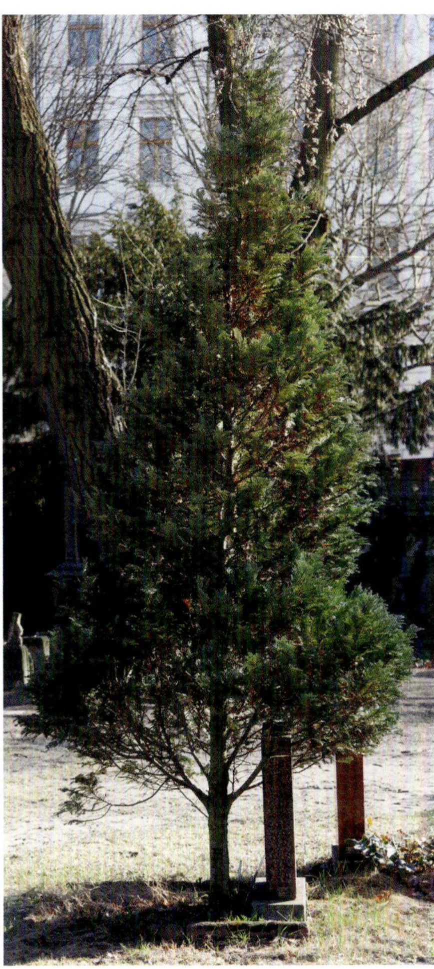

E1–S   E1–W   G: Thuja/Lebensbaum [Thuja]
o   ADR: Nostitzstrasse 60, 10961 Kreuzberg Berlin
                        GPS: 52.494522, 13.392146, HT: 160 cm, YR: 1978

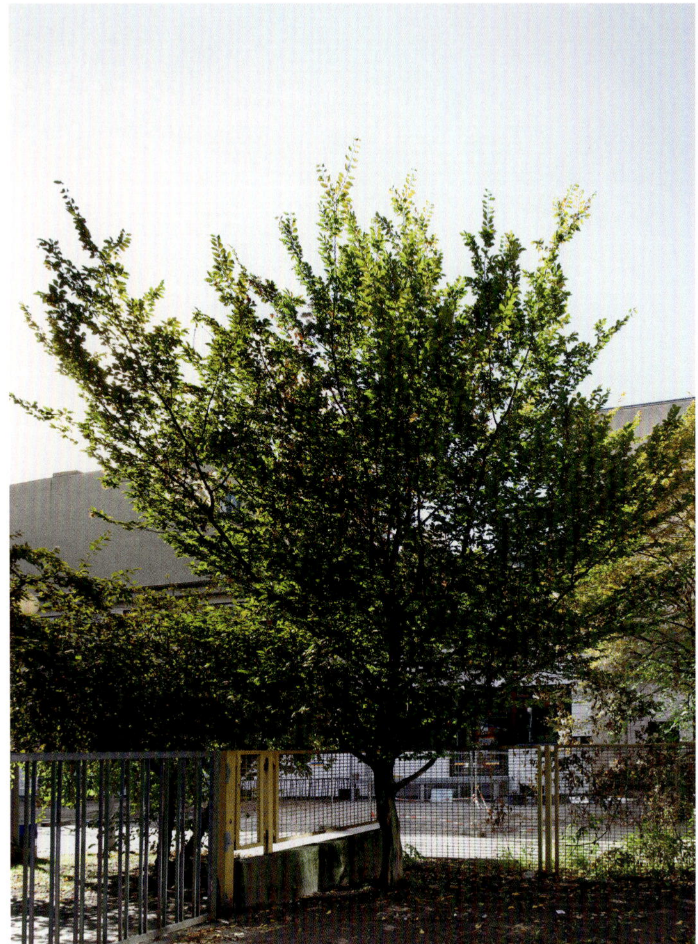 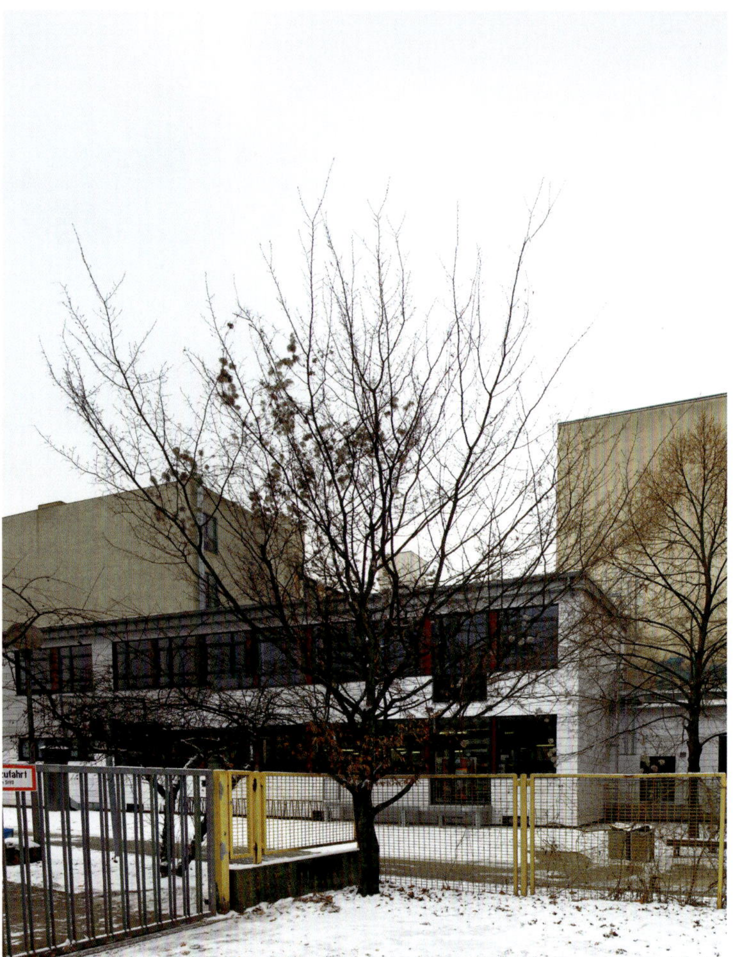

E2–S   E2–W   G: Hornbeam / Hainbuche [Carpinus betulus]
ADR: Alexandrinenstrasse 8, 10969 Kreuzberg Berlin
GPS: 52.499584, 13.401113, HT: 710 cm, YR: 1992

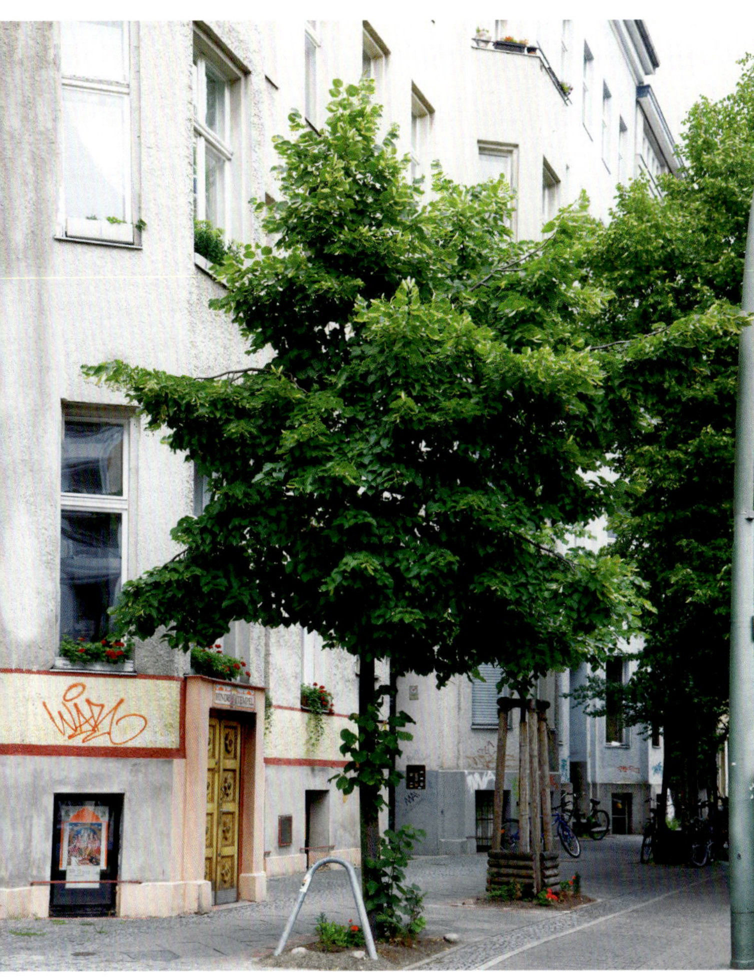
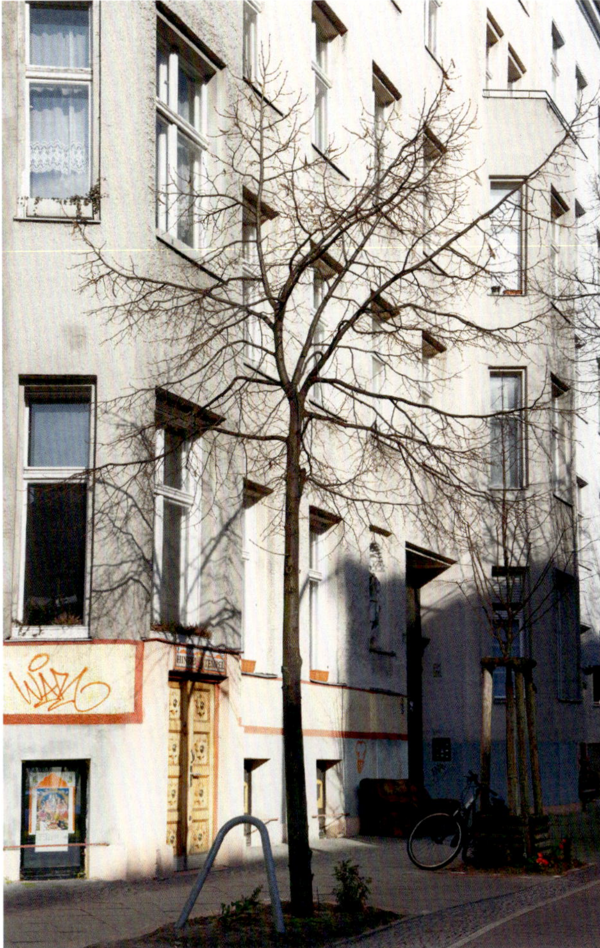

E3–S   E3–W   G: Linden/Linde [Tilia × europaea 'Pallida']
o   ADR: Urbanstrasse 177, 10961 Kreuzberg Berlin
                  GPS: 52.494237, 13.401892, HT: 750 cm, YR: 2008

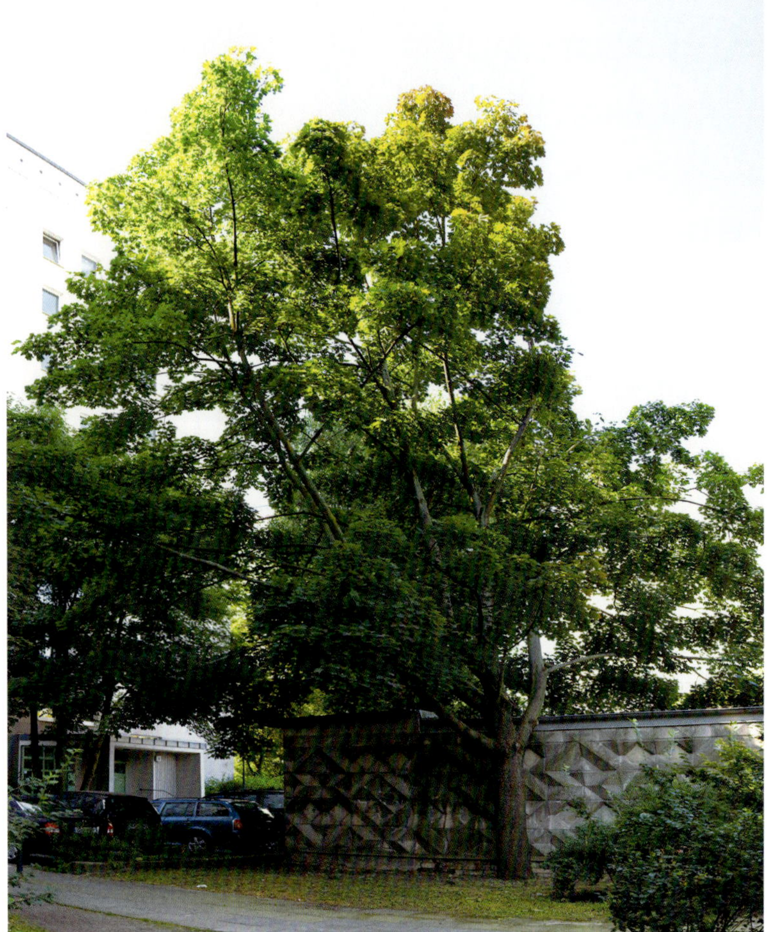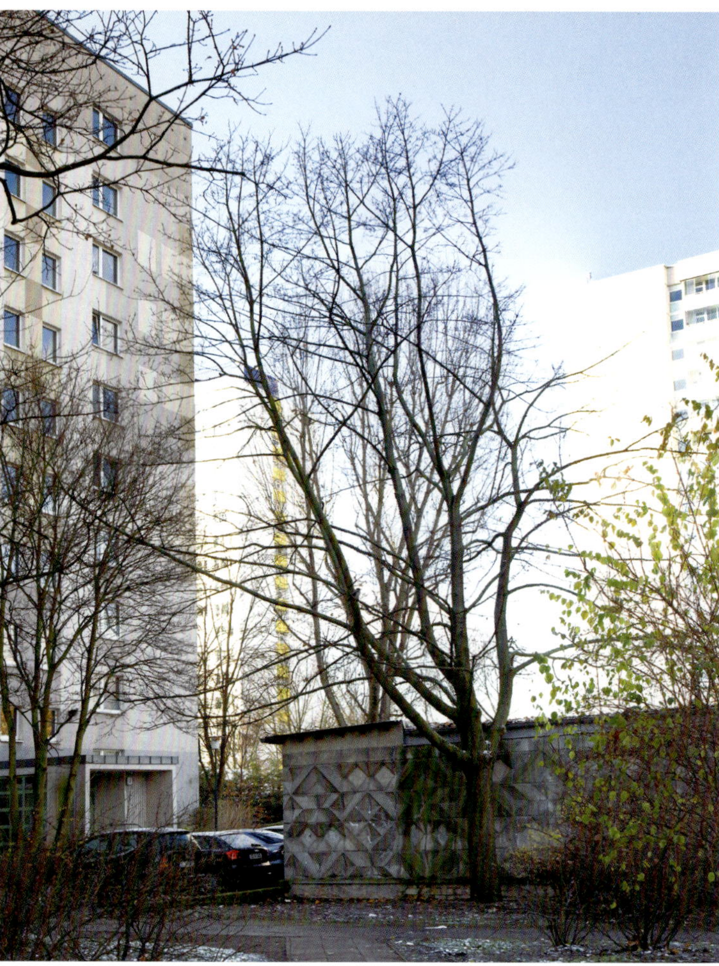

E4–S E4–W G: Maple/Ahorn [Acer]
o ADR: Ifflandstrasse 2, 10179 Mitte Berlin
GPS: 52.517037,13.421109, HT: 1590 cm, YR: 1993

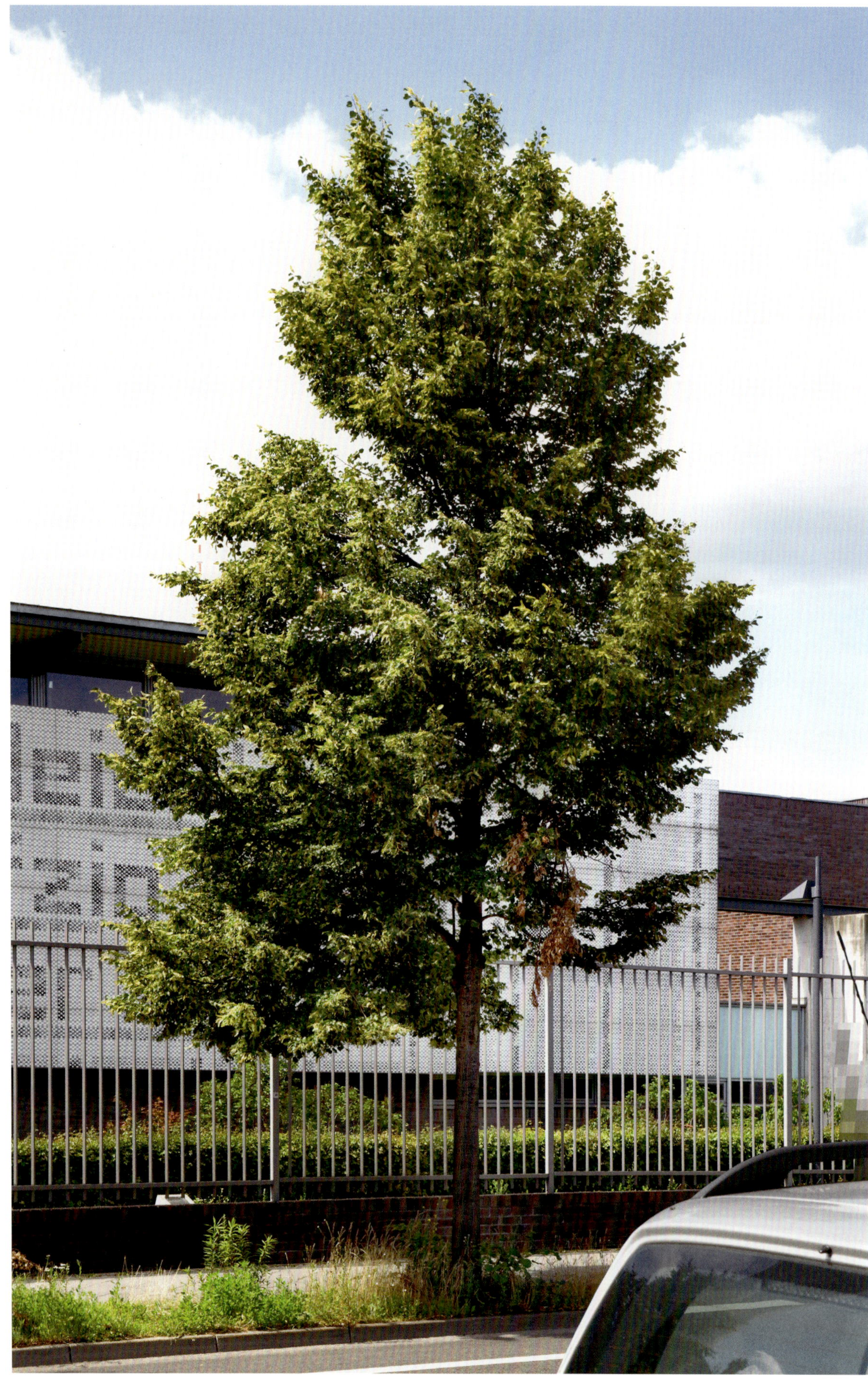

E5–S   E5–W   G: Linden/Linde [Tilia × europaea]
○   ○   ADR: Michaelkirchstrasse 27, 10179 Mitte Berlin
                            GPS: 52.51124, 13.42212, HT: 990 cm, YR: 1999

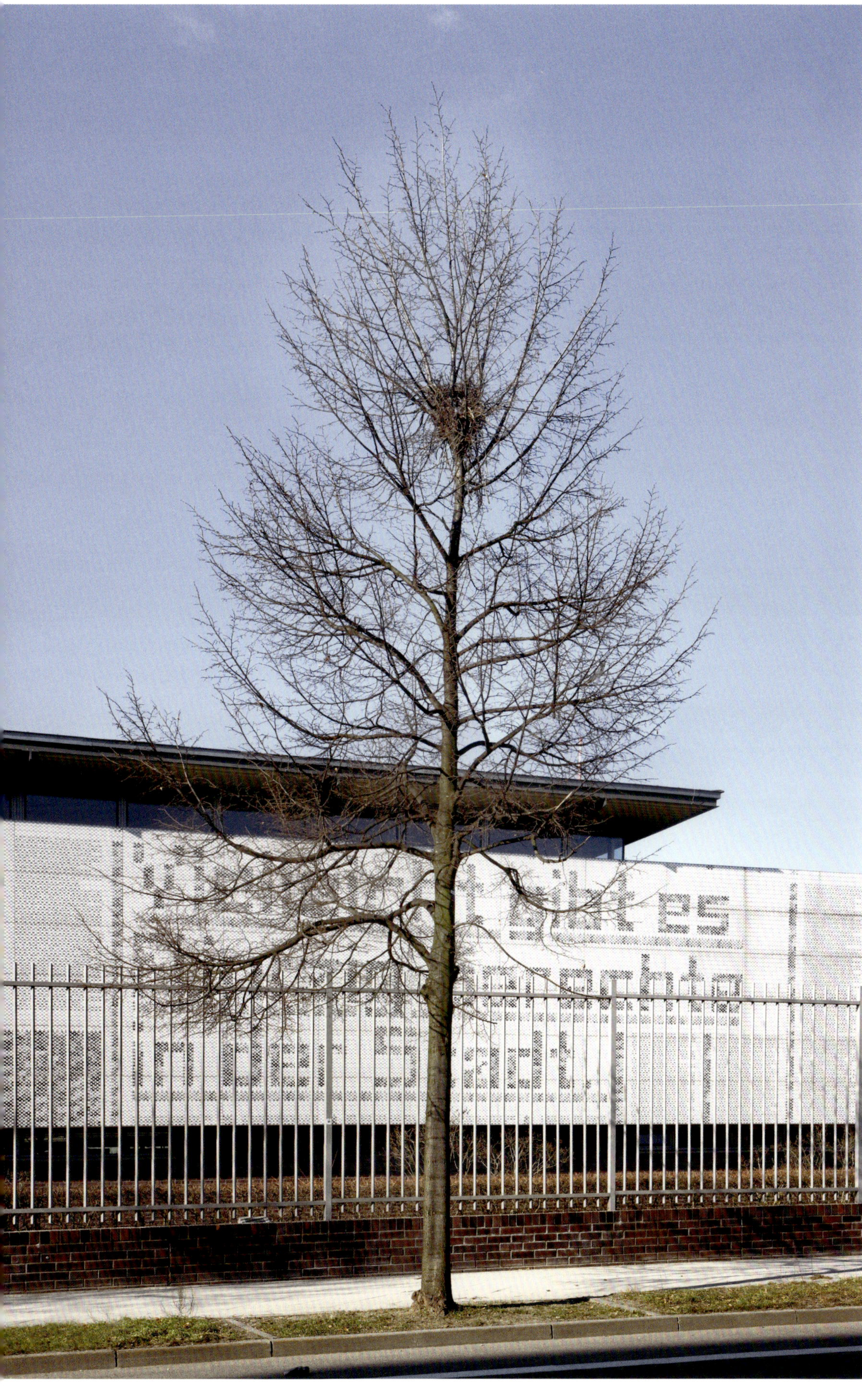

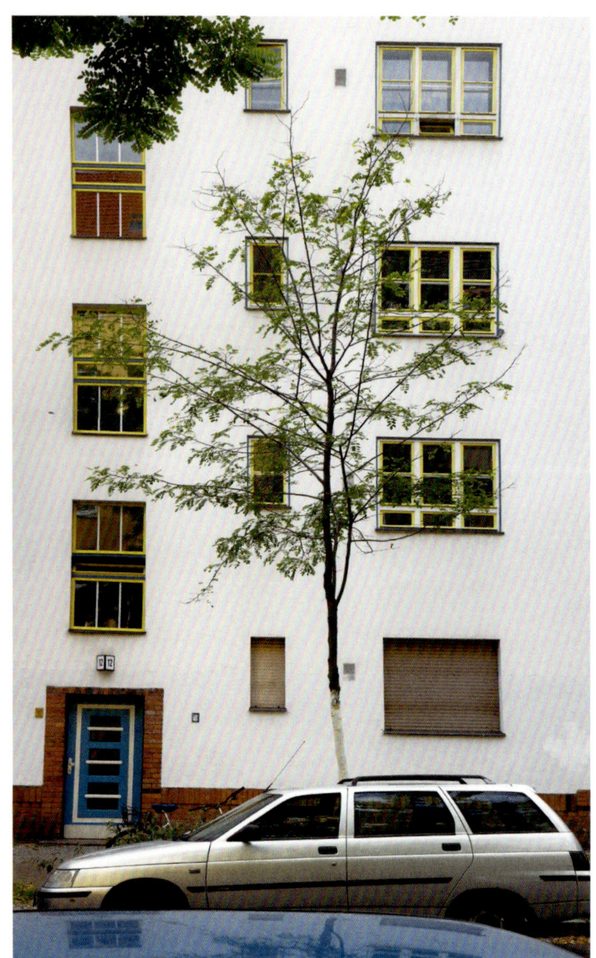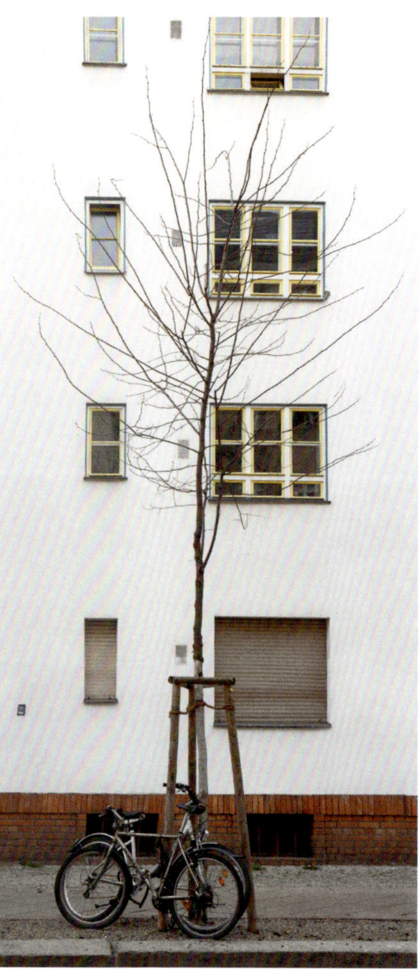

E6–S   E6–W   G: Locust/Robinie [Robinia × margaretta]
          o   ADR: Ossastrasse 13, 12045 Neukölln Berlin
                    GPS: 52.486683, 13.437661, HT: 700 cm, YR: 2008

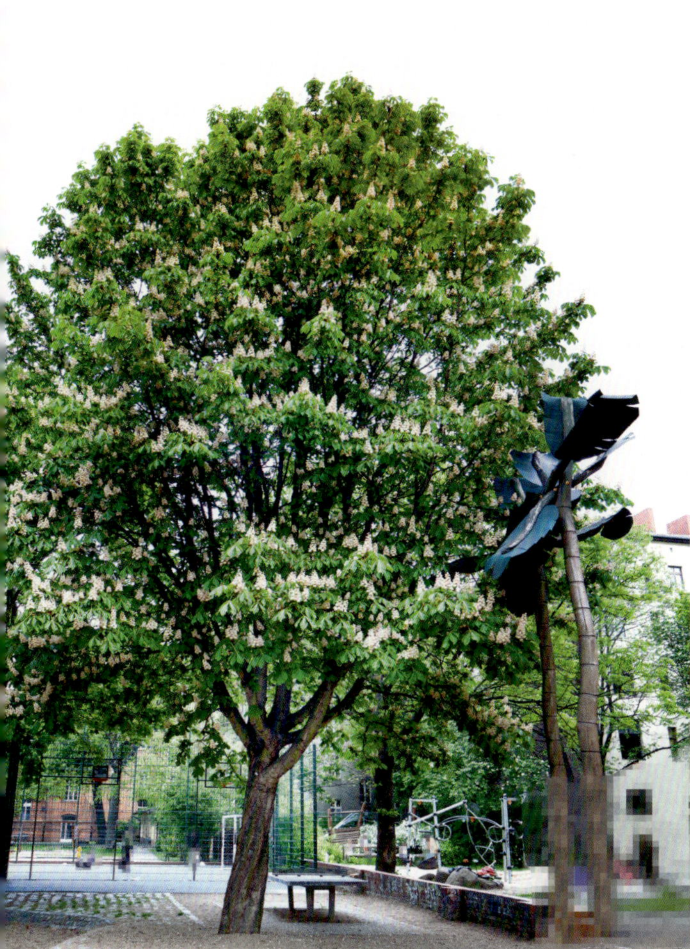

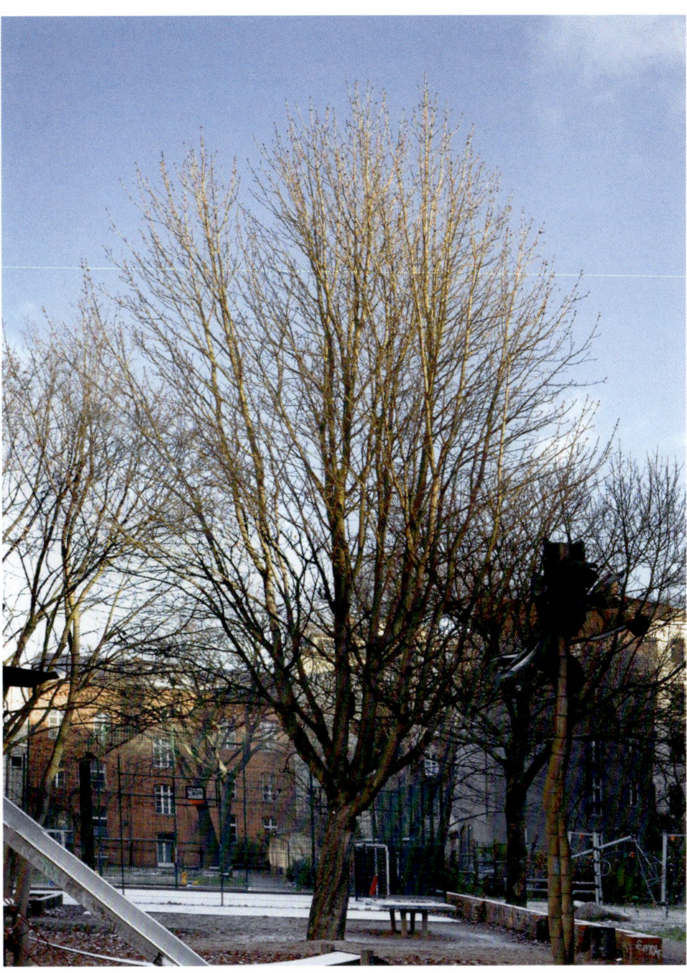

E7–S   E7–W   G: Chestnut/Kastanie [Aesculus × carnea]
                        ADR: Wrangelstrasse 84A, 10997 Kreuzberg Berlin
                        GPS: 52.499613, 13.442006, HT: 1600 cm, YR: 1983

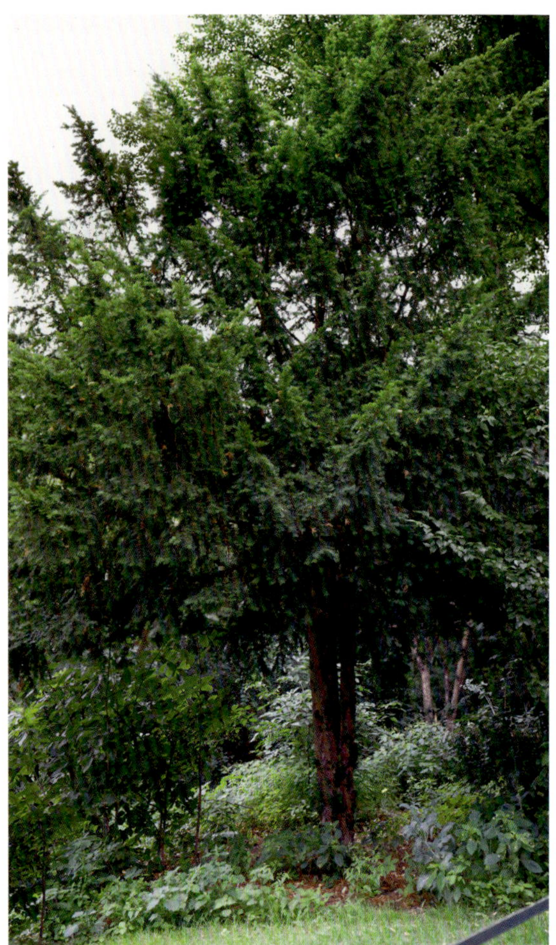 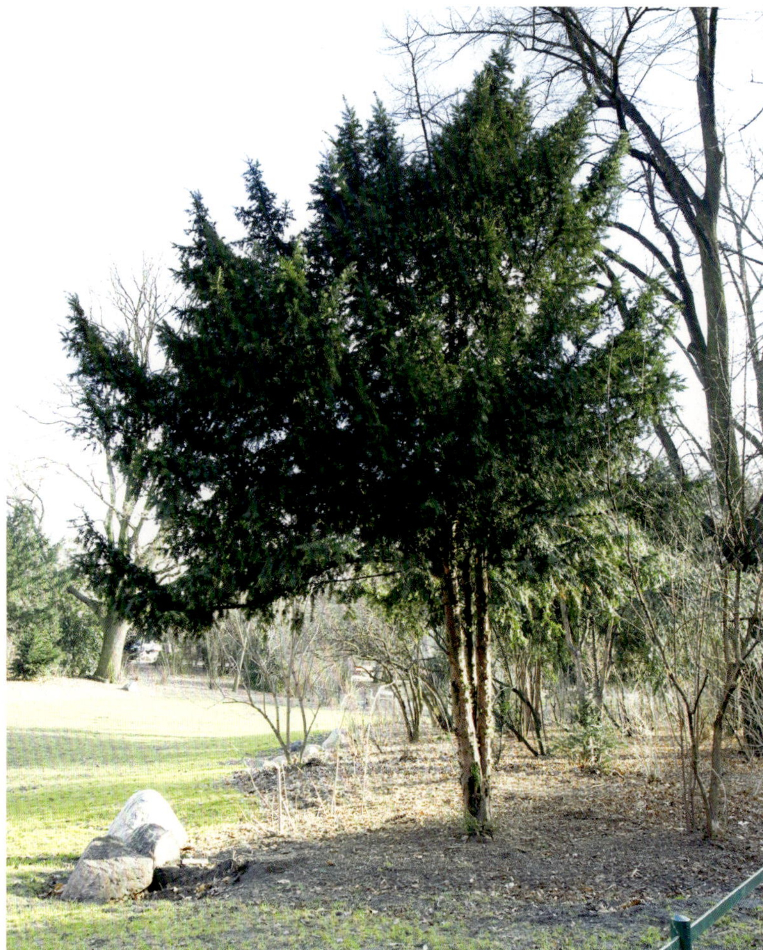

E8–S   E8–W   G: English yew/Eibe [Taxus baccata]
                            ADR: Wildenbruchplatz 5, 12045 Neukölln Berlin
                            GPS: 52.483561, 13.445086, HT: 440 cm YR: 2001

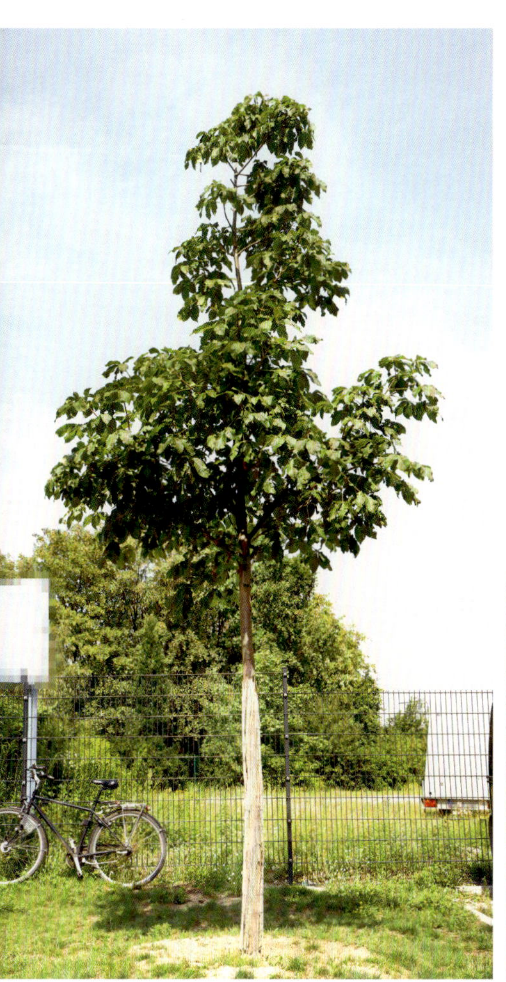
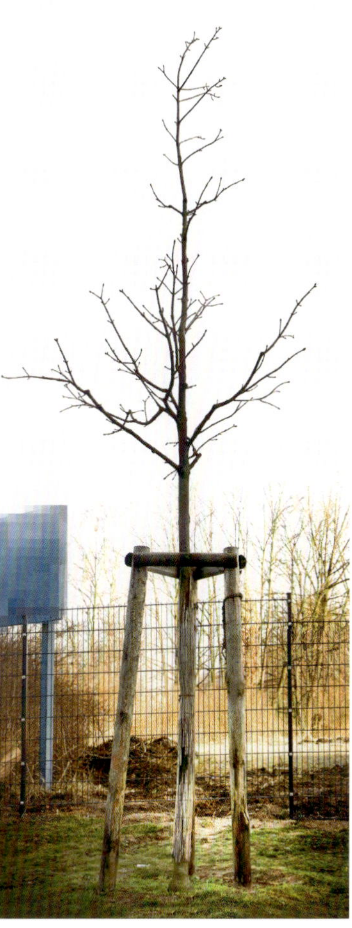

E9–S   E9–W   G: Chestnut/Kastanie [Aesculus × carnea]
○   ○   ADR: Jordanstrasse 36, 12435 Alt-Treptow Berlin
                GPS: 52.494310, 13.446560, HT: 430 cm, YR: 2008

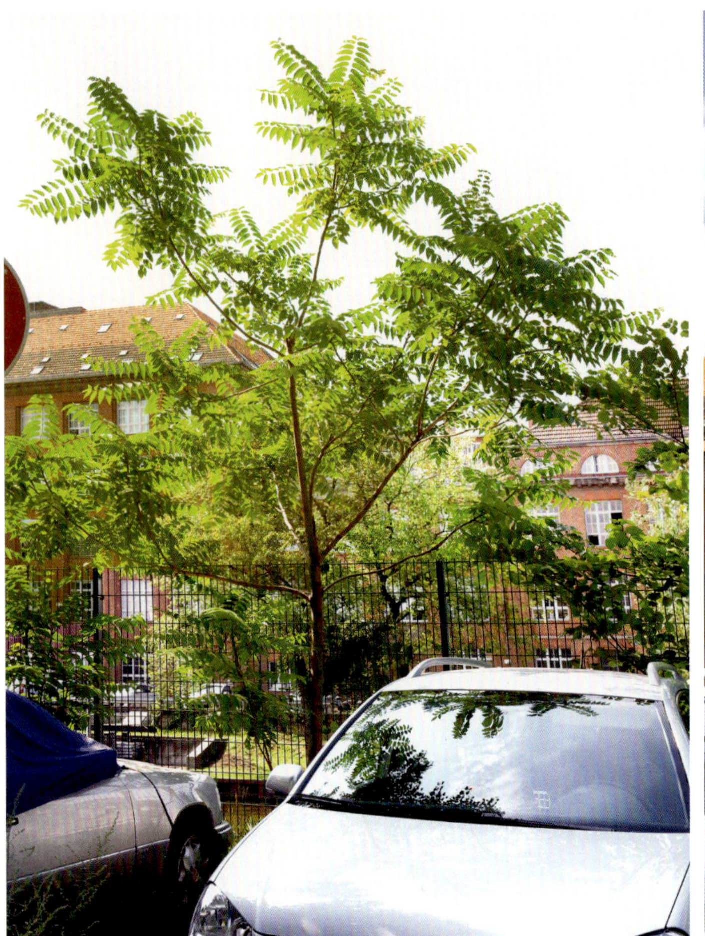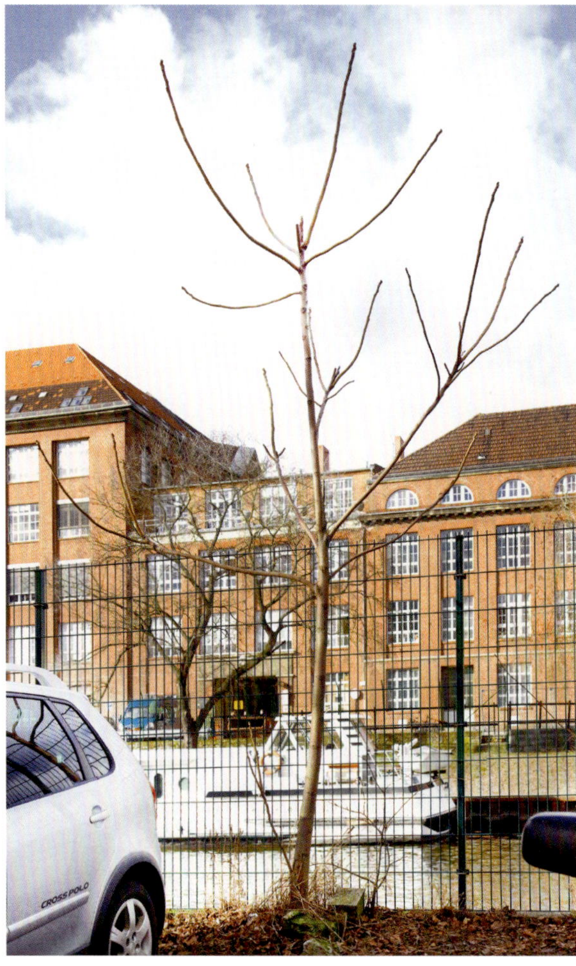

E10–S   E10–W   G: Tree of heaven/Götterbaum [Ailanthus altissima]
            o   ADR: Schleusenufer 6, 10997 Kreuzberg Berlin
                        GPS: 52.498760, 13.450850, HT: 410 cm, YR: 2007

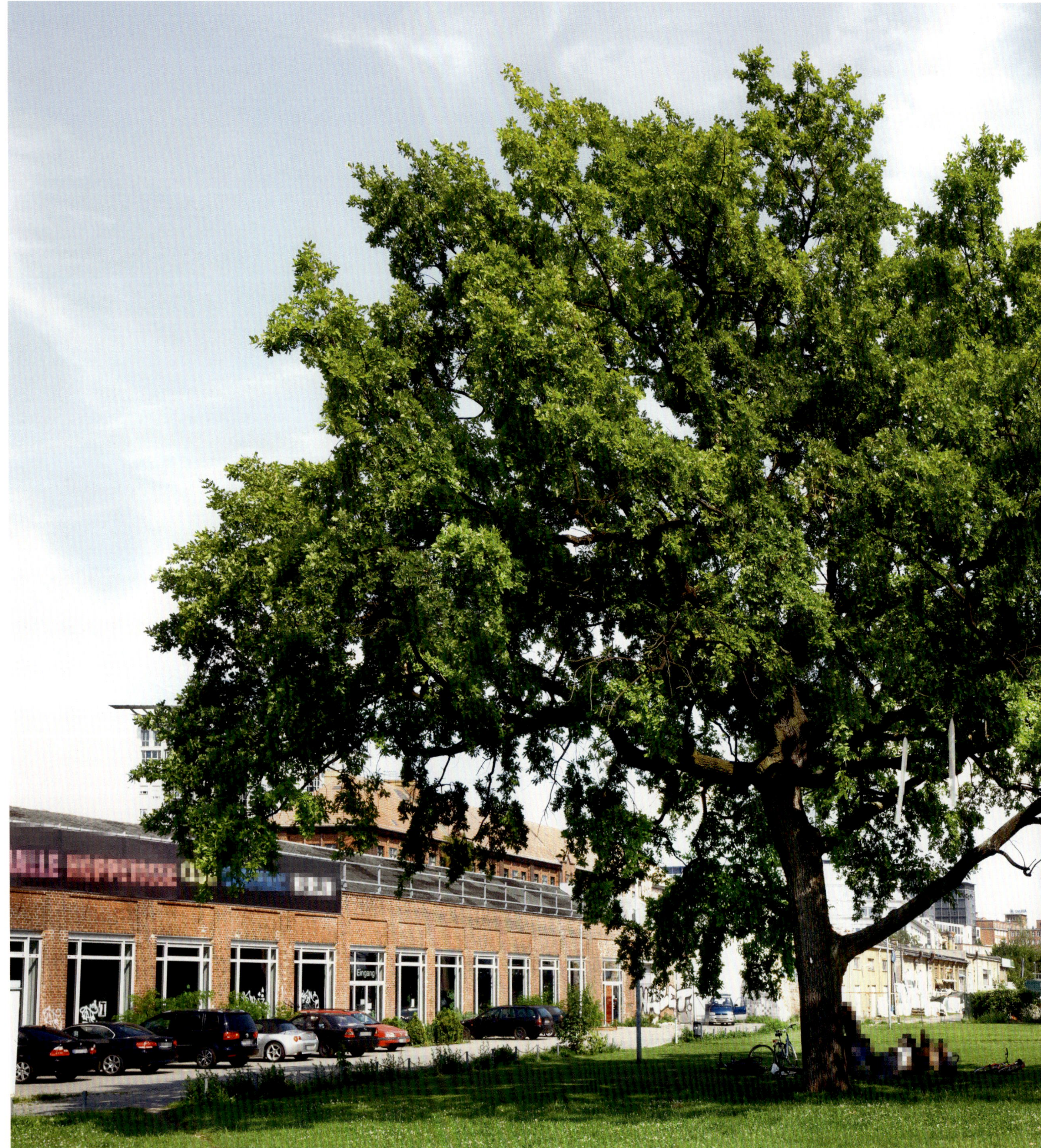

E11–S

G: British oak/Eiche [Quercus robur]
ADR: Am Flutgraben 1, 12435 Alt-Treptow Berlin
GPS: 52.496530, 13.451120, HT: 1800 cm, YR: 1998

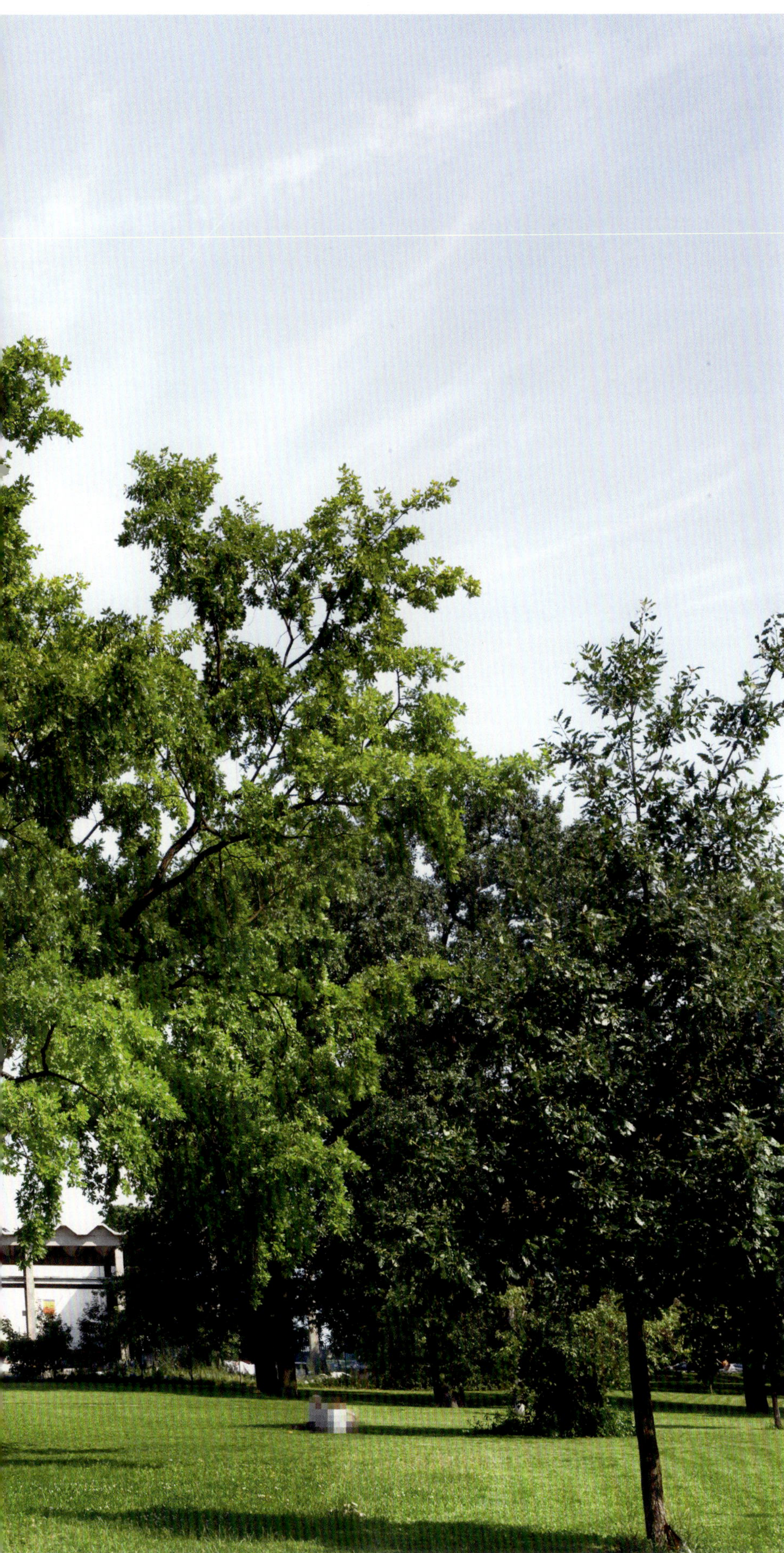

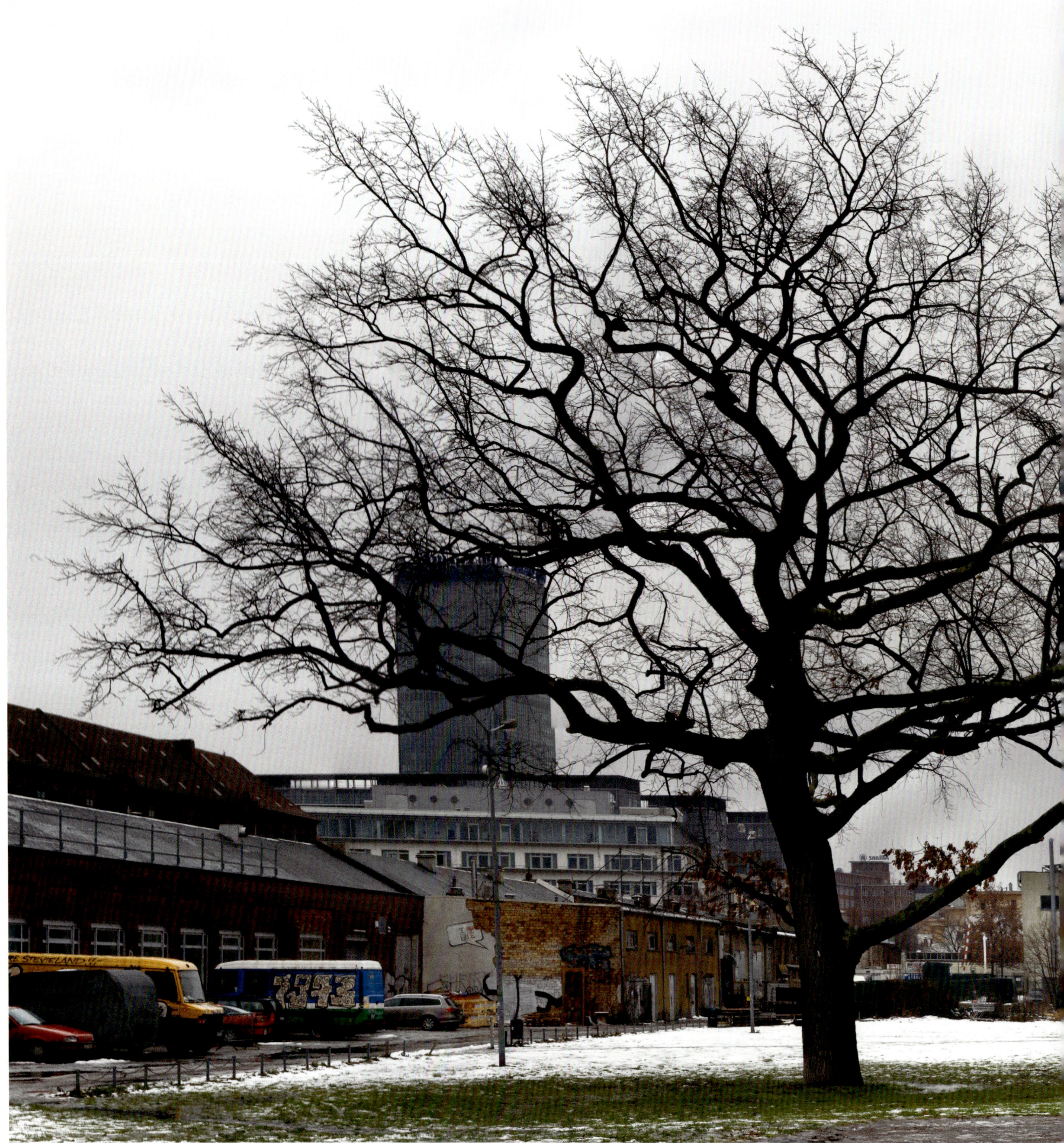

E11–W   G: British oak / Eiche [Quercus robur]
               ADR: Am Flutgraben 1, 12435 Alt-Treptow Berlin
               GPS: 52.496530, 13.451120, HT: 1800 cm, YR: 1998

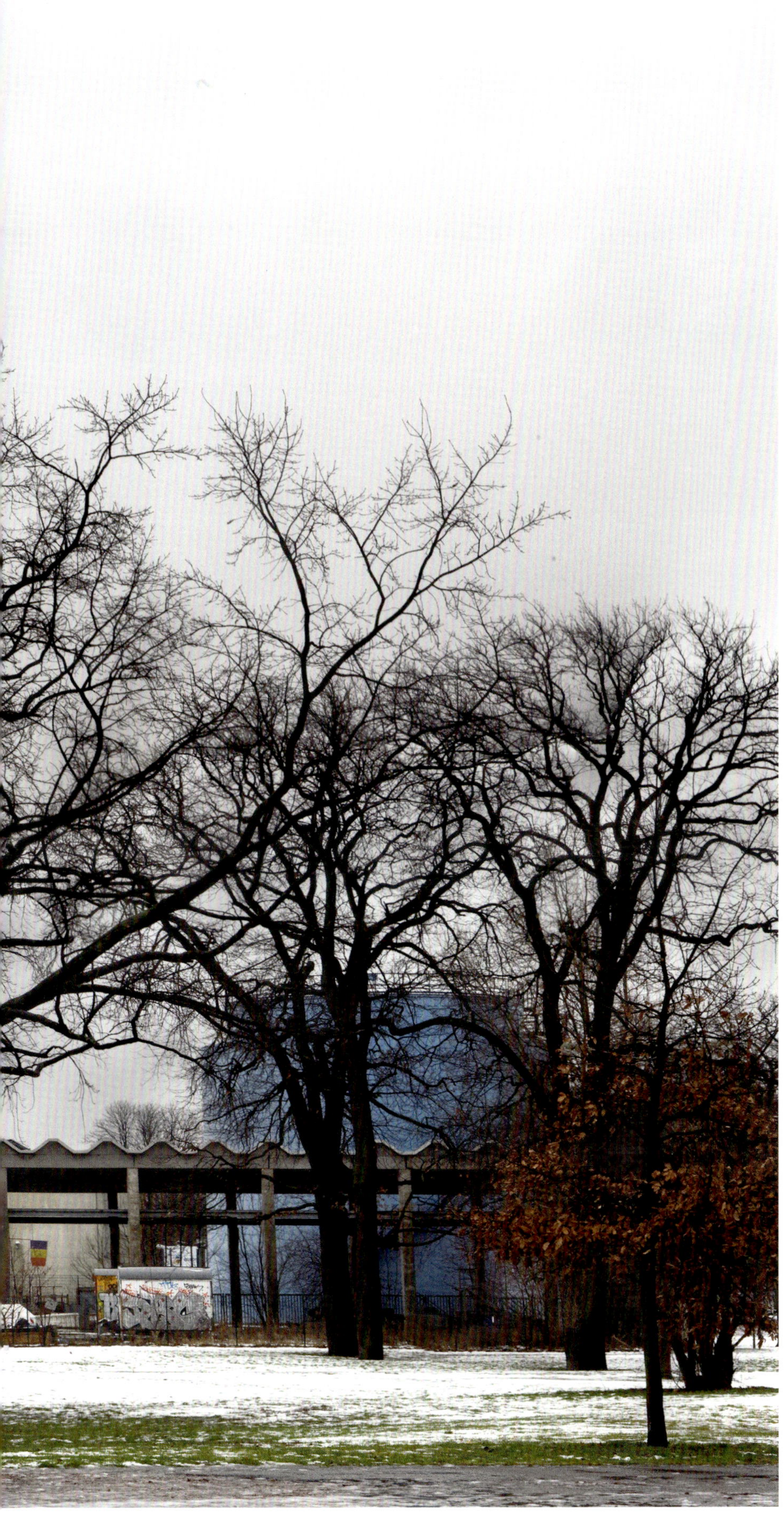

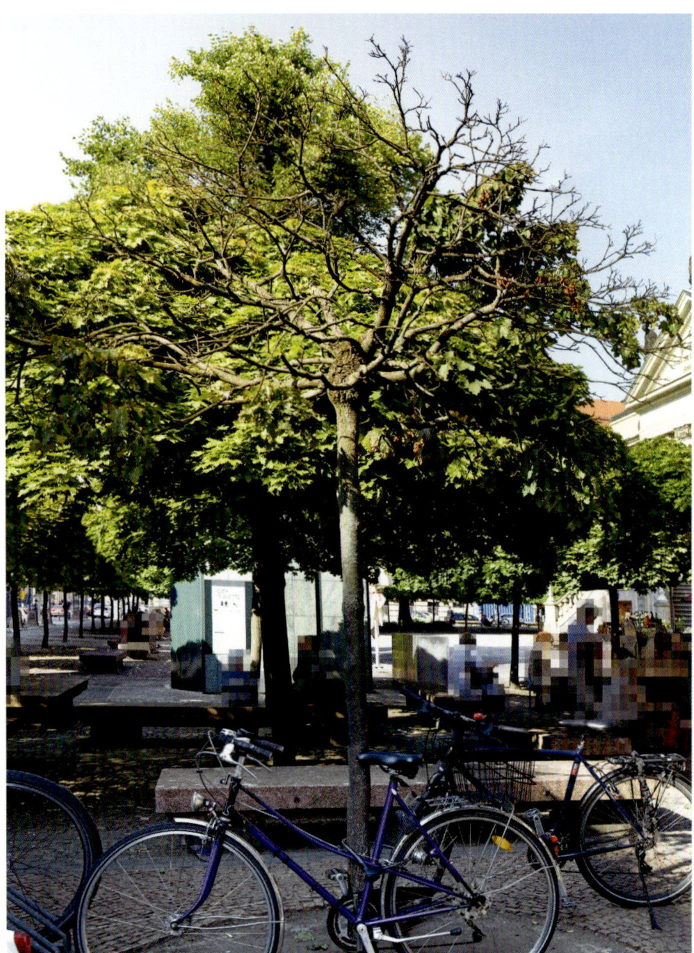
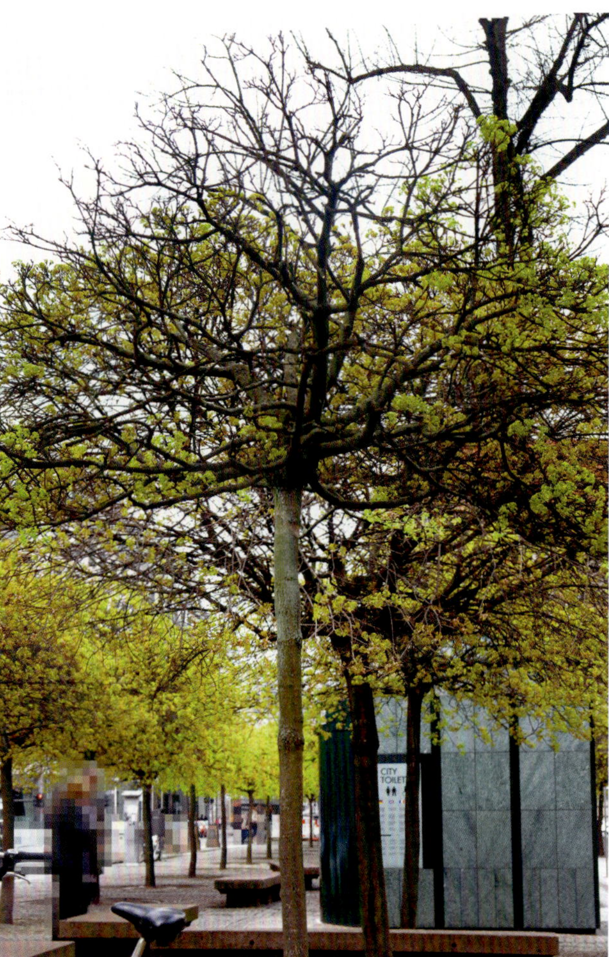

U1–S   U1–W   G: Maple/Ahorn [Acer platanoides 'Globosum']
ADR: Jägerstrasse 19, 10117 Mitte Berlin
GPS: 52.514043, 13.391481, HT: 390 cm, YR: 1990

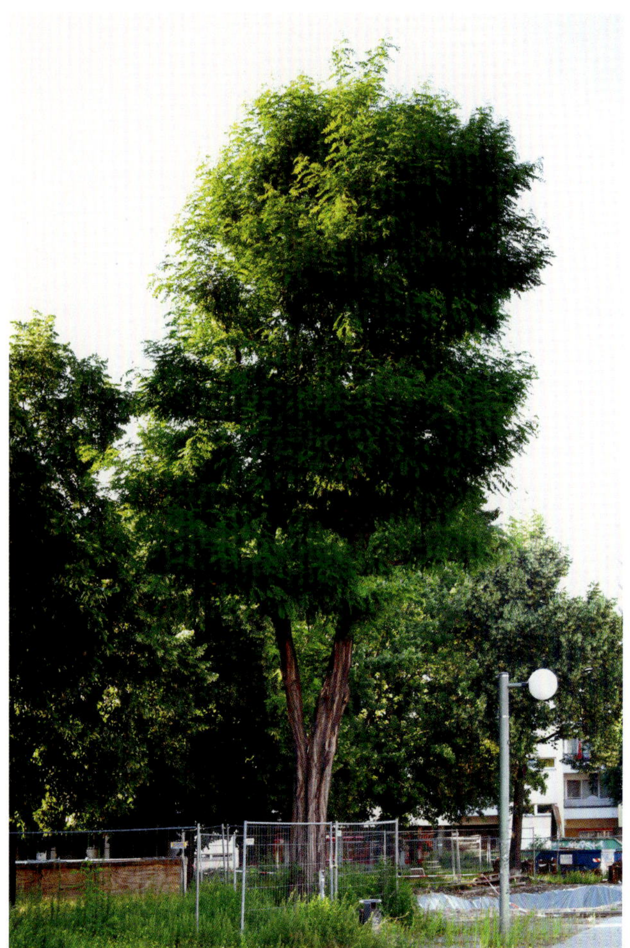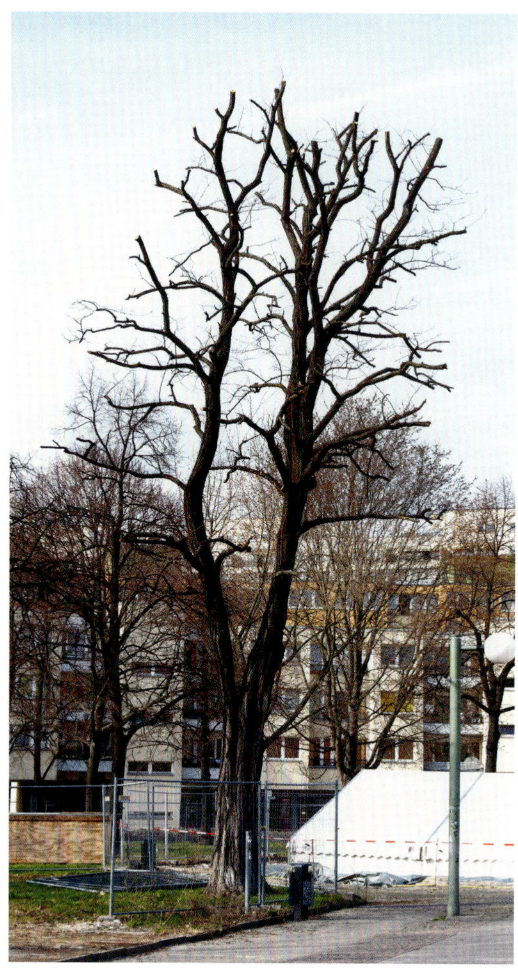

U2–S   U2–W   G: Locust/Robinie [Robinia pseudoacacia]
ADR: Mehringplatz 36, 10969 Kreuzberg Berlin
GPS: 52.498810, 13.391640, HT: 1200 cm, YR: 1965

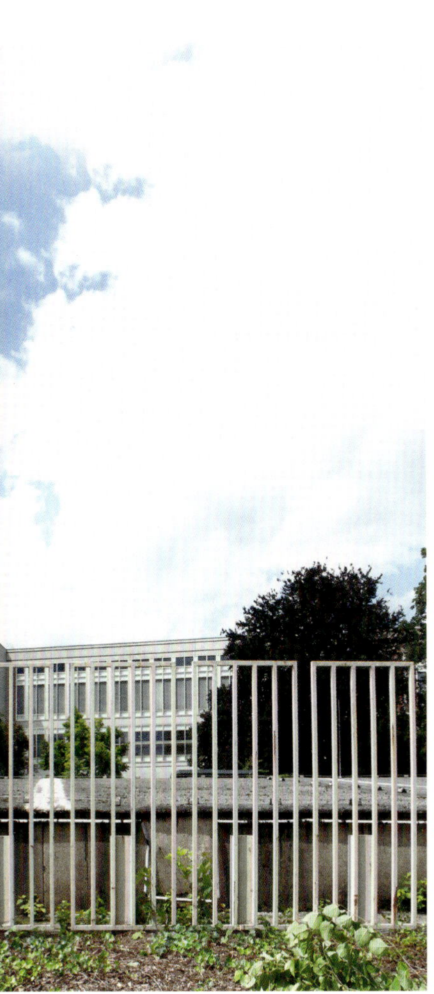
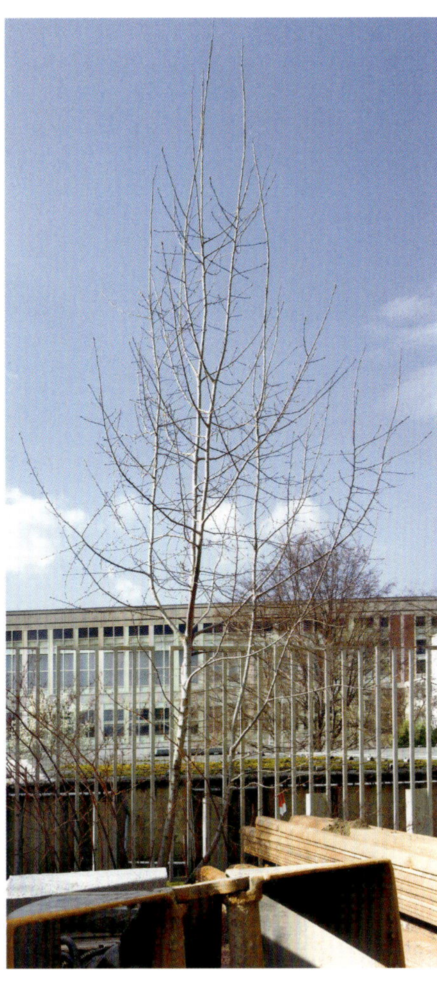

U3-S   U3-W   G: Maple/Ahorn [Acer]
ADR: Sperlingsgasse 1, 10178 Mitte Berlin
GPS: 52.514690, 13.402330, HT: 340 cm, YR: 1989

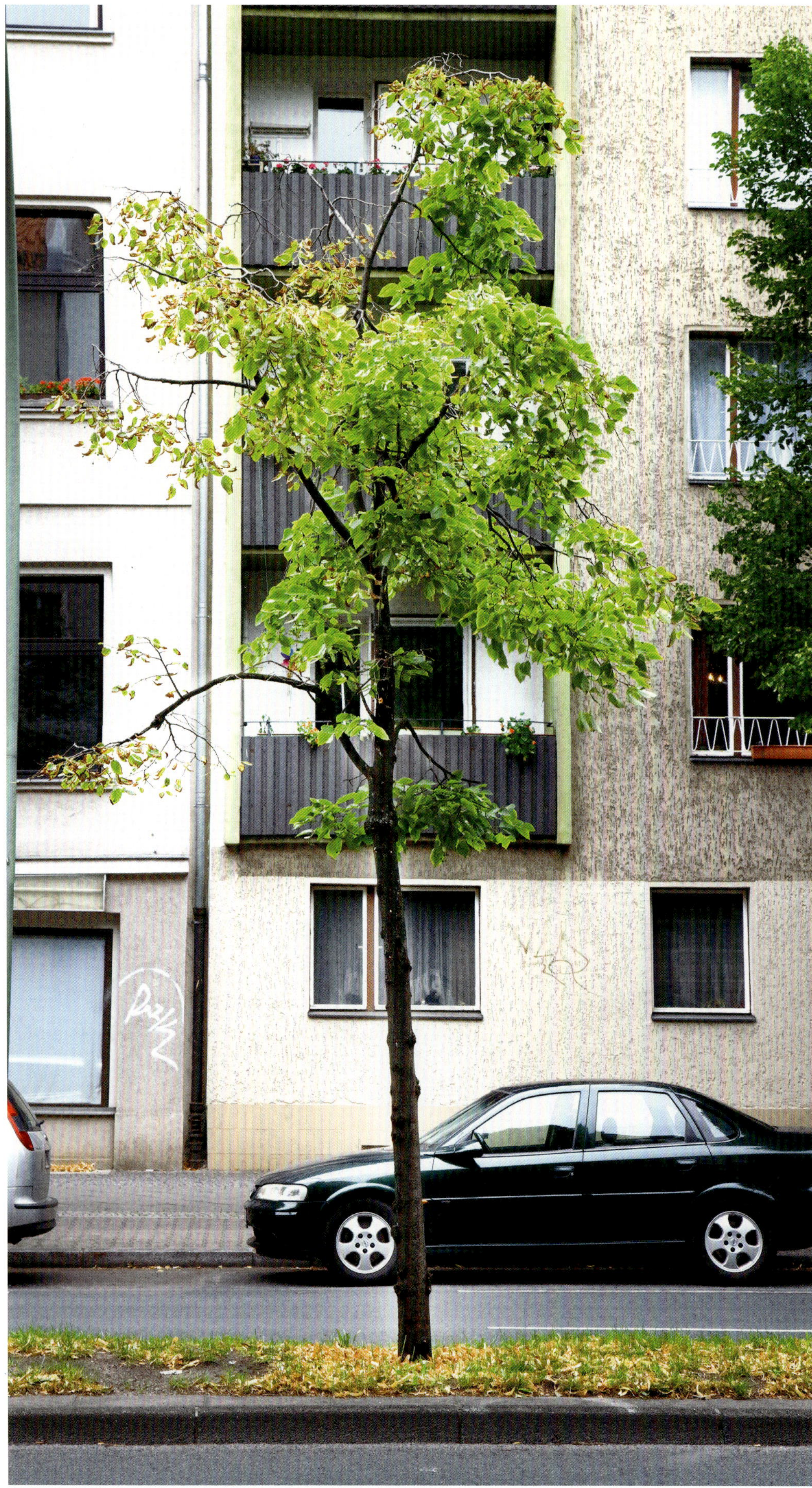

U4–S   U4–W   G: Linden/Linde [Tilia]
o   o   ADR: Urbanstrasse 4–5, 10961 Kreuzberg Berlin
                        GPS: 52.494263, 13.401095, HT: 550 cm, YR: 1959

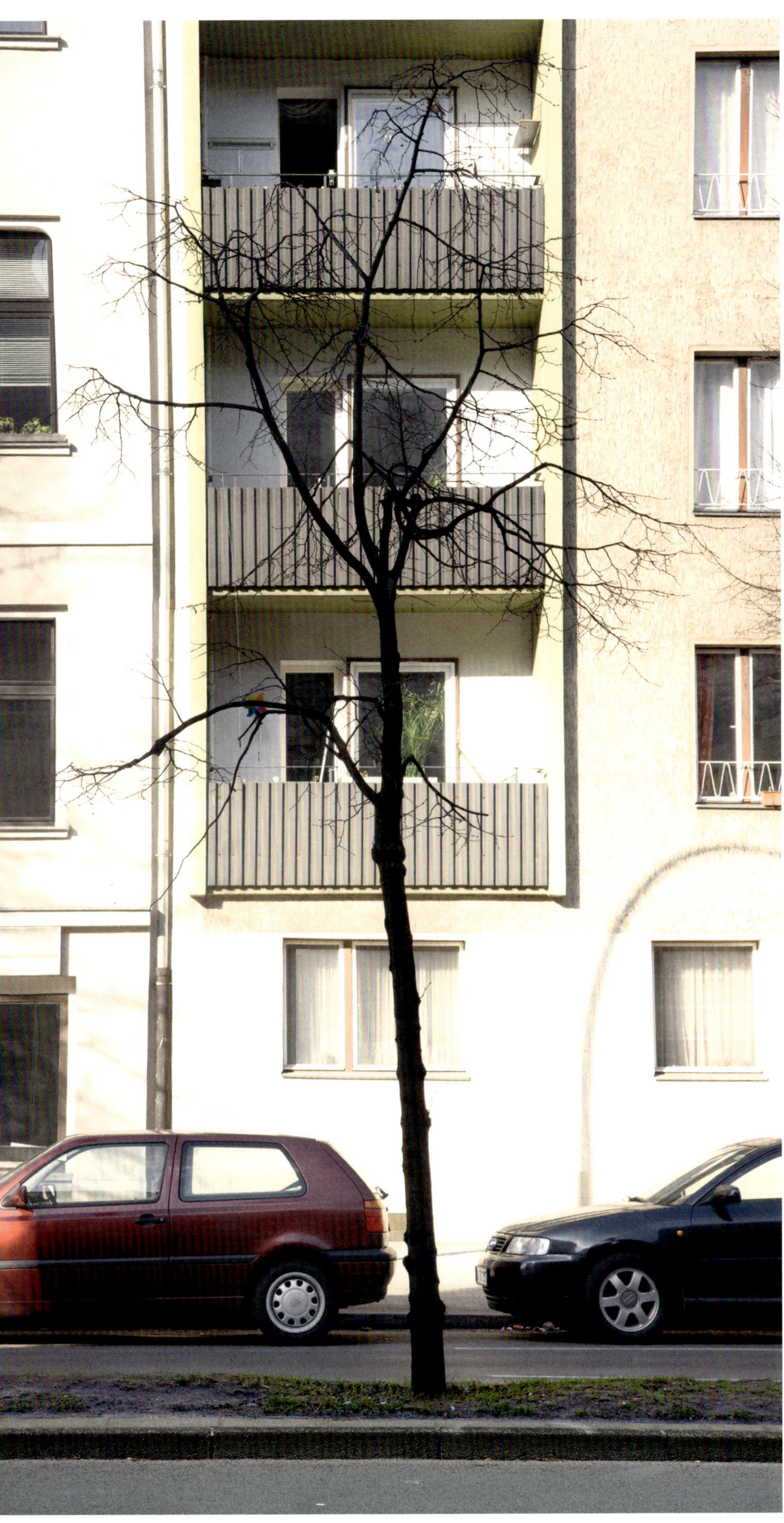

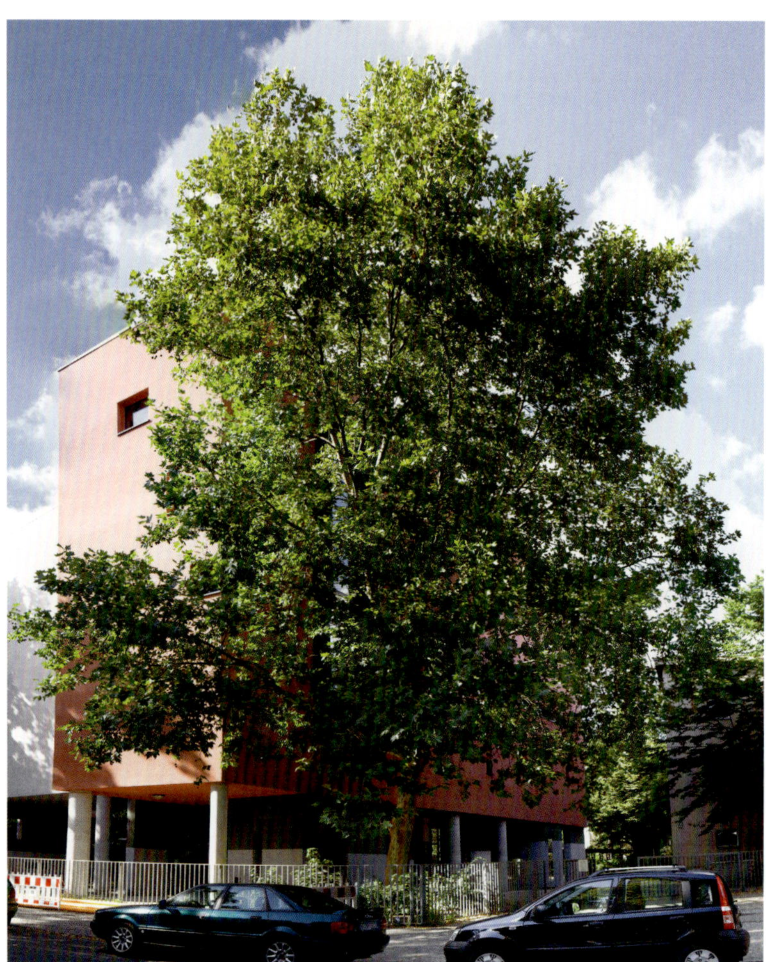
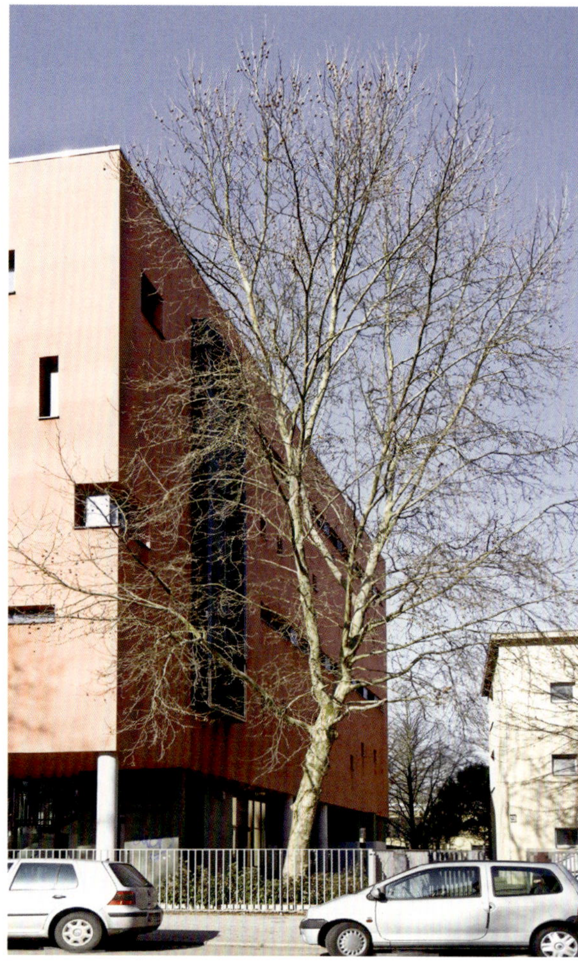

U5-S   U5-W   G: Plane/Platane [Platanus x acerifolia]
                            ADR: Karlsgartenstrasse 9, 12049 Neukölln Berlin
                            GPS: 52.482030, 13.421100, HT: 1630 cm, YR: 1982

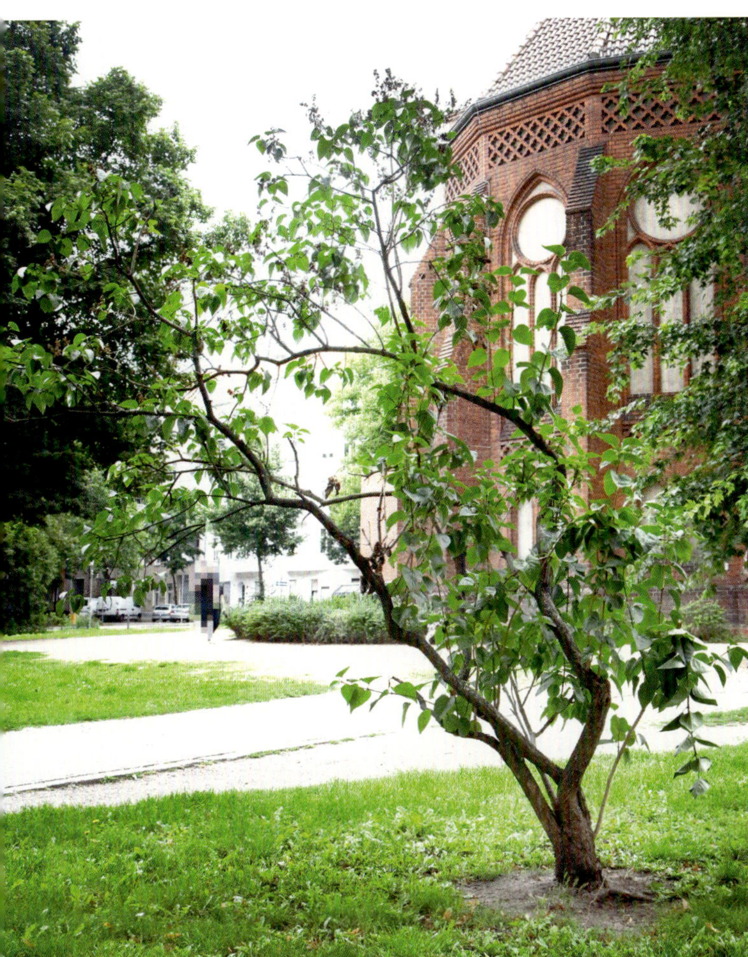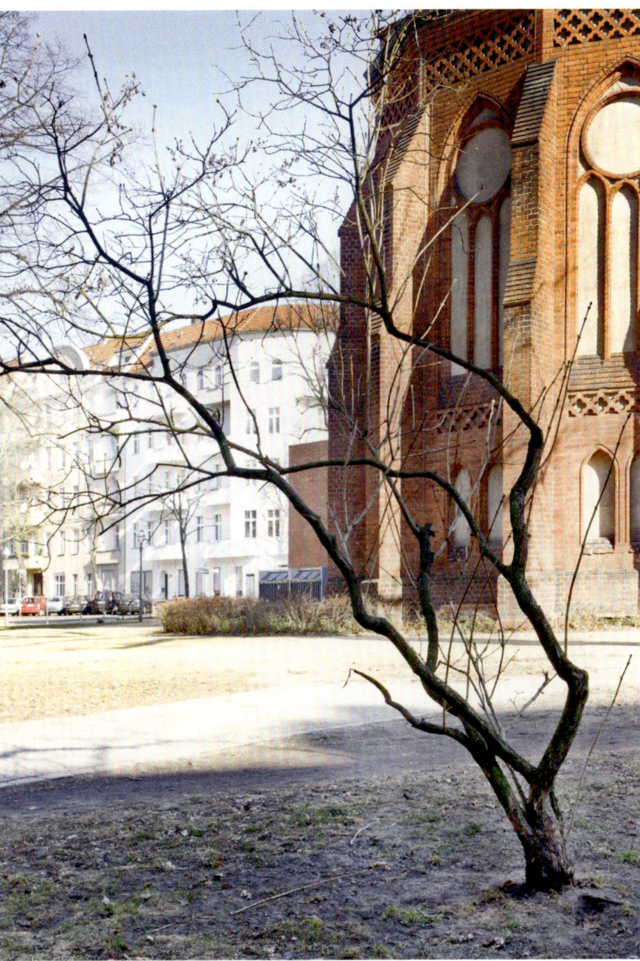

U6-S　　U6-W　　G: Lilac/Flieder [Syringa]
○　　　　○　　　ADR: Herrfurthplatz 7, 12049 Neukölln Berlin
　　　　　　　　　GPS: 52.476910, 13.421610, HT: 150 cm, YR: 2008

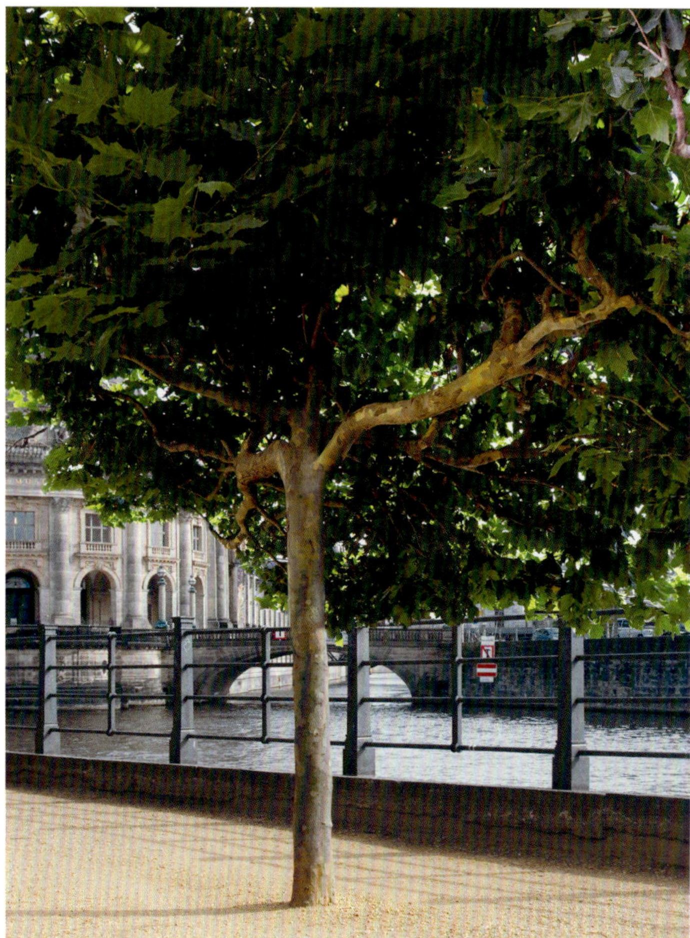 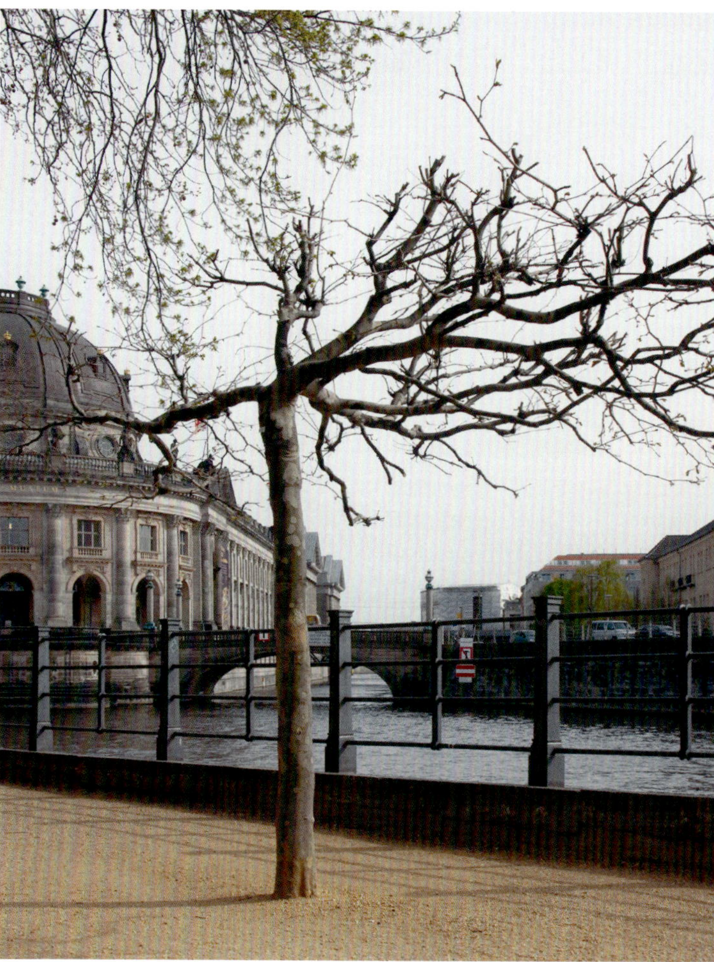

B1–S   B1–W   G: Plane/Platane [Platanus x acerifolia]
                            ADR: Tucholskystrasse 1, 10117 Mitte Berlin
                            GPS: 52.522680, 13.392360, HT: 420 cm YR: 1993

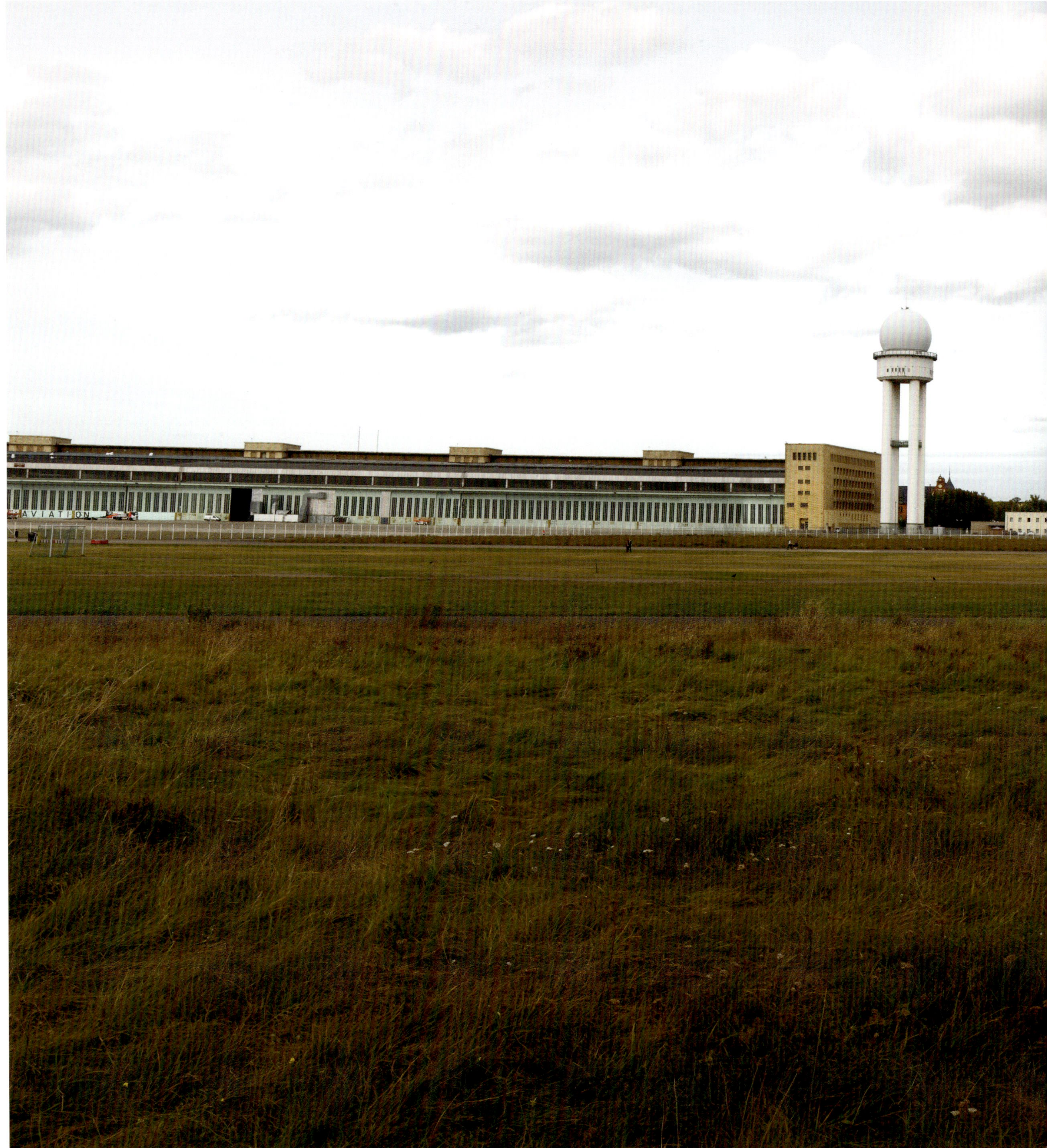

B2   Tempelhofer Feld
                     GPS: 52.47083, 13.38851

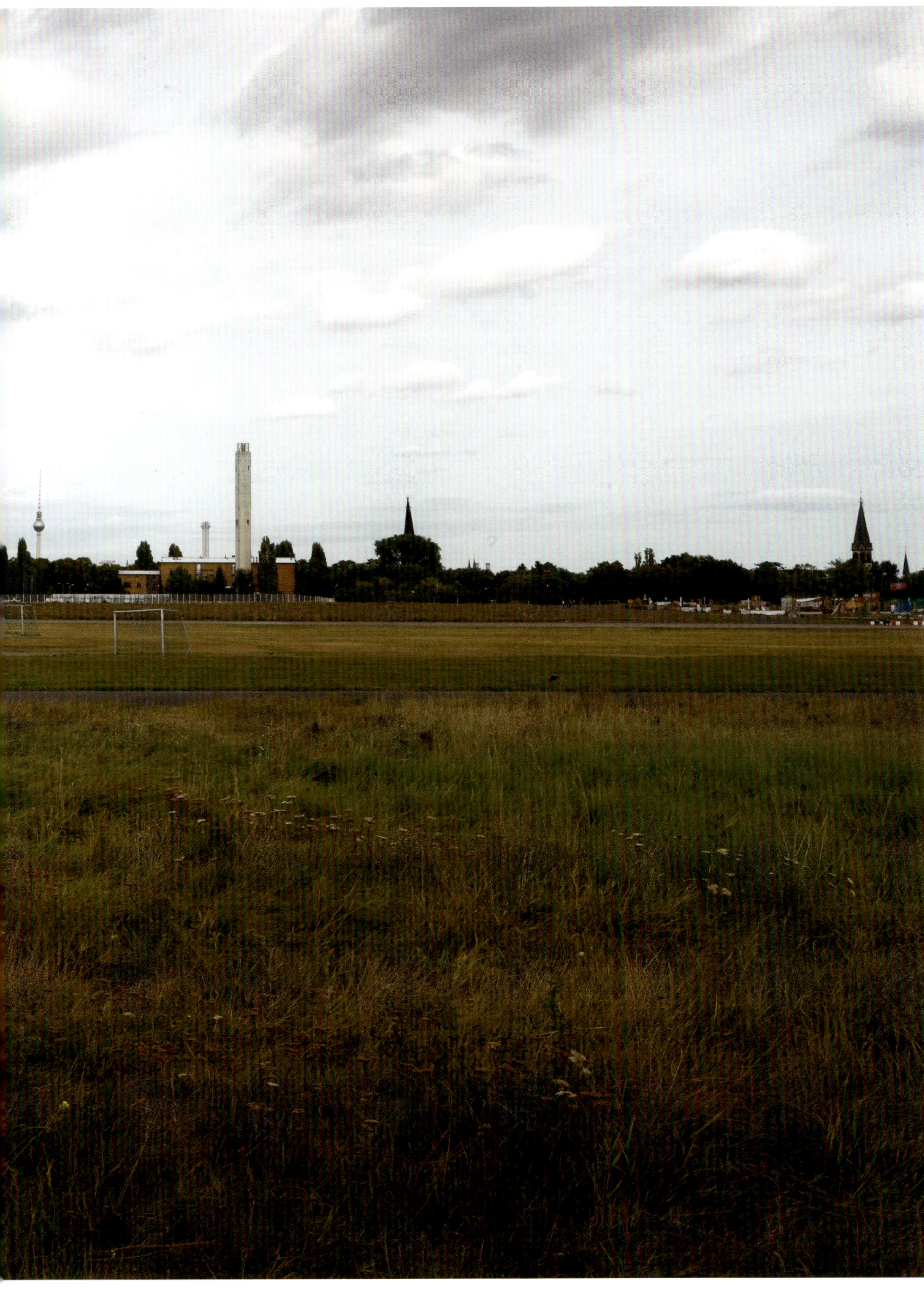

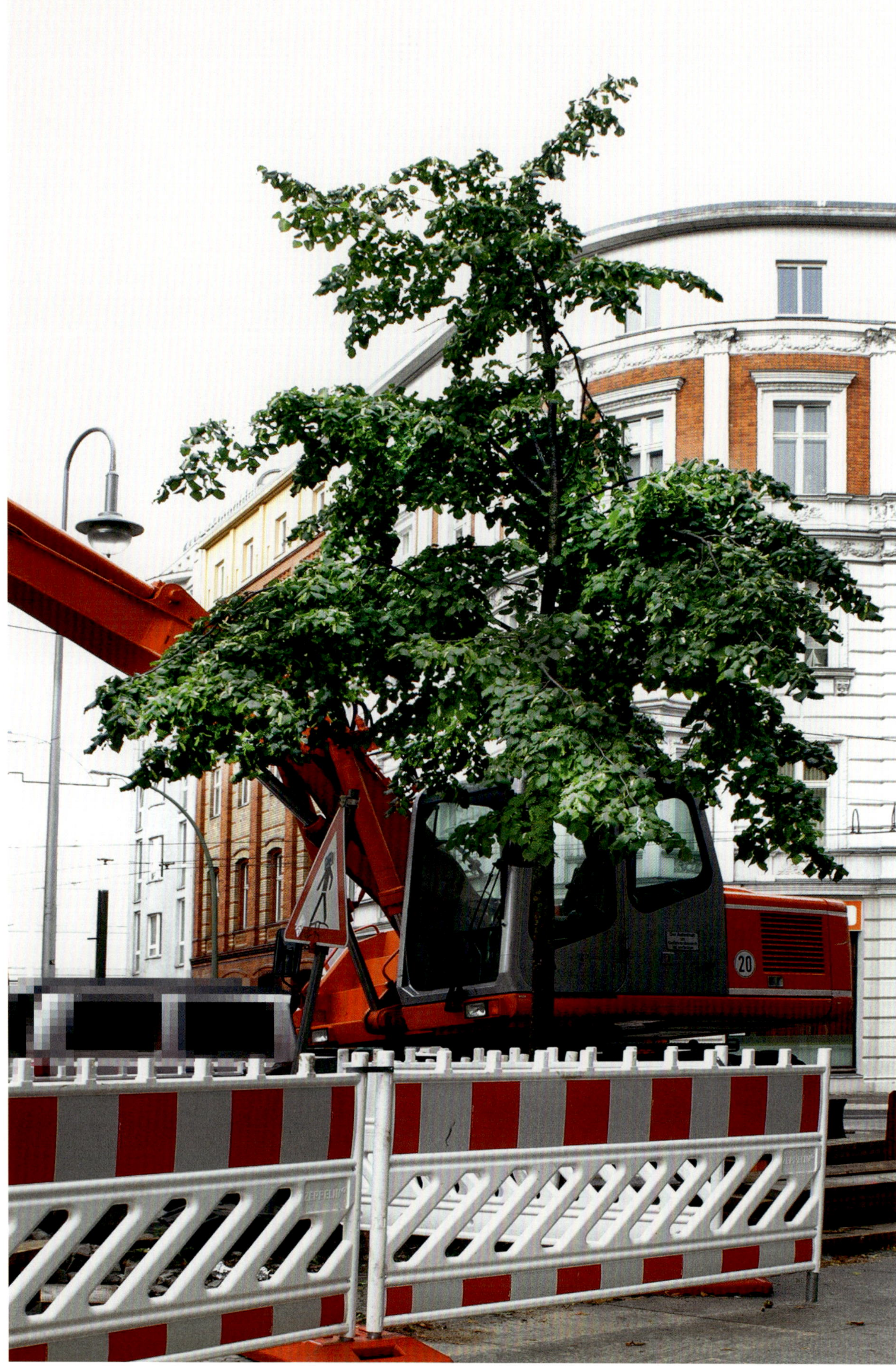

B3–S   B3–W   G: Linden/Linde [Tilia cordata]
○   ○   ADR: Monbijouplatz 12, 10178 Mitte Berlin
                              GPS: 52.522790, 13.399900, HT: 570 cm YR: 2001

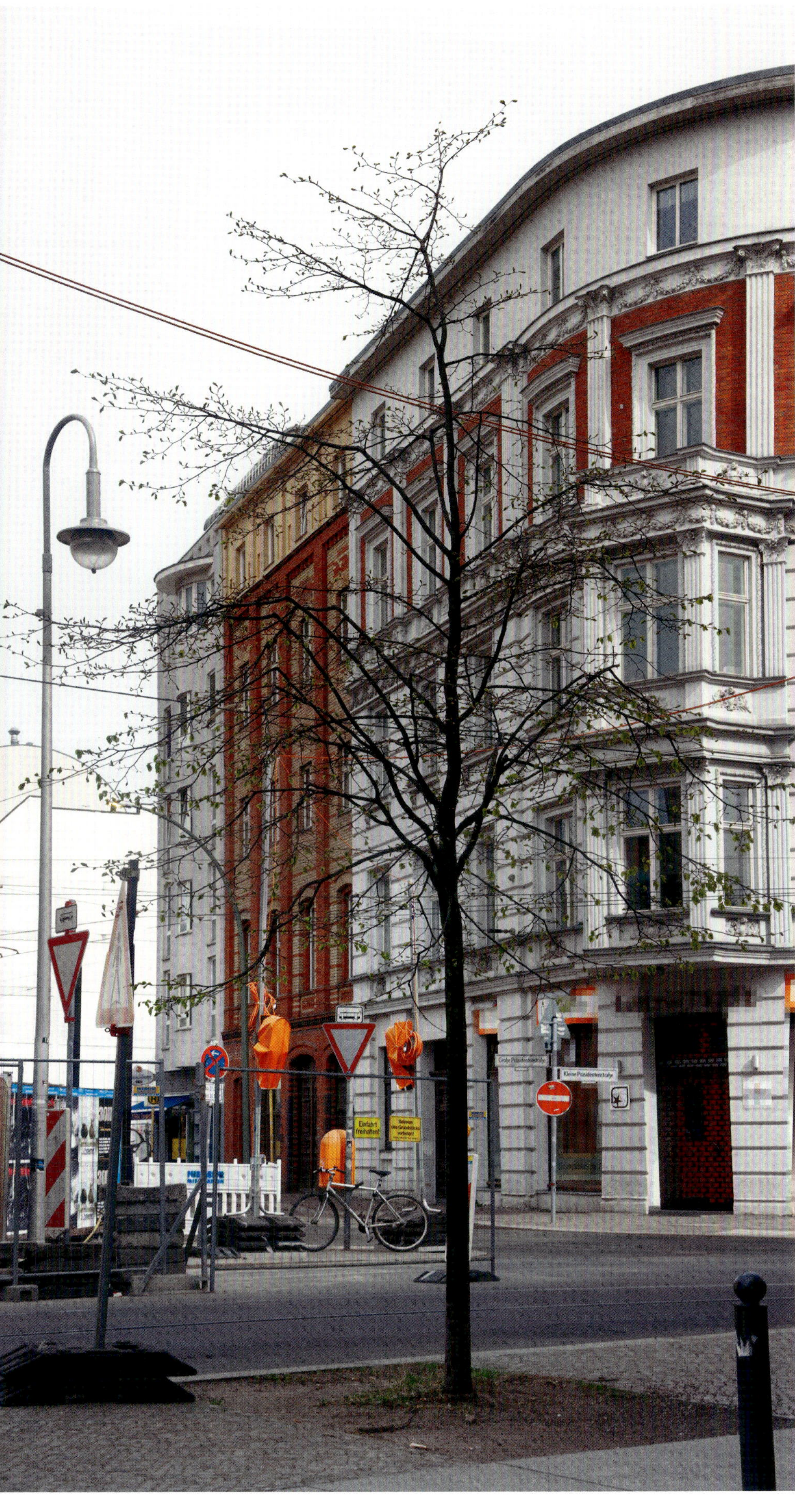

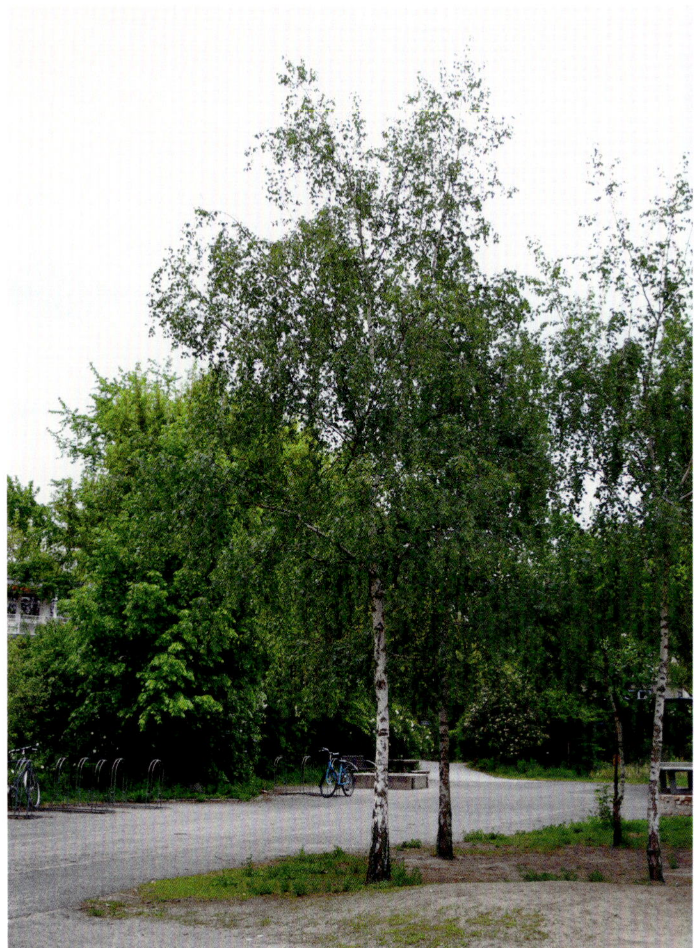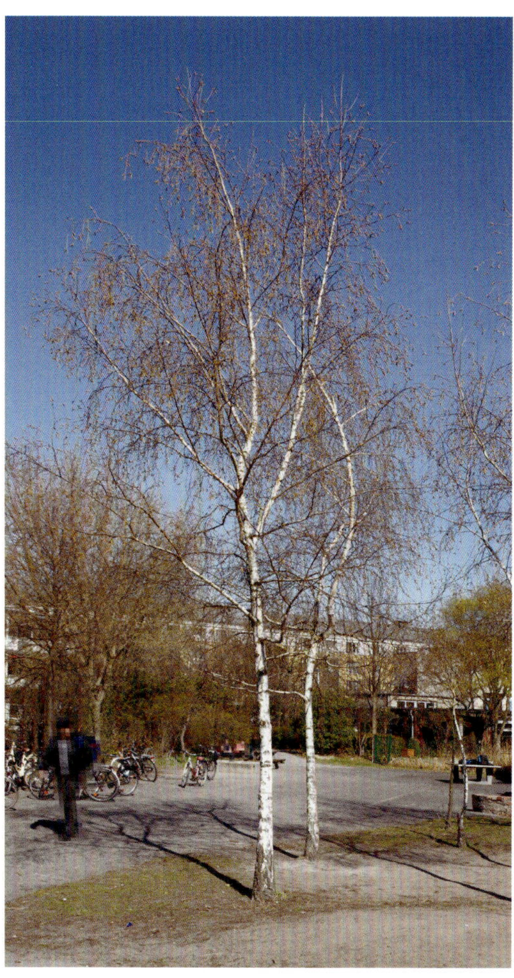

B4–S   B4–W   G: Silver birch/Hängebirke [Betula pendula]
ADR: Ritterstrasse 77, 10969 Kreuzberg Berlin
GPS: 52.503150, 13.400890, HT: 940 cm YR: 1997

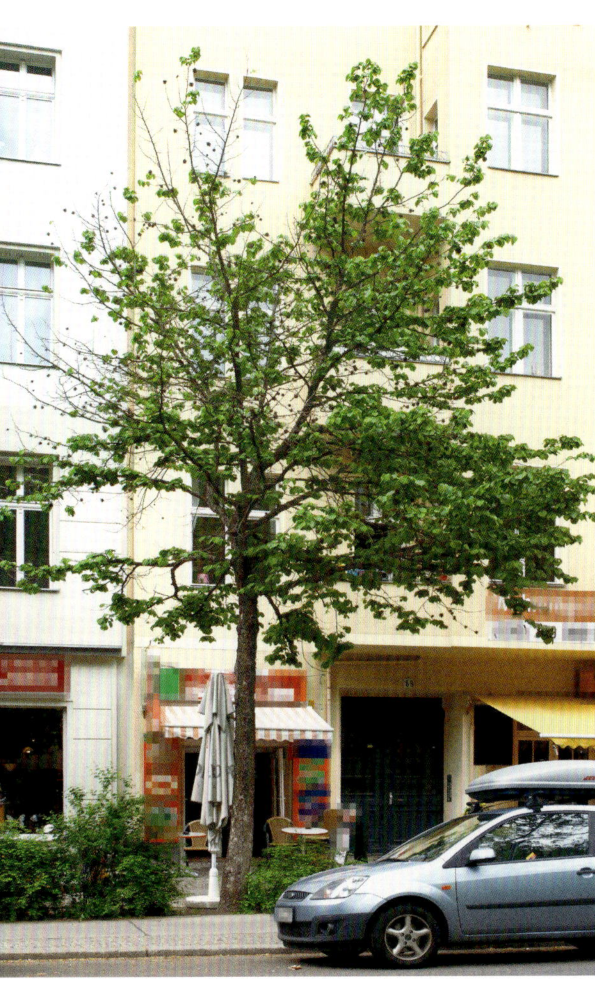
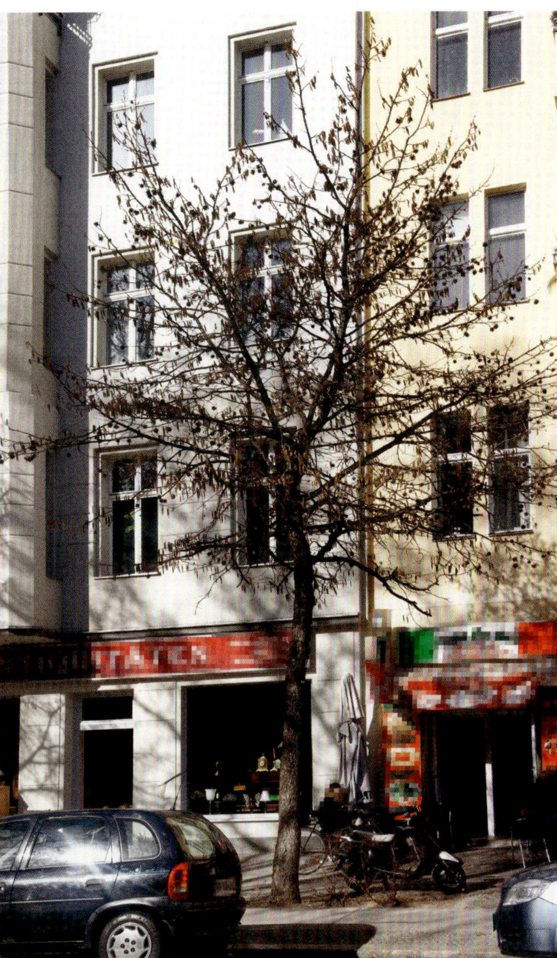

B5–S   B5–W   G: Hazel/Hasel [Corylus colurna]
                            ADR: Gneisenaustrasse 72, 10961 Kreuzberg Berlin
                            GPS: 52.490450, 13.401100, HT: 980 cm YR: 1978

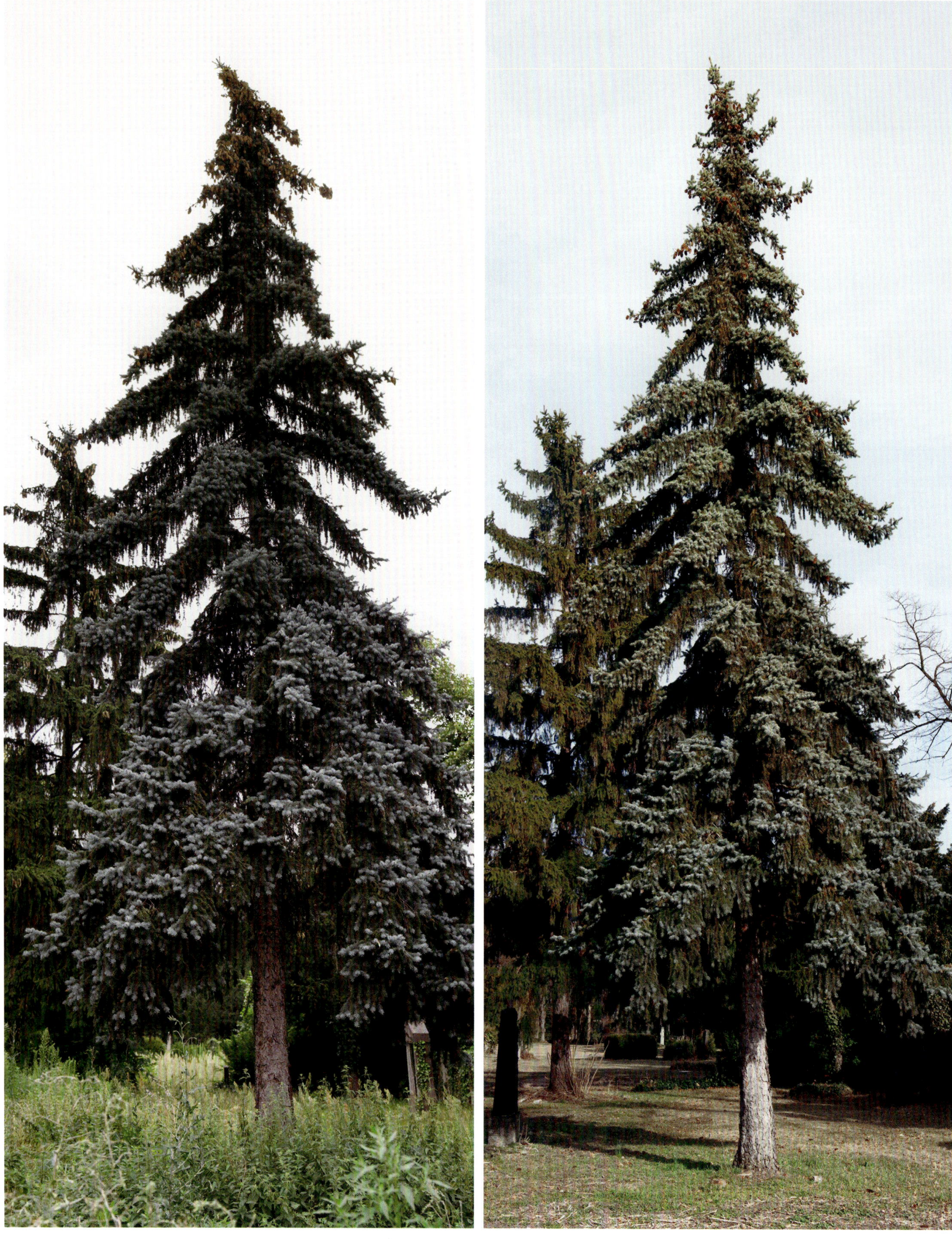

B6–S   B6–W   G: Blue spruce/Stechfichte [Picea Pungens]
ADR: Züllichauer Strasse 1, 10965 Kreuzberg Berlin
GPS: 52.485370, 13.401730, HT: 1020 cm YR: 1982

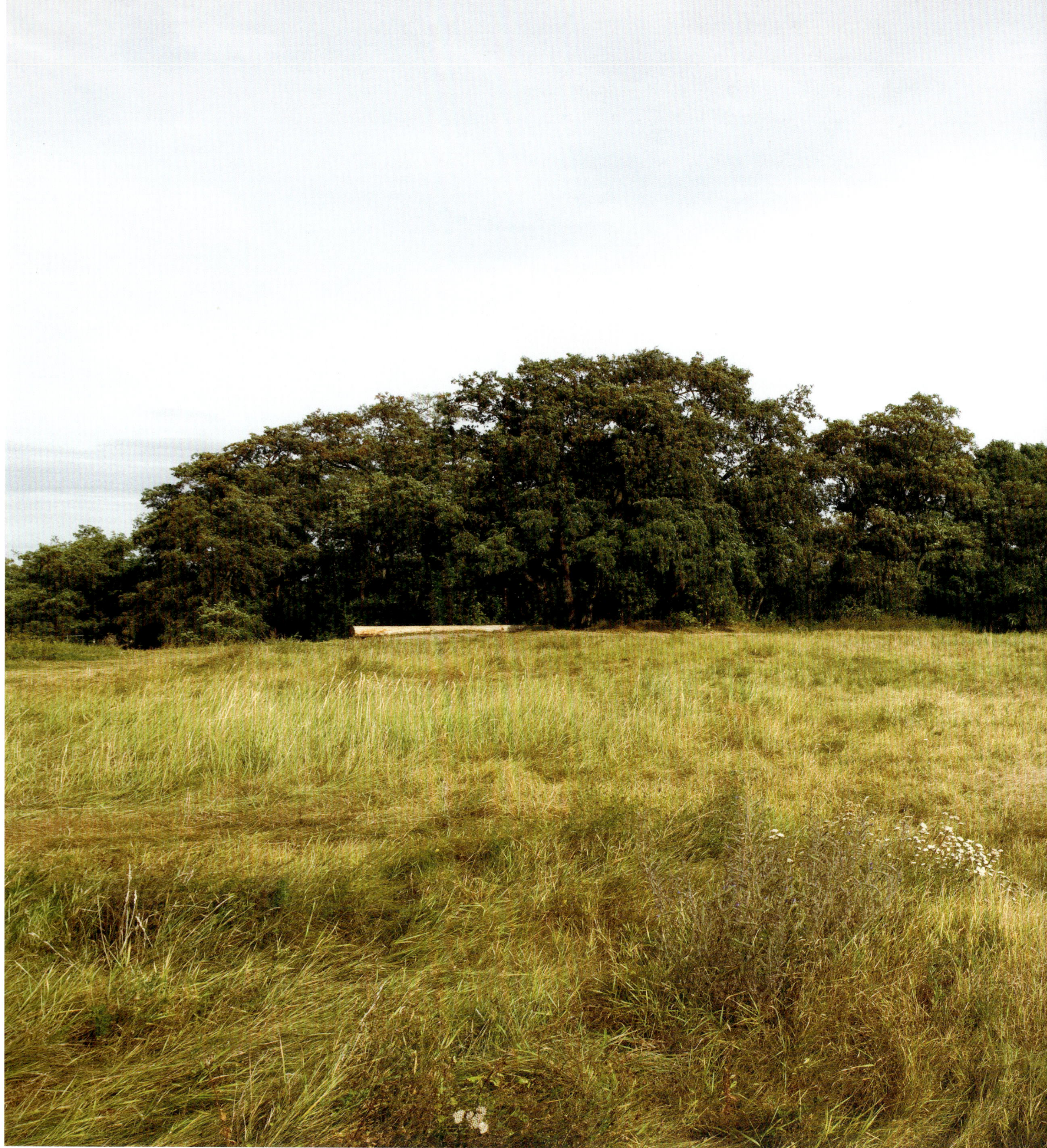

B7 Tempelhofer Feld Berlin
GPS: 52.47319, 13.40132

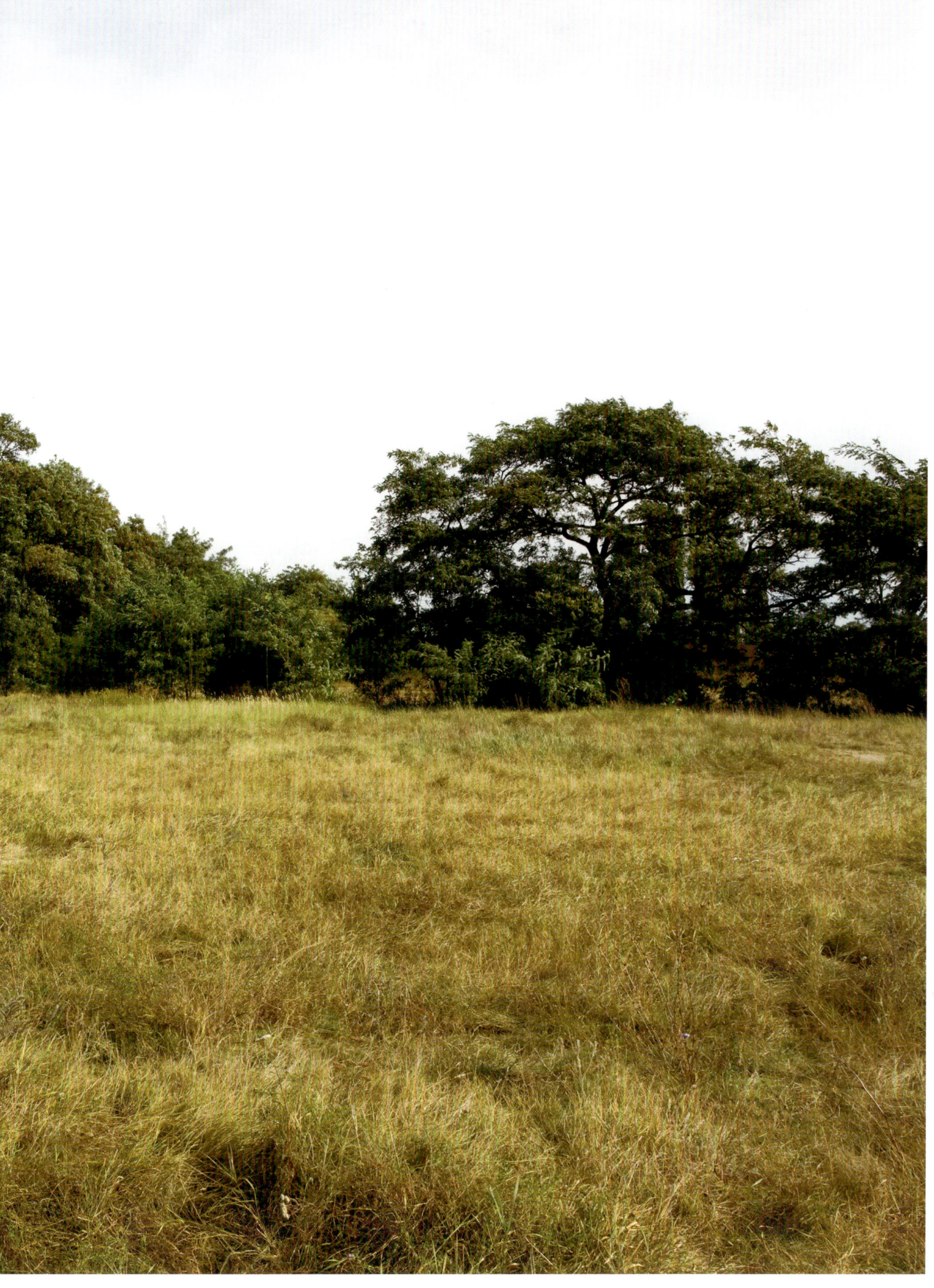

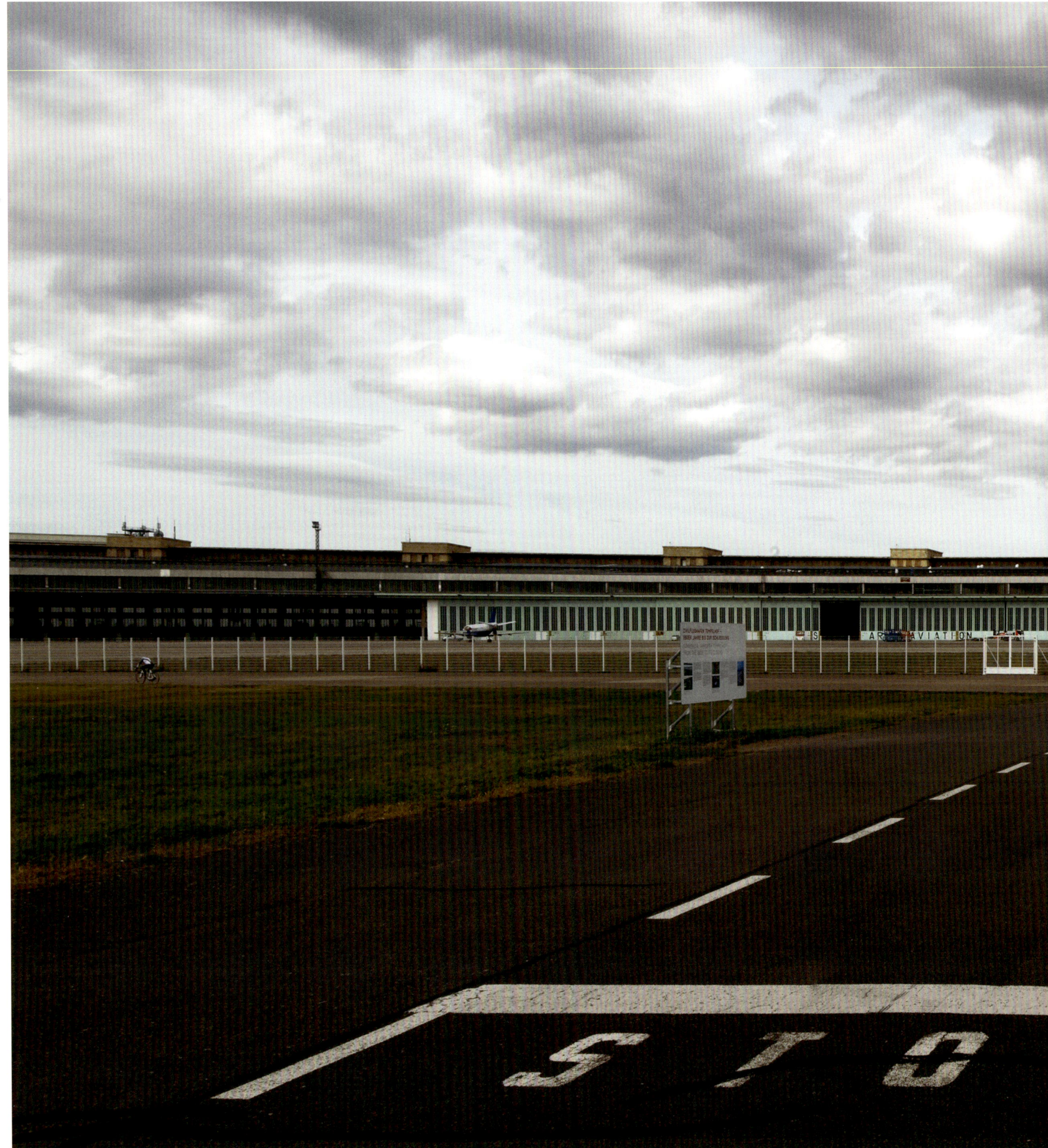

Tempelhofer Feld Berlin
GPS: 52.47090, 13.40115

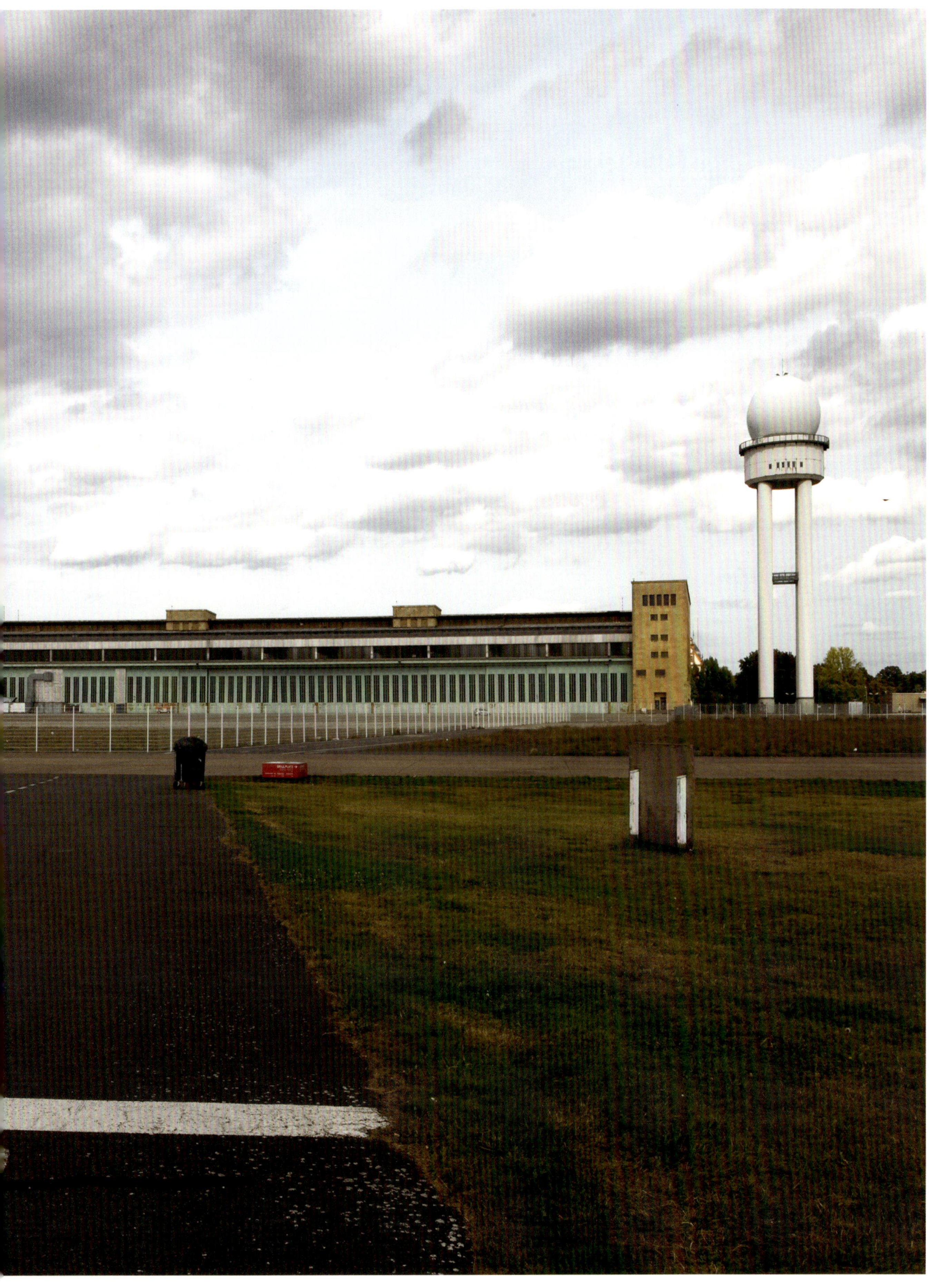

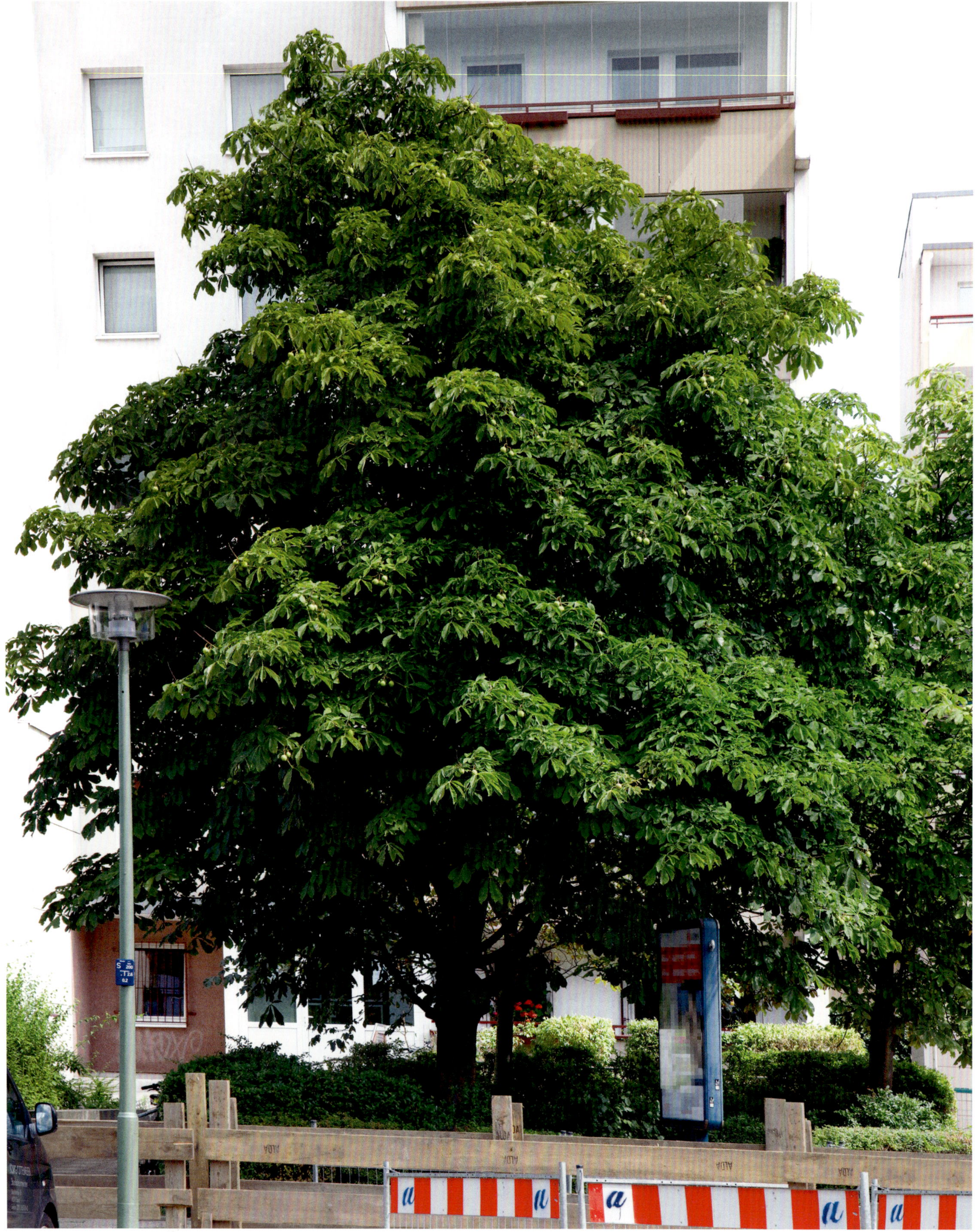

B9–S   B9–W   G: Chestnut / Kastanie [Aesculus × carnea]
o   ADR: Michaelkirchstrasse 2, 10179 Mitte Berlin
                                            GPS: 52.508130, 13.420210, HT: 1030 cm YR: 1968

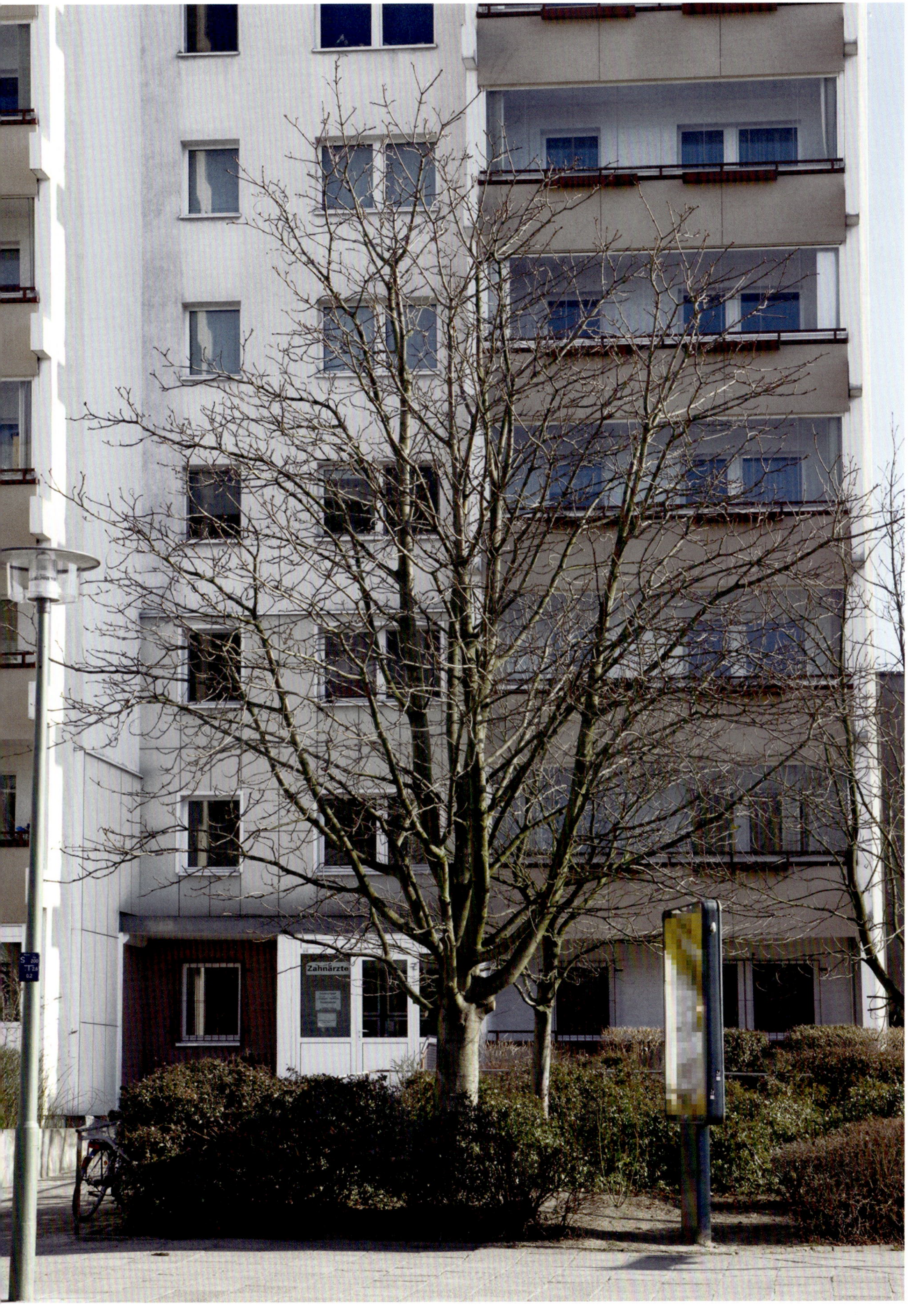

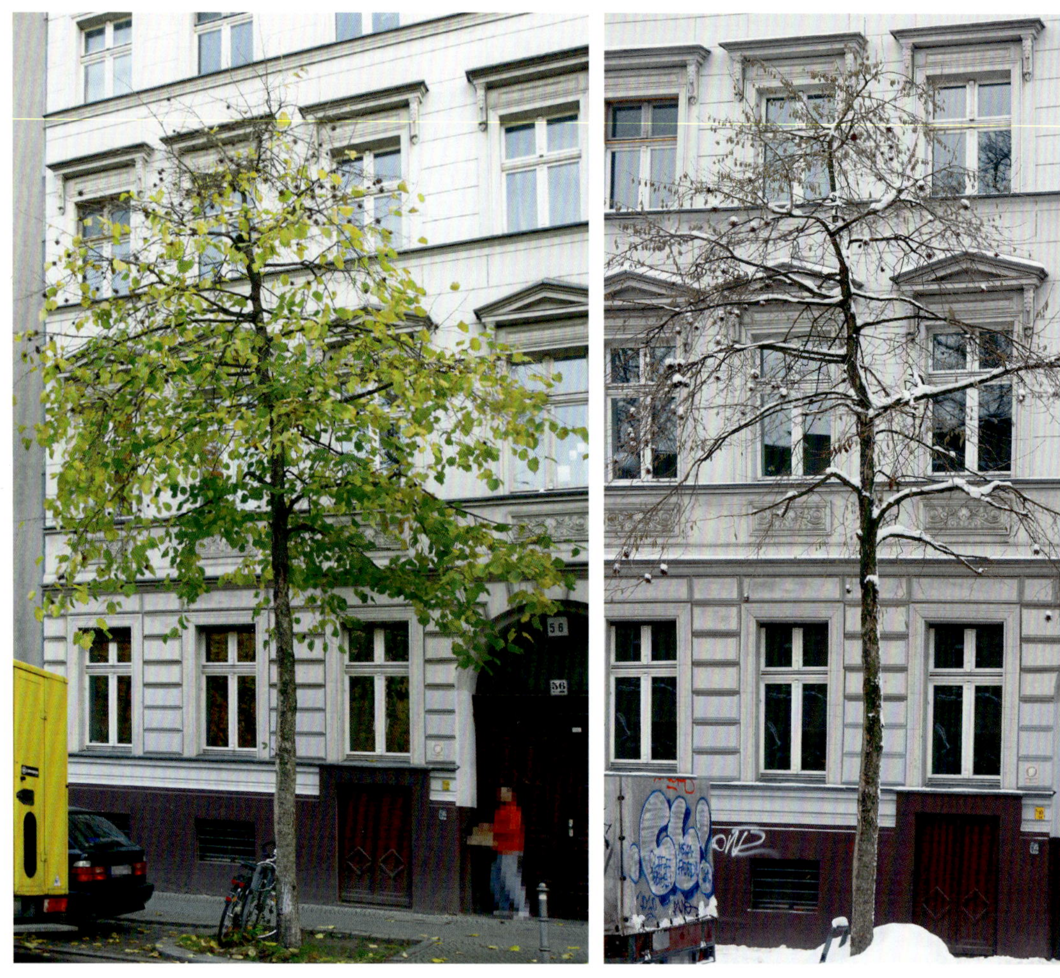

B10–S   B10–W   G: Hazel/Hasel [Corylus colurna]
                   o   ADR: Waldemarstrasse 60, 10997 Kreuzberg Berlin
                                   GPS: 52.502840, 13.421950, HT: 1030 cm YR: 1988

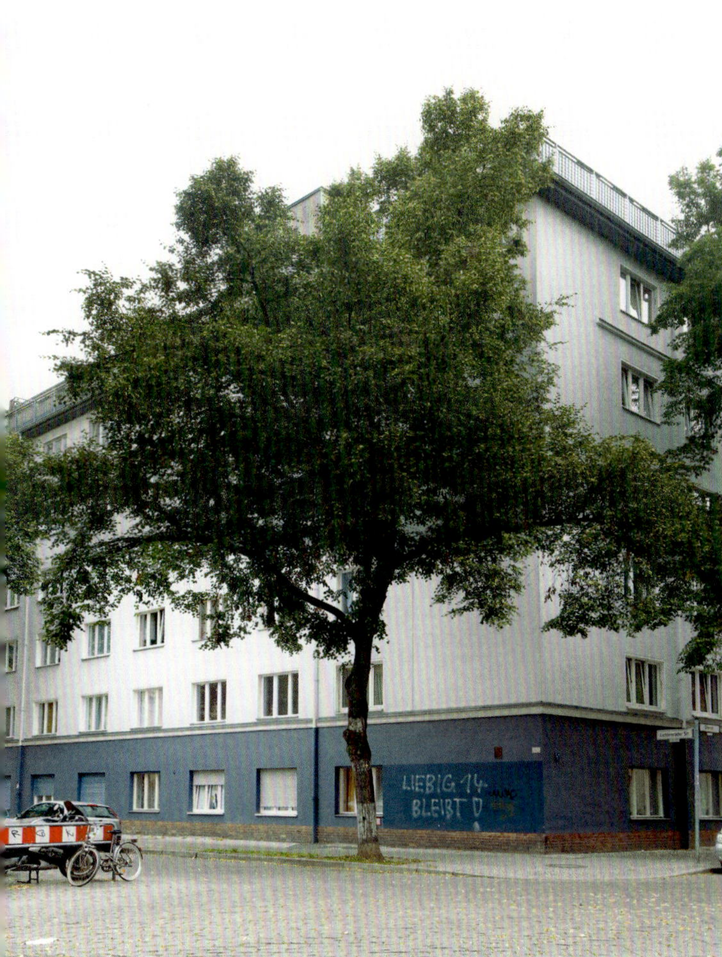

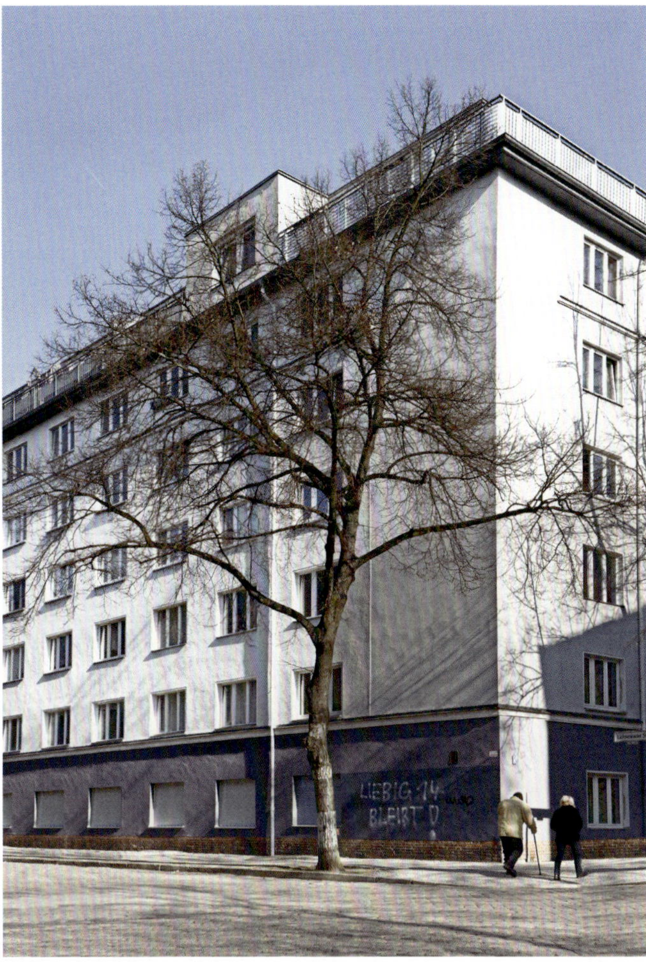

B11–S　　　　B11–W　　　　G: Linden/Linde [Tilia]
ADR: Lichtenrader Strasse 35, 12049 Neukölln Berlin
GPS: 52.473700, 13.421280, HT: 1340 cm YR: 1960

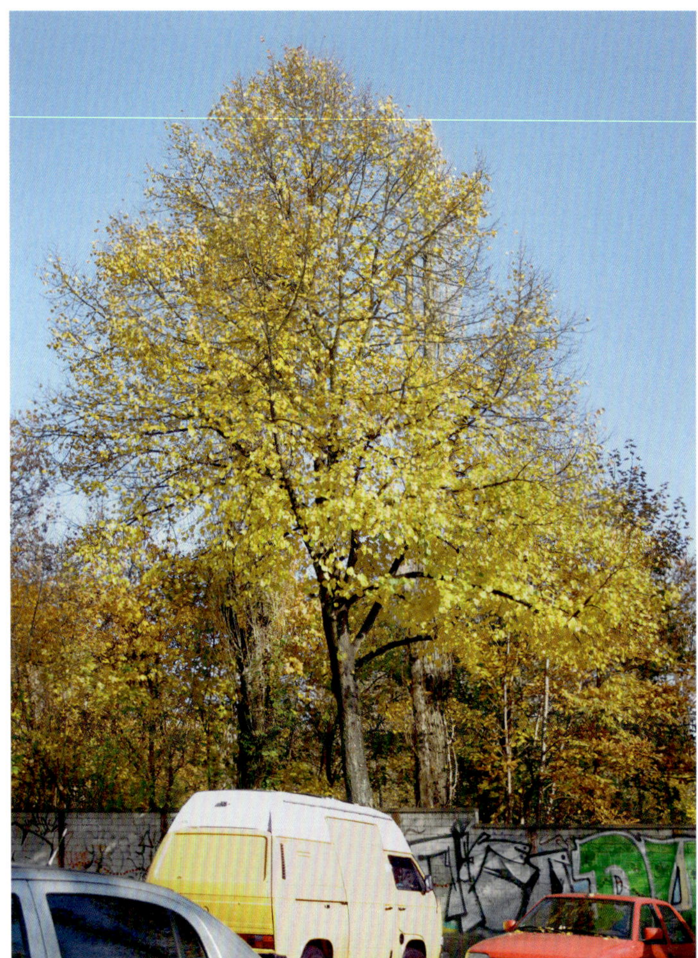 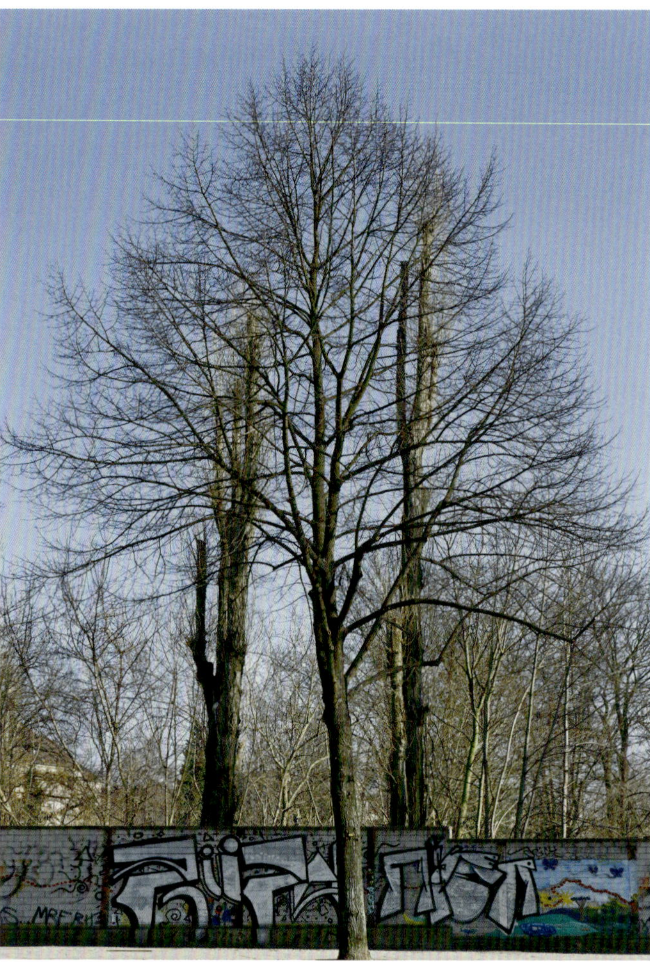

B12-S   B12-W   G: Linden/Linde [Tilia]
                              ADR: Oderstrasse 4, 12051 Neukölln Berlin
                              GPS: 52.468090, 13.420990, HT: 1020 cm YR: 1979

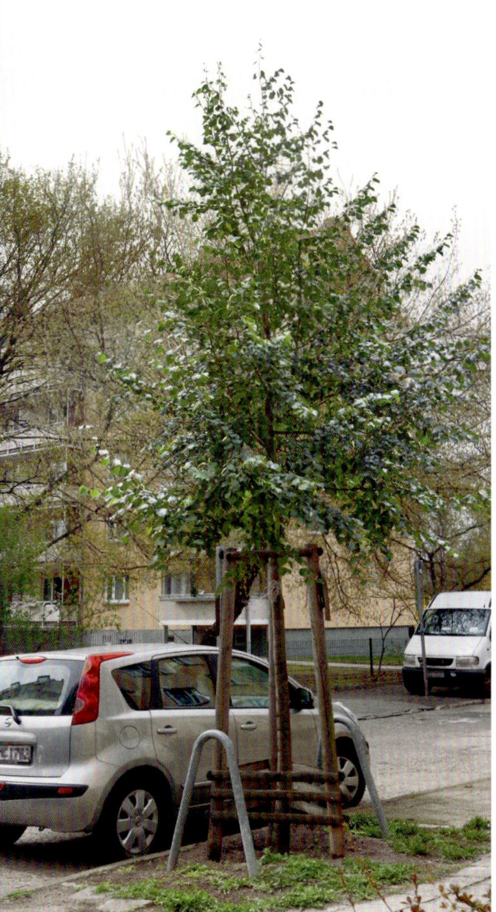
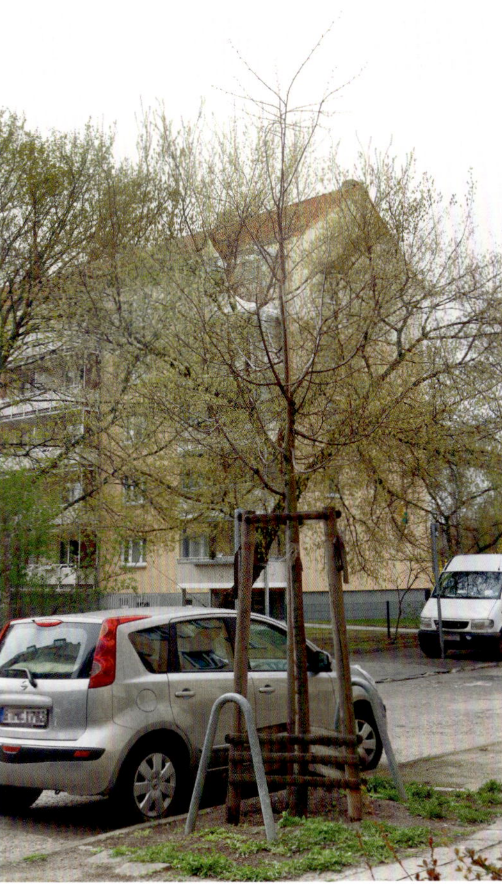

B13 – S   B13 – W   G: Linden / Linde [Tilia cordata]
  ○   ○   ADR: Lexisstrasse 3, 12435 Alt-Treptow Berlin
                              GPS: 52.49037, 13.44204, HT: 470 cm YR: 2006

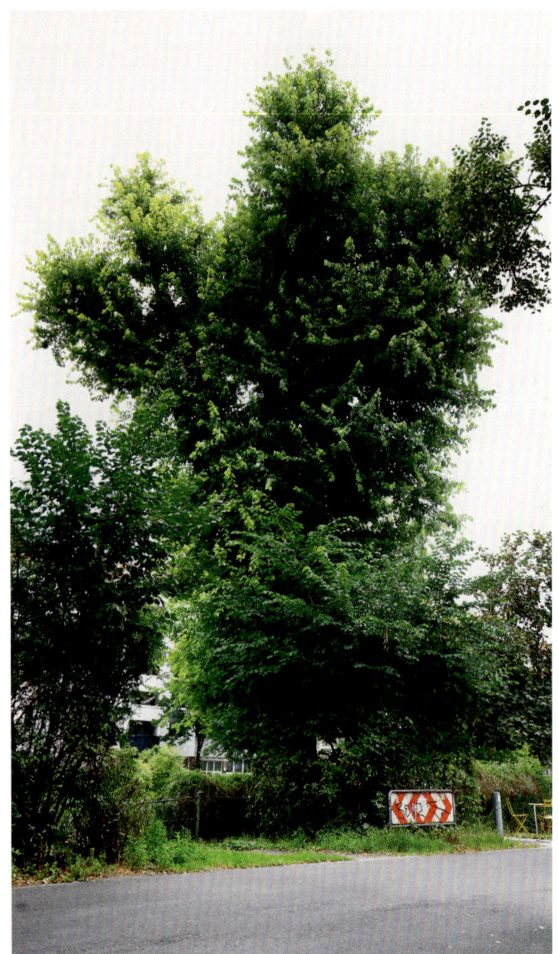 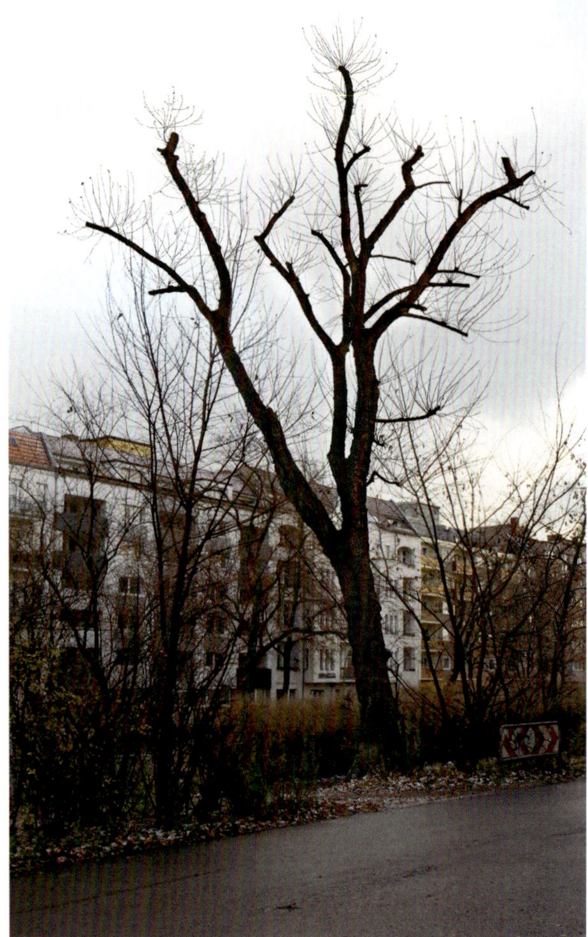

B14–S   B14–W   G: Silver maple/Silberahorn [Acer saccharinum]
            o   ADR: Weigandufer 9, 12045 Neukölln Berlin
                        GPS: 52.485850, 13.442280, HT: 1230 cm YR: 1870

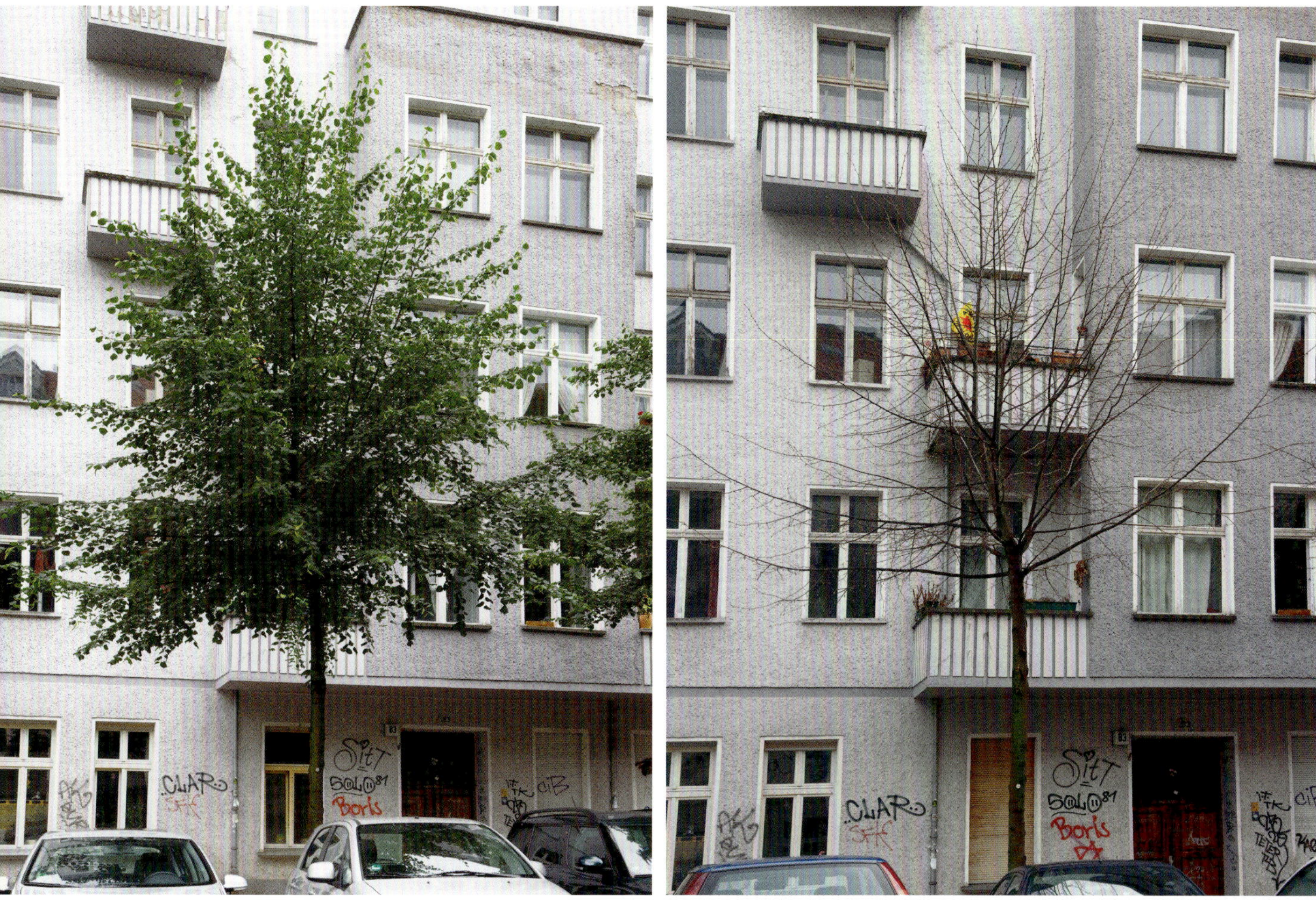

B15–S   B15–W   G: Linden/Linde [Tilia tomentosa]
○   ○   ADR: Bouchestrasse 83, 12435 Alt-Treptow Berlin
                    GPS: 52.490990, 13.449920, HT: 710 cm YR: 2000

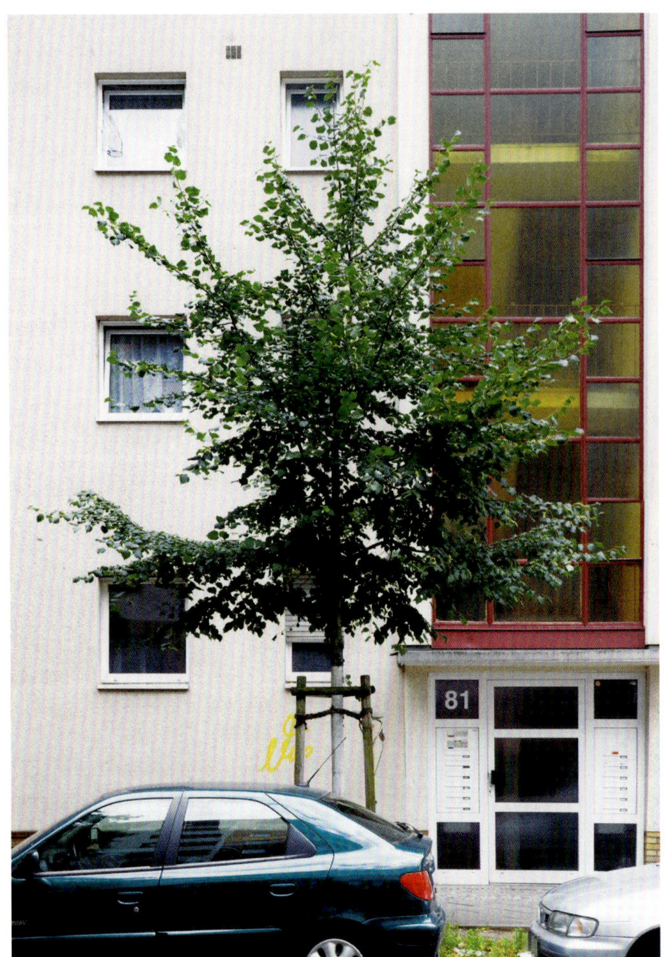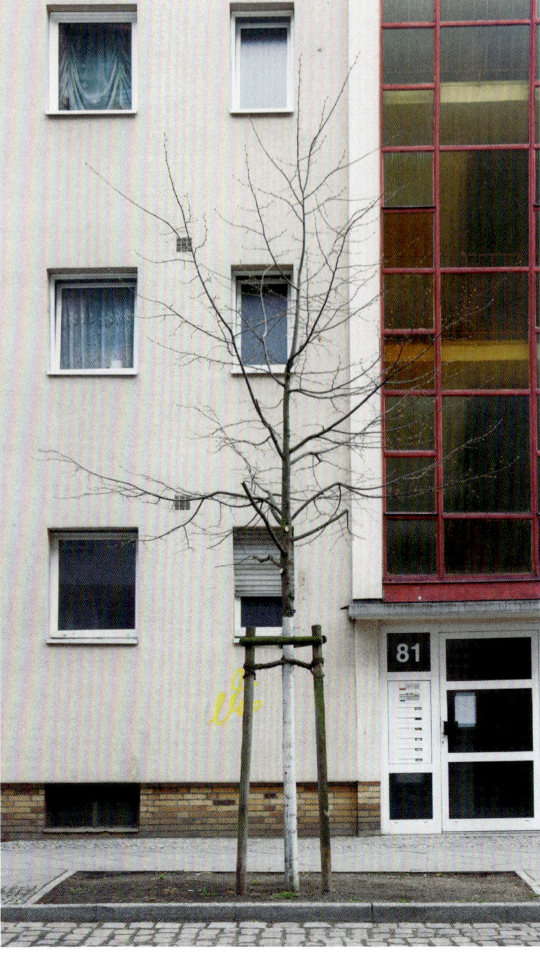

B16–S   B16–W   G: Linden/Linde [Tilia]
               o   ADR: Elsenstrasse 81, 12059 Neukölln Berlin
                         GPS: 52.486190, 13.450470, HT: 590 cm YR: 2005

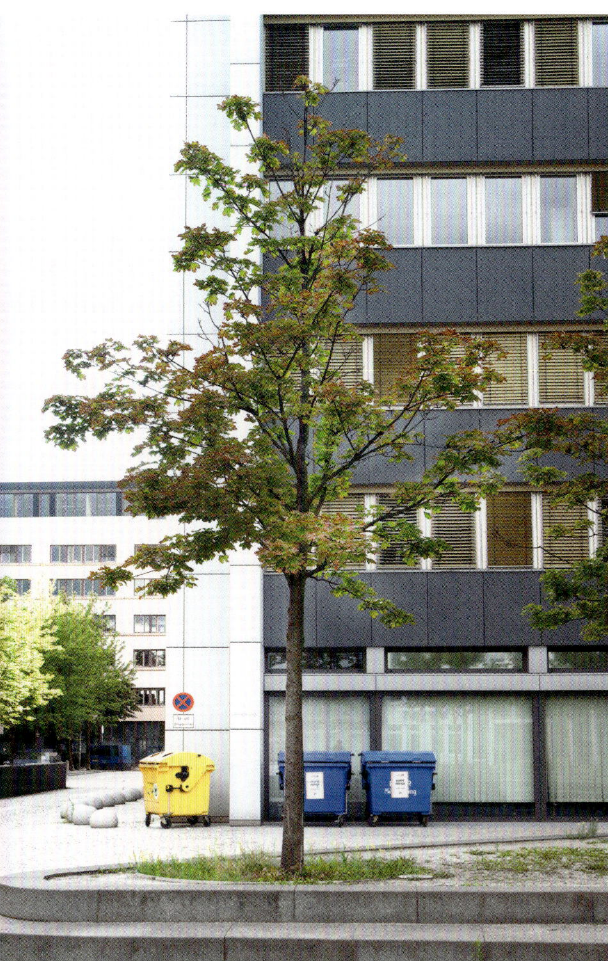 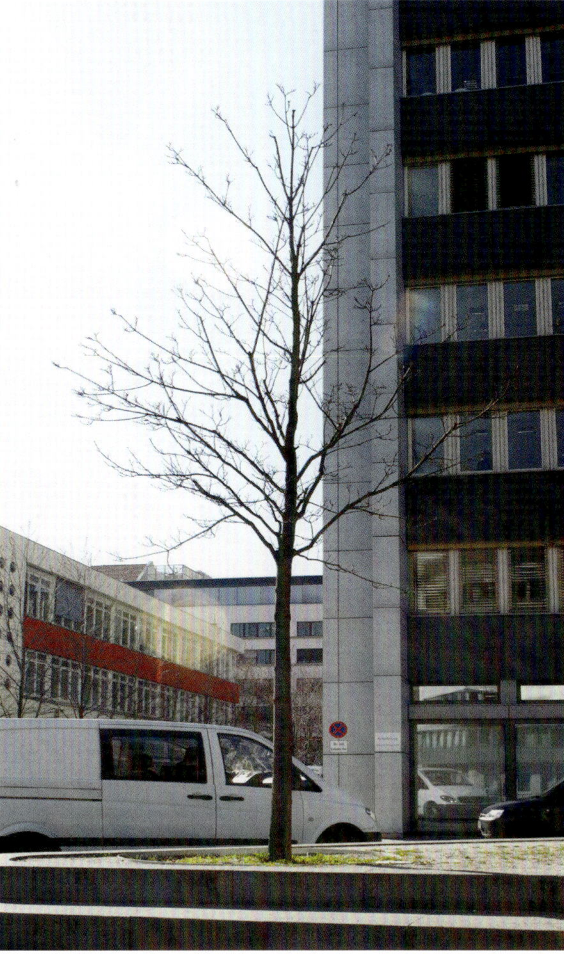

A1–S   A1–W   G: Maple/Ahorn [Acer platanoides]
                            ADR: Markgrafenstrasse 66, 10969 Kreuzberg Berlin
                            GPS: 52.506340, 13.393930, HT: 580 cm YR: 2000

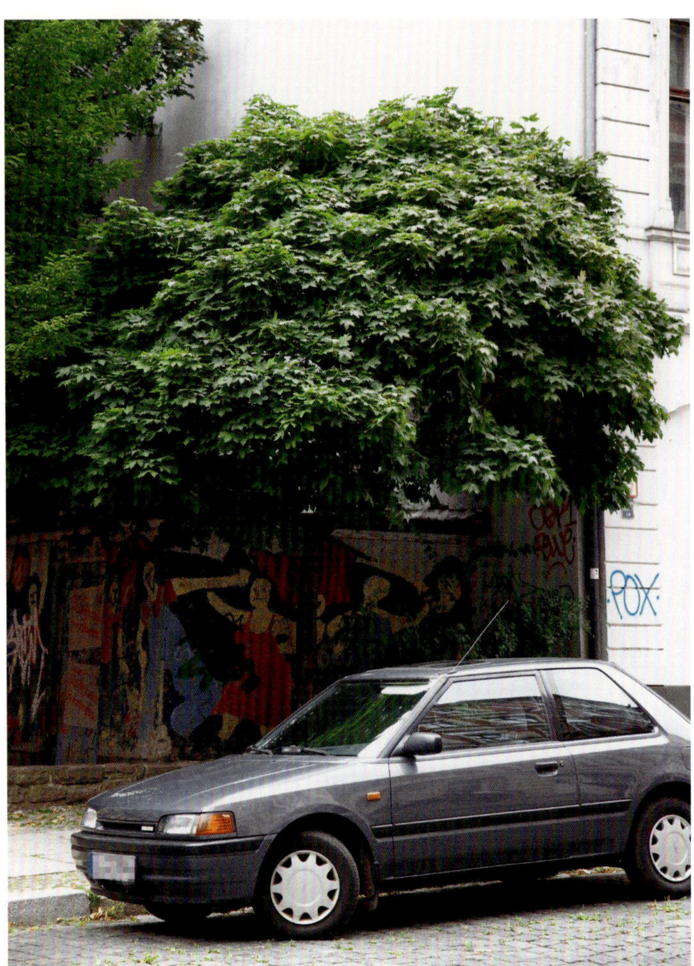 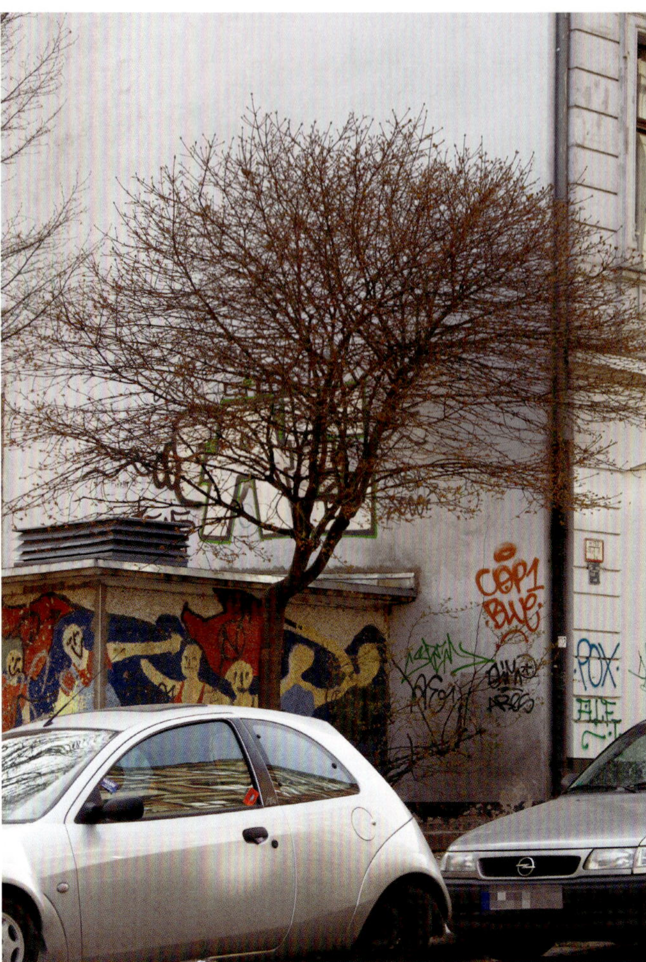

A2–S A2–W G: Maple / Ahorn [Acer platanoides]
o
ADR: Willibald‑Alexis‑Strasse 22, 10965 Kreuzberg Berlin
GPS: 52.487720, 13.390270, HT: 560 cm YR: 1946

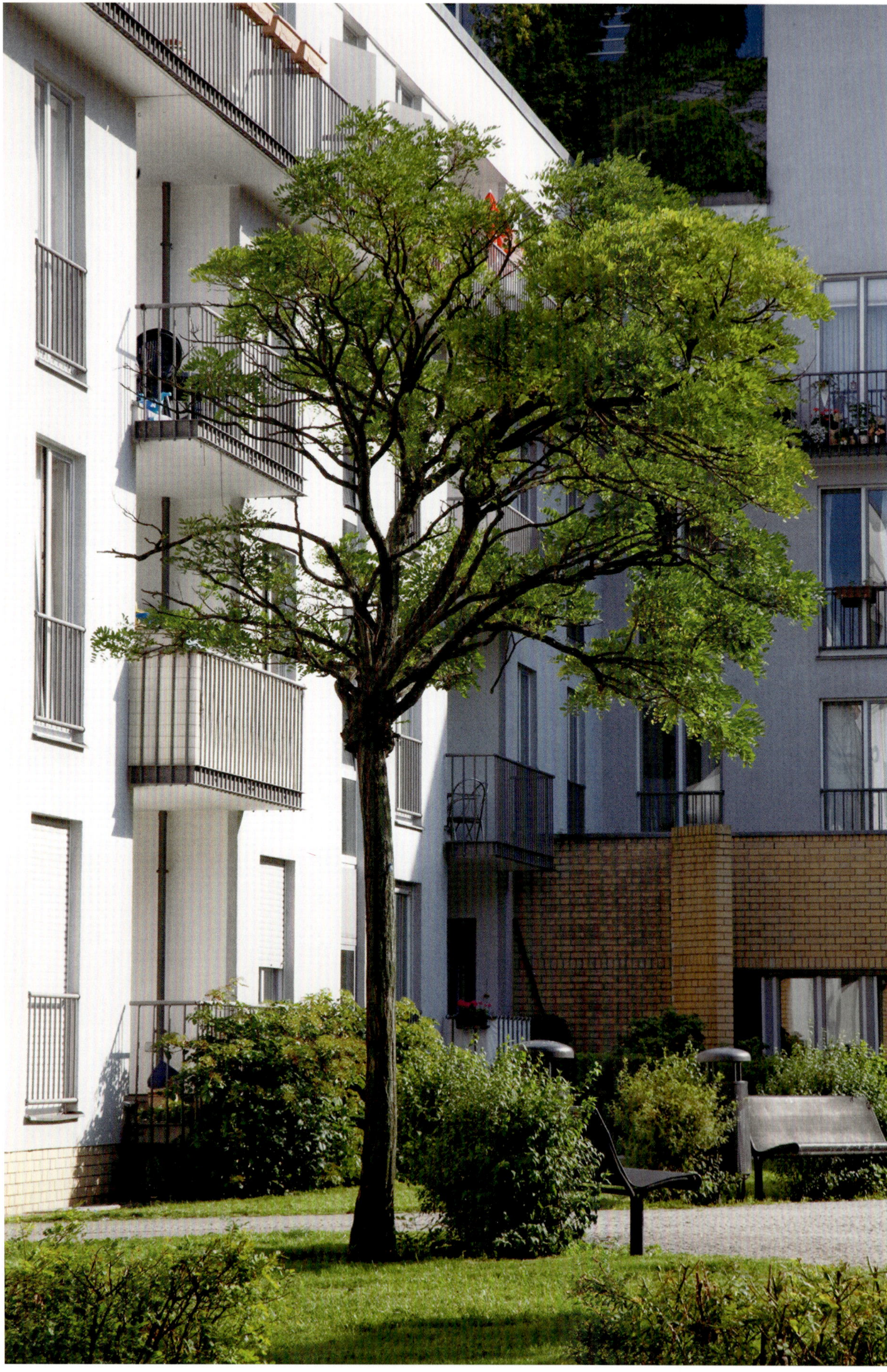

A3–S   A3–W   G: Honey locust/Lederhülsenbaum [Gleditsia triacanthos]
                            ADR: Ritterstrasse 44, 10969 Kreuzberg Berlin
                            GPS: 52.504340, 13.402380, HT: 620 cm YR: 1961

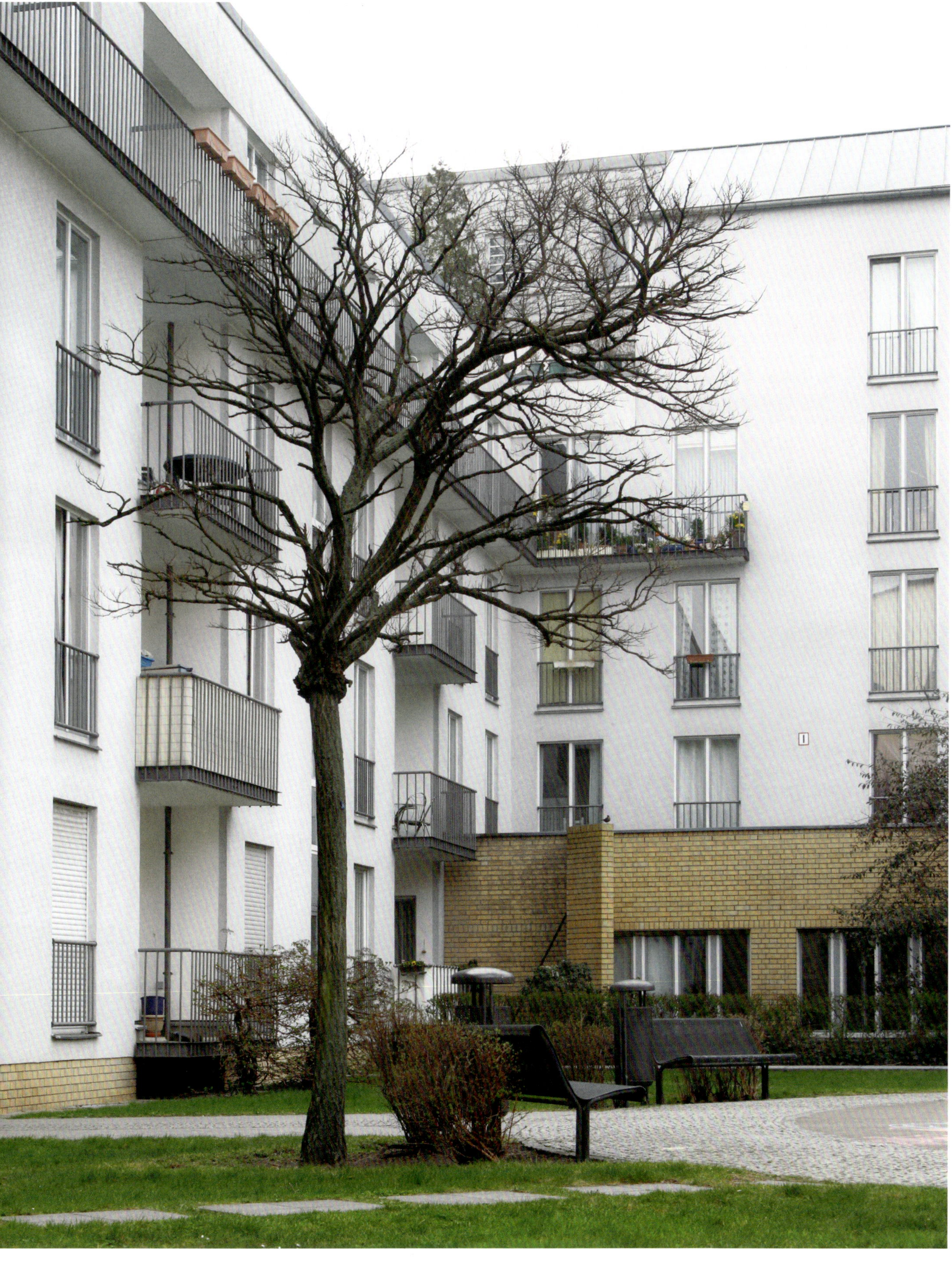

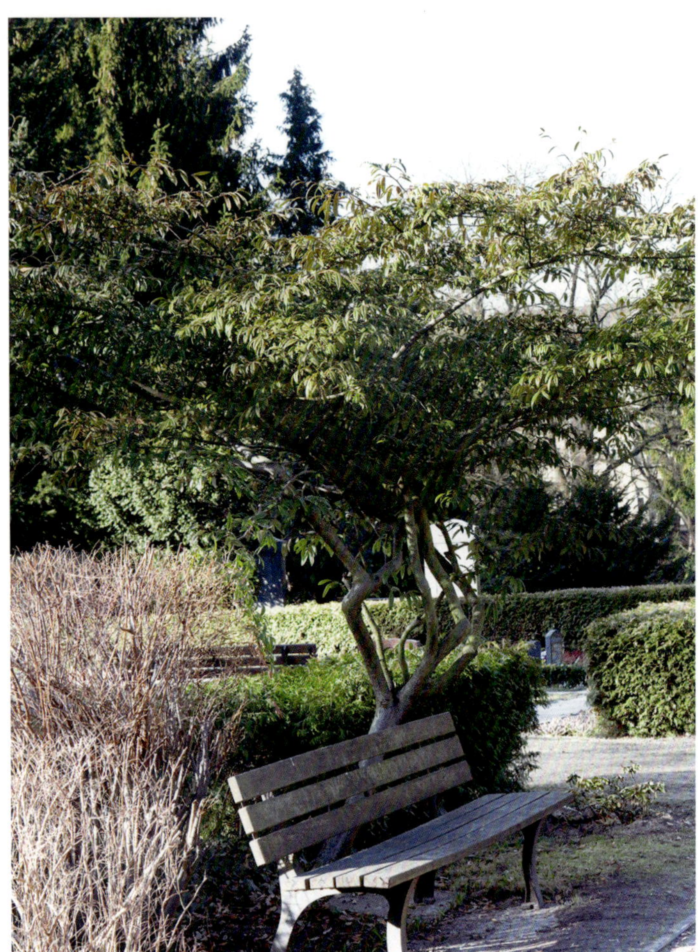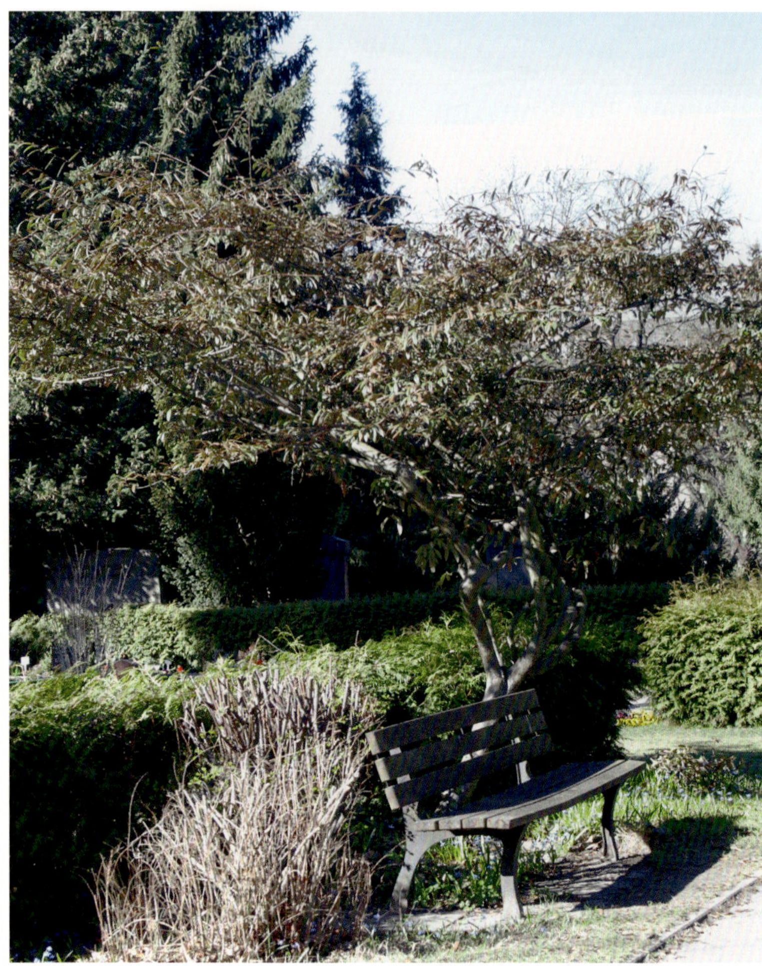

A4–S A4–W G: Mistletoe / Zwergmistel [Viscum minimum]
ADR: Jüterboger Strasse 3, 10965 Kreuzberg Berlin
GPS: 52.487120, 13.400710, HT: 310 cm YR: 1978

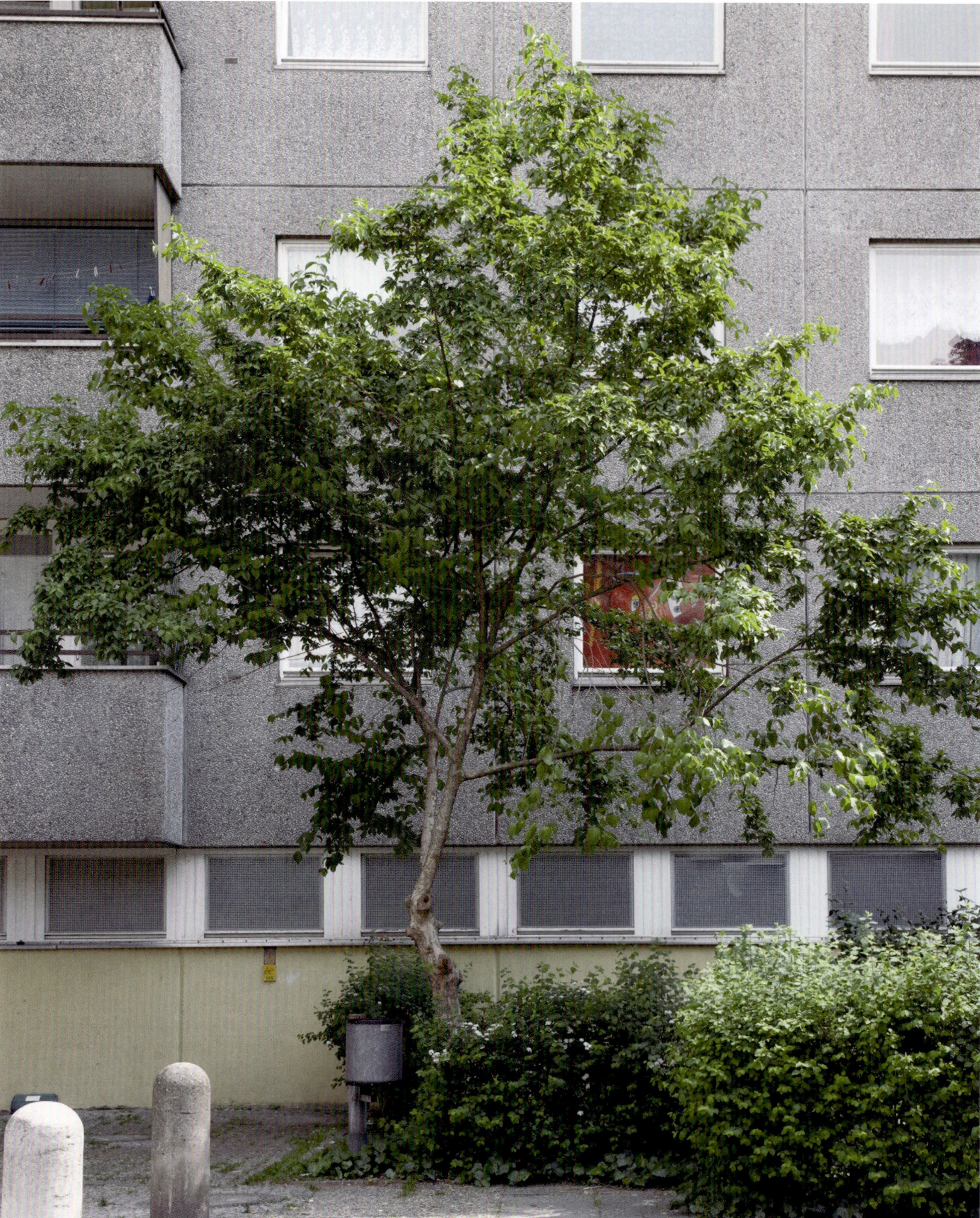

A5–S   A5–W   G: Cornelian cherry/Kornellkirsche [Cornus mas]
                        ADR: Bergfriedstrasse 9, 10969 Kreuzberg Berlin
                        GPS: 52.500330, 13.411750, HT: 690 cm YR: 1994

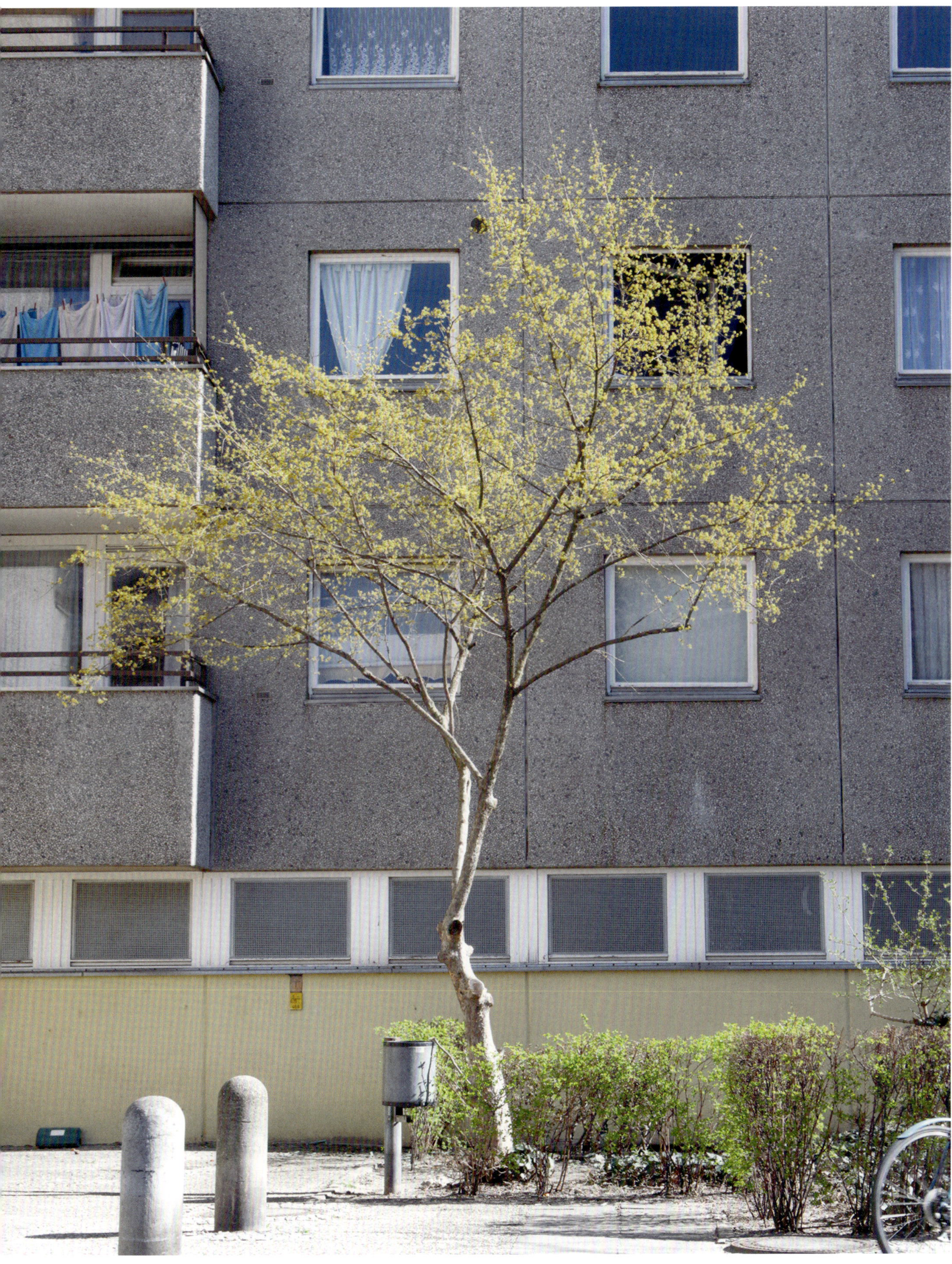

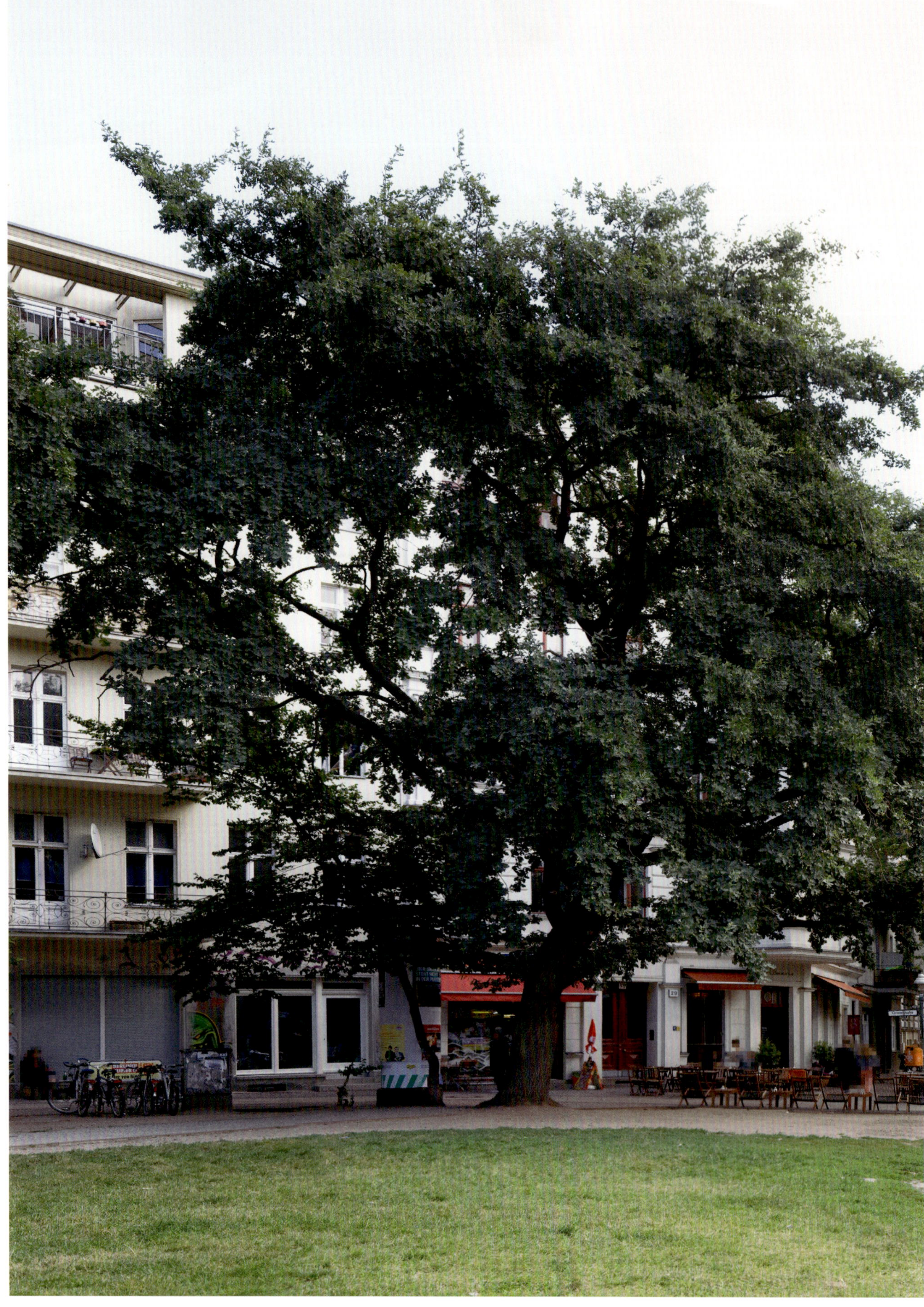

A6–S   A6–W   G: Oak / Eiche [Quercus robur]
              o   ADR: Böckhstrasse 54, 10967 Kreuzberg Berlin
                            GPS: 52.494750, 13.415390, HT: 1580 cm YR: 1988

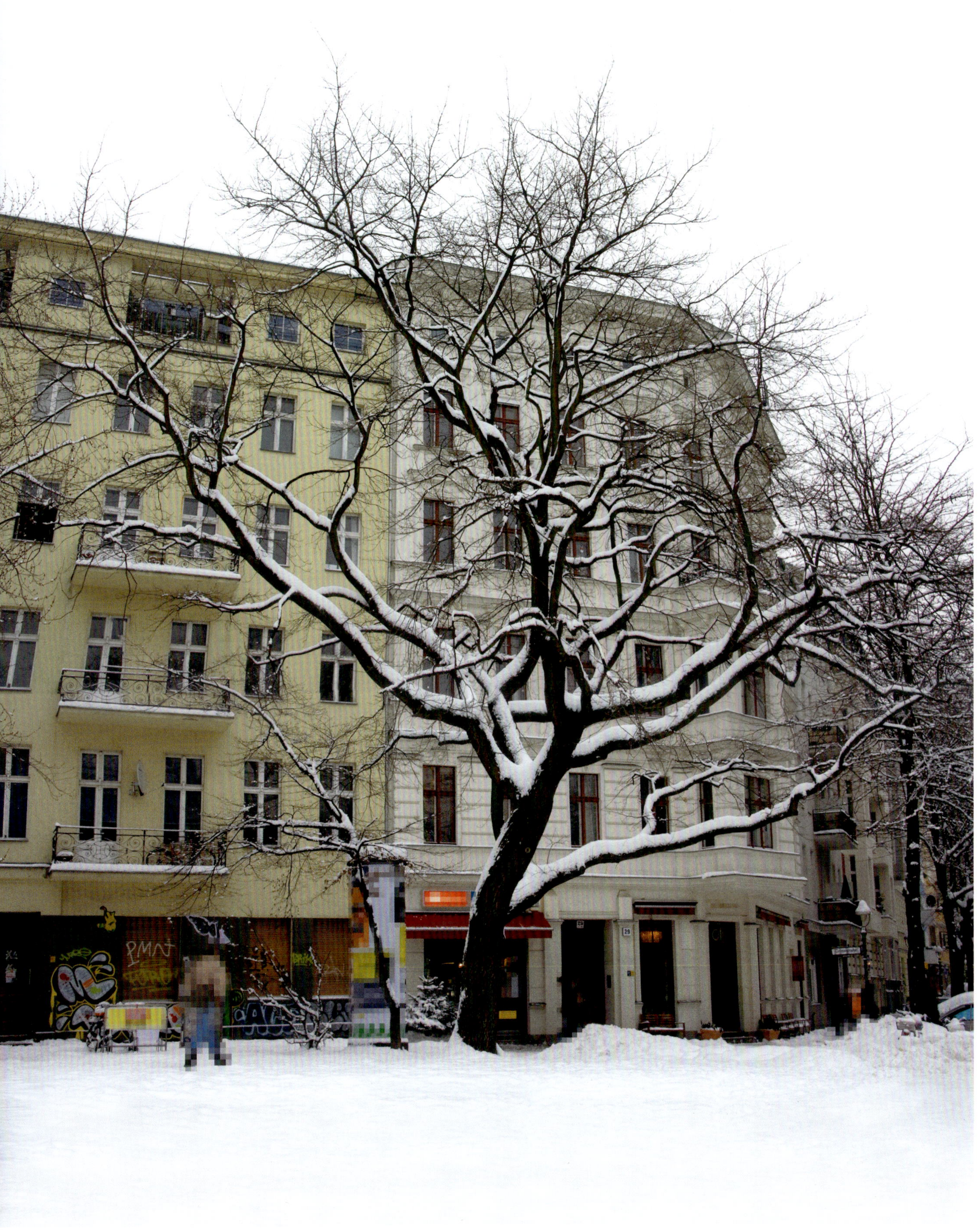

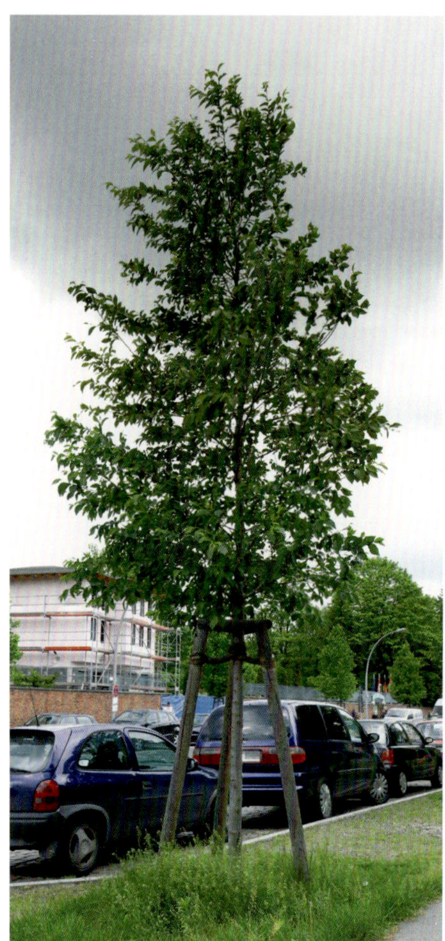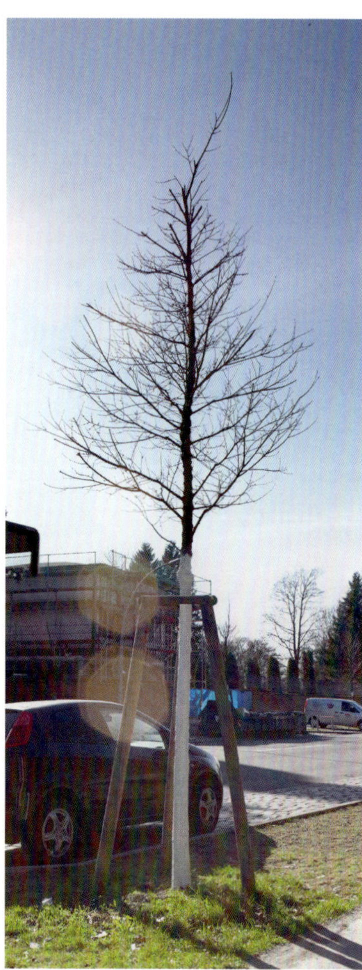

A7–S   A7–W   G: Elm / Ulme [Ulmus Resista]
ADR: Columbiadamm 128, 10965 Kreuzberg Berlin
GPS: 52.481830, 13.410530, HT: 460 cm YR: 2008

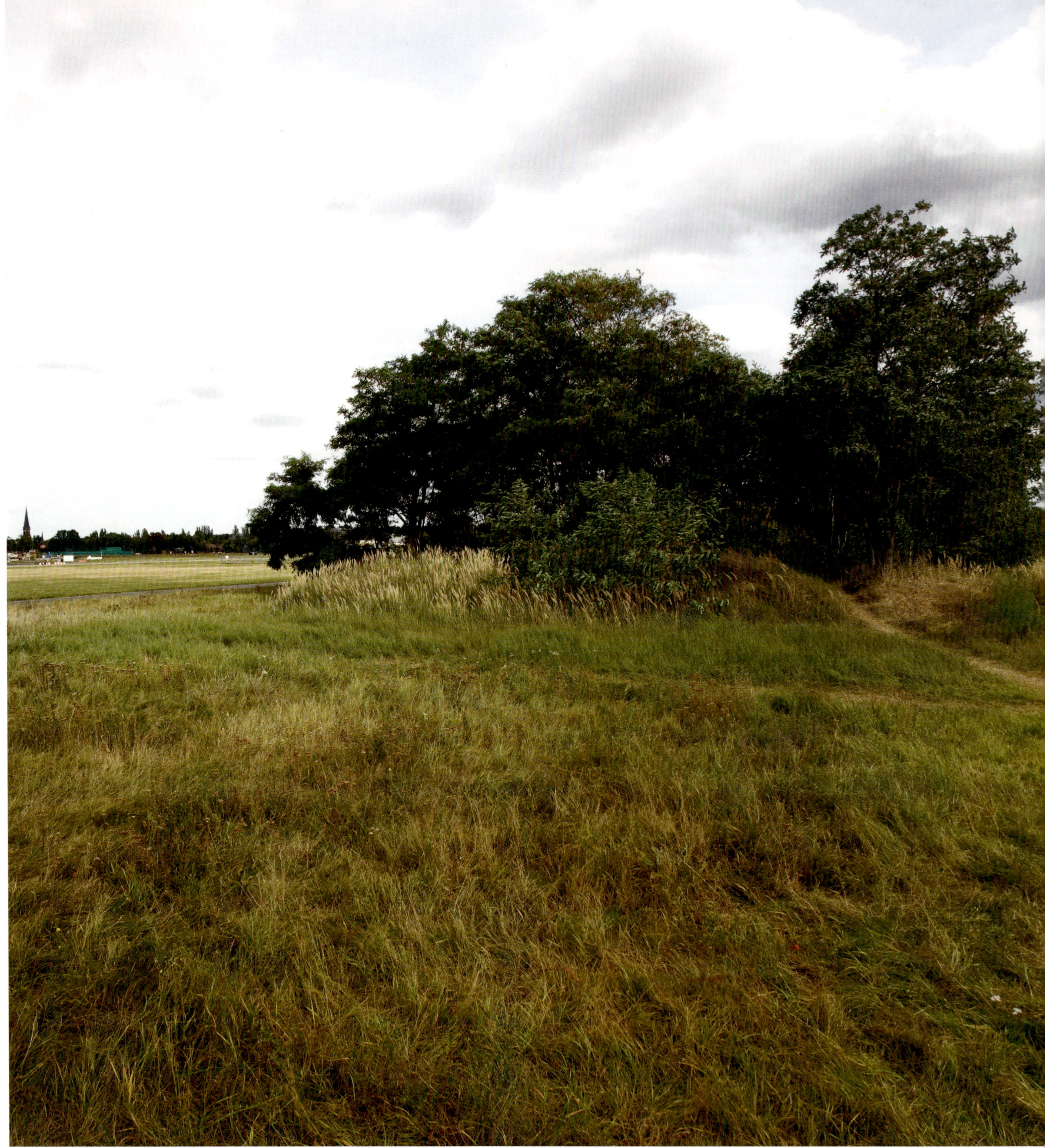

A8   Tempelhofer Feld Berlin
GPS: 52.47680, 13.41094

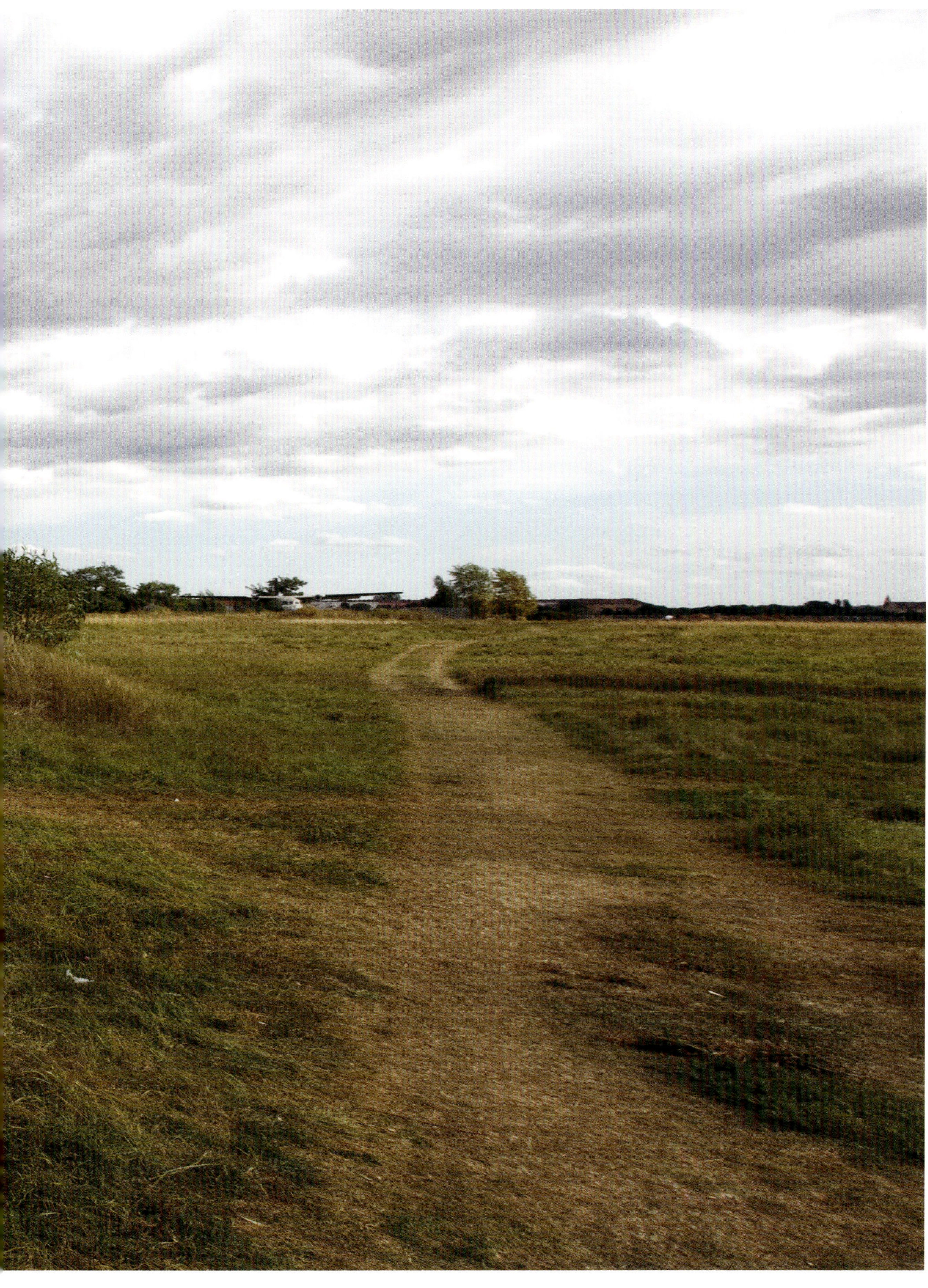

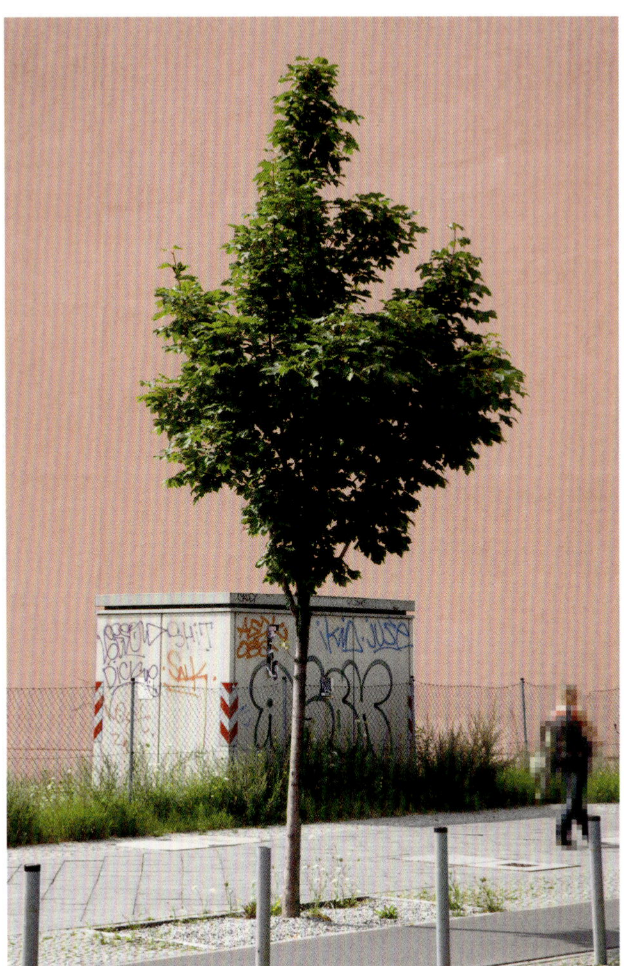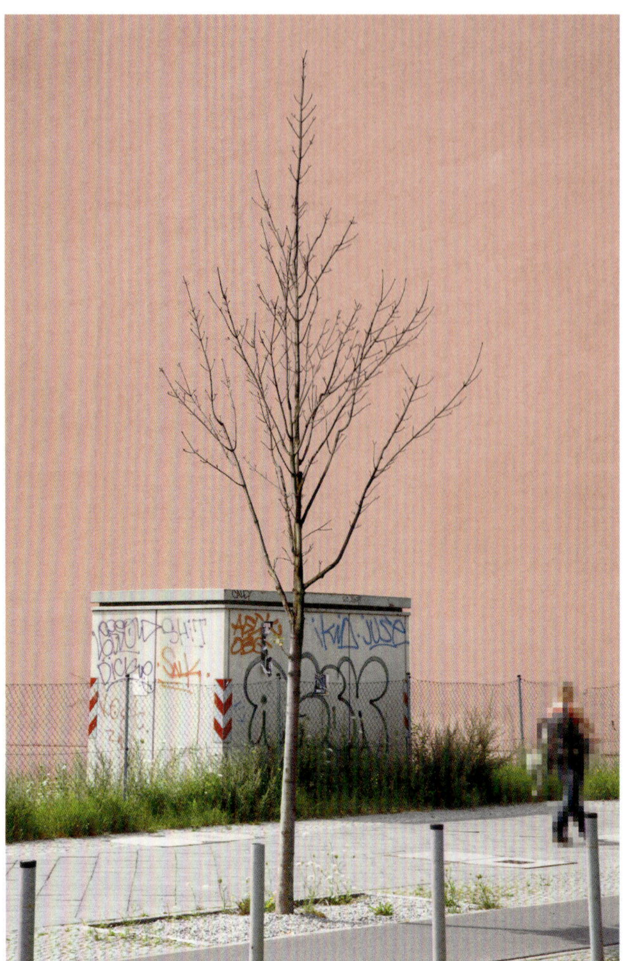

A9–S   A9–W   G: Maple / Ahorn [Acer platanoides]
o   o   ADR: Alexanderstrasse 31, 10179 Mitte Berlin
                        GPS: 52.518214, 13.417614, HT: 580 cm YR: 2007

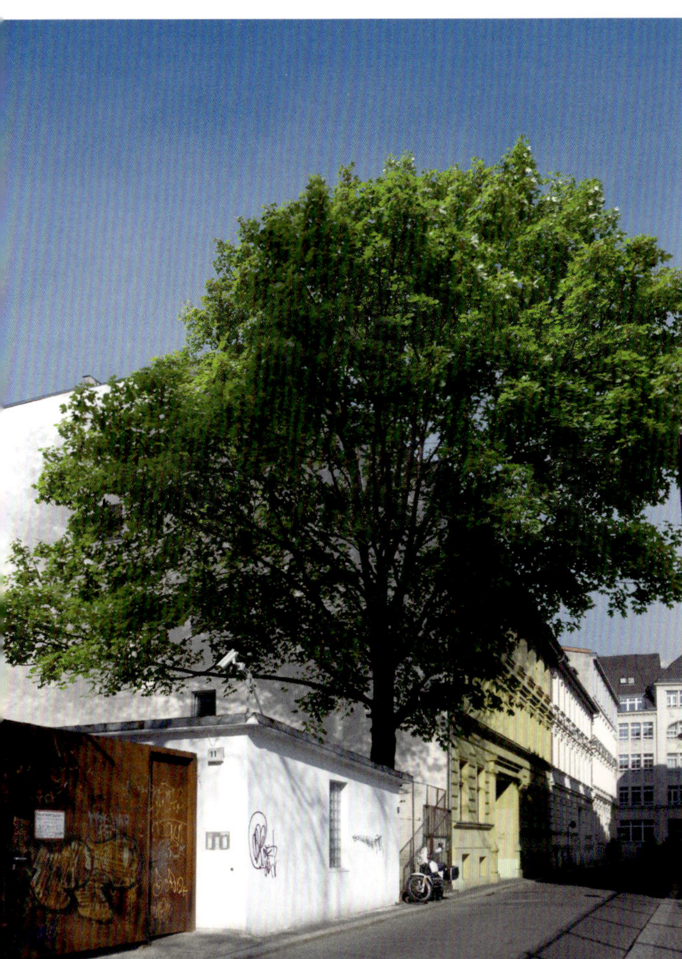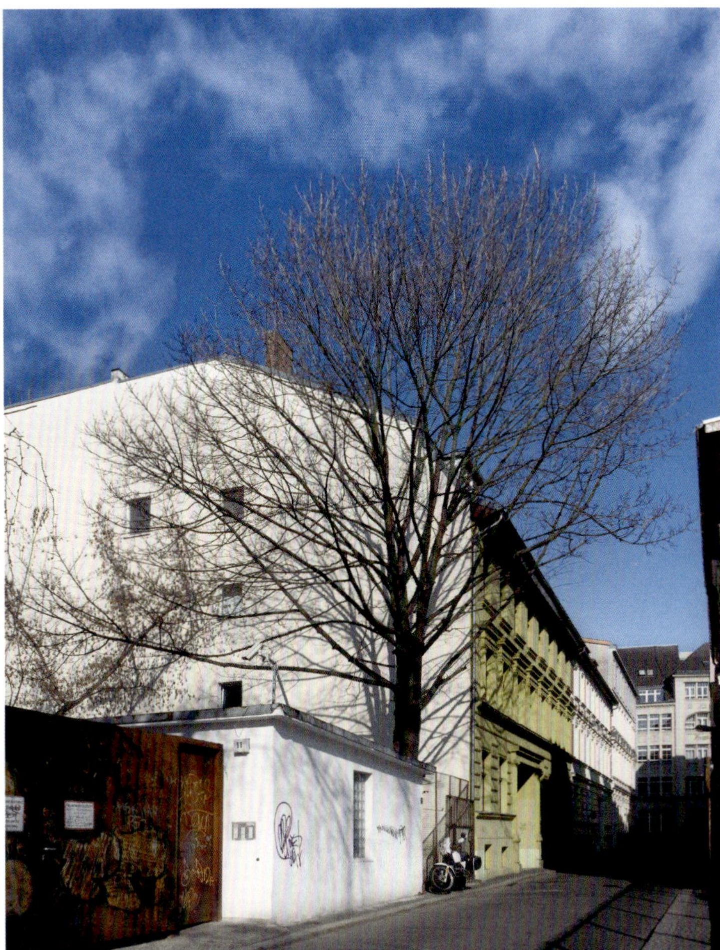

A10–S   A10–W   G: Maple / Ahorn [Acer]
○   ADR: Ohmstrasse 11, 10179 Mitte Berlin
                               GPS: 52.511690, 13.418060, HT: 1620 cm YR: 1982

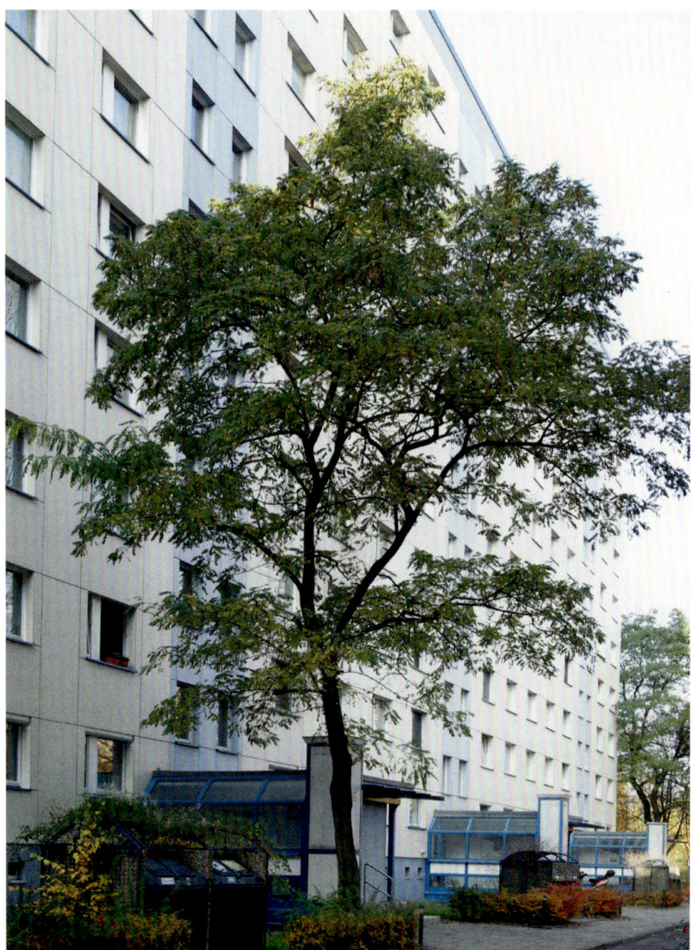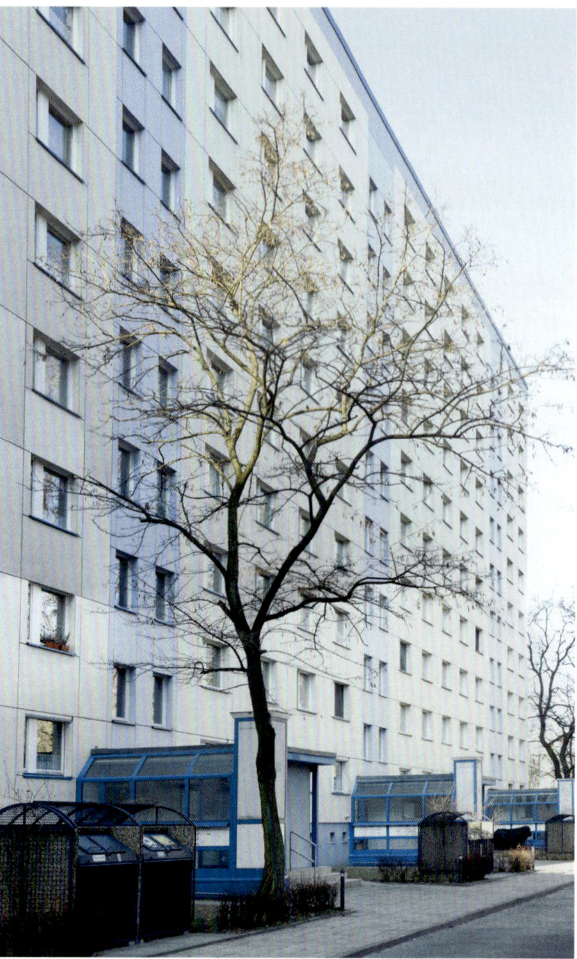

A11–S   A11–W   G: Locust/Robinie [Robinia]
                         ADR: Singerstrasse 115, 10179 Mitte Berlin
                         GPS: 52.517050, 13.425160, HT: 1350 cm YR: 1989

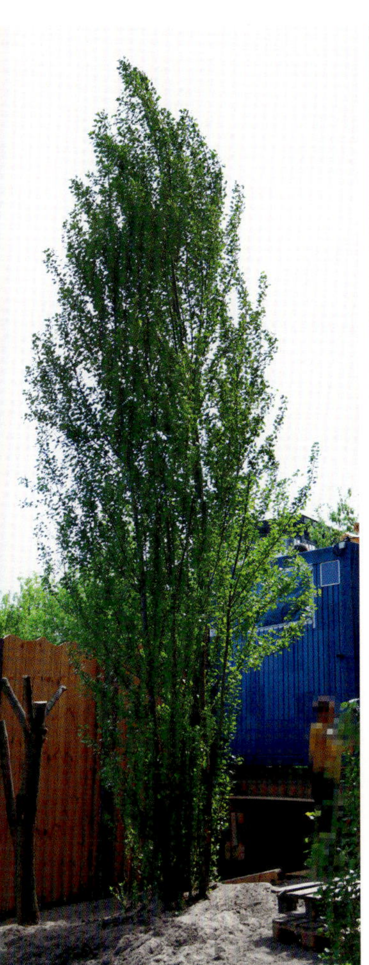
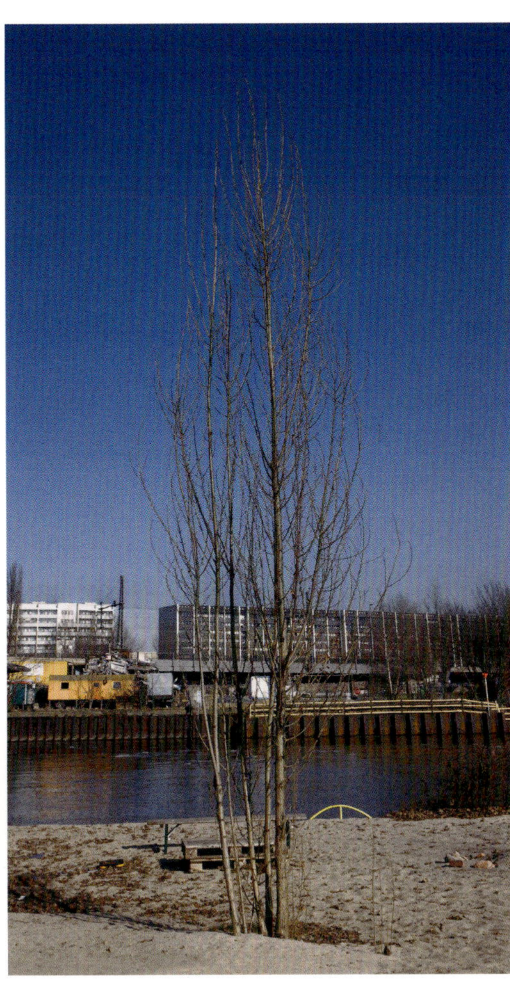

A12–S   A12–W
          o

G: Poplar / Pappel [Populus nigra 'Italica']
ADR: Michaelkirchstrasse 19, 10179 Mitte Berlin
GPS: 52.511030, 13.424990, HT: 710 cm YR: 2003

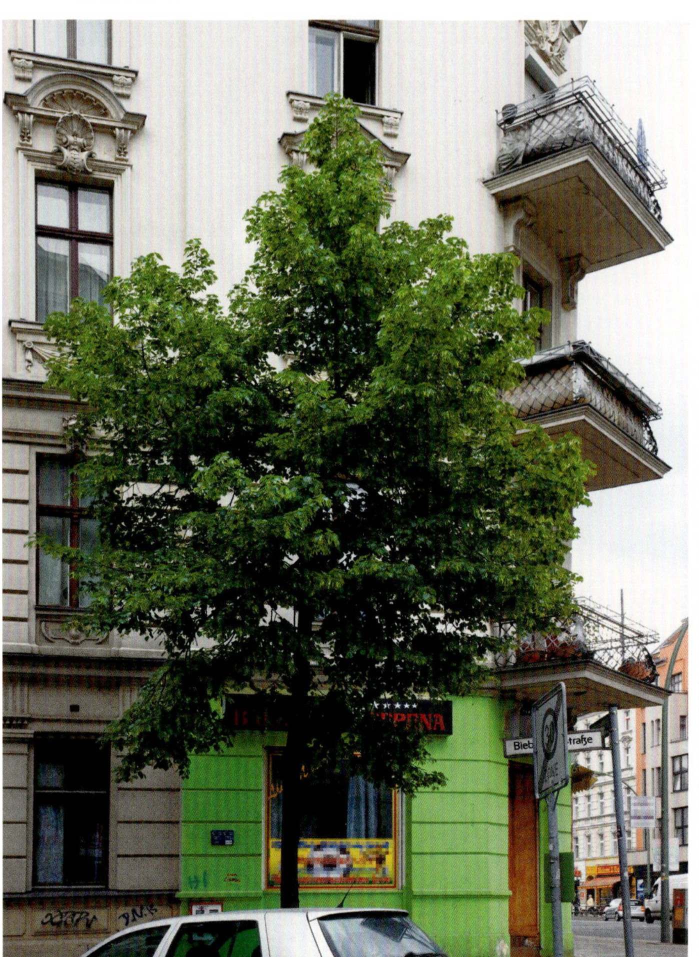
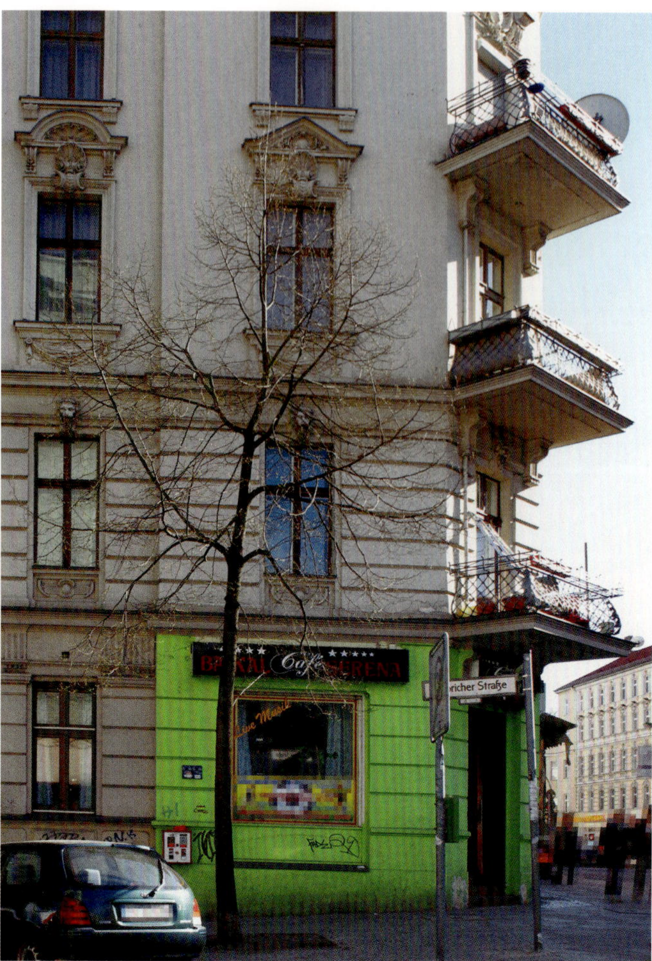

A13–S   A13–W   G: Linden/Linde [Tilia]
                              ADR: Karlsgartenstrasse 1, 12049 Neukölln Berlin
                              GPS: 52.482240, 13.424480, HT: 920 cm YR: 1980

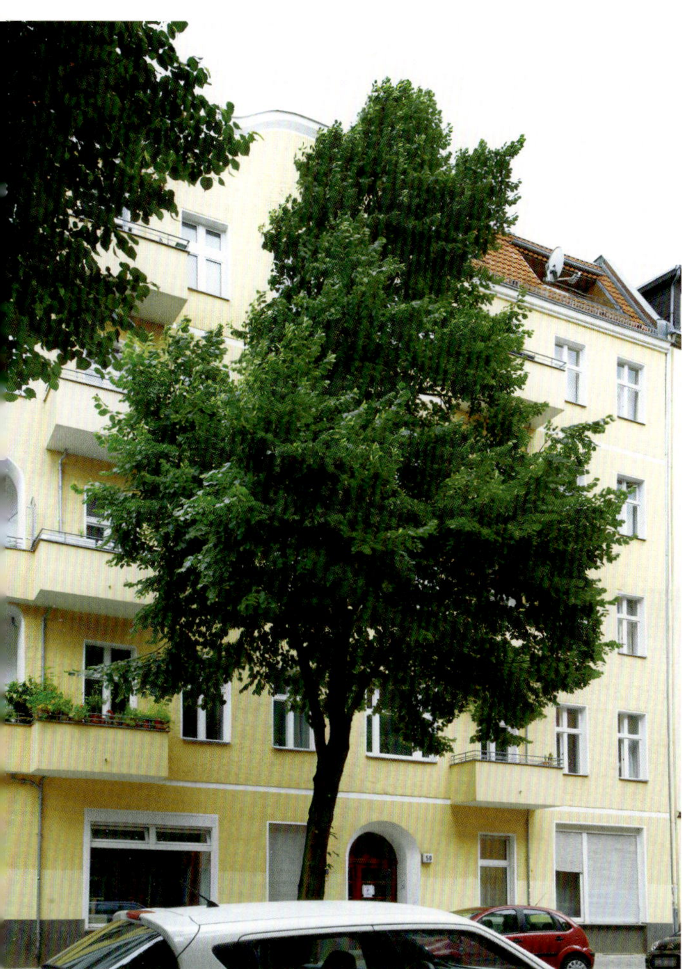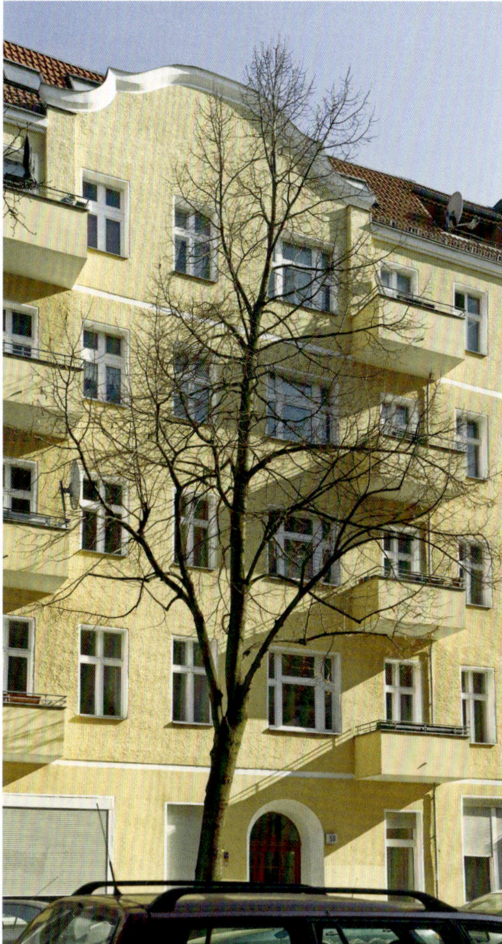

A14–S   A14–W   G: Linden/Amerikanische Linde [Tilia americana]
○   ○   ADR: Weisestrasse 51, 12049 Neukölln Berlin
                              GPS: 52.476900, 13.424200, HT: 1210 cm YR: 1975

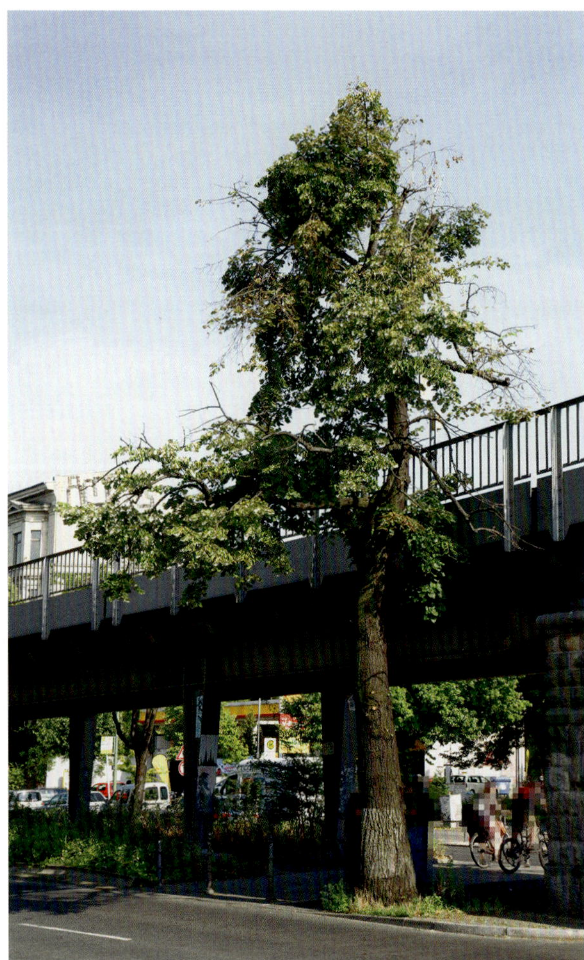 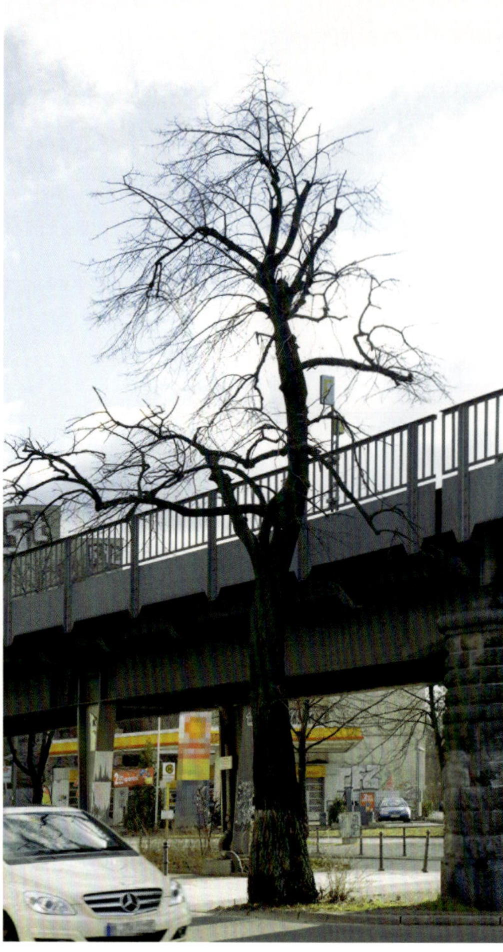

A15–S   A15–W   G: Silver lime / Silberlinde [Tilia tomentosa]
ADR: Skalitzer Strasse 95, 10997 Kreuzberg Berlin
GPS: 52.499470, 13.432120, HT: 1100 cm YR: 1983

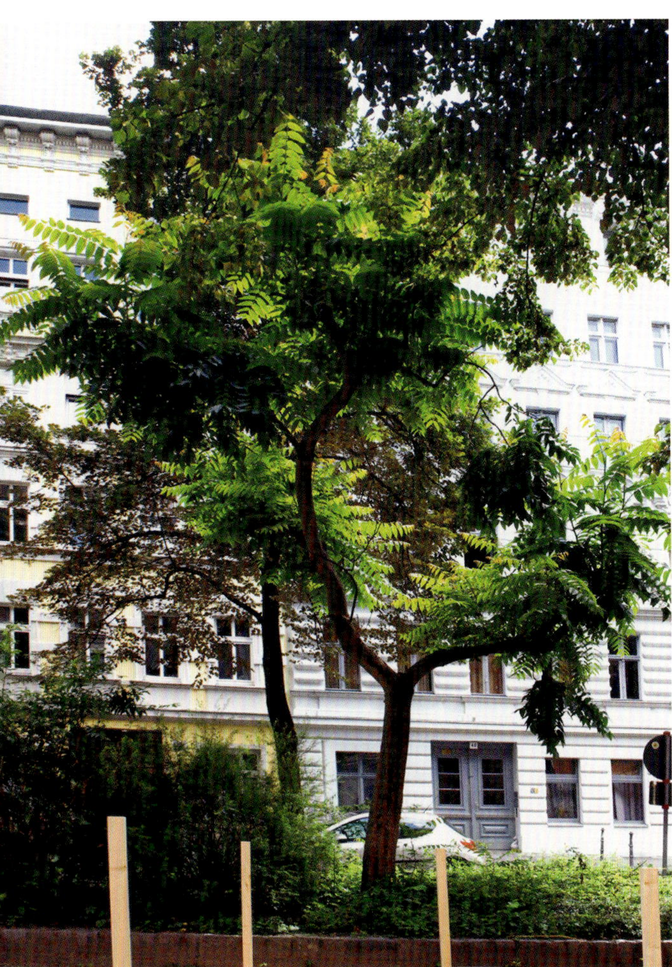 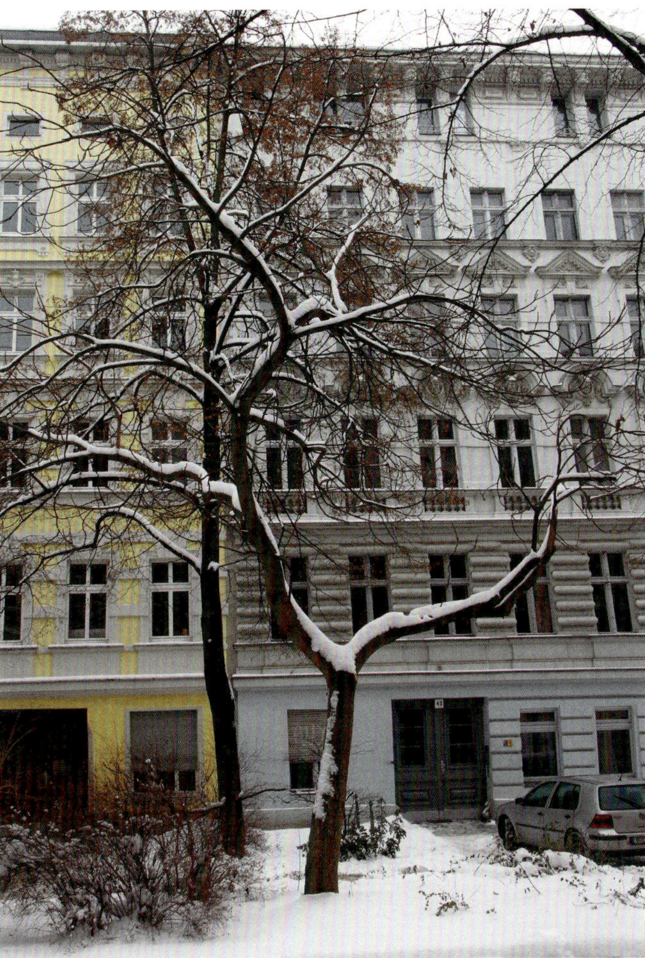

A16–S   A16–W
                 o

G: Tree of heaven/Götterbaum [Ailanthus altissima]
ADR: Reichenberger Strasse 95, 10999 Kreuzberg Berlin
GPS: 52.493950, 13.431980, HT: 620 cm YR: 2003

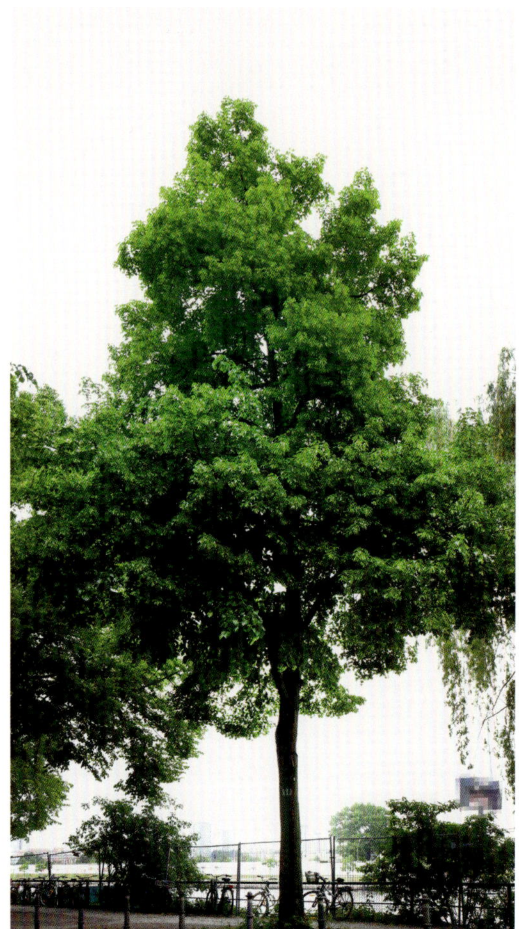 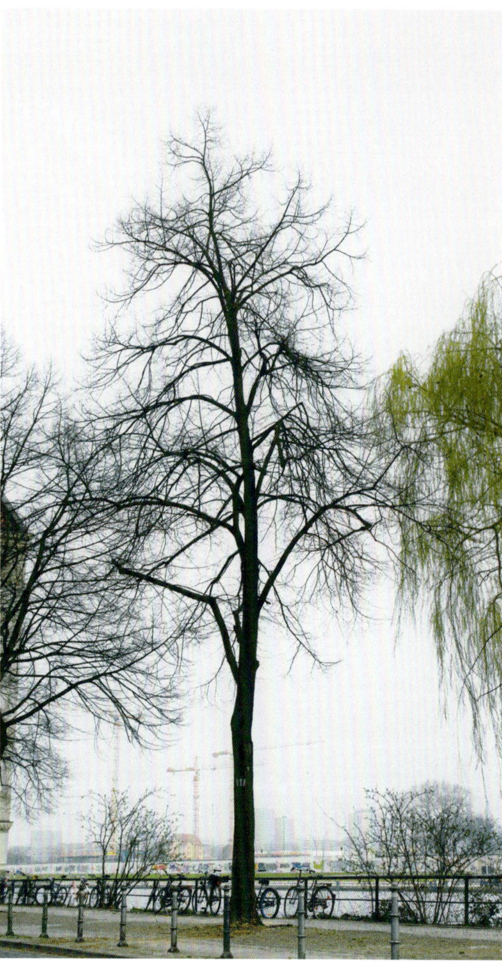

A17–S   A17–W   G: Linden/Linde [Tilia]
                         ADR: Gröbenufer 1, 10997 Kreuzberg Berlin
                         GPS: 52.502730, 13.441640, HT: 1210 cm, YR: 1949

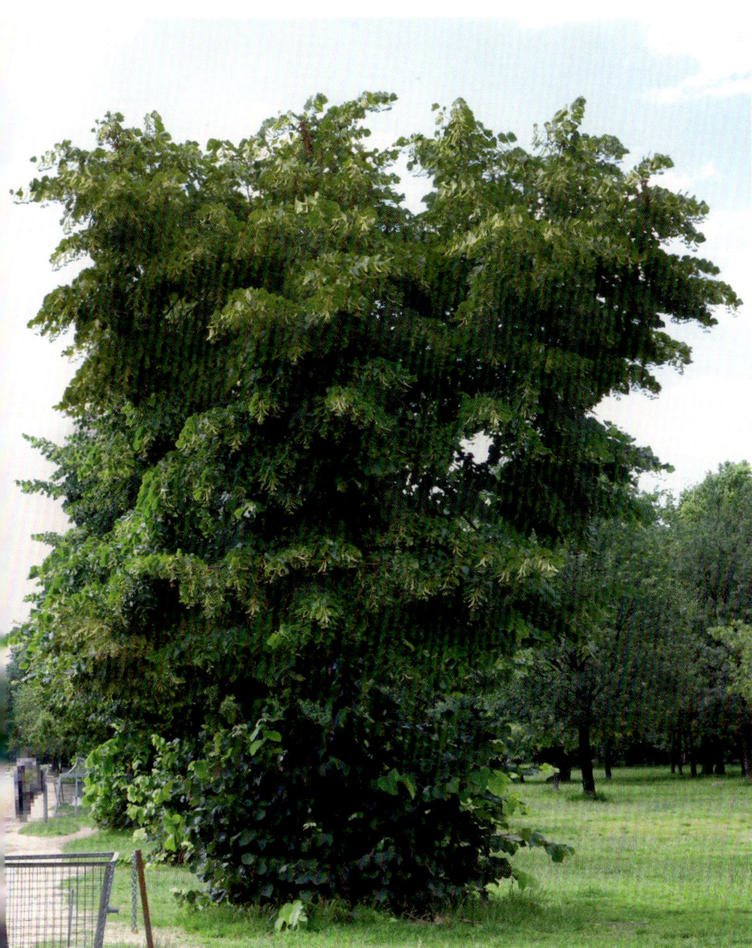 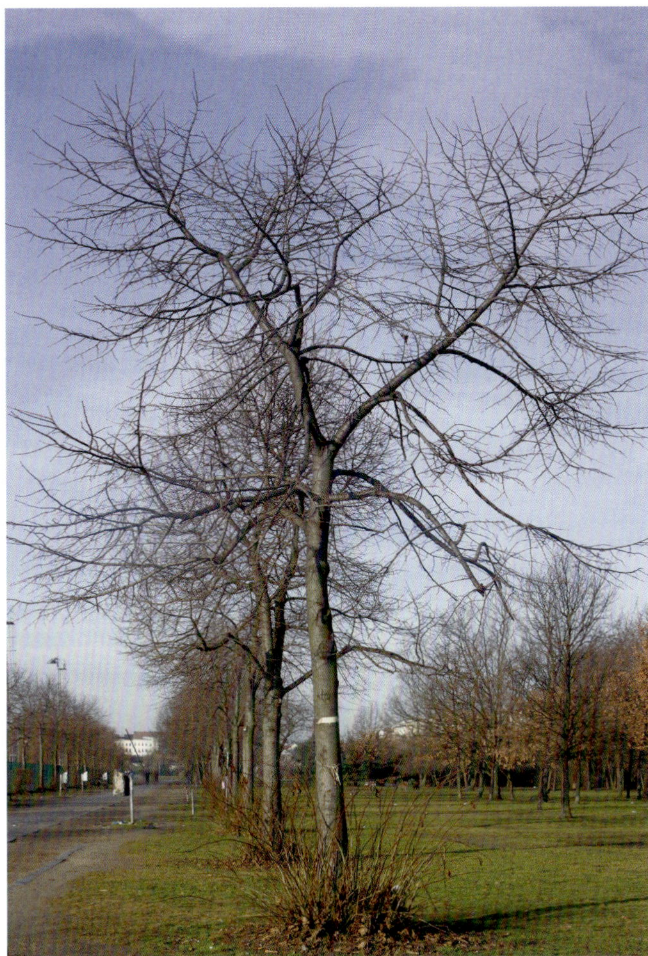

A18–S   A18–W   G: Linden/Holländische Linde [Tilia × intermedia]
o   ADR: Görlitzer Strasse 40, 10997 Kreuzberg Berlin
                              GPS: 52.495167, 13.441990, HT: 650 cm, YR: 1978

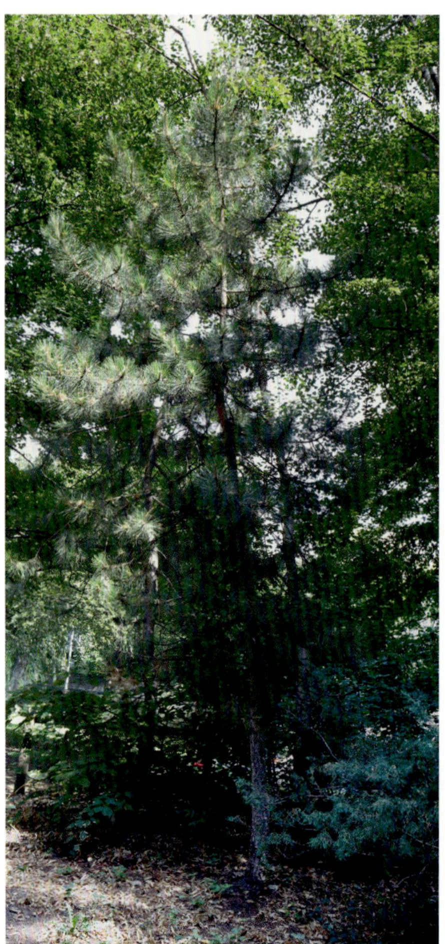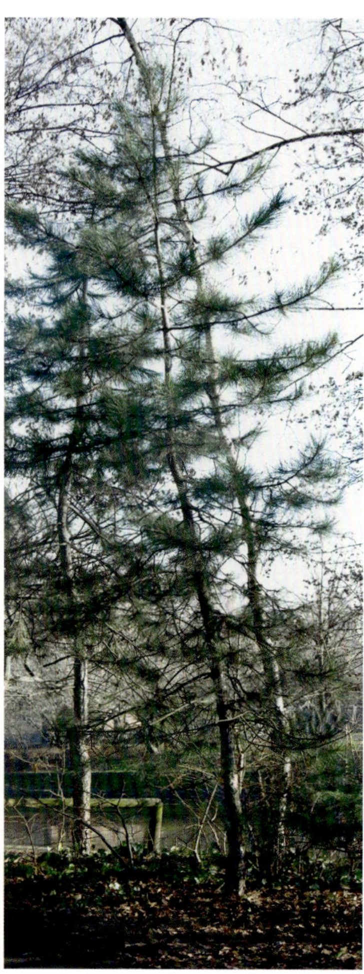

A19 – S   A19 – W   G: Pine / Kiefer [Pinus]
ADR: Lohmühlenstrasse 21, 10999 Kreuzberg Berlin
GPS: 52.492542, 13.441724, HT: 320 cm YR: 2001

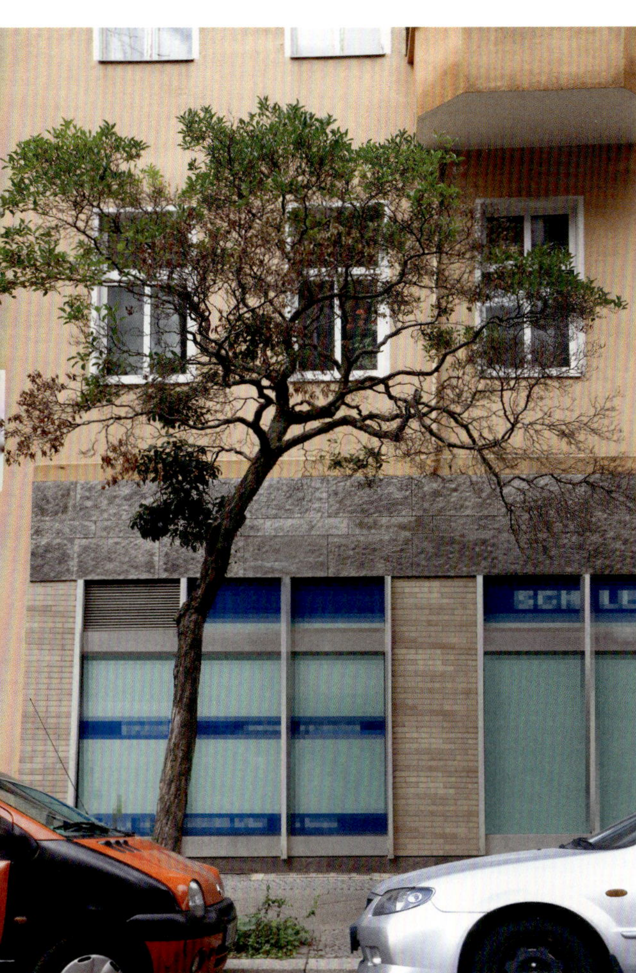
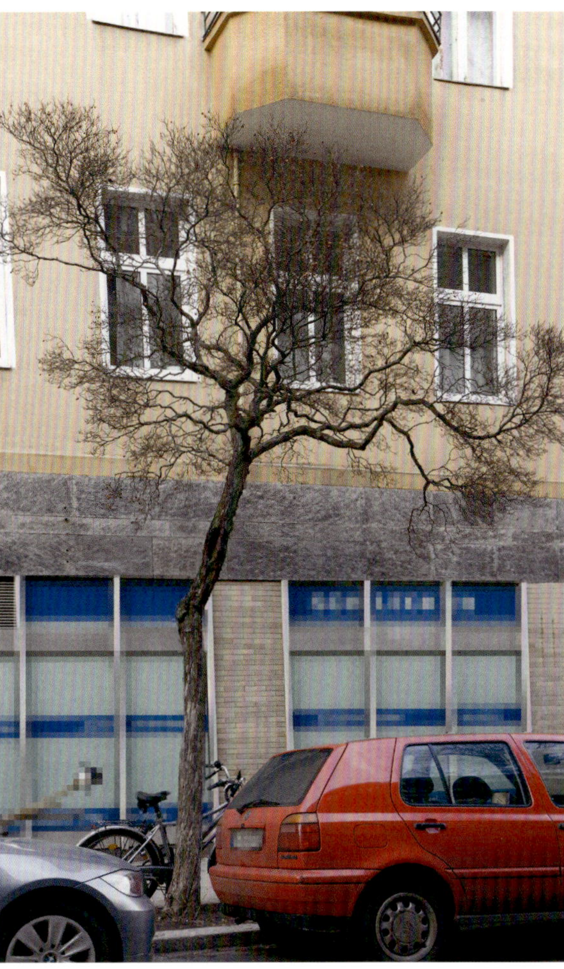

A20-S   A20-W   G: Hawthorn/Weissdorn [Crataegus prunifolia]
                         ADR: Anzengruberstrasse 14, 12043 Neukölln Berlin
                         GPS: 52.4808,13.441032, HT: 590 cm YR: 1980

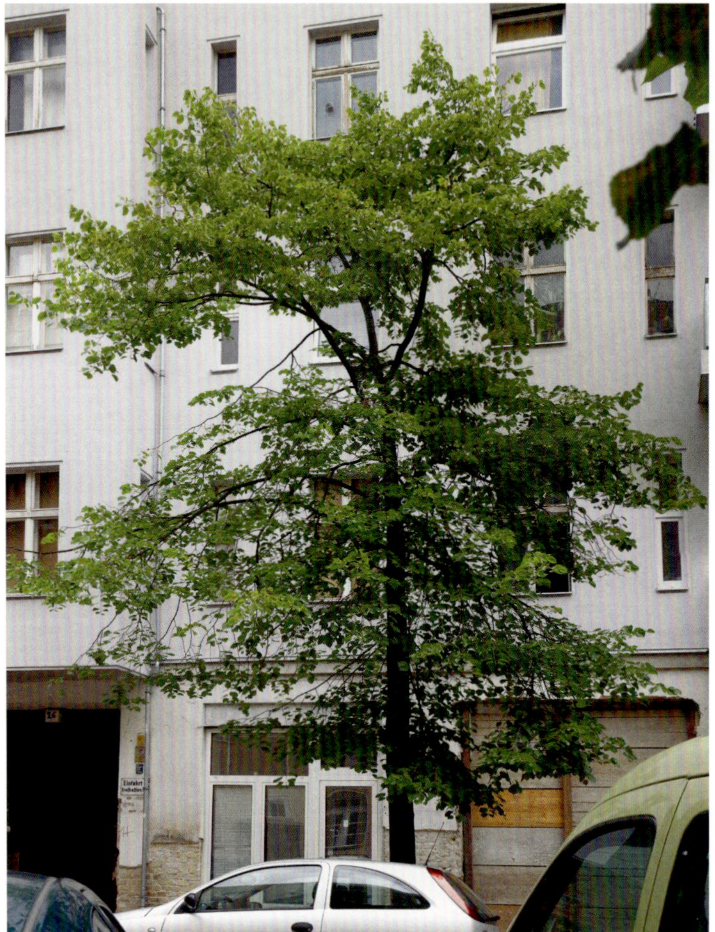 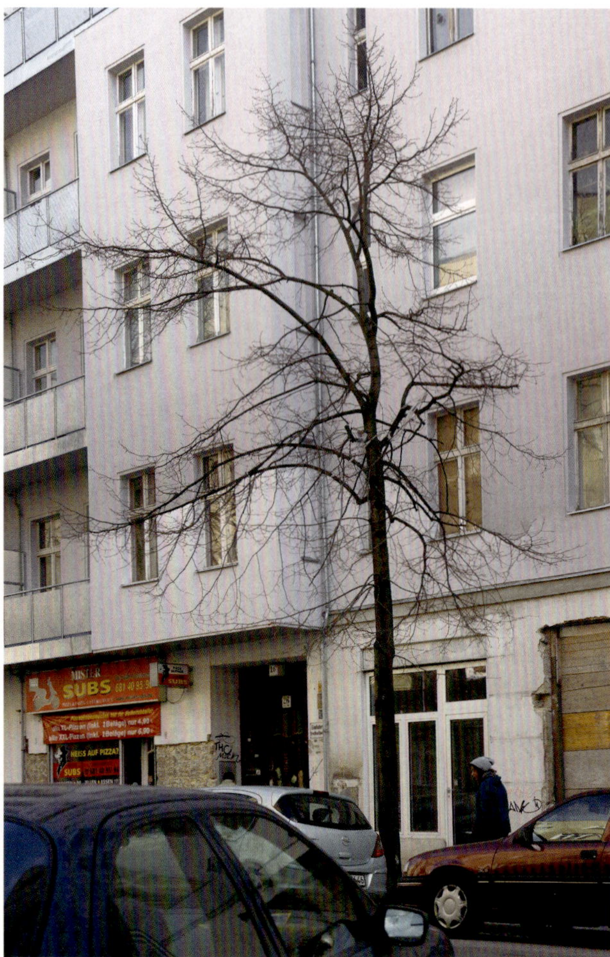

A21–S   A21–W   G: Linden/Linde [Tilia]
                          ADR: Innstrasse 24, 12059 Neukölln
                          GPS: 52.479765,13.449406   HT: 880 cm YR: 1990

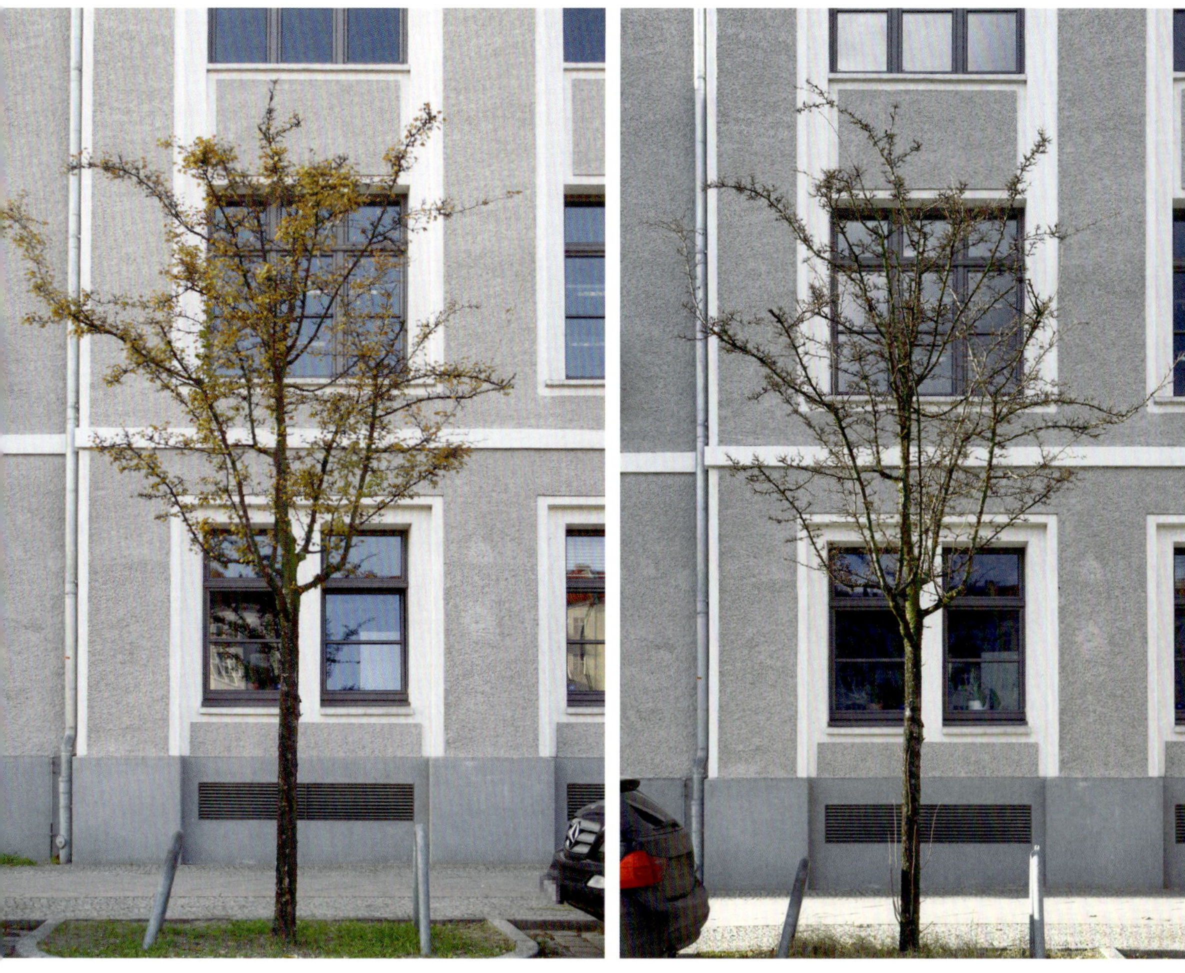

A22–S   A22–W   G: Hawthorn/Weissdorn [Crataegus laevigata]
                              ADR: Ehrenbergstrasse 20, 10245 Friedrichshain Berlin
                              GPS: 52.502750, 13.451350, HT: 520 cm YR: 1999

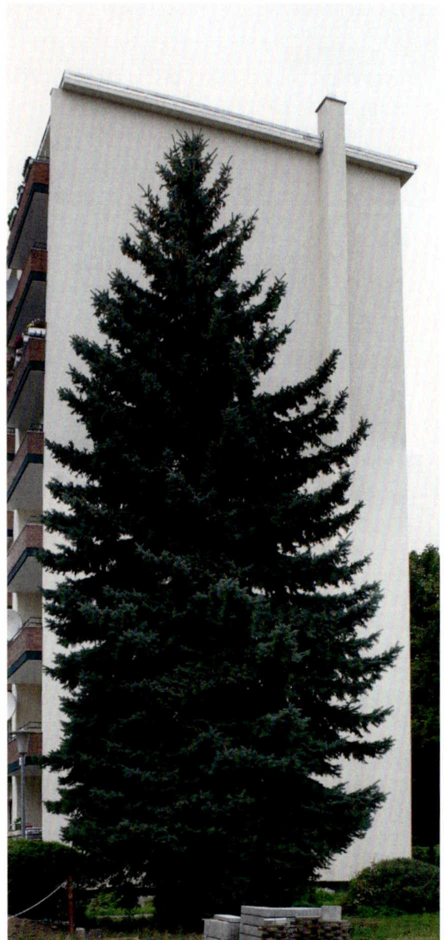 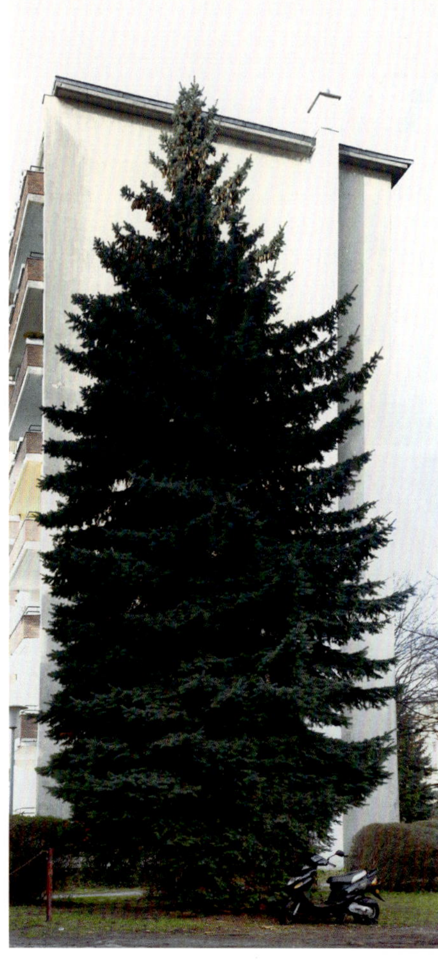

A23-S   A23-W   G: Spruce/Fichte [Picea]
                              ADR: Weserstrasse 133, 12059 Neukölln Berlin
                              GPS: 52.479765,13.449406, HT: 1430 cm YR: 1990

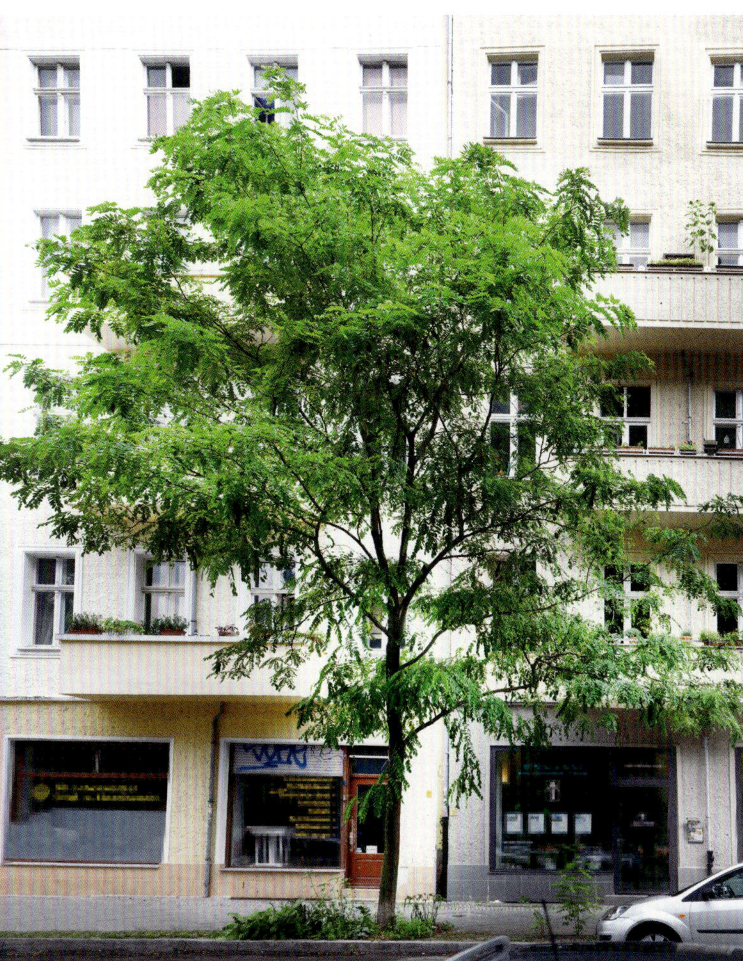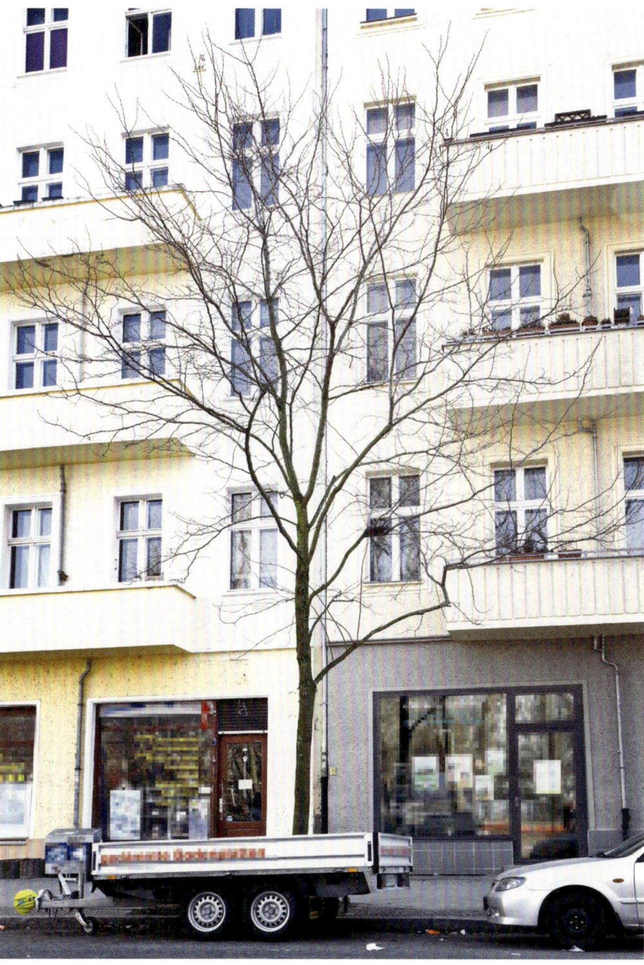

U7–S   U7–W   G: Locust/Robinie [Robinia pseudoacacia]
              o   ADR: Fredersdorfer Strasse 10, 10243 Friedrichshain Berlin
                     GPS: 52.514390, 13.442560, HT: 1200 cm, YR: 2002

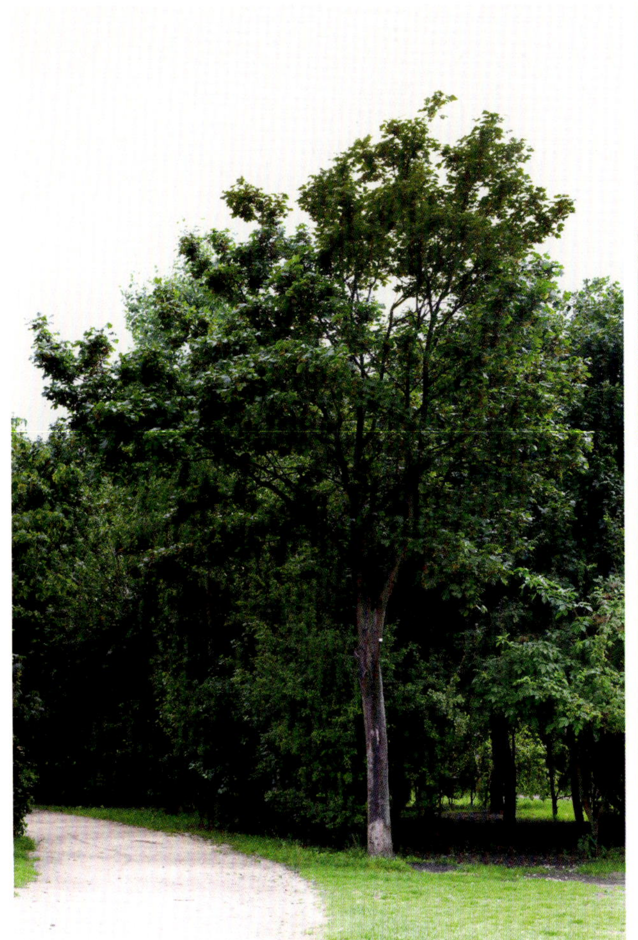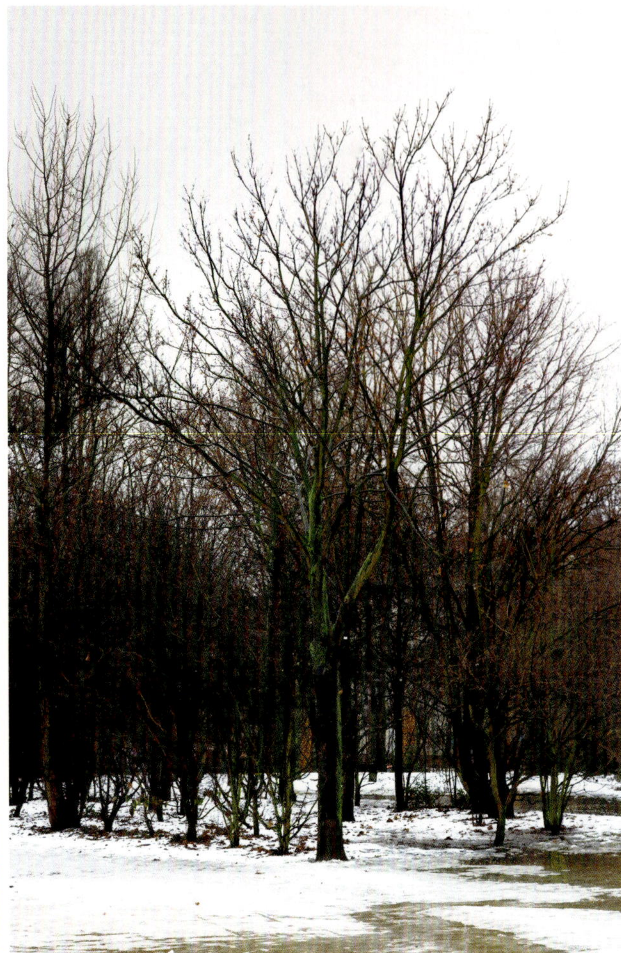

U8–S   U8–W   G: Maple/Ahorn [Acer platanoides]
                        ADR: Wiener Strasse 56, 10999 Kreuzberg Berlin
                        GPS: 52.494641,13.441928, HT: 980 cm, YR: 1981

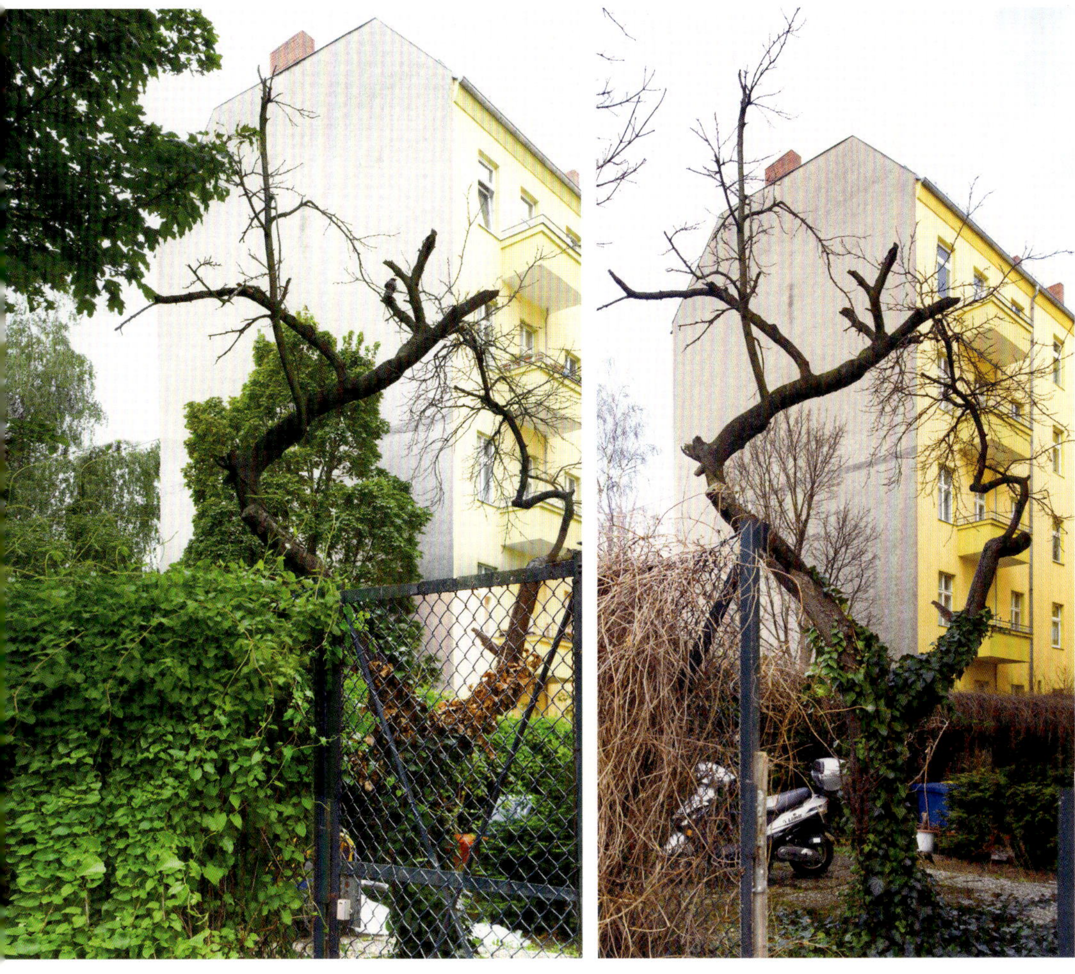

U9−S   U9−W   G: Morello Cherry/Sauerkirsche [Prunus]
          o   ADR: Finowstrasse 29, 12045 Neukölln Berlin
                     GPS: 52.481640, 13.441730, HT: 340 cm, YR: 1989

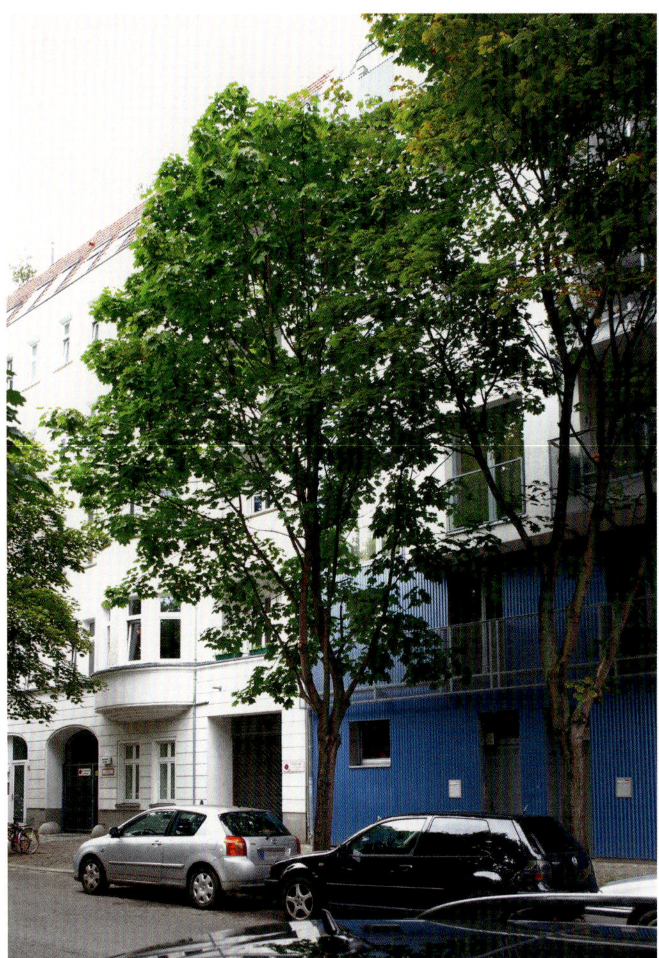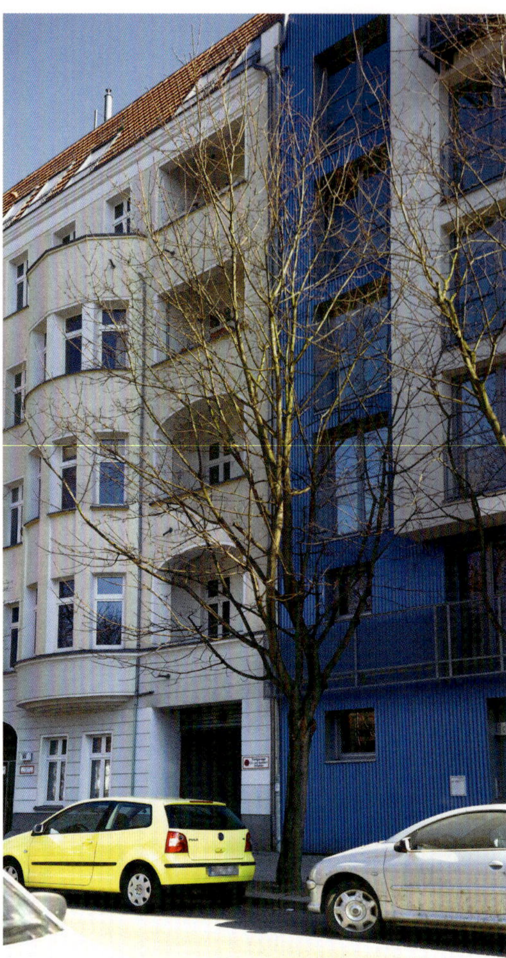

U10–S   U10–S   G: Maple / Ahorn [Acer platanoides]
                              ADR: Kadiner Strasse 19, 10243 Friedrichshain Berlin
                              GPS: 52.487720, 13.390270, HT: 1230 cm, YR: 1978

ADR	Address		MB	Megabyte
ANP	Anchor Points		S	Summer
CM	Centimeter		SM	Summer Module
EPS	Encapsulated Postscript		SV	Summer Vector File
G	Genus		W	Winter
GPS	Global Positioning System		WM	Winter Module
GSM	Grams per Square Meter		WV	Winter Vector File
HDV	High Definition Vector		YR	Planting Year
HT	Height		o	Vector Silhouette (indication)

Appendix

Vector Tree Index
Acknowledgements
Studio Notes
Imprint
Forst Data Download

Vector Tree Index

Reference Number	Anchorpoints Winter Tree	Anchorpoints Summer Tree	Actual Height (cm)	Maximum Height (cm)	Genus	Designer
N1	20,228	22,703	520	3000	Linden/Linde	Will Smith
N7	—	20,768	750	3000	Locust/Robinie	François Leherissier
N8	18,940	40,221	1700	2500	Plane/Platane	Benjamin Ganz
N11	21,243	—	1030	1200	Maple/Ahorn	Marine Stephane
N12	15,994	—	1100	2000	Hazel/Hasel	Marine Stephane
E1	28,671	—	160	1500	Thuja/Lebensbaum	Benjamin Ganz
E3	13,586	—	750	4000	Linden/Linde	Robert Loeber
E4	—	44,325	1590	3000	Maple/Ahorn	Akane Sakai
E5	42,950	138,695	990	4000	Linden/Linde	Thomas Holmes
E6	—	16,345	700	1000	Locust/Robinie	Thomas Holmes
E9	6,551	4,512	430	2200	Chestnut/Kastanie	Oriol Salles
E10	—	3,343	410	3000	Tree of heaven/Götterbaum	François Leherissier
U4	8,907	18,007	550	3000	Linden/Linde	Daniel Cottis
U6	13,816	15,650	150	600	Lilac/Flieder	David Pope
B3	19226	37,004	570	3000	Linden/Linde	Benjamin Ganz, David Pope
B9	18988	—	1030	2200	Chestnut/Kastanie	Benjamin Ganz
B10	—	56,537	1000	2000	Hazel/Hasel	Benjamin Ganz
B13	22,997	9,114	470	3000	Linden/Linde	Daniel Cottis
B14	—	20,928	1230	3600	Silver maple/Silberahorn	Daniel Cottis
B15	100,650	23,462	710	3000	Linden/Linde	Moritz Otten
B16		14,544	590	3000	Linden/Linde	Marine Stephane
A2	10'238	—	560	3000	Maple/Ahorn	Daniel Cottis
A9	7,302	7,986	580	3000	Maple/Ahorn	Daniel Cottis, David Pope
A10	49,403	—	1620	3000	Maple/Ahorn	Marine Stephane
A12	—	30,056	710	3000	Poplar/Pappel	François Leherissier
A14	27,451	59,837	1210	2500	Linden/Linde	Bhav Mistry
A16	—	18,303	620	3000	Linden/Linde	Cezanne Noordhoek
A18	12,969	—	560	3000	Linden/Holländische Linde	Maximilian Voormann
U7	—	51,854	1200	2000	Locust/Robinie	Akane Sakai
U9	—	20,247	340	2500	Morello Cherry/Sauerkirsche	François Leherissier

Stefan Gandl would like to extend a very special
thank you to the entire 'Neubau Forst' team:

A particular thanks to:

Akane Sakai (JP)
Bhav Mistry (UK)
Benjamin Ganz (CH)
Cezanne Noordhoek (NL)
Christoph Grünberger (DE)
Daniel Cottis (US)
David Pope (IR)
François Leherissier (FR)
Jeffrey Bowman (UK)
Joerg Petri (DE)
Lukas Reinhard (DE)
Marine Stephane (FR)
Margarida Castel-Branco (PT)
Marius Hanf (DE)
Maximilian Voormann (DE)
Miriam Busch (DE)
Moritz Otten (DE)
Oriol Salles (ES)
Paul Heys (UK)
Robert Loeber (UK)
Thomas Holmes (UK)
Will Smith (UK)

Barbara Gandl
Viktor Gandl
Theodor Gandl
Dr. Friederike Gandl
Rina Vrancic
Josip Vrancic
Michaela Wienerroither
Franz Wienerroither
Sibylle Ganz-Koechlin
Matthias Ganz
Julian Ganz
David Ganz
Christiane Gelzer
Bertrand Knobel
Laura Heys
Elijah Heys
Tobias Kestel
Paul McNeil
Prof. Alex Coles
Prof. Steve Swindells
Dr. Russell Bestley
Dr. Ian Massey
Dr. Lisa Stansbie
Dr. Verina Gfader
Joe McCullagh
Martina Mullis
Rebekka Kiesewetter
Lea Michel
Christian Hofer
Sebastian Navarro
Tim Wetter
Sebastian Bareis
Klaus Voormann
Wim Crouwel
Guido Fellhölter

Thanks for the support:
University of Huddersfield (UK)
University of Applied Sciences
FH Potsdam (DE)
Andreas Lutz
Angelique Spaninks
Gerrit Terstiege
Scott Belsky
Matias Corea
Eva Franch i Gilabert
Storefront (NY)

Bezirksamt Neukölln von Berlin
Tiefbau- und Landschaftsplanungsamt
Fachbereich Grün- und Freiflächen
Karl-Marx-Strasse 83

Neubau

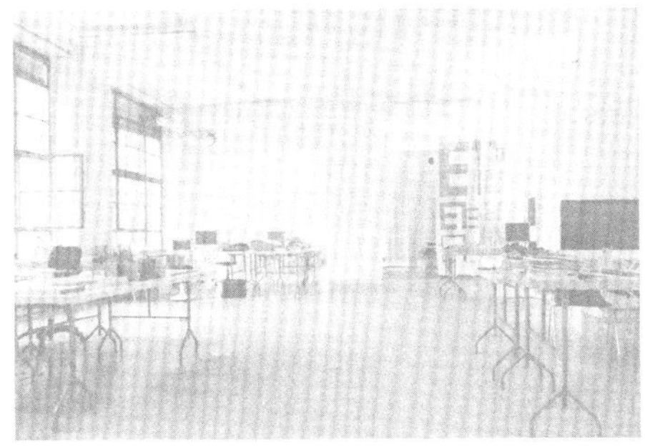

Austrian-born, Berlin-based designer Stefan Gandl formed the design studio Neubau in late 2001 before taking the world by storm with the release of two bestselling books 'Neubau Welt' (2005) and 'Neubau Modul' (2007). In 2008 Neubau's work was exhibited in the 'Neubauism' exhibition at MU (Eindhoven, NL), a perspicacious, kinetic journey through the world of Neubau.

Neubau's work has been exhibited and published in countless publications all over the world.

Neubau is defined by a systematic approach to type and designing for systems. Neubau operates through commissions, developing design and typography for print, screen and space.

Studio Address
Neubau, Paul-Lincke-Ufer 44A
2.H/Fabrik B, 10999 Berlin, Germany

Studio URL
neubauberlin.com

Studio Contact
abc@neubauberlin.com

Neubau Shop
neubauladen.com

Neubau Forst Promotional Website
neubauforst.com

Studio Notes

Neubau, 'Forst', and its exhaustive content, past, present (and future), endeavours to connect with its people, surroundings and a greater global network. 'Occupying and utilising (public) open space socially', and innovatively, offers the studio a privileged position concerning its asserted roll as a pragmatic and municipal graphic design studio, its creations and the distribution of its content.

Neubau endeavours to promote the power of collectivity within contemporary design cultures and advance the opportunity of global collaboration and digital distribution of accessible and affordable design products. Beyond the studio output, we observe the external and public usage of our efforts, all of which are executed admirably with a shared sense and technical precision and sensitivity; examples include written and printed matter, educational facilities, promotional music videos, fashion, global advertising, corporate branding and a wide range of consumer goods. Our work appears in feature films, and we are proud that it has contributed to positive political and social iconography. However, most reassuringly, it continues to appear and form an embedded reference within the work of our design contemporaries.

Neubau Forst Catalogue
Urban Tree Collection for the
Modern Architect & Designer

Editor:
Stefan Gandl

Concept:
Neubau

Editorial team:
Ganz, Gandl

Design & Typography:
Ganz, Gandl

Typeface:
NB International™
(Regular & Mono)

Coordination:
Neubau and
Lars Müller Publishers

Photography:
Benjamin Ganz, Stefan Gandl,
Akane Sakai, Daniel Cottis,
François Leherissier,
David Pope, Lukas Reinhard

Image retouching:
Benjamin Ganz,
Christoph Grünberger

Proofreading:
Keonaona Peterson

Translations:
Allison Plath-Moseley

Printing and binding:
Kösel, Altusried-Krugzell,
Germany

Paper:
Munken Print white 115 gsm
Multi Art gloss 150 gsm,
Hello Fat Matt 150 gsm
(FSC® Certified)

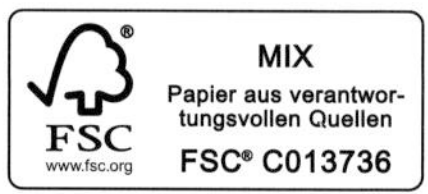

© 2014
Lars Müller Publishers
and Neubau

No part of this book may be
used or reproduced in any
form or manner whatsoever
without prior written permis-
sion, except in the case of
brief quotations embodied in
critical articles and reviews.

Lars Müller Publishers
Zürich, Switzerland
lars-mueller-publishers.com

ISBN 978-3-03778-435-8

Printed in Germany

Neubau Forst Data Download →

With 'Neubau Forst', Lars Müller Publishers and Neubau take pleasure in presenting the alliance of the analogue and the digital world in spectacular precision.

The physical sensation of the book in coalition with the virtual experience of data collection, represent a trendsetting perception of reality, which the authors and the publisher are deeply convinced of.

Being the proud owner of this book, you are invited to acquire the complete digital library (incl. 683 editable assets) at a preferential price.

Lars Müller
Stefan Gandl

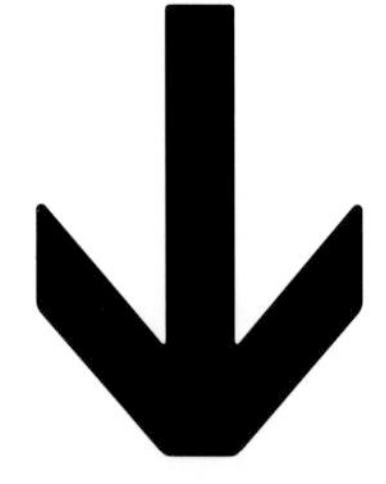

Buy the complete digital 'Neubau Forst' library at exclusive conditions by using this coupon code

[NBF-53f46157bef58]

at neubauladen.com